# Essentials of
# Global Marketing

Visit the Hollensen: *Essentials of Global Marketing* Companion Website at
www.pearsoned.co.uk/hollensen to find valuable **student** learning material
including:

- Full versions of the video case studies at the start of each part
- Self-assessment multiple choice questions for each chapter
- Annotated links to relevant, specific sites on the web
- Searchable online glossary
- Flashcards to test your knowledge of key terms and definitions

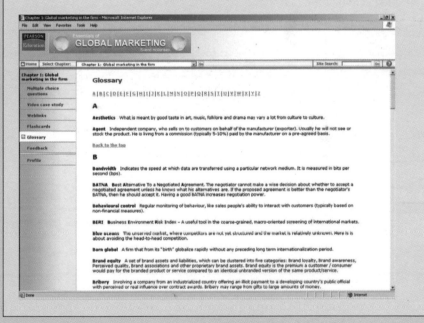

**PEARSON Education**

We work with leading authors to develop the strongest
educational materials in marketing, bringing cutting-edge
thinking and best learning practice to a global market.

Under a range of well-known imprints, including
Financial Times Prentice Hall, we craft high quality print
and electronic publications that help readers to
understand and apply their content, whether studying
or at work.

To find out more about the complete range of our
publishing, please visit us on the World Wide Web at:
www.pearsoned.co.uk

# ESSENTIALS OF GLOBAL MARKETING

Svend Hollensen

Prentice Hall

FINANCIAL TIMES

*An imprint of* **Pearson Education**

Harlow, England • London • New York • Boston • San Francisco • Toronto
Sydney • Tokyo • Singapore • Hong Kong • Seoul • Taipei • New Delhi
Cape Town • Madrid • Mexico City • Amsterdam • Munich • Paris • Milan

**Pearson Education Limited**

Edinburgh Gate
Harlow
Essex CM20 2JE
England

and Associated Companies throughout the world

*Visit us on the World Wide Web at:*
www.pearsoned.co.uk

———————————

First published 2008

ISBN: 978-0-273-71784-3

**British Library Cataloguing-in-Publication Data**
A catalogue record for this book is available from the British Library

**Library of Congress Cataloging-in-Publication Data**
Hollensen, Svend.
    Essentials of global marketing / Svend Hollensen.
        p.   cm.
    Shortened version of: Global marketing. 4th ed. 2007.
    Includes bibliographical references and index.
    ISBN 978-0-273-71784-3
    1. Export marketing.   2. Export marketing–case studies.   I. Hollensen, Svend.
Global marketing.   II. Title.
    HF1416.H65   2008
    658.8′4–dc22                                    2008017536

10   9   8   7   6   5   4   3   2
11   10

Typeset in 10.5/12.5pt Sabon by 35
Printed and bound by Graficas Estella, Spain

# Brief contents

# SUPPORTING RESOURCES

Visit www.pearsoned.co.uk/hollensen to find valuable online resources:

### Companion website for students
- Full versions of the video case studies at the end of each chapter
- Self-assessment multiple choice questions for each chapter
- Annotated links to relevant, specific sites on the web
- Searchable online glossary
- Flashcards to test your knowledge of key terms and definitions
- Classic extra case studies that help take your learning further
- An entire web-based chapter on global e-marketing, that helps keep you up-to-date in this fast-moving area
- Further reading for chapters 1–14

### For instructors
- Media-rich PowerPoint slides, including animated key figures from the book, video clips, audio and direct links to the web
- Extensive Instructor's Manual, with sample answers for all the case study question material, including the extra case studies on the book's website
- Answers to the questions in the book that accompany the video case studies integrated with the book
- A testbank (delivered in TestGen) of over 600 multiple choice questions

**Also:** The Companion Website provides the following features:
- Search tool to help locate specific items of content
- E-mail results and profile tools to send results of quizzes to instructors
- Online help and support to assist with website usage and troubleshooting

For more information please contact your local Pearson Education sales representative or visit www.pearsoned.co.uk/hollensen

# Contents

## Part IV
## DESIGNING THE GLOBAL MARKETING PROGRAMME    293

# Preface

The increase in world trade, an increasing integration of world's major economies, and the onward march on globalization, will mean that the global marketing strategy of the firm will continue to be an important issue. Within a relatively short time span, globalization and global marketing has emerged as a research discipline and it has enabled international marketing practitioners and academics to live up to the claim of the ancient Greek philosopher Socrates, who stated, 'I am a citizen, not of Athens of Greece, but of the world.'

The primary argument of the proponents of globalization rests on the assumption of a homogenization of demand worldwide. This homogenization of demand expresses itself in a worldwide consumer demand for high quality and low costs due to the impact of technology. In addition, Levitt (1983)* argued that firms could take advantage of technology by adopting a standardized approach that will result in products of high quality and low costs for the world market. Other researchers have pointed out that the international markets continue to be different in spite of the forces of globalization. They argue that the evidence for standardization is weak and that standardization of the strategy is not a must to compete in global markets. Even in markets or countries that are apparently culturally similar such as the European Union, differences in customer needs continue to persist. We also still see differences in the criteria that consumers used to make decisions. In addition, there are too many differences between countries and too many constraints in different markets for a standardized approach to be feasible.

The task of global marketing management is complex enough when the company operates in one foreign national market. It is much more complex when the company starts operations in several countries. Marketing programmes must, in these situations, adapt to the needs and preferences of customers that have different levels of purchasing power as well as different climates, languages and cultures. Moreover, patterns of competition and methods of doing business differ between nations and sometimes also within regions of the same nation. In spite of the many differences, however, it is important to hold on to similarities across borders. Some coordination of international activities will be required, but at the same time the company will gain synergy across borders, in the way that experience and learning acquired in one country can be transferred to another.

## Objectives

This book's value chain offers the reader an analytic decision-oriented framework for the development and implementation of global marketing programmes. Consequently, the reader should be able to analyse, select and evaluate the appropriate conceptual frameworks for approaching the five main management decisions connected with the global marketing process.

Having studied this book, the reader should be better equipped to understand how the firm can achieve global competitiveness through the design and implementation of market-responsive programmes.

---

* Levitt, T. (1983) 'The Globalization of Markets', *Harvard Business Review*, May–June, pp. 92–102.

## Target audience

This book is written for people who want to develop effective and decision-oriented global marketing programmes. It can be used as a textbook for undergraduate or graduate courses in global/international marketing. A second audience is the large group of people joining 'global marketing' or 'export' courses on non-university programmes. Finally, this book is of special interest to the manager who wishes to keep abreast of the most recent developments in the global marketing field.

## Prerequisites

An introductory course in marketing.

## Special features

This book has been written from the perspective of the firm competing in international markets, irrespective of its country of origin. It has the following key features:

- aims to be a 'true' global marketing book, with cases and exhibits from all parts of the world, including Europe, the Middle East, Africa, the Far East, and North and South America;
- many new up-to-date exhibits and cases illustrate the theory by showing practical applications. (Examples of the practice of global marketing by actual companies are used throughout the book, in the form of exhibits. Furthermore, each chapter and part end with cases, which include questions for students.)
- a focus on SMEs as global marketing players;
- a decision/'action'-oriented approach;
- a value chain approach (both the traditional product value chain and the service value chain);
- coverage of global buyer–seller relationships;
- extensive coverage of born globals and global account management (GAM), as an extension of the traditional key account management (KAM);
- presents new interesting theories in marketing, for example, service value chain, value innovation, blue ocean strategy, social marketing, global account management, viral branding, and sensory and celebrity branding;
- provides a complete and concentrated overview of the total international marketing planning process.

## Pedagogical/learning aids

One of the strengths of *Essentials of Global Marketing* is its strong pedagogical features.

- Chapter objectives tell the reader what they should be able to do after completing each chapter.
- Real-world examples and exhibits enliven the text and enable the reader to relate to marketing models.
- End-of-chapter summaries recap the main concepts.
- Each chapter ends with a case study, which helps the student relate the models presented in the chapter to a specific business situation.
- Questions for discussion allow students to probe further into important topics.
- Each part is introduced by a Video Case Study, where the students are encouraged to watch the video before answering the questions.

- Part cases studies – for each part there are two comprehensive end-of-part case studies covering the themes met in the part. To reinforce learning, all case studies are accompanied by questions. Case studies are based on real-life companies. Further information about these companies can be found on the Internet. Company cases are derived from many different countries representing all parts of the world. Tables 1 and 2 present the chapter and part case studies.
- Multiple choice questions.
- Video library, including questions.

Table 1 Chapter case studies: overview

| Chapter | Case study title, subtitle and related websites | Country/area of company headquarters | Geographical target area | Target market | |
|---|---|---|---|---|---|
| | | | | B2B | B2C |
| **Chapter 1**<br>**Global marketing in the firm** | Case study 1.1<br>**Bubba Gump Shrimp Co.**<br>A US-based restaurant chain is going international?<br>www.bubbagump.com | USA | USA, World | ✓ | ✓ |
| **Chapter 2**<br>**Initiation of internationalization** | Case study 2.1<br>**Elvis Presley Enterprises Inc. (EPE)**<br>Internationalization of a 'cult' icon<br>www.elvis.com | USA | World | | ✓ |
| **Chapter 3**<br>**Internationalization theories** | Case study 3.1<br>**Entertainment Rights**<br>The internationalization of 'Postman Pat'<br>www.entertainmentrights.com | UK | World | | ✓ |
| **Chapter 4**<br>**Development of the firm's international competitiveness** | Case study 4.1<br>**Wii**<br>Nintendo's Wii takes first place on the world market – can it last?<br>www.nintendo.co.jp | Japan | World | | ✓ |
| **Chapter 5**<br>**The political and economic environment** | Case study 5.1<br>**Sauer-Danfoss**<br>Which political/economic factor would affect a manufacturer of hydraulic components?<br>www.sauer-danfoss.com | Germany, Denmark, USA | World | ✓ | |
| **Chapter 6**<br>**The sociocultural environment** | Case study 6.1<br>**IKEA Catalogue**<br>Are there any cultural differences?<br>www.ikea.com | Sweden, Holland | World | | ✓ |
| **Chapter 7**<br>**The international market selection process** | Case study 7.1<br>**Philips Lighting**<br>Screening markets in the Middle East<br>www.philips.com | Holland | World | | ✓ |
| **Chapter 8**<br>**Some approaches to the choice of entry mode** | Case study 8.1<br>**Ansell condoms**<br>Is acquisition the right way for gaining market shares in the European market?<br>www.anselleurope.com | Australia | Europe, World | | ✓ |
| **Chapter 9**<br>**Export, intermediate and hierarchical modes** | Case study 9.1<br>**Lysholm Linie Aquavit**<br>International marketing of the Norwegian Aquavit brand<br>www.linie-aquavit.com | Norway | Germany, the rest of the World | ✓ | ✓ |

## Table 1 continued

| Chapter | Case study title, subtitle and related websites | Country/area of company headquarters | Geographical target area | Target market | |
|---|---|---|---|---|---|
| | | | | B2B | B2C |
| **Chapter 10 International buyer– seller relationships** | Case study 10.1 **YouTube** Can YouTube get too many marketing partners? www.youtube.com | USA | World China | ✓ | |
| **Chapter 11 Product and pricing decisions** | Case study 11.1 **Zippo Manufacturing Company** Has product diversification beyond the lighter gone too far? www.zippo.com | USA | World | | ✓ |
| **Chapter 12 Distribution and communication decisions** | Case study 12.1 **De Beers** Forward integration into the diamond industry value chain www.debeers.com | South Africa, UK | Europe, World | ✓ | ✓ |
| **Chapter 13 Cross-cultural sales negotiations** | Case study 13.1 **Mecca Cola** Marketing of a Muslim cola to the European market www.mecca-cola.com | United Arab Emirates (UAE) | Europe | ✓ | ✓ |
| **Chapter 14 Organization and control of the global marketing programme** | Case study 14.1 **iPhone** Apple's entry into the global mobile phone business www.apple.com/iphone | USA | World | ✓ | ✓ |

## Table 2  Part case studies: overview

(The video case studies can be downloaded at **www.pearsoned.co.uk/hollensen**)

| Part | Case study title, subtitle and related websites | Country/area of company headquarters | Geographical target area | Target market | |
|---|---|---|---|---|---|
| | | | | B2B | B2C |
| **Part I The decision to internationalize** | Part I Video case study **Acme Whistles Ltd.** A SME is globalizing its whistles sales www.acmewhistles.co.uk | UK | World | ✓ | ✓ |
| | Case study I.1 **Manchester United** Still trying to establish a global brand www.manutd.com | UK | World, USA | | ✓ |
| | Case study I.2 **Cereal Partners Worldwide (CPW)** The No. 2 world player is challenging the No. 1 – Kellogg www.cerealpartners.co.uk | Switzerland, USA | World | | ✓ |
| **Part II Deciding which markets to enter** | Part II Video case study **Land Rover** Which markets should be selected for the new Freelander 2 www.landrover.com | UK/USA | World | | ✓ |
| | Case study II.1 **Red Bull** The global market leader in energy drinks is considering further market expansion www.redbull.com | Austria | World | ✓ | ✓ |

Table 2 continued

| Part | Case study title, subtitle and related websites | Country/area of company headquarters | Geographical target area | Target market | |
|------|------|------|------|------|------|
| | | | | B2B | B2C |
| | Case study II.2 **Skagen Designs** Becoming an international player in designed watches www.skagendesigns.com | USA (Denmark) | World | ✓ | ✓ |
| **Part III Market entry strategies** | Part III Video case study **Tata** Which entry modes should be used for Tata Nano – the World's cheapest car www.tata.com | India | World | | ✓ |
| | Case study III.1 **IKEA** Expanding through franchising to the South American market? www.ikea.com | Sweden, Holland | South America (Brazil) | | ✓ |
| | Case study III.2 **Autoliv Air Bags** Transforming Autoliv into a global company www.autoliv.com | Sweden | World | ✓ | |
| **Part IV Designing the global marketing programme** | Part IV Video case study **Electrolux** Trying to establish a global brand identity www.electrolux.com | Sweden | World | ✓ | ✓ |
| | Case study IV.1 **Guinness** How can the Irish iconic beer brand compensate for the declining sales in the home market? www.diageo.com | UK, Ireland | World | ✓ | ✓ |
| | Case study IV.2 **Dyson Vacuum Cleaner** Shifting from domestic to international marketing with the famous bagless vacuum cleaner www.dyson.co.uk | UK | USA, the rest of the World | ✓ | ✓ |
| **Part V Implementing and coordinating the global marketing programme** | Part V Video case study **Royal Enfield** Trying to establish an international brand identity www.royalenfield.com | India/UK | Europe USA | | ✓ |
| | Case study V.1 **Sony BMG** New worldwide organizational structure and the marketing planning and budgeting of Dido's new album www.sonybmg.com | Germany, USA | World, UK | | ✓ |
| | Case study V.2 **Philips Shavers** Maintaining shaving leadership in the world market www.philips.com | Holland | World | ✓ | ✓ |

# Guided tour

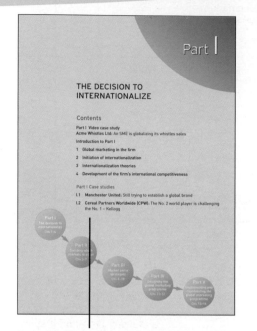

**Case Studies**, drawn from a wide range of countries, products and industries, enhance the end of each part of the book.

The **Exhibits** analyse and discuss specific companies to show how the theories in the chapter are used by well-known brands in the business world.

An **Overview** outlines the topics, Case Studies, and Learning objectives in each chapter, showcasing what you should expect to learn.

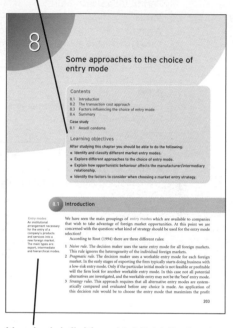

**Marginal definitions** highlight the key terms in each chapter. A full **Glossary** can be found at the end of the book and on the *Essentials of Global Marketing* website at **www.pearsoned.co.uk/hollensen**.

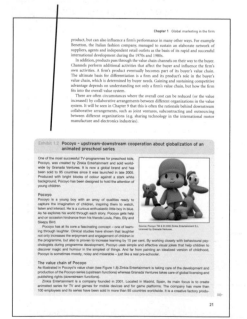

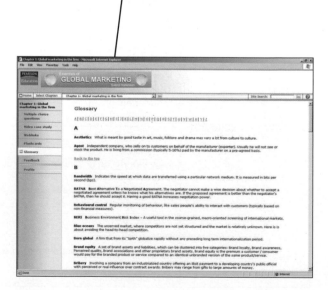

Each chapter concludes with a **Case Study,** providing a range of material for seminars and private study by illustrating the real life applications and implications of the topics covered in the chapter.

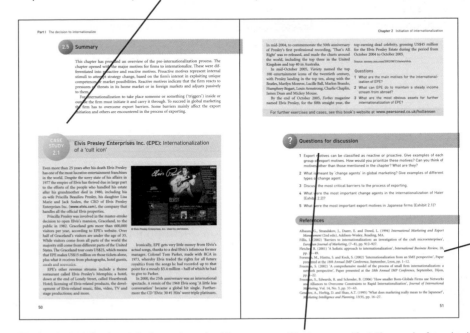

The **Reference** list sources – books, journal articles and websites – that will help develop your understanding and inspire independent learning.

Each part of the book is introduced with a **Video Case Study** demonstrating practical marketing issues with a variety of leading international companies.

Test yourself at the end of each chapter with a set of **Questions for Discussion**. Then try answering the self-assessment Multiple Choice Questions that accompany each chapter on the *Essentials of Global Marketing* Companion Website at **www.pearsoned.co.uk/hollensen**.

# Acknowledgements

Writing any book is a long-term commitment and involves time-consuming effort. The successful completion of a book depends on the support and generosity of many people and the realization of this book is certainly no exception.

I wish to thank the many scholars whose articles, books and other materials I have cited or quoted. However, it is not possible to acknowledge everyone by name. In particular I am deeply indebted to the following individuals and organizations. I thank you all for your help and contribution:

## University of Southern Denmark

- The management at University of Southern Denmark provided the best possible environment for writing and completing this project.
- Colleagues provided encouragement and support during the writing process.

## Reviewers

- Reviewers provided suggestions that were useful in improving many parts of the text. In particular: Alexandra Murcsan (London Metropolitan), John Thomson (Napier), Chris Rock (Greenwich), Graeme Stephen (Aberdeen), Joel Arnott (Sunderland), Sten Söderman (Stockholm) and Jonathan Wilson (Anglia).
- In the development of this text a number of reviewers have been involved, whom I would like to thank for their important and valuable contribution: Henrik Agndal, Jönköping International Business School; Grahame Fallon, University College Northampton; Ronald Salters, Fontys Eindhoven; Ola Feurst, Gotland University.
- Professor Alkis Magdalinos, contributed with many necessary corrections and suggestions for improvement in different sections of the book.

## Case contributors

- Wim Wilms, Fontys Eindhoven, for Case 7.1: Philips Lighting.
- Sjoerd Drost, Product manager, Philips Shavers, for Case V.2: Philips Shavers.

I also wish to acknowledge the help from the following firms whose managers have provided valuable material that has enabled me to write the following cases. I have been in direct personal contact with most of the following companies and thank the managers involved for their very useful comments.

*Chapter cases:*
- Entertainment Rights, London, UK for Case 3.1 on Postman Pat.
- IKEA, Sweden for Case 6.1 on the IKEA Catalogue.
- Arcus AS, Oslo, Norway for Case 9.1 on Lysholm Linie Aquavit.

*Part cases*:
- Skagen Designs, Reno, USA and Copenhagen, Denmark for Case II.2: Skagen Designs
- Autoliv AB, Stockholm, Sweden for Case III.2: Autoliv Air Bags
- Sony BMG, New York, USA for Case V.1: Sony BMG
- Philips Shavers, Eindhoven, Holland for Case V.2: Philips Shavers.

I would also like to thank Madame Tussaud Group, especially Global Marketing Director Nicky Marsh from London and Cathy Wong, External Affairs Consultant from Shanghai for their contribution to Exhibit 11.2.

I am also grateful to the following international advertising agencies, which have provided me with examples of standardized and/or localized advertising campaigns:

- J. Walter Thompson (JWT Europe), London who contributed with a European ad for LUX soap.
- Hindustan Thompson (HTA), Bombay, India who contributed with an ad for Kellogg's Basmati Flakes in India and an ad for LUX soap in India.
- Ammirati Puris Lintas, Hamburg, Germany who contributed with an ad from the 'Me and my Magnum' campaign.

I would also like to thank LEGO and Langnese (special thanks to Silke for her efforts to get the Magnum ad) for their contributions to different examples in the book.

I am grateful to my publisher, Pearson Education. I would like to thank Acquisitions Editor David Cox and Desk Editor Georgina Clark-Mazo for their help with this edition.

I also extend my greatest gratitude to my colleagues at the University of Southern Denmark for their constant help and inspiration.

Finally, I thank my family for their support through the process. I am pleased to dedicate this version to Jonna, Nanna and Julie.

*Svend Hollensen*
*University of Southern Denmark, Sønderborg, Denmark*
*June 2008*

svend@sam.sdu.dk

# Publisher's acknowledgements

We are grateful to the following for permission to reproduce copyright material:

Figure 1.2 from 'A framework for analysis of strategy development in globalizing markets', *Journal of International Marketing*, 5(1), reprinted by permission of the American Marketing Association (Solberg, C.A. 1997); Figure 1.6 adapted from *Competitive Advantage: Creating and Sustaining Superior Performance*, reprinted by permission of The Free Press, a Division of Simon & Schuster Adult Publishing Group (Porter, M.E. 1985); Table 2.1 adapted from *International Marketing and Export Management*, 2nd edn, Addison-Wesley, reprinted by permission of Pearson Education Ltd (Albaum, G. *et al.* 1994); Figure 3.1 adapted from *International føretagsekonomi*, Norstedts, reprinted by permission of Mats Forsgren (Forsgren, M. and Johanson, J. 1975); Figure 3.2 from 'Internationalization: evolution of a concept', *Journal of General Management*, 14(2), reprinted by permission of The Braybrooke Press Ltd (Welch, L.S. and Loustarinen, R. 1988); Figure 3.5 adapted from *Internationalization Handbook for the Software Business*, reprinted by permission of Centre of Expertise for Software Product Business (Âijö, T. *et al.* 2005); Table 4.1 from 'Composite strategy: the combination of collaboration and competition', *Journal of General Management*, 21(1), reprinted by permission of The Braybrooke Press Ltd (Burton, J. 1995); Figure 4.4 adapted from 'Competitive advantage: merging marketing and competence-based perspectives', *Journal of Business and Industrial Marketing*, 9(4), reprinted by permission of Hans P. Wehrli (Jüttner, U. and Wehrli, H.P. 1994); Figure 4.5 from 'Exploiting the core competences of your organization', *Long Range Planning*, 27(4), reprinted by permission of Elsevier (Tampoe, M. 1994); Table 5.1 'The Big Mac Index' from *The Economist* 25 March 2006, © The Economist Newspaper Ltd, London (25.3.06), reprinted by permission of The Economist Newspaper Ltd; Figure 5.2 from *Global Marketing*, 1st edn, reprinted with permission of South-Western, a part of Cengage Learning, Inc. (Czinkota, M.R. and Ronkainen, I.A. 1996); Table 6.2 adapted from *International Marketing Strategy: Analysis, Development and Implementation*, Thomson Learning, reprinted by permission of Thomson Publishing Services (Phillips, C. *et al.* 1994); Figure 6.3 from *International Marketing: A Cultural Approach*, reprinted by permission of Pearson Education Ltd (Usunier, J.-C. 2000); Table 6.4 from *Going International: How to Make Friends and Deal Effectively in the Global Marketplace*, Random House, reprinted by permission of The Sagalyn Agency (Copeland, L. and Griggs, L. 1985); Figure 7.6 from *European Business: An Issue-Based Approach*, 3rd edn, Pitman, reprinted by permission of Pearson Education Ltd (Welford, R. and Prescott, K. 1996); Figure 7.10 from *International Marketing Strategy*, 2nd edn, Prentice Hall, reprinted by permission of Pearson Education Ltd (Bradley, F. 1995); Figure 7.11 from 'Market expansion strategies in multinational marketing', *Journal of Marketing*, 43, Spring, reprinted by permission of the American Marketing Association (Ayal, I. and Zif, J. 1979); Case Study II.1 Table 1 from Red Bull GmbH – Softdrink – World, Global Company Profile, *Euromonitor International*, March, © Euromonitor International 2007 (Euromonitor 2007); Figure 9.8 adapted from *Strategiske allianser i globale strategier*, Norges Eksportråd, reprinted by permission of Index Publishing/Norwegian Trade Council (Lorange, P. and Roos, J. 1995); Figures 9.9 and

9.10 from *Joint Ventures, Alliances, and Corporate Strategy*, reprinted by permission of Beard Books (Harrigan, K.R. 2003); Figure 19.13 from 'Toward a theory of international new ventures', *Journal of International Business Studies*, 25(1), reprinted by permission from Macmillan Publishers Ltd (Oviatt, B. M. and McDougall, P. P. 1994); Figure 9.14 from 'Organisational dimensions of global marketing', *European Journal of Marketing*, 23(5), reprinted by permission of Emerald Publishing Ltd (Raffée, H. and Kreutzer, R. 1989); Figure 9.15 from 'Regional headquarters: the spearhead for Asian Pacific markets', *Long Range Planning*, 29(1), reprinted by permission of Elsevier (Lasserre, P. 1996); Figure 9.16 from 'Why are foreign subsidiaries divested? A conceptual framework' in *The Nature of the International Firm*, edited by I. Björkman and M. Forsgren, Handelshøjskolens Forlag/Copenhagen Business School Press, reprinted by permission of the author (Benito, G.R.G. 1997); Figure 10.1 adapted from 'Alihankintajarjestelma 1990-luvulla [subcontracting system in the 1990s]', *Publications of SITRA*, No. 114, reprinted by permission of SITRA (Lehtinen, U. 1991); Table 10.1 and Figure 10.6 from 'Relationship marketing from a value system perspective', *International Journal of Service Industry Management*, 5, reprinted by permission of Emerald Publishing Ltd (Jüttner, U. and Wehrli, H.P. 1994); Figure 10.3 reproduced with permission of Council of Supply Chain Management Professionals, from 'A total cost/value model for supply chain competitiveness', *Journal of Business Logistics*, J.L. Cavinato, 13(2), 1992, permission conveyed through Copyright Clearance Center, Inc. (Cavinato, J.L. 1992); Figure 10.4 adapted from 'Interactive strategies in supply chains: a double-edged portfolio approach to SME', *Subcontractors Positioning Paper* presented at the Eighth Nordic Conference on Small Business Research, reprinted by permission of Per Blenker (Blenker, P. and Christensen, P.R. 1994); Figure 10.5 from *Strategies for International Industrial Marketing*, Croom Helm, reprinted by permission of Taylor and Francis Books UK (Turnbull, P.W. and Valla, J.P. 1986); Part IV Figure 3, p. 298, from 'Marketing mix standardisation: an integrated approach to global marketing', *European Journal of Marketing*, 22(10), reprinted by permission of Emerald Group Publishing Ltd (Kreutzer, R. 1988); Table 11.2 adapted from 'The international dimension of branding: strategic considerations and decisions', *International Marketing Review*, 6(3), reprinted by permission of Emerald Publishing Ltd (Onkvisit, S. and Shaw, J.J. 1989); Table 11.3 from 'The future of consumer branding as seen from the picture today', *Journal of Consumer Marketing*, 12(4), reprinted by permission of Emerald Group Publishing Ltd (Boze, B.V. and Patton, C.R. 1995); Figure 11.4 adapted from *International Marketing: Analysis and Strategy*, 2nd edn, Macmillan, reprinted by permission of Sak Onkvisit (Onkvisit, S. and Shaw, J.J. 1993); Figure 11.13 from 'Pricing conditions in the European Common Market', *European Management Journal*, 12(2), reprinted by permission of Elsevier (Diller, H. and Bukhari, I. 1994); Figure 11.15 from 'The European pricing bomb – and how to cope with it', *Marketing and Research Today*, February, reprinted by permission of ESOMAR (Simon, H. and Kucher, E. 1993); Figure 12.2 from 'US–Japan distribution channel cost structures: is there a significant difference?', *International Journal of Physical Distribution and Logistics Management*, 27(1), reprinted by permission of Emerald Group Publishing Ltd (Pirog III, S.F. and Lancioni, R. 1997); Figure 12.3 from *Marketing Management: An Overview*, The Dryden Press, reprinted by permission of Dale M. Lewison (Lewison, D.M. 1996); Figure 12.4 adapted from *Marketing Management: An Overview*, The Dryden Press, reprinted by permission of Dale M. Lewison (Lewison, D.M. 1996); Table 12.4 from *International Marketing Strategy: Analysis, Development and Implementation*, Thomson Learning, reprinted by permission of Thomson Publishing Services (Phillips, C. *et al.* 1994); Table 12.6 from 'Guidelines for managing an international sales force', *Industrial Marketing Management*, 24(2), reprinted by permission of

Elsevier (Honeycutt, E.D. and Ford, J.B. 1995); Figure 12.7 from *International Marketing Management*, 5th edn, South-Western College Publishing, reprinted by permission of the author (Jain, S.C. 1996); Exhibit 14.1 Figure, p. 454, Sauer-Danfoss Production Locations reprinted by permission of Sauer-Danfoss Inc.; Table 14.1 adapted from *Principles and Practice of Marketing*, 3rd edn, reprinted by permission of the McGraw-Hill Publishing Company (Jobber, D. 1995).

We are grateful to the following for permission to reproduce Case Study material:

Case Study 2.1 screen shot from www.elvis.com, Elvis image used by permission, Elvis Presley Enterprises, Inc.; Case Study 3.1 screen shot from www.entertainmentrights.com and image, Postman Pat® © 1981 Woodland Animations Ltd, a division of Entertainment Rights plc., licensed by Entertainment Rights Distribution Limited, Original writer John Cunliffe, Royal Mail and Post Office imagery is used by kind permission of Royal Mail Group plc, all rights reserved; Case Study I.1 screen shot from www.ManUtd.com reprinted by permission of Manchester United Limited; Case Study 5.1 screen shot from www.sauer-danfoss.com reprinted by permission of Sauer-Danfoss Inc.; Case Study III.1 screen shot from www.ikea.com reprinted by permission of IKEA Ltd; Case Study III.2 screen shot from www.autoliv.com reprinted by permission of Autoliv Inc.; Case Study 11.1 screen shot from www.zippo.com reprinted by permission of Zippo Manufacturing Company; Case Study 13.1 screen shot from www.mecca-cola.com reprinted by permission of Mecca Cola World.

We are grateful to the following for permission to reproduce pictures:

Exhibit 1.1 images reprinted by permission of McDonald's Corporation; Exhibit 1.2 image Pocoyo TM & © 2005 Zinkia Entertainment S.L. Licensed by Granada Ventures; Case Study 1.1 image © Craig Lovell/Eagle Visions Photography/Alamy; Exhibit 2.2 image © Michael Reynolds/epa/Corbis; Exhibit 4.2 image Tony Souter, © Dorling Kindersley; Case Study 4.1 image Andrew Parsons/PA Archive/PA Photos; Case Study I.2 the 'Cheerios', 'Nesquik', 'Shreddies' and 'Shredded Wheat' name and image is reproduced with the kind permission of Société des Produits Nestlé S.A.; Exhibit 6.3 image reprinted by permission of Polaroid Corporation; Exhibit 6.4 screen shot from Pocari Sweat official website reprinted by permission of Otsuka Pharmaceutical Co., Ltd; Case Study 6.1 images used with the permission of Inter IKEA Systems B.V.; Exhibit 7.1 Sanex Global Brand image reprinted by permission of Sara Lee; Case Study 7.1 image reprinted by permission of Wim Wilms; Case Study II.1 p. 186 image (bottom) Michael Kunkel/Hochzwei/PA Photos; Case Study II.1 p. 187 image Serkan Senturk/AP/PA Photos; Case Study II.1 p. 188 image Evan Kafka/Getty Images Entertainment/Getty Images; Case Study II.2 images reprinted by permission of Skagen Designs A/S; Case Study 8.1 image reprinted by permission of Ansell Healthcare Europe; Case Study 9.1 Linie Aquavit advertisement reprinted by permission of Arcus AS; Case Study 10.1 image © Roberto Herrett/Alamy; Exhibit 12.3 Baileys® Irish Cream Liqueur bottle image reprinted by permission of Diageo; Chapter 12, p. 387, LEGO® FreeStyle in the Far East, © 1997 and LEGO® FreeStyle in Europe, © 1997 advertisements, © 2008 The LEGO Group, used by permission; Exhibit 12.4 image © Frank Trapper/Corbis; Case Study IV.1 Guinness® brand images reprinted by permission of Diageo; Case Study IV.2 image Matthew Fearn/PA/EMPICS; Case Study 14.1 Cathal McNaughton/PA Wire/PA Photos; Case Study V.1 image reprinted by permission of Sony BMG Music Entertainment (UK) Ltd.

We are grateful to the following for permission to reproduce texts:

Exhibit 10.1 from Network sourcing: A hybrid approach, *International Journal of Purchasing and Materials Management*, 31(2), Spring, reprinted by permission of Blackwell Publishing Ltd (Hines, P. 1995).

In some instances we have been unable to trace the owners of copyright material, and we would appreciate any information that would enable us to do so.

# Abbreviations

| | |
|---|---|
| ACs | advanced countries |
| APEC | Asia Pacific Economic Cooperation |
| ASEAN | Association of South East Asian Nations |
| B2B | business to business |
| B2C | business to consumer |
| BDA | before–during–after |
| BER | business environment risk |
| C2B | consumer to business |
| C2C | consumer to consumer |
| CATI | computer-assisted telephone interviews |
| CEO | chief executive officer |
| CRM | customer relationship management |
| DSS | decision support system |
| ECB | European Central Bank |
| ECO | ecology |
| ECSC | European Coal and Steel Community |
| EDI | electronic data interchange |
| EDLP | everyday low prices |
| EEA | European Economic Area |
| EEC | European Economic Community |
| EFTA | European Free Trade Area |
| EMC | Export Management Company |
| EMEA | Europe, Middle East and Africa |
| EMU | European Economic and Monetary Union |
| EU | European Union: title for the former EEC used since the ratification of the Maastricht Treaty in 1992 |
| FDI | foreign direct investment: a market entry strategy in which a company invests in a subsidiary or partnership in a foreign market (joint venture) |
| FMCG | fast-moving consumer goods |
| FSC | foreign sales corporation |
| GAM | global account management |
| GATT | General Agreement on Tariffs and Trade |
| GDP | gross domestic product |
| GNI | gross national income |
| GNP | gross national product: the total 'gross value' of all goods and services produced in the economy in one year |
| GPC | global pricing contract |
| GRP | gross rating point |
| HQ | headquarters |
| IDR | intermediation–disintermediation–reintermediation |
| IMF | International Monetary Fund |
| IMS | international market selection |
| IPLC | international product life cycle |
| ISO | International Standards Organization |
| ISP | internet service provider |

| | |
|---|---|
| IT | information technology |
| KAM | key account management |
| LDCs | less developed countries |
| LSEs | large-scale enterprises |
| LTO | long-term orientation |
| M&A | merger and acquisition |
| MIS | marketing information system |
| MNCs | multinational corporations |
| MNE | multi-national enterprise |
| NAFTA | North American Free Trade Agreement: a free trade agreement to establish an open market between the United States, Canada and Mexico |
| NICs | newly industrialized countries |
| OE | operational effectiveness |
| OECD | Organization for Economic Cooperation and Development: a multinational forum that allows the major industrialised nations to discuss economic policies and events |
| OEM | original equipment manufacturer (outsourcer) |
| OLI | ownership-location-internalization |
| OPEC | Organization of Petroleum Exporting Countries |
| OTS | opportunity to see |
| PDA | personal digital assistant |
| PEST | political/legal, economic, social/cultural, technological |
| PLC | product life cycle: a theory that characterises the sales history of products as passing through four stages: introduction, growth, maturity, decline |
| POS | point of sale |
| PPP | purchasing-power parity |
| PR | public relations |
| QDF | quality deployment function |
| R&D | research and development |
| RM | relationship management |
| RMC | regional management centre |
| ROA | return on assets |
| ROI | return on investment |
| SBU | strategic business unit: a single business or a collection of related businesses that can be planned separately from the rest of the company |
| SMEs | small and medium-sized enterprises |
| SMS | short message service |
| SRC | self-reference criterion |
| TC | transaction cost |
| TCA | transactional cost analysis |
| TF | trade fair |
| TQM | total quality management |
| URL | universal |
| USP | unique selling proposition |
| VAT | value added tax |
| WAP | wireless application protocol |
| WTO | World Trade Organization (successor to GATT) |

# About the author

**Svend Hollensen** is an Associate Professor of International Marketing at University of Southern Denmark. He is also Visiting Professor of London Metropolitan University. He holds an MSc (Business Administration) from Aarhus Business School. He has practical experience from a job as International Marketing Coordinator in a large Danish multinational enterprise as well as from being International Marketing Manager in a company producing agricultural machinery.

After working in industry Svend received his PhD in 1992 from Copenhagen Business School.

He has published articles in journals and is the author of two case books that focus on general marketing and international marketing (published by Copenhagen Business School Press).

With Pearson Education he has published *Global Marketing* (4th edition, which came out in April 2007) and *Marketing Management – A Relationship Approach* (a 2nd edition is planned for 2009) as well as *Marketing Research – An International Approach* (May 2006), together with Marcus Schmidt.

Svend has also worked as a business consultant for several multinational companies, as well as global organizations such as the World Bank.

The author may be contacted via:

University of Southern Denmark
Alsion 2
DK-6400 Sønderborg
Denmark
*e-mail*: svend@sam.sdu.dk

# Part I

# THE DECISION TO INTERNATIONALIZE

## Contents

**Part I**
The decision to internationalize
Chs 1–4

**Part II**
Deciding which markets to enter
Chs 5–7

**Part III**
Market entry strategies
Chs 8–10

**Part IV**
Designing the global marketing programme
Chs 11–12

**Part V**
Implementing and coordinating the global marketing programme
Chs 13–14

# Acme Whistles Ltd:
## An SME is globalizing its whistles sales

In 1883 Joseph Hudson, a toolmaker and violinist, began making gadgets to sell. One of the things he made was whistles. Prior to that time whistles had been used as musical instruments. After observing British Police having a hard time communicating with rattles, he realized that his whistle could be used as a tool.

Today Acme (**www.acmewhistles.co.uk**) is the world's largest and most famous producer of whistles. Its patented designs are standards in loud noise production. The name 'Acme' comes from the Greek word 'acme', meaning a high point. This indicates that the whistle is a tool for producing a very high decibel level.

**Acme Thunder 1**

Acme's first whistle for Scotland Yard was nicknamed the 'Thunderer' and it is still Acme's best-selling brand, with 200 million sold units. Acme is particularly famous for the production of the Titanic whistles, which were subsequently used in the film *Titanic*. This resulted in a significant number of orders for reproduction whistles manufactured using the original tooling.

Today Acme, employing about 50 people, sells about 6 million whistles per annum to about 120 countries world-wide. It has made over a billion whistles altogether. While most today are made of plastic, the original whistles were made from folded brass strips. In addition to the 'Thunderer', Acme makes varieties of bird calls, dog calls, safety whistles, sports whistles and party whoopers.

**Acme whistle website**

Acme Whistles has both B2C and B2B customers. Its B2B customers range from sporting bodies, safety organizations and security organizations, for example, NATO forces, the UN, Royal Life Saving Society, International Mountain Rescue Council, Boy Scouts of USA, Singapore Police, Canadian Hockey, Hong Kong Lifeguards Association and NFL.

*Watch the video before answering the questions.*

## Questions

1 Which parts of Acme Whistles' value chain are centralized (standardized) and which are decentralized (adapted)?

2 How is the internet (online) helping Acme Whistles to expand global sales of whistles?

3 Initial market research conducted by the company has shown that there could be a market opportunity for the production of a high value added jewelled whistle (e.g. a silent dog whistle covered in diamonds to hang around a girl's neck). Who might be potential customers for such a product? Where should Acme Whistles find these customers?

Source: Video accompanying the text, **www.acmewhistles.co.uk**

# Introduction to Part I

It is often the case that a firm going into an export adventure should have stayed in the home market because it did not have the necessary competences to start exporting. Chapter 1 discusses competences and global marketing strategies from the value chain perspective. Chapter 2 discusses the major motivations of the firm to internationalize. Chapter 3 concentrates on some central theories that explain firms' internationalization processes. Chapter 4 discusses the concept of 'international competitiveness' from a macro level to a micro level.

# 1

# Global marketing in the firm

## Contents

**Case study**

## Learning objectives

After studying this chapter you should be able to do the following:

● Characterize and compare the management style in SMEs (small and medium-sized enterprises) and LSEs (large-scale enterprises).

● Identify drivers for 'global integration' and 'market responsiveness'.

● Explain the role of global marketing in the firm from a holistic perspective.

● Describe and understand the concept of the value chain.

● Identify and discuss different ways of internationalizing the value chain.

## 1.1 The process of developing the global marketing plan

As the book has a clear decision-oriented approach, it is structured according to the five main decisions that marketing people in companies face in connection with the global marketing process. The 14 chapters are divided into five parts.

Part 1: The decision to internationalize (Chapters 1–4)
Part 2: Deciding which markets to enter (Chapters 5–7)
Part 3: Market entry strategies (Chapters 8–10)
Part 4: Designing the global marketing programme (Chapters 11–12)
Part 5: Implementing and coordinating the global marketing programme (Chapters 13–14).

In the end, the firm's global competitiveness is mainly dependent on the end-result of the global marketing stages: *the global marketing plan* (see Figure 1.1). The purpose of the marketing plan is to create sustainable competitive advantages in the global marketplace. Generally, firms go through some kind of mental process in developing global marketing plans. In SMEs this process is normally informal; in larger organizations it is often more systematized. Figure 1.1 offers a systematized approach to developing a global marketing plan – the stages are illustrated by the most important models and concepts that are explained and discussed throughout the chapters. It is advisable to return to this figure throughout the book.

## 1.2 Introduction to globalization

**Globalization**
Reflects the trend of firms buying, developing producing and selling products and services in most countries and regions of the world.

**Internationalization**
Doing business in many countries of the world, but often limited to a certain region (e.g. Europe).

In the face of globalization and an increasingly interconnected world many firms attempt to expand their sales into foreign markets. International expansion provides new and potentially more profitable markets; helps increase the firm's competitiveness; and facilitates access to new product ideas, manufacturing innovations and the latest technology. However, internationalization is unlikely to be successful unless the firm prepares in advance. Advance planning has often been regarded as important to the success of new international ventures (Knight, 2000).

Solberg (1997) discusses the conditions under which the company should 'stay at home' or further 'strengthen the global position' as two extremes (see Figure 1.2). The framework in Figure 1.2 is based on the following two dimensions:

### Industry globalism

In principle, the firm cannot influence the degree of industry globalism, as it is mainly determined by the international marketing environment. Here the strategic behaviour of firms depends on the international competitive structure within an industry. In the case of a high degree of industry globalism there are many interdependencies between markets, customers and suppliers, and the industry is dominated by a few large powerful players (*global*), whereas the other end (*local*) represents a multidomestic market environment, where markets exist independently from one another. Examples of very global industries are PCs, IT (software), records (CDs), movies and aircrafts (the two dominant players being Boeing and Airbus). Examples of more local industries are the more culture-bounded industries, like hairdressing, foods and dairies (e.g. brown cheese in Norway).

### Preparedness for internationalization

This dimension is mainly determined by the firm. The degree of preparedness is dependent on the firm's ability to carry out strategies in the international marketplace, i.e. the actual skills in international business operations. These skills or organizational capabilities may consist of personal skills (e.g. language, cultural sensitivity), the managers' international experience or financial resources. The well-prepared company (*mature*) has a good basis for dominating the international markets and consequently it would gain higher market shares.

In the global/international marketing literature the 'staying at home' alternative is not discussed thoroughly. However, Solberg (1997) argues that with limited international experience and a weak position in the home market there is little reason for a

Figure 1.1  Development of an international marketing plan

## Tools used in different stages (references to the book)

### PART I: THE DECISION TO INTERNATIONALIZE

The 'nine strategic windows' model:

> Chapter 1

Benchmarking – competence profile

### PART II: DECIDING WHICH MARKETS TO ENTER

> Chapter 4

See Screening process in Chapter 7

## Process stages

**Introduction:**
Purpose of the international marketing plan

**Should the company go international or not?**

**What are the competences of the firm and how should they be utilized internationally?**

**External analysis:**
- Political forces
- Economic forces
- Socio-cultural forces
- Market size

(Chapters 5 and 6)

**Internal analysis:**
Identifying firm competences ⇨ International competitiveness (Chapter 4)

Match

### SWOT-analysis

| | Weaknesses |
|---|---|
| Strengths | Threats |
| Opportunities | |

Internal          External

**IMS = International Market Selection**

## Description

**Introduction:**
The international marketing plan is based on a firm's mission (purpose of the business) and vision (where do we want to go). Developing an international marketing plan is the systematic process involving the assessment of market opportunities combined with the internal resources, the determination of marketing objectives, and the plan for implementation of the international marketing mix. The plan describes all the marketing activities that the firm should perform during a specified time period (usually one to three years).

**The 'nine strategic windows' model:**
This model uses industry globalism and the firm's preparedness as criteria for deciding if the firm should go abroad or rather stay at home

**Benchmarking – competence profile:**
The customer perceived value of the different competitor offerings along the value chain provide the necessary input for determining where the firm has got its core competence and where further capabilities should be developed

**SWOT-analysis:**
**Strengths and Weaknesses** (inside your company)
Identify internal strengths and weaknesses of your company. For example education-level, international experience and reputation in your area of expertise is most likely a strength

**Opportunities and Threats** (from outside)
Identify and rank by order of importance, any threats or opportunities your business may face from outside influences.

The whole issue is to find the right match between the internal and external analysis, i.e. where in the global market can we use our special firm competences?

**Estimation of total market:** Numbers of buyers x average consumption per year

**Segmentation:** Relevant segmentation/screening criteria
B-t-C markets: Demographic: age, income, occupation
Psychographic: lifestyle, preferences, etc.
Geographic: Countries, regions
Behavioural: heavy, medium, light users

B-t-B markets: Demographic: size of firm, type of industry
Economic: Buying power of customers

- Geographical market: region (Western Europe, Eastern Europe, Far East, North America etc.) country or area in a country
- Customer type: end-customer, middlemen, OEMs, Global Accounts (GAs)

**Competitor analysis:**

You'll discover your company's competitive advantage – the reason customers do business with you instead of your competition. By observing the actions of your competitors, you might learn more about your market. For example, does a successful competitor offer reduced prices in a specific market? If so, what might that tell you about the market's spending habits. If you find that your market is saturated with capable competitors ('red ocean'), you can avoid the costly mistake of selecting a target market without adequate demand for your offer. You can then redirect your efforts toward something that will generate more profit with the existing resources base in your company ('blue ocean strategy').

**Marketing objectives:**

Meeting marketing objectives should lead to sales. (If not, you need to set different marketing objectives). They should be clear, measurable, and have a stated time frame for achievement.

With other words the objectives should follow the SMART-concept: **S**pecific, **M**easurable, **A**chievable, **R**ealistic, **T**imeable

Setting your marketing objectives and finalizing the remaining components of your marketing plan may serve as a reality check: Do you have the resources and competences necessary to accomplish your objectives?

Example: Increase market share in target market from now ($t_0$) 5% to 15% in three years ($t_3$) – Is that realistic?

**Entry mode strategy:**

Once the firm has set its target objectives in target markets the next step is to choose the best way to enter the market. The chosen entry mode can be regarded as the first decision level in the vertical chain that will provide distribution to the next actors in the vertical chain at the national level.

Following characteristics are connected to the three types of entry modes (seen from the manufacturer's perspective):

- Export Modes (agent, distributor): Low control, low risk, high flexibility
- Intermediate mode (joint venture, strategic alliance): shared control and risk, split ownership
- Hierarchical modes (Own subsidiary): High control, high risk, low flexibility

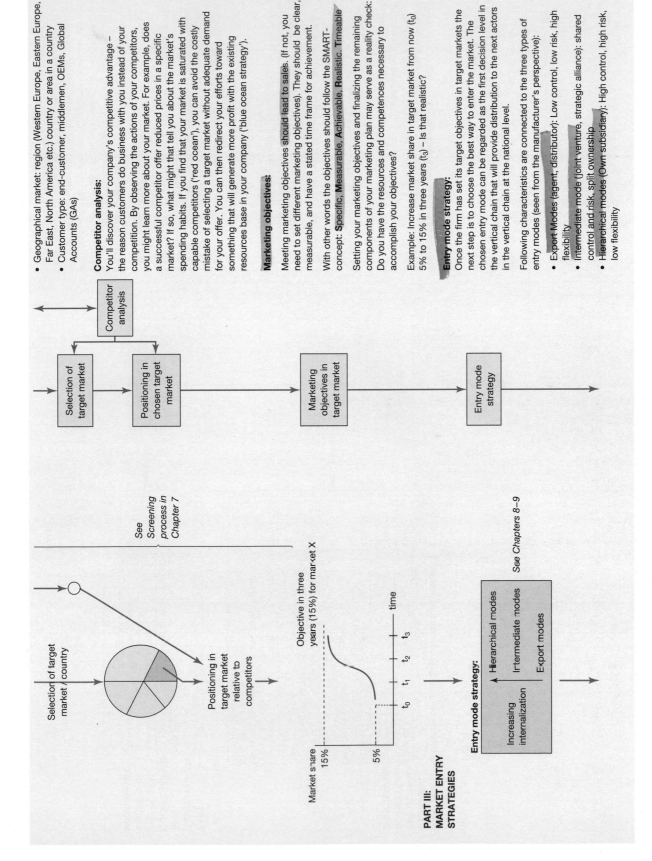

See *Screening process in Chapter 7*

Selection of target market / country

Positioning in target market relative to competitors

Market share

15%

5%

Objective in three years (15%) for market X

$t_0$  $t_1$  $t_2$  $t_3$  time

**PART III: MARKET ENTRY STRATEGIES**

**Entry mode strategy:**

Increasing internalization

Hierarchical modes

Intermediate modes

Export modes

*See Chapters 8–9*

Competitor analysis

Selection of target market

Positioning in chosen target market

Marketing objectives in target market

Entry mode strategy

Figure 1.1 continued

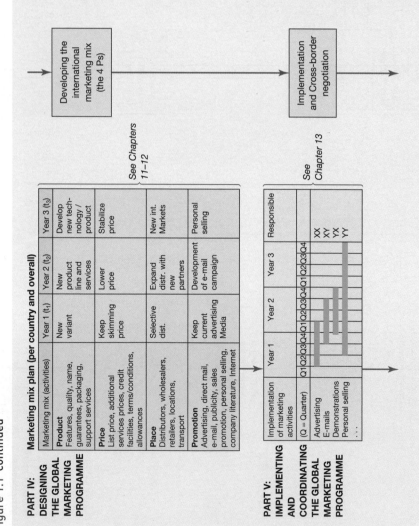

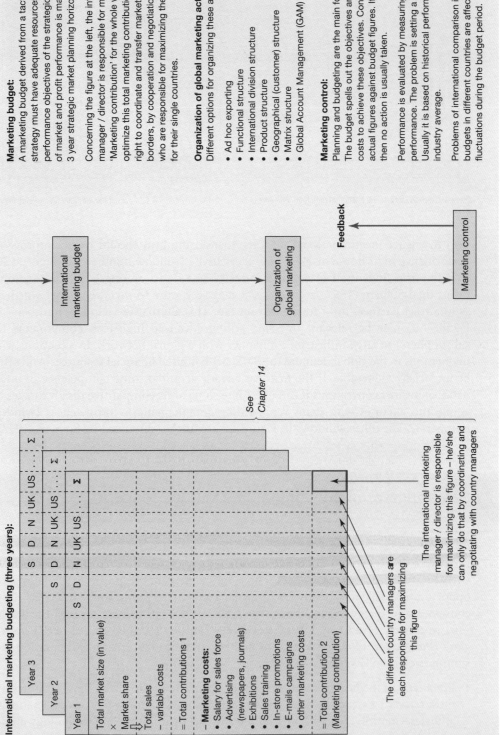

**Marketing budget:**

A marketing budget derived from a tactical marketing strategy must have adequate resources allocated to meet the performance objectives of the strategic market plan. An estimate of market and profit performance is made for each year of a 3 year strategic market planning horizon.

Concerning the figure at the left, the international marketing manager / director is responsible for maximizing the total 'Marketing contribution' for the whole world ($\Sigma$). In order to optimize this total marketing contribution ($\Sigma$), this person has the right to coordinate and transfer marketing resources across borders, by cooperation and negotiation with country managers, who are responsible for maximizing the 'Marketing contribution' for their single countries.

**Organization of global marketing activities:**

Different options for organizing these activities:

- Ad hoc exporting
- Functional structure
- International division structure
- Product structure
- Geographical (customer) structure
- Matrix structure
- Global Account Management (GAM)

**Marketing control:**

Planning and budgeting are the main formal control methods. The budget spells out the objectives and necessary marketing costs to achieve these objectives. Control consists of measuring actual figures against budget figures. If there is tolerable variance then no action is usually taken.

Performance is evaluated by measuring actual against planned performance. The problem is setting a performance standard. Usually it is based on historical performance with some kind of industry average.

Problems of international comparison inevitably occur like how budgets in different countries are affected by currency fluctuations during the budget period.

Figure 1.2  The nine strategic windows

| | | Industry globalism | | |
|---|---|---|---|---|
| | | *Local* | *Potentially global* | *Global* |
| **Preparedness for internationalization** | *Mature* | 3.   Enter new business | 6.   Prepare for globalization | 9. Strengthen your global position |
| | *Adolescent* | 2. Consolidate your export markets | 5.   Consider expansion in international markets | 8.   Seek global alliances |
| | *Immature* | 1.   Stay at home | 4.   Seek niches in international markets | 7.   Prepare for a buyout |

Source: Solberg, 1997, p. 11. Reprinted with kind permission. In the original article Solberg has used the concept 'globality' instead of 'globalism'.

**SMEs**
SME occurs commonly in the EU and in international organizations. The EU categorizes companies with fewer than 50 employees as 'small', and those with fewer than 250 as 'medium'. In the EU, SMEs (250 employees and less) comprise approximately 99 per cent of all firms.

firm to engage in international markets. Instead the firm should try to improve its performance in its home market. This alternative is window number 1 in Figure 1.2.

If the firm finds itself in a global industry as a dwarf among large multinational firms, then Solberg (1997) argues that it may seek ways to increase its net worth so as to attract partners for a future buyout bid. This alternative (window number 7 in Figure 1.2) may be relevant to SMEs selling advanced high-tech components (as subsuppliers) to large industrial companies with a global network. In situations with fluctuations in the global demand the SME (with limited financial resources) will often be financially vulnerable. If the firm has already acquired some competence in international business operations it can overcome some of its competitive disadvantages by going into alliances with firms representing complementary competences (window number 8). The other windows in Figure 1.2 are further discussed by Solberg (1997).

## 1.3   Development of the 'global marketing' concept

Basically 'global marketing' consists of finding and satisfying global customer needs better than the competition, and of coordinating marketing activities within the constraints of the global environment. The form of the firm's response to global market opportunities depends greatly on the management's assumptions or beliefs, both conscious and unconscious, about the nature of doing business around the world. This worldview of a firm's business activities can be described as the EPRG framework (Perlmutter, 1969; Chakravarthy and Perlmutter, 1985): its four orientations are summarized as follows:

1 *Ethnocentric*: the home country is superior and the needs of the home country are most relevant. Essentially headquarters extends ways of doing business to its foreign affiliates. Controls are highly centralized and the organization and technology implemented in foreign locations will essentially be the same as in the home country.

2 *Polycentric* (multidomestic): each country is unique and therefore should be targeted in a different way. The polycentric enterprise recognizes that there are different conditions of production and marketing in different locations and tries to adapt to those different conditions in order to maximize profits in each location. The control with affiliates is highly decentralized and communication between headquarters and affiliates is limited.

3 R*egiocentric*: the world consists of regions (e.g. Europe, Asia, the Middle East). The firm tries to integrate and coordinate its marketing programme within regions, but not across them.

4 G*eocentric* (global): the world is getting smaller and smaller. The firm may offer global product concepts but with local adaptation ('think global, act local').

The regio- and geocentric firm (in contrast to the ethnocentric and polycentric) seeks to organize and integrate production and marketing on a regional or global scale. Each international unit is an essential part of the overall multinational network, and communications and controls between headquarters and affiliates are less top-down than in the case of the ethnocentric firm.

This leads us to a definition of global marketing:

Global marketing is defined as the firm's commitment to coordinate its marketing activities across national boundaries in order to find and satisfy global customer needs better than the competition. This implies that the firm is able to:

- develop a global marketing strategy, based on similarities and differences between markets;
- exploit the knowledge of the headquarters (home organization) through worldwide diffusion (learning) and adaptations;
- transfer knowledge and 'best practices' from any of its markets and use them in other international markets.

There follows an explanation of some key terms:

- *Coordinate its marketing activities*: coordinating and integrating marketing strategies and implementing them across global markets, which involves centralization, delegation, standardization and local responsiveness.
- *Find global customer needs*: this involves carrying out international marketing research and analysing market segments, as well as seeking to understand similarities and differences in customer groups across countries.
- *Satisfy global customers*: adapting products, services and elements of the marketing mix to satisfy different customer needs across countries and regions.
- *Being better than the competition*: assessing, monitoring and responding to global competition by offering better value, low prices, high quality, superior distribution, great advertising strategies or superior brand image.

The second part of the global marketing definition is also illustrated in Figure 1.3 and further commented on below.

This global marketing strategy strives to achieve the slogan, 'think globally but act locally' (the so-called 'glocalization' framework), through dynamic interdependence between headquarters and subsidiaries. Organizations following such a strategy coordinate their efforts, ensuring local flexibility while exploiting the benefits of global integration and efficiencies, as well as ensuring worldwide diffusion of innovation. A key element in knowledge management is the continuous learning from experiences. In practical terms, the aim of knowledge management as a learning-focused activity across borders is to keep track of valuable capabilities used in one market that could

**Glocalization**
The development and selling of products or services intended for the global market, but adapted to suit local culture and behaviour. (Think globally, act locally.)

Figure 1.3 The principle of transferring knowledge and learning across borders

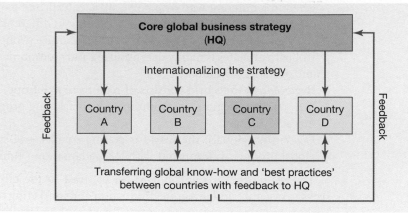

be used elsewhere (in other geographic markets), so that firms can continually update their knowledge. This is also illustrated in Figure 1.3 with the transfer of knowledge and 'best practices' from market to market. However, knowledge developed and used in one cultural context is not always easily transferred to another. The lack of personal relationships, the absence of trust and 'cultural distance', all conspire to create resistance, frictions and misunderstandings in cross-cultural knowledge management.

With globalization becoming a centrepiece in the business strategy of many firms – be they engaged in product development or providing services – the ability to manage the 'global knowledge engine' to achieve a competitive edge in today's knowledge-intensive economy is one of the keys to sustainable competitiveness. But in the context of global marketing the management of knowledge is *de facto* a cross-cultural activity, whose key task is to foster and continually upgrade collaborative cross-cultural learning (this will be further discussed in Chapter 14). Of course, the kind and/or type of knowledge that is strategic for an organization and which needs to be managed for competitiveness varies depending on the business context and the value of different types of knowledge associated with it.

## 1.4  Forces for 'global integration' and 'market responsiveness'

In Figure 1.4 it is assumed that SMEs (small and medium-sized enterprises) and LSEs (large-scale enterprises) are learning from each other.

The consequence of both movements may be an action-oriented approach, where firms use the strengths of both orientations. The following section will discuss the differences in the starting points of LSEs and SMEs in Figure 1.4. The result of the convergence movement of LSEs and SMEs into the upper-right corner can be illustrated by Figure 1.4.

An example of a LSEs movement from 'left' to 'right' is given in Figure 1.4, where McDonalds has adapted its menus to the local food cultures. SMEs have traditionally been strong on 'high degree of responsiveness', but their tendency to decentralization and local decision making has made them more vulnerable to a low degree of coordination across borders (which on the contrary is the strength of LSEs).

The terms 'glocal strategy' and 'glocalization' have been introduced to reflect and combine the two dimensions in Figure 1.4: 'Globalization' (*y*-axis) and 'Localization' (*x*-axis).

**Figure 1.4** The global integration/market responsiveness grid: the future orientation of LSEs and SMEs

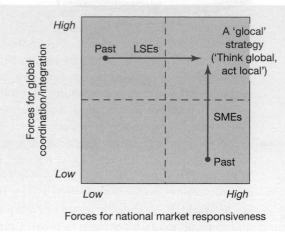

The glocal strategy approach reflects the aspirations of a global integrated strategy, while recognizing the importance of local adaptations/market responsiveness. In this way 'glocalization' tries to optimize the 'balance' between standardization and adaptation of the firm's international marketing activities (Svensson, 2001; Svensson, 2002).

First let us try to explain the underlying forces for global coordination/global integration and market responsiveness in Figure 1.4:

**Global integration**
Recognizing the similarities between international markets and integrating them into the overall global strategy.

**Market responsiveness**
Responding to each market's needs and wants.

## Forces for 'global coordination/integration'

In the shift towards integrated global marketing, greater importance will be attached to transnational similarities for target markets across national borders and less on cross-national differences. The major drivers for this shift are as follows (Sheth and Parvatiyar, 2001; Segal-Horn, 2002):

- *Removal of trade barriers (deregulation).* Removal of historic barriers, both tariff (such as import taxes) and non-tariff (such as safety regulations), which have constituted barriers to trade across national boundaries. Deregulation has occurred at all levels: national, regional (within national trading blocs) and international. Thus deregulation has an impact on globalization since it reduces the time, costs and complexity involved in trading across boundaries.
- *Global accounts/customers.* As customers become global and rationalize their procurement activities they demand suppliers provide them with global services to meet their unique global needs. Often this may consist of global delivery of products, assured supply and service systems, uniform characteristics and global pricing. Several LSEs such as IBM, Boeing, IKEA, Siemens and ABB make such 'global' demands on their smaller suppliers, typical SMEs. For these SMEs managing such global accounts requires cross-functional customer teams, in order to deploy quality consistency across all functional units.
- *Relationship management/network organization.* As we move towards global markets it is becoming increasingly necessary to rely on a network of relationships with external organizations; for example, customer and supplier relationships to pre-empt competition. The firm may also have to work with internal units (e.g. sales subsidiaries) located in many and various parts of the world. Business alliances and network relationships help to reduce market uncertainties, particularly in the

context of rapidly converging technologies and the need for higher amounts of resources to cover global markets. However, networked organizations need more coordination and communication.

- *Standardized worldwide technology.* Earlier differences in world market demand were due to the fact that advanced technological products were primarily developed for the defence and government sectors before being scaled down for consumer applications. However, today the desire for gaining scale and scope in production is so high that worldwide availability of products and services should escalate. As a consequence we may witness more homogeneity in the demand and usage of consumer electronics across nations.

- *Worldwide markets.* The concept of 'diffusions of innovations' from the home country to the rest of the world tend to be replaced by the concept of worldwide markets. Worldwide markets are likely to develop because they can rely on world demographics. For example, if a marketer targets its products or services to the teenagers of the world, it is relatively easy to develop a worldwide strategy for that segment and draw up operational plans to provide target market coverage on a global basis. This is becoming increasingly evident in soft drinks, clothing and sports shoes, especially in the Internet economy.

- *'Global village'.* The term 'global village' refers to the phenomenon in which the world's population shares commonly recognized cultural symbols. The business consequence of this is that similar products and similar services can be sold to similar groups of customers in almost any country in the world. Cultural homogenization therefore implies the potential for the worldwide convergence of markets and the emergence of a global marketplace, in which brands such as Coke, Nike and Levi's are universally aspired to.

- *Worldwide communication.* New Internet-based 'low-cost' communication methods (e-mailing, e-commerce, etc.) ease communication and trade across different parts of the world. As a result customers within national markets are able to buy similar products and similar services across parts of the world.

- *Global cost drivers.* These are categorized as 'economies of scale' and 'economies of scope'.

## Forces for 'market responsiveness'

These are as follows:

- *Cultural differences.* Despite the 'global village' cultural diversity clearly continues. Cultural differences often pose major difficulties in international negotiations and marketing management. These cultural differences reflect differences in personal values and in the assumptions people make about how business is organized. Every culture has its opposing values. Markets are people, not products. There may be global products, but there are not global people.

- *Regionalism/protectionism.* Regionalism is the grouping of countries into regional clusters based on geographic proximity. These regional clusters (such as the European Union or NAFTA) have formed regional trading blocs, which may represent a significant blockage to globalization, since regional trade is often seen as incompatible with global trade. In this case, trade barriers that are removed from individual countries are simply reproduced for a region and a set of countries. Thus all trading blocs create outsiders as well as insiders. Therefore one may argue that regionalism results in a situation where protectionism reappears around regions rather than individual countries.

**Deglobalization**
Moving away from the globalization trends and regarding each market as special, with its own economy, culture and religion.

*trend.* More than 2,500 years ago the Greek historian Herodotus (based on observations) claimed that everyone believes their native customs and religion are the best. Current movements in Arab countries, the big demonstrations accompanying conferences such as the World Economic Forum in Davos, or the World Trade Organization (WTO) meetings show that there could be a return to old values, promoting barriers to the further success of globalization. Rhetorical words such as 'McDonaldization' and 'Coca-Colonization' describe in a simple way fears of US cultural imperialism.

Exhibit 2.3 (p. 47) shows an example of British Telecommunications' (BTs) experience with de-internationalization of their American and Asian strategy (Gardiner and Turner, 2007).

Whether or not 11 September 2001 means that globalization will continue is debatable. Quelch (2002) argues that it will, because 11 September is motivating greater cross-border cooperation among national governments on security matters, and this cooperation will reinforce interaction in other areas.

---

## Exhibit 1.1 McDonald's is moving towards a higher degree of market responsiveness

McDonald's (www.mcdonalds.com) has now expanded to about 30,000 restaurants in over 100 countries. Executives at the headquarters of the McDonald's Corp. in Oak Brook, Illinois, have learned that despite the cost/savings inherent in standardization, success is often about being able to adapt to the local environment. Here are some examples.

### Japan

McDonald's first restaurant in Japan opened during 1971. At that time fast-food here was either a bowl of noodles or miso soup.

With its first mover advantage, McDonald's kept its lead in Japan. By 1997 McDonald's had over 1,000 outlets across that nation, and these sold more food in Japan than any other restaurant company. This includes 500 million burgers per annum.

Among the offerings of McDonald's Co. (Japan) Ltd are chicken tatsuta, teriyaki chicken, and the Teriyaki McBurger. Burgers are garnished with a fried egg. Beverages include iced coffee and corn soup.

McDonald's in Japan imports about 70 per cent of its food needs, including pickles from the United States and beef patties from Australia. High volumes facilitate bargaining with suppliers, in order to guarantee sourcing at a low cost.

Japan Tamago Burger

### India

McDonald's, which now has seven restaurants in India, was launched there in 1996. It has had to deal with a market that is 40 per cent vegetarian; with an aversion to either beef or pork among meateaters; with a hostility to frozen meat and fish; and with the general Indian fondness for spice with everything.

The Big Mac was replaced by the Maharaja Mac, made from mutton, and also on offer were vegetarian rice-patties flavoured with vegetables and spice.

### Other countries

In tropical markets, guava juice was added to the McDonald's product line. In Germany, McDonald's did well selling beer as well as

Rice Burger

McCroissants. Bananafruit pies became popular in Latin America and McSpaghetti noodles became a favourite in the Philippines. In Thailand, McDonald's introduced the Samurai Pork Burger with sweet sauce. Meanwhile, McDonald's in New Zealand launched the Kiwiburger served with beetroot sauce and optional apricot pie.

In Singapore, where fries came to be served with chilli sauce, the Kiasuburger chicken breakfast became a bestseller. Singapore was among the first markets in which McDonald's introduced delivery service.

As indicated, McDonald's has achieved 'economies of scale' and cost savings through standardization and in its packaging. In 2003, McDonald's announced that all its restaurants – 30,000 in over 100 countries – would soon be adopting the same brand packaging for menu items. According to a company press release, the new packaging would feature photographs of real people doing things they enjoy, such as listening to music, playing soccer and reading to their children.

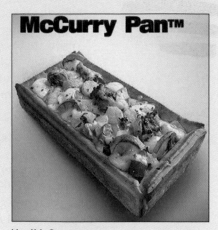

VegiMcCurry

McDonald's global chief marketing officer was quoted as saying, 'It is the first time in our history that a single set of brand packaging, with a single brand message, will be used concurrently around the world.' Two years later, in 2005, the company had to pull back when it announced plans to *localize* its packages (Frost, 2006).

Source: Adapted from a variety of public media. Images reprinted by permission of McDonald's Corporation.

## 1.5 The value chain as a framework for identifying international competitive advantage

### The concept of the value chain

**Value chain**
A categorization of the firm's activities providing value for the customers and profit for the company.

The value chain shown in Figure 1.5 provides a systematic means of displaying and categorizing activities. The activities performed by a firm in any industry can be grouped into the eight generic categories shown.

At each stage of the value chain there exists an opportunity to contribute positively to the firm's competitive strategy by performing some activity or process in a way that is better and/or different than the competitors' offer, and so provide some uniqueness or advantage. If a firm attains such a competitive advantage, which is sustainable, defensible, profitable and valued by the market, then it may earn high rates of return, even though the industry structure may be unfavourable and the average profitability of the industry modest.

In competitive terms, value is the amount that buyers are willing to pay for what a firm provides them with (perceived value). A firm is profitable if the value it commands exceeds the costs involved in creating the product. Creating value for buyers that exceeds the cost of doing so is the goal of any generic strategy. Value, instead of cost, must be used in analysing competitive position, since firms often deliberately raise their costs in order to command a premium price via differentiation. The concept of buyers' perceived value will be discussed further in Chapter 4.

The value chain displays total value and consists of value activities and margin. Value activities are the physically and technologically distinct activities that a firm performs. These are the building blocks by which a firm creates a product valuable to its

Figure 1.5 The value chain

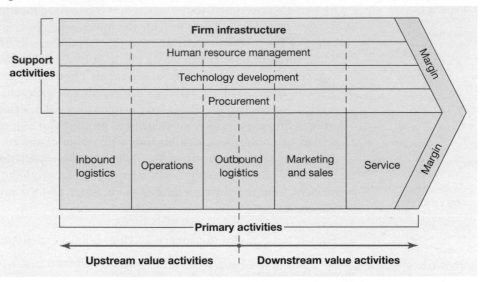

buyers. Margin is the difference between total value (price) and the collective cost of performing the value activities.

Competitive advantage is a function of either providing comparable buyer value more efficiently than competitors (lower cost), or performing activities at comparable cost but in unique ways that create more customer value than the competitors are able to offer and, hence, command a premium price (differentiation). The firm might be able to identify elements of the value chain that are not worth the costs. These can then be unbundled and produced outside the firm (outsourced) at a lower price.

Value activities can be divided into two broad types, primary activities and support activities. *Primary activities*, listed along the bottom of Figure 1.5, are the activities involved in the physical creation of the product, its sale and transfer to the buyer, as well as after-sales assistance. In any firm, primary activities can be divided into the five generic categories shown in the figure. *Support activities* support the primary activities and each other by providing purchased inputs, technology, human resources and various firm-wide functions. The dotted lines reflect the fact that procurement, technology development and human resource management can be associated with specific primary activities as well as supporting the entire chain. Firm infrastructure is not associated with particular primary activities, but supports the entire chain.

## Primary activities

The primary activities of the organization are grouped into five main areas: inbound logistics, operations, outbound logistics, marketing and sales, and service as follows:

1 *Inbound logistics.* The activities concerned with receiving, storing and distributing the inputs to the product/service. These include materials, handling, stock control, transport, etc.
2 *Operations.* The transformation of these various inputs into the final product or service: machining, packaging, assembly, testing, etc.
3 *Outbound logistics.* The collection, storage and distribution of the product to customers. For tangible products this would involve warehousing, material handling,

transport, etc.; in the case of services it may be more concerned with arrangements for bringing customers to the service if it is in a fixed location (e.g. sports events).

4 *Marketing and sales.* These provide the means whereby consumers/users are made aware of the product/service and are able to purchase it. This would include sales administration, advertising, selling, etc. In public services, communication networks that help users access a particular service are often important.

5 *Services.* These are all the activities that enhance or maintain the value of a product/service. Asugman *et al.* (1997) have defined after-sales service as 'those activities in which a firm engages after purchase of its product that minimize potential problems related to product use, and maximize the value of the consumption experience'. After-sales service consists of the following: the installation and start-up of the purchased product, the provision of spare parts for products, the provision of repair services, technical advice regarding the product, and the provision and support of warranties.

Each of these groups of primary activities is linked to support activities.

## Support activities

These can be divided into four areas:

1 *Procurement.* This refers to the process of acquiring the various resource inputs to the primary activities (not to the resources themselves). As such, it occurs in many parts of the organization.

2 *Technology development.* All value activities have a 'technology', even if it is simply 'know-how'. The key technologies may be concerned directly with the product (e.g. R&D, product design) or with processes (e.g. process development) or with a particular resource (e.g. raw material improvements).

3 *Human resource management.* This is a particularly important area that transcends all primary activities. It is concerned with the activities involved in recruiting, training, developing and rewarding people within the organization.

4 *Infrastructure.* The systems of planning, finance, quality control, etc., are crucially important to an organization's strategic capability in all primary activities. Infrastructure also consists of the structures and routines of the organization that sustain its culture.

As indicated in Figure 1.5, a distinction is also made between the production-oriented, 'upstream' activities and the more marketing-oriented, 'downstream' activities.

Having looked at Porter's original value chain model, a simplified version will be used in most parts of this book (Figure 1.6). This simplified version is characterized by the fact that it contains only the primary activities of the firm.

Although value activities are the building blocks of competitive advantage, the value chain is not a collection of independent activities, but a system of interdependent activities. Value activity is related by horizontal linkages within the value chain. Linkages are relationships between the way in which one value activity is dependent on the performance of another.

Furthermore, the chronological order of the activities in the value chain is not always as illustrated in Figure 1.6. In companies where orders are placed before production of the final product (build-to-order, e.g. seen at Dell) the sales and marketing function takes place before production.

In understanding the competitive advantage of an organization the strategic importance of the following types of linkage should be analysed in order to assess how they contribute to cost reduction or value added. There are two kinds of linkage:

Figure 1.6 A 'simplified' version of the value chain

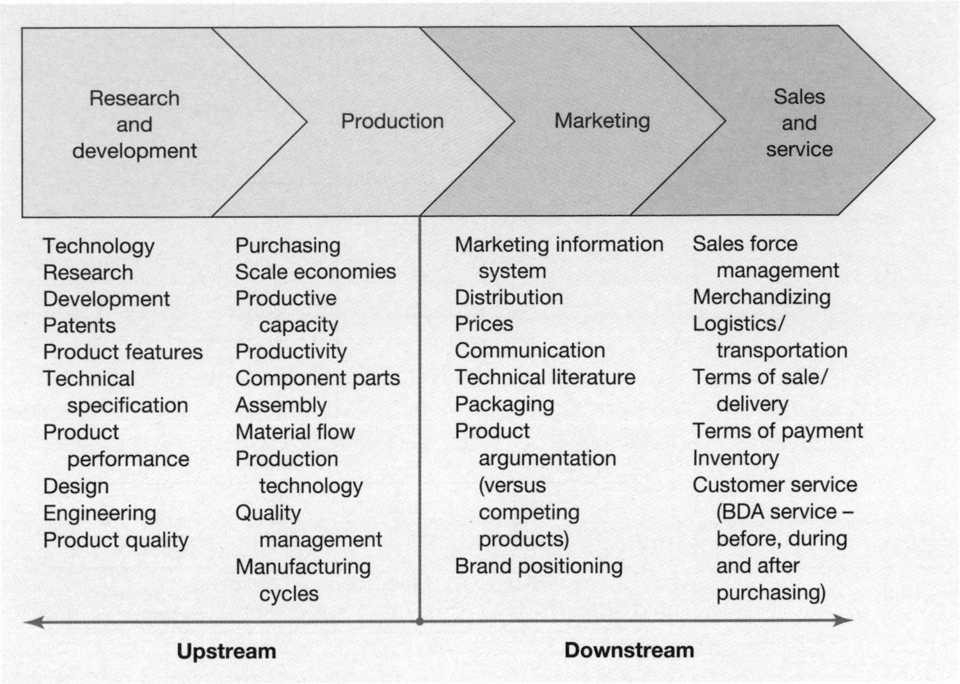

| Research and development | Production | Marketing | Sales and service |
|---|---|---|---|
| Technology | Purchasing | Marketing information | Sales force |
| Research | Scale economies | system | management |
| Development | Productive | Distribution | Merchandizing |
| Patents | capacity | Prices | Logistics/ |
| Product features | Productivity | Communication | transportation |
| Technical | Component parts | Technical literature | Terms of sale/ |
| specification | Assembly | Packaging | delivery |
| Product | Material flow | Product | Terms of payment |
| performance | Production | argumentation | Inventory |
| Design | technology | (versus | Customer service |
| Engineering | Quality | competing | (BDA service – |
| Product quality | management | products) | before, during |
| | Manufacturing | Brand positioning | and after |
| | cycles | | purchasing) |

**Upstream** ← → **Downstream**

1  *internal linkages* between activities within the same value chain, but perhaps on different planning levels within the firm;
2  *external linkages* between different value chains 'owned' by the different actors in the total value system.

## Internal linkages

There may be important links between the primary activities. In particular, choices will have been made about these relationships and how they influence value creation and strategic capability. For example, a decision to hold high levels of finished stock might ease production scheduling problems and provide a faster response time to the customer. However, it will probably add to the overall cost of operations. An assessment needs to be made of whether the added value of 'stocking' is greater than the added cost. Suboptimization of the single value chain activities should be avoided. It is easy to miss this point in an analysis if, for example, the marketing activities and operations are assessed separately. The operations may look good because they are geared to high-volume, low-variety, low-unit-cost production. However, at the same time the marketing team may be selling quickness, flexibility and variety to the customers. When put together these two potential strengths are weaknesses because they are not in harmony, which is what a value chain requires. The link between a primary activity and a support activity may be the basis of competitive advantage. For example, an organization may have a unique system for procuring materials. Many international hotels and travel companies use their computer systems to provide immediate 'real-time' quotations and bookings worldwide from local access points.

As a supplement to comments about the linkages between the different activities, it is also relevant to regard the value chain (illustrated in Figure 1.6 in a simplified form) as a thoroughgoing model on all three planning levels in the organization.

Figure 1.7 The value chain in relation to the strategic pyramid

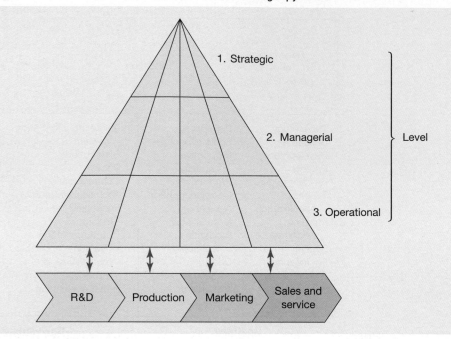

In purely conceptual terms, a firm can be described as a pyramid as illustrated in Figure 1.7. It consists of an intricate conglomeration of decision and activity levels, having three distinct levels, but the main value chain activities are connected to all three strategic levels in the firm:

1 The *strategic level* is responsible for formulation of the firm's mission statement, determining objectives, identifying the resources that will be required if the firm is to attain its objectives, and selecting the most appropriate corporate strategy for the firm to pursue.

2 The *managerial level* has the task of translating corporate objectives into functional and/or unit objectives and ensuring that resources placed at its disposal (e.g. in the marketing department) are used effectively in the pursuit of those activities that will make the achievement of the firm's goals possible.

3 The *operational level* is responsible for the effective performance of the tasks that underlie the achievement of unit/functional objectives. The achievement of operational objectives is what enables the firm to achieve its managerial and strategic aims. All three levels are interdependent, and clarity of purpose from the top enables everybody in the firm to work in an integrated fashion towards a common aim.

### External linkages

One of the key features of most industries is that a single organization rarely undertakes all value activities from product design to distribution to the final consumer. There is usually a specialization of roles, and any single organization usually participates in the wider value system that creates a product or service. In understanding how value is created it is not enough to look at the firm's internal value chain alone. Much of the value creation will occur in the supply and distribution chains, and this whole process needs to be analysed and understood.

Suppliers have value chains that create and deliver the purchased inputs used in a firm's chain (the upstream part of the value chain). Suppliers not only deliver a product, but can also influence a firm's performance in many other ways. For example Benetton, the Italian fashion company, managed to sustain an elaborate network of suppliers, agents and independent retail outlets as the basis of its rapid and successful international development during the 1970s and 1980s.

In addition, products pass through the value chain channels on their way to the buyer. Channels perform additional activities that affect the buyer and influence the firm's own activities. A firm's product eventually becomes part of its buyer's value chain. The ultimate basis for differentiation is a firm and its product's role in the buyer's value chain, which is determined by buyer needs. Gaining and sustaining competitive advantage depends on understanding not only a firm's value chain, but how the firm fits into the overall value system.

There are often circumstances where the overall cost can be reduced (or the value increased) by collaborative arrangements between different organizations in the value system. It will be seen in Chapter 9 that this is often the rationale behind downstream collaborative arrangements, such as joint ventures, subcontracting and outsourcing between different organizations (e.g. sharing technology in the international motor manufacture and electronics industries).

---

**Exhibit 1.2 Pocoyo – upstream-downstream cooperation about globalization of an animated preschool series**

One of the most successful TV-programmes for preschool kids, Pocoyo, was created by Zinkia Entertainment and sold worldwide by Granada Ventures. It is now a global brand and has been sold to 95 countries since it was launched in late 2005. Produced with bright blocks of colour against a stark white background, Pocoyo has been designed to hold the attention of young children.

### Pocoyo

Pocoyo is a young boy with an array of qualities ready to capture the imagination of children, inspiring them to watch, listen and interact. He is a curious enthusiastic little boy in blue. As he explores his world through each story, Pocoyo gets help and on occasion hindrance from his friends Loula, Pato, Elly and Sleepy Bird.

Source: Pocoyo TM & © 2005 Zinkia Entertainment S.L. Licensed by Granada Ventures.

Pocoyo has at its core a fascinating concept – one of learning through laughter. Clinical studies have shown that laughter not only increases the enjoyment and engagement of children in the programme, but also is proven to increase learning by 15 per cent. By working closely with behavioural psychologists during programme development, Pocoyo uses simple and effective visual jokes that help children to discover magic and humour in the simplest of things. And far from painting an idealized version of childhood, Pocoyo is sometimes moody, noisy and miserable – just like a real pre-schooler.

### The value chain of Pocoyo

As illustrated in Pocoyo's value chain (see Figure 1.8) Zinkia Entertainment is taking care of the development and production of the Pocoyo series (upstream functions) whereas Granada Ventures takes care of global licensing and publishing rights (downstream functions).

Zinkia Entertainment is a company founded in 2001. Located in Madrid, Spain, its main focus is to create animated series for TV and games for mobile devices and for game platforms. The company has more than 100 employees and its series have been sold in more than 95 countries worldwide. It is a creative factory

Exhibit 1.2 continued

Figure 1.8 **The Pocoyo value chain**

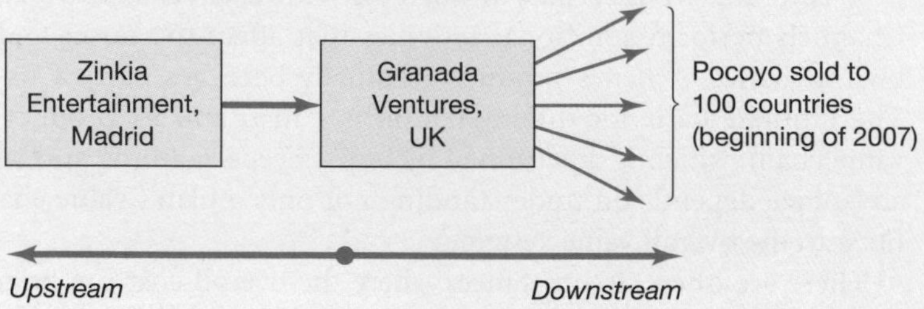

producing audiovisual content, focusing on animation and cinematic documentaries as well as interactive content for online communities, consoles and multi-player mobile games. Since the company was established, Zinkia's projects include, among others, Pocoyo (52 × 7 minutes), a 3D animated pre-school series. In June 2006, Pocoyo was awarded the Cristal award for the 'Best TV Series in the world' at the 30th International Festival of Annecy.

Zinkia Entertainment's partner in the Pocoyo value chain is Granada Ventures, the merchandise, licensing and publishing division of the UK-based television channel ITV plc. Established in October 2003, following the merger of Granada and Carlton, the company's remit is to drive secondary revenue streams for the corporation by moving brands beyond broadcast by selling them worldwide on a licensing basis, mainly to other TV channels. The company currently owns worldwide licensing and publishing rights of almost 1,000 products and 3,000 DVD titles in television, film and sports. This includes brands such as Pocoyo and Hell's Kitchen as well as established brands such as 'I'm A Celebrity . . . Get Me Out Of Here!'

## Cultural issues in the globalization of Pocoyo

Normally global branding is comprehensive and the cultural demands of the market are difficult to define. However it seems that the core themes of Pocoyo – learning, gentle humour, visual stimulus and play – cross all national borders.

Pocoyo was developed in Spain, with a great deal of input from the UK. In the original rushes, Pocoyo was often seen with a dummy in his mouth, which caused a few alarm bells to ring in Britain. The Madrid team had not even begun to consider that this might be the cause of any controversy, but in line with current cultural queries on the parental right and wrongs of using a 'pacifier' in other parts of the globe, the dummy had to go.

## Worldwide brand extensions

Brand extensions into merchandise are equally important for ensuring Pocoyo's world success and longevity. Granada Ventures has been able to give Pocoyo a life off-screen with books, bath toys and clothing. Children can play with the character, along with their parents and peers, around the clock. This creates a virtuous brand circle, increasing loyalty and affection.

Sources: Donohoe, G. (2006) 'How to reach children in every nation', *Brand Strategy*, June, p. 10; www.zinkia.com/; www.granadaventures.co.uk/.

# Internationalizing the value chain

## International configuration and coordination of activities

All internationally oriented firms must consider an eventual internationalization of the value chain's functions. The firm must decide whether the responsibility for the single value chain function is to be moved to the export markets or is best handled centrally from head office. Principally, the value chain function should be carried out where there is the highest competence (and the most cost effectiveness), and this is not necessarily at head office.

Figure 1.9 **Centralizing the upstream activities and decentralizing the downstream activities**

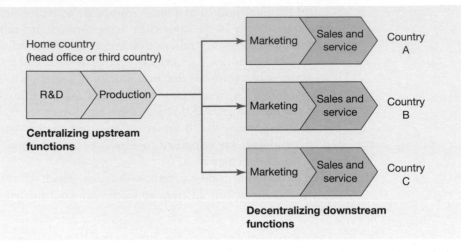

A distinction immediately arises between the activities labelled downstream in Figure 1.6 and those labelled upstream activities. The location of downstream activities, those more related to the buyer, is usually tied to where the buyer is located. If a firm is going to sell in Australia, for example, it must usually provide service in Australia, and it must have salespeople stationed in Australia. In some industries it is possible to have a single sales force that travels to the buyer's country and back again; other specific downstream activities, such as the production of advertising copy, can sometimes also be performed centrally. More typically, however, the firm must locate the capability to perform downstream activities in each of the countries in which it operates. In contrast, upstream activities and support activities are more independent of where the buyer is located (Figure 1.9). However, if the export markets are culturally close to the home market, it may be relevant to control the entire value chain from head office (home market).

This distinction carries some interesting implications. First, downstream activities create competitive advantages that are largely country specific: a firm's reputation, brand name and service network in a country grow largely out of its activities and create entry/mobility barriers largely in that country alone. Competitive advantage in upstream and support activities often grows more out of the entire system of countries in which a firm competes than from its position in any single country.

Second, in industries where downstream activities or other buyer-tied activities are vital to competitive advantage, there tends to be a more multidomestic pattern of international competition. In many service industries, for example, not only downstream activities but frequently upstream activities are tied to buyer location, and global strategies are comparatively less common. In industries where upstream and support activities such as technology development and operations are crucial to competitive advantage, global competition is more common. For example, there may be a large need in firms to centralize and coordinate the production function worldwide to be able to create rational production units that are able to exploit economies of scale. Today it is very popular among companies to outsource production to the Far East, e.g. China.

Furthermore, as customers increasingly join regional cooperative buying organizations, it is becoming more and more difficult to sustain a price differentiation across markets. This will put pressure on the firm to coordinate a European price policy. This will be discussed further in Chapter 11.

The distinctive issues of international strategies, in contrast to domestic, can be summarized in two key dimensions of how a firm competes internationally. The first is called the *configuration* of a firm's worldwide activities, or the location in the world where each activity in the value chain is performed, including the number of places. For example, a company can locate different parts of its value chain in different places – for instance, factories in China, call centres in India and retail shops in Europe. IBM is an example of a company that exploit wage differentials by increasing the number of employees in India from 9,000 in 2004 to 50,000 by mid-2007 and by planning for massive additional growth. Most of these employees are in IBM Global Services, the part of the company that is growing fastest but has the lowest margins – which the Indian employees are supposed to improve, by reducing (wage) costs rather than raising prices (Ghemawat, 2007).

The second dimension is called *coordination*, which refers to how identical or linked activities performed in different countries are coordinated with each other (Porter, 1986).

## 1.6   Value shop and the 'service value chain'

Michael Porter's value-chain model claims to identify the sequence of key generic activities that businesses perform in order to generate value for customers. Since its introduction in 1985, this model has dominated the thinking of business executives. Yet a growing number of services businesses, including banks, hospitals, insurance companies, business consulting services and telecommunications companies, have found that the traditional value-chain model does not fit the reality of their service industry sectors. Stabell and Fjeldstad (1998) identified two new models of value creation – value shops and value networks. Fjeldstad and Stabell argue that the value chain is a model for making products, while the value shop is a model for solving customer or client problems in a service environment. The value network is a model for mediating exchanges between customers. Each model utilizes a different set of core activities to create and deliver distinct forms of value to customers.

**Value shops**
A model for solving problems in a service environment. Similar to workshops. Value is created by mobilizing resources and deploying them to solve a specific customer problem.

**Value networks**
The formation of several firms' value chains into a network, where each company contributes a small part to the total value chain.

The main differences between the two types of value chains are illustrated in Table 1.1.

Value shops (as in workshops, not retail stores) create value by mobilizing resources (e.g. people, knowledge and skills) and deploying them to solve specific problems such as curing an illness, delivering airline services to the passengers or delivering a solution to a business problem. Shops are organized around making and executing decisions – identifying and assessing problems or opportunities, developing alternative solutions or approaches, choosing one, executing it and evaluating the results. This model applies to most service-oriented organizations such as building contractors, consultancies and legal organizations. However, it also applies to organizations that are primarily configured to identify and exploit specific market opportunities, such as developing a new drug, drilling a potential oilfield or designing a new aircraft.

Different parts of a typical business may exhibit characteristics of different configurations. For example, production and distribution may resemble a value chain; research and development a value shop.

Value shops make use of specialized knowledge-based systems to support the task of creating solutions to problems. However, the challenge is to provide an integrated set of applications that enable seamless execution across the entire problem-solving or opportunity-exploitation process. Several key technologies and applications are emerging in value shops – many focus on utilizing people and knowledge better.

**Table 1.1 The traditional value chain versus the service value chain**

| Traditional value chain model | Service value chain ('value shop') model |
|---|---|
| Value creation through transformation of inputs (raw material and components) to products. | Value creation through customer problem solving. Value is created by mobilizing resources and activities to resolve a particular and unique customer problem. Customer value is not related to the solution itself but to the value of solving the problem. |
| Sequential process ('first we develop the product, then we produce it, and finally we sell it'). | Cyclical and iterative process. |

| | |
|---|---|
| The traditional value chain consists of primary and support activities: **Primary activities** are directly involved in creating and bringing value to customers: Upstream (product development and production) and downstream activities (marketing and sales and service). **Support activities** that enable and improve the performance of the primary activities are procurement, technology development, human resource management and firm infrastructure. | The **primary activities** of a value shop are: <br> 1 *Problem finding*: Activities associated with the recording, reviewing and formulating of the problem to be solved and choosing the overall approach to solving the problem. <br> 2 *Problem solving*: Activities associated with generating and evaluating alternative solutions. <br> 3 *Choice*: Activities associated with choosing among alternative problem solutions. <br> 4 *Execution*: Activities associated with communicating, organizing, and implementing the chosen solution. <br> 5 *Control and evaluation*: Activities associated with measuring and evaluating to what extent implementation has solved the initial statement. |
| Examples: Production and sales of furniture, consumer food products, electronic products and other mass products. | Examples: Banks, hospitals, insurance companies, business consulting services and telecommunications companies. |

Source: Based on Stabell and Fjeldstad (1998).

Groupware, intranets, desktop videoconferencing and shared electronic workspaces enhance communication and collaboration between people, essential to mobilizing people and knowledge across value shops. Integrating project planning with execution is proving crucial, for example, in pharmaceutical development, where bringing a new drug through the long, complex approval process a few months early can mean millions of dollars in revenue. Technologies such as inference engines and neural networks can help to make knowledge about problems and the process for solving them explicit and accessible.

The term 'value network' is widely used but imprecisely defined. It often refers to a group of companies, each specializing in one piece of the value chain, and linked together in some virtual way to create and deliver products and services. Stabell and Fjelstad (1998) define value networks quite differently – not as networks of affiliated companies, but as a business model for a single company that mediates interactions and exchanges across a network of its customers. This model clearly applies best to telecommunications companies, but also to insurance companies and banks, whose business, essentially, is mediating between customers with different financial needs – some saving, some borrowing, for example. Key activities include operating the customer-connecting infrastructure, promoting the network, managing contracts and relationships, and providing services.

Some of the most IT-intensive businesses in the world are value networks – banks, airlines and telecommunications companies, for instance. Most of their technology provides the basic infrastructure of the 'network' to mediate exchanges between customers. But the competitive landscape is now shifting beyond automation and efficient transaction processing to monitoring and exploiting information about customer behaviour.

The aim is to add more value to customer exchanges through better understanding of usage patterns, exchange opportunities, shared interests and so on. Data mining and visualization tools, for example, can be used to identify both positive and negative connections between customers.

Competitive success often depends on more than simply performing your primary model well. It may also require the delivery of additional kinds of complementary value. Adopting attributes of a second value configuration model can be a powerful way to differentiate your value proposition or defend it against competitors pursuing a value model different to your own. It is essential, however, to pursue another model only in ways that leverage the primary model. For example, Harley-Davidson's primary model is the chain – it makes and sells products. Forming the Harley Owners Group (HOG) – a network of customers – added value to the primary model by reinforcing the brand identity, building loyalty, and providing valuable information and feedback about customers' behaviours and preferences. Amazon.com is a value chain like other book distributors, and initially used technology to make the process vastly more efficient. Now, with its book recommendations and special interest groups, it is adding the characteristics of a value network. Our research suggests that the value network in particular offers opportunities for many existing businesses to add more value to their customers, and for new entrants to capture market share from those who offer less value to their customers.

## Combining the 'product value chain' and the 'service value chain'

Blomstermo *et al.* (2006) make a distinction between *hard* and *soft services*. Hard services are those where production and consumption can be decoupled. For example software services can be transferred into a CD or some other tangible medium, which can be mass-produced, making standardization possible. With soft services, where production and consumption occur simultaneously, the customer acts as a coproducer, and decoupling is not viable. The soft-service provider must be present abroad from its first day of foreign operations. Figure 1.10 is mainly valid for soft services, but at the same time in more and more industries we see that physical products and services are combined (see Figure 1.10).

Most product companies offer services to protect or enhance the value of their product businesses. Cisco, for instance, built its installation, maintenance and network-design service business to ensure high-quality product support and to strengthen relationships with enterprise and telecom customers. A company may also find itself drawn into services when it realizes that competitors use its products to offer services of value. If it does nothing, it risks not only the commoditization of its own products – something that is occurring in most product markets, irrespective of the services on offer – but also the loss of customer relationships. To make existing service groups

Figure 1.10 **Combining the 'product value chain' and the 'service value chain'**

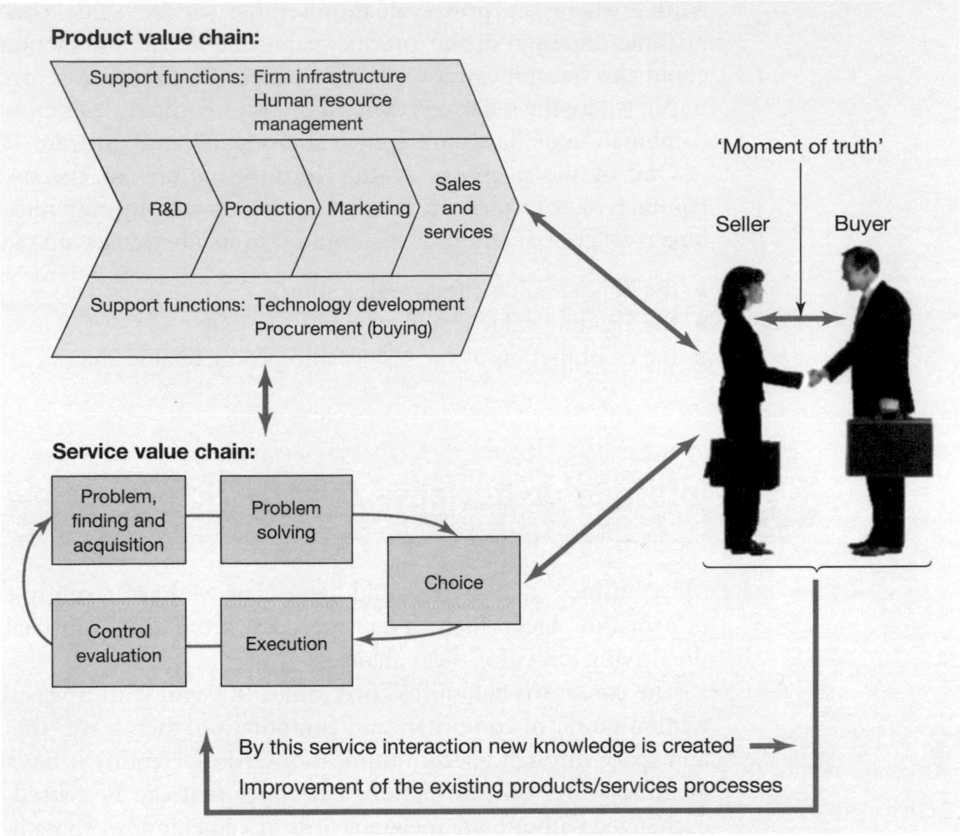

profitable – or to succeed in launching a new embedded service business – executives of product companies must decide whether the primary focus of service units should be to support existing product businesses or to grow as a new and independent platform.

When a company chooses a business design for delivering embedded *services* to customers, it should remember that its strategic intent affects which elements of the delivery life cycle are most important. If the aim is to protect or enhance the *value* of a product, the company should integrate the system for delivering it and the associated *services* in order to promote the development of product designs that simplify the task of *service* (e.g. by using fewer subsystems or integrating diagnostic software). This approach involves minimizing the footprint of *service* delivery and incorporating support into the product whenever possible. If the company wants the *service* business to be an independent growth platform, however, it should focus most of its delivery efforts on constantly reducing unit costs and making the *services* more productive (Auguste *et al.*, 2006).

In the 'moment of truth' (e.g. in a consultancy service situation), the seller represents all the functions of the focal company's 'product' and 'service' value chain – at the same time. The seller (the product and service provider) and the buyer create a service in an interaction process: 'The service is being created and consumed as it is produced.' Good representatives on the seller's side are vital to service brands' successes, being ultimately responsible for delivering the seller's promise. As such a shared understanding of the service brand's values needs to be anchored in their minds and hearts to encourage brand-supporting behaviour. This internal brand-building process becomes more challenging as service brands expand internationally drawing on workers from different global domains.

Figure 1.10 also shows the cyclic nature of the service interaction ('moment of truth') where the post-evaluation of the service value chain gives input for the possible re-design of the 'product value chain'. The interaction shown in Figure 1.10 could also be an illustration or a snapshot of a negotiation process between seller and buyer, where the seller represents a branded company, which is selling its projects as a combination of 'hardware' (physical products) and 'software' (services).

One of the purposes of the 'learning nature' of the overall decision cycle in Figure 1.10 is to pick up the 'best practices' among different kinds of international buyer–seller interactions. This would lead to a better set-up of:

- the 'service value chain' (value shop);
- the 'product value chain';
- the combination of the service and product value chain.

## 1.7 Information business and the virtual value chain

Most business managers would agree that we have recently entered a new era, 'the information age', which differs markedly from the industrial age. What have been the driving forces for these changes?

The consensus has shifted over time. To begin with it was thought to be the automation power of computers and computation; then it was the ability to collapse time and space through telecommunications. More recently it has been seen as the value-creating power of information, a resource that can be reused, shared, distributed or exchanged without any inevitable loss of value; indeed value is sometimes multiplied. Today's fascination with competing on invisible assets means that people now see knowledge and its relationship with intellectual capital as the critical resource, because it underpins innovation and renewal.

**Virtual value chain**
An extension of the conventional value chain, where the information processing itself can create value for customers.

One way of understanding the strategic opportunities and threats of information is to consider the virtual value chain as a supplement to the physical value chain (Figure 1.11).

By introducing the *virtual value chain* Rayport and Sviokla (1996) have made an extension to the conventional value chain model, which treats information as a

Figure 1.11 The virtual value chain as a supplement to the physical value chain

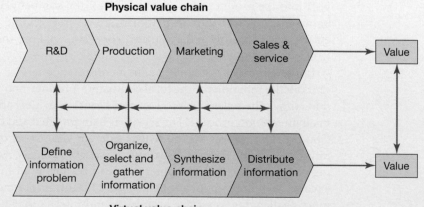

supporting element in the value-adding process. Rayport and Sviokla (1996) show how information in itself can be used to create value.

Fundamentally, there are four ways of using information to create business value (Marchand, 1999):

1 *Managing risks.* In the twentieth century the evolution of risk management stimulated the growth of functions and professions such as finance, accounting, auditing and controlling. These information-intensive functions tend to be major consumers of IT resources and people's time.

2 *Reducing costs.* Here the focus is on using information as efficiently as possible to achieve the outputs required from business processes and transactions. This process view of information management is closely linked with the re-engineering and continuous improvement movements of the 1990s. The common elements are focused on eliminating unnecessary and wasteful steps and activities, especially paperwork and information movements, and then simplifying and, if possible, automating the remaining processes.

3 *Offering products and services.* Here the focus is on knowing one's customers, and sharing information with partners and suppliers to enhance customer satisfaction. Many service and manufacturing companies focus on building relationships with customers and on demand management as ways of using information. Such strategies have led companies to invest in point-of-sale systems, account management, customer profiling and service management systems.

4 *Inventing new products.* Finally, companies can use information to innovate – to invent new products, provide different services and use emerging technologies. Companies such as Intel and Microsoft are learning to operate in 'continuous discovery mode', inventing new products more quickly and using market intelligence to retain a competitive edge. Here, information management is about mobilizing people and collaborative work processes to share information and promote discovery throughout the company.

Every company pursues some combination of the above strategies.

In relation to Figure 1.11 each of the physical value-chain activities might make use of one or all four information-processing stages of the virtual value chain, in order to create extra value for the customer. That is the reason for the horizontal double arrows (in Figure 1.11) between the different physical and virtual value-chain activities. In this way information can be captured at all stages of the physical value chain. Obviously such information can be used to improve performance at each stage of the physical value chain and to coordinate elements across it. However, it can also be analysed and repackaged to build content-based products or to create new lines of businesses.

A company can use its information to reach out to other companies' customers or operations, thereby rearranging the value system of an industry. The result might be that traditional industry sector boundaries disappear. The CEO of Amazon.com, Bezos, clearly sees his business as not in the book-selling business but in the information-broker business.

## 1.8 Summary

*Global marketing* is defined as the firm's commitment to coordinate its marketing activities across national boundaries in order to find and satisfy global customer needs better than the competition does. This implies that the firm is able to:

- develop a global marketing strategy based on similarities and differences between markets;
- exploit the knowledge of the headquarters (home organization) through worldwide diffusion (learning) and adaptations;
- transfer knowledge and 'best practices' from any of its markets and use them in other international markets.

SMEs are often characterized by an entrepreneurial and action-oriented decision-making model, where drastic changes in strategy are possible because decision making is intuitive, sporadic and unstructured. On the other hand SMEs are more flexible than LSEs and are able to react more quickly to sudden changes in the international environment.

However, as a consequence of LSEs often acting as a confederation of SMEs, there seems to be a convergence of the marketing behaviour in SMEs and LSEs towards a market-responsiveness approach.

Porter's original value chain model was introduced as a framework model for major parts of this book. In understanding how value is created it is not enough to look at the firm's internal value chain alone. In most cases the supply and distribution value chains are interconnected, and this whole process needs to be analysed and understood before considering an eventual internationalization of value chain activities. This also involves decisions about configuration and coordination of the worldwide value-chain activities.

As a supplement to the traditional (Porter) value chain, the service value chain (based on the so-called 'value shop' concept) has been introduced. Value shops create value by mobilizing resources (people, knowledge and skills,) and deploying them to solve specific problems. Value shops are organized around making and executing decisions in the specific service interaction situation with a customer – identifying and assessing service problems or opportunities, developing alternative solutions or approaches, choosing one, executing it and evaluating the results. This model applies to most service-oriented organizations.

Many product companies want to succeed with embedded services: as competitive pressures increasingly commoditize product markets, services will become the main differentiator of *value* creation in coming years. However, companies will need a clearer understanding of the strategic rules of this new game – and will have to integrate the rules into their operations – to realize the promise of these fast-growing businesses.

At the end of this chapter the 'virtual value chain' was introduced as a supplement to the 'physical value chain', thus using information to create further business value.

---

CASE STUDY 1.1

# Bubba Gump Shrimp Co.: A US-based restaurant chain is going international

### Background

Originally Bubba Gump Shrimp Co. (hereafter abbreviated to Bubba Gump) started out in 1972 with the launch of Rusti Pelican Restaurants in California, USA. In 1986 Winston Groom published his novel *Forrest Gump*. When the film was launched in 1994, *Forrest Gump* (with Tom Hanks in the title role) immediately became a box office smash hit and later won six Academy Awards.

In 1995 the *Forrest Gump* film makers, Paramount Pictures, approached Rusty Pelican Restaurants, which at the time was looking for developing a concept for a mid-market seafood restaurant. While there was no actual restaurant in the film, the main character, Forrest Gump, ran a shrimp boat business called Bubba Gump Shrimp Co. together with his 'best good friend' Bubba, who wore an iconic hat representing the operation. This served as the launching point for the restaurant brand. Taking on the name of Bubba Gump provided instant brand identification at the consumer level.

In 1996 the restaurant company Bubba Gump Shrimp Co. (holding company) started up in San Clemente as a licensing partnership between the *Forrest Gump* film makers, Paramount Pictures, and Rusty Pelican. The first restaurant opened at Cannery Row in Monterey, California. The promotional material for the opening of Bubba Gump in Cancun (Mexico) is shown above.

Source: © Craig Lovell/Eagle Visions Photography/Alamy.

## The concept

Bubba Gump's own research revealed that the name brought instant recognition and association with the movie. The research showed that there was a 94 per cent unaided awareness of Bubba Gump because of its association with the film. *Forrest Gump* was in the all-time top five grossing films when the concept launched, so the resulting restaurant brand had instant appeal. On the one hand, Bubba Gump learned from its market research that there was an unforced translation from the movie to a restaurant. It made sense in the consumers' minds that such a thing would exist. On the other hand, the restaurant chain also realized that if the brand did not deliver on the quality of the product, it would not have much chance in the market.

The restaurant brand connected with the film property. The theme of Bubba Gump from the film was carried through in decor and menu with items including Bubba's Far Out Dip and Run Across America Sampler, echoing scenes that took place on screen. However, to ensure that it was a brand that could stands on its own, Rusty Pelican's experience of running a seafood restaurant was crucial. The name would bring people in but it would be the restaurant experience – hot food, hot and cold food, cold, and service with a smile in pleasant, clean and interesting surroundings – that would create the brand equity in the long term.

For the Paramount Picture licensing division this has been the single most successful restaurant brand to have emerged from a film property to date. The value has been based on the brand extension after the movie's initial success. It is also worth noting that the success of the restaurants has, in turn, supported the franchise of the film *Forrest Gump* in the marketplace, including sales of DVDs, videos, books and numerous branded products such as the familiar 'box of chocolates'.

The restaurants are positioned in places that have a high footfall of traffic and are very visible, such as the largest shopping malls and tourist destinations in the United States, like Times Square, New York. The typical restaurant sizes vary from 6,300 to 10,000 square feet.

## Importance of the HR policy

One of the most important success factors in a restaurant is the quality of the personnel. Bubba Gump must constantly ask itself what it can do to be a better employer. The following are some of the current initiatives (Berta, 2005):

- Employees who put in more than 30 hours a week are eligible for medical, dental and life insurance.
- They receive one week of vacation after a year and two weeks after two years.
- Hourly employees who become certified trainers keep their benefits even if they drop to part-time status.
- There are retirement plans for salaried workers.
- Managers meet every year in exotic locations for ongoing training and development programmes.
- All managers have regular one-on-one meetings with their immediate supervisors to discuss development goals and management issues.

- Ongoing training and development occurs at all levels of the organization and includes such things as English or Spanish language instruction and self-paced management and leadership development courses.
- Bonuses and recognition programmes also are a standard practice at Bubba Gump.
- Twenty-five per cent of a manager's bonus is based on achieving personal goals, and the rest is based on a store's fiscal performance.
- Each store is given a budget for 'Employee Benefit', which is used to reward and recognize workers.

### Sales and internationalization

The company currently has 35 restaurants (as of May 2008). In the United States the restaurants are company-owned, but abroad the international expansion of Bubba Gump is mainly based on franchising agreements, where Bubba Gump Shrimp Co. (USA) is the franchisor and the local restaurant owners are the franchisees.

The internationalization process started in Osaka, Japan, and continued over the years. In May 2008 Bubba Gump had nine restaurants outside the United States: three in Japan (one in Osaka and two in Tokyo); one in Indonesia (Bali); one in the Philippines (Makati City); one in China (Hong Kong); and one in Malaysia (Kuala Lumpur).

In 2007 Bubba Gump secured a franchise agreement with Middle East-based Mubarak Al-Hassawi Restaurant Development Group, which plans to open 12 restaurants in key Middle East cities.

The average bill (per person/per family) is $17 for lunch and $22 for dinner. In 2007 this resulted in a total turnover for Bubba Gump of over $150 million.

Sources: Hosea, M. (2007) 'Fantasy brands on a reality check', *Brand Strategy*, May, pp. 25–29; Berta, D. (2005) 'Bubba Gump nets low turnover with incentives', *Nation's Restaurant News*, 12 September, p. 58; Hume, S. (2007) 'Strategic Planning – Top 400 Chains', *Restaurants & Institutions*, 1 July, p. 50; www.bubbagump.com.

### Questions

1 What are Bubba Gump's 'Key Success Factors' when going international?

2 Should Bubba Gump Shrimp Co. further internationalize its concept? Why or why not?

3 Over the next five years, Bubba Gump plans to open 35 to 50 new restaurants. What should be its main criteria for selecting locations for these new restaurants?

For further exercises and cases, see this book's website at **www.pearsoned.co.uk/hollensen**

 ## Questions for discussion

1 How can an SME compensate for its lack of resources and expertise in global marketing when trying to enter export markets?

2 What are the main differences between global marketing and marketing in the domestic context?

3 Explain the main advantages of centralizing upstream activities and decentralizing downstream activities.

4 How is the 'virtual value chain' different from the 'conventional value chain'?

# References

Asugman, G., Johnson, J.L. and McCullough, J. (1997) 'The role of after-sales service in international marketing', *Journal of International Marketing*, 5(4), pp. 11–28.

Auguste, B.G., Harmon, E.P., Pandit, V. (2006) 'The right service strategies for product companies', *McKinsey Quarterly*, 1 March, pp. 10–15.

Blomstermo, A., Sharma, D.D. and Sallis, J. (2006) 'Choice of foreign market entry mode in service firms', *International Marketing Review*, 23(2), pp. 211–229.

Chakravarthy, B.S. and Perlmutter, H.V. (1985) 'Strategic Planning for a Global Business', *Columbia Journal of World Business*, 20(2), pp. 3–10.

Frost, R. (2006) 'Global Packaging: What's the difference?', www.Brandchannel.com, 16 January 2006.

Ghemawat, P. (2007) 'Managing Differences – The Central Challenge of Global Strategy', *Harvard Business Review*, March, pp. 59–68.

Knight, G. (2000) 'Entrepreneurship and marketing strategy: the SME under globalization', *Journal of International Marketing*, 8(2), pp. 12–32.

Marchand, D.A. (1999) 'Hard IM choices for senior managers', Part 10 of 'Your guide to mastering information management', *Financial Times*, 5 April.

Perlmutter, H.V. (1969) 'The tortuous evolution of the multinational corporation', *Columbia Journal of World Business*, 9 (January–February), pp. 9–18.

Porter, M.E. (1985) *Competitive Advantage: Creating and Sustaining Superior Performance*, The Free Press, New York.

Porter, M.E. (1986) 'Competition in global industries: a conceptual framework', in Porter, M.E. (ed.), *Competition in Global Industries*, Harvard Business School Press, Boston, MA.

Quelch, J.A. (2002) 'Does globalization have staying power?', *Marketing Management*, March/April, pp. 18–23.

Rayport, J.F. and Sviokla, J.J. (1996) 'Exploiting the virtual value chain', *McKinsey Quarterly*, 1, pp. 21–36.

Segal-Horn, S. (2002) 'Global firms: heroes or villains? How and why companies globalize', *European Business Journal*, 14(1), pp. 8–19.

Sheth, J.N. and Parvatiyar, A. (2001) 'The antecedents and consequences of integrated global marketing', *International Marketing Review*, 18(1), pp. 16–29.

Solberg, C.A. (1997) 'A framework for analysis of strategy development in globalizing markets', *Journal of International Marketing*, 5(1), pp. 9–30.

Stabell, C.B. and Fjeldstad, Ø.B. (1998) 'Configuring value for competetive advantage: on chains, shops, and networks', *Strategic Management Journal*, 19, pp. 413–437.

Svensson, G. (2001) '"Glocalization" of business activities: a "glocal strategy" approach', *Management Decision*, 39(1), pp. 6–18.

Svensson, G. (2002) 'Beyond global marketing and the globalization of marketing activities', *Management Decision*, 40(6), pp. 574–583.

# 2

# Initiation of internationalization

## Contents

## Learning objectives

After studying this chapter you should be able to do the following:

- Discuss the reason (motives) why firms go international.
- Explain the difference between proactive and reactive motives.
- Analyse the triggers of export initiation.
- Explain the difference between internal and external triggers of export initiation.
- Describe different factors hindering export initiation.
- Discuss the critical barriers in the process of exporting.

## 2.1 Introduction

Internationalization occurs when the firm expands its R&D, production, selling and other business activities into international markets. In many larger firms internationalization may occur in a relatively continuous fashion, with the firm undertaking various internationalization stages on various foreign expansion projects simultaneously, in incremental steps, over a period of time. However, for SMEs, internationalization is often a relatively discrete process; that is, one in which management regards each internationalization venture as distinct and individual.

In the pre-internationalization stages, SME managers use information to achieve enough relevant knowledge to initiate internationalization (Freeman, 2002). Figure 2.1 illustrates the different stages in pre-internationalization, and the rest of this chapter refers to the stages in this figure.

Figure 2.1 Pre-internationalization: initiation of SME internationalization

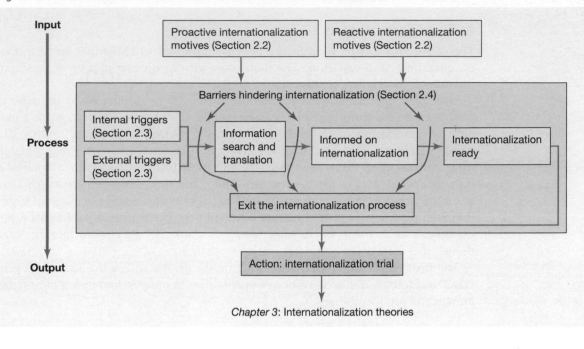

## 2.2 Internationalization motives

*Slides 15*

The fundamental reason for exporting, in most firms, is to make money. But, as in most business activities, one factor alone rarely accounts for any given action. Usually a mixture of factors results in firms taking steps in a given direction.

**Internationalization motives**
The fundamental reasons – proactive and reactive – for internationalization.

Table 2.1 provides an overview of the major internationalization motives. They are differentiated into proactive and reactive motives. *Proactive* motives represent stimuli to attempt strategy change, based on the firm's interest in exploiting unique competences (e.g. a special technological knowledge) or market possibilities. *Reactive* motives indicate that the firm reacts to pressures or threats in its home market or in foreign markets and adjusts passively to them by changing its activities over time.

Let us take a closer look at each export motive.

Table 2.1 Major motives for starting export

| Proactive motives | Reactive motives |
|---|---|
| ● Profit and growth goals | ● Competitive pressures |
| ● Managerial urge | ● Domestic market: small and saturated |
| ● Technology competence/unique product | ● Overproduction/excess capacity |
| ● Foreign market opportunities/market information | ● Unsolicited foreign orders |
| ● Economies of scale | ● Extend sales of seasonal products |
| ● Tax benefits | ● Proximity to international customers/psychological distance |

Source: adapted from Albaum *et al.*, 1994, p. 31.

## Proactive motives

### Profit and growth goals

The desire for short-term profit is especially important to SMEs that are at a stage of initial interest in exporting. The motivation for growth may also be of particular importance for the firm's export start.

Over time, the firm's attitude towards growth will be influenced by the type of feedback received from past efforts. For example, the profitability of exporting may determine management's attitude towards it. Of course the perceived profitability, when planning to enter international markets, is often quite different from profitability actually attained. Initial profitability may be quite low, particularly in international start-up operations. The gap between perception and reality may be particularly large when the firm has not previously engaged in international market activities. Despite thorough planning, sudden influences often shift the profit picture substantially. For example, a sudden shift in exchange rates may drastically alter profit forecasts even though they were based on careful market evaluation.

The stronger the firm's motivation to grow, the greater will be the activities it generates, including search activity for new possibilities, in order to find means of fulfilling growth and profit ambitions.

### Managerial urge

**Managerial urge**
Managers' motivation that reflects the desire and enthusiasm to drive internationalization forward.

Managerial urge is a motivation that reflects the desire, drive and enthusiasm of management towards global marketing activities. This enthusiasm can exist simply because managers like to be part of a firm that operates internationally. Further, it can often provide a good reason for international travel. Often, however, the managerial urge to internationalize is simply a reflection of general entrepreneurial motivation – of a desire for continuous growth and market expansion.

Managerial attitudes play a critical role in determining the exporting activities of the firm. In SMEs export decisions may be the province of a single decision maker; in LSEs they can be made by a decision-making unit. Irrespective of the number of people involved in the export decision-making process, the choice of a foreign market entry strategy is still dependent on the decision maker's perceptions of foreign markets, expectations concerning these markets and the company's capability of entering them.

The internationalization process may also be encouraged by the cultural socialization of the managers. Managers who either were born or have the experience of living or travelling abroad may be expected to be more internationally minded than other managers. Prior occupation in exporting companies, or membership in trade and professional associations, may also reinforce key decision makers' perceptions and evaluations of foreign environments.

### Technology competence/unique product

A firm may produce goods or services that are not widely available from international competitors or may have made technological advances in a specialized field. Again, real and perceived advantages should be differentiated. Many firms believe that theirs are unique products or services, even though this may not be the case in the international market. If products or technology are unique, however, they can certainly provide a sustainable competitive edge and result in major business success abroad. One issue to consider is how long such a technological or product advantage will continue.

Historically, a firm with a competitive edge could count on being the sole supplier to foreign markets for years to come. This type of advantage, however, has shrunk dramatically because of competing technologies and a frequent lack of international patent protection.

However, a firm producing superior products is more likely to receive enquiries from foreign markets because of the perceived competence of its offerings. Several dimensions in the product offering affect the probability that a potential buyer will be exposed to export stimuli. Furthermore, if a company has developed unique competences in its domestic market, the possibilities of spreading unique assets to overseas markets may be very high because the opportunity costs of exploiting these assets in other markets will be very low.

## Foreign market opportunities/market information

It is evident that market opportunities act as stimuli only if the firm has or is capable of securing those resources necessary to respond to the opportunities. In general, decision makers are likely to consider a rather limited number of foreign market opportunities in planning their foreign entry. Moreover, such decision makers are likely to explore first those overseas market opportunities perceived as having some similarity with the opportunities in their home market.

From time to time certain overseas markets grow spectacularly, providing tempting opportunities for expansion-minded firms. The attraction of the south-east Asian markets is based on their economic successes, while the attraction of the eastern European markets is rooted in their new-found political freedoms and desire to develop trade and economic relationships with countries in western Europe, North America and Japan. Other countries that are likely to increase in market attractiveness as key internal changes occur include the People's Republic of China and South Africa.

Specialized marketing knowledge or access to information can distinguish an exporting firm from its competitors. This includes knowledge about foreign customers, marketplaces or market situations that is not widely shared by other firms. Such specialized knowledge may result from particular insights based on a firm's international research, special contacts a firm may have, or simply being in the right place at the right time (e.g. recognizing a good business situation during a vacation trip). Past marketing success can be a strong motivator for future marketing behaviour. Competence in one or more of the major marketing activities will often be a sufficient catalyst for a company to begin or expand exports.

## Economies of scale - learning curve

Becoming a participant in global marketing activities may enable the firm to increase its output and therefore climb more rapidly on the learning curve. Ever since the Boston Consulting Group showed that a doubling of output can reduce production costs by up to 30 per cent this effect has been very much sought. Increased production for the international market can therefore also help in reducing the cost of production for domestic sales and make the firm more competitive domestically as well. This effect often results in seeking market share as a primary objective of firms. (See Exhibits 1.2 and 2.1 as examples of this.) At an initial level of internationalization it may mean an increased search for export markets; later on it can result in opening foreign subsidiaries and foreign production facilities.

---

### Exhibit 2.1  Global marketing and economics of scale in Japanese firms

Japanese firms exploit foreign market opportunities by using a penetration pricing strategy – a low-entry price to build up market share and establish a long-term dominant market position. They do accept losses in the early years, as they view it as an investment in long-term market development. This can be achieved because much of Japanese industry (especially the *keiretsu* type of organization) is supported or owned by banks or other financial institutions with a much lower cost of capital.

Furthermore, because of the lifetime employment system, labour cost is regarded as a fixed expense, not a variable as it is in the West. Since all marginal labour cost will be at the entry salary level, raising volume is the only way to increase productivity rapidly. As a result market share, not profitability, is the primary concept in Japanese firms, where scale of operation and experience allow economies of scale, which also help to reduce distribution costs. The international trading companies typically take care of international sales and marketing, allowing the Japanese firm to concentrate on economies of scale, resulting in lower cost per unit.

Source: Genestre *et al.*, 1995.

---

Through exporting, fixed costs arising from administration, facilities, equipment, staff work and R&D can be spread over more units. For some companies a condition for exploiting scale effects on foreign markets to the fullest extent is the possibility of standardizing the marketing mix internationally. For others, however, standardized marketing is not necessary for scale economies.

### Tax benefits

Tax benefits can also play a major motivating role. In the United States a tax mechanism called the Foreign Sales Corporation (FSC) has been instituted to assist exporters. It is in conformity with international agreements and provides firms with certain tax deferrals. Tax benefits allow the firm either to offer its products at a lower cost in foreign markets or to accumulate a higher profit. This may therefore tie in closely with the profit motivation.

However, antidumping laws enforced by the WTO (the World Trade Organization) punish foreign producers for selling their products on local markets at very low prices, in order to protect local producers. This is the law that every country that has signed the WTO agreement (and most countries have signed) must abide by.

## Reactive motives

### Competitive pressures

A prime form of reactive motivation is reaction to competitive pressures. A firm may fear losing domestic market share to competing firms that have benefited from economies of scale gained by global marketing activities. Further, it may fear losing foreign markets permanently to domestic competitors that decide to focus on these markets, knowing that market share is most easily retained by the firm that obtains it initially. Quick entry may result in similarly quick withdrawal once the firm recognizes that its preparations have been insufficient. In addition to this, knowing that other firms, particularly competitors, are internationalizing provides a strong incentive to internationalize. Competitors are an important external factor stimulating internationalization. Coca-Cola became international much earlier than Pepsi did, but there is no doubt whatever that Coca-Cola's move into overseas markets influenced Pepsi to move in the same direction.

## Domestic market: small and saturated

A company may be pushed into exporting because of a small home market potential. For some firms, domestic markets may be unable to sustain sufficient economies of scale and scope, and these companies automatically include export markets as part of their market entry strategy. This type of behaviour is likely for industrial products that have few, easily identified customers located throughout the world, or for producers of specialized consumer goods with small national segments in many countries.

A saturated domestic market, whether measured in sales volume or market share, has a similar motivating effect. Products marketed domestically by the firm may be at the declining stage of the product life cycle. Instead of attempting a push-back of the life cycle process, or in addition to such an effort, firms may opt to prolong the product life cycle by expanding the market. In the past such efforts were often met with success as customers in many developing countries only gradually reached a level of need and sophistication already attained by customers in industrialized nations. Some developing nations are still often in need of products for which the demand in the industrialized world is already on the decline. In this way firms can use the international market to prolong the life cycle of their product. (See also Chapter 11 for further discussion.)

Many US appliance and car manufacturers initially entered international markets because of what they viewed as near-saturated domestic markets. US producers of asbestos products found the domestic market legally closed to them, but because some overseas markets had more lenient consumer protection laws they continued to produce for overseas markets.

Another perspective on market saturation is also relevant for understanding why firms may expand overseas. Home market saturation suggests that unused productive resources (such as production and managerial slack) exist within the firm. Production slack is a stimulus for securing new market opportunities, and managerial slack can provide those knowledge resources required for collecting, interpreting and using market information.

## Overproduction/excess capacity

If a firm's domestic sales of a product are below expectation the inventory can be above desired levels. This situation can be the trigger for starting export sales via short-term price cuts on inventory products. As soon as the domestic market demand returns to previous levels global marketing activities are curtailed or even terminated. Firms that have used such a strategy may encounter difficulties when trying to employ it again because many foreign customers are not interested in temporary or sporadic business relationships. This reaction from abroad may well lead to a decrease in the importance of this motivation over time.

In some situations, however, excess capacity can be a powerful motivation. If equipment for production is not fully utilized firms may see expansion into the international market as an ideal possibility for achieving broader distribution of fixed costs. Alternatively, if all fixed costs are assigned to domestic production, the firm can penetrate international markets with a pricing scheme that focuses mainly on variable costs. Although such a strategy may be useful in the short term it may result in the offering of products abroad at a lower cost than at home, which in turn may stimulate parallel importing. In the long run, fixed costs have to be recovered to ensure replacement of production equipment. A market penetration strategy based on variable cost alone is therefore not feasible over the long term.

Sometimes excess production capacity arises because of changing demand in the domestic market. As domestic markets switch to new and substitute products companies making older product versions develop excess capacity and look for overseas market opportunities.

## Unsolicited foreign orders

Many small companies have become aware of opportunities in export markets because their products generated enquiries from overseas. These enquiries can result from advertising in trade journals that have a worldwide circulation, through exhibitions and by other means. As a result a large percentage of exporting firms' initial orders were unsolicited.

## Extend sales of seasonal products

Seasonality in demand conditions may be different in the domestic market from other international markets. This can act as a persistent stimulus for foreign market exploration that may result in a more stable demand over the year.

A producer of agricultural machinery in Europe had demand from its domestic market primarily in the spring months of the year. In an attempt to achieve a more stable demand over the year it directed its market orientation towards the southern hemisphere (e.g. Australia, South Africa), where it is summer when the northern hemisphere is winter and vice versa.

## Proximity to international customers/psychological distance

Physical and psychological closeness to the international market can often play a major role in the export activities of a firm. For example, German firms established near the Austrian border may not even perceive their market activities in Austria as global marketing. Rather, they are simply an extension of domestic activities, without any particular attention being paid to the fact that some of the products go abroad.

Unlike US firms, most European firms automatically become international marketers simply because their neighbours are so close. As an example, a European firm operating in Belgium needs to go only 100 kilometres to be in multiple foreign markets. Geographic closeness to foreign markets may not necessarily translate into real or perceived closeness to the foreign customer. Sometimes cultural variables, legal factors and other societal norms make a foreign market that is geographically close seem psychologically distant. For example, research has shown that US firms perceive Canada as psychologically much closer than Mexico. Even England, mainly because of similarity in language, is perceived by many US firms as much closer than Mexico or other Latin American countries, despite the geographic distances. The recent extensive expansion of many Greek firms (especially banks) into the Balkans is another example of proximity to international customers.

In a study of small UK firms' motives for going abroad, Westhead *et al.* (2002) found the following main reasons for starting exporting of firms' products/services:

- being contacted by foreign customers that place orders;
- one-off order (no continuous exporting);
- the availability of foreign market information;
- part of growth objective of the firm;
- export markets actively targeted by key founder/owner/manager.

The results in the Westhead *et al.* (2002) study also showed that the bigger the firm the more likely that it would have cited *proactive* stimuli/motives.

---

Exhibit 2.2　**Internationalization of Haier – proactive and reactive motives**

The Chinese manufacturer of home appliances (e.g. refrigerators), Haier Group, was near bankruptcy when Mr Zhang Ruimin was appointed plant director in 1984, the fourth one that year. It is Zhang Ruimin who has led the company to stand up and grow to the world's sixth largest home appliance manufacturer.

**China, consumer goods production, Haier**
© Michael Reynolds/epa/Corbis.

### Proactive motives

Zhang Ruimin had an internationalization mindset for the initial stage of Haier's development. In 1984, soon after having joined the plant, he introduced technology and equipment from Liebherr, a German company, to produce several popular refrigerator brands in China. At the same time he actively expanded cooperation with Liebherr by manufacturing refrigerators based on its standards which were then sold to Liebherr, as a way of entering the German market. In 1986 the value of Haier's exports reached US$3 million for the first time. Zhang Ruimin later commented on this strategy: 'Exporting to earn foreign exchange was necessary at that time.'

When Haier invested in a plant in the United States, Zhang Ruimin thought it gained location advantage by setting up plants overseas to avoid tariffs and reduce transportation costs. Internalization advantage had been attained through controlling services and marketing/distribution, and ownership advantage had been achieved by developing design and R&D capabilities through utilizing high-quality local human resources.

### Reactive motives

The entry of global home appliance manufacturers into the Chinese market forced Haier to seek international expansion. In particular, since China joined the WTO almost every international competitor has invested in China, establishing wholly-owned companies. The best defensive strategy for Haier would be to have a presence in its competitors' home markets.

The saturation of the Chinese home appliance market, with intensifying competition, has been a major motive. After the mid-1990s price wars broke out one after another in various categories of the market. At the end of 2000, Haier's market shares in China of refrigerators, freezers, air conditioners and washing machines had reached 33, 42, 31 and 31 per cent, respectively. The potential for further development in the domestic market was therefore limited.

One of the important external triggers for the internationalization of Haier has been the Chinese government. Being an international player, Haier gained some special conditions that other Chinese companies could not obtain. For instance, Haier had already been approved to establish a financial company, to be the majority shareholder of a regional commercial bank, and to form a joint venture with a US insurance company. Without its active pursuit of internationalization, as well as a dominant position in home appliance sectors, it would normally be impossible for a manufacturer to get approval to enter the financial sector.

Source: adapted from Liu and Li, 2002.

---

The results of Suárez-Ortega and Alamo-Vera (2005) suggest that the main driving forces motivating internationalization are found within the firm, and therefore they are based on the management's strengths and weaknesses. They conclude that it is not the external environment that mainly influence the internationalization activities, but the pool of resources and capabilities within the firm that might be appropriately combined to succeed in international markets. Consequently, the speed and intensity of internationalization can be emphasized through programmes aimed at enhancing managers' skills and capabilities. Also export promotion programmes aiming to get more non-exporters to become interested in exporting should emphasize activities that increase managers' awareness of export advantages.

## 2.3   Triggers of export initiation (change agents)

**Internationalization triggers**
Internal or external events taking place to initiate internationalization

For internationalization to take place someone or something within or outside the firm (so-called change agents) must initiate the process and carry it through to implementation (see Table 2.2). These are known as internationalization triggers. One conclusion from the research done in this area is that it is rare that an isolated factor will trigger the firm's internationalization process. In most cases it is a combination of factors that initiates the internationalization process (Rundh, 2007).

### Internal triggers

#### Perceptive management

Perceptive managers gain early awareness of developing opportunities in overseas markets. They make it their business to become knowledgeable about these markets, and maintain a sense of open-mindedness about where and when their companies should expand overseas. Perceptive managers include many cosmopolitans in their ranks.

A trigger factor is frequently foreign travel, during which new business opportunities are discovered or information received which makes management believe that such opportunities exist. Managers who have lived abroad, have learned foreign languages or are particularly interested in foreign cultures are likely, sooner rather than later, to investigate whether global marketing opportunities would be appropriate for their firm.

Often managers enter a firm having already had some global marketing experience in previous jobs and try to use this experience to further the business activities of their new firm. In developing their goals in the new job managers frequently consider an entirely new set of options, one of which may be global marketing activities.

#### Specific internal event

A significant event can be another major change agent. A new employee who firmly believes that the firm should undertake global marketing may find ways to motivate management. Overproduction or a reduction in domestic market size can serve as such an event, as can the receipt of new information about current product uses. For instance, a company's research activity may develop a by-product suitable for sale overseas, as happened with a food-processing firm that discovered a low-cost protein ideal for helping to relieve food shortages in some parts of Africa.

Research has shown that in SMEs the initial decision to export is usually made by the chief executive, with substantial input provided by the marketing department. The

**Table 2.2  Triggers of export initiation**

| Internal triggers | External triggers |
| --- | --- |
| ● Perceptive management<br>● Specific internal event<br>● Importing as inward internationalization | ● Market demand<br>● Competing firms<br>● Trade associations<br>● Outside experts |

carrying out of the decision – that is, the initiation of actual global marketing activities and the implementation of these activities – is then primarily the responsibility of marketing personnel. Only in the final decision stage of evaluating global marketing activities does the major emphasis rest again with the chief executive of the firm. In order to influence a firm internally, it therefore appears that the major emphasis should be placed first on convincing the chief executive to enter the international marketplace and then on convincing the marketing department that global marketing is an important activity. Conversely, the marketing department is a good place to be if one wants to become active in international business.

In a recent study of internationalization behaviour in Finnish SMEs, Forsman *et al.* (2002) found that the three most important triggers for starting up operations internationally were as follows:

1  management's interest in internationalization;
2  foreign enquiries about the company's products/services;
3  inadequate demand in the home market.

In this study it is interesting to note that companies do not regard contacts from Chambers of Commerce or other support organizations as important for getting their international activities going. However, Chambers of Commerce are often used for obtaining further information about a foreign country after an initial trigger has led to the consideration of going international.

## Inward/outward internationalization

Internationalization has traditionally been regarded as an outward flow and most internationalization models have not dealt explicitly with how earlier inward activities, and thereby gained knowledge, can influence later outward activities. A natural way of internationalizing would be first to get involved in inward activities (imports) and thereafter in outward activities (exports). Relationships and knowledge gathered from import activities could thus be used when the firm engages in export activities (Welch *et al.*, 2001).

Welch and Loustarinen (1993) claim that inward internationalization (importing) may precede and influence outward internationalization (international market entry and marketing activities) – see Figure 2.2.

A direct relationship exists between inward and outward internationalization in the way that effective inward activities can determine the success of outward activities, especially in the early stages of internationalization. The inward internationalization may be initiated by one of the following:

- *the buyer*: active international search of different foreign sources (buyer initiative = reverse marketing); or
- *the seller*: initiation by the foreign supplier (traditional seller perspective).

During the process from inward to outward internationalization the buyer's role (in country A) shifts to that of seller, both to domestic customers (in country A) and to foreign customers. Through interaction with the foreign supplier the buyer (importer) gets access to the network of the supplier, so that at some later time there may be an outward export to members of this network.

Inward international operations thus usually cover a variety of different forms used to strengthen a firm's resources. Of course inward flows imply importing products needed for the production process, such as raw materials and machinery. But inward operations can also include finances and technology through different operational forms, such as franchising, direct investments and alliances (Forsman *et al.*, 2002). In some cases inward foreign licensing may be followed by outward technology sales.

**Inward internationalization** Imports as a preceding activity for the later market entries in foreign markets.

**Outward internationalization** Imports as a preceding activity for the later market entries in foreign markets.

Figure 2.2 Inward/outward internationalization: a network example

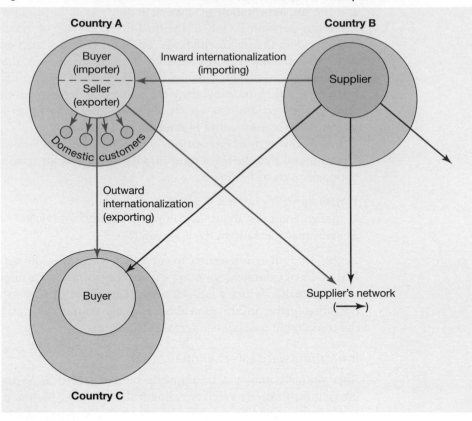

According to Fletcher (2001) and Freeman (2002), inward and outward activities and the links between them can develop in different ways. The links are most tangible in counter-trade arrangements (where the focal firm initiates exporting to the same market from which importing takes place), but they can also be found in the networks of relationships between subunits within a multinational enterprise and in strategic alliances.

## External triggers

### Market demand

Growth in international markets also causes the demand for the products of some companies also to grow, pushing the makers of these products into internationalization. Many pharmaceutical companies entered international markets when growth in the international demand for their products was first getting under way. The US-based company Squibb entered the Turkish market before it was large enough to be profitable; but the market was growing rapidly, which encouraged Squibb to internationalize further.

### Competing firms

Information that an executive in a competing firm considers certain international markets to be valuable and worthwhile developing captures the attention of management. Such statements not only have source credibility but are also viewed with a certain amount of fear because the competitor may eventually infringe on the firm's business.

## Trade associations

Formal and informal meetings among managers from different firms at trade association meetings, conventions or business round tables often serve as a major change agent. It has even been suggested that the decision to export may be made by small firms on the basis of the collective experience of the group of firms to which they belong.

### Outside experts

Several outside experts encourage internationalization. Among them are export agents, governments, Chambers of Commerce and banks.

- *Export agents* Export agents as well as export trading companies and export management firms generally qualify as experts in global marketing. They are already dealing internationally with other products, have overseas contacts and are set up to handle other exportable products. Many of these trade intermediaries approach prospective exporters directly if they think that their products have potential markets overseas.
- *Governments* In nearly all countries governments try to stimulate international business through providing global marketing expertise (export assistance programmes). For example, government stimulation measures can have a positive influence not only in terms of any direct financial effects that they may have, but also in relation to the provision of information.
- *Chambers of Commerce* Chambers of Commerce and similar export production organizations are interested in stimulating international business, both exports and imports. These organizations seek to motivate individual companies to get involved in global marketing and provide incentives for them to do so. These incentives include putting the prospective exporter or importer in touch with overseas business, providing overseas market information, and referring the prospective exporter or importer to financial institutions capable of financing global marketing activity.
- *Banks* Banks and other financial institutions are often instrumental in getting companies to internationalize. They alert their domestic clients to international opportunities and help them to capitalize on these opportunities. Of course, they look forward to their services being used more extensively as domestic clients expand internationally.

## Information search and translation

Of all resources, information and knowledge are perhaps the most critical factor in the initiation of the internationalization process in the SME (see also Figure 2.1 earlier).

Because each international opportunity constitutes a potential innovation for the SME its management must acquire appropriate information. This is especially important to SMEs that typically lack the resources to internationalize in the manner of LSEs. Consequently management launches an *information search* and aquires relevant information from a number of sources, such as internal written reports, government agencies, trade associations, personal contacts or the Internet, relevant to the intended internationalization project. In the *information translation* stage the internationalization information is transformed by managers into knowledge within the firm. It is through the information search and translation into knowledge that management becomes informed on internationalization. At this stage the firm has entered a cycle of continuous search and translation into internationalization knowledge. This cycle continues until management is satisfied that it has sufficiently reduced the uncertainty associated with the internationalization project to ensure a relatively high probability of success. Once sufficient information has been acquired and translated into usable knowledge the firm leaves the cycle, becoming *internationalization ready*. It is here that the firm proceeds to action, that is, *internationalization trial*. 'Action' refers to behaviours and activities that management executes based on the knowledge that it has acquired. At this stage the firm could be said to have an embedded internationalization culture, where even the most challenging foreign markets can be overcome, leading to further internationalization and 'storage' of actual internationalization knowledge in the heads of the managers. The above description represents the firm more or less in isolation. However, the network theory recognizes the importance of the firm's membership in a constellation of firms and organizations. By interacting within such a constellation the firm derives advantages well beyond what it could obtain in isolation.

At the most fine-grained level, knowledge is created by individuals. Individuals acquire explicit knowledge via specific means and tacit knowledge through 'hands-on' experience (experiential learning).

The nature of the pre-internationalization process (illustrated in Figure 2.1) will be unique in each firm because of several factors at the organization and individual levels within the firm (Knight and Liesch, 2002). For example, for SMEs it seems that the managers' personal networks tend to speed up the pre-internationalization process. These personal networks are used for creating cross-border alliances with suppliers, distributors and other international partners (Freeman *et al.*, 2006).

Throughout the process depicted in Figure 2.1 the firm may exit from the pre-internationalization process at any time, as a result of the barriers hindering internationalization. The manager may decide to 'do nothing', an outcome that implies exiting from pre-internationalization.

## 2.4   Internationalization barriers/risks

A wide variety of barriers to successful export operations can be identified. Some problems mainly affect the export start; others are encountered in the process of exporting.

### Barriers hindering internationalization initiation

Critical factors hindering *internationalization initiation* include the following (mainly internal) barriers:

- insufficient finances;
- insufficient knowledge;
- lack of foreign market connections;
- lack of export commitment;
- lack of capital to finance expansion into foreign markets;
- lack of productive capacity to dedicate to foreign markets;
- lack of foreign channels of distribution;
- management emphasis on developing domestic markets;
- cost escalation due to high export manufacturing, distribution and financing expenditures.

Inadequate information on potential foreign customers, competition and foreign business practices are key barriers facing active and prospective exporters. Obtaining adequate representation for overseas distribution and service, ensuring payment, import tariffs and quotas, and difficulties in communicating with foreign distributors and customers are also major concerns. Serious problems can also arise from production disruptions resulting from a requirement for non-standard export products. This will increase the cost of manufacturing and distribution.

In a study of craft micro-enterprises (less than ten employees) in the United Kingdom and Ireland, Fillis (2002) found that having sufficient business in the domestic market was the major factor in the decision not to export. Other reasons of above-average importance were: lack of export inquiries, relating to the reactive approach to business; complicated exporting procedures; poor levels of exporting assistance; and limited government incentives. Similar results were supported by a study by Westhead *et al.* (2002), who found that for small firms 'focus on local market' was the main reason for not exporting any of their products.

The internationalization process can also go in another direction than expected – see Exhibit 2.3.

---

### Exhibit 2.3  De-internationalization at British Telecommunications (BT)

BT started its internationalization from the mid-1990s. Over the the next years BT built a global strategy seeking to position itself as a leading supplier of telecommunication services to multinational companies in different countries. However the percentage increase in international activities has slowed down over the years. In 1994 less than 1 per cent of total turnover came from international activities. In 2002 this increased to 11 per cent, and in 2007 it increased to 15 per cent of its £20 billion turnover. So though BT overall has experienced a sharp increase in turnover from international activities it has also experienced some setbacks in the internationalization process, especially in the beginning, as indicated in Figure 2.3.

In the beginning of the internationalization process BT built its international strategy around three guiding principles:

1  Not over-committing itself by building its own infrastructure based on uncertatain traffic flows.
2  Achieving quick and reliable access to targeted marketplaces by entering distribution partnerships and equity joint ventures. This strategy involved relatively low risk and allowed speedy access into marketplaces with partners who had intimate knowledge of local market conditions.
3  Ensuring that the strategy gave BT sufficient strategic flexibility to be able to adjust rapidly to changing market conditions

At its height in 1999, BT had 25 equity joint ventures and 44 distribution partnerships. Within the equity joint ventures, BT took a minority stake with the stated intention to gradually upgrade this stake to a controlling investment over time. BT would also often take a stake in its distribution partners as a means of giving them incentives to sell the BT products.

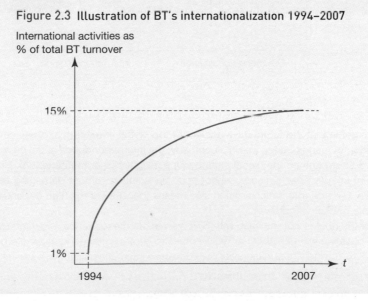

**Figure 2.3 Illustration of BT's internationalization 1994–2007**

International activities as % of total BT turnover

Exhibit 2.3 continued

## De-internationalization at BT

In 2002, BT launched a new corporate strategy that was considerably more defensive than its predecessor. There were mainly two problems with the series of joint ventures and partnerships:

1  BT needed different skills and competences for different partners. This made coordination of activities between partners very complex. As a consequence, BT found itself on a steep learning curve with this large number of partners.
2  The strategy of only taking a minority stake in the joint ventures rebounded on BT. Furthermore, there was little imperative by partners to fully support the roll out of BT products especially where they were in competition with their own offerings. When BT attempted to increase its financial stake within the partnership, it often found that the other shareholders had exactly the same intent.

Subsequently, BT made divestments, both in North America and in Asia.

## What can we learn from the BT case?

BT's de-internationalization was driven by the financial situation, where the high cost of market entry combined with falling prices (driven by excess capacity in the telecommunication sector) led to declining profits throughout the 1990s. Consequently, the new defensive strategy represented a process of de-internationalization as BT retreated from the US and Asian markets ('Multiple withdrawal' in Figure 2.4). BT's new international strategy is based on the European market where there are interdependencies with the core UK business. This means that BT tries to own and control all aspects of the delivery mechanism within the European market.

Figure 2.4  **Global strategy options**

This BT case demonstrates that the future development of the global marketing strategy can work in both directions. If the globalization of markets goes well in a company, the interdependence and synergies between markets can be further utilized to strengthen the global strategy (upper-right corner in Figure 2.4). However the case also shows that divestment in individual locations cannot occur in isolation without damaging the firm's global value proposition. Therefore, BT's de-internationalization also means (because of the high dependence of markets) that it had to make multiple market withdrawals.

If we talk about SMEs (that is not the case with BT!) we will often experience a low interdependence between markets, and in that case we will talk about a 'multi-domestic' strategy if we increase internationalization (lower-right corner in Figure 2.4) and individual withdrawal if we decrease internationalization (lower-left corner in Figure 2.4).

Source: Adapted from Turner and Gardiner, 2007; BT Financial Report 2007.

## Barriers hindering the further process of internationalization

Critical barriers in the *process of internationalization* may generally be divided into three groups: general market risks, commercial risks and political risks.

### General market risks

General market risks include the following:

- comparative market distance;
- competition from other firms in foreign markets;
- differences in product usage in foreign markets;
- language and cultural differences;
- difficulties in finding the right distributor in the foreign market;
- differences in product specifications in foreign markets;
- complexity of shipping services to overseas buyers.

### Commercial risks

The following fall into the commercial risks group:

- exchange rate fluctuations when contracts are made in a foreign currency;
- failure of export customers to pay due to contract dispute, bankruptcy, refusal to accept the product or fraud;
- delays and/or damage in the export shipment and distribution process;
- difficulties in obtaining export financing.

### Political risks

Among the political risks resulting from intervention by home and host country governments are the following:

- foreign government restrictions;
- national export policy;
- foreign exchange controls imposed by host governments that limit the opportunities for foreign customers to make payment;
- lack of governmental assistance in overcoming export barriers;
- lack of tax incentives for companies that export;
- high value of the domestic currency relative to those in export markets;
- high foreign tariffs on imported products;
- confusing foreign import regulations and procedures;
- complexity of trade documentation;
- enforcement of national legal codes regulating exports;
- civil strife, revolution and wars disrupting foreign markets.

The importance of these risks must not be overemphasised, and various risk-management strategies are open to exporters. These include the following:

- Avoid exporting to high-risk markets.
- Diversify overseas markets and ensure that the firm is not overdependent on any single country.
- Insure risks when possible. Government schemes are particularly attractive.
- Structure export business so that the buyer bears most of the risk. For example, price in a hard currency and demand cash in advance.

In Fillis (2002) over one-third of the exporting craft firms indicated that they encountered problems once they entered export markets. The most common problem was connected with the choice of a reliable distributor, followed by difficulties in promoting the product and matching competitors' prices.

Summary

This chapter has provided an overview of the pre-internationalization process. The chapter opened with the major motives for firms to internationalize. These were differentiated into proactive and reactive motives. Proactive motives represent internal stimuli to attempt strategy change, based on the firm's interest in exploiting unique competences or market possibilities. Reactive motives indicate that the firm reacts to pressures or threats in its home market or in foreign markets and adjusts passively to them.

For internationalization to take place someone or something ('triggers') inside or outside the firm must initiate it and carry it through. To succeed in global marketing the firm has to overcome export barriers. Some barriers mainly affect the export initiation and others are encountered in the process of exporting.

CASE STUDY 2.1

## Elvis Presley Enterprises Inc. (EPE): Internationalization of a 'cult icon'

Even more than 25 years after his death Elvis Presley has one of the most lucrative entertainment franchises in the world. Despite the sorry state of his affairs in 1977 the empire of Elvis has thrived due in large part to the efforts of the people who handled his estate after his grandmother died in 1980, including his ex-wife Priscilla Beaulieu Presley, his daughter Lisa Marie and Jack Soden, the CEO of Elvis Presley Enterprises Inc. (**www.elvis.com**), the company that handles all the official Elvis properties.

Priscilla Presley was involved in the master-stroke decision to open Elvis's mansion, Graceland, to the public in 1982. Graceland gets more than 600,000 visitors per year, according to EPE's website. Over half of Graceland's visitors are under the age of 35. While visitors come from all parts of the world the majority still come from different parts of the United States. The Graceland tour costs US$25, which means that EPE makes US$15 million on those tickets alone, plus what it receives from photographs, hotel guests, meals and souvenirs.

EPE's other revenue streams include a theme restaurant called Elvis Presley's Memphis; a hotel, down at the end of Lonely Street, called Heartbreak Hotel; licensing of Elvis-related products, the development of Elvis-related music, film, video, TV and stage productions; and more.

© Used by permission, Elvis Presley Enterprises, Inc.

Ironically, EPE gets very little money from Elvis's actual songs, thanks to a deal Elvis's infamous former manager, Colonel Tom Parker, made with RCA in 1973, whereby Elvis traded the rights for all future royalties from the songs he had recorded up to that point for a measly $5.4 million – half of which he had to give to Parker.

In 2000, the 25th anniversary was an international spectacle. A remix of the 1968 Elvis song 'A little less conversation' became a global hit single. Furthermore the CD 'Elvis: 30 #1 Hits' went triple platinum.

In mid-2004, to commemorate the 50th anniversary of Presley's first professional recording, 'That's All Right' was re-released, and made the charts around the world, including the top three in the United Kingdom and top 40 in Australia.

In mid-October 2005, *Variety* named the top 100 entertainment icons of the twentieth century, with Presley landing in the top ten, along with the Beatles, Marilyn Monroe, Lucille Ball, Marlon Brando, Humphrey Bogart, Louis Armstrong, Charlie Chaplin, James Dean and Mickey Mouse.

By the end of October 2005, *Forbes* magazine named Elvis Presley, for the fifth straight year, the top-earning dead celebrity, grossing US$45 million for the Elvis Presley Estate during the period from October 2004 to October 2005.

Source: money.cnn.com/2002/08/15/news/elvis.

### Questions

1 What are the main motives for the internationalization of EPE?

2 What can EPE do to maintain a steady income stream from abroad?

3 What are the most obvious assets for further internationalization of EPE?

For further exercises and cases, see this book's website at **www.pearsoned.co.uk/hollensen**

## Questions for discussion

1 Export motives can be classified as reactive or proactive. Give examples of each group of export motives. How would you prioritize these motives? Can you think of motives other than those mentioned in the chapter? What are they?

2 What is meant by 'change agents' in global marketing? Give examples of different types of change agent.

3 Discuss the most critical barriers to the process of exporting.

4 What were the most important change agents in the internationalization of Haier (Exhibit 2.2)?

5 What were the most important export motives in Japanese firms (Exhibit 2.1)?

## References

Albaum, G., Strandskov, J., Duerr, E. and Dowd, L. (1994) *International Marketing and Export Management* (2nd edn), Addison-Wesley, Reading, MA.

Fillis, I. (2002) 'Barriers to internationalization: an investigation of the craft microenterprises', *European Journal of Marketing*, (7–8), pp. 912–927.

Fletcher, R. (2001) 'A holistic approach to internationalization', *International Business Review*, 10, pp. 25–49.

Forsman, M., Hinttu, S. and Kock, S. (2002) 'Internationalization from an SME perspective', Paper presented at the *18th Annual IMP Conference*, September, Lyon, pp. 1–12.

Freeman, S. (2002) 'A comprehensive model of the process of small firm internationalization: a network perspective', Paper presented at the *18th Annual IMP Conference*, September, Dijon, pp. 1–22.

Freeman, S., Edwards, R. and Schroder, B. (2006) 'How smaller Born-Globals Firms use Networks and Alliances to Overcome Constraints to Rapid Internationalization', *Journal of International Marketing*, Vol. 14, No. 3, pp. 33–63.

Genestre, A., Herbig, D. and Shao, A.T. (1995) 'What does marketing really mean to the Japanese?', *Marketing Intelligence and Planning*, 13(9), pp. 16–27.

Knight, G.A. and Liesch, P.W. (2002) 'Information internalization in internationalizing the firm', *Journal of Business Research*, 55, pp. 981–995.

Liu, H. and Li, K. (2002) 'Strategic implications of emerging Chinese multinationals: the Haier case study', *European Management Journal*, 20(6), pp. 699–706.

Rundh, B. (2007) 'International Marketing Behaviour Amongst Exporting Firms', *European Journal of Marketing*, Vol. 41, No. 1/2, pp. 181–198.

Suárez-Ortega, S.M. and Àlamo-Vera, F.R. (2005) 'SMES' internationalization: firms and managerial factors', *International Journal of Entrepreneurial Behavior & Research*, 11(4), pp. 258–279.

Turner, C. and Gardiner, P.D. (2007) 'De-internationalisation and global strategy: the case of British Telecommunications (BT)', *Journal of Business & Industrial Marketing*, Vol. 22, No. 7, pp. 489–497.

Welch, L.S., Benito, G.R.G., Silseth, P.R. and Karlsen, T. (2001) 'Exploring inward–outward linkages in firms' internationalization: a knowledge and network perspective', Paper presented at the *17th Annual IMP Conference*, September, Oslo, pp. 1–26.

Welch, L.S. and Loustarinen, R.K. (1993) 'Inward–outward connections in internationalization', *Journal of International Marketing*, 1(1), pp. 44–56.

Westhead, P., Wright, M. and Ucbasaran, D. (2002) 'International market selection strategies selected by "micro" and "small" firms', *Omega – The International Journal of Management Science*, 30, pp. 51–68.

# 3

# Internationalization theories

## Contents

**Case study**

## Learning objectives

After studying this chapter you should be able to do the following:

- Analyse and compare the three theories explaining a firm's internationalization process:
  1 the Uppsala internationalization model;
  2 the transaction cost theory; and
  3 the network model.
- Explain the most important determinants for the internationalization process of SMEs.
- Discuss the different factors which influence internationalization of services.
- Explain and discuss the relevance of the network model for an SME serving as a subcontractor.
- Explain the term 'Born Global' and its connection to Internet marketing.

## 3.1 Introduction

Having discussed the barriers to starting internationalization in Chapter 2, we will begin this chapter by presenting the different theoretical approaches to international marketing and then choose three models for further discussion in sections 3.2, 3.3 and 3.4.

# Historical development of internationalization

Much of the early literature on internationalization was inspired by general marketing theories. Later on, internationalization dealt with the choice between exporting and FDI (foreign direct investment). During the past 10–15 years there has been much focus on internationalization in networks, by which the firm has different relationships not only with customers but also with other actors in the environment.

## The traditional marketing approach

The Penrosian tradition (Penrose, 1959; Prahalad and Hamel, 1990) reflects the traditional marketing focus on the firm's core competences combined with opportunities in the foreign environment.

The cost-based view of this tradition suggested that the firm must possess a 'compensating advantage' in order to overcome the 'cost of foreignness' (Kindleberger, 1969; Hymer, 1976). This led to the identification of technological and marketing skills as the key elements in successful foreign entry.

## 'Life cycle' concept for international trade

Sequential modes of internationalization were introduced by Vernon's 'product cycle hypothesis' (1966), in which firms go through an exporting phase before switching first to market-seeking FDI, and then to cost-oriented FDI. Technology and marketing factors combine to explain standardization, which drives location decisions.

Vernon's hypothesis is that producers in advanced countries (ACs) are 'closer' to the markets than producers elsewhere; consequently the first production facilities for these products will be in the ACs. As demand expands a certain degree of standardization usually takes place. 'Economies of scale', through mass production, become more important. Concern about production cost replaces concern about product adaptations. With standardized products the less developed countries (LDCs) may offer competitive advantages as production locations. One example of this is the movement of production locations for personal computers from ACs to LDCs.

## The Uppsala Internationalization model

The Scandinavian 'stages' models of entry suggest a sequential pattern of entry into successive foreign markets, coupled with a progressive deepening of commitment to each market. Increasing commitment is particularly important in the thinking of the Uppsala School (Johanson and Wiedersheim-Paul, 1975; Johanson and Vahlne, 1977). The main consequence of this Uppsala Internationalization model is that firms tend to intensify their commitment towards foreign markets as their experience grows. See also Section 3.2.

**Uppsala Internationalization model**
Additional market commitments are made in small incremental steps: choosing additional geographic markets with small psychic distances, combined with choosing entry modes with few additional risks.

## The internationalization/transaction cost approach

In the early 1970s intermediate forms of internationalization such as licensing were not considered interesting. Buckley and Casson (1976) expanded the choice to include licensing as a means of reaching customers abroad. But in their perspective the multinational firm would usually prefer to 'internalize' transactions via direct equity investment rather than license its capability. Joint ventures were not explicitly considered to be in the spectrum of governance choices until the mid-1980s (Contractor and Lorange, 1988; Kogut, 1988).

Buckley and Casson's focus on market-based (externalization) versus firm-based (internalization) solutions highlighted the strategic significance of licensing in market entry. Internationalization involves two interdependent decisions – location and mode of control.

The internalization perspective is closely related to the transaction cost (TC) theory (Williamson, 1975). The paradigmatic question in internalization theory is that, upon deciding to enter a foreign market, should a firm do so through internalization within its own boundaries (a subsidiary) or through some form of collaboration with an external partner (externalization)? The internalization and TC perspectives are both concerned with the minimization of TC and the conditions underlying market failure. The intention is to analyse the characteristics of a transaction in order to decide on the most efficient, i.e. TC minimizing, governance mode. The internalization theory can be considered the TC theory of the multinational corporation (Rugman, 1986; Madhok, 1998).

### Dunning's eclectic approach

In his eclectic Ownership-Location-Internalization (OLI) framework Dunning (1988) discussed the importance of locational variables in foreign investment decisions. The word 'eclectic' represents the idea that a full explanation of the transnational activities of firms needs to draw on several strands of economic theory. According to Dunning the propensity of a firm to engage itself in international production increases if the following three conditions are being satisfied:

1 *Ownership advantages*: A firm that owns foreign production facilities has bigger ownership advantages compared to firms of other nationalities. These 'advantages' may consist of intangible assets, such as know-how.
2 *Locational advantages*: It must be profitable for the firm to continue these assets with factor endowments (labour, energy, materials, components, transport and communication channels) in the foreign markets. If not, the foreign markets would be served by exports.
3 *Internalization advantages*: It must be more profitable for the firm to use its advantages rather than selling them, or the right to use them, to a foreign firm.

### The network approach

The basic assumption in the network approach is that the international firm cannot be analysed as an isolated actor but has to be viewed in relation to other actors in the international environment. Thus the individual firm is dependent on resources controlled by others. The relationships of a firm within a domestic network can be used as connections to other networks in other countries (Johanson and Mattson, 1988).

In the following three sections (sections 3.2 to 3.4) we will concentrate on three of the approaches presented above.

### The difference between 'cultural distance' and 'psychic distance'

Cultural distance (used in Chapter 6) refers to the (macro) cultural level of a country and is defined as the degree to which (factual) cultural values in one country are different from those in another country, i.e. 'distance' between countries.

**Psychic distance**
Differences in language, culture and political system, which disturb the flow between the firm and the market.

Psychic distance (used in this chapter) can be defined as the individual manager's perception of the differences between the home and the foreign market and it is a highly subjective interpretation of reality. Therefore, psychic distance cannot be measured with factual indicators, such as publicly available statistics on level of education, religion, language and so forth. The distinction between the two concepts is important for managers. By assessing psychic distance at the individual level, it is possible to take appropriate steps to reduce the manager's psychic distance towards foreign markets (Sousa and Bradley, 2005, 2006).

## 3.2  The Uppsala internationalization model

### The stage model

During the 1970s a number of Swedish researchers at the University of Uppsala (Johanson and Wiedersheim-Paul, 1975; Johanson and Vahlne, 1977) focused their interest on the internationalization process. Studying the internationalization of Swedish manufacturing firms, they developed a model of the firm's choice of market and form of entry when going abroad. Their work was influenced by Aharoni's seminal (1966) study.

With these basic assumptions in mind, the Uppsala researchers interpreted the patterns in the internationalization process they had observed in Swedish manufacturing firms. They had noted, first of all, that companies appeared to begin their operations abroad in fairly nearby markets and only gradually penetrated more far-flung markets. Second, it appeared that companies entered new markets through exports. It was very rare for companies to enter new markets with sales organizations or manufacturing subsidiaries of their own. Wholly-owned or majority-owned operations were established only after several years of exports to the same market.

Johanson and Wiedersheim-Paul (1975) distinguish between four different modes of entering an international market, where the successive stages represent higher degrees of international involvement/market commitment:

- Stage 1: No regular export activities (sporadic export).
- Stage 2: Export via independent representatives (export modes).
- Stage 3: Establishment of a foreign sales subsidiary.
- Stage 4: Foreign production/manufacturing units.

The assumption that the internationalization of a firm develops step by step was originally supported by evidence from a case study of four Swedish firms. The sequence of stages was restricted to a specific country market. This market commitment dimension is shown in Figure 3.1.

The concept of market commitment is assumed to contain two factors – the amount of resources committed and the degree of commitment. The amount of resources could be operationalized to the size of investment in the market (marketing, organization, personnel, etc.), while the degree of commitment refers to the difficulty of finding an alternative use for the resources and transferring them to the alternative use.

International activities require both general knowledge and market-specific knowledge. Market-specific knowledge is assumed to be gained mainly through experience in the market, whereas knowledge of the operations can be transferred from one country to another; the latter will thus facilitate the geographic diversification in Figure 3.1. A direct relation between market knowledge and market commitment is postulated: knowledge can be considered as a dimension of human resources. Consequently, the better knowledge about a market, the more valuable are the resources and the stronger the commitment to the market.

Figure 3.1 implies that additional market commitment as a rule will be made in small incremental steps, both in the market commitment dimension and in the geographical dimension. There are, however, three exceptions. First, firms that have large resources experience small consequences of their commitments and can take larger internationalization steps. Second, when market conditions are stable and homogeneous, relevant market knowledge can be gained in ways other than experience. Third, when the firm has considerable experience from markets with similar conditions, it

Figure 3.1 **Internationalization of the firm: an incremental (organic) approach**

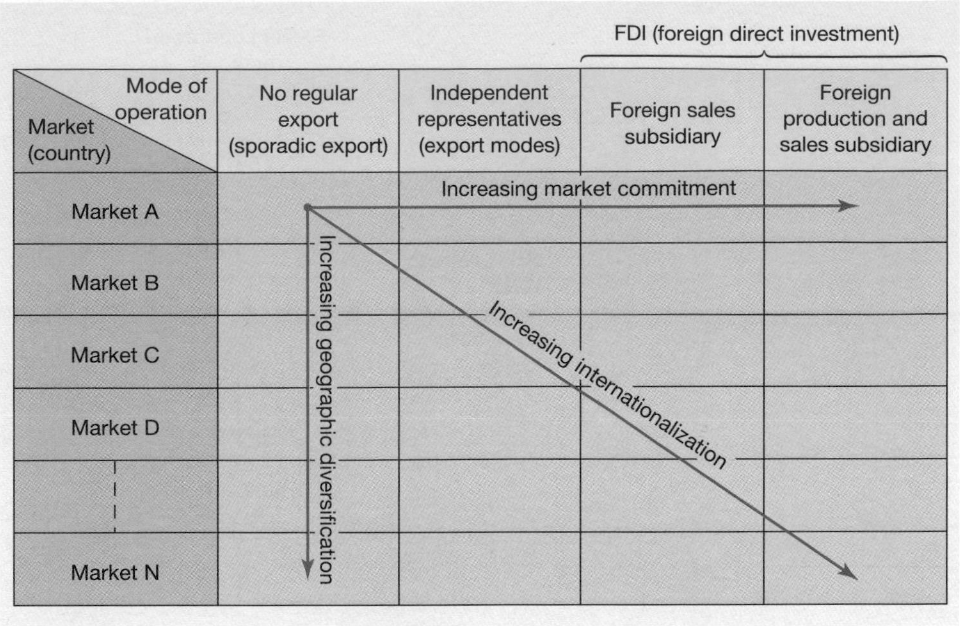

| | | | FDI (foreign direct investment) | |
|---|---|---|---|---|
| Market (country) — Mode of operation | No regular export (sporadic export) | Independent representatives (export modes) | Foreign sales subsidiary | Foreign production and sales subsidiary |
| Market A | | | | |
| Market B | | | | |
| Market C | | | | |
| Market D | | | | |
| | | | | |
| Market N | | | | |

*Increasing market commitment →*

*Increasing geographic diversification ↓*

*Increasing internationalization*

Source: Adapted from Forsgren and Johanson, 1975, p. 16.

may be able to generalize this experience to any specific market (Johanson and Vahlne, 1990).

The geographical dimension in Figure 3.1 shows that firms enter new markets with successively greater psychic distance. Psychic distance is defined in terms of factors such as differences in language, culture and political systems, which disturb the flow of information between the firm and the market. Thus firms start internationalization by going to those markets they can most easily understand. There they will see opportunities, and there the perceived market uncertainty is low (Brewer, 2007).

The original stage model has been extended by Welch and Loustarinen (1988), who operate with six dimensions of internationalization (see Figure 3.2):

1  *sales objects* (what?): goods, services, know-how and systems;
2  *operations methods* (how?): agents, subsidiaries, licensing, franchising management contracts;
3  *markets* (where?): political/cultural/psychic/physical distance differences between markets;
4  *organizational structure*: export department, international division;
5  *finance*: availability of international finance sources to support the international activities;
6  *personnel*: international skills, experience and training.

## 3.3 The transaction cost analysis (TCA) model

The foundation for this model was made by Coase (1937). He argued that 'a firm will tend to expand until the cost of organizing an extra transaction within the firm will become equal to the cost of carrying out the same transaction by means of an exchange on the open market' (p. 395). It is a theory which predicts that a firm will perform

### Figure 3.2 Dimensions of internationalization

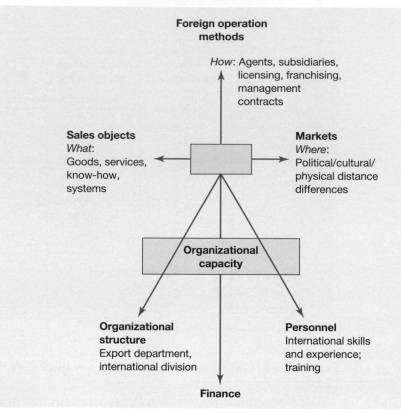

Source: Welch and Loustarinen, 1988. Reproduced with permission from The Braybrooke Press Ltd.

internally those activities it can undertake at lower cost through establishing an internal ('hierarchical') management control and implementation system while relying on the market for activities in which independent outsiders (such as export intermediaries, agents or distributors) have a cost advantage.

Transaction costs emerge when markets fail to operate under the requirements of perfect competition ('friction free'); the cost of operating in such markets (i.e. the transaction cost) would be zero, and there would be little or no incentive to impose any impediments to free market exchange. However, in the real world there is always some kind of 'friction' between buyer and seller, resulting in transaction costs (see Figure 3.3).

The friction between buyer and seller can often be explained by opportunistic behaviour. Williamson (1985) defines it as a 'self-interest seeking with guile'. It includes methods of misleading, distortion, disguise, and confusion. To protect against the hazards of opportunism, the parties may employ a variety of safeguards or governance structures. The term 'safeguard' (or alternatively 'governance structure') as used here can be defined as a control mechanism, which has the objective of bringing about the perception of fairness or equity among transactors. The purpose of safeguards is to provide, at minimum cost, the control and 'trust' that is necessary for transactors to believe that engaging in the exchange will make them better off. The most prominent safeguard is the legal contract. A legal contract specifies the obligations of each party and allows a transactor to go to a third party (i.e. a court) to sanction an opportunistic trading partner.

The transaction cost analysis (TCA) framework argues that cost minimization explains structural decisions. Firms internalize, that is, integrate vertically, to reduce

**Transaction costs**
The 'friction' between buyer and seller, which is explained by opportunistic behaviour.

**Opportunistic behaviour**
Self-interest with guile – misleading, distortion, disguise and confusion.

**Transaction cost analysis**
Transaction cost analysis concludes that if the 'friction' between buyer and seller is higher than through an internal hierarchical system then the firm should internalize.

**Internalize**
Integrate an external partner into one's own organization.

**Figure 3.3 The principles of the TCA model**

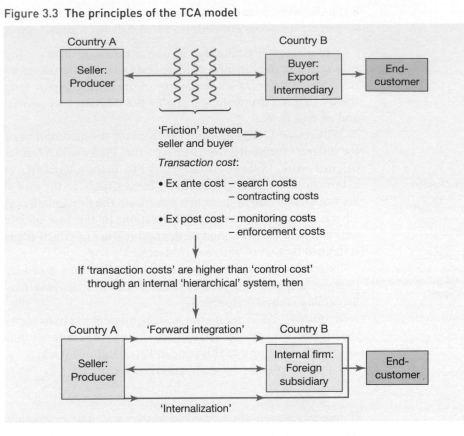

transaction costs. Transaction costs can be divided into *different forms of costs* related to the transactional relationship between buyer and seller. The underlying condition for the following description of the cost elements is this equation:

$$\text{transaction cost} = \text{ex ante costs} + \text{ex post costs} = (\text{search costs} + \text{contracting costs}) + (\text{monitoring costs} + \text{enforcement costs})$$

## Ex ante costs

- *Search costs*: include the cost of gathering information to identify and evaluate potential export intermediaries. Although such costs can be prohibitive to many exporters, knowledge about foreign markets is critical to export success. The search costs for distant, unfamiliar markets, where available (published) market information is lacking and organizational forms are different, can be especially prohibitive (e.g. exports from the United Kingdom to China). In comparison, the search costs for nearby, familiar markets may be more acceptable (e.g. export from United Kingdom to Germany).
- *Contracting costs*: refer to the costs associated with negotiating and writing an agreement between seller (producer) and buyer (export intermediary).

## Ex post costs

- *Monitoring costs*: refer to the costs associated with monitoring the agreement to ensure that both seller and buyer fulfil the predetermined set of obligations.

- *Enforcement costs*: refer to the costs associated with the sanctioning of a trading partner who does not perform in accordance with the agreement.

A fundamental assumption of transaction cost theory is that firms will attempt to minimize the combination of these costs when undertaking transactions. Thus, when considering the most efficient form of organizing export functions, transaction cost theory suggests that firms will choose the solution that minimizes the sum of ex ante and ex post costs.

Williamson (1975) based his analysis on the assumption of transaction costs and the different forms of governance structure under which transactions take place. In his original work, Williamson identified two main alternatives of governance markets: externalization and internalization ('hierarchies'). In the case of externalization, market transactions are by definition external to the firm and the price mechanism conveys all the necessary governance information. In the case of internalization, the international firm creates a kind of internal market in which the hierarchical governance is defined by a set of 'internal' contracts.

**Externalization**
Doing business through an external partner (importer, agent, distributor).

**Internalization**
Doing business through own internal system (own subsidiaries).

Externalization and internalization of transactions are equated with intermediaries (agents, distributors) and sales subsidiaries (or other governance structures involving ownership control) respectively.

In this way, Williamson's framework provides the basis for a variety of research into the organization of international activity and the choice of international market entry mode. We will return to this issue in Part III of this book.

The conclusion of the transaction cost theory is:

If the transaction costs (defined above) through externalization (e.g. through an importer or agent) are higher than the control cost through an internal hierarchical system, then the firm should seek internalization of activities, i.e. implementing the global marketing strategy in wholly-owned subsidiaries. Or more popularly explained: if the 'friction' between buyer and seller is too high then the firm should rather internalize, in the form of its own subsidiaries.

## Limitations of the TCA framework

### Narrow assumptions of human nature

Ghoshal and Moran (1996) have criticized the original work of Williamson as having too narrow assumptions of human nature (opportunism and its equally narrow interpretation of economic objectives). They also wonder why the theory's mainstream development has remained immune to such important contributions as Ouchi's (1980) insight on social control. Ouchi (1980) points to the relevance of intermediate forms (between markets and hierarchies), such as the clan, where governance is based on a win–win situation (in contrast to a zero-sum game situation).

Sometimes firms would even build trust with their externalized agents and distributors by turning them into partners. In this way the firms would avoid large investments in subsidiaries around the world.

### Excluding 'internal' transaction costs

The TCA framework also seems to ignore the 'internal' transaction cost, assuming zero friction within a multinational firm. One can imagine severe friction (resulting in transaction cost) between the head office of a firm and its sales subsidiaries when internal transfer prices have to be settled.

### Relevance of 'intermediate' forms for SMEs

One can also question the relevance of the TCA framework to the internationalization process of SMEs (Christensen and Lindmark, 1993). The lack of resources and knowledge in SMEs is a major force for the externalization of activities. But since the use of markets often raises contractual problems, markets in many instances are not real alternatives to hierarchies for SMEs. Instead, the SMEs have to rely on intermediate forms of governance, such as contractual relations and relations based on clan-like systems created by a mutual orientation of investments, skills and trust building. Therefore SMEs are often highly dependent on the cooperative environment available. Such an approach will be presented and discussed in the next section.

### Importance of 'production cost' is understated

It can be argued that the importance of transaction cost is overstated and that the importance of production cost has not been taken into consideration. Production cost is the cost of performing a particular task/function in the value chain, such as R&D costs, manufacturing costs and marketing costs. According to Williamson (1985), the most efficient choice of internationalization mode is one that will help *minimize the sum of production and transaction costs*.

---

## 3.4 The network model

### Basic concept

**Business networks**
Actors are autonomous and linked to each other through relationships, which are flexible and may alter accordingly to rapid changes in the environment. The 'glue' that keeps the relationships together are based on technical, economic, legal and especially personal ties.

**Network model**
The relationships of a firm in a domestic network can be used as bridges to other networks in other countries.

**Business networks** are a mode of handling activity interdependences between several business actors. As we have seen, other modes of handling or governing interdependences in a business field are markets and hierarchies.

The **network model** differs from the market with regard to relations between actors. In a market model, actors have no specific relations to each other. The interdependences are regulated through the market price mechanism. In contrast, in the business network the actors are linked to each other through exchange relationships, and their needs and capabilities are mediated through the interaction taking place in the relationships.

The industrial network differs from the hierarchy in the way that the actors are autonomous and handle their interdependences bilaterally rather than via a coordinating unit on a higher level. Whereas a hierarchy is organized and controlled as one unit from the top, the business network is organized by each actor's willingness to engage in exchange relationships with some of the other actors in the network. The networks are more loosely coupled than are hierarchies; they can change shape more easily. Any actor in the network can engage in new relationships or break off old ones, thereby modifying its structure. Thus business networks can be expected to be more flexible in response to changing conditions in turbulent business fields, such as those where technical change is very rapid.

It can be concluded that business networks will emerge in fields where coordination between specific actors can give strong gains and where conditions are changing rapidly. Thus the network approach implies a move away from the firm as the unit of analysis, towards exchange between firms and between a group of firms and other groups of firms as the main object of study. However, it also implies a move away from transactions towards more lasting exchange relationships constituting a structure within which international business takes place and evolves.

Evidently, business relationships and consequently industrial networks are subtle phenomena, which cannot easily be observed by an outsider: that is, a potential entrant. The actors are tied to each other through a number of different bonds: technical, social, cognitive, administrative, legal, economic, etc.

A basic assumption in the network model is that the individual firm is dependent on resources controlled by other firms. The companies get access to these external resources through their network positions. Since the development of positions takes time and depends on resource accumulations, a firm must establish and develop positions in relation to counterparts in foreign networks.

To enter a network from outside requires that other actors be motivated to engage in interaction, something which is resource demanding and may require several firms to make adaptations in their ways of performing business. Thus foreign market or network entry of the firm may very well be the result of interaction initiatives taken by other firms that are insiders in the network in the specific country. However, the chances of being the object of such initiatives are much greater for an insider.

The networks in a country may well extend far beyond country borders. In relation to the internationalization of the firm, the network view argues that the internationalizing firm is initially engaged in a network which is primarily domestic.

The relationships of a firm in a domestic network can be used as bridges to other networks in other countries. In some cases the customer demands that the supplier follows it abroad if the supplier wants to keep the business at home. An example of an international network is shown in Figure 3.4. It appears that one of the subsuppliers

**Figure 3.4 An example of an international network**

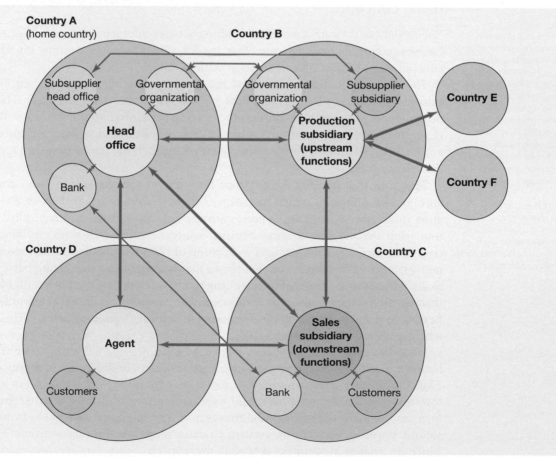

established a subsidiary in Country B. Here the production subsidiary is served by the local company of the subsupplier. Countries E and F, and partly Country C, are sourced from the production subsidiary in Country B. Generally it can be assumed that direct or indirect bridges exist between firms and different country networks. Such bridges can be important both in the initial steps abroad and in the subsequent entry of new markets.

The character of the ties in a network is partly a matter of the firms involved. This is primarily the case with technical, economic and legal ties. To an important extent, however, the ties are formed between the persons engaged in the business relationships. This is the case with social and cognitive ties. Industries as well as countries may differ with regard to the relative importance of firm and personal relationships. But it can be expected that the personal influence on relationships is strongest in the early establishment of relationships. Later in the process routines and systems will become more important.

When entering a network, the internationalization process of the firm will often proceed more quickly. In particular, SMEs in high-tech industries tend to go directly to more distant markets and to set up their own subsidiaries more rapidly. One reason seems to be that the entrepreneurs behind those companies have networks of colleagues dealing with the new technology. Internationalization, in these cases, is an exploitation of the advantage that this network constitutes.

## 3.5 Born globals

### Introduction

In recent years research has identified an increasing number of firms that certainly do not follow the traditional stages pattern in their internationalization process. In contrast, they aim at international markets or maybe even the global market right from their birth.

**Born global**
A firm that from its 'birth' globalizes rapidly without any preceding long term internationalization period.

A 'born global' can be defined as: 'a firm that from its inception pursue a vision of becoming global and globalize rapidly without any preceding long term domestic or internationalization period' (Oviatt and McDougall, 1994; Gabrielsson and Kirpalani, 2004).

Born globals represent an interesting case of firms operating under time and space compression conditions that have allowed them to assume a global geographic scope since their start up. This 'time–space compression' phenomenon (Harvey, 1996) means that geographical processes can be reduced and compressed into 'here and now' trade and information exchange over the globe – if available infrastructure, communication and IT devices are put in place together with skilled people. The global financial market is a good example of the phenomenon (Törnroos, 2002).

Oviatt and McDougall (1994) grouped born globals (or 'international new ventures' as they call them) into four different categories, dependent on the number of value chain activities performed combined with the number of countries involved. For example, they distinguish the 'export/import start-up' from the 'global start-up', whereby the latter – contrary to the former – involves many activities coordinated across many countries.

Born globals are typically characterized by being SMEs with less than 500 employees and annual sales under $100 million – and reliance on cutting-edge technology in the development of relatively unique product or process innovations. But the most distinguishing feature of born global firms is that they tend to be managed by entrepreneurial visionaries who view the world as a single, borderless marketplace from the time of the firm's founding. Born globals are small, technology-oriented companies that operate in international markets from the earliest days of their establishment. There is growing evidence of the emergence of born globals in numerous countries of the developed world.

More recently the concept of *born-again global firms* has been proposed, i.e. long-established firms that previously focused on their domestic markets but that suddenly embrace rapid and dedicated internationalization (Bell *et al.*, 2001). Furthermore, it seems that there can be *true-born globals* (focusing on both low- and high distance markets) and apparently born-globals, that is *born-internationals*, which are mainly focusing on low-distance markets (Kuivalainen *et al.*, 2007).

The born global phenomenon suggests a new challenge to traditional theories of internationalization.

## Born globals are challenging traditional theories

Born globals may be similar to the 'late starter' or the 'international among others' (Johanson and Mattson, 1988). In the latter situation both the environment and the firm are highly internationalized. Johanson and Mattson (1988) point out that internationalization processes of firms will be much faster in internationalized market conditions, among other reasons because the need for coordination and integration across borders is high. Since relevant partners/distributors will often be occupied in neighbouring markets, firms do not necessarily follow a 'rings in the water' approach to market selection. In the same vein their 'establishment chain' need not follow the traditional picture because strategic alliances, joint ventures, etc., are much more prevalent; firms seek partners with supplementary skills and resources. In other words internationalization processes of firms will be much more individual and situation specific in internationalized markets.

Many industries are characterized by *global sourcing activities* and also by networks across borders. The consequence is that innovative products can very quickly spread to new markets all over the world – because the needs and wants of buyers become more homogeneous. Hence the internationalization process of subcontractors may be quite diverse and different from the stages models. In other words, the new market conditions pull the firms into many markets very fast. Finally, financial markets have also become international, which means that an entrepreneur in any country may seek financial sources all over the world.

In the case of born globals we may argue that the background of the decision maker (founder) has a large influence on the internationalization path followed (Freeman and Cavusgil, 2007). Market knowledge, personal networking of the entrepreneur or international contacts and experience transmitted from former occupations, relations and education are examples of such international skills obtained prior to the birth of the firm. Factors such as education, experience from living abroad, experience of other internationally oriented jobs, etc., mould the mind of the founder and decrease the psychic distances to specific product markets significantly; the previous experience and knowledge of the founder extends the network across national borders, opening possibilities for new business ventures (Madsen and Servais, 1997).

Often born globals govern their sales and marketing activities through a specialized network in which they seek partners that complement their own competences; this is necessary because of their limited resources.

In many ways the slow organic (Uppsala-model) process and the accelerated 'born global' pathways are the opposites of one another, at the two extremes of a spectrum (see Figure 3.5). They also often represent the choice of doing it alone (the organic

**Figure 3.5 Two extreme pathways of internationalization: the 'organic' versus 'born global'**

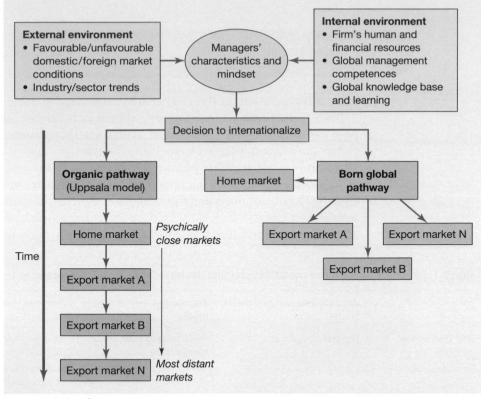

Source: Adapted from Âijö *et al.* (2005), p. 6.

pathway), while the 'born global' pathway is based on different types of cooperation and partnerships in order to facilitate rapid growth and internationalization.

In spite of the different time frames and prerequisites for the pathways, there are also some common characteristics in all models. Internationalization is seen as a process where knowledge and learning go hand in hand, even in rapid internationalization. Past knowledge contributes to current knowledge of the company. Firms aiming for the 'born global' pathway do not have time to develop these skills in the organic way (inside the firm), they need to possess them beforehand or to be able to acquire them underway, i.e. through collaborating with other firms already possessing these supplementary competences.

Most often 'born globals' must choose a business area with homogeneous and minimal adaptation of the marketing mix. The argument is that these small firms cannot take a multi-domestic approach as can large firms, simply because they do not have sufficient scale in operations worldwide. They are vulnerable because they are dependent on a single product (niche market) that they have to commercialize in lead markets first, no matter where such markets are situated geographically. The reason is that such markets are the key to broad and rapid market access, which is important because these firms often incur relatively high fixed R&D costs, which occur 'up front', i.e. before any sales are made. Since this is the key factor influencing the choice of the initial market the importance of psychic distance as a market selection criterion is reduced. In order to survive, firms must quickly catch the growth track to cover the initial expenses. Finally, competition for a typical 'born global' is very intense and its products may become obsolete rather quickly (e.g. in the case of software). If a company is to take full advantage of the market potential during its 'global window of opportunity', it may be forced to penetrate simultaneously all major markets (Âijö *et al.*, 2005).

## 3.6    Summary

The main conclusions of this chapter are summarized in Table 3.1.

Born globals represent a relatively new research field in international marketing. Born globals share some fundamental similarities: they possess unique assets, focus on narrow global market segments, are strongly customer oriented, and the entrepreneur's vision and competences are of crucial importance. In the end, for these firms, being global does not seem to be an option but a necessity. They are pushed into globalization by global customers and too small national/regional market segments. They can sustain their immediate global reach thanks to entrepreneurial vision and competences, and a deep awareness and knowledge of their competitive advantage in foreign markets.

**Table 3.1  Summary of the three models explaining the internationalization process of the firm**

|  | Uppsala internationalization model | Transaction cost analysis model | Network model |
|---|---|---|---|
| *Unit of analysis* | The firm | The transaction or set of transactions | Multiple interorganizational relationships between firms<br><br>Relationships between one group of firms and other groups of firms |
| *Basic assumptions about firms' behaviour* | The model is based on behavioural theories and an incremental decision-making process with little influence from competitive market factors. A gradual learning-by-doing process from simple export to Foreign Direct Investment (FDI) | In the real world there is 'friction'/transactional difficulties between buyer and seller. This friction is mainly caused by opportunistic behaviour: the self-conscious attention of the single manager (i.e. seeking of self-interest with guile) | The 'glue' that keeps the network (relationships) together is based on technical, economic, legal and especially personal ties. Managers' personal influence on relationships is strongest in the early phases of the establishment of relationships. Later in the process routines and systems will become more important |
| *Explanatory variables affecting the development process* | The firm's knowledge/market commitment<br><br>Psychic distance between home country and the firm's international markets | Transactional difficulties and transaction costs increase when transactions are characterized by asset specificity, uncertainty, frequency of transaction | The individual firms are autonomous. The individual firm is dependent on resources controlled by other firms<br><br>Business networks will emerge in fields where there is frequent coordination between specific actors and where conditions are changing rapidly |
| *Normative implications for international marketers* | Additional market commitments should be made in small incremental steps:<br>– Choose new geographic markets with small psychic distances from existing markets<br>– Choose an 'entry mode' with few marginal risks | Under the above-mentioned conditions (i.e. prohibitively high transaction costs), firms should seek internalization of activities (i.e. implement the global marketing strategy in wholly-owned subsidiaries). Overall, the firm should select the entry mode for which transaction costs are minimized | The relationships of a firm in a domestic network can be used as bridges to other networks in other countries. Such direct or indirect bridges to different country networks can be important in the initial steps abroad and in the subsequent entry of new markets. Sometimes an SME can be forced to enter foreign networks: for example, if a customer requires that the subsupplier (an SME) follows it abroad. |

CASE
STUDY
3.1

# Entertainment Rights: Internationalization of 'Postman Pat'

Entertainment Rights (ER) (**www.entertainmentrights. com**) is a global media group focusing on the ownership and development of children's brands. ER maintains a portfolio of more than 4,300 episodes of live-action and animated children's television programming (Postman Pat, Basil Brush, Rupert Bear – Follow the Magic, Jim Jam & Sunny). ER's wholly-owned subsidiary Tell-Tale Productions, created and produced *The Tweenies*, one of the UK's most successful pre-school brands. Through Tell-Tale Productions (acquired in 2004) ER also produces such original programming as Fun Song Factory and BB3B. That same year ER acquired the Filmation library of classic contemporary programming including Fat Albert, She-Ra Princess of Power and He-Man and the Masters of the Universe. Entertainment Rights also has Licensing and Merchandising operations as well as its own Home Entertainment division.

In 2005 ER acquired a majority interest in the classic Rupert Bear character from Express Newspapers, a unit of Northern and Shell.

More recently, in January 2007, ER announced the acquisition of Classic Media Inc., the US-based owner of an extensive children's portfolio of children's and family brands such as Rudolph the Red Nose Reindeer, Lassie, Caspar the Friendly Ghost and the award-winning Veggie Tales. This adds a further 4,400 episodes to the programme library.

ER has grown rapidly. Annual revenues have increased from £1.8 million in 1999 to £30.7 million in 2005, the last reported financial year. The financial development of ER in the last three years is shown in Table 1.

In 2005 the total revenues across regions were as follows:

|  | % of total revenues in 2005 |
| --- | --- |
| Europe: |  |
| UK | 59 |
| Rest of Europe | 26 |
| North & South America | 8 |
| Rest of World | 7 |
| Total | 100 |

Table 1 Financial development in the last three years (£000)

|  | 2006 | 2005 | 2004 |
| --- | --- | --- | --- |
| Operating revenue (revenue/sales) | 29,747 | 30,735 | 25,467 |
| Gross operating profit | 16,949 | 14,270 | 9,967 |
| Total income (EBIT) | 10,227 | 7,502 | 3,203 |
| Pre-tax income (EBT) | 7,829 | 5,956 | 2,186 |
| Total net income | 6,203 | 5,387 | 2,202 |

Source: Financial reports of Entertainment Rights and CoreData, Inc., International Institutional Database.

The total revenues across products were as follows:

| | % of total revenues in 2004 |
|---|---|
| Television & production | 57 |
| Home entertainment | 34 |
| Consumer products | 9 |
| Total | 100 |

The total number of employees is around 80.

## Postman Pat

Set in the fictional Yorkshire village of Greendale, Postman Pat and his faithful companion, Jess the Cat, began delivering post on BBC1 25 years ago in September 1981. Postman Pat continues to air on the BBC in the United Kingdom with episodes licensed and the broadcast platform secured beyond 2010. The target viewer group for the show is the pre-school age (2–6 years).

Postman Pat and the TV shows have now been shown in more than 100 countries around the world. With sales in so many international markets, it is important that the brand awareness created by the TV platform is leveraged through the development of a strong licensing and merchandising line – a business imperative for ER. For example, in the United Kingdom ER has succeeded in the licensing of toy lines to leading retailers. In 2004 Marks & Spencer acquired the rights for using the characters in 70 of its top stores. The programme included a range of nightwear, underwear, slippers, watches

and puzzles for children aged 3–6. Postman Pat and Jess the Cat proved to be an irresistible gift buy for parents, grandparents, guardians and others.

Source: www.entertainmentrights.com; 'Marks & Spencer takes on Postman Pat', Weekly E-news, Issue 76, 14 September 2004, www.licensmag.com.

### Questions

1  List the criteria, that Entertainment Rights should use for choosing new international markets.

2  If you were to advise ER would you recommend them to use the 'organic' or 'born global' pathway for the internationalization of Postman Pat?

3  What values/benefits can ER transfer to the license partners for consumer products apart from using the Postman Pat characters?

For further exercises and cases, see this book's website at **www.pearsoned.co.uk/hollensen**

## ? Questions for discussion

1  Explain why internationalization is an ongoing process in constant need of evaluation.

2  Explain the main differences between the three theories of internationalization: the Uppsala model, the transaction cost theory and the network model.

3  What is meant by the concept of 'psychological' or 'psychic distance'?

# References

Aharoni, Y. (1966) *The Foreign Investment Decision Process*, Harvard Business School Press, Boston, MA.

Âijö, T., Kuivalainen, O., Saarenketo, S., Lindqvist, J. and Hanninen, H. (2005) *Internationalization Handbook for the Software Business*, Centre of Expertise for Software Product Business, Espoo, Finland.

Bell, J., McNaughton, R. and Young, S. (2001) 'Born-Again global firms: an extension to the born global phenomenon', *Journal of International Management*, 7(3), pp. 173–190.

Brewer, P.A. (2007) 'Operationalizing Phychic Distance: A Revised Approach', *Journal of International Marketing*, Vol. 15, No. 1, pp. 44–66.

Buckley, P.J. and Casson, M. (1976) *The Future of the Multinational Enterprise*. Holmes & Meier, New York.

Christensen, P.R. and Lindmark, L.L. (1993) 'Location and internationalization of small firms', in Lindquist, L. and Persson, L.O. (eds) *Visions and Strategies in European Integration*, Springer Verlag, Berlin and Heidelberg.

Coase, R.H. (1937) 'The nature of the firm', *Economica*, pp. 386–405.

Contractor, F.J. and Lorange, P. (eds) (1998) *Cooperative Strategies in International Business*. Lexington Books, Lexington, MA.

Dunning, J.H. (1988) *Explaining International Production*, Unwin, London.

Forsgren, M. and Johansen, J. (1975) *International føretagsekonomi*, Norstedts.

Forsgren, M. and Johanson, J. (1975) *International føretagsekonomi*, Norstedts, Stockholm.

Freeman, S. and Cavusgil, S.T. (2007) 'Towards a Typology of Commitment States among Managers of Born-Global Firms: A study of Accelerated Internationalization', *Journal of International Marketing*, Vol. 15, No. 4, pp. 1–40.

Gabrielson, M. and Kirpalani, M.V.H. (2004) 'Born Globals; how to reach new business space rapidly', *International Business Review*, 13, pp. 555–571.

Ghoshal, S. and Moran, P. (1996) 'Bad for practice: a critique of the transaction cost theory', *Academy of Management Review*, 21(1), pp. 13–47.

Harvey, D. (1996) Justice, Nature and the Geography of Difference, Basil Blackwell, Oxford.

Hymer, S.H. (1976) The International Operations of National Firms: A study of direct foreign investment, unpublished 1960 PhD thesis, MIT Press, Cambridge, MA.

Johanson, J. and Mattson, L.G. (1988) 'Internationalization in industrial systems', in Hood, N. and Vahlne, J.E. (eds), *Strategies in Global Competition*, Croom Helm, Beckenham (UK).

Johanson, J. and Vahlne, J.E. (1977) 'The internationalization process of the firm: a model of knowledge development and increasing foreign market commitment', *Journal of International Business Studies*, 8(1), pp. 23–32.

Johanson, J. and Vahlne, J.E. (1990) 'The mechanism of internationalization', *International Marketing Review*, 7(4), pp. 11–24.

Johanson, J. and Wiedersheim-Paul, F. (1975) 'The internationalization of the firm: four Swedish cases', *Journal of Management Studies*, October, pp. 305–322.

Kindleberger, C.P. (1969) *American Business Abroad*, Yale University Press, New Haven, CT.

Kogut, B. (1988) 'Joint ventures: theoretical and empirical perspective', *Strategic Management Journal*, 9, pp. 319–332.

Kuivalainen, O., Sundqvist, S. and Servais, P. (2007) 'Firms' degree of born-globalness, international entrepreneurial orientation and export performance', *Journal of World Business*, Vol. 42, pp. 253–267.

Madhok, A. (1998) 'The nature of multinational firm boundaries: transaction cost, firm capabilities and foreign market entry mode', *International Business Review*, 7, pp. 259–290.

Madsen, T.K. and Servais, P. (1997) 'The internationalization of Born Globals: an evolutionary process?', *International Business Review*, 6(6), pp. 561–583.

Ouchi, W.G. (1980) 'Markets, bureaucracies and clans', *Administrative Science Quarterly*, 25, pp. 129–142.

Oviatt, B. and McDougall, P. (1994) 'Towards a theory of international new ventures', *Journal of International Business Studies*, 25(1), pp. 45–64.

Penrose, E. (1959) *The Theory of the Growth of the Firm*. Blackwell, London.

Prahalad, C.K. and Hamel, G. (1990) 'The core competence and the corporation', *Harvard Business Review*, May, pp. 71–97.

Rugman, A.M. (1986) 'New theories of the multinational enterprise: an assessment of internationalization theory', *Bulletin of Economic Research*, 38(2), pp. 101–118.

Sousa, C.M.P. and Bradley, F. (2005) 'Global markets: does psychic distance matter?' *Journal of Strategic Marketing*, 13, March, pp. 43–59.

Sousa, C.M.P. and Bradley, F. (2006) 'Cultural distance and psychic distance: two peas in a pod?', *Journal of International Marketing*, 14(1), pp. 49–70.

Törnroos, J.-Å. (2002) 'Internationalization of the firm: a theoretical review with implications for business network research', Paper presented at the *18th Annual IMP Conference*, September, Lyon, pp. 1–21.

Vernon, R. (1966) 'International investment and international trade in the product cycle', *Quarterly Journal of Economics*, 80, pp. 190–207.

Welch, L.S. and Loustarinen, R. (1988) 'Internationalization: evolution of a concept', *Journal of General Management*, 14(2), pp. 36–64.

Williamson, O.E. (1975) Markets and Hierarchies: Analysis and antitrust implications, The Free Press, New York.

Williamson, O.E. (1985) *The Economic Institutions of Capitalization*, The Free Press, New York.

# 4

# Development of the firm's international competitiveness

## Contents

## Learning objectives

After studying this chapter you should be able to do the following:

- Define the concept 'international competitiveness' in a broader perspective from a macro level to a micro level.
- Discuss the factors influencing the firm's international competitiveness.
- Explain how Porter's traditional competitive-based five forces model can be extended to a collaborative (five sources) model.
- Explore the idea behind the 'competitive triangle'.
- Analyse the basic sources of competitive advantage.
- Explain the steps in competitive benchmarking.

## 4.1 Introduction

The topic of this chapter is how the firm creates and develops competitive advantages in the international market. Development of a firm's international competitiveness takes place interactively with the environment. The firm must be able to adjust to customers, competitors and public authorities. To be able to participate in the international competitive arena the firm must have established a competitive basis consisting of resources, competences and relations to others in the international arena.

To enable an understanding of the development of a firm's international competitiveness in a broader perspective, a model in three stages (see Figure 4.1) will be presented:

1 analysis of national competitiveness (the Porter diamond) – macro level;
2 competition analysis in an industry (Porter's five forces) – meso level;

Figure 4.1  Development of a firm's international competitiveness

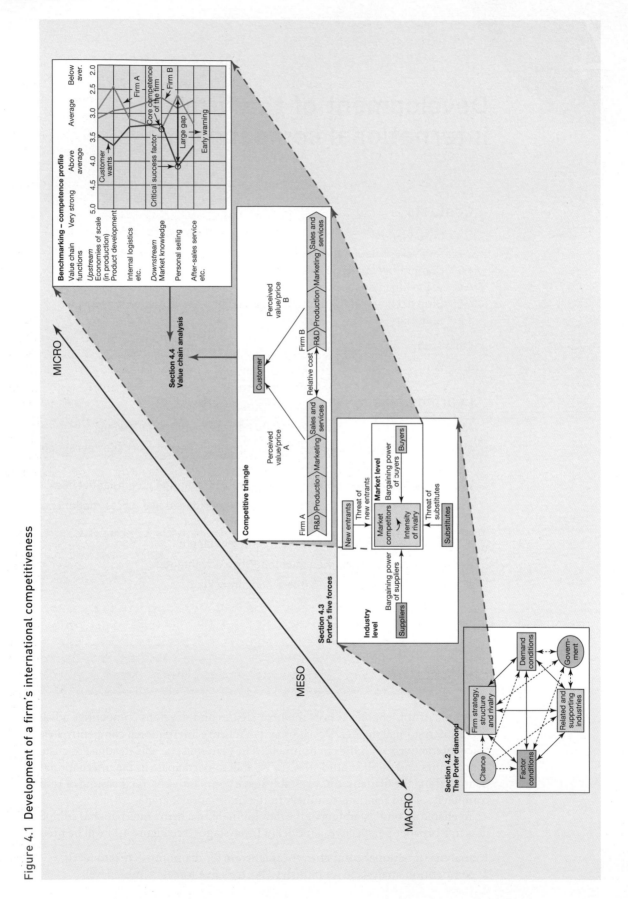

3 value chain analysis – micro level:
   (a) competitive triangle;
   (b) benchmarking.

The analysis starts at the macro level and then moves into the firm's competitive arena through Porter's five forces framework. Based on the firm's value chain, the analysis is concluded with a discussion of which activities/functions in the value chain are the firm's core competences (and must be developed internally in the firm) and which competences must be placed with others through alliances and market relations.

The graphical system used in Figure 4.1 (which will be referred to throughout this chapter) places the models after each other in a hierarchical windows logic, where you get from stage 1 to stage 2 by clicking on the icon box: 'Firm strategy, structure and rivalry'. Here Porter's five forces model appears. From stage 2 to 3 we click the middle box labelled 'Market competitors/Intensity of rivalry' and the model for a value chain analysis/competitive triangle appears.

### Individual competitiveness and time-based competition

In this chapter the analysis ends at the firm level but it is possible to go a step further by analysing individual competitiveness (Veliyath and Zahra, 2000). The factors influencing the capacity of an individual to become competitive would include intrinsic abilities, skills, motivation levels and the amount of effort involved. Traditional decision-making perspectives maintain that uncertainty leads executives to search for more additional information with which to increase certainty. However Kedia *et al.* (2002) showed that some executives increase competitiveness by using tactics to accelerate analysis of information and alternatives during the decision-making process. For example, these executives examine several alternatives simultaneously. The comparison process speeds their analysis of the strengths and weaknesses of options.

## 4.2   Analysis of national competitiveness (the Porter diamond)

Analysis of national competitiveness represents the highest level in the entire model (Figure 4.1). Michael E. Porter called his work *The Competitive Advantage of Nations* (1990), but as a starting point it is important to say that it is firms which are competing in the international arena, not nations. Yet the characteristics of the home nation play a central role in a firm's international success. The home base shapes a company's capacity to innovate rapidly in technology and methods, and to do so in the proper directions. It is the place from which competitive advantage ultimately emanates and from which it must be sustained. Competitive advantage ultimately results from an effective combination of national circumstances and company strategy. Conditions in a nation may create an environment in which firms can attain international competitive advantage, but it is up to a company to seize the opportunity. The national diamond becomes central to choosing the industries to compete with, as well as the appropriate strategy. The home base is an important determinant of a firm's strengths and weaknesses relative to foreign rivals.

Understanding the home base of foreign competitors is essential in analysing them. Their home nation yields them advantages and disadvantages. It also shapes their likely future strategies.

Porter (1990) describes a concentration of firms within a certain industry as industrial clusters. Within such industrial clusters firms have a network of relations to other firms in the industry: customers (including firms that work on semi-manufactured goods), suppliers and competitors. These industrial clusters may go worldwide, but they will usually have their starting point and location in a certain country or region of a country.

A firm gains important competitive advantages from the presence in its home nation of world-class buyers, suppliers and related industries. They provide insight into future market needs and technological developments. They contribute to a climate for change and improvement, and become partners and allies in the innovation process. Having a strong cluster at home unblocks the flow of information and allows deeper and more open contact than is possible when dealing with foreign firms. Being part of a cluster localized in a small geographic area can be even more valuable, so the central question we can ask is: what accounts for the national location of a particular global industry? The answer begins, as does all classical trade theory, with the match between the factor endowments of the country and the needs of the industry.

Let us now take a closer look at the different elements in Porter's diamond. Throughout the analysis the Indian IT/software industry (especially illustrated by the Bangalore area) will be used as an example (Nair *et al.*, 2007).

**Porter's diamond**
The characteristics of the 'home base' play a central role in explaining the international competitiveness of the firm – the explaining elements consist of factor conditions, demand conditions, related and supporting industries, firm strategy – structure and rivalry, chance and government.

## Factor conditions

We can make a distinction between 'basic and advanced' factors. Basic factors include natural resources (climate, minerals, oil) where the mobility of the factors is low. These factors can also create the ground for international competitiveness, but they can never turn into real value creation without the advanced factors, like sophisticated human resources (skills) and research capabilities. Such advanced factors also tend to be specific to the industry.

In the Indian software industry, Bangalore has several engineering- and science-oriented educational institutions. Also the Indian Institute of Science (a research-oriented graduate school) can be identified as essential in the development of the software industry in the region. The presence of the public-sector engineering firms and the private engineering colleges has attracted young people from the country to Bangalore and it has created a diverse, multilingual, tolerant and cosmopolitan culture. One of the most critical success factors of the industry was the availability of advanced- and higher-educated people, but with generalized skills. These generalists (rather than specialists in software or programming) could be trained into problem solvers in specific areas based on industry needs.

## Demand conditions

These factors are represented in the right-hand box of Porter's diamond (Figure 4.1). The characteristics of this element that drive industry success include the presence of early home demand, market size, its rate of growth and sophistication.

There is an interaction between scale economies, transportation costs and the size of the home market. Given sufficiently strong economies of scale, each producer wants to serve a geographically extensive market from a single location. To minimize transportation costs the producer chooses a location with large local demand. When scale economies limit the number of production locations the size of a market will be an important determinant of its attractiveness. Large home markets will also ensure that firms located at that site develop a cost advantage based on scale and often on experience as well.

An interesting pattern is that an early large home market that has become saturated forces efficient firms to look abroad for new business. For example, the Japanese motorcycle industry with its large home market used its scale advantages in the global marketplace after an early start in Japan. The composition of demand also plays an important role.

A product's fundamental or core design nearly always reflects home market needs. In electrical transmission equipment, for example, Sweden dominates the world in the high-voltage distribution market. In Sweden there is a relatively large demand for transporting high voltage over long distances, as a consequence of the location of population and industry clusters. Here the needs of the home market shaped the industry that was later able to respond to global markets (with ABB as one of the leading producers in the world market).

The sophistication of the buyer is also important. The US government was the first buyer of chips and remained the only customer for many years. The price inelasticity of government encouraged firms to develop technically advanced products without worrying too much about costs. Under these conditions the technological frontier was clearly pushed much further and much faster than it would have been had the buyer been either less sophisticated or more price sensitive.

The Indian software industry was kicked off as a result of the Y2K problem (a problem caused due to a coding convention in older systems that assigned only two digits for the year count, thereby creating a potential disruption as the calendar year turned 2000) because US firms contracted with Indian software firms that had employees who were skilled in older programming languages such as Cobol and Fortran. As their experience with US firms increased and the Y2K problems were solved, Indian-based software firms began diversifying and offering more value-added products and service. Serving demanding US customers forced the Indian software firms to develop high-quality products and services. Later on this experience helped to address the needs of IT customers in Germany, Japan and other markets.

## Related and supporting industries

The success of an industry is associated with the presence of suppliers and related industries within a region. In many cases competitive advantages come from being able to use labour that is attracted to an area to serve the core industry, but which is available and skilled enough to support this industry. Coordination of technology is also eased by geographic proximity. Porter argues that Italian world leadership in gold and silver jewellery has been sustained in part by the local presence of manufacturers of jewellery-making machinery. Here the advantage of clustering is not so much transportation cost reductions but technical and marketing cooperation. In the semiconductor industry, the strength of the electronics industry in Japan (which buys the semiconductors) is a strong incentive to the location of semiconductors in the same area. It should be noted that clustering is not independent of scale economies. If there were no scale economies in the production of intermediate inputs, then the small-scale centres of production could rival the large-scale centres. It is the fact that there are scale economies in both semiconductors and electronics, coupled with the technological and marketing connections between the two, that give rise to clustering advantages.

In the beginning, Bangalore's lack of reliable supporting industries, like telecommunications and power supplies, was a problem, but many software firms installed their own generators and satellite communication equipment. Recently, firms that provide venture capital, recruitment assistance, network, hardware maintenance and marketing/accounting support have emerged in the Bangalore area to support the software firms. Also the presence of consulting firms like KPMG, PricewaterhouseCoopers and

Ernst & Young assist incoming multinational companies to enter the Indian market, by solving problems linked to currency, location, etc. Consequently, a whole system of support has now evolved around the software industry.

## Firm strategy, structure and rivalry

This fairly broad element includes how companies are organized and managed, their objectives, and the nature of domestic rivalry.

One of the most compelling results of Porter's study of successful industries in ten different nations is the powerful and positive effect that domestic competition has on the ability to compete in the global marketplace. In Germany, the fierce domestic rivalry among BASF, Hoechst and Bayer in the pharmaceutical industry is well known. Furthermore, the process of competition weeds out inferior technologies, products and management practices, and leaves as survivors only the most efficient firms. When domestic competition is vigorous firms are forced to become more efficient, adopt new cost-saving technologies, reduce product development time, and learn to motivate and control workers more effectively. Domestic rivalry is especially important in stimulating technological developments among global firms.

The small country of Denmark has three producers of hearing-aids (William Demant, Widex and GN Resound/Danavox), which are all among the top ten of the world's largest producers of hearing-aids. In 1996 Oticon (the earlier William Demant) and Widex fought a violent technological battle to be the first in the world to launch a 100 per cent digitalized hearing-aid. Widex (the smaller of the two producers) won, but forced Oticon at the same time to keep a leading edge in technological development.

In relation to the Indian software industry, most firms in the Bangalore area experience fierce competition. The competition about future customers is not just with local firms, but also with firms outside Bangalore and multinational companies such as IBM and Accenture. Competition has resulted in a pressure on firms to deliver quality products and services, but also to be cost-effective. It has also encouraged firms to seek international certifications, with a rating in software development. Today the Bangalore area has the world's highest concentration of companies with the so-called CMM-SEI (Carnegie Mellon University's Software Engineering Institute) Level 5 certification (the highest quality rating).

## Government

According to Porter's diamond-model, governments can influence and be influenced by each of the four main factors. Governments can play a powerful role in encouraging the development of industries within their own borders that will assume global positions. Governments finance and construct infrastructure, providing roads, airports, education and health care, and can support use of alternative energy (e.g. wind turbines) or other environmental systems that affect factors of production.

In relation to the Indian software industry, the federal government in Delhi had already in the 1970s targeted software as a growth area, because of its high skill requirements and labour intensity. Through the 1970s and 1980s the industry was mainly dominated by public-sector companies like CMC. In 1984 the government started liberalizing industrial and investment policies, which gave access to IT-companies from abroad (e.g. Texas Instruments). One of the new initiatives was also setting up 'technology parks', for example, the Software Technology Park (STP) in Bangalore. The liberation policy continued throughout the 1980s and 1990s. In 1988 NASSCOM (the National Association of Software and Service Companies) was formed. NASSCOM is an association of IT-firms, which acts as a catalyst for industry growth by supporting

IT research and education in India. In 1999 the Ministry of Information Technology was set up to coordinate the IT-initiatives at government, academic and business levels. Thus Bangalore's success in becoming a software hub was contributed to by the state government's active role in the early and later stages of the industry's evolution.

## Chance

According to Porter's diamond, national/regional competitiveness may also be triggered by random events.

When we look at the history of most industries we also see the role played by chance. Perhaps the most important instance of chance involves the question of who comes up with a major new idea first. For reasons having little to do with economics, entrepreneurs will typically start their new operations in their home countries. Once the industry begins in a given country scale and clustering effects can cement the industry's position in that country.

In relation to the development of competitiveness of the Indian software industry (especially in Bangalore) two essential events can be identified:

1 The Y2K problems (described earlier), which created an increased demand for services of Indian software firms.
2 The collapse of the dotcom boom in 2001 in the United States and Europe, resulting in a search for ways to cut costs by outsourcing software functions to India.

From the firm's point of view the last two variables, chance and government, can be regarded as exogenous variables that the firm must adjust to. Alternatively, the government may be considered susceptible through lobbying, interest organizations and mass media.

## Summary

In summary, we have identified six factors that influence the location of global industries: factors of production, home demand, the location of supporting industries, the internal structure of the domestic industry, chance and government. We have also suggested that these factors are interconnected. As industries evolve their dependence on particular locations may also change. For example, the shift in users of semiconductors from the military to the electronics industry has had a profound effect on the shape of the national diamond in that industry. To the extent that governments and firms recognize the source of any locational advantages that they have, they will be better able to both exploit those differences and anticipate their shifts.

In relation to the software industry in India (Bangalore), which was used throughout the diamond model, the following conclusions may be arrived at (Nair *et al.*, 2007):

● The software industry in Bangalore started off by serving not only its domestic customers but the demanding North American customers. Also the rivals for software firms tend not to be so much local but global.
● The support needed for software services is much less sophisticated than for manufacturing. For the manufacturing sector it is also important to have access to a well-functioning physical infrastructure (transport, logistics, etc.), which is not necessary for the software industry where most of the logistic can be done over the Internet. That is one of the reasons why Bangalore's software industry created international competitiveness, but the manufacturing sector did not.
● The software industry is very much dependent on advanced and well-educated human resources as the key factor input.

While the Bangalore-based firms started off at the low end of the value chain (performing coding work for the Y2K problem) they have continuously moved in the direction of delivering more value-added services in emerging areas.

## 4.3   Competition analysis in an industry

The next step in understanding the firm's competitiveness is to look at the competitive arena in an industry, which is the top box in the diamond model (see Figure 4.1).

One of the most useful frameworks for analysing the competitive structure has been developed by Porter. Porter (1980) suggests that competition in an industry is rooted in its underlying economic structure and goes beyond the behaviour of current competitors. The state of competition depends upon five basic competitive forces, as shown in Figure 4.1. Together these factors determine the ultimate profit potential in an industry, where profit is measured in terms of long-run return on invested capital. The profit potential will differ from industry to industry.

To make things clearer we need to define a number of key terms. An *industry* is a group of firms that offer a product or class of products which are close substitutes for each other. Examples are the car industry and the pharmaceutical industry (Kotler, 1997, p. 230). A *market* is a set of actual and potential buyers of a product and sellers. A distinction will be made between industry and market level, as we assume that the industry may contain several different markets. This is why the outer box in Figure 4.1 is designated 'industry level' and the inner box 'market level'.

*Porter's five-forces model*
The state of competition and profit potential in an industry depends on five basic competitive forces: new entrants, suppliers, buyers, substitutes, buyers and market competitors.

Thus the *industry level* (Porter's five-forces model) consists of all types of actors (new entrants, suppliers, substitutes, buyers and market competitors) that have a potential or current interest in the industry.

The *market level* consists of actors with a current interest in the market: that is, buyers and sellers (market competitors). In section 4.4 (value chain analysis) this market level will be further elaborated on as the buyers' perceived value of different competitor offerings will be discussed.

Although division into the above-mentioned two levels is appropriate for this approach, Levitt (1960) pointed out the danger of 'marketing myopia', where the seller defines the competition field (i.e. the market) too narrowly. For example, European luxury car manufacturers showed this myopia with their focus on each other rather than on the Japanese mass manufacturers, who were new entrants into the luxury car market.

The goal of competition analysis is to find a position in industry where the company can best defend itself against the five forces, or can influence them in its favour. Knowledge of these underlying pressures highlights the critical strengths and weaknesses of the company, shows its position in the industry, and clarifies areas where strategy changes yield the greatest pay-off. Structure analysis is fundamental for formulating competitive strategy.

Each of the five forces in the Porter model in turn comprises a number of elements that combine to determine the strength of each force, and its effect on the degree of competition. Each force is now discussed.

### Market competitors

The intensity of rivalry between existing competitors in the market depends on a number of factors:

- *The concentration of the industry*. Numerous competitors of equal size will lead to more intense rivalry. There will be less rivalry when a clear leader (at least 50 per cent larger than the second) exists with a large cost advantage.
- *Rate of market growth*. Slow growth will tend towards greater rivalry.
- *Structure of costs*. High fixed costs encourage price cutting to fill capacity.
- *Degree of differentiation*. Commodity products encourage rivalry, while highly differentiated products, which are hard to copy, are associated with less intense rivalry.
- *Switching costs*. When switching costs are high because the product is specialized, the customer has invested a lot of resources in learning how to use the product or has made tailor-made investments that are worthless with other products and suppliers (high asset specificity), rivalry is reduced.
- *Exit barriers*. When barriers to leaving a market are high due to such factors as lack of opportunities elsewhere, high vertical integration, emotional barriers or the high cost of closing down plant, rivalry will be more intense than when exit barriers are low.

Firms need to be careful not to spoil a situation of competitive stability. They need to balance their own position against the well-being of the industry as a whole. For example, an intense price or promotional war may gain a few percentage points in market share, but lead to an overall fall in long-run industry profitability as competitors respond to these moves. It is sometimes better to protect industry structure than to follow short-term self-interest.

## Suppliers

The cost of raw materials and components can have a major bearing on a firm's profitability. The higher the bargaining power of suppliers, the higher the costs. The bargaining power of suppliers will be higher in the following circumstances:

- Supply is dominated by few companies and they are more concentrated than the industry they sell to.
- Their products are unique or differentiated, or they have built up switching costs.
- They are not obliged to contend with other products for sale to the industry.
- They pose a credible threat of integrating forwards into the industry's business.
- Buyers do not threaten to integrate backwards into supply.
- The market is not an important customer to the supplier group.

A firm can reduce the bargaining power of suppliers by seeking new sources of supply, threatening to integrate backwards into supply, and designing standardized components so that many suppliers are capable of producing them.

## Buyers

The bargaining power of buyers is higher in the following circumstances:

- Buyers are concentrated and/or purchase in large volumes.
- Buyers pose a credible threat of integrating backwards to manufacture the industry's product.
- Products they purchase are standard or undifferentiated.
- There are many suppliers (sellers) of the product.
- Buyers earn low profits, which create a great incentive to lower purchasing costs.
- The industry's product is unimportant to the quality of the buyer's products, but price is very important.

Firms in the industry can attempt to lower buyer power by increasing the number of buyers they sell to, threatening to integrate forward into the buyer's industry, and producing highly valued, differentiated products. In supermarket retailing, the brand leader normally achieves the highest profitability, partially because being number one means that supermarkets need to stock the brand, thereby reducing buyer power in price negotiations.

Customers who purchase the product but are not the end user (such as OEMs or distributors) can be analysed in the same way as other buyers. Non end-customers can gain significant bargaining power when they can influence the purchasing decision of customers downstream (Porter, 2008). Over the years ingredient supplier, DuPont, has created enormous clout by advertising its 'Teflon' brand not only to the manufacturers of cooking equipment, but also to downstream end-customers (households). See also section 11.4 about ingredient branding.

## Substitutes

The presence of substitute products can reduce industry attractiveness and profitability because they put a constraint on price levels.

If the industry is successful and earning high profits it is more likely that competitors will enter the market via substitute products in order to obtain a share of the potential profits available. The threat of substitute products depends on the following factors:

- the buyer's willingness to substitute;
- the relative price and performance of substitutes;
- the costs of switching to substitutes.

The threat of substitute products can be lowered by building up switching costs. These costs may be psychological. Examples are the creation of strong, distinctive brand personalities, and maintaining a price differential commensurate with perceived customer values.

## New entrants

New entrants can serve to increase the degree of competition in an industry. In turn, the threat of new entrants is largely a function of the extent to which barriers to entry exist in the market. Some key factors affecting these entry barriers include the following:

- economies of scale;
- product differentiation and brand identity, which give existing firms customer loyalty;
- capital requirements in production;
- switching costs – the cost of switching from one supplier to another;
- access to distribution channels.

Because high barriers to entry can make even a potentially lucrative market unattractive (or even impossible) to enter for new competitors, the marketing planner should not take a passive approach but should actively pursue ways of raising barriers to new competitors.

High promotional and R&D expenditures and clearly communicated retaliatory actions to entry are some methods of raising barriers. Some managerial actions can unwittingly lower barriers. For example, new product designs that dramatically lower manufacturing costs can make entry by newcomers easier.

## The collaborative 'five-sources' model

Porter's original model is based on the hypothesis that the competitive advantage of the firm is best developed in a very competitive market with intense rivalry relations.

The five-forces framework thus provides an analysis for considering how to squeeze the maximum competitive gain out of the context in which the business is located – or how to minimize the prospect of being squeezed by it – on the five competitive dimensions that it confronts.

Over the past decade, however, an alternative school (e.g. Reve, 1990; Kanter, 1994; Burton, 1995) has emerged which emphasises the positive role of cooperative (rather than competitive) arrangements between industry participants, and the consequent importance of what Kanter (1994) has termed 'collaborative advantage' as a foundation of superior business performance.

An all-or-nothing choice between a single-minded striving for either competitive or collaborative advantage would, however, be a false one. The real strategic choice problem that all businesses face is where (and how much) to collaborate, and where (and how intensely) to act competitively.

Put another way, the basic questions that firms must deal with in respect of these matters are as follows:

- choosing the combination of competitive and collaborative strategies that are appropriate in the various dimensions of the industry environment of the firm;
- blending the two elements together so that they interact in a mutually consistent and reinforcing, and not counterproductive, manner;
- in this way, optimizing the firm's overall position, drawing upon the foundation and utilization of both collaborative and competitive advantage.

This points to the imperative in the contemporary context of complementing the competitive strategy model with a sister framework that focuses on the assessment of collaborative advantage and strategy. Such a complementary analysis, which is called the *five-sources framework* (Burton, 1995), is outlined below.

Corresponding to the array of five competitive forces that surround a company – as elaborated in Porter's treatment – there are also five potential sources for the building of collaborative advantage in the industrial environments of the firm (the five-sources model). These sources are listed in Table 4.1.

**Five sources model**
Corresponding to Porter's five competitive forces there are also five potential sources for building collaborative advantages together with the firm's surrounding actors.

In order to forge an effective and coherent business strategy, a firm must evaluate and formulate its collaborative and competitive policies side by side. It should do this for two purposes:

1 to achieve the appropriate balance between collaboration and competition in each dimension of its industry environment (e.g. relations with suppliers, policies towards customers/channels);
2 to integrate them in a way that avoids potential clashes and possibly destructive inconsistencies between them.

This is the terrain of composite strategy, which concerns the bringing together of competitive and collaborative endeavours.

Table 4.1  The five sources model and the corresponding five forces in the Porter model

| Porter's five-forces model | The five-sources model |
|---|---|
| *Market competitors* | Horizontal collaborations with other enterprises operating at the same stage of the production process/producing the same group of closely related products (e.g. contemporary global partnering arrangements among car manufacturers). |
| *Suppliers* | Vertical collaborations with suppliers of components or services to the firm – sometimes termed vertical quasi-integration arrangements (e.g. the *keiretsu* formations between suppliers and assemblers that typify the car, electronics and other industries in Japan). |
| *Buyers* | Selective partnering arrangements with specific channels or customers (e.g. lead users) that involve collaboration extending beyond standard, purely transactional relationships. |
| *Substitutes* | Related diversification alliances with producers of both complements and substitutes. Producers of substitutes are not 'natural allies', but such alliances are not inconceivable (e.g. collaborations between fixed-wire and mobile telephone firms in order to grow their joint network size). |
| *New entrants* | Diversification alliances with firms based in previously unrelated sectors, but between which a 'blurring' of industry borders is potentially occurring, or a process (commonly due to new technological possibilities) that opens up the prospect of cross-industry fertilization of technologies/business that did not exist before (e.g. the collaborations in the emerging multimedia field). |

Source: Burton, 1995. Reproduced with permission from The Braybrooke Press Ltd.

## 4.4  Value chain analysis

Until now we have discussed the firm's international competitiveness from a strategic point of view. To get closer to the firm's core competences we will now look at the market-level box in Porter's five-forces model, which treats buyers and sellers (market competitors). Here we will look more closely at what creates a competitive advantage among market competitors towards customers at the same competitive level.

### The competitive triangle

Success in the marketplace is dependent not only upon identifying and responding to customer needs, but also upon our ability to ensure that our response is judged by customers to be superior to that of competitors (i.e. high perceived value). Several writers (e.g. Porter, 1980; Day and Wensley, 1988) have argued that causes of difference in performance within a market can be analysed at various levels. The immediate causes of differences in the performance of different firms, these writers argue, can be reduced to two basic factors (D'Aveni, 2007):

1 The *perceived value* of the product/services offered, compared to the perceived sacrifice. The *perceived sacrifice* includes all the 'costs' the buyer faces when making a purchase, primarily the *purchase price*, but also acquisition costs, transportation,

Figure 4.2 Perceived value, relative costs and competitive advantage

| | | Perceived value (compared to the purchase price) | |
| --- | --- | --- | --- |
| | | *Higher for A* | *Higher for B* |
| **Relative costs** | *Lower for A* | I | II |
| | *Lower for B* | III | IV |

installation, handling, repairs and maintenance (Ravald and Grönroos, 1996). In the models presented the (purchase) price will be used as a representative of the perceived sacrifice. D'Aveni (2007) presents a strategic tool for evaluating how much a customer is willing to pay for a perceived benefit of a product/service.

2  The firm-related *costs* incurred in creating this perceived value.

These two basic factors will be further discussed later in this section.

The more value customers perceive in a market offering relative to competing offerings, and the lower the costs in producing the value relative to competing producers, the higher the performance of the business. Hence firms producing offerings with a higher perceived value and/or lower relative costs than competing firms are said to have a competitive advantage in that market.

This can be illustrated by the 'competitive triangle' (see Figure 4.1, earlier). There is no one-dimensional measure of competitive advantage, and perceived value (compared to the price) and relative costs have to be assessed simultaneously. Given this two-dimensional nature of competitive advantage it will not always be clear which of the two businesses will have a competitive advantage over the other.

Looking at Figure 4.2, firm A will clearly have an advantage over firm B in case I, and clearly have a disadvantage in case IV, while cases II and III do not immediately allow such a conclusion. Firm B may have an advantage in case II, if customers in the market are highly quality conscious and have differentiated needs and low price elasticity, while firm A may have a similar advantage in case II when customers have homogeneous needs and high price elasticity. The opposite will take place in case III.

Even if firm A has a clear competitive advantage over firm B, this may not necessarily result in a higher return on investment for A, if A has a growth and B a hold policy. Thus performance would have to be measured by a combination of return on investment and capacity expansion, which can be regarded as postponed return on investment.

While the relationship between perceived value, relative costs and performance is rather intricate, we can retain the basic statement that these two variables are the cornerstone of competitive advantage. Let us take a closer look at these two fundamental sources of competitive advantage.

### Perceived value advantage

We have already observed that customers do not buy products, they buy benefits. Put another way, the product is purchased not for itself but for the promise of what it

**Competitive triangle**
Consists of a customer, the firm and a competitor (the 'triangle'). The firm or competitor 'winning' the customer's favour depends on perceived value offered to the customer compared to the relative costs between the firm and the competitor.

**Perceived value**
The customer's overall evaluation of the product/service offered by a firm.

will 'deliver'. These benefits may be intangible: that is, they may relate not to specific product features but rather to such things as image or reputation. Alternatively, the delivered offering may be seen to outperform its rivals in some functional aspect.

Perceived value is the customer's overall evaluation of the product/service offered. So, establishing what value the customer is actually seeking from the firm's offering (value chain) is the starting point for being able to deliver the correct mix of value-providing activities. It may be some combination of physical attributes, service attributes and technical support available in relation to the particular use of the product. This also requires an understanding of the activities that constitute the customer's value chain.

Unless the product or service we offer can be distinguished in some way from its competitors there is a strong likelihood that the marketplace will view it as a 'commodity', and so the sale will tend to go to the cheapest supplier. Hence the importance of seeking to attach additional values to our offering to mark it out from the competition.

What are the means by which such value differentiation may be gained?

If we start in the value chain perspective (see section 1.6), we can say that each activity in the business system adds perceived value to the product or service. Value, for the customer, is the perceived stream of benefits that accrue from obtaining the product or service. Price is what the customer is willing to pay for that stream of benefits. If the price of a good or service is high it must provide high value, otherwise it is driven out of the market. If the value of a good or service is low its price must be low, otherwise it is also driven out of the market. Hence, in a competitive situation, and over a period of time, the price that customers are willing to pay for a good or service is a good proxy measure of its value.

If we look especially at the downstream functions of the value chain, a differential advantage can be created with any aspect of the traditional 4-P marketing mix: product, distribution, promotion and price are all capable of creating added customer perceived value. The key to whether improving an aspect of marketing is worthwhile is to know if the potential benefit provides value to the customer.

If we extend this model particular emphasis must be placed upon the following (see Booms and Bitner, 1981; Magrath, 1986; Rafiq and Ahmed, 1995):

- *People.* These include both consumers, who must be educated to participate in the service, and employees (personnel), who must be motivated and well trained in order to ensure that high standards of service are maintained. Customers identify and associate the traits of service personnel with the firms they work for.
- *Physical aspects.* These include the appearance of the delivery location and the elements provided to make the service more tangible. For example, visitors experience Disneyland by what they see, but the hidden, below-ground support machinery is essential for the park's fantasy fulfilment.
- *Process.* The service is dependent on a well-designed method of delivery. Process management assures service availability and consistent quality in the face of simultaneous consumption and production of the service offered. Without sound process management balancing service demand with service supply is extremely difficult.

Of these three additional Ps, the firm's *personnel* occupy a key position in influencing customer perception of product quality. As a consequence the *image* of the firm is very much influenced by the personnel. It is therefore important to pay particular attention to the quality of employees and to monitor their performance. Marketing managers need to manage not only the service provider – customer interface – but also the actions of other customers; for example, the number, type and behaviour of other people will influence a meal at a restaurant.

## Relative cost advantage

Each activity in the value chain is performed at a cost. Getting the stream of benefits that accrue from the good or service to the customer is thus done at a certain 'delivered cost', which sets a lower limit to the price of the good or service if the business system is to remain profitable. Decreasing the price will thus imply that the delivered cost be first decreased by adjusting the business system. As mentioned earlier, the rules of the game may be described as *providing the highest possible perceived value to the final customer, at the lowest possible delivered cost.*

A firm's cost position depends on the configuration of the activities in its value chain versus that of competitors and its relative location on the cost drivers of each activity. A cost advantage is gained when the cumulative cost of performing all the activities is lower than competitors' costs. This evaluation of the relative cost position requires an identification of each important competitor's value chain. In practice, this step is extremely difficult because the firm does not have direct information on the costs of competitors' value activities. However, some costs can be estimated from public data or interviews with suppliers and distributors.

Creating a relative cost advantage requires an understanding of the factors that affect costs. It is often said that 'big is beautiful'. This is partly due to economies of scale, which enable fixed costs to be spread over a greater output, but more particularly it is due to the impact of the *experience curve.*

The experience curve is a phenomenon that has its roots in the earlier notion of the learning curve. The effects of learning on costs were seen in the manufacture of fighter planes for the Second World War. The time taken to produce each plane gradually fell as learning took place. The combined effect of economies of scale and learning on cumulative output has been termed the experience curve. The Boston Consulting Group estimated that costs reduced on average by approximately 15–20 per cent each time cumulative output doubled.

Subsequent work by Bruce Henderson, founder of the Boston Consulting Group, extended this concept by demonstrating that all costs, not just production costs, would decline at a given rate as volume increased. In fact, to be precise, the relationship that the experience curve describes is between real unit costs and cumulative volume.

This suggests that firms with greater market share will have a cost advantage through the experience curve effect, assuming that all companies are operating on the same curve. However, a move towards a new manufacturing technology can lower the experience curve for adopting companies, allowing them to leapfrog over more traditional firms and thereby gain a cost advantage even though cumulative output may be lower.

The general form of the experience curve and the above-mentioned leapfrogging to another curve are shown in Figure 4.3.

Leapfrogging the experience curve by investing in new technology is a special opportunity for SMEs and newcomers to a market, since they will (as a starting point) have only a small market share and thereby a small cumulative output.

The implications of the experience curve for the pricing strategy will be discussed further in Chapter 16. According to Porter (1980) there are other cost drivers that determine the costs in value chains:

- *Capacity utilization.* Underutilization incurs costs.
- *Linkages.* Costs of activities are affected by how other activities are performed. For example, improving quality assurance can reduce after-sales service costs.
- *Interrelationships.* For example, different SBUs' sharing of R&D, purchasing and marketing will lower costs.
- *Integration.* For example, deintegration (outsourcing) of activities to subsuppliers can lower costs and raise flexibility.

**Relative cost advantage**
A firm's cost position depends on the configuration of the activities in its value chain versus that of the competitors.

Figure 4.3 Leapfrogging the experience curve

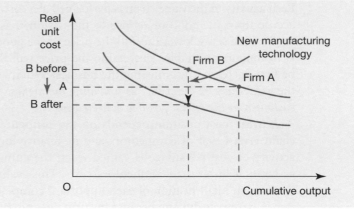

- *Timing*. For example, first movers in a market can gain cost advantage. It is cheaper to establish a brand name in the minds of the customers if there are no competitors.
- *Policy decisions*. Product width, level of service and channel decisions are examples of policy decisions that affect costs.
- *Location*. Locating near suppliers reduces in-bound distribution costs. Locating near customers can lower out-bound distribution costs. Some producers locate their production activities in eastern Europe or the Far East to take advantage of low wage costs.
- *Institutional factors*. Government regulations, tariffs, local content rules, etc., will affect costs.

## The basic sources of competitive advantage

**Resources**
Basic units of analysis – financial, technological, human and organizational resources – found in the firm's different departments.

**Competences**
Combination of different resources into capabilities and later competences – being something that the firm is really good at.

The perceived value created and the costs incurred will depend on the firm's resources and its competences (see Figure 4.4).

Figure 4.4 The roots of performance and competitive advantage

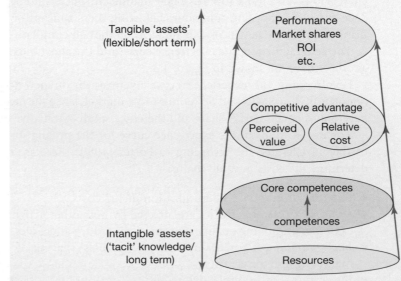

Source: Adapted from Jüttner and Wehrli, 1994.

## Resources

Resources are the basic units of analysis. They include all inputs into the business processes – that is, financial, technological, human and organizational resources. Although resources provide the basis for competence building, on their own they are barely productive.

Resources are necessary in order to participate in the market. The competitors in a market will thus not usually be very different with regard to these skills and resources, and the latter will not explain differences in created perceived value, relative costs and the resulting performance. They are failure preventers, but not success producers. They may, however, act as barriers to entry for potential new competitors, and hence raise the average level of performance in the market.

## CSR (corporate social responsibility)

The traditional corporate paradigm has always supported a strong external customer relationship, because customers buy the firm's product and ultimately deliver profits to the stockholders. The concept of corporate social responsibility (CSR) has become a relatively visible phenomenon in the marketing literature, shifting the narrow notion of customer-based marketing to a broader corporate-level marketing concept.

A prevailing understanding of CSR is based on the notion of stakeholders' expectations, which are of important concern to corporate marketing. This means that an organization operates within a network of different stakeholders who can influence it directly or indirectly. Therefore, the scope of CSR should focus on the organization's commitment to avoid harm and improve stakeholders' and society's well-being.

Definitions of CSR, and the very actions of CSR, vary among countries, regions, societies and communities. One very broad definition of CSR may be what a business puts back in to the local or state economy in return for what it takes out. Many definitions of CSR include management practices, linking the inner circle of management with the outer circle of community-at-large. Managers have a direct impact on companies' abilities to manage the business processes in a way that produces an overall positive impact on society.

Thus the concept of CSR refers to the belief that modern businesses have a responsibility to society that extends beyond delivering profits to the stockholders or investors in the firm. These other societal stakeholders typically include consumers, employees, the community at large, government and the natural environment. The CSR concept applies to organizations of all sizes, but discussions have tended to focus on large organizations because they tend to be more visible and have more power. And, as many have observed, with power comes responsibility.

CSR must be rooted deep in the company's resource base (see also Figure 4.4), which means that short-term gain must take a clear second place to long-term thinking. Exhibit 4.1 shows a company (Chiquita), which managed to integrate this long-term view into its resource base and improve its international competitiveness as a result.

---

**Exhibit 4.1   Chiquita – integrating CSR in the resource base**

The time it can take to embed successfully CSR into a brand, then see a return on that investment, is illustrated by US-based fruit and vegetable producer Chiquita Brands Inc., one of the world's biggest importers of bananas that oversees a maze of local labour partnerships. Anticipating that its European business was going to be threatened by lower-priced competitors, Chiquita began overhauling its entire sourcing infrastructure around ethical credentials. This process, which cost the firm $20 million, began in 1992, and culminated with certification by the Rainforest Alliance in 2000. However, it only began actively to communicate a sustainability and responsibility message to consumers in 2005.

## Exhibit 4.1 continued

Many strategies suffer from a failure in perhaps one of the most critical aspects of their deployment – making the resource base visible and tangible to the external stakeholders. CSR is no different. Adopting CSR is one thing, but like all business tools, in order to bring success it must be adequately monitored. As for Chiquita, this ongoing assessment process is a vital part of the chain.

In 1998, executives at Chiquita were horrified to see their company splashed all over the newspapers after an undercover investigation into 'dangerous and illegal business practices' throughout its Latin American operations. Chiquita had to make a dramatic review of its entire business.

Whilst it would be relatively easy for a CEO to declare commitment to CSR on a philosophical level, but take very little positive action, Chiquita has followed through on its promises and continues to raise the standards. For instance, official company assessments highlighted numerous challenges faced by the Guatemalan division. Chiquita responded by installing a new management team that introduced important policy changes and helped to improve workers' perceptions of the company. The CSR report also includes a section that plots the company's CSR objectives against a timescale of 'achieved', 'on target to achieve' and significantly 'unlikely to achieve by target date'. For Chiquita, transparency is a commendable part of its overall CSR strategy and demonstrates a very public commitment to performance assessment.

Chiquita's CEO declared his commitment to breaking new ground in responsible management and pledged that the company would do much more than merely repair the damage brought about by the media. Ten years after, and despite changes at the corporate management level, Chiquita's CSR policy is still in full flight and its long-term international competitiveness has been improved as a result.

'Our motto was "Create facts first",' says George Jaksch, Chiquita's senior director of corporate responsibility and public affairs. 'We were not going to promote an ethical message until we were absolutely sure we had built a solid foundation. In Europe it has been a highly effective strategy.'

Source: Curtis (2006).

## Competences

Competences – being components of a higher level – result from a combination of the various resources. Their formation and quality depend on two factors. The first factor is the specific capabilities of the firm in integrating resources. These capabilities are developed and improved in a collective learning process. On the other hand, the basis for the quality of a competence is the resource assortment. This forms a potential for competences, which should be exploited to the maximum extent.

Cardy and Selvarajan (2006) classify competences into two broad categories: *personal* or *corporate*. Personal competences are possessed by individuals and include characteristics such as knowledge, skills, abilities, experience, and personality. Corporate competences belong to the organization and are embedded processes and structures that tend to reside within the organization, even when individuals leave. These two categories are not entirely independent. The collection of personal competences can form a way of doing things or a culture that becomes embedded in the organization. In addition, corporate characteristics can determine the type of personal competences that will best work or fit in the organization.

**Core competences**
Value chain activities in which the firm is regarded as better than its competitors.

A firm can have a lot of competences but only a few of them are core competences: that is, a value chain activity in which the firm is regarded as a better performer than any of its competitors (see Figure 4.5).

In Figure 4.5 a core competence is represented by a strategic resource (asset) that competitors cannot easily imitate and which has the potential to earn long-term profit. The objective of the firm will be to place products and services at the top-right corner. The top-left corner also represents profit possibilities, but the competitive advantage is easier to imitate, so the high profit will only be short term. The bottom-left corner represents the position of the price-sensitive commodity supplier. Here the profits are

Figure 4.5 Illustration of the core competence

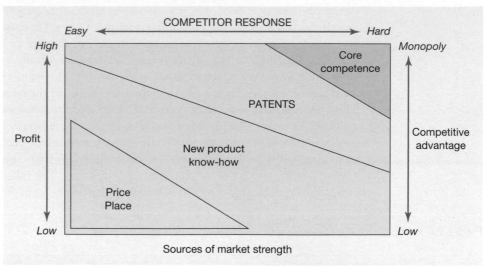

Source: Reprinted from *Long Range Planning*, Vol. 27, No. 4, Tampoe, M. (1994) 'Exploiting the core competences of your organization', p. 74, Copyright 1994, with permission from Elsevier.

likely to be low because the product is primarily differentiated by place (distribution) and especially price.

## Competitive benchmarking

The ultimate test of the efficiency of any marketing strategy has to be in terms of profit. Those companies that strive for market share, but measure market share in terms of volume sales, may be deluding themselves to the extent that volume is bought at the expense of profit.

Because market share is an 'after the event' measure, we need to utilize continuing indicators of competitive performance. This will highlight areas where improvements in the marketing mix can be made.

In recent years a number of companies have developed a technique for assessing relative marketplace performance, which has come to be known as competitive benchmarking. Originally the idea of competitive benchmarking was literally to take apart a competitor's product, component by component, and compare its performance in a value engineering sense with your own product. This approach has often been attributed to the Japanese, but many western companies have also found the value of such detailed comparisons.

The concept of competitive benchmarking is similar to what Porter (1996) calls operational effectiveness (OE), meaning performing similar activities better than competitors perform them. However, Porter (1996) also thinks that OE is a necessary but not a sufficient condition for outperforming rivals. Firms also have to consider strategic (or market) positioning, meaning the performance of *different* activities from rivals or performing similar activities in different ways. Only a few firms have competed successfully on the basis of OE over a long period. The main reason is the rapid diffusion of best practices. Competitors can rapidly imitate management techniques and new technologies with support from consultants.

However, the idea of benchmarking is capable of extension beyond this simple comparison of technology and cost effectiveness. Because the battle in the marketplace is for 'share of mind', it is customers' perceptions that we must measure.

**Competitive benchmarking**
A technique for assessing relative marketplace performance compared with main competitors.

The measures that can be used in this type of benchmarking programme include delivery reliability, ease of ordering, after-sales service, the quality of sales representation and the accuracy of invoices and other documentation. These measures are not chosen at random, but are selected because of their importance to the customer. Market research, often based on in-depth interviews, would typically be employed to identify what these 'key success factors' are. The elements that customers identify as being the most important (see Figure 4.6) then form the basis for the benchmark questionnaire. This questionnaire is administered to a sample of customers on a regular basis: for example, German Telecom carries out a daily telephone survey of a random sample of its domestic and business customers to measure customers' perceptions of service. For most companies an annual survey might suffice; in other cases, perhaps a quarterly survey, particularly if market conditions are dynamic. The output these surveys might typically be presented in the form of a competitive profile, as in the example in Figure 4.6.

**Figure 4.6  Competitive benchmarking (example with only a few criteria)**

| Examples of value chain functions (mainly downstream functions) | Customer Importance to customer (key success factors) | | | | | Own firm (Firm A) How do customers rate performance of our firm? | | | | | Key competitor (Firm B) How do customers rate performance of key competitor? | | | | |
|---|---|---|---|---|---|---|---|---|---|---|---|---|---|---|---|
| | *High importance* | | | | *Low importance* | *Good* | | | | *Bad* | *Good* | | | | *Bad* |
| | 5 | 4 | 3 | 2 | 1 | 5 | 4 | 3 | 2 | 1 | 5 | 4 | 3 | 2 | 1 |
| Uses new technology | | | | | | | | | | | | | | | |
| High technical quality and competence | | | | | | | | | | | | | | | |
| Uses proven technology | | | | | | | | | | | | | | | |
| Easy to buy from | | | | | | | | | | | | | | | |
| Understands what customers want | | | | | | | | | | | | | | | |
| Low price | | | | | | | | | | | | | | | |
| Delivery on schedule | | | | | | | | | | | | | | | |
| Accessible for enquiries | | | | | | | | | | | | | | | |
| Takes full responsibility | | | | | | | | | | | | | | | |
| Flexible and quick | | | | | | | | | | | | | | | |
| Known contact person | | | | | | | | | | | | | | | |
| Provides customer training | | | | | | | | | | | | | | | |
| Take account of future requirements | | | | | | | | | | | | | | | |
| Courteous and helpful | | | | | | | | | | | | | | | |
| Specified invoices | | | | | | | | | | | | | | | |
| Gives guarantees | | | | | | | | | | | | | | | |
| ISO 9000 certified | | | | | | | | | | | | | | | |
| Right first time | | | | | | | | | | | | | | | |
| Can give references | | | | | | | | | | | | | | | |
| Environment conscious | | | | | | | | | | | | | | | |

Most of the criteria mentioned above relate to downstream functions in the value chain. Concurrently with closer relations between buyers and suppliers, especially in the industrial market, there will be more focus on the supplier's competences in the upstream functions.

## Development of a dynamic benchmarking model

On the basis of the value chain's functions, we will suggest a model for the development of a firm's competitiveness in a defined market. The model will be based on a specific market as the market demands are assumed to differ from market to market, and from country to country.

Before presenting the basic model for development of international competitiveness we will first define two key terms:

1 *Critical success factors*. Those value chain functions where the customer demands/ expects the supplier (firm X) to have a strong competence.
2 *Core competences*. Those value chain functions where firm X has a strong competitive position.

## The strategy process

The model for the strategy process is shown in Figure 4.7.

### Stage 1: Analysis of situation (identification of competence gaps)

We will not go into detail here about the problems there have been in measuring the value chain functions. The measurements cannot be objective in the traditional way of thinking, but must rely on internal assessments from firm representatives (interviews with relevant managers) supplemented by external experts ('key informants') who are able to judge the market's (customers') demand now and in the future.

The competence profile for firm A in Figure 4.1 (top-right diagram) is an example of how a firm is not in accordance with the market (= customer) demand. The company has its core competences in parts of the value chain's functions where customers place little importance (market knowledge in Figure 4.1).

Figure 4.7 **Model for development of core competences**

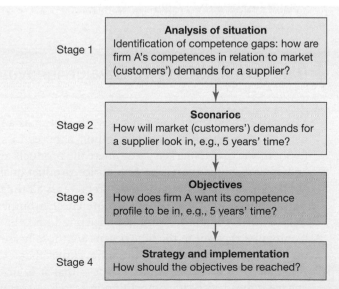

If there is a generally good match between the critical success factors and firm A's initial position, it is important to concentrate resources and improve this core competence to create sustainable competitive advantages.

If, on the other hand, there is a large gap between customers' demands and the firm's initial position in critical success factors in Figure 4.1 (as with the personal selling functions), it may give rise to the following alternatives:

- Improve the position of the critical success factor(s).
- Find business areas where firm A's competence profile better suits the market demand and expectations.

As a new business area involves risk, it is often important to identify an eventual gap in a critical success factor as early as possible. In other words, an 'early warning' system must be established that continuously monitors the critical competitive factors so that it is possible to start initiatives that limit an eventual gap as early as possible.

In Figure 4.1 the competence profile of firm B is also shown.

### Stages 2 and 3: Scenarios and objectives

To be able to estimate future market demand different scenarios are made of the possible future development. These trends are first described generally, then the effect of the market's future demand/expectations on a supplier's value chain function is concretized.

By this procedure the described 'gap' between market expectations and firm A's initial position becomes more clear. At the same time the biggest gap for firm A may have moved from personal sales to, for example, product development. From knowledge of the market leader's strategy it is possible to complete scenarios of the market leader's future competence profile.

These scenarios may be the foundation for a discussion of objectives and of which competence profile the company wants in, say, five years' time. Objectives must be set realistically and with due consideration of the organization's resources (the scenarios are not shown in Figure 4.1).

### Stage 4: Strategy and implementation

Depending on which of firm A's value chain functions are to be developed, a strategy is prepared. This results in implementation plans that include the adjustment of the organization's current competence level.

## 4.5  Blue ocean strategy and value innovation

**Red oceans**
Tough head-to-head competition in mature industries often results in nothing but a bloody red ocean of rivals fighting over a shrinking profit pool.

**Blue oceans**
The unserved market, where competitors are not yet structured and the market is relatively unknown. Here it is about avoiding head-to-head competition.

Kim and Mauborgne (2005a, b, c) use the ocean as a metaphor to describe the competitive space in which an organization chooses to swim. Red oceans refer to the frequently accessed marketspaces where the products are well-defined, competitors are known and competition is based on price, product quality and service. In other words, red oceans are an old paradigm that represents all the industries in existence today.

In contrast, the blue oceans denote an environment where products are not yet well-defined, competitors are not structured and the market is relatively unknown. Companies that sail in the blue oceans are those beating the competition by focusing on developing compelling value innovations that create uncontested marketspace. Adopters of blue ocean strategy believe that it is no longer valid for companies to engage in head-to-head competition in search of sustained, profitable growth.

In Michael Porter (1980, 1985) companies are fighting for competitive advantage, battling for market share and struggling for differentiation, blue ocean strategists argue that cut-throat competition results in nothing but a bloody red ocean of rivals fighting over a shrinking profit pool.

Blue ocean is a marketspace that is created by identifying an unserved set of customers, then delivering to them a compelling new value proposition. This is done by reconfiguring what is on offer to better balance customer needs with the economic costs of doing so. This is as opposed to a red ocean, where the market is well defined and heavily populated by the competition.

Blue-ocean strategy should not be a static process but a dynamic one. Consider The Body Shop. In the 1980s, The Body Shop was highly successful, and rather than compete head on with large cosmetics companies, it invented a whole new marketspace for natural beauty products. During the 1990s The Body Shop also struggled, but that does not diminish the excellence of its original strategic move. Its genius lay in creating a new marketspace in an intensely competitive industry that historically competed on glamour (Kim and Mauborgne, 2005b).

Kim and Mauborgne (2005a) is based on a study of 150 strategic moves that spanned more than 100 years (1880–2000) and 30 industries. Kim and Mauborgne's first point in distinguishing this strategy from the traditional strategic frameworks is that in the traditional business literature, the company forms the basic unit of analysis, and the industry analysis is the means of positioning the company. Their hypothesis is that since markets are constantly changing in their levels of attractiveness, and companies over time vary in their level of performance, it is the particular *strategic move of the company*, and not the company itself or the industry, which is the correct criterion for evaluating the difference between red and blue ocean strategies.

## Value innovation

Kim and Mauborgne (2005a) argue that tomorrow's leading companies will succeed not by battling competitors, but by making strategic moves, which they call *value innovation*.

The combination of value with innovation is not just marketing and taxonomic positioning. It has consequences. Value without innovation tends to focus on value creation on an incremental scale, and innovation without value tends to be technology driven, market pioneering, or futuristic, often overshooting what buyers are ready to accept and pay for. Conventional Porter logic (1980, 1985) leads companies only to compete at the margin for incremental share. The logic of value innovation starts with an ambition to dominate the market by offering a tremendous leap in value. Many companies seek growth by retaining and expanding their customer base. This often leads to finer segmentation and greater customization of offerings to meet specialized needs. Instead of focusing on the differences between customers, value innovators build on the powerful commonalities in the features that customers value (Kim and Mauborgne, 1997).

Value innovation is intensely customer focused, but not exclusively so. Like value chain analysis it balances costs of delivering the value proposition with what the buyer values are, and then resolves the trade-off dilemma between the value delivered and the costs involved. Instead of compromising the value wanted by the customer because of the high costs associated with delivering it, costs are eliminated or reduced if there is no or less value placed on the offering by the customer. This is a real win–win resolution that creates the compelling proposition. Customers get what they really want for less, and sellers get a higher rate of return on invested capital by reducing start-up and/or operational delivery costs. The combination of these two is the catalyst of blue ocean market creation. Exhibit 4.2 illustrates this by using the case of Formule 1.

The output of the value innovation analysis is the value curves of the different marketers in the industry (also called the 'strategy canvas' in Kim and Mauborgne (2005a) – see Exhibit 4.1). These different value curves raise four basic questions for the focal firm:

1  Which factors should be reduced well below the industry standard?
2  Which of the factors that the industry takes for granted should be eliminated?
3  Which factors should be raised well above the industry standard?
4  Which factors should be created that the industry has never offered?

The resulting new value curve should then determine if the firm is on its way into the 'blue ocean'.

---

### Exhibit 4.2    Value innovation at Hotel Chain Formule 1

When Accor launched Formule 1 (a line of French budget hotels) in 1985, the budget hotel industry was suffering from stagnation and overcapacity. The top management urged the managers to forget everything they knew of the existing rules, practices and traditions of the industry. There were two distinct market segments in the industry. One segment consisted of no-star and one star (very cheap, around €20 per room per night) and the other segment was two-star hotels, with an average price €40 per room. These more expensive two-star hotels attracted customers by offering better sleeping facilities than the cheap segment. Accor's management undertook market research and found out what most customers of all budget hotels wanted: a good night's sleep at a low price. Then they asked themselves (and answered) the four fundamental questions:

#### 1 Which of the factors that the budget hotel industry took for granted should be eliminated?

The Accor management eliminated such standard hotel features as costly restaurants and appealing lounges. Accor reckoned that they might lose some customers by this, but they also knew that most customers could live without these features.

#### 2 Which factors should be reduced well below the industry standard?

Accor also believed that budget hotels were over-performing along other dimensions. For example, at Formule 1 receptionists are on hand only during peak checkin and checkout hours. At all other times, customers use an automated teller. The

Source: Tony Souter © Dorling Kindersley.

rooms at Formule 1 are small and equipped only with a bed and bare necessities – no desks or decorations. Instead of closets there are a few shelves for clothing.

#### 3 Which factors should be raised well above the industry standard?

As seen in Formule 1's value curve (Figure 4.8) the following factors:

- the bed quality,
- hygiene and
- room quietness,

were raised above the relative level of the low budget hotels (the one-star and two-star hotels). The price performance was perceived as being at the same level as the average one-star hotels.

**Figure 4.8 Formule 1's value curve**

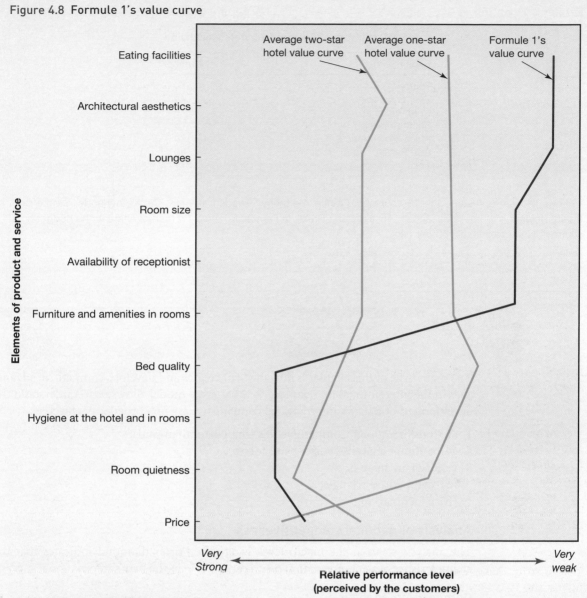

Source: Adapted from Kim and Mauborgne (1997).

## 4 Which new factors (that the industry had never offered) should be developed?

These covered cost-minimizing factors such as the availability of room keys via an automated teller. The rooms themselves are modular blocks manufactured in a factory. That is a method which may not result in the nicest architectural aesthetics but give economies of scale in production and considerable cost advantages. Formule 1 has cut in half the average cost of building a room and its staff costs (in relation to total sales) dropped below the industry average (approximately 30 per cent) to between 20 per cent and 23 per cent. These cost savings have allowed Accor to improve the features, that customers value most ('a good night's sleep at a low price').

Note that in Figure 4.8 if the price is perceived as relatively low, it is regarded as a strong performance.

## What has happened with Accor and Formule 1?

Today Accor is owner of several hotel chains (besides Formule 1), for example, Mercure, Sofitel, Novotel, Ibis and Motel 6. In 2005 the sales of Accor Group were €7.6 billion. As of 1 January 2006 Fomule 1 has the following number of hotels in the following regions of the world:

Exhibit 4.2 continued

Table 4.2  **Number of Formule 1 hotels worldwide**

| Region | Number |
| --- | --- |
| France | 284 |
| Rest of Europe | 44 |
| North America | – |
| South America | 5 |
| Africa (South Africa) | 24 |
| Asia Pacific | 20 |
| Total | 377 |

Formule 1 is represented in 12 countries: France, Germany, Sweden, the UK, the Netherlands, Switzerland, Spain, Belgium, South Africa, Japan, Australia and Brazil. In France, Formule 1's market share in the budget hotel segment is approximately 50 per cent.

Source: www.accor.com, www.hotelformule1.com; Kim and Mauborgne, 1997.

## 4.6  Summary

The main issue of this chapter is how the firm creates and develops competitive advantages in the international marketplace. A three-stage model allows us to understand the development of a firm's international competitiveness in a broader perspective:

1 analysis of national competitiveness (the Porter diamond);
2 competition analysis (Porter's five forces);
3 value chain analysis:
   (a) competitive triangle;
   (b) benchmarking.

### Analysis of national competitiveness

The analysis starts at the macro level, where the Porter diamond indicates that the characteristics of the home nation play a central role in the firm's international success.

### Competition analysis

The next stage is to move to the competitive arena where the firm is the unit of analysis. Porter's five-forces model suggests that competition in an industry is rooted in its underlying economic structure and goes beyond the behaviour of current competitors. The state of competition depends upon five basic competitive forces, which determine the profit potential in an industry.

### Value chain analysis

Here we look at what creates a competitive advantage at the same competitive level (among industry competitors). According to the *competitive triangle*, it can be concluded that firms have a competitive advantage in a market if they offer products with the following:

● a higher perceived value to the customers;
● lower relative costs than competing firms.

A firm can find out its competitive advantages or core competences by using *competitive benchmarking*, which is a technique where customers measure marketplace performance of the firm compared to a 'first-class' competitor. The measures in the value chain that can be used include delivery reliability, ease of ordering, after-sales service and quality of sales representation. These value chain activities are chosen on the basis of their importance to the customer. As customers' perceptions change over time, it may be relevant to try and estimate customers' future demands on a supplier of particular products.

According to the blue ocean strategy, the red oceans represent all the industries in existence today. This is *known* marketspace. Blue oceans denote all the industries not in existence today. This is *unknown* marketspace.

In the red oceans, industry boundaries are defined and accepted, and the competitive rules of the game are known. Here companies try to outperform their rivals to grab a greater share of existing demand. As the marketspace gets more and more crowded, prospects for profits and growth are reduced. Products become commodities, and cut-throat competition turns the red ocean bloody.

Blue oceans, in contrast, are defined by untapped marketspace, demand creation and the opportunity for highly profitable growth. While blue oceans are occasionally created well beyond existing industry boundaries, most are created by expanding existing industry boundaries. In blue oceans, competition is irrelevant as the rules of the game are waiting to be set.

Once a company has created a blue ocean, it should prolong its profit and growth sanctuary by swimming as far as possible in the blue ocean, making itself a moving target, distancing itself from potential imitators, and discouraging them in the process. The aim here is to dominate the blue ocean over imitators for as long as possible. But, as other companies' strategies converge on your market, and the blue ocean turns red with intense competition, companies need to reach out to create a new blue ocean to break away from the competition yet again.

---

**CASE STUDY 4.1**

## Wii: Nintendo's Wii takes first place on the world market – can it last?

A few years ago, very few analysts would have predicted that Nintendo's Wii would be market leader in the games console market against the established Playstation 3 (PS 3) and Xbox 360 brands. But analysts can be in error. In the week ending 23 August 20007 **www.Vgchartz.com** data, which are based on sample data from retailers all over the world, indicated that Nintendo's Wii (which was released in November 2006, one year after the Xbox 360), passed Xbox 360 lifetime units sales, making Nintendo the new world market leader in both the games console businesses. This will have a large impact on third-party publishers and will undoubtedly influence the decisions that the three major players (Microsft, Sony and Nintendo) will make in future.

One factor that has no doubt helped Nintendo's Wii to gain popularity so quickly is the console's broad appeal across all age groups, demographics and countries.

**The Nintendo Wii**

Source: Andrew Parsons/PA Archive/PA Photos.

### Nintendo – key facts and financial data

Nintendo Co. was founded in 1889 as the Marufuku Company to make and sell 'hanafuda', Japanese game cards. It became the Nintendo Playing Card Company in 1951 and began making theme cards under a licensing agreement with Disney in 1959.

During the 1980s Nintendo sought new products, releasing Game Boy in 1989 and the Super Family Computer game system (Super NES in the United States) in 1991. The company broke with tradition in 1994 by making design alliances with companies like Silicon Graphics. After creating a 32-bit product in 1995, Nintendo launched the much-touted N64 game system in 1996. It also teamed with Microsoft and Nomura Research Institute on a satellite-delivered Internet system for Japan. Price wars between the top contenders continued in the US and Japan.

In 1998 Nintendo released Pokémon, which involves trading and training virtual monsters (it had been popular in Japan since 1996), in the United States. The company also launched the video game *The Legend of Zelda: Ocarina of Time*, which sold 2.5 million units in about six weeks. Nintendo issued 50 new games for 1998, compared to Sony's 131.

Nintendo announced in 1999 that its next-generation game system, Dolphin (later renamed GameCube), would use IBM's PowerPC microprocessor and Matsushita's DVD players.

In September 2001, Nintendo launched its long-awaited GameCube console system (which retailed at $100 less than its console rivals, Sony's PlayStation 2 and Microsoft's XBox). The system debuted in North America in November. In addition, the company came out with Game Boy Advance, its newest handheld model with a bigger screen and faster chip.

In 2003 Nintendo bought a stake (about 3 per cent) in game developer and toy maker Bandai, a move expected to solidify cooperation between the two companies in marketing game software.

Today Nintendo (**www.nintendo.co.jp**) is engaged in the creation of interactive entertainment products. It manufactures and markets hardware and software for its home video game systems. The company primarily operates in Japan, Europe and America. It is headquartered in Kyoto, Japan, and employs about 3,400 people.

In the fiscal year 2007, Nintendo's recorded revenue was $8,189.4 million, an increase of 90 per cent over 2006. The operating profit of the company was $1,916.2 million during fiscal year 2007, compared to $773.7 million in 2006. Approximately 67 per cent of the company's revenue is generated from regions outside Japan. The net profit was $1,478.2 million in fiscal year 2007, an increase of 77.2 per cent over 2006. Nintendo has managed to achieve higher returns on its investments, assets and equity as compared to the industry average.

Nintendo has not raised any capital through debt in the past few years. The company's total debt to equity ratio at the beginning of 2007 is zero compared to the industry average of 12 per cent. Debt free status indicates the company's ability to finance its operations efficiently. Additionally, no debt obligation provides the company with significant liquidity and financial flexibility.

## The video game console industry

The interactive entertainment software market is characterized by short product life cycles and frequent introductions of new products.

The game consoles are relatively expensive in the beginning of their product life cycles. Hard-core game freaks pay dearly to have a console early, but sales really jump in years two and three as Moore's law and economies of scale drive prices down and third-party developers release must-have games. By year four the buzz has begun about the next generation and then the games consoles can be found at the local grocery store at discount prices.

Nintendo has been operating in the video game console market since 1977 with colour television games, and is considered the oldest company in this market. It is one of the largest console manufacturers in the world, and a leader in the handheld console market. The company had released four generations of consoles over the past two decades, which include Nintendo Entertainment System, Super Nintendo Entertainment System, Nintendo 64 and GameCube. Nintendo has dominated the handheld games market since its release of the original Game Boy handheld system in 1989. In fiscal year 2007, Nintendo sold 79.5 millions units of Game Boy Advance (GBA). Nintendo DS, another handheld console of Nintendo, sold 40.3 millions units in fiscal 2007.

## Nintendo launches Wii

The company's latest console Wii was launched in November 2006. Nintendo's arguments for using this brandname were:

- Wii sounds like 'we', which emphasizes this console is for everyone.
- Wii can easily be remembered by people around the world, no matter what language they speak.
- Wii has a distinctive 'ii' spelling that symbolizes both the unique controllers and the image of people gathering to play.

The Wii's success has done little to convince Microsoft executives they are on the wrong course. The company is positioning itself for a world where people play multiplayer games, download movies and control their TVs through one box. 'Nintendo has created a unique and innovative experience,' says Peter Moore, who runs Microsoft's Xbox business. 'I love the experience, the price point, and Nintendo content.' But Moore adds, 'Microsoft provides experiences that Nintendo cannot provide' (O'Brian, 2007).

Of course Microsoft has little more to lose than money, and there's plenty of that to go around. Sony is another matter. Gaming has been the company's profit centre for years. Suddenly, when everyone thought the PS3 would solidify Sony's dominance, along came the Wii. With an unheard-of price and few quality games to choose from, the PS3 has produced disappointing sales. The father of the PlayStation, Ken Kutaragi, was recently forced to resign his post as chairman of Sony Computer Entertainment (O'Brian, 2007).

But while he acknowledges a slow start, Jack Tretton, the president and CEO of Sony Computer Entertainment America, thinks it's too early to start talking winners. 'You have to give Nintendo credit for what they've accomplished,' says Tretton, who is quick to point out that Sony has come out with some innovative controllers too, 'but if you look at the industry, any industry, it doesn't typically go backwards technologically. The controller is innovative, but the Wii is basically a repurposed GameCube. If you've built your console on an innovative controller, you have to ask yourself, Is that long term?' (O'Brian, 2007).

## Wii's Blue Ocean Strategy

Nintendo is attempting to create a blue ocean by creating a unique gaming experience and keeping the cost of its system lower than Sony's and Microsoft's. In a recent Forbes.com interview, Perrin Kaplan, vice president of marketing and corporate affairs for Nintendo of America, discusses its implementation of Blue Ocean:

*Inside Nintendo, we call our strategy 'Blue Ocean'. This is in contrast to a 'Red Ocean'. Seeing a Blue Ocean is the notion of creating a market where there initially was none – going out where nobody has yet gone. Red Ocean is what our competitors do – heated competition where sales are finite and the product is fairly predictable. We're making games that are expanding our base of consumers in Japan and America. Yes, those who've always played games are still playing, but we've got people who've never played to start loving it with titles like Nintendogs, Animal Crossing and Brain Games. These games are Blue Ocean in action.* (Forbes, 2006)

Part of blue ocean strategy involves creating a strategy canvas that depicts the current market space and relative offering level for major attributes that companies compete on. It helps visualize which offerings cost more to compete on. It also helps companies identify which values to eliminate, reduce and/or raise. And finally, it helps identify new values that are not currently competed on. Figure 1 shows a strategy canvas for the new Nintendo Wii when compared to Microsoft's Xbox 360 and Sony's PlayStation 3. Nintendo's value curve is in blue:

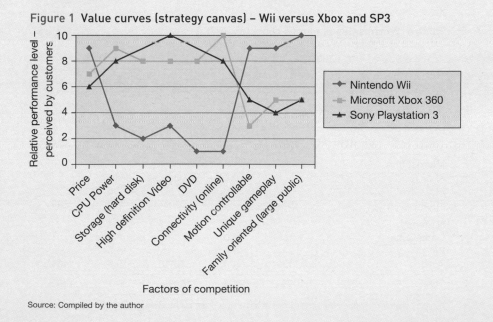

**Figure 1 Value curves (strategy canvas) – Wii versus Xbox and SP3**

Source: Compiled by the author

The bottom of the graph lists the primary sources of competitive advantages:

- *Price*: Wii is 20–30 per cent cheaper than Xbox 360 and Sony Playstation 3, therefore Wii is offering a higher perceived value to the consumer on this parameter, all other things being equal.
- *CPU power*: Wii has comparatively low processor speed, it has no Dolby 5.1 (sound system). Both PS3 and Xbox 360 have processors that are far more powerful than you will find in most PCs.
- *Storage (hard disk)*: In the basic model Wii has no hard disk.
- *High definition video*: Both PS3 and Xbox 360 use high-end graphics chips that support high-definition games and are prepared for high definition TV. Wii's graphics are marginally better than the PS2 and the original Xbox, but Wii pales next to the PS3 and Xbox 360.
- *DVD*: Both Sony and Microsoft provide the DVD opportunity. Sony even includes a Blu-Ray DVD drive.
- *Connectivity (online)*: The Xbox has positioned itself primarily as the online games console with multi-player functions
- *Motion controllable*: With its innovative motion control stick Wii adds new value to game playing. The stick integrates the movements of a player directly into the video game (tennis, golf, sword fights, etc.)
- *Unique gameplay*: The new Wii gaming console senses depth and motion from players thus adding a whole new element to the play experience.

- *Family oriented (large public)*: With the motion control stick Nintendo opens up the console world to a completely new public of untapped non-gamers from the age of about 30 onwards. Parents to teens and even grandparents are having fun on the Wii.

### Wii's market share compared to Microsoft (Xbox) and Sony (SP3)

Table 1 shows the worldwide sales of games consoles from 2005 to 2007, together with their corresponding market share.

Current Wii sales are pretty evenly split between the three major markets – 30 per cent have been sold in Japan, the American market (including Canada and South America) accounts for 40 per cent and other markets (including Europe and Australia and a few niche markets) accounts for the remaining 30 per cent sold. The sales of Sony (PS2 and PS3) and Microsoft (Xbox and Xbox 360) has been more unequally distributed: Microsoft sells most Xbox and Xbox 360 products in North America, whereas Sony's biggest markets for PS2 and PS3 are Japan, China and the rest of Asia.

### Nintendo's dependence on subsuppliers

Nintendo is highly dependent on subsuppliers. The company commissions a number of subsuppliers and contract manufacturers to produce the key components of game consoles or assemble finished products. The company is not able to meet the growing demand for its the new Wii console, which was

Table 1  World sales of games consoles (units)

|  | 2005 | | 2006 | | 2007 | |
|---|---|---|---|---|---|---|
|  | Units (m) | % | Units (m) | % | Units (m) | % |
| **Sony:** | | | | | | |
| PS2 | 16.8 | | 11.7 | | 8.6 | |
| PS3 | – | | 1.2 | | 7.2 | |
| Total | 16.8 | 69% | 12.9 | 53% | 15.8 | 40% |
| **Microsoft:** | | | | | | |
| Xbox | 3.6 | | 0.7 | | – | |
| Xbox 360 | 1.2 | | 6.8 | | 7.8 | |
| Total | 4.8 | 20% | 7.5 | 31% | 7.8 | 20% |
| **Nintendo:** | | | | | | |
| GameCube | 2.7 | | 1.0 | | – | |
| Wii | – | | 3.0 | | 15.5 | |
| Total | 2.7 | 11% | 4.0 | 16% | 15.5 | 40% |
| Total | 24.3 | 100% | 24.4 | 100% | 39.1 | 100% |

Source: Adapted from http://www.vgchartz.com data and other public media sources.

launched in November 2006, as its contract manufacturers have not been able to ramp up their production to meet the demand. A shortage of key components or the finished products could have a significant affect on the company's revenues.

Sources: **www.Vgchartz.com**; O'Brian, J.M. (2007) 'Wii will rock you', *Fortune*, 4 June 2007 **http://money.cnn.com/magazines/fortune/fortune_archive/2007/06/11/100083454/index.ht**; Forbes interview, 7 June 2006, **http://www.forbes.com/technology/cionetwork/2006/02/07/xbox-ps3-revolution-cx_rr_0207nintendo.html**); Gamespot (2006) 'Microsoft to ship 13–15 million 360s by June 2007', **www.gamespot.com**, 21 July; *Financial Times* (2000) 'Companies and Markets: Microsoft to take on video game leaders', 10 March; *New*

*Media Age* (2000) 'Let the games begin', 8 March; BBC News (2002) 'Works starts on new Xbox', 26 June; BBC News (2002) 'Price cut boosts Xbox sales', 24 July; CNN News (2002) 'Console wars: Round two', 22 May.

### Questions

1 What were Microsoft's motives in entering the games console market with Xbox?

2 What are the competitive advantages in the business model of Wii?

3 What do you think are Nintendo's chances of creating a long-term blue ocean with Wii?

For further exercises and cases, see this book's website at **www.pearsoned.co.uk/hollensen**

## ? Questions for discussion

1 How can analysis of national competitiveness explain the competitive advantage of the single firm?

2 Identify the major dimensions used to analyse a competitor's strengths and weaknesses profile. Do local, regional and global competitors need to be analysed separately?

3 How can a country with high labour costs improve its national competitiveness?

4 As the global marketing manager for Coca-Cola, how would you monitor reactions around the world to a major competitor such as Pepsi?

## References

Booms, B.H. and Bitner, M.J. (1981) 'Marketing strategies and organization structures for service firms', in Donnelly, J.H. and George, W.R. (eds), *Marketing of Services*, American Marketing Association, Chicago, IL.

Burton, J. (1995) 'Composite strategy: the combination of collaboration and competition', *Journal of General Management*, 21(1), pp. 1–23.

Cardy, R.L. and Selvarajan, T.T. (2006) 'Competencies: alternative frameworks for competitive advantage', *Business Horizons*, 49, pp. 235–245.

Curtis, J. (2006) 'Why don't they trust you with CSR?', *Marketing*, 13 September, pp. 30–31.

Day, G.S. and Wensley, R. (1988) 'Assessing advantage: a framework for diagnosing competitive superiority', *Journal of Marketing*, 52(2), pp. 1–20.

D'Aveni, R.A. (2007) 'Mapping your Competitive Position', *Harvard Business Review*, November, pp. 111–120.

Jüttner, U and Wehrli, H.P. (1994) 'Competitive advantage: merging markcting and competence-based perspective', *Journal of Business and Industrial Marketing*, 9(4), pp. 42–53.

Kanter, R.M. (1994) 'Collaborative advantage: the art of alliances', *Harvard Business Review*, July–August, pp. 96–108.

Kedia, B.L., Nordtvedt, R., Perez, L.M. (2002) 'International business strategies, decision-making theories, and leadership styles: an integrated framework', *CR*, 12(1), pp. 38–52.

Kim, W.C. and Mauborgne, R. (1997) 'Value innovation: the strategic logic of high growth', *Harvard Business Review*, 75(1) (January/February), pp. 102–112.

Kim, W.C. and Mauborgne, R. (2005a), *Blue Ocean Strategy: How to Create Market Space and Make the Competition Irrelevant*, Harvard Business School Publishing Corporation, Boston.

Kim, W.C. and Mauborgne, R. (2005b) 'Value innovation: a leap into the blue ocean', *Journal of Business Strategy*, 26(4), pp. 22–28.

Kim, W.C. and Mauborgne, R. (2005c) 'Blue ocean strategy – from theory to practice', *California Review*, 47(3), Spring, pp. 105–121.

Kotler, P. (1997) *Marketing Management: Analysis, planning, implementation, and control* (9th edn), Prentice-Hall, Englewood Cliffs, NJ.

Levitt, T. (1960) 'Marketing myopia', *Harvard Business Review*, July–August, pp. 45–56.

Magrath, A.J. (1986) 'When marketing service's 4 Ps are not enough', *Business Horizons*, May–June, pp. 44–50.

Nair, A., Ahlstrom, D. and Filer, L. (2007) 'Localized Advantage in a Global Economy: The Case of Bangalore', *Thunderbird International Business Review*, Vol. 49, No. 5, September–October, pp. 591–618.

Porter, M.E. (1980) *Competitive Strategy*, The Free Press, New York.

Porter, M. (1985), *Competitive Advantage: Creating and Sustaining Superior Performance*, The Free Press, New York.

Porter, M.E. (1990) *The Competitive Advantage of Nations*, The Free Press, New York.

Porter, M.E. (1996) 'What is strategy?', *Harvard Business Review*, November–December, pp. 61–78.

Porter, M.E. (2008) 'The competitive forces that shape strategy', *Harvard Business Review*, January, pp. 78–93.

Rafiq, M. and Ahmed, P.K. (1995) 'Using the 7Ps as a generic marketing mix', *Marketing Intelligence and Planning*, 13(9), pp. 4–15.

Ravald, A. and Grönroos, C. (1996) 'The value concept and relationship marketing', *European Journal of Marketing*, 30(2), pp. 19–30.

Reve, T. (1990) 'The firm as a nexus of internal and external contracts', in Aoki, M., Gustafsson, M. and Williamson, O.E. (eds), *The Firm as a Nexus of Treaties*, Sage, London.

Tampoe, M. (1994) 'Exploiting the core competencies of your organization', *Long Range Planning*, 27(4), pp. 66–77.

Veliyath. R. and Zahra, S.A. (2000) 'Competitiveness in the 21st century: reflections on the growing debate about globalization', *ACR*, 8(1), pp. 14–33.

# Manchester United:
## Still trying to establish a global brand

Manchester United (abbreviated as ManUtd, www.manutd.com) has developed into one of the most famous and financially successful football clubs in the world, being recognized in virtually every country, even those with little interest in the sport. Real Madrid has displaced ManUtd from the pole position in Deloitte's football money league. The list, which has been running for the last nine years, identifies the top 20 clubs by value.

The top five in 2006 were: Real Madrid with €275.7 million, Manchester United (€246.4 million), AC Milan (€234 million), Juventus (€229.4 million) and Chelsea (€220.8 million) (*Accountancy*, 2006). The most valuable US sport teams, the National Football League's Washington Redskins and Baseball's New York Yankees are both worth somewhat more, but more than any US sports team, ManUtd has built a global brand.

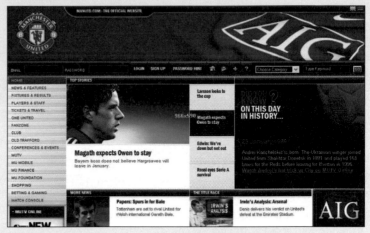

Source: www.ManUtd.com. Manchester United Limited.

### The intangible assets of ManUtd

ManUtd has developed a huge fan base. In 2005, its global fan base reached 75 million. Europe had 24 million, Asia (including Australia) had 40 million, Southern Africa had 6 million, and the Americas had 5 million. Expanding this base and developing life-long allegiances is critical to ManUtd's long-term growth. And providing international fans with a taste of the excitement at a game, through TV and Internet coverage, is key to maintaining and building the brand.

### Brand assets

ManUtd's brand assets includes (1) the physical aspects of logos, colours, names, and facilities, and (2) the intangible aspects of reputation, image, and perception. The official mascot of the team is the Red Devil. Although centrally featured in ManUtd's logo, the mascot doesn't play a prominent role in promotions. The team's nickname is the Reds, which seems logical enough, given the dominant colour of its home jerseys, but unfortunately, Liverpool, another top team in the Premier League, is also referred to as the Reds.

### International brand evolution

For British fans of ManUtd, passions run deep. Although the brand is solidly entrenched in British soccer fans' psyches, it is in transition. ManUtd is no longer simply a British brand; it is a world brand. It boasts incredible number of fans in China. A survey of China's 12 largest markets shows that 42 per cent of fans are between 15 and 24, and that 26 per cent are between 25 and 34. The team is positioned to take advantage of China's growing middle class, with members who are anxious to enjoy the good life and associate themselves with successful Western brands. As an early entrant, ManUtd has the chance to establish itself as one of Asia's dominant brands (Olson *et al.*, 2006).

Although the absolute numbers are much smaller, the United States also represents fertile ground. Of course, international soccer must compete with established groups such as the Major League Baseball, National Football League, the National Basketball Association and the National Hockey League. But soccer has become a staple at schools across the country. A recent, unprompted awareness study of European soccer teams revealed that among North American fans, the most frequently mentioned team was ManUtd, at 10 per cent; Liverpool, Real Madrid, and Barcelona each generated 3 per cent, and Arsenal generated 2 per cent. The study also showed that awareness of ManUtd is strongest in the North-Eastern and Western parts of the United States.

In order to be successful in foreign markets, ManUtd must generate memberships, sell kits and other merchandise, have access to media markets (including TV, Internet, mobile phones, and publishing), set up soccer schools, form licensing agreements with strong local sponsors, and embark on tours to create halo effects.

The challenge ManUtd faces is accomplishing this transition without destroying what made it distinctly British and highly successful. Today's team is composed of players from around the globe. (Although ManUtd still has British players, the Premier League is no longer dominated by them.) And that raises another concern: strong teams employ strong players who become brands themselves. Most notable for ManUtd was the rise of David Beckham to the ranks of superstar, on the pitch and in the media, for example., through his marriage to Victoria, previously one of the Spice Girls. ManUtd considered that Beckham's market value was greater than they could afford, so they sold him to Real Madrid one year before the contract expired. But now the brand building of ManUtd depends on new and upcoming stars such as Wayne Rooney, Cristiano Ronaldo and Rio Ferdinand. At the same time as they are ManUtd brand builders, it also allows them to build their own personal brand.

## Brand challenges

ManUtd is in the enviable position of market leader, during a time of dramatic media growth in the world's most popular game. But leaders can stumble and the team is not immune to the sensitive nature of sports fans. To address this concern, ManUtd has developed a customer relationship management (CRM) database of more than 2.5 million fans. Many of these database members are game-day customers.

A substantial group of US ManUtd fans are not loyal. They climb on the bandwagon of team, when it has success, only to climb off the instant it stumbles. With the number of US soccer players holding steady at 18 million, the market is relatively small.

Chinese fans don't possess the same level of experience with professional teams as US fans and might not be as fickle. Nevertheless, cultural and physical barriers exist between British and Chinese fans. To develop deeper loyalties in Chinese markets, ManUtd established a Mandarin website, started a soccer school in Hong Kong, and is constantly planning Asian tours while looking to add Asian players to the roster (e.g. Ji-Sung Park, who joined the ManUtd team in July 2005). Although these are sound moves to build brand loyalty, well-funded competitors such as Chelsea or Liverpool can copy ManUtd.

Even in England, ManUtd faces significant challenges. Especially after the Glazer invasion (see below) it generates a love-them-or-hate-them mentality. Fans of opposing teams were thrilled to see Chelsea, Arsenal and Liverpool secure the three major championships – leaving ManUtd without a major trophy in the last two years.

## Then Glazer came . . .

In the late 1990s and early part of the 2000s, an increasing source of concern for many United supporters was the possibility of the club being taken over. The supporters' group IMUSA (Independent Manchester United Supporters' Association) were extremely active in opposing a proposed takeover by Rupert Murdoch in 1998. However, they could not do anything in May 2005 when the US sports tycoon Malcolm Glazer (who also owns the American Football team Tampa Bay Buccaneers) paid $1.4 billion for a 98 per cent stake in ManUtd, following a nearly year-long takeover battle. So is the ManUtd brand worth $1.5 billion? Glazer seemed to think so, as he paid roughly $200 million more than the team's open-market stock valuation.

It was a hostile takeover of the club which plunged the club into massive debt as his bid was heavily funded by borrowing on the assets owned already by ManUtd. The takeover was fiercely opposed by many fans of ManUtd. Many supporters were outraged and some formed a new club called F.C. United of Manchester. This club entered the second division of the North West Counties Football League and were confirmed as champions on 15 April 2006. They will play in the first division in the 2006–07 season.

After the takeover the Glazer family (Malcolm Glazer and his three sons) took big steps to shore up the club's finances. They cut more than 20 staff members, including some executives. They also plan to raise ticket prices and have been lending 23 players to other clubs, saving ManUtd more than $20 million in fees and salaries. In general, they have been cutting expenses everywhere they can.

The 2004–05 season was characterized by a failure to score goals, and ManUtd finished the season trophyless and in third place in the Premier League.

ManUtd made a poor start to the 2005–06 season, with midfielder Roy Keane leaving the club to join his boyhood heroes Celtic after publicly criticizing several of his teammates, and the club failed to qualify for the knock-out phase of the UEFA Champions League for the first time in over a decade after losing to Portuguese team Benfica Lissabon. ManUtd also ensured a second-place finish in the Premier League and automatic Champions League qualification.

## Sponsorships

On 23 November 2005 Vodafone ended their £36 million, four-year shirt sponsorship deal with ManUtd. On

6 April 2006, ManUtd announced AIG as its new shirt sponsors ManUtd in a British record shirt sponsorship deal worth £56.5 million to be paid over four years (£14.1 million a year). ManUtd will have the largest sponsorship in the world ahead of Italian side Juventus, who have a £12.8 million a year sponsorship deal with Tamoil. The four-year agreement has been heralded as the largest sponsorship deal in British history, eclipsing Chelsea's deal with Samsung.

In 2006 ManUtd also finalized a four-year sponsorship deal with US-based financial services giant American International Group for a record $56 million. The deal replaces Vodafone, which had previously had its name emblazoned on ManUtd's famous red jerseys.

Besides these sponsorships there still exists a few others: the 13-year, £303 million ($527.2 million) deal with Nike also provides ManUtd with two vital advantages. First, it calls for Nike to pay the team a fixed fee for merchandise rights to its kits (shirts, shorts, and so on), generating a guaranteed revenue base for ManUtd while transferring product development and merchandising to a firm with proven international expertise. Second, the team links its brand with a market leader in a complementary industry (sporting goods apparel, shoes and equipment). In the first 22 months of the agreement, Nike sold 3.8 million replica shirts.

ManUtd retains eight second-tier sponsors: Pepsi, Budweiser, Audi, Wilkinson Sword, Dimension Data, Lycos.co.uk, Fuji and Century Radio. In 2004, as part of this relationship, the team invested £2 million ($3.5 million) in light-emitting diode digital-advertising boards around three sides of the pitch. Future plans call for a reduction in licensing agreements to two principals (Vodafone and Nike) and four platinum firms (to be determined). Under this arrangement, these six major sponsors will have expanded international opportunities and a stronger presence at Old Trafford. The team will then sell additional local licensing agreements with restricted rights for specific geographic markets.

Besides licensing, ManUtd generates revenues from additional secondary business lines, predominantly financial. Fans now can finance their houses or cars with a ManUtd mortgage or loan, buy tickets with a ManUtd credit card, insure their homes/cars/travel plans with ManUtd insurance, invest in ManUtd bonds, gamble in ManUtd Super Pool lotteries, or see a movie at the Red Cinema in Salford, Greater Manchester. Of course, other firms manage these lines; nevertheless, these businesses generate additional revenues while promoting the team and developing lifelong fans.

## Financial situation

|  | 2005 | 2004 | 2003 |
|---|---|---|---|
| Revenues ($m) | 286 | 308 | 230 |
| Net profits ($m) | 13 | 35 | 48 |
| Employees (number) | 480 | 504 | 493 |

In 2005, ManUtd blamed a drop in television revenues following the negotiation of a new UK broadcast rights deal, and a decline in the club's share of Champion's League media earnings as a result of its weaker performance in the tournament. The football club also incurred one-off costs in fees relating to its takeover by Glazer.

In a statement to the 2005 financial report, chief executive David Gill said, in a statement published on the club's website. 'Manchester United continues to be the world's biggest football club based on its global brand revenues and profits' (www.manutd.com).

Although current international revenues account for only 1–2 per cent of total revenues, this segment of the business holds tremendous potential.

Sources: Cohn, L. and Holmes, S. (2005) 'ManU Gets Kicked In the Head – Again', *Business Week*, 12 December, pp. 34–35; *Accountancy* (2006) 'Manchester United loses top spot in Deloitte football league', March, 137(1351), p. 16; Olson, E.M., Slater, S.F., Cooper R.D. and Reddy V. (2006) 'Good Sport: Manchester United is no longer just a British brand', *Marketing Management*, 15(1) (January/February), pp. 14–16.

## Questions

1 How do you evaluate the international competitiveness of ManUtd after the takeover of Malcolm Glazer?

2 Discuss and explain how the different alliances can increase the competitiveness of ManUtd.

3 What are the main threats to retaining 'Manchester United' as a global brand?

# Cereal Partners Worldwide (CPW): The No. 2 world player is challenging the No. 1 - Kellogg

On a lovely spring morning in April 2007, while giving her kids some Cheerios, the CEO of Cereal Partners Worldwide S.A. (CPW), Carol Smith thinks about how CPW might expand international sales and/or capture further market shares in the saturated breakfast cereals market. Right now, CPW is the clear No. 2 in the world market for breakfast cereals, but it is a tough competition, primarily with the Kellogg Company, which is the world market leader.

Maybe there would be other ways of gaining new sales in this competitive market? Carol has just read the business bestseller *Blue Ocean Strategy* and she is fascinated by the thought of moving competition in the cereals breakfast market from the 'red ocean' to the 'blue ocean'. The question is just how?

Maybe it would be better just to take the 'head-on' battle with Kellogg Company. After all, CPW has managed to beat Kellogg in several minor international markets (e.g. in Middle and Far East).

The children have finished their Cheerios and it is time to drive them to the kindergarten in Lausanne, Switzerland where CPW has its HQ.

Later that day, Carol has to present the long-term global strategy for CPW, so she hurries to her office, and starts preparing the presentation. One of her marketing managers has prepared a background report about CPW and its position in the world breakfast cereals market. The following shows some important parts of the report.

## History of breakfast cereals

Ready-to-eat cereals first appeared during the late 1800s. According to one account, John Kellogg, a doctor who belonged to a vegetarian group, developed wheat and corn flakes to extend the group's dietary choices. John's brother, Will Kellogg, saw potential in the innovative grain products and initiated commercial production and marketing. Patients at a Battle Creek, Michigan, sanitarium were among Kellogg's first customers.

Another cereal producer with roots in the nineteenth century was the Quaker Oats Company. In 1873, the North Star Oatmeal Mill built an oatmeal plant in Cedar Rapids, Iowa. North Star reorganized with other enterprises and together they formed Quaker Oats in 1901.

The Washburn Crosby Company, a predecessor to General Mills, entered the market during the 1920s. The company's first ready-to-eat cereal, Wheaties, was introduced to the American public in 1924. According to General Mills, Wheaties was developed when a Minneapolis clinician spilled a mixture of gruel that he was making for his patients on a hot stove.

## Cereal Partners Worldwide (CPW)

Cereal Partners Worldwide (CPW) was formed in 1990 as a 50:50 joint venture between Nestlé and General Mills (see Figure 1).

### General Mills

General Mills, a leading global manufacturer of consumer food products, operates in more than 30 global markets and exports to over 100 countries. General Mills has 66 production facilities: 34 are located in the United States; 15 in the Asia/Pacific region; six in Canada; five in Europe; five in Latin America and Mexico; and one in South Africa. The company is headquartered in Minneapolis, Minnesota. In financial year 2006 the total net sales were US$11.6 of which 16 per cent came from outside the United States.

In October 2001 General Mills completed the largest acquisition in its history when it purchased The Pillsbury Company from Diageo. The US$10.4 billion deal almost doubled the size of the company, and consequently boosted General Mills's worldwide ranking, making General Mills one of the world's largest food companies. However, the company is heavily debt-laden

Figure 1 The CPW joint venture

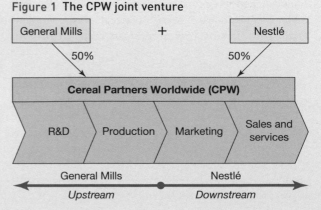

following its Pillsbury acquisition, which will continue to eat into operating and net profits for the next few years.

The company now has more than 100 US consumer brands, including Betty Crocker, Cheerios, Yoplait, Pillsbury Doughboy, Green Giant and Old El Paso.

Integral to the successes of General Mills has been its ability to build and sustain huge brand names and maintain continued net growth. Betty Crocker, origin-

ally a pen name invented in 1921 by an employee in the consumer response department, has become an umbrella brand for products as diverse as cookie mixes to ready meals. The Cheerios cereal brand, which grew rapidly in the US post-war generation, remains one of the top cereal brands worldwide.

However, heavy domestic dependence leaves the company vulnerable to variations in that market, such as supermarket price-cutting or sluggish sales in prominent product types such as breakfast cereals.

Internationally, General Mills uses its 50 per cent stake in Cereal Partners Worldwide (CPW) to sell its breakfast cereals abroad. Cereal sales have faced tough competition recently leading to significant drops in sales, particularly tough competition from private labels.

### Nestlé

Founded in 1866, Nestlé is the world's largest food and beverage company in terms of sales. The company began in the field of dairy-based products and later diversified to food and beverages in the 1930s. Nestlé is headquartered in Vevey, Switzerland and the company has 500 factories in 83 countries. It has about 406 subsidiaries located across the world. The company employs 247,000 people around the world, of which 131,000 employees work in factories, while the remaining employees work in administration and sales.

Nestlé's businesses are classified into six divisions based on product groups, which include Beverages; Milk Products, Nutrition and Ice Cream; Prepared Dishes and Cooking Aids; Chocolate, Confectionery and Biscuits; PetCare; and Pharmaceutical Products. Nestlé's global brands include Nescafé, Taster's Choice, Nestlé Pure Life, Perrier, Nestea, Nesquik, Milo, Carnation, Nido, Nestlé, Milkmaid, Sveltesse, Yoco, Mövenpick, Lactogen, Beba, Nestogen, Cerelac, Nestum, PowerBar, Pria, Nutren, Maggi, Buitoni, Toll House, Crunch, Kit-Kat, Polo, Chef, Purina, Alcon, and L'Oréal (equity stake).

Nestlé reported net sales of $83 billion for the fiscal year 2005.

### CPW

CPW markets cereals in more than 130 countries, except for the United States and Canada, where the two companies market themselves seperately. The joint venture was established in 1990 and the agreement also extends to the production of private label cereals in the UK. Volume growth for CPW was 4 per cent in 2005. The company's cereals are sold under the Nestlé brand, although many originated from General Mills. Brand names manufactured (primarily by General Mills) under the Nestlé name under this agreement include Corn Flakes, Crunch, Fitness, Cheerios and Nesquik. Shredded Wheat and Shreddies were once made by Nabisco, but are now marketed by CPW.

The CPW turnover in 2005 was a little less than US$2 billion.

When CPW was established in 1990 each partner was bringing distinctive competences into the joint venture:

### General Mills:

- proven cereal marketing expertise;
- technical excellence in products and production processes;
- broad portfolio of successful brand.

### Nestlé:

- world's largest food company;
- strong worldwide organization;
- deep marketing and distribution knowledge.

CPW is No. 2 in most international markets, but it is also market leader in some of the smaller breakfast cereal markets like China (80 per cent market share), Poland (70 per cent market share), Turkey (70 per cent market share), East/Central Europe (50 per cent market share) and South East Asia (50 per cent market share).

## The world market for breakfast cereals

In the early 2000s breakfast cereal makers were facing stagnant, if not declining, sales. Gone are the days of the family breakfast, of which a bowl of cereal was standard fare. The fast-paced American lifestyle has more and more consumers eating breakfast on the go. Quick-serve restaurants like McDonald's, ready-to-eat breakfast bars, bagels and muffins offer consumers less labour-intensive alternatives to cereal. Although the value of product shipped by cereal manufacturers has grown in absolute figures, increased revenues came primarily from price hikes rather than market growth.

English-speaking nations represented the largest cereal markets. Consumption in non-English markets was estimated at only one-fourth the amount consumed by English speakers (see Table 1), where the breakfast cereal consumption per capita is 6 kg in UK, but only 1.5 kg in South-west Europe (France, Spain and Portugal). On the European continent, consumption per capita averaged 1.5 kg per year.

Growth in the cereal industry has been slow to non-existent in this century. The question at hand for the industry is how to remake cereal's image in light of the

**Table 1 Breakfast cereal consumption per capita per year – 2005**

| Region | Per capita consumption per year (kg) |
| --- | --- |
| Sweden | 9.0 |
| Canada | 7.0 |
| UK | 6.0 |
| Australia | 6.0 |
| USA | 5.0 |
| South West Europe (France, Spain) | 1.5 |
| South East Asia | 0.1 |
| Russia | 0.1 |

**Table 2 World market for breakfast cereals by region – 2005**

| Region | Billion US$ | % |
|---|---|---|
| North America | 10 | 50 |
| Europe | 6 | 30 |
| Rest of the World | 4 | 20 |
| Total | 20 | 100 |

new culture. Tinkering with flavourings and offerings, such as the recent trend toward the addition of dried fresh fruit, proves some relief, but with over 150 different choices on store shelves and 20 new offerings added annually, variety has done more to overwhelm than excite consumers. In addition, cereal companies are committing fewer dollars to their marketing budgets.

## Development in geographical regions
As seen in Table 2, the United States is by far the largest breakfast cereals market in the world. In total North America accounts for 50 per cent of the global sales of $20 billion in 2005. The United States accounts for about 90 per cent of the North American market.

The European region accounts for 30 per cent of global sales, at US$6 billion in 2005. By far the largest market is the UK, contributing nearly 40 per cent of the regional total, with France and Germany other key, if notably smaller, players. Eastern Europe is a minor breakfast cereal market, reflecting the product's generally new status in the region. It contributed just 3 per cent of world sales in 2005. However, the market is vibrant as new lifestyles born from growing urbanization and westernization – key themes in emerging market development – have fuelled steady sales growth. Despite its low level of per capita spending, Russia is the largest market in Eastern Europe, accounting for over 40 per cent of regional sales in 2005. The continued steady growth of this market underpinned overall regional development over the review period. Cereals remain a niche market in Russia, as they do across the region, with the product benefiting from a perception of novelty. A key target for manufacturers has been children and young women, at which advertising has been aimed.

The Australasian breakfast cereals sector, like Western Europe and North America, dominated by a single nation, Australia, is becoming increasingly polarized. In common with the key US and UK markets, breakfast cereals in Australia are suffering from a high degree of maturity, with annual growth at a low single-digit level.

The Latin American breakfast cereals sector is the third largest in the world, but at US$2 billion in 2005, it is notably overshadowed by the vastly larger North American and Western European markets. However, in common with these developed regions, one country plays a dominant role in the regional make-up, Mexico, accounting for nearly 60 per cent of the overall breakfast cereal markets in Latin America.

In common with Eastern Europe, breakfast cereal sales, whilst small in Africa and the Middle East, have displayed marked growth in recent years as a direct result of greater urbanization and a growing trend (in some areas) towards westernization. Given the overriding influence of this factor on market development, sales are largely concentrated in the more developed regional markets, such as Israel and South Africa, where the investment by multinationals has been at its highest.

In Asia the concept of breakfast cereals is relatively new, with the growing influence of Western culture fostering a notable increase in consumption in major urban cities. Market development has been rapid in China, reflecting the overall rate of industry expansion in the country, with breakfast cereals sales rising by 19 per cent in 2005. In the region's developed markets, in particular Japan, market performance is broadly similar, although the key growth driver is different, in that it is health. Overall, in both developed and developing markets, breakfast cereals are in their infancy.

## Health trend
With regards to health, breakfast cereals have been hurt by the rise of fad diets such as Atkins and South Beach, which have heaped much scorn on carbohydrate-based products. The influence of these diets is on the wane but their footprint remains highly visible on national eating trends. In addition, the high sugar content of children's cereals has come under intense scrutiny, which caused a downturn in this sector, although the industry is now coming back with a range of 'better for you' variants.

Regarding convenience, this trend, once a growth driver for breakfast cereals, has now become a threat, with an increasing number of consumers opting to skip breakfast. Portability has become a key facet of convenience, a development that has fed the emergence and expansion of breakfast bars at the expense of traditional foods, such as breakfast cereals. In an increasingly cash-rich, time-poor society, consumers are opting to abandon a formal breakfast meal and instead are relying on an 'on-the-go' solution, such as breakfast bars or pastries. These latter products, in particular breakfast bars, are taking share from cereals, a trend that looks set to gather pace in the short term.

## Trends in product development
Consumer awareness of health and nutrition also played a major part in shaping the industry in recent years. Cereal manufacturers began to tout the benefits

of eating breakfast cereal right on the package – vitamin-fortified, low in fat, and a good source of fibre. Another trend, begun in the 1990s and picking up steam in the 2000s, is adding dehydrated whole fruits to cereal, which provides colour, flavour, and nutritional value. Yet touting health benefits to adults and marketing film characters to children have not been sufficient to reinvigorate this mature industry.

Under the difficult market conditions, cereal packaging is receiving new attention. Packaging was a secondary consideration, other than throwing in special offers to tempt kids. But these days, with meal occasions boiled down to their bare essentials, packaging and delivery have emerged as key weapons in the cereal marketer's arsenal. New ideas circulating in the industry usually include doing away with the traditional cereal box, which has undergone little change in its lifetime. Alternatives range from clear plastic containers to a return of the small variety six-packs.

## Trends in distribution
Supermarkets tend to be the dominant distribution format for breakfast cereals. The discounter format is dominated by mass merchandisers, the most famous example of which is Wal-Mart in the United States. This discounter format tends to favour shelf-stable, packaged products and as a result they are increasingly viewed as direct competitors to supermarkets.

Independent food stores have suffered a decline during the past years. They have been at a competitive disadvantage compared to their larger and better resourced chained competitors.

## Trends in advertising
Advertising expenditures of most cereal companies were down in recent years due to decreases in consumer spending. However there are still a lot of marketing activities going on.

General Mills has a comprehensive marketing programme for each of its core brands, from traditional television and print advertisements to in-store promotions, coupons and free gifts. In 2002, the company teamed up with US publisher Simon & Schuster to include books or audio CDs with the purchase of its Oatmeal Crisp Raisin and Basic 4 cereals.

Other promotions have included free Hasbro computer games included in boxes, promotion of new millennium pennies and golden dollars in 2000, and the inclusion of scale models of the Cheerios-sponsored NASCAR.

In response to Kellogg's 2001 launch of Special K Red Berries, General Mills countered with the introduction of freeze dried fruit in Cheerios, with Berry Burst and Triple Berry Burst product extensions from February 2003. The introduction is a response to the need for the packaging to communicate the inclusion of real berries in the box and not just flavouring. Consequently, the chosen designs consisted of vibrant red and purple boxes, each featuring a spoonful of Cheerios and fruit splashing in milk. Since freeze-dried fruit tends to absorb moisture, the company was also compelled to develop a more moisture-resistant package liner.

The introduction of Berry Burst Cheerios was supported by a US$40 million advertising and promotional campaign that included TV advertising, consumer couponing, outdoor advertising, in-store sampling and merchandising.

## Celebrity glamour
Celebrity endorsements continue to play a critical part of General Mills's marketing strategies, in particular its association with sporting personalities dating back to the 1930s with baseball sponsorship. One of the main lines of celebrity endorsement involves Wheaties boxes and a long line of sports people have appeared on the box since the 1930s. In 2001, Tiger Woods, spokesman for the Wheaties brand, appeared on special edition packaging for Wheaties to commemorate his victory of four Grand Slam golf titles.

## Distribution
General Mills distributes the majority of its products directly through its own sales organization to retailers, cooperatives and wholesalers. In Europe and Asia-Pacific the company licenses products for local production, but it also exports to over 100 different countries.

## New products, new channels
New products and new product innovations have helped create new distribution channels for General Mills recently. The success of General Mills's snack products has helped create a large demand for products in convenience stores and the company has actively developed products to meet the demands of the convenience store consumer such as its healthy Chex Mex range. A new chocolate-flavoured Chex Mex was added to the product line in 2005.

The development of cereal-in-a-bowl range has helped create new outlets for General Mills's products in college cafeterias and hotel restaurants. This may see the development of additional products to compliment these channels.

## Traditional channels
Traditional retailers such as supermarkets continue to play a major role in the distribution of General Mills's products, and the company has an extensive number of

Table 3 The world market for breakfast cereals, by company – 2005

| Manufacturer | Germany % market share | UK % market share | USA % market share | World % market share |
|---|---|---|---|---|
| Kellogg Company | 27 | 30 | 30 | 30 |
| CPW (General Mills + Nestlé) | 12 | 15 | 30[1] | 20 |
| PepsiCo (Quaker) | – | 6 | 14 | 10 |
| Weetabix | – | 10 | – | 5 |
| Private label | 35 | 15 | 10 | 15 |
| Others | 26 | 24 | 16 | 20 |
| Total | 100 | 100 | 100 | 100 |

[1] In the United States General Mills and Nestlé market each of their breakfast cereal products independently, because the CPW only covers international markets outside the United States.

cereal, snack, meal and yoghurt brands to maintain shelf space in major retail outlets.

## Private label competition intensifies

Across many categories, rising costs have led to price increases in branded products which have not been matched by any pricing actions taken in private labels. As a result, the price gaps between branded and private label products have increased dramatically and in some cases can be as much as 30 per cent.

This creates intense competitive environments for branded products, particularly in categories such as cereals which is one of General Mills's biggest markets, as consumers have started to focus more on price than brand identity. This shift in focus is partly the result of private labels' increased quality as they compete for consumer loyalty and confidence in their label products.

## Competitors

### Kellogg's

The company that makes breakfast foods and snacks for millions began with only 25 employees in Battle Creek in 1906. Today, Kellogg Company employs more than 25,000 people, manufactures in 17 countries and sells its products in more than 180 countries.

Kellogg was the first American company to enter the foreign market for ready-to-eat breakfast cereals. Company founder Will Keith (W.K.) Kellogg was an early believer in the potential of international growth and began establishing Kellogg's as a global brand with the introduction of *Kellogg's Corn Flakes*® in Canada in 1914. As success followed and demand grew, Kellogg Company continued to build manufacturing facilities

around the world, including Sydney, Australia (1924), Manchester, England (1938), Queretaro, Mexico (1951), Takasaki, Japan (1963), Bombay, India (1994) and Toluca, Mexico (2004).

Kellogg Company is the leader among global breakfast cereal manufacturers with 2005 sales revenue of $10.2 billion (net earnings were $980 million). Wal-Mart Stores, Inc. and its affiliates, accounted for approximately 17 per cent of consolidated net sales during 2005.

Established in 1906, Kellogg Company was the world's market leader in ready-to-eat cereals throughout most of the twentieth century. In 2005, Kellogg had 30 per cent of the world market share for breakfast cereals (see Table 3). Canada, the United Kingdom, and Australia represented Kellogg's three largest overseas markets.

A few well-known Kellogg products are Corn Flakes, Frosted Mini-Wheats, Corn Pops, and Fruit Loops.

### PepsiCo

In August 2001, PepsiCo merged with Quaker Foods, thereby expanding its existing portfolio. Quaker's family of brands includes Quaker Oatmeal, Cap'n Crunch and Life cereals, Rice-A-Roni and Near East side dishes, and Aunt Jemima pancake mixes and syrups.

The Quaker Food's first puffed product, 'Puffed Rice', was introduced in 1905. In 1992, Quaker Oats held an 8.9 per cent share of the ready-to-eat cereal market, and its principal product was Cap'n Crunch. Within the smaller hot cereal segment, however, the company held approximately 60 per cent of the market. In addition to cereal products, Quaker Oats produced Aunt Jemima Pancake mix and Gatorade sports drinks.

The PepsiCo brands in the breakfast cereal sector include Cap'n Crunch, Puffed Wheat, Crunchy Bran, Frosted Mini Wheats and Quaker.

Despite recent moves to extend its presence into new markets, PepsiCo tends to focus on its North American operations.

### Weetabix

Weetabix is an UK manufacturer, with a relatively high market share (10 per cent) in United Kingdom. The company is owned by a private investment group – Lion Capital. The company sells its cereals in over 80 countries and has a product line that includes Weetabix, Weetos, and Alpen. Weetabix is headquartered in Northamptonshire, UK. In 2005 Weetabix has an estimated turnover of US$1 billion.

Sources: www.cerealpartners.co.uk; www.generalmills.com; www.nestle.com; www.euromonitor.com; www.datamonitor.com; www.marketwatch.com; Bowery, J. (2006) 'Kellogg broadens healthy cereals portfolio', *Marketing*, 8 February, p. 5; Sanders, T. (2006) 'Cereals spark debate', *Food Manufacture*; August, 81(8), p. 4; Reyes, S. (2006) 'Saving Private Label',

*Brandweek*, 5 August, 47(19), pp. 30–34; Hanson, P. (2005) 'Market focus breakfast cereals', *Brand Strategy*, March, 190, p. 50; Pehanich, M. (2003) 'Cereals Run Sweet and Healthy', *Prepared Foods*, March, pp. 75–76; Vignali, C. (2001) 'Kellogg's – internationalisation versus globalisation of the marketing mix', *British Food Journal*, 103(2), pp. 112–130.

## Questions

Carol has heard that you are the new global marketing specialist so you are called in as a 'last-minute' consultant before the presentation to the board of directors.

You are confronted with the following questions, which you are supposed to answer as best you can.

1 How can General Mills and Nestlé create international competitiveness by joining forces in CPW?

2 Evaluate the international competitiveness of CPW compared to the Kellogg Company.

3 Suggest how CPW can create a blue ocean strategy.

4 Where and how can CPW create further international sales growth?

# Part II

# DECIDING WHICH MARKETS TO ENTER

## Contents

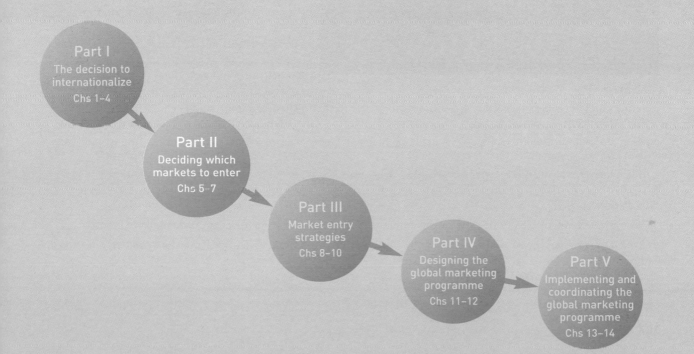

Part I
The decision to internationalize
Chs 1–4

Part II
Deciding which markets to enter
Chs 5–7

Part III
Market entry strategies
Chs 8–10

Part IV
Designing the global marketing programme
Chs 11–12

Part V
Implementing and coordinating the global marketing programme
Chs 13–14

# Land Rover:
## Which markets should be selected for the new Freelander 2

Land Rover (**www.landrover.com**) is a British all-terrain and multi-purpose vehicle (MPV) manufacturer based in the UK. Originally the term 'Land Rover' referred to one specific vehicle, a pioneering civilian all-terrain utility vehicle launched in 1948, but it was later used as a brand for several distinct models, all four-wheel drive versions.

Land Rovers, particularly the commercial and military models, became popular throughout rural areas and in the developing world. Since the 1970s in most remote areas of Africa, South America, Asia and in the Australian outback the Toyota Land Cruiser and Mitsubishi Pajaro has overtaken the Land Rover as the utility four-wheel drive of choice, probably because they are cheaper to buy and a better parts network service is offered by Japanese competitors. However, in many of these remote areas Land Rover is trying to regain lost sales and in many places succeeding, even with a higher purchase price compared to its Japanese competitors.

**Land Rover Freelander 2**

Since Ford bought Land Rover from BMW in 2000, Land Rover has been closely associated with Jaguar. In many countries the two share a common sales and distribution network (including shared dealerships), and some models now share components and production facilities.

In 2007, Land Rover achieved its third successive record sales year with 226,395 vehicles sold around the world. That is an increase of 18 per cent compared to 2006. In the UK, Land Rover sold over 50,000 vehicles for the first time in its 60-year history. In 2007, the four-wheel drive specialist sold 50,664 cars – an increase of 7 per cent on the previous year, making the UK Land Rover's biggest market. The US market was Land Rover's second largest market. The £22,300 Freelander 2 got off to an impressive start in its first full year of production with sales in the UK of just under 19,000.

**Land Rover Masai advertisement**

Today Land Rover employs 8,000 people and supports a further 30,000 jobs in its supply chain.

In June 2007, Ford announced that it planned to sell Land Rover, along with Jaguar. On 26 March 2008 it was announced that Ford Motor Company had sold Jaguar and Land Rover to Indian conglomorate Tata Group (Tata Motors) for £1.15 billion.

*Watch the video before answering the questions.*

## Questions

1 Which environmental factors would mostly influence future sales of Land Rover four-wheel drive models?

2 Which screening criteria would you recommend for Land Rover's future market (country) selection after they have been taken over by Tata Motors?

Source: Video accompanying the text, **www.landrover.com**

# Introduction to Part II

After considering the initial phase (Part I, The decision to internationalize) the structure of this part follows the process of selecting the 'right' international market. The
political and environment (Chapter 5) and the sociocultural environment (Chapter 6)
are used as inputs to the process from which the output is the target market(s) that
the firm should select as a basis for development of the international marketing mix
(see Part IV). The structure of Part II is shown in Figure 1.

As Figure 1 shows, the environmental forces presented in Chapters 6 and 7, provide
the environmental framework that is necessary for the following:

● the selection of the right market(s) (Chapter 7);
● the subsequent development of the global marketing mix.

The discussion following Chapters 5 and 6 will be limited to the major macroenvironmental dimensions affecting market and buyer behaviour and thus the global
marketing mix of the firm.

Figure 1 **The structure and process of Part II**

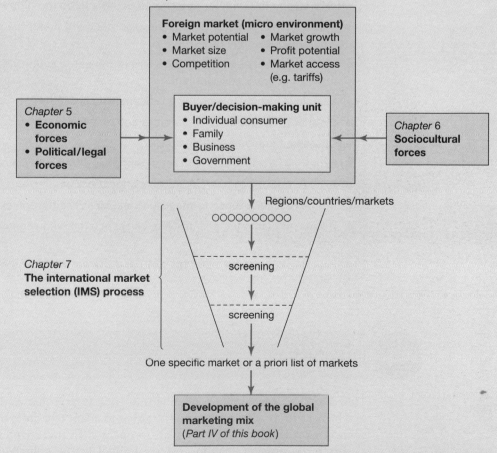

# 5

# The political and economic environment

## Contents

**Case study**

## Learning objectives

After studying this chapter you should be able to do the following:

- Discuss how the political/legal environment will affect the attractiveness of a potential foreign market.
- Distinguish between political factors in the home country environment and the host country environment.
- Explain the steps in a political risk analysis procedure.
- Distinguish between tariff barriers and non-tariff barriers.
- Describe the major trading blocs.
- Explore why the structure of consumption is different from country to country.
- Explain how managers can influence local politics.
- Define regional economic integration and identify different levels of integration.
- Discuss the benefits and drawbacks associated with regional economic integration.
- Evaluate consequences of the EMU and the euro on European business.

## 5.1 Introduction

This chapter is devoted to macroenvironmental factors that explain the many forces to which a firm is exposed. The marketer has to adapt to a more or less uncontrollable environment within which they plan to operate. In this chapter the environmental factors in the foreign environment are limited to the political/legal forces and the economic forces.

## 5.2    The political/legal environment

This section will concentrate mainly on political issues. The political/legal environment comprises primarily two dimensions:

1   the home country environment;
2   the host country environment.

*slide Pag.*

Besides these two dimensions there is also a third:

3   The general international environment (see Figure 5.1).

### Home country environment

A firm's home country political environment can constrain its international operations as well as its domestic operations. It can limit the countries that the international firm may enter.

The best-known example of the home country political environment affecting international operations was South Africa. Home country political pressure induced some firms to leave the country altogether. After US companies left South Africa the Germans and the Japanese remained as the major foreign presence. German firms did not face the same political pressure at home that US firms had. However, the Japanese government was embarrassed when Japan became South Africa's leading trading partner. As a result some Japanese companies reduced their South African activity.

One challenge facing multinationals is the triple-threat political environment. Even if the home country and the host country do not present problems, they may face threats in third markets. Firms that did not have problems with their home government or the South African government, for example, could be troubled or boycotted about their South African operations in third countries, such as the United States. Today European firms face problems in the United States if they do business in Cuba. Nestlé's problems with its infant formula controversy were most serious, not at home in Switzerland, or in African host countries, but in a third market – the United States.

A third area in which some governments regulate global marketing concerns bribery and corruption. In many countries payments or favours are a way of life, and an 'oiling of the wheels' is expected in return for government services. In the past many companies doing business internationally routinely paid bribes or did favours for foreign officials in order to gain contracts.

Many business managers argue that their home country should not apply its moral principles to other societies and cultures in which bribery and corruption are endemic.

Figure 5.1  Barriers in the political/legal environment

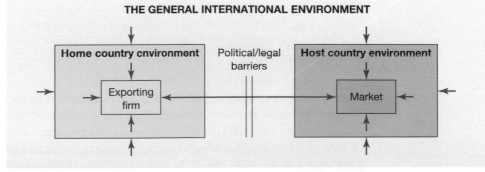

If they are to compete globally, these managers argue, they must be free to use the most common methods of competition in the host country. Particularly in industries that face limited or even shrinking markets, such stiff competition forces firms to find any edge possible to obtain a contract.

On the other hand, applying different standards to management and firms, depending on whether they do business abroad or domestically, is difficult to envisage. Also, bribes may open the way for shoddy performance and loose moral standards among managers and employees, and may result in a concentration on how best to bribe rather than on how best to produce and market products.

The global marketer must carefully distinguish between reasonable ways of doing business internationally – including compliance with foreign expectations – and outright bribery and corruption.

## Promotional activities (sponsored by governmental organizations)

The programmes adopted by governmental organizations to promote exporting are an increasingly important force in the international environment. Many of the activities involve implementation and sponsorship by government alone, while others are the results of the joint efforts of government and business.

Furthermore, so-called regulatory supportive activities are direct government attempts to make its country's products more competitive in world markets. Also, there are attempts to encourage greater participation in exporting, particularly by smaller companies.

The granting of subsidies is of special interest: export subsidies are to the export industries what tariffs are to domestic industries. In both cases the aim is to ensure the profitability of industries and individual firms that might well succumb if exposed to the full force of competition. For export industries, revenue is supplemented by subsidies, or costs are reduced by subsidies to certain input factors. Subsidies can be given through lower taxes on profits attributable to export sales, refunding of various indirect taxes, etc. Furthermore, a subsidy may take the form of a direct grant, which enables the recipient to compete against companies from other countries that enjoy cost advantages, or may be used for special promotion by recipient companies.

In a broader sense, government export promotion programmes, and programmes for global marketing activities in general, are designed to deal with the following internal barriers (Albaum *et al.*, 2002):

- lack of motivation, as global marketing is viewed as more time consuming, costly and risky, and less profitable, than domestic business;
- lack of adequate information;
- operational/resource-based limitations.

Some of these programmes are quite popular in developing countries, especially if they enjoy the support of the business community. Exhibit 5.1 highlights the role of the home government in the internationalization process of Huawei Technologies Corporation, China's biggest telecommunications equipment and service provider.

## Financial activities

Through the membership of international financial organizations such as the International Monetary Fund (IMF) and the World Bank the national government can assume its role as an international banker. The granting of subsidies is another financially based promotional activity of national governments.

One of the most vital determinants of the results of a company's export marketing programme is its credit policy. The supplier that can offer better payment terms and

## Exhibit 5.1 Huawei Technologies Corporation: The role of home government in the internationalization process

Huawei Technologies Corporation is now the largest telecom vendor in China, with reported 2006 revenues of US$ 8.5 billion. While Huawei has a strong national identity, it is seeking international expansion at a time when global telecommunication giants have already established their global brands in major trading blocs.

Government-run corporations remain the main driver for the Chinese national economy. Historically, the telecommunication sector in China has been closely controlled by the central government through the Ministry of Information Industry (MII). However, it is apparent that the Chinese telecommunication sector is in a process of transformation from a centrally controlled sector to a semi-capitalist industry. This transformation process is also as a result of China's commitment to the principles of the WTO. China will have to open up to more foreign investments. But China's central government will

Huawei home page screenshot.

continue to play a central role in stimulating technical progress through alliances, mergers and acquisitions. The political and business leaders see the global telecommunication giants (like Motorola, Nokia, Alcatel and Siemens) as catalysts for China's development and huge concessions have already been made to these companies, in cases where they have invested in China. Also Huawei receives plenty of state support, including soft loans to help with its international expansion. The China Development Bank (CDB) extended a credit facility of US$10 billion to help overseas customers to fund the purchase of Huawei's products.

MII also continued to encourage local Chinese operators like China Mobile and China Telecom to purchase telecommunications equipment from Chinese manufacturers (e.g. Huawei, ZTE (Zhongxing), Datang and Great Dragon).

So the key future challenge for Huawei is competing in two market environmental structures – one local and the other global.

Source: www.huawei.com, Low (2007).

financing conditions may make a sale, even though its price may be higher or the quality of its product inferior to that of its competitors.

If the credit terms are extended, the risks of non-payment increase, and many exporters are reluctant to assume the risks. Consequently, it may be necessary to offer exporters the opportunity of transferring some of the risk to governmental organizations through credit insurance. *Export credit insurance* and guarantees cover certain commercial and political risks that might be associated with any given export transaction.

### Information services

Many large companies can collect the information they need themselves. Other firms, even if they do not possess the expertise to do their own research, can afford to hire outside research agencies to do the necessary research. However, a large number of companies are not in a position to take either of these approaches. For these firms, generally smaller companies or newcomers to global marketing, their national government is the major source of basic marketing information.

Although the information relevant for international/export marketers varies from country to country, the following kinds are typically available (Albaum *et al.*, 2002, pp. 119–120):

- economic, social and political data on individual countries, including their infrastructure;
- summary and detailed information on aggregate global marketing transactions;
- individual reports on foreign firms;
- specific export opportunities;
- lists of potential overseas buyers, distributors and agents for various products in different countries;
- information on relevant government regulations both at home and abroad;
- sources of various kinds of information not always available from the government: for example, foreign credit information;
- information that will help the company manage its operation: for example, information on export procedures and techniques.

Most types of information are made available to firms through published reports or through the Internet. In addition, government officials often participate in seminars and workshops aimed at helping the international marketer.

## Export-facilitating activities

A number of national government activities can stimulate export. These include the following (Albaum *et al.*, 2002, pp. 119–120):

- Trade development offices abroad, either as a separate entity or as part of the normal operations of an embassy or consulate.
- Government-sponsored trade fairs and exhibitions. A trade fair is a convenient marketplace in which buyers and sellers can meet, and in which an exporter can display products.
- Sponsoring trade missions of businesspeople who go abroad for the purpose of making sales and/or establishing agencies and other foreign representation.
- Operating permanent trade centres in foreign market areas, which run trade shows often concentrating on a single industry.

From the national government's point of view, each of these activities represents a different approach to stimulating the growth of exports. From the point of view of an individual company, these activities provide relatively low-cost ways of making direct contact with potential buyers in overseas markets.

## Promotion by private organizations

Various non-governmental organizations play a role in the promotion of global marketing. These include the following (Albaum *et al.*, 2002, p. 120):

- industry and trade associations, national, regional and sectoral industry associations, associations of trading houses, mixed associations of manufacturers and traders, and other bodies;
- chambers of commerce: local chambers of commerce, national chambers, national and international associations of chambers, national chambers abroad and binational chambers;
- other organizations concerned with trade promotion: organizations carrying out export research, regional export promotion organizations, world trade centres, geographically oriented trade promotion organizations, export associations and clubs, international business associations, world trade clubs and organizations concerned with commercial arbitration;

- export service organizations, banks, transport companies, freight forwarders, export merchants and trading companies.

The type of assistance available to firms includes information and publications, education and assistance in 'technical' details, and promotion in foreign countries.

### State trading

Many of the former communist countries are now allowing some private trading activities, either through joint ventures or as a result of privatization of state-owned enterprises. However, there are still countries with active state trading, such as Cuba and to some extent China.

Private businesses are concerned about state trading for two reasons. First, the establishment of import monopolies means that exporters have to make substantial adjustments in their export marketing programmes. Second, if state traders wish to utilize the monopolistic power they possess, private international marketers will have a difficult time.

## Host country environment

Managers must continually monitor the government, its policies and its stability to determine the potential for political change that could adversely affect operations of the firm.

### Political risks

There is political risk in every nation, but the range of risks varies widely from country to country. In general, political risk is lowest in countries that have a history of stability and consistency. Three major types of political risk can be encountered:

1 *ownership risk*, which exposes property and life;
2 *operating risk*, which refers to interference with the ongoing operations of a firm;
3 *transfer risk*, which is mainly encountered when companies want to transfer capital between countries.

Political risk can be the result of government action, but it can also be outside the control of government. The types of action and their effects can be classified as follows:

- *Import restrictions.* Selective restrictions on the import of raw materials, machines and spare parts are fairly common strategies to force foreign industry to purchase more supplies within the host country and thereby create markets for local industry. Although this is done in an attempt to support the development of domestic industry, the result is often to hamstring and sometimes interrupt the operations of established industries. The problem then becomes critical when there are no adequately developed sources of supply within the country.
- *Local-content laws.* In addition to restricting imports of essential supplies to force local purchase, countries often require a portion of any product sold within the country to have local content: that is, to contain locally made parts. This requirement is often imposed on foreign companies that assemble products from foreign-made components. Local-content requirements are not restricted to developing countries. The European Union (EU) has a 45 per cent local-content requirement for foreign-owned assemblers. This requirement has been important for Far East car producers.
- *Exchange controls.* Exchange controls stem from shortages of foreign exchange held by a country. When a nation faces shortages of foreign exchange, controls may be

levied over all movements of capital or, selectively, against the most politically vulnerable companies to conserve the supply of foreign exchange for the most essential uses. A problem for the foreign investor is getting profits and investments into the currency of the home country (transfer risks).

- *Market control.* The government of a country sometimes imposes control to prevent foreign companies from competing in certain markets. Some years ago the US government threatened to boycott foreign firms trading with Cuba. The EU countries have protested against this threat.

- *Price controls.* Essential products that command considerable public interest, such as pharmaceuticals, food, petrol and cars, are often subjected to price controls. Such controls can be used by a government during inflationary periods to control the environmental behaviour of consumers or the cost of living.

- *Tax controls.* Taxes must be classified as a political risk when used as a means of controlling foreign investments. In many cases they are raised without warning and in violation of formal agreements. In underdeveloped countries, where the economy is constantly threatened with a shortage of funds, unreasonable taxation of successful foreign investments appeals to some governments as the most convenient and quickest way of finding operating funds.

- *Labour restrictions.* In many nations labour unions are very strong and have great political influence. Using their strength, unions may be able to persuade the government to pass very restrictive laws that support labour at heavy cost to business. Traditionally labour unions in Latin America have been able to prevent lay-offs and plant shutdowns. Labour unions are gradually becoming strong in western Europe as well. For example, Germany and a number of other European nations require labour representation on boards of directors.

- *Change of government party.* A new government may not honour an agreement that the previous government has made with the company. This is especially an issue in the developing countries, where the governing party changes quite often.

- *Nationalization (Expropriation).* Defined as official seizure of foreign property, this is the ultimate government tool for controlling foreign firms. This most drastic action against foreign firms is fortunately occurring less often as developing countries begin to see foreign direct investment as desirable.

- *Domestication.* This can be thought of as creeping expropriation and is a process by which controls and restrictions placed on the foreign firm gradually reduce the control of the owners. The firm continues to operate in the country while the host government is able to maintain leverage on the foreign firm through imposing different controls. These controls include: greater decision-making powers accorded to nationals; more products produced locally rather than imported for assembly; gradual transfer of ownership to nationals (demand for local participation in joint ventures); and promotion of a large number of nationals to higher levels of management. Domestication provides the host country with enough control to regulate the activities of the foreign firm carefully. In this way, any truly negative effects of the firm's operations in the country are discovered and prompt corrective action may be taken.

**Nationalization**
Takeover of foreign companies by the host government.

## Trade barriers from home country to host country

Free trade between nations permits international specialization. It also enables efficient firms to increase output to levels far greater than would be possible if sales were limited to their own domestic markets, thus permitting significant economies of scale. Competition increases, prices of goods in importing countries fall, while profits increase in the exporting country.

While countries have many reasons for wishing to trade with each other, it is also true to say that all too frequently an importing nation will take steps to inhibit the inward flow of goods and services by effecting trade barriers.

One of the reasons why international trade is different from domestic trade is that it is carried on between different political units, each one a sovereign nation exercising control over its own trade. Although all nations control their foreign trade, they vary in the degree of control. Each nation or trading bloc invariably establishes trade laws that favour its indigenous companies and discriminate against foreign ones.

There are two main reasons why countries levy tariffs:

1 *To protect domestic producers*. First, tariffs are a way of protecting domestic producers of a product. Because import tariffs raise the effective cost of an imported good, domestically produced goods can appear more attractive to buyers. In this way domestic producers gain a protective barrier against imports. Although producers receiving tariff protection can gain a price advantage, protection can keep them from increasing efficiency in the long run. A protected industry can be destroyed if protection encourages complacency and inefficiency when it is later thrown into the lion's den of international competition.

2 *To generate revenue*. Second, tariffs are a source of government revenue. Using tariffs to generate government revenue is most common among relatively less-developed nations. The main reason is that less-developed nations tend to have less formal domestic economies that presently lack the capability to record domestic transactions accurately. The lack of accurate record keeping makes the collection of sales taxes within the country extremely difficult. Nations solve the problem by simply raising their needed revenue through import and export tariffs. Those nations obtaining a greater portion of their total revenue from taxes on international trade are mainly the poorer nations.

Trade distortion practices can be grouped into two basic categories: tariff and non-tariff barriers.

## Tariff barriers

Tariffs are direct taxes and charges imposed on imports. They are generally simple, straightforward and easy for the country to administer. While they are a barrier to trade they are a visible and known quantity and so can be accounted for by companies when developing their marketing strategies.

Tariffs are used by poorer nations as the easiest means of collecting revenue and protecting certain home industries. They are a useful tool for politicians to show indigenous manufacturers that they are actively trying to protect their home markets.

The most common forms of tariffs are as follows:

- *Specific*. Charges are imposed on particular products, by either weight or volume, and usually stated in the local currency.
- *Ad valorem*. The charge is a straight percentage of the value of the goods (the import price).
- *Discriminatory*. In this case the tariff is charged against goods coming from a particular country, either where there is a trade imbalance or for political purposes.

## Non-tariff barriers

In the past 40 years the world has seen a gradual reduction in tariff barriers in most developed nations. However, in parallel to this, non-tariff barriers have substantially increased. Non-tariff barriers are much more elusive and can be more easily disguised. However, in some ways the effect can be more devastating because they are an unknown quantity and are much less predictable.

**Trade barriers**
Trade laws (often tariffs) that favour local firms and discriminate against foreign ones.

**Tariffs**
A tool that is used by governments to protect local companies from outside competition. The most common forms are: quotas, ad valorem and discriminatory.

Among non-tariff barriers the most important (not mentioned earlier) are as follows.

### Quotas

A restriction on the amount (measured in units or weight) of a good that can enter or leave a country during a certain period of time is called a *quota*. After tariffs, a quota is the second most common type of trade barrier. Governments typically administer their quota systems by granting quota licences to the companies or governments of other nations (in the case of import quotas), and domestic producers (in the case of export quotas). Governments normally grant such licences on a year-by-year basis.

There are two reasons why a government imposes *import quotas*:

1 It may wish to protect its domestic producers by placing a limit on the amount of goods allowed to enter the country. This helps domestic producers maintain their market shares and prices because competitive forces are restrained. In this case, domestic producers win because of the protection of their markets. Consumers lose because of higher prices and less selection due to lower competition. Other losers include domestic producers whose own production requires the import to be slapped with a quota. Companies relying on the importation of so-called 'intermediate' goods will find the final cost of their own products increases.
2 It may impose import quotas to force the companies of other nations to compete against one another for the limited amount of imports allowed. Thus those wishing to get a piece of the action will likely lower the price that they are asking for their goods. In this case, consumers win from the resulting lower prices. Domestic producers of competing goods win if external producers do not undercut their prices, but lose if they do.

Likewise, there are at least two reasons why a country imposes *export quotas* on its domestic producers:

1 It may wish to maintain adequate supplies of a product in the home market. This motive is most common among countries exporting natural resources that are essential to domestic business or the long-term survival of a nation.
2 It may restrict exports to restrict supply on world markets, thereby increasing the international price of the good. This is the motive behind the formation and activities of the Organization of Petroleum Exporting Countries (OPEC). This group of nations from the Middle East and Latin America attempts to restrict the world's supply of crude oil to earn greater profits.

A unique version of the export quota is called a *voluntary export restraint* (VER) – a quota that a nation imposes on its exports usually at the request of another nation. Countries normally self-impose a voluntary export restraint in response to the threat of an import quota or total ban on the product by an importing nation. The classic example of the use of a voluntary export restraint is the automobile industry in the 1980s. Japanese carmakers were making significant market share gains in the US market. The closing of US carmakers' production facilities in the United States was creating a volatile anti-Japan sentiment among the population and the US Congress. Fearing punitive legislation in Congress if Japan did not limit its auto exports to the United States, the Japanese government and its carmakers self-imposed a voluntary export restraint on cars headed for the United States.

Consumers in the country that imposes an export quota benefit from greater supply and the resulting lower prices if domestic producers do not curtail production. Producers in an importing country benefit because the goods of producers from the exporting country are restrained, which may allow them to increase prices. Export quotas hurt consumers in the importing nation because of reduced selection and perhaps higher prices. However, export quotas might allow these same consumers to retain their jobs if imports were threatening to put domestic producers out of business. Again, detailed economic studies are needed to determine the winners and losers in any particular export quota case.

### Embargoes

A complete ban on trade (imports and exports) in one or more products with a particular country is called an *embargo*. An embargo may be placed on one or a few goods or completely ban trade in all goods. It is the most restrictive non-tariff trade barrier available and is typically applied to accomplish political goals. Embargoes can be decreed by individual nations or by supranational organizations such as the United Nations. Because they can be very difficult to enforce, embargoes are used less today than in the past. One example of a total ban on trade with another country has been the United States' embargo on trade with Cuba.

### Administrative delays

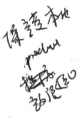

Regulatory controls or bureaucratic rules designed to impair the rapid flow of imports into a country are called *administrative delays*. This non-tariff barrier includes a wide range of government actions such as requiring international air carriers to land at 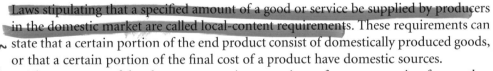 inconvenient airports; requiring product inspections that damage the product itself; purposely understaffing customs offices to cause unusual time delays; and requiring special licences that take a long time to obtain. The objective of such administrative delays for a country is to discriminate against imported products – in a word, it is protectionism.

Although Japan has removed some of its trade barriers many subtle obstacles to imports remain. Products ranging from cold pills and vitamins to farm products and building materials find it hard to penetrate the Japanese market.

### Local-content requirements

Laws stipulating that a specified amount of a good or service be supplied by producers in the domestic market are called local-content requirements. These requirements can state that a certain portion of the end product consist of domestically produced goods, or that a certain portion of the final cost of a product have domestic sources.

The purpose of local-content requirements is to force companies from other nations to employ local resources in their production processes – particularly labour. Similar to other restraints on imports, such requirements help protect domestic producers from the price advantage of companies based in other, low-wage countries. Today companies can circumvent local-content requirements by locating production facilities inside the nation stipulating such restrictions.

## Historical development of barriers

Non-tariff barriers become much more prevalent in times of recession. The United States and Europe have witnessed the mobilisation of quite strong political lobby groups as indigenous industries, which have come under threat, lobby their governments to take measures to protect them from international competition. The last major era of protectionism was in the 1930s. During that decade, under the impact of the most disastrous trade depression in history, most countries of the world adopted high tariffs.

After the Second World War there was a reaction against the high tariff policy of the 1930s and significant efforts were made to move the world back to free trade. World organizations (such as GATT and its successor, WTO) have been developed to foster international trade and provide a trade climate in which such barriers can be reduced.

## The general international environment

In addition to the politics and laws of both the home and the host countries, the marketer must consider the overall international political and legal environment. Relations between countries can have a profound impact on firms trying to do business internationally.

The international political environment involves political relationships between two or more countries. This is in contrast to our previous concern for what happens only within a given foreign country. The international firm almost inevitably becomes somewhat involved with the host country's international relations, no matter how neutral it may try to be. It does so because its operations in a country are frequently related to operations in other countries, either on the supply or the demand side or both. East–West relations are a good example of a situation in the international political environment that is continually evolving.

The effect of politics on global marketing is determined by both the bilateral political relations between home and host countries and the multilateral agreements governing the relations among groups of countries. One aspect of a country's international relations is its relationship with the firm's home country.

A second critical element affecting the political environment is the host country's relations with other nations. If a country is a member of a regional group, such as the European Union or ASEAN, this influences the firm's evaluation of the country. If a nation has particular friends or enemies among other nations, the firm must modify its international logistics to comply with how that market is supplied and to whom it can sell.

Another clue to a nation's international behaviour is its membership of international organizations. Membership of the IMF or the World Bank may aid a country's financial situation, but it also puts constraints on the country's behaviour. Many other international agreements impose rules on their members. These agreements may affect, for example, patents, communication, transportation and other items of interest to the international marketer. As a rule, the more international organizations a country belongs to, the more regulations it accepts, and the more dependable is its behaviour.

## 5.3  The economic environment

Market size and growth are influenced by many forces, but the total buying power in the country and the availability or non-availability of electricity, telephone systems, modern roads and other types of infrastructure will influence the direction of that spending.

Economic development results from one of three types of economic activity:

1 *Primary*. These activities are concerned with agriculture and extractive processes (e.g. coal, iron ore, gold, fishing).
2 *Secondary*. These are manufacturing activities. There are several evolutions. Typically countries will start manufacturing through processing the output of primary products.
3 *Tertiary*. These activities are based upon *services* – for example, tourism, insurance and health care. As the average family income in a country rises the percentage of income spent on food declines, the percentage spent on housing and household activities remains constant, and the percentage spent on service activities (e.g. education, transport and leisure) will increase.

## How exchange rates influence business activities

Times of crisis are not the only occasions during which companies are affected by exchange rates. In fact movement in a currency's exchange rate affects the activities of both domestic and international companies. Let us now examine how exchange rate changes affect the business decisions of companies, and why stable and predictable rates are desirable.

Exchange rates affect demand for a company's products in the global marketplace. When a country's currency is *weak* (valued low relative to other currencies), the price of its exports on world markets declines and the price of imports increases. Lower prices make the country's exports more appealing on world markets. They also give companies the opportunity to take market share away from companies whose products are highly priced in comparison.

Furthermore, a company selling in a country with a *strong* currency (one that is valued high relative to other currencies) while paying workers in a country with a weak currency improves its profits.

The international lowering of the value of a currency by the nation's government is called devaluation. The reverse, the intentional raising of its value by the nation's government, is called revaluation. These concepts are not to be confused with the terms *weak* and *strong* currencies, although their effects are similar.

*Devaluation* lowers the price of a country's exports on world markets and increases the price of imports because the country's currency is now worth less on world markets. Thus a government might devalue its currency to give its domestic companies an edge over competition from other countries. It might also devalue to boost exports so that a trade deficit can be eliminated. However, such a policy is not wise because devaluation reduces consumers' buying power. It also allows inefficiencies to persist in domestic companies because there is now less pressure to be concerned with production costs. In such a case, increasing inflation may be the result. *Revaluation* has the opposite effect: it increases the price of exports and reduces the price of imports.

As we have seen, unfavourable movements in exchange rates can be costly for both domestic and international companies. Therefore, managers prefer that exchange rates be *stable*. Stable exchange rates improve the accuracy of financial planning, including cash flow forecasts. Although methods do exist for insuring against potentially adverse exchange rate movements, most of these are too expensive for small and medium-sized businesses. Moreover, as the unpredictability of exchange rates increases, so too does the cost of insuring against the accompanying risk.

## Law of one price

An exchange rate tells us how much of one currency we must pay to receive a certain amount of another. But it does not tell us whether a specific product will actually cost us more or less in a particular country (as measured in our own currency). When we travel to another country we discover that our own currency buys more or less than it does at home. In other words, we quickly learn that exchange rates do not guarantee or stabilize the buying power of our currency. Thus we can lose purchasing power in some countries while gaining it in others.

The law of one price stipulates that an identical product must have an identical price in all countries when price is expressed in a common-denominator currency. For this principle to apply products must be identical in quality and content in all countries, and must be entirely produced within each particular country.

### Big Mac Index/Big MacCurrencies

The usefulness of the law of one price is that it helps us determine whether a currency is overvalued or undervalued. Each year *The Economist* magazine publishes what it calls its 'Big MacCurrencies' exchange-rate index (see Table 5.1).

The index is based on the theory of purchasing-power parity (PPP), the notion that a dollar should buy the same amount in all countries. The theory naturally relies on certain assumptions, such as negligible transportation costs, that goods and services must be 'tradable', and that a good in one country does not differ substantially from the same good in another country. Thus, in the long run, the exchange rate between two currencies should move towards the rate that equalizes the prices of an identical basket of goods and services in each country. In this case the 'basket' is a McDonald's Big Mac, which is produced in about 120 countries. The Big Mac PPP is the exchange rate that would mean hamburgers cost the same in the United States as abroad. Comparing actual exchange rates with PPP indicates whether a currency is under- or overvalued.

This index uses the law of one price to determine the exchange rate that should exist between the US dollar and other major currencies. It employs the McDonald's Big Mac as its single product to test the law of one price. Why the Big Mac? Because each Big Mac is fairly identical in quality and content across national markets and almost entirely produced within the nation in which it is sold. The underlying assumption is that the price of a Big Mac in any world currency should, after being converted to dollars, equal

**Table 5.1  The hamburger standard (based on 25 March 2006 Big Mac prices)**

| Country | Big Mac price | | Implied PPP of the $ (local price divided by price in US) | Actual Exchange Rate 1 USD = | Over(+) / Under(−) valuation against the dollar, % |
|---|---|---|---|---|---|
| | in local currency | in US dollars | | | |
| United States | $3.10 | 3.10 | – | 1.00 | – |
| Argentina | Peso7.00 | 2.27 | 2.26 | 3.08 | −27 |
| Australia | A$3.25 | 2.49 | 1.05 | 1.30 | −19 |
| Brazil | Real6.40 | 2.94 | 2.06 | 2.17 | −5 |
| Britain | £1.94 | 3.68 | 1.60* | 1.90* | +19 |
| Canada | C$3.52 | 3.13 | 1.14 | 1.12 | +2 |
| China | Yuan10.50 | 1.31 | 3.39 | 7.98 | −58 |
| Euro area | €2.94 | 3.77 | 0.95 | 0.77 | +22 |
| Hong Kong | HK$12.00 | 1.54 | 3.87 | 7.77 | −50 |
| Hungary | Forint560 | 2.65 | 181.00 | 210.74 | −14 |
| Indonesia | Rupiah14,600 | 1.60 | 4.71 | 9,090.91 | −48 |
| Japan | ¥250 | 2.17 | 80.6 | 115.18 | −30 |
| Malaysia | M$5.50 | 1.49 | 1.77 | 3.67 | −52 |
| Mexico | Peso29.0 | 2.66 | 9.35 | 10.87 | −14 |
| New Zealand | NZ$4.45 | 2.81 | 1.44 | 1.58 | −9 |
| Poland | Zloty6.50 | 2.15 | 2.10 | 3.02 | −30 |
| Russia | Rouble48.00 | 1.79 | 15.5 | 26.72 | −42 |
| Singapore | S$3.60 | 2.29 | 1.16 | 1.57 | −26 |
| South Africa | Rand13.95 | 2.06 | 4.50 | 6.76 | −33 |
| South Korea | Won2,500 | 2.57 | 806 | 970.40 | −17 |
| Sweden | Skr33.0 | 4.60 | 10.6 | 7.16 | +48 |
| Switzerland | SFr6.30 | 5.12 | 2.03 | 1.22 | +65 |
| Taiwan | NT$75.00 | 2.29 | 24.2 | 32.65 | −26 |
| Thailand | Baht60.0 | 1.59 | 19.4 | 37.52 | −48 |

* Dollars per pound.

Source: *The Economist*, 25 March 2006 © The Economist Newspaper Limited, London (25.04.06).

the price of a Big Mac in the United States. A country's currency would be overvalued if the Big Mac price (converted to dollars) is higher than the US price. Conversely, a country's currency would be undervalued if the converted Big Mac price was lower than the US price.

Such large discrepancies between a currency's exchange rate on currency markets and the rate predicted by the Big Mac Index are not surprising, for several reasons. For one thing, the selling price of food is affected by subsidies for agricultural products in most countries. Also, the Big Mac is not a 'traded' product in the sense that one can buy Big Macs in low-priced countries and sell them in high-priced countries. Prices can also be affected because Big Macs are subject to different marketing strategies in different countries. Finally, countries impose different levels of sales tax on restaurant meals.

The drawbacks of the Big Mac Index reflect the fact that applying the law of one price to a single product is too simplistic a method for estimation of exchange rates. Nonetheless, a recent study finds that currency values in eight out of 12 industrial countries do tend to change in the direction suggested by the Big Mac Index. And for six out of seven currencies that change more than 10 per cent the Big Mac Index was as good a predictor as more sophisticated methods.

Table 5.1 also uses the concept of purchasing-power parity (PPP), which economists use when adjusting national income data (GNP, etc.) to improve comparability. PPPs are the rates of currency conversion that equalize the purchasing power of different currencies by eliminating the differences in price levels between countries. In their simplest form PPPs are simply price relatives that show the ratio of the prices in national currencies of the same good or service in different countries.

The easiest way to see how a PPP is calculated is to consider Table 5.1 for a product that is identical in several countries. For example, a Big Mac costs Peso7.00 in Argentina. If we divide 7.00 with the price in the United States, $3.10, the result will be the PPP of the dollar = 2.26 (the 'theoretical' exchange rate of the Peso). Then if we divide 2.26 with the actual exchange rate, 3.08, we find that the Argentina Peso is undervalued by $1 - (2.26/3.08) \times 100 = 27$ per cent.

However, the easiest way to calculate the over- or under-valuation of the local currency against the US$ is to divide the local Big Mac price (in US$) with the US Big Mac Price. So, for example, the Indonesian Rupiah is undervalued with $1 - (1.60/3.10) \times 100 = 48$ per cent.

PPPs are not only calculated for individual products; they are calculated for a 'basket' of products, and PPP is meaningful only when applied to such a 'basket'.

## Classification by income

**GNP**
Gross national product is the value of all goods and services produced by the domestic economy over a one-year period, including income generated by the country's international activities.

**GNP per capita**
Total GNP divided by its population.

Countries can be classified in a variety of ways. Most classifications are based on national income (GDP or GNP per capita) and the degree of industrialization. The broadcast measure of economic development is gross national product (GNP) – the value of all goods and services produced by a country during a one-year period. This figure includes income generated both by domestic production and by the country's international activities. *Gross domestic product* (GDP) is the value of all goods and services produced by the domestic economy over a one-year period. In other words, when we add to GDP the income generated from exports, imports and the international operations of a nation's companies, we get GNP. A country's GNP per capita is simply its GNP divided by its population. GDP per capita is calculated similarly.

Both GNP per capita and GDP per capita measure a nation's income per person. In this regard GNI (Gross National Income) can be regarded as the same as GNP.

## Less developed countries (LDCs)

This group includes underdeveloped countries and developing countries. The main features are a low GDP per capita (less than $3,000), limited amount of manufacturing activity and a very poor and fragmented infrastructure. Typical infrastructure weaknesses are in transport, communications, education and health care. In addition, the public sector is often slow moving and bureaucratic.

It is common to find that LDCs are heavily reliant on one product and often on one trading partner. The typical pattern for single-product dependence is the reliance on one agricultural crop or on mining. Colombia (coffee) and Cuba (sugar) are examples of extreme dependence upon agriculture. The risks posed to the LDC by changing patterns of supply and demand are great. Falling commodity prices can result in large decreases in earnings for the whole country. The resultant economic and political adjustments may affect exporters to that country through possible changes in tariff and non-tariff barriers.

A wide range of economic circumstances influences the development of the LDCs in the world. Without real prospects for rapid economic development private sources of capital are reluctant to invest in such countries. This is particularly the case for long-term infrastructure projects. As a result, important capital spending projects rely heavily on world aid programmes.

The quality of distribution channels varies considerably between countries. There are often great differences between the small-scale, undercapitalized distribution intermediaries in LDCs and the distributors in more advanced countries. Retailers, for example, are more likely to be market traders. The incidence of large-scale self-service outlets will be comparatively low.

## Newly industrialised countries (NICs)

NICs are countries with an emerging industrial base: one that is capable of exporting. Examples of NICs are the 'tigers' of south-east Asia: Hong Kong, Singapore, South Korea and Taiwan. Brazil and Mexico are examples of NICs in South America. In NICs, although the infrastructure shows considerable development, high growth in the economy results in difficulties with producing what is demanded by domestic and foreign customers.

## Advanced industrialized countries

These countries have considerable GDP per capita, a wide industrial base, considerable development in the services sector and substantial investment in the infrastructure of the country.

This attempt to classify the economies of the world into neat divisions is not completely successful. For example, some of the advanced industrialized countries (e.g. the United States and France) have important agricultural sectors.

## Regional economic integration

Economic integration has been one of the main economic developments affecting world markets since the Second World War. Countries have wanted to engage in economic cooperation to use their respective resources more effectively and to provide large markets for member-country producers.

Some integration efforts have had quite ambitious goals, such as political integration; some have failed as a result of perceptions of unequal benefits from the arrangement or a parting of the ways politically. Figure 5.2, a summary of the major forms of econ-

**Figure 5.2 Forms of economic integration in regional markets**

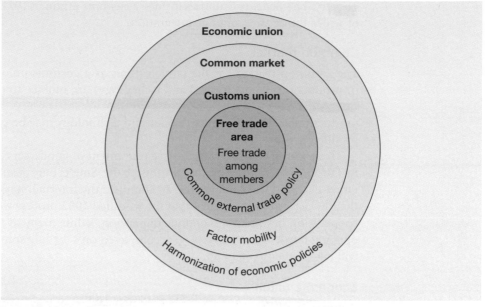

Source: From Czinkota/Ronkainen. *Global Marketing*, 1e. © 1996 South-Western, a part of Cengage Learning, Inc. Reproduced by permission. www.cengage.com/permissions.

omic cooperation in regional markets, shows the varying degrees of formality with which integration can take place. These economic integration efforts are dividing the world into trading blocs.

The levels of economic integration will now be described.

## Free trade area

The free trade area is the least restrictive and loosest form of economic integration among nations. In a free trade area all barriers to trade among member countries are removed. Each member country maintains its own trade barriers vis-à-vis non-members.

The European Free Trade Area (EFTA) was formed in 1960 with an agreement by eight European countries. Since that time EFTA has lost much of its original significance due to its members joining the European Union. All EFTA countries have cooperated with the European Union through bilateral free trade agreements, and since 1994 through the European Economic Area (EEA) arrangement that allows for free movement of people, products, services and capital within the combined area of the European Union and EFTA. Of the EFTA countries, Iceland and Liechtenstein have decided not to apply for membership of the European Union and Norway turned down membership after a referendum in 1994. Switzerland has also decided to stay out of the European Union.

After three failed tries during the last century the United States and Canada signed a free trade agreement that went into effect in 1989. North American free trade expanded in 1994 with the inclusion of Mexico in the North American Free Trade Agreement (NAFTA).

## Customs union

The customs union is one step further along the spectrum of economic integration. As in the free trade area, goods and services are freely traded among members. In addition, however, the customs union establishes a common trade policy with respect to non-members. Typically this takes the form of a common external tariff, whereby

131

imports from non-members are subject to the same tariff when sold to any member country. The Benelux countries formed a customs union in 1921 that later became part of wider European economic integration.

## Common market

The common market has the same features as a customs union. In addition, factors of production (labour, capital and technology) are mobile among members. Restrictions on immigration and cross-border investment are abolished. When factors of production are mobile capital, labour and technology may be employed in their most productive uses.

The removal of barriers to the free movement of goods, services, capital and people in Europe was ratified by the passing of the Single European Act in 1987 with the target date of 31 December 1992 to complete the internal market. In December 1991 the EEC agreed in Maastricht that the so-called 1992 process would be a step towards cooperation beyond the economic dimension. While many of the directives aimed at opening borders and markets were completed on schedule some sectors, such as cars, will take longer to open up.

## Economic union

The creation of true economic union requires integration of economic policies in addition to the free movement of goods, services and factors of production across borders. Under an economic union members harmonize monetary policies, taxation and government spending. In addition, a common currency is used by members and this could involve a system of fixed exchange rates. The ratification of the Maastricht Treaty in late 1993 resulted in the European Union being effective from 1 January 1994. Clearly the formation of a full economic union requires the surrender of a large measure of national sovereignty to a supranational body. Such a union is only a short step away from political unification, but many countries in the European Union (especially in the northern part of Europe) are sceptical about this development because they fear a loss of national identity.

## Enlargement of the EU

The EU can already look back on a history of successful enlargements. The Treaties of Paris (1951), establishing the European Coal and Steel Community (ECSC), and Rome (1957), establishing the European Economic Community (EEC) and EURATOM, were signed by six founding members: Belgium, France, Germany, Italy, Luxembourg and the Netherlands. The EU then underwent four successive enlargements: 1973, Denmark, Ireland and the United Kingdom; 1981, Greece; 1986, Portugal and Spain; 1995, Austria, Finland and Sweden.

After growing from six to 15 members, the European Union is now preparing for its biggest enlargement ever in terms of scope and diversity. Thirteen countries have applied to become new members and ten of these – Cyprus, the Czech Republic, Estonia, Hungary, Latvia, Lithuania, Malta, Poland, the Slovak Republic and Slovenia – joined on 1 May 2004. Bulgaria and Romania joined on 1 January 2007, while Turkey is not currently negotiating its membership. However, Turkey wants to be a member of the EU and the issue will be taken up again in the future.

The current 27 member states of the European Union as on 1 January 2007 are: Austria, Belgium, Bulgaria, Cyprus, Czech Republic, Denmark, Estonia, Finland, France, Germany, Greece, Hungary, Ireland, Italy, Latvia, Lithuania, Luxembourg, Malta, Netherlands, Poland, Portugal, Romania, Spain, Slovakia, Slovenia, Sweden and the United Kingdom.

New countries wanting to join the EU, need to fulfil the economic and political conditions known as the 'Copenhagen criteria', according to which a prospective member must (http://europa.eu.int/comm/enlargement): be a stable democracy, respecting human rights, the rule of law, and the protection of minorities; have a functioning market economy; and adopt the common rules, standards and policies that make up the body of EU law.

## 5.4 The European Economic and Monetary Union and the euro

The Maastricht Treaty resulted in the European Economic and Monetary Union (EMU), which also included the new common European currency, the euro. Although the EMU is currently limited to 12 of the 25 member states, it nevertheless involves the extension of the 'law of one price' across a market comprising 300 million consumers, representing one-fifth of the world economy, which should promote increased trade and stimulate greater competition. Consequently the development of this 'new' Europe has an importance beyond the relatively small group of nations currently involved in its creation. The former eastern European nations, eager to gain full EU membership, for political and economic reasons, will be required to accept full participation in EMU. Unaided, this could conceivably preoccupy their economies for decades (Whyman, 2002).

The consequences of European economic integration will not be restricted to so-called 'European' business. Most obviously the developments associated with the EMU will have a direct impact upon all foreign subsidiaries located within the new euro market. These companies will be forced to adapt their accounting, personnel and financial processes to accommodate the new currency.

The EMU will also affect the international competitiveness of European companies. Reductions in transaction costs, exchange rate risk, intensified domestic competition and the possibilities of gleaning additional economies of scale should all facilitate reductions in the cost structures of European firms, with inevitable consequences upon their external competitors. However, this may be negated by the impact of demands for wage equalization and restrictions imposed by regulations.

With so many important issues in the EMU there is no single economic consensus concerning the likely development of the European economy.

Supporters of EMU claim that the greater nominal exchange rate stability, lower transaction costs (by the introduction of the euro) and price transparency (across European borders) resulting in reduction of information costs will increase the international competitiveness of European business, raising consumer welfare together with the demand for cheaper products. The establishment of an independent European Central Bank (ECB) is anticipated to ensure a low level of inflation, reduce real interest rates and thereby stimulate investment, output and employment.

Opponents of the EMU claim the following:

- The loss of national economic policy tools will have a destabilizing impact.
- The lack of 'real' convergence of participating economies is likely to increase the problem of asymmetric shocks.
- The ECB's attempts at stabilization by the use of a single instrument, a common interest rate, are likely to prove insufficient because the common monetary policy affects EU members differently due to differences in factors, including the concentration of owner-occupation and variable interest borrowing.

## Major trading blocs

Table 5.2 shows the major trading blocs together with their population, GNI (gross national income) and GNI per capita. GNI (= GNP) is the current income indicator used by the World Bank. Previously the World Bank used gross domestic product (GDP) which is the total value of all goods and services produced by capital and workers in a country. GNI is GDP plus net income from assets abroad (e.g. subsidiaries). This means that GNI is the total value of all goods and services produced by a country's residents or corporations, regardless of their location (World Bank, 2005).

The size and economic importance of the EU, USA and Japan stand out. The affluence of Luxembourg and Denmark – both small countries – is marked by high values of GNI per capita.

> **Gross domestic product**
> Plus/minus net income from assets (e.g. subsidiaries abroad) is GNI (= GNP).

### 5.5 Summary

In this chapter we have concentrated on analysing the political/legal and the economic environment as it affects the firm in international markets. Most companies are unable to influence the environment of their markets directly, but their opportunities for successful business conduct largely depend on the structure and content of that environment. A marketer serving international markets or planning to do so, therefore, has to assess carefully the political and legal environments of the markets served or under consideration to draw the appropriate managerial consequences.

### Political environment

The international marketer's political environment is complex because of the interaction among domestic, foreign and international politics. When investing in a foreign country firms have to be sensitive to that country's political concerns. The firm should prepare a monitoring system that allows it systematically to evaluate the political risks – such as expropriation, nationalization and restrictions against exports and/or imports. Through skilful adaptation and control political risks can be reduced or neutralized.

Tariffs have traditionally been used as barriers to international trade. International trade liberalization during the last decade of the twentieth century led to a significant reduction of tariff barriers. Therefore governments have been increasingly using non-tariff barriers to protect those of their countries' industries that they think are unable to sustain free international competition. A government may also support or deter international business through its investment policy, that is, the general rules governing legislation concerning domestic as well as foreign participation in the equity or ownership of businesses and other organizations of the country.

There are various trade barriers that can inhibit global marketing. Although nations have used the WTO to lessen many of the restrictions several of these barriers will undoubtedly remain.

The political risk perspective of a nation can be studied using factors such as:

- a change in government policy;
- the stability of the government;
- the quality of the host government's economic management;
- the host country's attitude towards foreign investment;
- the host country's relationship with the rest of the world;

Table 5.2 Major trading blocs as of 1 January 2007 (figures are from 2005 – World Bank)

| Organization | Type | Members | Population (million) | GNI ($bn) | GNI per capita ($) |
|---|---|---|---|---|---|
| European Union | Political and economic union | Belgium | 10.5 | 373.8 | 35,700 |
| | | Luxembourg | 0.5 | 30.0 | 65,630 |
| | | Denmark | 5.4 | 256.8 | 47,390 |
| | | France | 60.7 | 2,177.7 | 34,810 |
| | | Germany | 82.5 | 2,852.3 | 34,580 |
| | | Ireland | 4.2 | 166.6 | 40,150 |
| | | Italy | 57.5 | 1,724.9 | 30,010 |
| | | UK | 60.2 | 2,263.7 | 37,600 |
| | | Netherlands | 16.3 | 598.0 | 36,620 |
| | | Greece | 11.1 | 218.1 | 19,670 |
| | | Portugal | 10.6 | 170.7 | 16,170 |
| | | Spain | 43.4 | 1,100.1 | 25,360 |
| | | Sweden | 9.0 | 370.5 | 41,060 |
| | | Austria | 8.2 | 303.6 | 36,980 |
| | | Finland | 5.2 | 196.5 | 37,460 |
| | | Bulgaria | 7.7 | 26.7 | 3,450 |
| | | Cyprus | 0.8 | 13.6 | 16,510 |
| | | Czech Republic | 10.2 | 109.2 | 10,710 |
| | | Estonia | 1.3 | 12.2 | 9,100 |
| | | Latvia | 2.3 | 15.5 | 6,760 |
| | | Lithuania | 3.4 | 24.0 | 7,050 |
| | | Hungary | 10.1 | 101.2 | 10,030 |
| | | Malta | 0.4 | 5.5 | 13,590 |
| | | Poland | 38.1 | 271.4 | 7,110 |
| | | Romania | 21.6 | 82.9 | 3,830 |
| | | Slovakia | 5.4 | 42.8 | 7,950 |
| | | Slovenia | 2.0 | 34.7 | 17,350 |
| | | Total | 488.6 | 13,543.0 | 27,718 |
| Association of South East Asian Nations (ASEAN) | Limited trade and cooperation agreement | Indonesia | 220.6 | 282.2 | 1,280 |
| | | Brunei | n.a. | n.a. | n.a. |
| | | Vietnam | 83.0 | 51.7 | 620 |
| | | Malaysia | 25.3 | 125.8 | 4,960 |
| | | Singapore | 4.4 | 119.6 | 27,490 |
| | | Philippines | 83.1 | 108.3 | 1,300 |
| | | Thailand | 64.2 | 176.9 | 2,750 |
| | | Laos | 5.9 | 2.6 | 440 |
| | | Myanmar | n.a. | n.a. | n.a. |
| | | Cambodia | 14.1 | 5.3 | 380 |
| | | Total | 500.6 | 872.4 | 1,743 |
| Asia Pacific Economic Cooperation (APEC, excl. ASEAN, USA and Canada) | Formal institution | China | 1,304.5 | 2,263.8 | 1,740 |
| | | Japan | 128.0 | 4,988.6 | 38,980 |
| | | South Korea | 48.3 | 764.7 | 15,830 |
| | | Taiwan* | 23.0 | 337.1 | 14,630 |
| | | Australia | 20.3 | 654.6 | 32,220 |
| | | New Zealand | 4.1 | 106.7 | 25,960 |
| | | Total | 1,528.2 | 9,115.5 | 5,965 |
| North American Free Trade Area (NAFTA) | Free trade area | US | 296.5 | 12,969.6 | 43,740 |
| | | Canada | 32.3 | 1,051.9 | 32,600 |
| | | Mexico | 103.1 | 753.4 | 7,310 |
| | | Total | 431.9 | 14,774.9 | 34,209 |

* Estimated from different sources as Taiwan is not in the World Bank Statistics.

Source: Adapted from *World Bank* (2006).

- the host country's relationship with the parent company's home government;
- the attitude towards the assignment of foreign personnel;
- the closeness between the government and people;
- the fairness and honesty of administrative procedures.

The importance of these factors varies from country to country and from firm to firm. Nevertheless, it is desirable to consider them all to ensure a complete knowledge of the political outlook for doing business in a particular country.

International terrorism is an increasing problem for companies, but with appropriate strategic and operational thinking, the effects of terrorism can be anticipated and planned for. While new procedures intended to minimize terrorism's harm may prove costly, they must be weighed against the substantial savings afforded by corporate preparedness for both the direct and indirect effects of terrorism. In the long run, manufacturers should increasingly incorporate product value chains that facilitate rapid switching to alternative parts and components in the event of supply shocks to critical input goods.

## Economic environment

The economic environment is a major determinant of market potential and opportunity. Significant variations in national markets originate in economic differences. Population characteristics, of course, represent one major dimension. The income and wealth of the nation's people are also extremely important because these key figures determine people's purchasing power. Countries and markets may be at different stages of economic development, each stage having different characteristics.

The Maastricht Treaty resulted in the European Economic and Monetary Union (EMU), which also included the new common European currency, the euro. Although the EMU is currently limited to 12 of the 15 member states it nevertheless involves the extension of the 'law of one price' across a market comprising 300 million consumers, representing one-fifth of the world economy, which should promote increased trade and stimulate greater competition. Consequently the development of this 'new' Europe has an importance beyond the relatively small group of nations currently involved in its creation.

Formal methods for gauging economic development in other nations include: (a) national production, such measures as gross national product and gross domestic product; (b) purchasing-power parity, or the relative ability of two countries' currencies to buy the same 'basket' of goods in those two countries. This index is used to correct comparisons that are made.

# Sauer-Danfoss: Which political/economic factors would affect a manufacturer of hydraulic components?

Sauer-Danfoss (**www.sauer-danfoss. com**) is a comprehensive subsupplier of mobile hydraulic solutions as either components or integrated systems to manufacturers of mobile equipment in agriculture, construction, material handling and road building, as well as specialty vehicles in forestry and on-highway. With more than 7,000 employees and 24 factories in North America, Europe and East Asia, Sauer-Danfoss is among the largest manufacturers and suppliers of mobile hydraulics in the world today. Sauer-Danfoss has its principal business centres in Ames, Iowa (US), Neumünster (Germany) and Nordborg (Denmark).

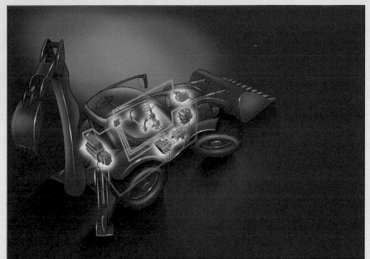

## Questions

1 Which political and economic factors in the global environment would have the biggest effect on the future global sales of Sauer-Danfoss hydraulic components/ systems to:

  (a) manufacturers of construction and mining equipment (e.g. Caterpillar)?

  (b) manufacturers of agricultural machinery (e.g. John Deere)?

2 What are the biggest problems in forecasting future demand for a subsupplier such as Sauer-Danfoss?

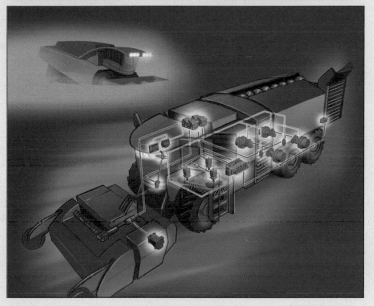

The two blue images represent the agricultural market (combine harvester) and construction market (excavator)

For further exercises and cases, see this book's website at www.pearsoned.co.uk/hollensen

## ? Questions for discussion

1 Identify different types of barrier to the free movement of goods and services.

2 Explain the importance of a common European currency to firms selling goods to the European market.

3 How useful is GNP when undertaking a comparative analysis of world markets? What other approaches would you recommend?

4 Discuss the limitations of per capita income in evaluating market potential.

5 Distinguish between: (a) free trade area, (b) customs union, (c) common market, (d) economic and monetary union and (e) political union.

6 Why is the international marketer interested in the age distribution of the population in a market?

7 Describe the ways in which foreign exchange fluctuations affect: (a) trade, (b) investments, (c) tourism.

8 Why is political stability so important for international marketers? Find some recent examples from the press to underline your points.

9 How can the change of major political goals in a country have an impact on the potential for success of an international marketer?

10 A country's natural environment influences its attractiveness to an international marketer of industrial products. Discuss.

11 Explain why a country's balance of trade may be of interest to an international marketer.

## References

Albaum, G., Strandskov, J. and Duerr, E. (2002) *International Marketing and Export Management* (4th edn), Financial Times/Pearson Education, Harlow.

Czinkota, M.R. and Ronkainen, I.A. (1996) *Global Marketing*, 1st edn, South-Western.

Low, B. (2007) 'Huawei Technologies Corporation: from local dominance to global challenge?', *Journal of Business & Industrial Marketing*, Vol. 22, No. 2, pp. 138–144

Whyman, P. (2002) 'Living with the euro: the consequences for world business', *Journal of World Business*, 37(3), Autumn, pp. 208–215.

World Bank (2005) *Data & Statistics – Quick Reference Tables*, Washington, DC (http://web.worldbank.org/).

World Bank (2006) World Development Indicators database, 1 July 2006, www.worldbank.org.

# 6

# The sociocultural environment

## Contents

## Learning objectives

After studying this chapter you should be able to do the following

- Discuss how the sociocultural environment will affect the attractiveness of a potential market.

- Define culture and name some of its elements.

- Explain the '4 + 1' dimensions in Hofstede's model.

- Discuss the strengths and weaknesses of Hofstede's model.

- Discuss whether the world's cultures are converging or diverging.

## 6.1 Introduction

The importance of culture to the international marketer is profound. Culture is a pervasive influence which underlies all facets of social behaviour and interaction. It is embodied in the objects used in everyday life and in modes of communication in society. The complexity of culture is reflected in the multitude of definitions of culture (Craig and Douglas, 2006). Every author who has dealt with culture has given a different definition. Tylor's (1881) definition is one of the most widely accepted: 'Culture is a complex whole which includes knowledge, belief, art, morals, law, custom and any other capabilities and habits acquired by man as a member of the society'.

Culture is an obvious source of differentiation between international markets. Some cultural differences are easier to manage than others. In tackling markets in which buyers speak different languages or follow other religions, for instance, the international marketer can plan in advance how to manage specific points of difference. Often a greater problem is to understand the underlying attitudes and values of buyers in different countries.

The concept of culture is broad and extremely complex. It encompasses virtually every part of a person's life. The way in which people live together in a society is influenced by religion, education, family and reference groups. It is also influenced by legal, economic, political and technological forces. There are various interactions between these influences. We can look for cultural differences in the ways different societies communicate: different spoken languages are used, and the importance of spoken and other methods of communication (e.g. the use of space between people) will vary. The importance of work, the use of leisure, and the types of reward and recognition that people value vary from culture to culture. In some countries people are highly motivated by monetary rewards, while in other countries and cultures social position and recognition are more important.

Culture develops through recurrent social relationships which form patterns that are eventually internalized by members of the entire group. In other words, a culture does not stand still, but changes slowly over time. Finally, cultural differences are not necessarily visible but can be quite subtle, and can surface in situations where one would never notice them.

It is commonly agreed that a culture must have these three characteristics:

1 *It is learned*: that is, acquired by people over time through their membership of a group that transmits culture from generation to generation. In the case of a national culture, you learn most intensively in the early years of life. By the age of five you are already an expert in using your language. You have internalized values associated with such functions as:
   (a) interacting with other members of your family;
   (b) eliciting rewards and avoiding punishments;
   (c) negotiating for what you wanted;
   (d) causing and avoiding conflict.
2 *It is interrelated*: that is, one part of the culture is deeply connected with another part such as religion and marriage, business and social status.
3 *It is shared*: that is, tenets of a culture extend to other members of the group. The cultural values are passed on to an individual by other members of the culture group. These include parents, other adults, family, institutions such as schools, and friends.

Culture can be thought of as having three other levels (Figure 6.1). The tangible aspects of a culture – things you can see, hear, smell, taste or touch – are artefacts or manifestations of underlying values and assumptions that a group of people share. The structure of these elements is like that of an iceberg.

The part of the iceberg that you see above the water is only a small fraction of what is there. What you cannot see are the values and assumptions that can sink your ship if you mistakenly run into them. Daily behaviour is influenced by values and social morals that work closer to the surface than the basic cultural assumptions. The values and social norms help people to make adjustments to their short-term daily behaviour; these standards change over shorter periods of time (ten or 20 years), whereas the basic cultural assumptions are probably formed over centuries.

For the purposes of this book we will define culture as the learned ways in which a society understands, decides and communicates.

**Culture**
The learned ways in which a society understands, decides and communicates.

Figure 6.1 **The visible and invisible parts of culture**

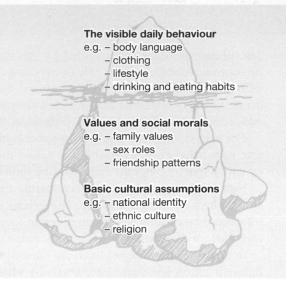

**The visible daily behaviour**
e.g. – body language
– clothing
– lifestyle
– drinking and eating habits

**Values and social morals**
e.g. – family values
– sex roles
– friendship patterns

**Basic cultural assumptions**
e.g. – national identity
– ethnic culture
– religion

One way to approach the analysis of cultural influences is to examine cultures by means of a high context/low context analysis. Because languages are an important component of culture and an important means of communication we will look at both spoken languages and silent languages.

The differences between some cultures may be large. Language and value differences between the Swiss and Chinese cultures, for instance, are considerable. There are also differences between the Spanish and Italian cultures, but they are much fewer. Both have languages based on Latin – they use the same written form of communication and they have similar, although not identical, values and norms.

---

**Exhibit 6.1    Scotch whisky crossing international borders**

Scotch whisky is consumed globally but bought for many different reasons. The right image has to be communicated for each culture, without of course losing any of the product's core brand values. The key value for Scotch generally is status.

In the United Kingdom this tends to be underplayed, never brash or 'in-your-face'. In Italy the image is more tied to machismo and any Scotch ad would have to show a man with a woman on his arm, flaunting the status the drink confers. In Japan, however, the status value is all about going with the majority. It is not aspirational to be individualistic in Japan.

Thus the understated drinker image that might work in the United Kingdom is inappropriate in other countries.

Source: Adapted from Boundary Commission, *Marketing Week*, London, 29 January 1998; Sophie MacKenzie.

---

The use of communication techniques varies in different cultures. In some languages communication is based strictly on the words that are said or written; in others the more ambiguous elements such as surroundings or the social status of the message giver are important variables in the transmission of understanding. Hall (1960a) used this finding to make a generalized division between what he referred to as 'low-context cultures' and 'high-context cultures'.

## 6.2 Layers of culture

The norms of behaviour accepted by the members of the company organization become increasingly important with the company's internationalization. When people with increasingly diverse national cultural backgrounds are hired by international firms the layers of culture can provide a common framework to understand the various individuals' behaviour and their decision-making process of how to do business.

The behaviour of the individual person is influenced by different layers of culture. The national culture determines the values that influence business/industry culture, which then determines the culture of the individual company.

Figure 6.2 illustrates a typical negotiation situation between a seller in one country and a buyer in another country. The behaviour of the individual buyer or seller is influenced by cultural aspects on different levels, which are interrelated in a complex way. Each of the different levels influences the individual's probable behaviour.

In Figure 6.2 the different levels are looked at from a 'nesting' perspective, where the different culture levels are nested into each other in order to grasp the cultural interplay between the levels. The total nest consists of the following levels:

- *National culture.* This gives the overall framework of cultural concepts and legislation for business activities.
- *Business/industry culture.* Every business is conducted within a certain competitive framework and within a specific industry (or service sector). Sometimes these may overlap but, in general, a firm should be able to articulate quite clearly what business it is in. This level has its own cultural roots and history, and the players within this level know the rules of the game. Industry culture is very much related to a branch of industry, and this culture of business behaviour and ethics is similar across borders. For example, shipping, the oil business, international trading and electronics have similar characteristics across national borders.

**Figure 6.2 The different layers of culture**

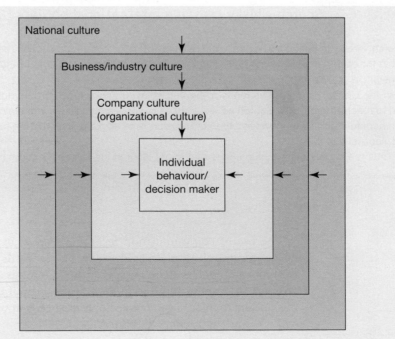

- *Company culture (organizational culture).* The total organization often contains subcultures of various functions. Functional culture is expressed through the shared values, beliefs, meanings and behaviours of the members of a function within an organization (e.g. marketing, finance, shipping, purchasing, top management and blue-collar workers).
- *Individual behaviour.* The individual is affected by the other cultural levels. In the interaction environment the individual becomes the core person who 'interacts' with the other actors in industrial marketing settings. The individual is seen as important because there are individual differences in perceiving the world. Culture is learned; it is not innate. The learning process creates individuals due to different environments in learning and different individual characteristics.

## 6.3 High- and low-context cultures

Edward T. Hall (1960a) introduced the concept of high and low contexts as a way of understanding different cultural orientation. Table 6.1 summarizes some of the ways in which high- and low-context cultures differ.

**Low-context cultures**
Rely only on spoken and written language ('get everything down in the written contract'). Low degree of complexity in communication.

- Low-context cultures rely on spoken and written language for meaning. Senders of messages encode their messages, expecting that the receivers will accurately decode the words used to gain a good understanding of the intended message.

Table 6.1 **General comparative characteristics of cultures**

| Characteristic | Low-context/individualistic (e.g. western Europe, US) | High-context/collectivistic (e.g. Japan, China, Saudi Arabia) |
|---|---|---|
| *Communication and language* | Explicit, direct | Implicit, indirect |
| *Sense of self and space* | Informal handshakes | Formal hugs, bows and handshakes |
| *Dress and appearance* | Dress for individual success, wide variety | Indication of position in society, religious rule |
| *Food and eating habits* | Eating is a necessity, fast food | Eating is social event |
| *Time consciousness* | Linear, exact, promptness is valued, time = money | Elastic, relative, time spent on enjoyment, time = relationships |
| *Family and friends* | Nuclear family, self-oriented, value youth | Extended family, other oriented, loyalty and responsibility, respect for old age |
| *Values and norms* | Independence, confrontation of conflict | Group conformity, harmony |
| *Beliefs and attitudes* | Egalitarian, challenge authority, individuals control destiny, gender equity | Hierarchical, respect for authority, individuals accept destiny, gender roles |
| *Mental process and learning* | Lateral, holistic, simultaneous, accepting life's difficulties | Linear, logical, sequential, problem solving |
| *Business/work habits* | Deal oriented ('quickly getting down to business'), rewards based on achievement, work has value | Relationship oriented ('first you make a friend, then you make a deal'), rewards based on seniority, work is a necessity |

Figure 6.3 The contextual continuum of differing cultures

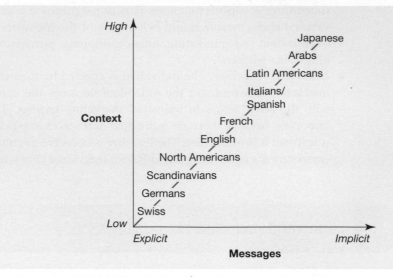

Source: Usunier, J.-C., 2000, *International Marketing*. Reprinted by permission of Pearson Education Limited.

**High-context cultures**
Use more elements surrounding the message. The cultural context in where the message is communicated has a lot to say. High degree of complexity in communication.

- **High-context cultures** use and interpret more of the elements surrounding the message to develop their understanding of the message. In high-context cultures the social importance and knowledge of the person and the social setting add extra information, and will be perceived by the message receiver.

Figure 6.3 shows the contextual differences in the cultures around the world. At one extreme are the low-context cultures of northern Europe. At the other extreme are the high-context cultures. The Japanese and Arabs have a complex way of communicating with people according to their sociodemographic background.

In an analysis of industrial buyer behaviour in Arab countries Solberg (2002) found that building trust with partners willing to endorse one's products takes more time in Arab countries than is customary in the West. Networking – using the power of other partners – seems to play a far greater role for Arab buyers. In Arab countries the position of the agent and his network with prominent families may be critical for success. 'Falling in love' with the wrong agent may therefore spoil the exporter's chances of spending a long period of time in the market.

The greater the context difference between those trying to communicate, the greater the difficulty in achieving accurate communication.

## 6.4 Elements of culture

There are varying definitions of the elements of culture, including one (Murdoch, 1945) that counts 73 'cultural universals'.

The following elements are usually included in the concept of culture.

### Language

A country's language is the key to its culture and can be described as the mirror of the culture. Thus, if one is to work extensively with any one culture, it is imperative to learn the language. Learning a language well means learning the culture because the words of the language are merely concepts reflecting the culture from which it derives.

Language can be divided into two major elements. The verbal language of vocal sounds in patterns that have meaning is the obvious element. Non-verbal language is less obvious, but it is a powerful communicator through body language, silences and social distance.

## Verbal language

Verbal language is an important means of communication. In various forms, such as plays and poetry, the written word is regarded as part of the culture of a group of people. In the spoken form, the actual words spoken and the ways in which the words are pronounced provide clues to the receiver about the type of person who is speaking.

Language capability plays four distinct roles in global marketing:

1 Language is important in information gathering and evaluation efforts. Rather than rely completely on the opinions of others, the manager is able to see and hear personally what is going on. People are far more comfortable speaking their own language, and this should be treated as an advantage. The best intelligence is gathered on a market by becoming part of the market rather than observing it from the outside. For example, local managers of a global corporation should be the firm's primary source of political information to assess potential risk. But take care, they may also be biased.
2 Language provides access to local society. Although English may be widely spoken, and may even be the official company language, speaking the local language may make a dramatic difference. For example, firms that translate promotional materials and information are seen as being serious about doing business in the country.
3 Language capability is increasingly important in company communications, whether within the corporate family or with channel members. Imagine the difficulties encountered by a country manager who must communicate with employees through an interpreter.
4 Language provides more than the ability to communicate; it extends beyond mechanics to the interpretation of contexts.

A very important dimension of the language that can vary by culture is the extent to which communication is explicit or implicit. In explicit-language cultures managers are taught that to communicate effectively you should 'say what you mean, and mean what you say'. Vague directives and instructions are seen as a sign of poor communication abilities. The assumption in explicit-language cultures is that the burden of effective communication is on the speaker. In contrast, in implicit-language cultures (mostly high context) the assumption is that the speaker and listener both share the burden of effective communication. Implicit communication also helps avoid unpleasant and direct confrontations and disagreements.

Estimates of the main spoken languages around the world are given in Table 6.2.

Chinese is spoken as the mother tongue (or first language) by three times more people than the next largest language, English. However, Chinese is overtaken by English when spoken business-language population numbers are taken into account.

It should be noted that official languages are not always spoken by the whole population of a country. For example, French is an official language in Canada, but many Canadians have little or no fluency in French.

Hence English is often, but by no means always, the common language between businesspeople of different nationalities.

**Non-verbal language**
More important in high-context cultures: time, space (conversational distance between people), material possessions, friendship patterns and business agreements.

## Non-verbal language

Non-verbal language is a powerful means of communication, according to Hall (1960a). The importance of non-verbal communication is greater in high-context countries. In

Table 6.2　Official languages and spoken languages in the world

| Mother tongue (first language) | No. of speakers (million) |
| --- | --- |
| Chinese | 1,000 |
| English | 350 |
| Spanish | 250 |
| Hindi | 200 |
| Arabic | 150 |
| Bengali | 150 |
| Russian | 150 |
| Portuguese | 135 |
| Japanese | 120 |
| German | 100 |
| French | 70 |
| Punjabi | 70 |

Note: Chinese is composed of a number of dialects of which Mandarin is the largest.

Source: Adapted from Phillips *et al.*, 1994, p. 96.

these cultures people are more sensitive to a variety of different message systems, while in the low-context Anglo-Germanic cultures many of these non-verbal language messages would not be noticed.

Non-verbal language messages, according to Hall (1960b), communicate up to 90 per cent of the meaning in high-context cultures. Table 6.3 describes some of the main non-verbal languages.

Table 6.3　The main non-verbal languages in international business

| Non-verbal language | Implications for global marketing and business |
| --- | --- |
| *Time* | The importance of being 'on time'. In the high-context cultures (Middle East, Latin America), time is flexible and not seen as a limited commodity. |
| *Space* | Conversational distance between people. |
| | *Example*: |
| | Individuals vary in the amount of space they want separating them from others. Arabs and Latin Americans like to stand close to people they are talking with. If an American, who may not be comfortable with such close range, backs away from an Arab, this might be taken incorrectly as a negative reaction. |
| *Material possessions* | The relevance of material possessions and interest in the latest technology. This can have a certain importance in both low-context and high-context countries. |
| *Friendship patterns* | The significance of trusted friends as a social insurance in times of stress and emergency. |
| | *Example*: |
| | In high-context countries extended social acquaintance and the establishment of appropriate personal relations are essential to conducting business. The feeling is that one should often know one's business partner on a personal level before transactions occur. |
| *Business agreements* | Rules of negotiations based on laws, moral practices or informal customs. |
| | *Example*: |
| | Rushing straight to business will not be rewarded in high-context cultures because deals are made not only on the basis of the best product or price, but also on the entity or person deemed most trustworthy. Contracts may be bound by handshakes, not complex agreements – a fact that makes some, especially western, businesspeople uneasy. |

Exhibit 6.2  **Sensuality and touch culture in Saudi Arabian versus European advertising**

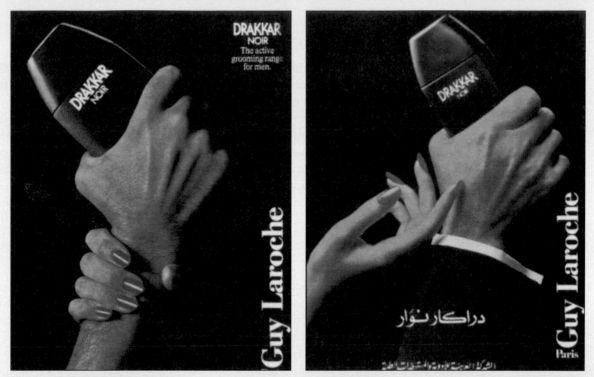

Drakkar Noir: Sensuality and touch culture in Europe and Saudi Arabia          Source: Field, 1986.

Although Saudi Arabia has a population of only about 9 million people (including 2 million immigrants) the country is the sixth biggest fragrance market in the world behind the United States, Japan, Germany, France and Italy. Saudi Arabia also has the world's highest per capita consumption of fragrance, leaving all other countries far behind.

In promoting perfumes the big importers generally use the same advertising materials used by marketers in Europe. What is specifically Arabian in the campaigns is often dictated by Arabian morals.

Normally Saudi Arabia is a high-touch culture, but inappropriate use of touch in advertising messages may cause problems. The Drakkar Noir pictures show two advertisements for the men's perfume, in which Guy Laroche (via the advertising agency Mirabelle) tones down the sensuality for the Arab version. The European ad (left) shows a man's hand clutching the perfume bottle and a woman's hand seizing his bare forearm. In the Saudi version (right), the man's arm is clothed in a dark jacket sleeve, and the woman is touching the man's hand only with her fingertip.

## Manners and customs

Changes occurring in manners and customs must be carefully monitored, especially in cases that seem to indicate a narrowing of cultural differences between peoples. Phenomena such as McDonald's and Coca-Cola have met with success around the world.

Understanding manners and customs is especially important in negotiations because interpretations based on one's own frame of reference may lead to a totally incorrect conclusion. To negotiate effectively abroad one needs to read correctly all types of communication.

In many cultures certain basic customs must be observed by the foreign business person. One of them concerns the use of the right and left hands. In so-called right-hand societies the left hand is the 'toilet hand' and using it to eat, for example, is considered impolite.

## Technology and material culture

Material culture results from technology and is directly related to how a society organizes its economic activity. It is manifested in the availability and adequacy of the basic economic, social, financial and marketing infrastructures.

With technological advancement comes cultural convergence. Black-and-white television sets extensively penetrated the US market more than a decade before they reached similar levels in Europe and Japan. With colour television, the lag was reduced to five years. With videocassette recorders, the difference was only three years, but this time the Europeans and the Japanese led the way, while Americans concentrated on cable systems. With the compact disc, penetration rates were even after only one year. Today, with the Internet or MTV available by satellite across Europe, no lag exists at all.

## Social institutions

Social institutions – business, political, family or class related – influence the behaviour of people and the ways in which people relate to each other. In some countries, for example, the family is the most important social group, and family relationships sometimes influence the work environment and employment practices.

In Latin America and the Arab world a manager who gives special treatment to a relative is considered to be fulfilling an obligation. From the Latin point of view, it makes sense only to hire someone you can trust. In the United States and Europe, however, it is considered favouritism and nepotism. In India there is a fair amount of nepotism. But there too it is consistent with the norms of the culture. By knowing the importance of family relationships in the workplace and in business transactions embarrassing questions about nepotism can be avoided.

An important part of the socialization process of consumers worldwide is *reference groups*. These groups provide the values and attitudes that become influential in shaping behaviour. Primary reference groups include the family, co-workers and other intimate groupings, whereas secondary groups are social organizations in which less continuous interaction takes place, such as professional associations and trade organizations.

Social organizations also determine the roles of managers and subordinates and how they relate to one another. In some cultures managers and subordinates are separated. In other cultures managers and subordinates are on a more common level, and work together in teams.

## Education

Education includes the process of transmitting skills, ideas and attitudes, as well as training in particular disciplines. Even primitive peoples have been educated in this broader sense. For example, the Bushmen of South Africa are well educated for the culture in which they live.

One function of education is the transmission of the existing culture and traditions to the new generation. However, education can also be used for cultural change. The promotion of a communist culture in the People's Republic of China is a notable example, but this, too, is an aspect of education in most nations. Educational levels will have an impact on various business functions. Training programmes for a production facility will have to take the educational backgrounds of trainees into account.

The global marketing manager may also have to be prepared to overcome obstacles in recruiting a suitable sales force or support personnel. For example, Japanese culture places a premium on loyalty, and employees consider themselves to be members of the corporate family. If a foreign firm decides to leave Japan employees may find themselves stranded in mid-career, unable to find a place in the Japanese business system. University graduates are therefore reluctant to join all but the largest and most well known of foreign firms.

If technology is marketed the level of sophistication of the product will depend on the educational level of future users. Product adaptation decisions are often influenced by the extent to which targeted customers are able to use the product or service properly.

## Values and attitudes

Our attitudes and values help determine what we think is right or appropriate, what is important, and what is desirable. Some relate to marketing, and these are the ones we will look at here.

The more rooted values and attitudes are in central beliefs (such as religion), the more cautiously the global marketing manager has to move. Attitude towards change is basically positive in industrialized countries, whereas in more tradition-bound societies change is viewed with great suspicion, especially when it comes from a foreign entity.

In a conservative society there is generally a greater reluctance to take such risks. Therefore the marketer must also seek to reduce the risk involved in trying a new product as perceived by customers or distributors. In part this can be accomplished through education; guarantees, consignment selling or other marketing techniques can also be used.

## Aesthetics

**Aesthetics**
What is meant by good taste in art, music, folklore and drama may vary a lot from culture to culture.

**Aesthetics** refers to attitudes towards beauty and good taste in the art, music, folklore and drama of a culture. The aesthetics of a particular culture can be important in the interpretation of symbolic meanings of various artistic expressions. What is and what is not acceptable may vary dramatically even in otherwise highly similar markets. Sex in advertising is an example.

It is important for companies to evaluate in depth such aesthetic factors as product and package design, colour, brand name and symbols. For instance, some conventional brand names that communicate positive messages in the United States have a totally different meaning in another country, which may substantially damage corporate image and marketing effectiveness (see Table 6.4).

## Religion

The major religions are shared by a number of national cultures:

- Christianity is the most widely practised. The majority of Christians live in Europe and the Americas, and numbers are growing rapidly in Africa.
- Islam is practised mainly in Africa, the Arab countries and around the Mediterranean, and in Indonesia. There has been a recent rise in Islamic fundamentalism in Iran, Pakistan, Algeria and elsewhere.

**Table 6.4 US brand names and slogans with offensive foreign translations**

| Company | Product | Brand name or slogan | Country | Meaning |
|---------|---------|---------------------|---------|---------|
| ENCO | Petroleum | Former name of EXXON | Japan | 'Stalled car' |
| American Motors | Automobile | Matador | Spain | 'Killer' |
| Ford | Truck | Fiera | Spain | 'Ugly old woman' |
| Pepsi | Soft drink | 'Come alive with Pepsi' | Germany | 'Come out of the grave' |

Source: *Going International: How to Make Friends and Deal Effectively in the Global Marketplace*, Copyright © Lennie Copeland and Lewis Griggs (Random House, 1985); all rights reserved.

- Hinduism is most common in India. Beliefs emphasize the spiritual progress of each person's soul rather than hard work and wealth creation.
- Buddhism has adherents in central and south-east Asia, China, Korea and Japan. Like Hinduism it stresses spiritual achievement rather than wealth, although the continuing development of these regions shows that it does not necessarily impede economic activity.
- Confucianism has adherents mainly in China, Korea and Japan. The emphasis on loyalty and obligation between superiors and subordinates has influenced the development of family companies in these regions.

Religion can provide the basis for transcultural similarities under shared beliefs in Islam, Buddhism or Christianity, for example. Religion is of utmost importance in many countries. In the United States and Europe substantial efforts are made to keep government and church matters separate. Nevertheless there remains a healthy respect for individual religious differences. In some countries, such as Lebanon and Iran, religion may be the very foundation of the government and a dominant factor in business, political and educational decisions.

Religion may affect the global marketing strategy directly in the following ways:

- Religious holidays vary greatly among countries, not only from Christian to Muslim, but even from one Christian country to another. In general, Sundays are a religious holiday in all nations where Christianity is an important religion. In the Muslim world, however, the entire month of Ramadan is a religious holiday for all practical purposes.

  In Saudi Arabia, for example, during the month of Ramadan, Muslims fast from sunrise to sunset. As a consequence worker production drops. Many Muslims rise earlier in the morning to eat before sunrise and may eat what they perceive to be enough to last until sunset. This affects their strength and stamina during the working day. An effort by management to maintain normal productivity levels will probably be rejected, so managers must learn to be sensitive to this and similar customs.

- Consumption patterns may be affected by religious requirements or taboos. Fish on Friday for Catholics used to be the classic example. Taboos against beef for Hindus and pork for Muslims and Jews are other examples. The pork restriction exists in Israel as well as in Islamic countries in the Middle East such as Saudi Arabia, Iraq and Iran, and south-east Asian countries such as Indonesia and Malaysia.

- Islamic worshippers pray facing the holy city of Mecca five times each day. Visiting westerners must be aware of this religious ritual. In Saudi Arabia and Iran it is not unusual for managers and workers to place carpets on the floor and kneel to pray several times during the day.

- The economic role of women varies from culture to culture, and religious beliefs are an important cause. In the Middle East women may be restricted in their capacity as consumers, as workers or as respondents in a marketing study. These differences can require major adjustments in the approach of a management conditioned to western markets. Women are, among other things, required to dress in such a way that their arms, legs, torso and faces are concealed. An American female would be expected to honour this dress code while in the host country.

---

**Exhibit 6.3  Polaroid's success in Muslim markets**

During the past 30 years Polaroid's instant photography has been largely responsible for breaking down taboos against picture taking in the Arab world, especially those concerning women revealing their faces.

When Polaroid entered the market in the mid-1960s it discovered that instant photography had a special appeal. Because of religious constraints there were only a few photo-processing laboratories. But with Polaroid's instant cameras Arab men were able to photograph their wives and daughters without fear of a stranger in a film laboratory seeing the women unveiled and without the risk of someone making duplicates.

Source: Harper, 1986.

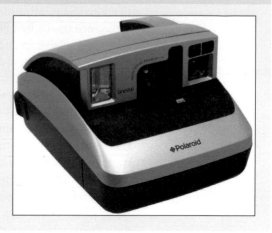

---

## 6.5 Hofstede's original work on national cultures (the '4 + 1' dimensions model)

While an international manager may have neither the time nor the resources to obtain a comprehensive knowledge of a particular culture, a familiarity with the most pervasive cultural 'differentiators' can provide useful guidance for corporate strategy development. One approach to identifying these pervasive fundamental differences of national cultures is provided by Hofstede (1983). Hofstede tried to find an explanation for the fact that some concepts of motivation did not work in the same way in all countries. Hofstede based his research on an extensive IBM database from which – between 1967 and 1973 – 116,000 questionnaires (from IBM employees) were used in 72 countries and in 20 languages.

According to Hofstede, the way people in different countries perceive and interpret their world varies along four dimensions: power distance, uncertainty avoidance, individualism and masculinity.

1  *Power distance* refers to the degree of inequality between people in physical and educational terms (i.e. from relatively equal to extremely unequal). In high power distance societies power is concentrated among a few people at the top who make all the decisions. People at the other end simply carry these decisions out. They accept differences in power and wealth more readily. In low power distance societies, on the other hand, power is widely dispersed and relations among people are more egalitarian. The lower the power distance the more individuals will expect to participate in the organizational decision-making process. A high power distance score was observed in Japan. The United States and Canada record a middle-level rating on power distance, but countries such as Denmark, Austria and Israel exhibit much lower ratings.

2 *Uncertainty avoidance* concerns the degree to which people in a country prefer formal rules and fixed patterns of life, such as career structures and laws, as means of enhancing security. Another important dimension of uncertainty avoidance is risk taking. High uncertainty avoidance is probably associated with risk aversion. Organization personnel in low uncertainty avoidance societies face the future as it takes shape without experiencing undue stress. In high uncertainty avoidance cultures managers engage in activities such as long-range planning to establish protective barriers to minimize the anxiety associated with future events. On uncertainty avoidance the United States and Canada score quite low, indicating an ability to be more responsive in coping with future changes. But Japan, Greece, Portugal and Belgium score high, indicating their desire to meet the future in a more structured and planned fashion.

3 *Individualism* denotes the degree to which people in a country learn to act as individuals rather than as members of groups. In individualistic societies people are self-centred and feel little need for dependency on others. They seek fulfilment of their own goals over the group's. In collectivistic societies members have a group mentality. They are interdependent on each other and seek mutual accommodation to maintain group harmony. Collectivistic managers have high loyalty to their organizations, and subscribe to joint decision making. The United Kingdom, Australia, Canada and the United States show very similar high ratings on individualism, while Japan, Brazil, Colombia, Chile and Venezuela exhibit very low ratings.

4 *Masculinity* relates to the degree to which 'masculine' values, such as achievement, performance, success, money and competition, prevail over 'feminine' values, such as quality of life, maintaining warm personal relationships, service, care for the weak, preserving the environment and solidarity. Masculine cultures exhibit different roles for men and women, and perceive anything big as important. The feminine cultures value 'small as beautiful', and stress quality of life and environment over materialistic ends. A relatively high masculinity index was observed for the United States, Italy and Japan. In low-masculinity societies such as Denmark and Sweden people are basically motivated by a more qualitative goal set as a means to job enrichment. Differences on masculinity scores are also reflected in the types of career opportunity available in organizations and associated job mobility.

5 *Time perspective* In a 23-country study, some years after Hofstede's original work, Hofstede and Bond (1988) identified a fifth dimension that they first termed Confucian Dynamism and then renamed 'time orientation'. This time orientation is defined as the way members in an organization exhibit a pragmatic future-oriented perspective rather than a conventional history or short-term point of view. The consequences of a high score on the long-term orientation (LTO) index are: persistence, ordering relationships by status and observing this order. The opposite is short-term orientation, which includes personal steadiness and stability.

Most south-east Asian markets, such as China, Hong Kong, Taiwan and South Korea, score high on the LTO index. This tendency has something to do with the Confucian traditions prevalent there. On the other hand many European countries are short-term oriented, believing in preserving history and continuing past traditions. In countries scoring high on the LTO index the respondents said they valued thrift, and in fact these countries have higher saving rates than countries scoring more short-term. More savings means more money for future productive investment (Hofstede, 2007).

## Exhibit 6.4  Pocari Sweat – A Japanese soft drink expands sales in Asia

Pocari Sweat is a popular Japanese soft and sports drink, manufactured by Otsuka Pharmaceutical Co. Ltd. The brand started selling in Japan in 1980 and has secured a good foothold for international expansion. The drink is now distributed in other countries in the region including China (Hong Kong), South Korea, Taiwan, Thailand, Indonesia, and the United Arab Emirates. In addition it can be obtained in the 'Chinatown' areas of many cities around the world.

Pocari Sweat's slogan runs as follows:

'Pocari Sweat – A drink with Properties to your Body's own Fluids'

'60 per cent of the Human Body is made up of Body Fluids' is also included in advertising.

Contrary to the odd name and its translucent-grey colour, Pocari Sweat does not taste like sweat; it is a mild-tasting, relatively light, sweet drink.

- What do you think about the brand name (Pocari Sweat) and its slogan?

Sources: Otsuka Pharmaceutical Co. Ltd. www.otsuka.co.jp/poc/.Pocari Sweat's official website.

## 6.6  Managing cultural differences

Having identified the most important factors of influence from the cultural environment on the firm's business and having analysed those factors, the international marketer is able to take decisions about how to react to the results of the analysis.

In accordance with Chapter 7 (The international market selection process) less attractive markets will not be considered further. On the other hand, in the more attractive markets, marketing management must decide to what extent adaptions to the given cultural specifics are needed.

For example, consider *punctuality*. In the most low-context cultures – the Germans, Swiss and Austrians, for example – punctuality is considered extremely important. If you have a meeting scheduled for 9.00 a.m. and you arrive at 9.07 a.m. you are considered 'late'. Punctuality is highly valued within these cultures, and to arrive late for a meeting (thus 'wasting' the time of those forced to wait for you) is not appreciated.

By contrast, in some southern European nations, and within Latin America, a somewhat 'looser' approach to time may pertain. This does not imply that one group is 'wrong' and the other 'right'. It simply illustrates that different approaches to the concept of time have evolved for a variety of reasons, over many centuries, within different cultural groups. Culture can and does influence the business sector in different parts of the world to function in distinct ways.

Another example of how cultural differences influence the business sector concerns the presentation of business cards. Within the United States – which has a very 'informal' culture – business cards are typically presented in a very casual manner. Cards are often handed out quickly and are just as quickly placed into the recipient's pocket or wallet for future reference.

In Japan, however – which has a comparatively 'formal' culture – the presentation of a business card is a more carefully orchestrated event. There, business cards are presented by holding the card up with two hands while the recipient carefully scrutinizes the information it contains. This procedure ensures that one's title is clearly understood: an important factor for the Japanese, where one's official position within one's organizational 'hierarchy' is of great significance.

To simply take the card of a Japanese and immediately place it in one's card holder could well be viewed (from a Japanese perspective) in a negative light. However, within the United States, to take several moments to carefully and deliberately scrutinize an American's business card might also be taken in a negative way, perhaps suggesting that one's credibility is in doubt.

These examples – the sense of time/punctuality and the presentation of the business card – illustrate just two of the many ways in which cultural factors can influence business relationships.

In attempting to understand another culture we inevitably interpret our new cultural surroundings on the basis of our existing knowledge of our own culture.

In global marketing it is particularly important to understand new markets in the same terms as buyers or potential buyers in that marketplace. For the marketing concept to be truly operational the international marketer needs to understand buyers in each marketplace and be able to use marketing research in an effective way.

Lee (1966) used the term *self-reference criterion* (SRC) to characterize our unconscious reference to our own cultural values. He suggested a four-step approach to eliminate SRC:

1  Define the problem or goal in terms of home country culture, traits, habits and norms.
2  Define the problems or goals in terms of the foreign culture, traits, habits and norms.
3  Isolate the SRC influence in the problem and examine it carefully to see how it complicates the problem.
4  Redefine the problem without the SRC influence and solve for the foreign market situation.

It is therefore of crucial importance that the culture of the country is seen in the context of that country. It is better to regard the culture as different from, rather than better or worse than, the home culture. In this way differences and similarities can be explored and the reasons for differences can be sought and explained.

##  6.7  Convergence or divergence of the world's cultures

As we have seen earlier in this book the right mix between local knowledge of different cultures and globalization/integration of national marketing strategies is the key to success in global marketing.

There seems to be a great difference in attitude towards the globalization of cultures among different age groups, the youth culture being more international/global than other age groups (Smith, 2000).

### Youth culture

Countries may be at different stages in the evolution of particular product and service categories, but in most cases youth is becoming more homogeneous across national markets. Youth cultures are more international than national. There are still some strong national characteristics and beliefs, but they are being eroded. The McDonald's culture is spreading into southern Europe, and at the same time we can see satellite TV taking the values of MTV, *The Simpsons* and Ricky Lake all over the world, with English language culture in their wake.

Differences between youth and adult markets are changing in several key respects, the professionals agree. Younger consumers differ from adults in emphasizing quality and being both discerning and technically literate. Younger consumers are now much more self-reliant and take responsibility far earlier. They are sensible, sophisticated and grown-up at an early age.

Generational barriers are now very blurred. The style leaders for many young people – musicians, sports stars and so on – are often in their 30s and 40s. Cultural and family influences remain very strong throughout Europe and the rest of the world. Few young people have 'role models', but they respect achievers particularly in music and sport – and their parents, particularly if their parents have succeeded from humble beginnings.

The lack of clarity in age-group targeting has to be weighed against a growth in cross-border consistencies. But marketers should beware of strategies aimed too blatantly at younger consumers. Young people tend to reject marketing and promotions that are obviously targeted at 'youth'. They perceive these to be false and hypocritical (Smith, 1998).

Today's young people have greater freedom than previous generations had. They are more culturally aware and are reluctant to take anything – or anyone – at face value. Pasco (2000) argues that getting youngsters to relate to celebrities is increasingly difficult. Celebrities often fail or disappoint young people, and again they 'sell out', giving up the integrity for which they were admired in the first place.

Disillusion with celebrities has led young people to look elsewhere for inspiration. They select values from a range of individuals rather than buy wholesale into one. Despite their mistrust of corporations the young increasingly aspire to, and engage with, brands. It appears safer to invest emotionally in brands than in celebrities.

## 6.8 The effects of cultural dimensions on ethical decision making

As more and more firms operate globally an understanding of the effects of cultural differences on ethical decision making becomes increasingly important for avoiding potential business pitfalls and for designing effective *international marketing* management programmes.

Culture is a fundamental determinant of ethical decision-making. It directly affects how an individual perceives ethical problems, alternatives and consequences. In order to succeed in today's international markets managers must recognize and understand how ideas, values and moral standards differ across cultures, and how these in turn influence marketing decision making.

Some countries, such as India, are well known for 'requiring' small payments if customs officials are to allow goods to enter the country. While this may indeed be a bribe and illegal, the ethics of that country seem to allow it (at least to a certain extent). The company is then left with a problem: does it bribe the official, or does it wait for normal clearance and let its products sit in the customs warehouse for a considerably longer time?

Fees and commissions paid to a firm's foreign intermediate or to consultant firms for their services are a particular problem – when does the legal fee become a bribe? One reason for employing a foreign representative or consultants is to benefit from their contacts with decision makers, especially in a foreign administration. If the export intermediary uses part of the fee to bribe administrators there is little that the firm can do.

Thus every culture – national, industry, organizational or professional – establishes a set of moral standards for business behaviour, that is, a code of business ethics. This set of standards influences all decisions and actions in a company, including, for example, what and how to manufacture (or not), what wages are appropriate to pay, how many hours personnel should work under what conditions, how to compete, and what communication guidelines to follow. Which actions are considered right or wrong, fair or unfair, in the conduct of business and which are particularly susceptible to ethical norms is heavily influenced by the culture in which they take place (the bribery theme is further discussed in Chapter 14).

The ethical commitment of an international company is illustrated in Figure 6.4 as a continuum from unacceptable ethical behaviour to most ethical decision making.

The adherence only to the letter of the law reflects minimally acceptable ethical behaviour. A classification of a company as 'most ethical' requires that the firm's code of ethics should address the following six major issues:

1 *Organizational relations*, including competition, strategic alliances and local sourcing.
2 *Economic relations*, including financing, taxation, transfer prices, local reinvestment, equity participation.
3 *Employee relations*, including compensation, safety, human rights, non-discrimination, collective bargaining, training, and sexual harassment.
4 *Customer relations*, including pricing, quality and advertising.
5 *Industrial relations*, including technology transfer, research and development, infrastructure development and organizational stability/longevity.
6 *Political relations*, including legal compliance, bribery and other corrupt activities, subsidies, tax incentives, environmental protection and political involvement.

Figure 6.4 Ethical decision making

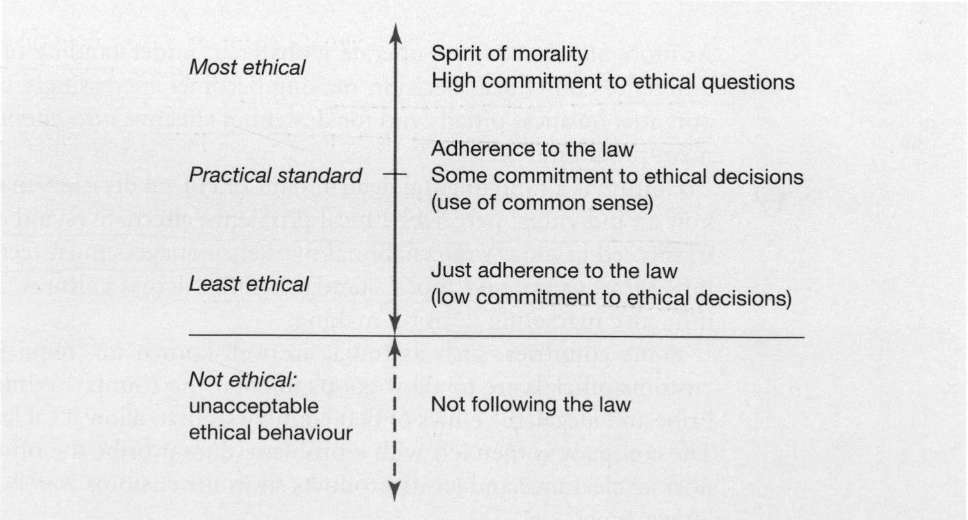

> **Exhibit 6.5   Levi Strauss: An example of a multinational company's ethics code**
>
> Levi Strauss's policy of being a responsible employer in developing countries, where poverty and social problems are endemic, is not something it shouts about. But it is at least partly designed to maintain that good image. Levi's is better able to pursue such a policy because it remains a private, family-run business. That means it does not have to answer to big shareholders on Wall Street, who might want a greater emphasis on short-term profitability. But finding the balance between efficiency and social responsibility is a challenge to Levi's.
>
> In May 1993 Levi's announced that it planned to end most of its business in the People's Republic of China. This meant phasing out the use of Chinese subcontractors, which at that time accounted for about 2 per cent of total production (approximately $50 million a year). The reason given was China's record of 'pervasive human rights abuses'.
>
> The decision to leave China reflected principles embodied in the company's organizational culture. This culture was expressed in sets of standards for doing business abroad, which emphasized a commitment to fair working conditions. If the company could not operate in a country without compromising its principles it should withdraw – as it had done in Myanmar and had threatened in Bangladesh.
>
> Source: Various public media.

It is easy to generalize about the ethics of political payoffs and other types of payments; it is much more difficult to make the decision to withhold payment of money when the consequences of not making the payment may affect the company's ability to do business profitably or at all. With the variety of ethical standards and levels of morality that exist in different cultures the dilemma of ethics and pragmatism which faces international business cannot be resolved until more countries decide to deal effectively with the issue.

## 6.9   Summary

For international marketers it is important to understand customers' personal values and accepted norms of behaviour in order to market to them properly. At the same time marketers must search for groups with shared cognitions that result in shared views of the marketer's offerings and in similar product-related behaviour to simplify their task. Such groups may even exist across country borders.

How we perceive other cultures stems from our own cultural mind-set and it is very difficult not to take the ethnocentric point of view when classifying other cultures. Classification of cultures is necessary to develop marketing and advertising strategies in the global marketplace. Classifying cultures on dimensions has proved to be the most constructive method. It helps in vocalizing and labelling cultural differences and similarities. Many of the cultural differences are reflected in the type of communication culture used. In this chapter different models for classification have been discussed.

### High/low context cultures

The difference between high- and low-context communication cultures helps us understand why, for example, Asian (high-context) and western (low-context) styles are so different, and why the Asians prefer indirect verbal communication and symbolism over the direct assertive communication approaches used by western people. Other dimensions, such as different concepts of time, can also explain major differences between East and West.

## Hofstede's model

In order to construct a more refined classification system, Hofstede developed a model of '4 + 1' dimensions for comparing work-related values, based on data collected in an extensive study. This model also proves useful for comparing cultures with respect to consumption-related values. As a result it can explain the variety of values and motivations used in marketing and advertising across cultures.

It can also explain differences in actual consumption behaviour and product use and can thus assist in predicting consumer behaviour or effectiveness of marketing strategies for cultures other than one's own. This will be particularly useful for companies that want to develop global marketing and advertising strategies.

The problem of business ethics is infinitely more complex in the international marketplace because value judgements differ widely among culturally diverse groups. What is commonly accepted as right in one country may be completely unacceptable in another. Giving business gifts of high value, for example, is generally condemned in western countries, but in many countries of the world gifts are not only accepted but expected.

Social marketing can be defined as the planning and implementation of programmes designed to generate social change (e.g. stopping smoking is a life style change). It is a system that can be used to change the way people think or behave. Social marketing is still based on concepts of commercial marketing and, like commercial marketing, it utilizes research to tailor messages to a particular target audience. The goal of social marketing is to get people to think differently about old ideas and focus on new concepts that will add values to their lives. Social marketing is especially prevalent among non-profit-making organizations, government agencies, community-based organizations, private foundations, social/health issue coalitions and indeed any entity that wants to effect social change.

---

**CASE STUDY 6.1**

# IKEA Catalogue: Are there any cultural differences?

IKEA was founded in Älmhult, Sweden in 1943 by Ingvar Kamprad. The company name is a composite of the first letters in his name in addition to the first letters of the names of the property and the village in which he grew up: Ingvar Kamprad Elmtaryd Agunnaryd.

The IKEA business philosophy is: 'We shall offer a wide range of well-designed, functional home furnishing products at prices so low that as many people as possible will be able to afford them.'

In the late 1940s, the first IKEA advertisements appeared in local newspapers. Demand for IKEA products soared, and Ingvar Kamprad quickly outgrew his ability to make individual sales calls. As a result, he began operating a mail order catalogue and distributed his products via the county milk van. This resourceful solution to a difficult problem led to the annual IKEA catalogue.

First published in Swedish in 1951, the IKEA catalogue was, in 2006, published each summer in 47 different editions, in 24 languages for 32 countries, and is considered to be the main marketing tool of the retail giant, consuming 70 per cent of the company's annual marketing budget. In terms of publishing quantity, the catalogue has surpassed the Bible as the world's most published work – at an estimated 160 million copies (in 2006) worldwide – triple that of its less materialistic counterpart. However, since the catalogue is free of charge, the Bible continues to be the most purchased non-fiction work.

In Europe alone the catalogue reaches more than 200 million people annually. Containing over 300 pages and about 12,000 products, it is distributed free of charge both in stores and by mail. The annual catalogue is distributed in August/September of each year and is valid for a full year. Prices in the catalogue

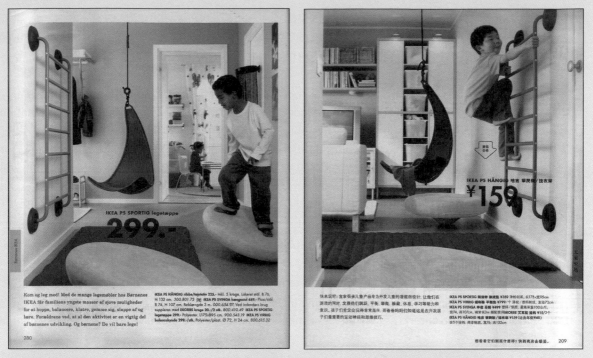

**Illustration of the same product in the IKEA Catalogue in Denmark and Shanghai**

Source: IKEA Catalogue, Denmark and Shanghai, 2005. © Inter IKEA Systems B.V.

are guaranteed not to increase while the catalogue is valid. Most of the catalogue is produced by IKEA Catalogue Services AB in IKEA's home town of Älmhult, Sweden.

At the beginning of 2006 there were 221 IKEA stores operating under a franchise from Inter IKEA Systems BV. Total IKEA turnover in 2005 was €15.2 billion.

IKEA accounts for just 5 to 10 per cent of the furniture market in each country in which it operates. More important is that the awareness of the IKEA brand is much bigger than the size of the company. That is because IKEA is far more than a furniture merchant. It sells a Scandinavian lifestyle that customers around the world embrace.

### Cultural difference

There are about 12,000 products in the total IKEA product range. Each store carries a selection of these 12,000 products depending on store size. The core range is the same worldwide, but as shown there are

differences in how the IKEA catalogue displays its products in the different national editions. Here we have two different illustrations featuring the same product. In this case the two illustrations for the same product are taken from the Danish and the Chinese catalogues.

Source: www.ikea.com.

### Questions

1 Discuss the advantages and disadvantages of having the same product range shown in all IKEA catalogues around the world?

2 The catalogue is the most important element in IKEA's global marketing planning. Discuss if there could be some cultural differences in the effectiveness of the catalogue as a marketing tool.

3 Explain some cultural differences which are illustrated by the two different illustrations of the same product (from the Danish and Chinese IKEA catalogues).

For further exercises and cases, see this book's website at **www.pearsoned.co.uk/hollensen**

## ? Questions for discussion

1 Because English is the world language of business, is it necessary for UK managers to learn a foreign language?

2 According to Hofstede and Hall, Asians are (a) more group oriented, (b) more family oriented and (c) more concerned with social status. How might such orientations affect the way you market your product to Asian consumers?

3 Do you think that cultural differences between nations are more or less important than cultural variations within nations? Under what circumstances is each important?

4 Identify some constraints in marketing to a traditional Muslim society. Use some of the examples in the chapter.

5 What layers of culture have the strongest influence on business people's behaviour?

6 The focus of this chapter has mainly been the influence of culture on international marketing strategies. Try also to discuss the potential influences of marketing on cultures.

7 What role does the self-reference criterion play in international business ethics?

8 Compare the role of women in your country to their role in other cultures. How do the different roles affect women's behaviour as consumers and as business people?

## References

Copeland, L. and Griggs, L. (1985) *Going International*, Random House, New York.

Craig, C.S. and Douglas, S.P. (2006) 'Beyond national culture: implications of cultural dynamics for consumer research', *International Marketing Review*, Vol. 23, No. 3, pp. 322–342.

Field, M. (1986) 'Fragrance marketers sniff out rich aroma', *Advertising Age* (special report on 'marketing to the Arab world'), 30 January, p. 10.

Hall, E.T. (1960a) *The Silent Language*. Garden City, NY: Doubleday.

Hall, E.T. (1960b) 'The silent language in overseas business', *Harvard Business Review*, May–June, pp. 87–97.

Harper, T. (1986) 'Polaroid clicks instantly in Moslem market', *Advertising Age* (special report on 'Marketing to the Arab world'), 30 January, p. 12.

Hofstede, G. (1983) 'The cultural relativity of organizational practices and theories', *Journal of International Business Studies*, Fall, pp. 75–89.

Hofstede, G. (2007) 'Asian Management in the 21st century', *Asia Pacific Journal of Management*, Vol. 24, pp. 411–420.

Hofstede, G. and Bond, M.R. (1988) 'The Confucius connection: from cultural roots to economic growth', *Organizational Dynamics*, 16(4), pp. 4–21.

Lee, J. (1966) 'Cultural analysis in overseas operations', *Harvard Business Review*, March–April, pp. 106–114.

MacKenzie, S. (1998) 'Boundary commission', *Marketing Week*, London, 29 January.

Murdoch, G.P. (1945) 'The common denominator of cultures', in Linton, R. (ed.), *The Science of Man in the World Crises*, Columbia University Press, New York.

Pasco, M. (2000) 'Brands are replacing celebrities as role models for today's youth', *Kids Marketing Report*, 27 January.

Phillips, C. *et al.* (1994) *International Marketing Strategy*, Thomson Learning.

Phillips, C., Doole, I. and Lowe, R. (1994) *International Marketing Strategy: Analysis, development and implementation*, London: Routledge.

Smith, D.S. (1998) 'Europe's youth is our future', *Marketing*, London, 22 January.

Smith, K.V. (2000) 'Why SFA is a tough sell in Latin America', *Marketing News*, Chicago, 3 January.

Solberg, C.A. (2002) 'Culture and industrial buyer behaviour: the Arab experience', Paper presented at the 18th *IMP Conference*, pp. 1–34.

Tylor, E.B. (1881) *Anthropology: An Introduction to the study of Man and Civilization*, D. Appleton, New York.

Usunier, J.-C. (2000) *International Marketing: A Cultural Approach*, Pearson Education, Harlow.

# 7

# The international market selection process

## Contents

## Learning objectives

After studying this chapter you should be able to do the following:

- Define international market selection and identify the problems in achieving it.
- Explore how international marketers screen potential markets/countries using secondary and primary data (criteria).
- Distinguish between preliminary and 'fine-grained' screening.
- Realize the importance of segmentation in the formulation of the global marketing strategy.
- Choose among alternative market expansion strategies.
- Distinguish between concentration and diversification in market expansion.

## 7.1 Introduction

Identifying the 'right' market(s) to enter is important for a number of reasons:

- It can be a major determinant of success or failure, especially in the early stages of internationalization.
- This decision influences the nature of foreign marketing programmes in the selected countries.
- The nature of geographic location of selected markets affects the firm's ability to coordinate foreign operations.

In this chapter a systematic approach to international market selection (IMS) is presented. A study of recently internationalized US firms showed that on average firms do not follow a highly systematic approach. However, those firms using a systematic sequence of steps in IMS showed a better performance (Yip *et al.*, 2000).

## 7.2  International market selection: SMEs versus LSEs

The international market selection process is different in small and medium-sized enterprises (SMEs) and large-scale enterprises (LSEs).

In the SME, the IMS is often simply a reaction to a stimulus provided by a change agent. This agent can appear in the form of an unsolicited order. Government agencies, chambers of commerce and other change agents may also bring foreign opportunities to the firm's attention. Such cases constitute an externally driven decision in which the exporter simply responds to an opportunity in a given market.

In other cases, the IMS of SMEs is based on the following criteria (Johanson and Vahlne, 1977):

- Low 'psychic' distance: low uncertainty about foreign markets and low perceived difficulty of acquiring information about them. 'Psychic' distance has been defined as differences in language, culture, political system, level of education or level of industrial development.
- Low 'cultural' distance: low perceived differences between the home and destination cultures ('cultural' distance is normally regarded as part of 'psychic' distance).
- Low geographic distance.

Using any one of these criteria often results in firms entering new markets with successively greater psychic distance. The choice is often limited to the SMEs' immediate neighbours, since geographic proximity is likely to reflect cultural similarity, more knowledge about foreign markets and greater ease in obtaining information. When using this model the decision maker will focus on decision making based on incrementalism where the firm is predicted to start the internationalization by moving into those markets they can most easily understand. It is generally believed that SMEs and firms which are early in their internationalization process are more likely to use a 'psychic' distance or other 'rules of thumb' procedures than LSEs with international experience (Andersen and Buvik, 2002).

By limiting their consideration to a nearby country, SMEs effectively narrow the IMS into one decision: to go or not to go to a nearby country. The reason for this behaviour can be that SME executives, usually being short of human and financial resources, find it hard to resist the temptation of selecting target markets intuitively.

In a study of internationalization in Danish SMEs Sylvest and Lindholm (1997) found that the IMS process was very different in 'old' SMEs (established before 1960) from that in 'young' SMEs (established in 1989 or later). The young SMEs entered more distant markets much earlier than the older SMEs, which followed the more traditional 'step-by-step' IMS process. The reason for the more rapid internationalization of young SMEs may be their status as subsuppliers to larger firms, where they are 'pulled out' to international markets by their large customers and their international networks.

While SMEs must make first entry decisions by selecting targets among largely unknown markets, LSEs with existing operations in many countries have to decide in which of them to introduce new products. By drawing on existing operations, LSEs have easier access to product-specific data in the form of primary information that is more accurate than any secondary database. As a result of this the LSEs can be more proactive. Although selecting markets based on intuition and pragmatism can be a satisfying way for SMEs, the following will be based on a more proactive IMS process, organized in a systematic and step-by-step analysis.

However, in 'real life' the IMS process will not always be a logical and gradual sequence of activities, but an iterative process involving multiple feedback loops (Andersen and Strandskov, 1998). Koch (2001) suggests that the IMS and the entry mode decision (see Chapter 8) should be considered as two aspects of one decision – the MEMS model (Market and Entry Mode Selection).

Another 'real life' example is found in many small subcontracting firms when they do not actively select their foreign markets. The decision about IMS is made by the partner obtaining the main contract (main contractor), thus pulling the SME into international markets (Brewer, 2001; Westhead *et al.*, 2002).

## 7.3  Building a model for international market selection

Research from the Uppsala school on the internationalization process of the firm has suggested several potential determinants of the firm's choice of foreign markets. These can be classified into two groups: (1) environmental and (2) firm characteristics (see Figure 7.1). This approach of integrating both internal and external variables in the IMS is supported by new research results (see e.g. Sakarya *et al.*, 2007).

Let us look first at the environment. How do we define 'international markets'? The following approach suggests two dimensions:

1  The international market as a country or a group of countries.
2  The international market as a group of customers with nearly the same characteristics. According to this latter definition a market can consist of customers from several countries.

Most books and studies in global marketing have attempted to segment the world market into the different countries or groups of countries. This has been done for two principal reasons:

**Figure 7.1  Potential determinants of the firm's choice of foreign markets**

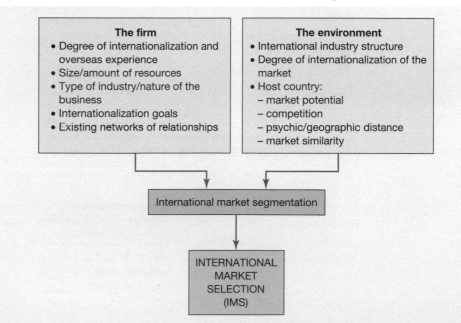

1  International data are more easily (and sometimes exclusively) available on a nation-by-nation basis. It is very difficult to acquire accurate cross-national statistical data.
2  Distribution management and media have also been organized on a nation-by-nation basis. Most agents/distributors still represent their manufacturers only in one single country. Few agents sell their products on a cross-national basis.

However, country markets or multicountry markets are not quite adequate. In many cases boundary lines are the result of political agreement or war and do not reflect a similar separation in buyer characteristics among people on either side of the border.

## Presentation of a market-screening model

In Figure 7.1 an outline model for IMS was presented. In the following we will look in more detail at the box labelled 'international market segmentation'. The elements of IMS are shown in Figure 7.2.

## Steps 1 and 2: Defining criteria

In general, the criteria for effective segmentation are as follows:

- *measurability*: the degree to which the size and purchasing power of resulting segments can be measured;
- *accessibility*: the degree to which the resulting segments can be effectively reached and served;
- *substantiality/profitability*: the degree to which segments are sufficiently large and/or profitable;
- *actionability*: the degree to which the organization has sufficient resources to formulate effective marketing programmes and 'make things happen'.

**Figure 7.2 International market segmentation**

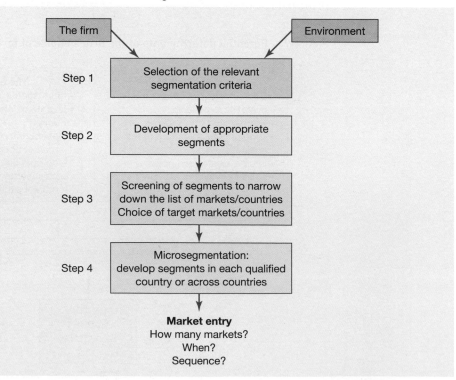

## Figure 7.3 The basis of international market segmentation

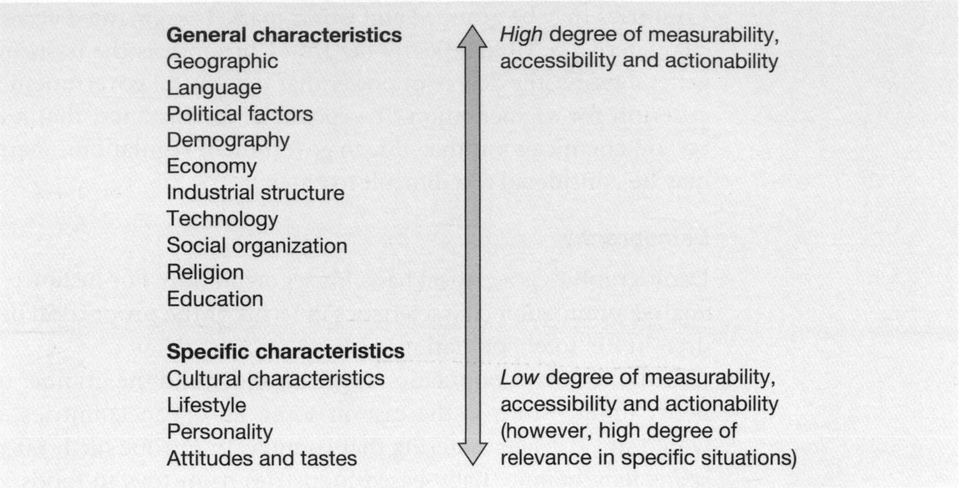

**General characteristics**
Geographic
Language
Political factors
Demography
Economy
Industrial structure
Technology
Social organization
Religion
Education

*High* degree of measurability, accessibility and actionability

**Specific characteristics**
Cultural characteristics
Lifestyle
Personality
Attitudes and tastes

*Low* degree of measurability, accessibility and actionability (however, high degree of relevance in specific situations)

A high degree of measurability and accessibility indicates more general characteristics as criteria (at the top of Figure 7.3) and vice versa.

It is important to realize that more than one measure can be used simultaneously in the segmentation process.

In Chapters 5 and 6 the different segmentation criteria in the international environment were discussed and structured according to the following PEST approach:

- political/legal;
- economic;
- social/cultural;
- technological.

We will now describe in more detail the general and specific criteria mentioned in Figure 7.3.

## General characteristics

### Geographic location

The location of the market can be critical in terms of segmenting world markets. Scandinavian countries or Middle Eastern countries may be clustered not only according to their geographic proximity, but also according to other types of similarity. However, the geographic location alone could be a critical factor. For instance, air conditioning needs in some of the Arab countries could make a manufacturer consider these countries as specific clusters.

### Language

Language has been described as the mirror of the culture. On one level its implications for the international marketer are self-evident: advertising must be translated; brand names must be vetted for international acceptability; business negotiations must often be conducted through expensive interpreters or through the yet more expensive acquisition of a foreign translator. In the latter case genuine fluency is essential; persuasion and contract negotiation present enough difficulties even in a mother tongue.

Less obvious is the fact that foreign language may imply different patterns of thought and different customer motivations. In such cases a knowledge – again, a good knowledge – of the language will do more than facilitate communication; it provides automatic insight into the relevant culture.

### Political factors

Countries may be grouped and world markets segmented according to broad political characteristics. Until recently the Iron Curtain was the basis of one such division. In general terms, the degree of power that the central government has may be the general criterion for segmentation. It is possible, for instance, that a company is producing certain chemicals but that, due to government regulations, many of the world markets may be considered too difficult to enter.

### Demography

Demographics is a critical basis for segmentation. For instance, it is often necessary to analyse population characteristics in terms of the proportion of elderly people or children in the total population.

If the country's population is getting older and the number of infants per thousand is declining, which is the case in some European countries, a baby food company would not consider entering that country. In Europe birth rates are tumbling and life spans lengthening. Baby-based industries from toys to foods and nappies face sharp competition. Consumer electronics and housing may also be affected.

### Economy

As the earlier studies have indicated, economic development level could be a critical variable for international market segmentation. Electric dishwashers or washer–dryers require a certain level of economic development. There is not a good market for these products in India. However, in western European countries these products are becoming almost a basic necessity. On the basis of the level of economic development certain specific consumption patterns emerge. Societies with high personal income spend more time and money on services, education and recreation. Thus it may be possible to arrange certain income groups from different countries into certain clusters.

### Industrial structure

A country's industrial structure is depicted by the characteristics of its business population. One country may have many small retailers; another country may rely on a large number of department stores for retail distribution. One country may be thriving on small manufacturers; another may have very concentrated and large-scale manufacturing activity. The type of competition that exists at the wholesale level may be the critical specific factor for clustering international markets. The international marketer may wish to work with a series of strong wholesalers.

### Technology

The degree of technological advancement or the degree of agricultural technology may easily be the basis for segmentation. A software company planning to enter international markets may wish to segment them on the basis of the number of PCs per thousand of the population. It may not be worthwhile for this company to enter markets below a certain number of PCs per thousand of the population. For example, it may find Pakistan, Iran and most Arab countries, all of Africa and all of eastern Europe less than satisfactory for entry.

### Social organization

The family is an important purchasing group in any society. In Europe marketers are accustomed to either the so-called nuclear family, with father, mother and children all living together under one roof, or, increasingly as society changes, the single-parent family. In other countries the key unit is the extended family, with three or four generations all in the same house.

In the United States, for instance, socioeconomic groupings have been used extensively as segmentation tools. A six-category classification is used: upper upper class, lower upper, upper middle, lower middle, upper lower and lower lower. The US high-income professionals are relegated to the lower upper class, described as those 'who have earned their position rather than inherited it', the *nouveaux riches*.

In contrast, it would have been hard to find useful socioeconomic groupings in Russia beyond white-collar worker, blue-collar worker and farm worker.

### Religion

Religious customs are a major factor in marketing. The most obvious example, perhaps, is the Christian tradition of present giving at Christmas, yet even in this simple matter pitfalls lie in wait for the international marketer: in some Christian countries the traditional exchange of presents takes place not on Christmas Day but on other days in December or early January.

The impact of religion on marketing becomes most evident in the case of Islam. Islamic laws, based on the Koran, provide guidance for a whole range of human activities, including economic activity.

### Education

Educational levels are of importance to the international marketer from two main standpoints: the economic potential of the youth market and, in developing countries, the level of literacy.

Educational systems vary a lot from country to country. The compensation for on-the-job training also varies a great deal. As a result the economic potential of the youth market is very different from country to country.

In most industrialized countries literacy levels are close to 100 per cent and the whole range of communications media is open to the marketer. In developing countries literacy rates can be as low as 25 per cent, and in one or two 15 per cent or less, although at such low levels the figures can be no more than estimates. In those same countries television sets and even radios are economically beyond the reach of most of the population, although communal television sets are sometimes available. The consumer marketer faces a real challenge in deciding on promotional policies in these countries, and the use of visual material is more relevant.

## Specific characteristics

### Cultural characteristics

Cultural characteristics may play a significant role in segmenting world markets. To take advantage of global markets or global segments firms require a thorough understanding of what drives customer behaviour in different markets. They must learn to detect the extent to which similarities exist or can be achieved through marketing activities. The cultural behaviour of the members of a given society is constantly shaped by a set of dynamic variables that can also be used as segmentation criteria: language, religion, values and attitudes, material elements and technology, aesthetics, education and social institutions. These different elements were dealt with more extensively in Chapters 5 and 6.

### Lifestyles

Typically activity, interest and opinion research is used as the tool for analysing lifestyles. However, such a research tool has not quite been developed for international purposes. Perhaps certain consumption habits or practices may be used as an indication of the lifestyle that is being studied. Food consumption habits can be used as one such general indicator. Types of food eaten can easily indicate lifestyles that an international food company should be ready to consider. For example, Indian-style hot curries are not likely to be very popular in Germany given its rather bland cooking. Very hot Arab dishes are not likely to be very popular in western Europe.

### Personality

Personality is reflected in certain types of behaviour. A general characteristic may be temper, so that segmentation may be based on the general temper of people. Latin Americans or Mediterranean people are known to have certain personality traits. Perhaps those traits are a suitable basis for the segmentation of world markets. One example is the tendency to haggle. In pricing, for instance, the international firm will have to use a substantial degree of flexibility where haggling is widespread. Haggling in a country such as Turkey is almost a national pastime. In the underground bazaars of Istanbul the vendor would be almost offended if the customer accepted the first asking price.

### Attitudes, tastes or predispositions

These are all complex concepts, but it is reasonable to say that they can be utilized for segmentation. Status symbols can be used as indicators of what some people in a culture consider would enhance their own self-concept as well as their perception among other people.

## Step 3: Screening of markets/countries

This screening process can be divided in two:

1 *Preliminary screening.* This is where markets/countries are screened primarily according to external screening criteria (the state of the market). In the case of SMEs the limited internal resources (e.g. financial resources) must also be taken into account. There will be a number of countries that can be excluded in advance as potential markets.
2 *Fine-grained screening.* This is where the firm's competitive power (and special competences) in the different markets can be taken into account.

### Preliminary screening

The number of markets is reduced by 'coarse-grained', macro-oriented screening methods based on criteria such as the following:

- restrictions in the export of goods from one country to another;
- gross national product per capita;
- cars owned per 1,000 of the population;
- government spending as a percentage of GNP;
- population per hospital bed.

When screening countries it is particularly important to assess the political risk of entering a country. Over recent years marketers have developed various indices to help assess the risk factors in the evaluation of potential market opportunities. One of these indices is the Business Environment Risk Index (BERI). An alternative for BERI is e.g. BMI (Business Monitor International). Users of country risk analysis at the two websites (www.Geri.com and www.businessmonitor.com) will normally have to pay for the services.

BMI and BERI measure the general quality of a country's business climate. They assess countries several times a year on different economic, political and financial

**BERI**
Business Environment Risk Index – a useful tool in the coarse-grained, macrooriented screening of international markets.

Table 7.1 Criteria included in the overall BERI index

| Criteria | Weights | Multiplied with the score (rating) on a scale of 0–4[a] | Overall BERI index[b] |
|---|---|---|---|
| Political stability | 3 | | |
| Economic growth | 2.5 | | |
| Currency convertibility | 2.5 | | |
| Labour cost/productivity | 2 | | |
| Short-term credit | 2 | | |
| Long-term loans/venture capital | 2 | | |
| Attitude towards the foreign investor and profits | 1.5 | | |
| Nationalization | 1.5 | | |
| Monetary inflation | 1.5 | | |
| Balance of payments | 1.5 | | |
| Enforceability of contracts | 1.5 | | |
| Bureaucratic delays | 1 | | |
| Communications: phone, fax, internet-access | 1 | | |
| Local management and partner | 1 | | |
| Professional services and contractors | 0.5 | | |
| Total | 25 | × 4 (max.) | = Max. 100 |

[a] 0 = unacceptable; 1 = poor; 2 = average conditions; 3 = above average conditions; 4 = superior conditions.

[b] Total points: >80 favourable environment for investors, advanced economy. 70–79 not so favourable, but still an advanced economy. 55–69 an immature economy with investment potential, probably an NIC. 40–54 a high-risk country, probably an LDC. Quality of management has to be superior to realize potential. <40 very high risk. Would only commit capital if some extraordinary justification.

factors, typically on a scale from 0 to 4. The overall index ranges from 0 to 100 (see Table 7.1).

The BERI and BMI index has been questioned as a general management decision tool and should therefore be supplemented by in-depth country reports (e.g. from www.state.gov/misc/list) before final market entry decisions are made.

Among other macro oriented screening methods is the *shift-share approach* (Green and Allaway, 1985; Papadopoulos and Denis, 1988; Papadopoulos *et al.*, 2002). This approach is based upon the identification of relative changes in international import shares among various countries. The average growth rate of imports for a particular product for a 'basket' of countries is calculated and then each country's actual growth rate is compared with the average growth rate. The difference, called the 'net shift', identifies growing or declining markets. This procedure has the advantage that it takes into account both the absolute level of a country's imports and their relative growth rate. On the other hand, it examines only those criteria and does not take into account other macro-oriented criteria.

### 'Fine-grained' screening

As the BERI index focuses only on the political risk of entering new markets a broader approach that includes the competences of the firm is often needed.

For this purpose a powerful aid to the identification of the 'best opportunity' target countries is the application of the market attractiveness/competitive strength matrix (Figure 7.4). This market portfolio model replaces the two single dimensions in the

Figure 7.4  The market attractiveness/competitive strength matrix

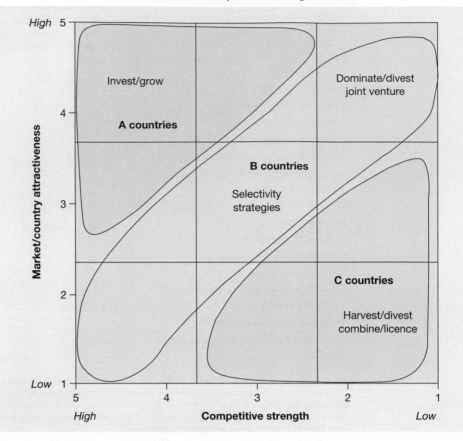

BCG growth–share matrix with two composite dimensions applied to global marketing issues. Measures on these two dimensions are built up from a large number of possible variables, as listed in Table 7.2. In the following, one of the important dimensions will be described and commented upon.

Table 7.2  Dimensions of market/country attractiveness and competitive strength

| Market/country attractiveness | Competitive strength |
| --- | --- |
| Market size (total and segments) | Market share |
| Market growth (total and segments) | Marketing ability and capacity (country-specific know-how) |
| Buying power of customers | Products fit to market demands |
| Market seasons and fluctuations | Price |
| Average industry margin | Contribution margin |
| Competitive conditions (concentration, intensity, entry barriers, etc.) | Image |
| Market prohibitive conditions (tariff/non-tariff barriers, import restrictions, etc.) | Technology position |
| Government regulations (price controls, local content, compensatory exports, etc.) | Product quality |
| Infrastructure | Market support |
| Economic and political stability | Quality of distributors and service |
| Psychic distance (from home base to foreign market) | Financial resources |
|  | Access to distribution channels |

*Market size*

The total market volume per year for a certain country/market can be calculated as:

> Production (of a product in a country)
> \+ import
> − export
> —————————————————
> \= theoretical market size
> +/− changes in stock size
> —————————————————
> \= effective market size

Production, import and export figures can usually be found in the specific country's statistics, if it is a standardized product with an identifiable customs position.

A more precise location of a particular country (in Figure 7.4) may be determined by using the questionnaire in Figure 7.5.

As seen from Figure 7.4 one of the results of this process is a prioritzied classification of countries/markets into distinct categories:

- *A countries*. These are the primary markets (i.e. the key markets), which offer the best opportunities for long-term strategic development. Here companies may want to establish a permanent presence and should therefore embark on a thorough research programme.
- *B countries*. These are the secondary markets, where opportunities are identified but political or economic risk is perceived as being too high to make long-term irrevocable commitments. These markets would be handled in a more pragmatic way due to the potential risks identified. A comprehensive marketing information system would be needed.
- *C countries*. These are the tertiary or 'catch what you can' markets. They will be perceived as high risk, and so the allocation of resources will be minimal. Objectives in such countries would be short term and opportunistic; companies would give no real commitment. No significant research would be carried out.

## Step 4: Develop subsegments in each qualified country and across countries

Once the prime markets have been identified firms then use standard techniques to segment markets within countries, using variables such as the following:

- demographic/economic factors;
- lifestyles;
- consumer motivations;
- geography;
- buyer behaviour;
- psychographics, etc.

Thus the prime segmentation basis is geographic (by country) and the secondary is within countries. The problem here is that, depending on the information basis, it may be difficult to formulate fully secondary segmentation bases. Furthermore, such an approach can run the risk of leading to a differentiated marketing approach, which may leave the company with a very fragmented international strategy.

The drawback of traditional approaches lies in the difficulty of applying them consistently across markets. If a company is to try to achieve a consistent and controlled marketing strategy across all its markets it needs a transnational approach to its segmentation strategy.

Figure 7.5  **Underlying questionnaire for locating countries on a market attractiveness/competitive strength matrix**

Time of analysis:
Analysis of product area:
In country:

**A. Market attractiveness**

| | 1<br>Very poor | 2<br>Poor | 3<br>Medium | 4<br>Good | 5<br>Very good | %<br>Weight factor | Result<br>(grading × weight) |
|---|---|---|---|---|---|---|---|
| Market size | | | | | | | |
| Market growth | | | | | | | |
| Buying structure | | | | | | | |
| Prices | | | | | | | |
| Buying power | | | | | | | |
| Market access | | | | | | | |
| Competitive intensity | | | | | | | |
| Political/economic risks | | | | | | | |
| etc. | | | | | | | |
| Total | | | | | | 100 | |

Market attractiveness = Result : 100 = ................

**B. Relative competitive strength**
with regard to the strongest competitor = ................

| | 1<br>Very poor | 2<br>Poor | 3<br>Medium | 4<br>Good | 5<br>Very good | %<br>Weight factor | Result<br>(grading × weight) |
|---|---|---|---|---|---|---|---|
| Products fit to market demands | | | | | | | |
| Prices and conditions | | | | | | | |
| Market presence | | | | | | | |
| Marketing | | | | | | | |
| Communication | | | | | | | |
| Obtainable market share | | | | | | | |
| Financial results | | | | | | | |
| etc. | | | | | | | |
| Total | | | | | | 100 | |

Relative competitive strength = Result : 100 = ................

**Figure 7.6 Transnational clustering of the western European market**

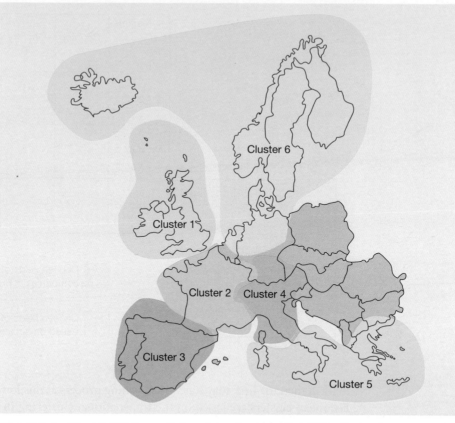

Source: Welford and Prescott, 1996. *European Business: An issue-based approach*, 3rd Edition. Reprinted by permission of Pearson Education Ltd.

It can be argued that companies competing internationally should segment markets on the basis of consumers, not countries. Segmentation by purely geographical factors leads to national stereotyping. It ignores the differences between customers within a nation and ignores similarities across boundaries.

Cluster analysis can be used to identify meaningful cross-national segments, each of which is expected to evoke a similar response to any marketing mix strategy. Figure 7.6 shows an attempt to segment the western European market into six clusters.

Once the firm has chosen a certain country as a target market the next stage in the micro segmentation process is to decide with which products or services the company wishes to become active in the individual countries. Here it is necessary to make a careful market segmentation, especially in the larger and more important foreign markets, in order to be in a position to exhaust the market potential in a differentiated manner (Figure 7.7).

In this context it is necessary to draw attention to a specific strategic procedure, which is oriented worldwide towards similar market segments. Here it is not the country-specific market attractiveness that influences the decision on specific markets, but the recognition of the existence of similar structures of demand and similar consumer habits in segments (and perhaps only in small segments) of different markets.

An illustration of the whole international market segmentation/screening process (steps 1–4 in Figure 7.2) is seen in Figure 7.8.

The model in Figure 7.8 begins by regarding the world market as the potential market for a firm's product. However, if the firm only regards western Europe as a possible

Figure 7.7 Micromarket segmentation

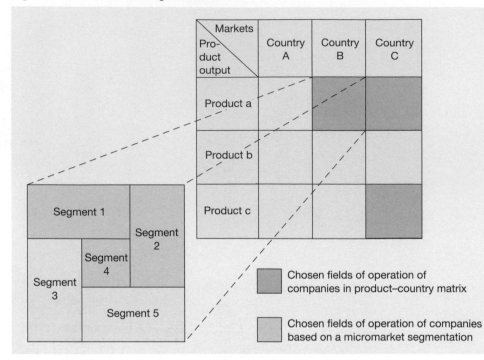

market, then the firm may start the screening process at this lower level. The six western European clusters are based on the transnational clustering in Figure 7.6. The further down in the model, the greater the use of primary data (personal interviews, field research, etc.), as well as screening from internal criteria. Furthermore, the firm may discover a *high market potential* in some geographic segments. However, this is not the same as a *high sales potential* for the firm's product. There may be some restrictions (e.g. trade barriers) on the exporting of products to a particular country. Also the management of the company may have a certain policy to select only markets that are culturally similar to the home market. This may exclude far distant countries from being selected as target markets, though they may have a high market potential. Furthermore, to be able to transform a high market potential into a high sales potential, there must be a harmony between the firm's competences (internal criteria) and the value-chain functions that customers rate as important to them. Only in this situation will a customer regard the firm as a possible supplier, equal to other possible suppliers. In other words, in making the IMS, the firm must seek synergy between the possible new target market and its own strengths, objectives, and strategy. The firm's choice of new international markets is very much influenced by the existence of complementary markets and marketing skills gained in these markets.

In general, Figure 7.8 is based on proactive and systematic decision-making behaviour by the firm. This is not always a realistic condition, especially not in SMEs, where a *pragmatic approach* is required. Often firms are not able to segment from their own criteria but must expect to be evaluated and chosen (as subsuppliers) by much larger firms. The pragmatic approach to IMS can also give rise to the firm choosing customers and markets with a background similar to the managers' own personal network and cultural background. Contingencies, serendipity and 'management feel' play an important role in both early and late phases of IMS. In a qualitative study of Australian firms Rahman (2003) found, that an important factor that firms take into consideration at

**Figure 7.8 The international market segmentation/screening process: an example of the proactive and systematic approach**

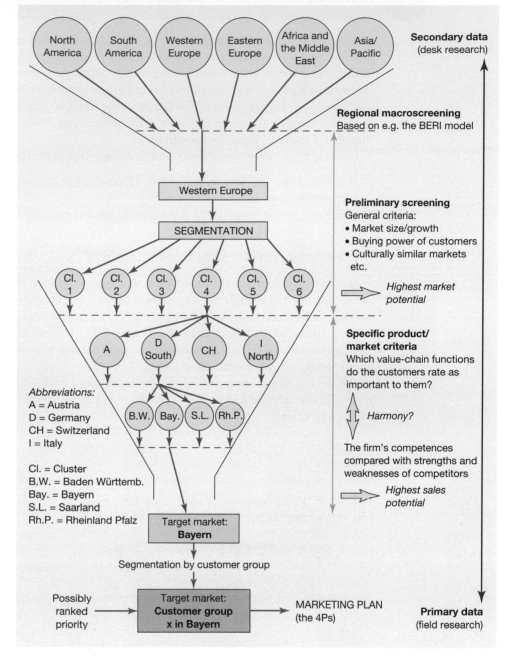

the final stage of evaluating the attractiveness of foreign markets is 'management feel'. One of the companies said:

> At the end of the day much of the decision depends on the management's feel about the market. There will always be some uncertainties in the market, particularly when you are deciding about the future, and international markets are no exception in this regard. So, we managers will have to make the decision within the limited information available to us, and 'gut feel' plays a big role in that (Rahman, 2003, p. 124).

### 7.4 Market expansion strategies

The choice of a market expansion strategy is a key decision in export marketing. First, different patterns are likely to cause development of different competitive conditions in different markets over time. For example, a fast rate of growth into new markets characterized by short product life cycles can create entry barriers towards competitors and give rise to higher profitability. On the other hand, a purposeful selection of relatively few markets for more intensive development can create higher market shares, implying stronger competitive positions.

In designing their strategy firms have to answer two underlying questions:

1 Will they enter markets incrementally (the waterfall approach) or simultaneously (the shower approach) (see Figure 7.9)?
2 Will entry be concentrated or diversified across international markets?

### Incremental versus simultaneous entry

A firm may decide to enter international markets on an incremental or experimental basis, entering first a single key market in order to build up experience in international operations, and then subsequently entering other markets one after the other. Alternatively, a firm may decide to enter a number of markets simultaneously in order to leverage its core competence and resources rapidly across a broader market base. (Read about Sanex's shower approach in Exhibit 7.1)

For the big global company the two strategies can be translated into the concept of the *international product life cycle* (Vernon, 1966), as illustrated in Figure 7.8. See also Figure 11.14, later.

**Figure 7.9** The incremental strategy (waterfall approach) and simultaneous strategy (the shower approach)

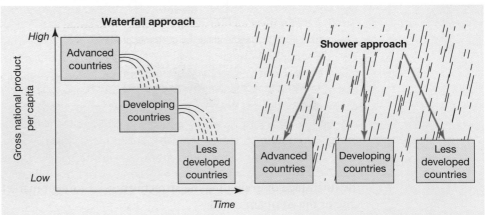

Source: *Global Marketing Management*, 5th edn, by Keegan, Warren J. © Pub. Pearson Education, Inc., Upper Saddle River, NJ 42–43.

## Exhibit 7.1 Sanex's aggressive search for cross-border niches: an example of the diversification approach

Sanex was developed as a liquid personal soap in 1984. Its success was established quickly – within a year it had gained market leadership in Spain. Soon afterwards it was bought by the US consumer giant Sara Lee, which has four main product sectors:

1 packaged meats and bakery products;
2 personal products;
3 coffee and groceries;
4 household and personal care products.

Source: © Sanex Global Brand.

The market basis for Sanex was the growing shower gel market in Europe. Consumers were moving from the ritual of bathing to the more hygienic routine of showering. The Sanex concept of healthy skin fitted perfectly with this trend. The word 'Sanex' is derived from sano, which is Spanish for 'healthy'. The idea behind the positioning was to build up a cross-border (European) concept of health in consumers' minds. This positioning strategy was in contrast to the positioning of the established players such as Procter & Gamble, Unilever, Colgate-Palmolive and Henkel. They were marketing their products under the cosmetic umbrella with strong perfume and colours, and high levels of detergents, supported by the sort of advertising familiar in the cosmetic industry, using beautiful women and exotic surroundings.

The market expansion strategy of Sanex was to launch the product simultaneously on a number of European markets (the 'shower approach' in Figure 7.9). The idea behind this strategy was that Sanex should obtain a 'first-mover advantage', which meant that the big competitors did not have time to copy the product concept before Sanex had product extensions ready for international market launching. The concept of Sanex's shower gel was well understood in most countries, but the potential for the brand would be different. If the habit of showering was well established, the opportunity for Sanex would be better. But in the United Kingdom, for example, baths are still very important, although the frequency of showering has increased. In another big potential market, the United States, people use bars of soap, although they have recently begun to switch to liquid soap.

In a relatively short time Sanex succeeded in developing and launching a broad range of products, including deodorants, colognes and body milk. With 1995 revenues of almost $100 million a year, Sanex is now marketed throughout Europe and the Far East.

Sources: Mazur and Lannon, 1993, p. 23.

Entry on an incremental basis, especially into small markets, may be preferred where a firm lacks experience in foreign markets and wishes to edge gradually into international operations. Information about, and familiarity with, operating in foreign markets are thus acquired step by step. This strategy may be preferable if a company is entering international markets late and faces entrenched local competition. Equally, if a firm is small and has limited resources, or is highly risk averse, it may prefer to enter a single or a limited number of markets and gradually expand in a series of incremental moves rather than making a major commitment to international expansion immediately.

Some companies prefer a rapid entry into world markets in order to seize an emerging opportunity or forestall competition. Rapid entry facilitates early market penetration across a number of markets and enables the firm to build up experience rapidly. It also enables a firm to achieve economies of scale in production and marketing by integrating and consolidating operations across these markets. This may be especially desirable if the product or service involved is innovative or represents a significant technological advance, in order to forestall pre-emption or limitation by other competitors. While increasingly feasible due to developments in global information technology, simultaneous entry into multiple markets typically requires substantial financial and management resources and entails higher operating risk.

Figure 7.10 **Appropriate global marketing strategies for SMEs**

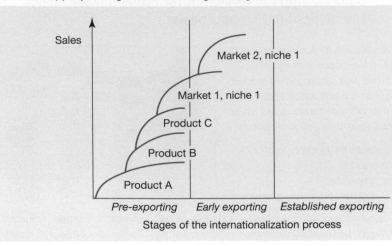

Source: Bradley, 1995. *International Marketing Strategy*, 2nd Edition. Reproduced by permission of Pearson Education Ltd.

## The appropriate expansion strategy for the SME

The SME often exploits domestic market opportunities to build up company resources, which later may be used in international markets (Figure 7.10).

The company strategy for market expansion should be concentrated on the product-market segment where the core competences of the company give it a competitive advantage (here product A, B, C and market 1, 2).

The process might evolve step by step, taking one market at a time, market 1, niche 1, learning from it, and then using it as a bridgehead to transfer that competence to the same niche in the next market (market 2, niche 1). The company may develop its international operations by continuing to develop new markets in a step-by-step process, ensuring consolidation and profitability before moving on.

## Concentration versus diversification

The firm must also decide whether to concentrate resources on a limited number of similar markets, or alternatively to diversify across a number of different markets. A company may concentrate its efforts by entering countries that are highly similar in terms of market characteristics and infrastructure to the domestic market. Management could also focus on a group of proximate countries. Alternatively, a company may prefer to diversify risk by entering countries that differ in terms of environmental or market characteristics. An economic recession in one country could be counterbalanced by growth in another market. The strength of competition also often varies from one market to another, and profits in a relatively protected or less competitive market may be funnelled into more fiercely competitive markets. Spreading out operations over a broader geographic base, and investing in different regions throughout the world, may also diversify risk, since in some industries markets in different regions are not interdependent (i.e. trends in one region will not spill over into another).

The question of concentrating or diversifying on the country level can be combined with concentration or diversification on the customer (segment) level. The resulting matrix (Figure 7.11) illustrates the four possible strategies.

**Figure 7.11** The market expansion matrix

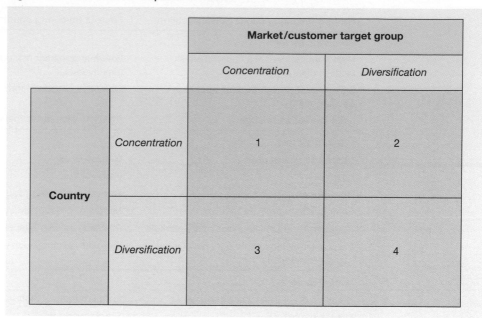

Source: Ayal and Zif, 1979, p. 84.

From Figure 7.11 four expansion alternatives can be identified:

1 few customer groups/segments in few countries;
2 many customer groups/segments in few countries;
3 few customer groups/segments in many countries;
4 many customer groups/segments in many countries.

A company can calculate its degree of export concentration and compare it over time or with other firms, using the Herfindahl index. This index is defined as the sum of the squares of the percentage of sales in each foreign country.

$$C = \sum S_i^2 \quad i = 1, 2, 3, 4 \ldots n \text{ countries}$$

where   $C$ = the export concentration index of the firm
        $S_i$ = exports to country $i$ as a percentage (measured in decimal numbers from 0 to 1) of the firm's total exports

$$\sum S_i = 1$$

Maximum concentration ($C = 1$) occurs when all the export is made to one country only, and minimum concentration ($C = 1/n$) exists when exports are equally distributed over a large number of countries.

The factors favouring country diversification versus concentration are shown in Table 7.3.

## 7.5 The global product/market portfolio

The corporate portfolio analysis provides an important tool to assess how to allocate resources, not only across geographic areas but also across the different product business (Douglas and Craig, 1995). The global corporate portfolio represents the most

Table 7.3 International market diversification versus market concentration

| Factors favouring country diversification | Factors favouring country concentration |
|---|---|
| *Company factors* | |
| High management risk consciousness (accept risk) | Low management risk consciousness (risk averse) |
| Objective of growth through market development | Objective of growth through market penetration |
| Little market knowledge | Ability to pick 'best' markets |
| *Product factors* | |
| Limited specialist uses | General uses |
| Low volume | High volume |
| Non-repeat | Repeat-purchase product |
| Early or late in product life cycle | Middle of product life cycle |
| Standard product saleable in many markets | Product requires adaptation to different markets |
| Radical innovation can trigger new global customer solutions | Incremental innovation – narrow market scope |
| *Market factors* | |
| Small markets – specialized segments | Large markets – high-volume segments |
| Unstable markets | Stable markets |
| Many similar markets | Limited number of markets |
| New or declining markets | Mature markets |
| Low growth rate in each market | High growth rate in each market |
| Large markets are very competitive | Large markets are not excessively competitive |
| Established competitors have large share of key markets | Key markets are divided among many competitors |
| Low customer loyalty | High customer loyalty |
| High synergy effects between countries | Low synergy effect between countries |
| Learning can be transferred across markets | Lack of awareness of global opportunities and threats |
| Short competitive lead time | Long competitive lead time |
| *Marketing factors* | |
| Low communication costs for additional markets | High communication costs for additional markets |
| Low order-handling costs for additional markets | High order-handling costs for additional markets |
| Low physical distribution costs for additional markets | High physical distribution costs for additional markets |
| Standardized communication in many markets | Communication requires adaptation to different markets |

Source: Adapted from Ayal and Zif, 1979; Piercy, 1981; Katsikea *et al.* (2005).

aggregate level of analysis and it might consist of operations by product businesses or by geographic areas.

As illustrated in Figure 7.12 (based on the market attractiveness/competitive strength matrix of Figure 7.4), Unilever's most aggregate level of analysis is its different product businesses. With this global corporate portfolio as a starting point, the further analysis of single corporate product business can go in a product dimension, a geographic dimension or a combination of the two.

It appears from the global corporate portfolio in Figure 7.12 that Unilever's 'foods' business is characterized by high market attractiveness and high competitive strengths.

Figure 7.12 Unilever's global portfolio

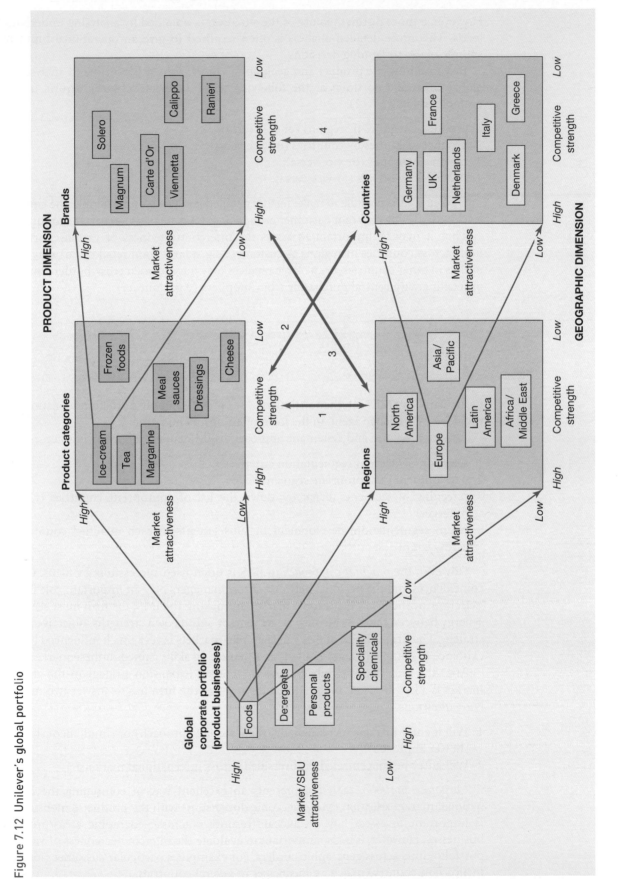

However, a more distinct picture of the situation is obtained by analysing underlying levels. This more detailed analysis is often required to give an operational input to specific market-planning decisions.

By combining the product and geographic dimensions it is possible to analyse the global corporate portfolio at the following levels (indicated by the arrows in the example of Figure 7.12):

1  product categories by regions (or vice versa);
2  product categories by countries (or vice versa);
3  regions by brands (or vice versa);
4  countries by brands (or vice versa).

Of course, it is possible to make further detailed analysis of, for example, the country level by analysing different customer groups (e.g. food retailers) in certain countries.

Thus it may be important to assess the interconnectedness of various portfolio units across countries or regions. A customer (e.g. a large food retail chain) may have outlets in other countries, or the large retailers may have formed cross-border alliances in retailing with central purchasing from suppliers (e.g. Unilever).

## 7.6  Summary

Particularly in SMEs international market selection is simply a reaction to a stimulus provided by a change agent, in the form of an unsolicited order.

A more proactive and systematic approach to IMS entails the following steps:

1  selection of relevant segmentation criteria;
2  development of appropriate segments;
3  screening of segments to narrow down the list of appropriate countries (choice of target);
4  micro segmentation: development of subsegments in each qualified country or across countries.

However, the *pragmatic approach* to IMS is often used successfully by firms. Often coincidences and the personal network of top managers play an important role in the 'selection' of the firm's first export market. In making the IMS, the firm must seek the synergy between the possible new target market and its own strengths, objectives, and strategy. The firm's choice of new international markets is very much influenced by the existence of complementary markets and marketing skills gained in these markets.

After the four steps described above the market expansion strategy of the chosen market is a key decision. In designing this strategy the firm has to answer two under-lying questions:

1  Will it enter markets incrementally (the waterfall approach) or simultaneously (the shower approach)?
2  Will entry be concentrated or diversified across international markets?

*Corporate portfolio analysis* represents an excellent way of combining the inter-national market selection (the geographic dimension) with the product dimension. It is important to assess how to allocate resources across geographic areas/product businesses. However, it is also important to evaluate the interconnectedness of various portfolio units across geographic borders. For example, a particular customer (located in a certain country) may have businesses in several countries.

# Philips Lighting: Screening markets in the Middle East

Royal Philips Electronics of the Netherlands is one of the world's biggest electronics companies, as well as the largest in Europe, with 161,500 employees in over 60 countries and sales in 2005 of €30.395 billion.

In 1891 the Dutch mechanical engineer Gerard Philips starts the production of carbon-filament lamps in a former buckskin factory in Eindhoven. Among his first major clients are early electricity companies who are including the provision of lamps in their power supply contracts.

Today Philips is number 1 in the world market for lighting. Philips lighting products (light bulbs and lamps) are found all around the world: not only everywhere in the home, but also in a multitude of professional applications, for example, in 30 per cent of offices, 65 per cent of the world's top airports, 30 per cent of hospitals, 35 per cent of cars and 55 per cent of major football stadiums.

**Outdoor advertising for Philips Lighting in Iraq (Bagdad)**
Source: Photo taken by one of the Philips distributors, Leadstay.

## Competition

Philips Lighting is world leader in lighting products manufacturing. Its market shares are 50 per cent in Europe, 36 per cent in North America and 14 per cent in the rest of the world. Since the 80s, Philips has participated intensively to the concentration of this industrial sector by purchasing smaller national companies such as Companie des Lampes (FR), AEG (GE) or Polam Pila (Poland). It has also developed joint ventures with Westinghouse Lamps, Kono Sylvania and EBT China.

### GE

General Electric Lighting (GEL) holds a 50 per cent share of the US market but had only a 2 per cent market share in Europe in 1988. In order to reach a 30 per cent market share in 2010, GEL has acquired several European national companies as Tungsram (Czechoslovakia), Thorn Emi (UK), Sivi (IT) and Linder Licht (GE). In 1994 GEL built a logistic unit in France to supply France, Germany, Benelux, Switzerland, Italy and Austria. It now intends to reduce prices in connection with supermarket chains.

### OSRAM

A 100 per cent subsidiary of the giant German holding SIEMENS, OSRAM achieves a 86 per cent share

of its turnover by exporting (46 per cent in North America, 41 per cent in EU, 6 per cent in South America and 6 per cent in Asia). Strategy for the next coming years is to increase Asian market shares by doubling its turnover in Asia.

Other significant manufacturers are Sylvania Lighting International and Panasonic.

## Philips Lighting market screening in Middle East

At the beginning of the twenty-first century Philips needed a coherent marketing strategy for the whole Middle East region. The first task was to select the most attractive markets in the region. Over the years Philips has developed a model which shows a correlation between a country's demand for lighting and its GDP per capita. During discussions with agents/distributors in many countries, Philips was completely dependent on its information about market size. If Philips underestimated market size, it missed market opportunities. That was the main reason why this model was developed, so that Philips could cross-check market estimations of its agents/distributors.

Figure 7.13 shows that lighting (demand for lamps and bulbs) is a basic need for a country and as soon as a country starts developing this basic need increases. But as the country's wealth increases the growth in the demand slows down, because at later stages of economic development basic lighting needs are covered, as we can observe in the case of Israel.

Figure 7.13 The relationship between the wealth of a country and the demand for lighting

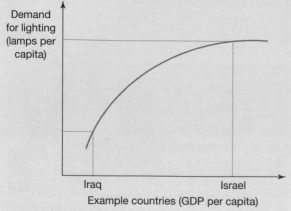

Example countries (GDP per capita)

Table 1 Basic demographic data in the Middle East (2003)

| Markets | Population (million) | GNP 2003 (% growth) | GNP per cap (US$) |
|---|---|---|---|
| Bahrain | 0.6 | 3.0 | 8,420 |
| Egypt | 61.9 | 5.0 | 1,032 |
| Iran | 66.0 | 3.0 | 1,470 |
| Iraq | 19.7 | −5.0 | 558 |
| Israel | 5.5 | 7.1 | 15,500 |
| Jordan | 4.6 | 5.0 | 2,159 |
| Kuwait | 2.2 | 3.5 | 15,670 |
| Lebanon | 3.2 | 4.0 | 3,845 |
| Libya | 5.5 | 3.5 | 4,882 |
| Oman | 2.4 | 4.3 | 6,268 |
| Palestine | 2.1 | −5.0 | 430 |
| Qatar | 0.6 | 2.0 | 13,120 |
| Saudi Arabia | 20.6 | 3.5 | 5,643 |
| Syria | 17.0 | 6.0 | 882 |
| UAE | 2.5 | 0.5 | 17,440 |
| Yemen | 15.0 | 3.0 | 693 |
| Middle East | 229.4 | – | – |

Source: Wim Wilms, Eindhoven, Fontys Export Day, 13 October 2004.

Basically, in order to find the most attractive markets Philips Lighting used the model (shown in Figure 7.13 and Table 1) in combination. The demand for lighting per capita has to be multiplied by the number of inhabitants in a country. Israel and Kuwait have the highest GDP/capita but their population size is small. On the other hand Iraq and Iran were (and still are) large markets for lighting, but they are very tough to enter because of their politically chaotic situations.

However, the Philips Lighting Middle East managers did not use market size as the only market selection criterion for priority, but the models were used as a starting point for discussions with agents and distributors in the countries. If the Philips sales in large lighting markets were very low, this would indicate a low Philips market share (unless the market size was also low). This would lead to a discussion with the local agents and distributors about how to increase the local Philips market shares in cooperation with the local distributor.

Sources: PowerPoint presentation from Wim Wilms, Eindhoven, Fontys Export Day, 13 October 2004; www.philips.com.

## Questions

1 Discuss the appropriateness of the screening model used in this case.

2 Suggest another screening model that could be relevant for Philips Lighting to use in the Middle East.

For further exercises and cases, see this book's website at **www.pearsoned.co.uk/hollensen**

 ## Questions for discussion

1 Why is screening of foreign markets important? Outline the reasons why many firms do not systematically screen countries/markets.

2 Explore the factors which influence the international market selection process.

3 Discuss the advantages and disadvantages of using only secondary data as screening criteria in the IMS process.

4 What are the advantages and disadvantages of an opportunistic selection of international markets?

5 What are the differences between a global market segment and a national market segment? What are the marketing implications of these differences for a firm serving segments on a worldwide basis?

6 Discuss the possible implications that the firm's choice of geographic expansion strategy may have on the ability of a local marketing manager of a foreign subsidiary to develop and implement marketing programmes.

## References

Andersen, O. and Buvik, A. (2002) 'Firms' internationalization and alternative approaches to the international customer/market selection', *International Business Review*, 11, pp. 347–363.

Andersen, P.H. and Strandskov, J. (1998) 'International market selection', *Journal of Global Marketing*, 11(3), pp. 65–84.

Ayal, I. and Zif, J. (1979) 'Market expansion strategies in multinational marketing', *Journal of Marketing*, 43, Spring, pp. 84–94.

Bradley, F. (1995) *International Marketing Strategy*, 2nd edn, Prentice-Hall, London.

Brewer, P. (2001) 'International market selection: developing a model from Australian case studies', *International Business Review*, 10, pp. 155–174.

Douglas, S. and Craig, C.A. (1995) *Global Marketing Strategy*, McGraw-Hill, New York.

Green, R.T. and Allaway, A.W. (1985) 'Identification of export opportunities: a shift-share approach', *Journal of Marketing*, 49, Winter, pp. 83–88.

Johanson, J. and Vahlne, J.E. (1977) 'The internationalization process of the firm: a model of knowledge development and increasing foreign market commitment', *Journal of International Business Studies*, 8(1), pp. 23–32.

Koch, A. (2001) 'Factors influencing market and entry mode selection: developing the MEMS model', *Marketing Intelligence & Planning*, Vol. 19, No. 5, pp. 351–361.

Katsikea, E.S., Theodosiou, M., Morgan, R.E. and Papavassiliou, N. (2005) 'Export market Expansion strategies of direct-selling small and medium-sized firms: Implications for export activities', *Journal of International Marketing*, 13(2), pp. 57–92.

Mazur, L. and Lannon, J. (1993) 'Crossborder marketing lessons from 25 European success stories', *EIU Research Report*, the Economist Intelligence Unit Limited, London, pp. 17–19.

Papadopoulos, N.G. and Denis, J.E. (1988) 'Inventory, taxonomy and assessment of methods for international market selection', *International Marketing Review*, Autumn, pp. 38–51.

Papadopoulos, N., Chen, H. and Thomas, D.R. (2002) 'Toward a tradeoff model for international market selection', *International Business Review*, 11, pp. 165–192.

Piercy, N. (1981) 'Company internationalization: active and reactive exporting', *European Journal of Marketing*, 15(3), pp. 26–40.

Rahman, S.H. (2003), 'Modelling of international market selection process: a qualitative study of successful Australian international businesses', *Qualitative Market Research: An International Journal*, 6(2), pp. 119–132.

Sakarya, S., Eckman, M. and Hyllegard, K.H. (2007) 'Market selection for international expansion – Assessing opportunities in emerging markets', *International Marketing Review*, Vol. 24, No. 2, pp. 208–238.

Sylvest, J. and Lindholm, C. (1997) 'Små globale virksomheder', *Ledelse & Erhvervsøkonomi*, 61, April, pp. 131–143.

Vernon, R. (1966) 'International investment and international trade in product cycle', *Quarterly Journal of Economics*, 80, pp. 190–208.

Welford, R. and Prescott, K. (1996) *European Business: An issue-based approach*, Pitman, London.

Westhead, P., Wright, M. and Ucbasaran, D. (2002) 'International market selection strategies selected by "micro" and small firms', *Omega*, 30, pp. 51–68.

Yip, G.S., Biscarri, J.G. and Monti, J.A. (2000), 'The role of the internationalization process in the performance of newly internationalizing firms', *Journal of International Marketing*, 8(3), pp. 10–35.

# Red Bull:
## The global market leader in energy drinks is considering further market expansion

### The beginning

Energy drinks may well have come from Scotland in the form of Irn-Bru, first produced in the form of 'Iron Brew' in 1901. In Japan, the energy drink phenomenon dates at least as far back as the early 1960s, with the release of the Lipovitan. Most such products in Japan bear little resemblance to soft drinks, and are sold instead in small brown glass medicine bottles or cans styled to resemble such containers. These so-called 'genki drinks', which are also produced in South Korea, helped employees to work long hours or to stay awake on the late commute home.

In UK, Lucozade Energy was originally introduced in 1929 as a hospital drink for 'aiding the recovery' in the early 1980s, it was promoted as an energy drink for 'replenishing lost energy'.

The origin of Red Bull dates back to 1962 where the original formula was developed by Chaleo Yoovidhya, a Thai businessman, and sold under the name Krating Daeng by a local pharmaceutical company to treat jetlag and boost energy for truck drivers.

Serkan Senturk/AP/PA Photos.

### The marketing man

Mateschitz grew up in a small village in Styria, Austria. When he turned 18, he went to the University of Vienna.

**Dietrich Mateschiz**
Source: Michael Kunkel/Hochzwei/PA Photos.

It took Mateschitz ten years to finally graduate with a degree in World Trade. His friends said that Mateschitz liked to play, party and pursue pretty women. After graduation he decided to get serious and become a 'really good marketing man'. His natural charm helped him land a training position at Unilever, and soon he was promoting dishwashing detergents and soap all over Europe. Colleagues described him as 'funny, full of ambition and always filled with crazy ideas'.

Mateschitz had a natural talent for selling. He was creative and had a knack for getting things done. He soon got promoted to the position of marketing director for a leading, international toothpaste brand called Blendax.

After years of travelling and selling toothpaste around the globe, Mateschitz became obsessed with the idea of creating his own business. In the summer of 1982 he read a story about the top ten taxpayers in Japan. He was surprised that a certain Mr Taisho, who had introduced a high-energy drink to Japan, made the top of the list. On the next stop of his sales trip – in Thailand – he learned from a local toothpaste distributor that energy drinks were a hot item among tired drivers stopping at gas stations. The top brand was Kratindaeng, meaning *water buffalo*. The ingredients were clearly written on the can. Like the original *Yellow Pages*, there was no trademark or patent to protect the formula.

Dietrich Mateschitz met up with Chaleo Yoovidhya at the beginning of 1980s and they decided to start an energy drink company together. Each partner would contribute about a half a million dollars in start-up capital. Chaleo Yoovidhya provided the beverage formula and his partner contributed the marketing flair. Red Bull was thus founded in 1984 by Dietrich Mateschitz and Chaleo Yoovidhya, and was headquartered in Austria. Today, Dietrich Mateschitz and Chaleo Yovidhya each own 49 per cent of the company. The remaining 2 per cent belongs to Yovidhya's son, Chalerm.

## The start-up in Austria and the further international expansion

The optimistic 40-year-old Mateschitz quit his job and applied for a licence to sell the high-energy drink in Austria. However, the Austrian bureaucracy would not allow the drink to be sold without scientific tests. It took three years and many sales calls to get a licence to sell. While waiting for the official licence, Mateschitz asked his old school friend Johannes Kastner, who ran an advertising agency in Frankfurt, Germany, to design the can and logo. Mateschitz rejected dozens of samples before settling on a macho logo with two red bulls charging each other. Kastner worked diligently on a snappy slogan, but Mateschitz rejected one after the other, each time saying, 'Not good enough.'

Kastner told Mateschitz to find someone else to come up with a better slogan, but Mateschitz pleaded, 'Sleep on it, and give me one more tag line.' The next morning Kastner called and said, 'Red Bull – gives you wings.' The slogan turned into a prophecy for the Red Bull brand, which continues to soar around the globe.

Mateschitz still had to find a bottler to produce his drink. Every bottler he called told him that Red Bull had no chance of success. Finally, Mateschitz found a sympathetic ear in Roman Rauch, the leading soft-drink bottler in Austria, and soon the shiny silver cans rolled off the production line. Within two years, and after many creative promotions, sales began to grow, but so did his losses. While a million-dollar loss in two years may scare an entrepreneur into closing the business, Mateschitz was undaunted. He financed everything without outside capital, and by 1990 Red Bull was in the black again. He soon realized that Austria was not a big enough market, and in 1993 he expanded to neighbouring Hungary and then focused his energies on conquering the German market.

Once the news of Red Bull's advancing sales spread in Europe, dozens of copycat competitors came on the market. Red Bull's initial move into the German market was highly successful. However, after three months of increasing demand, Mateschitz could not get enough aluminum to produce the cans anywhere in Europe, and sales of Red Bull dropped fast. A competitor named Flying Horse became the market leader. It took Red Bull four years to reclaim the top spot in the German market.

In 1995, Red Bull hit Britain; in 1997, the United States, starting in California. There, in a marketing trick typical of his unusual style, he hired students to drive around in liveried Minis with a Red Bull can on the roof to promote the drink.

The rest is history. Red Bull has become extremely popular over recent years increasing from almost a billion 250 ml cans sold in 2000 to more than 3 billion cans sold in 2006, in over 130 countries. In 2006, Red Bull generated over €2.6 billion in turnover throughout the world with the help of its 3,900 employees.

## Marketing orientation and consumers

Red Bull devised an innovative marketing approach to target mainly the young adult and consumers seeking an energy boost. It targets young adult consumers aged 16 to 29, young urban professionals, and post secondary school students. Red Bull created strategic programmes to attract post-secondary students by providing them free cases of drink and convincing them to give parties and targeting club goers by stocking Red Bull at night-clubs. This viral campaign created a noticeable effect by boosting sales. Supported by sleek advertising, it came out with a small silver blue can to attract young urban professionals who prefer a stylish life. The company also set about promoting the Red Bull brand directly to Generation Y, the so-called *millennials*, people born after 1981 who were believed to be cynical of traditional marketing strategies. Part of this idea involved recruiting 'student brand managers' who would be used to promote Red Bull on university campuses. The students would be encouraged to give parties at which cases of Red Bull would be distributed. The brand managers would then report back to the company, giving the firm a low cost form of market research data.

Red Bull tries to portray its products as drinks for energetic, physically active and health-conscious consumers, characterized by the sugar-free version. People in need of energy boosts include, but are not limited to, club-hoppers, truck drivers and students.

## The 'Red Bull' marketing strategy

Red Bull essentially threw the traditional marketing book out of the window. Its highly acclaimed strategy has been described as: grassroots, guerilla, word-of-mouth, viral marketing, underground, buzz-marketing and without a doubt, successful.

The first marketing trials of Red Bull failed miserably. The respondents didn't like the taste, colour or the 'stimulates mind and body' concept. At this point, many companies would have abandoned their plan or reformulated to make it more appealing to the consumer. However, Mateschitz rejected that these trials should be the basis for their marketing strategy. In this he meant that Red Bull was not selling a beverage but selling a 'way of life'. *Red Bull will give you wiiings ...* Red Bull is an enabler for what you desire. Red Bull needed to be enjoyed in the right context, where an energy boost was needed.

One effective brand builder was not initiated by the company but by Urban myth. Red Bull faced many obstacles in gaining regulatory approval in several countries because of its unique ingredients. During this time a rumour circulated that the taurine used came from bull's testicles and Red Bull was 'liquid Viagra', which made the drink even more mystic. Adding to the allure was the fact that the beverage has actually been banned in several countries such as France and Denmark.

## The product

Red Bull is sold as an energy drink to combat mental and physical fatigue. Active ingredients include 27g of sugar, B-complex vitamins, and 80mg of caffeine, which is a little less than the amount of caffeine found in an average cup of coffee and about two times as much caffeine as many leading cola drinks. Besides water, sugar and caffeine the drink contains an ingredient named taurine, an amino acid that, according to Japanese studies, benefits the cardiovascular system.

A sugar-free version has been available since the beginning of 2003. The drink tastes of citrus and herbs, and is commonly used as a mixer in alcoholic drinks such as Red Bull Wings (Red Bull and vodka) or as a base ingredient in the famous Jägerbomb (a cocktail combining one shot of Jägermeister dropped into a glass of Red Bull).

The company specializes in energy drinks and because Red Bull is the company's main brand (with only two flavour varieties and one packaging size), this allows it to focus its efforts and expand its footprint quickly while leveraging marketing and promotions used in other regions. In most countries and regions, Red Bull was the first energy drinks brand and as a result is the leading brand in almost all regions where it is sold.

Red Bull distinguishes itself from a lot of the beverage market by only offering its product in one size, 8.3 ounce (250 ml) cans, which is smaller than a typical soft drink. The cans are small, sleek vessels with distinctive printing, which have been described as more 'European' styling. With the exception of mandated warning labels the can design does not vary by country. Furthermore, unlike soft drinks or vodka, Red Bull is only offered in two varieties: original and sugar-free. This recognizable packaging provides Red Bull with an advantage, and

Source: Evan Kafka/Getty Images Entertainment/Getty Images.

the one size that is used worldwide creates production efficiencies.

## Price

This clear positioning has created a foothold in key markets such as the United Kingdom, Germany and the United States. Sales in key markets help drive the global positioning of the company, as well as providing the opportunity to sell Red Bull at a premium price over other brands. A single can generally retails for about €2 which is up to five times the cost of name-branded soft drinks.

Premium pricing is a feature of the energy drinks category. Since its inception the category has been positioned as providing products that not only refresh you, but give you the energy and related brain power to make the most of your time. While it could never be said that energy drinks position themselves as healthy, there is little doubt that they claim to provide a functional benefit to the consumer, which is the main reason why they can command a premium price. In 2006, the average price per litre for an energy drink across the world was US$5.78, almost four times the average price of a litre of carbonates (US$1.54), and similarly ahead of the average price per litre in the soft drinks category as a whole (US$1.50).

## Distribution

A key growth strategy at Red Bull has been increased international distribution. It has consistently worked on growing international sales, first making moves outside its domestic market in 1992, only five years after the first cans of Red Bull appeared in Austria. Now available in over 100 countries worldwide, Red Bull has a well-developed network of local subsidiaries set up in key markets to oversee distribution in any given region. These subsidiaries are responsible for importing Red Bull from Red Bull GmbH in Austria and either setting up an independent distribution network or working with a partner, such as in Australia where Red Bull Australia uses the Cadbury Schweppes's distribution network. In this case, Red Bull Australia imports and sells on to Cadbury Schweppes, which then sells to vendors in its network.

The typical Red Bull national distribution strategy for new markets is, like all else, atypical. Instead of targeting the largest distributors with the greatest reach Red Bull targets small distributors who often became exclusively Red Bull distributors. They even went to the extreme of hiring teenagers and college students and giving them vans to distribute the product.

Small independent venues are also the first targets. Red Bull would find the small bars, restaurants and stores and give them a small cooler to sell the beverage from. This is preferred rather than dealing with the demands of the larger stores, who eventually were begging to sell the product.

## Promotion/advertising

Many product launches are coupled with large advertising campaigns both in print and TV, taste test, give-aways and celebrity endorsements to get the brand and product out into the public. This is not a technique that is used by Red Bull.

Red Bull does not use traditional advertising to enter a market. Only after the product is in the market does advertising serve as a reminder. Furthermore, they never use print media since it is too dull and flat to express the product. Television ads often are cartoon drawings using the 'Red Bull gives you wiiings' slogan and are very carefully placed. Stations and programming are carefully selected to maximize exposure to the target audience such as late-night TV shows.

Red Bull does not hire celebrity endorsers, but they do enable celebrity endorsers. Some of the earliest deliveries of Red Bull in the United States were to Hollywood movie sets for consumption during long days of filming, even before the beverage was readily available. This created a scheme where the celebrities were doing what they could to get Red Bull and instantly became endorsers for the brand to the masses. Celebrities are not the only ones who were enabled for endorsements. Again, before the product was widely available, the company made it available to bar tenders in New York's trendiest spots for their own consumption. This led to an unpaid endorsement to the club patrons by the bar tenders.

Every year the company sponsors dozens of extreme sporting events, like the climbing of iced-down silos in Iowa or kite sailing in Hawaii, as well as cultural events like break-dancing contests and rock music jam sessions. Red Bull sponsors a DJ camp where some of the up and coming DJs get a chance to learn from some of the masters courtesy of Red Bull. Red Bull also sponsors some 500 athletes around the world, the type who would surf in Nova Scotia in January or jump out of a plane to 'fly' across the English Channel.

The local subsidiaries are also responsible for local marketing content such as buzz marketing, local sponsorships and arranging media including TV, billboards and radio. In addition to local marketing and advertising, local subsidiaries also acquire marketing material from Red Bull GmbH and its exclusive advertiser Kastner & Partner

All in all, Red Bull spends relatively little on traditional print and TV advertising, instead relying on sponsorships of extreme sports or giving away samples at local events. Since its introduction Red Bull has invested heavily in building the brand. It spends about 30 per cent of revenue on marketing: as a comparison, Coca-Cola spends 9 per cent.

## Competition

Red Bull operates within the **functional drinks market**, which is mostly made up of sales from **energy drinks** and **sports drinks** – Red Bull is only active in the energy drinks market. Sports drinks are not to be confused with energy drinks. Sports drinks are intended to replenish electrolytes, sugar, water and other nutrients, and are usually isotonic (containing the same proportions as found in the human body) after strenuous training or competition. Energy drinks, on the other hand, mainly provide sugar and caffeine, in order to increase concentration or mental and physical strain. The most well-known sports drink is Gatorade (Quaker Oats Co.), which was introduced in 1966.

Red Bull, despite being widely known as an energy drink, has other uses such as a coffee, tea and soda substitute: vitamin/energy supplement and mixer for alcohol. The majority of consumers are using Red Bull as a vitamin supplement or energy stimulant in place of preferred stimulants such as ginseng. Red Bull, with its liquid B-vitamin supplement, competes in the niche market for vitamins and is competing with the larger pharmaceutical companies. It is also competing indirectly with various drink mixers such as juice, sour mix and tonic. Red Bull initially marketed its energy drink mixed with alcohol to the average club-goers. However, due to various health concerns and fatal incidents associated with Red Bull when mixed with alcohol, explicit warnings have been placed on product labels discouraging improper use.

The market for energy drinks is characterized by the presence of specialized manufacturers as well as food and beverage powerhouses. Key players in the marketplace include Pepsi, Coca-Cola, Danone, Hansen Beverage Co., Monarch Beverage Co., Red Bull, Dark Dog, GlaxoSmithkline, Extreme Beverages, Taisho Pharmaceuticals and Otsuka Pharmaceuticals. In terms of market share, Gatorade and Red Bull lead the sports and energy drinks segments, respectively. Most of the soft drink multinationals (like Pepsi, Coca-Cola, Danone, GlaxoSmithKline) also cover the functional drinks market.

## The total market for functional drinks (including energy drinks)

Today's 24/7 lifestyle is driving the sales of functional drinks (including sports and energy drinks – see definition above), with volume having increased by impressive figures. Functional drinks have now clearly moved from niche to mass-market, having seen significant growth every year since their introduction. In order to get the most out of every day, consumers are increasingly looking at products with an extra kick, which is one reason why so many people are reaching for these kinds of drinks.

In the overall functional drinks market, Red Bull is increasingly being challenged by new innovative brands. With the global sales of 3 billion cans in 2006 Red Bull reached a 45 per cent market share of the world market in energy drinks. This has made it a clear world market leader in this segment. Higher per litre revenue in 'energy drinks' has attracted brands from all the major players into the market, such as Coca-Cola's Burn, and Pepsi's Adrenaline, but so far they have not come close to dislodging Red Bull from its position as global market leader.

In the overall global soft drink market the Red Bull market share is small. According to Euromonitor (2007) it is only 0.8 per cent. The overall Red Bull market shares in the 'functional drinks market' are shown in Table 1.

## The market development in the 'global energy drinks' market

Asia dominates the consumption volume of energy drinks, accounting for about 40 per cent of all energy drinks volumes. However, at a per capita level it is North America and Australia/New Zealand that lead the way. In almost all regions, the concept of energy drinks has been established and accepted by the consumer. The only two regions that remain exceptions in part are eastern Europe and Central and South America, where lower levels of disposable income remain a barrier.

**Table 1 Red Bull market shares (value) in the functional drinks market (2006)**

| Region | Red Bull Market share in the functional drinks market (%) |
| --- | --- |
| Western Europe | 26.8 |
| Eastern Europe | 31.4 |
| North America | 10.0 |
| Latin America | 11.7 |
| Asia (excluding Aus/NZ) | 2.8 |
| Aus / NZ | 13.6 |
| Africa / Middle East | 22.7 |
| Total World | 10.9 |
| Total world market (functional drinks market) | US$24,250m |

Source: Euromonitor (2007). © Euromonitor International 2007.

Not surprisingly, the United States is the largest country market, ahead of Japan, Indonesia and China. Three other Asian countries also appear in the top ten markets for energy drinks, namely Thailand, South Korea and Vietnam. While still accounting for nearly half of all energy drinks consumed worldwide, Asian dominance is starting to slowly slip as other regions begin to catch up. In fact, worldwide growth in consumption is beginning to slow. Following year-on-year growth of 31 per cent in 2004 and 24 per cent in 2005, growth slowed to 17 per cent in 2006.

In western Europe, the United Kingdom leads the way in volume terms, accounting for nearly half of the energy drinks consumed in the region. However, the Republic of Ireland and Austria have a far higher per capita consumption figure, with Irish consumers drinking an average of just under 8 litres of energy drinks per year, hugely more than the regional average of 1.6 litres per capita. Higher per capita figures in Austria can perhaps be explained by the fact that Red Bull and other energy drinks companies originated there.

In western Europe, many energy drinks are banned from sale due to certain ingredients, including Red Bull which is banned in France and Denmark. This obviously has a marked effect on the market when comparing it to other geographic regions.

Although Red Bull was originally targeted at the on-trade market (bars, disco, etc.), off-trade (retail) has now become the principal channel for energy drinks, with approximately two thirds of worldwide volume being sold through these channels. This picture is pretty consistent worldwide, other than in Central and South America where the split is far more even, and North America where the emphasis is far heavier on the retail channels (85 per cent). In many markets, the United Kingdom being a good example, the volume sold through on-premise channels is heavily impacted by energy drinks being sold as mixers with spirits, primarily vodka.

Sources: Hosea, M. (2007), 'Running with bulls', *Brand Strategy*, September, pp. 20–23; Datamonitor (2007), Red Bull GmbH, *Datamonitor Company Profile*, 25 April 2007; Gschwandtner, G. (2004), The Powerful Sales Strategy behind Red Bull, *Selling Power Magazine*, September 2004; Euromonitor (2007), Red Bull GmbH – Softdrink – World, Global Company Profile, *Euromonitor International*, March, pp. 1–15; Euromonitor (2006), Functional Drinks – Japan, *Euromonitor International*, October, pp. 1–11; Lerner, M. (2007), 'Running with "Red Bull" and an arena of speciality drinks', *American Metal Market*, August, pp. 20–22; *Marketing Week* (2006), 'Red Bull spreads its wings', 1 June 2006, p. 33.

## Questions

The top management team of Red Bull is considering placing the focus of its further expansion on new markets like Turkey, Russia, Mexico, Japan, China or the Middle East. In order to get an external evaluation of the market opportunities they have contacted you, and during the next week you are supposed to deliver a small report with the answers to the following questions.

1  How will you characterize the overall Red Bull's global marketing strategy (global, glocal or local)?

2  Argue for the most relevant segmentation (screening) criteria to be used in the international market selection (IMS) process.

3  What changes would you suggest for Red Bull's future global marketing mix, in order to meet its future challenges?

# Skagen Designs:
## Becoming an international player in designed watches

Towards the end of 2006 Charlotte and Henrik Jorst can look back at 15 hectic, but successful years. Their company was founded in an apartment in New York, from where its first marketing efforts took place. The two entrepreneurs started selling relatively expensive watches bearing a logo that American companies might use as company presents. During the Gulf Crisis it was, however, very difficult to sell watches in that price range. Therefore, in 1990 Charlotte and Henrik visited a watch fair in Basel in order to find a manufacturer who was able to produce the watches at a lower cost price. They found a Danish owned company, Comtech Watches, with headquarters in Aarhus and clock-and-watch factory in Hong Kong.

In 1992 Charlotte and Henrik had an annual turnover of US$800,000, primarily through an advertisement on the back page of a big mail-order catalogue for Father's Day. Since then events followed each other in quick succession. In 1995 the chain, Bloomingdale's, included the Skagen Design watches in its assortment and other retail chains like Macy's, Nordstrom and Watch World have followed. In addition, the watches are sold in big gift and design shops.

In 1998 Skagen Designs had an annual turnover of almost US$30 million; in 2005 turnover had increased to approximately US$70 million.

## Skagen designs – the story in brief

**1986:** Party at Carlsberg. Even though Henrik Jorst has brought his girlfriend, he manages to make Charlotte Kjølbye his neighbour at dinner, and they fall head over heels in love. Shortly after the party Carlsberg sends Henrik to New York. From New York Henrik manages Carlsberg's USA sales. Charlotte stays on for a year and a half in Denmark keeping in close contact with Henrik on the phone.

**1988:** Charlotte joins Henrik in the United States and reigns as Miss Carlsberg for the summer and fall months. After a Danish colleague sends them a few of his sample corporate watches to sell in the United States, Charlotte and Henrik embark on their dream of starting their own business and begin working in the world of watches. Charlotte and Henrik are married in May.

**1990:** Henrik quits his job at Carlsberg. Charlotte walks about the streets of New York trying to sell the Danish

Charlotte and Henrik Jorst considering different watch designs

Jacob Jensen watches to watchmakers. They have hardly any money. Charlotte gives birth to their daughter Christine.

**1991:** The Jorsts design a few sample corporate watches and exhibit them at the New York Premium and Incentive Show in the Spring. At this fair, several retailers notice the watches and wonder why the two Danes present them as corporate watches and not branded goods. The retailers state that if the watches were available without the corporate logos they would purchase them for their stores. During the summer they produce 800 copies of four different watches with the name *Skagen Denmark*. Few months later all watches are sold out and an additional amount was produced.

**1992:** Sitting at the dinner table Henrik and Charlotte design 30 different models, all labelled 'Skagen Denmark'. In a New York street Charlotte meets one of the managers from the mail order giant 'The Sharper Image'. She takes a chance, and yes, he features the Skagen watches on the back page of the Father's Day catalogue. Everything is sold out. From the apartment in New York Henrik and Charlotte have a turnover of US$800,000.

**1993:** There are not many states in the United States where business taxes are almost equal to zero. In Florida and Nevada this is, however, the case. One day they fly to Incline Village at Lake Tahoe – one of the world's best ski resorts. They lose their hearts and buy a house that is much too expensive, but big. The company moves into every room from kitchen cupboards to garage. They still do it all by themselves. Charlotte gives birth to their daughter Camilla.

**1995:** Five years after starting the company. Now, it becomes *really* big. Bloomingdale's takes the watches on trial. Sold out – on one single day. They engage employees in a small, rented office not far from their home at the lake. After a year the office is too small, and after another year the same happens again.

**1998:** The Magazine, Inc. puts Skagen Designs on the list of the 250 fastest growing, privately-owned companies. During five years the turnover has increased by almost 1,200 per cent. Finally, the rest of the company moves out of the villa at Lake Tahoe. New headquarters are opened in Reno, Nevada. An office is opened in Denmark to handle European distribution and an additional 80 stores throughout Denmark begin selling the Skagen Denmark line.

**1999:** The number of employees is approaching 100. Inc. Magazine's 'Inc. 500' lists the company as one of the fastest-growing companies in the United States. Henrik gives Charlotte a horse as present for their ten year wedding anniversary. The family moves from Lake Tahoe to a large house of 650 square metres on the outskirts of Reno. It is situated on the top of a hill with a beautiful view of the Sierra Nevada Mountains. Skagen begins its ongoing presence in major magazines such as *InStyle* and *GQ*. Distribution begins in the United Kingdom.

**2000:** Distribution begins in Germany and the Netherlands.

**2001:** Skagen Designs exhibits for the first time at BaselWorld – The Watch and Jewellery Show in Basel, Switzerland.

**2002:** Distribution begins in additional countries including Finland, Iceland, Ukraine and Kuwait.

**2003:** More countries join the Skagen Designs team and distribution begins in Belgium, Serbia, Montenegro, United Arab Emirates, Norway, France and Italy.

**2004:** To handle increasing growth, the European HQ office in Copenhagen moves to a larger facility. The European HQ targets large department stores in Germany and France.

**2005:** The former Director of Sales & Product Development, Scott Szybala is appointed as President. Scott's responsibilities are to oversee the daily oper-ations as well as the strategic direction for Skagen Designs, reporting directly to Charlotte and Henrik, who continue to be closely involved in the company's product development and sales.

**2006:** Skagen Designs becomes an official sponsor of Team CSC, one of the best teams in professional cycling, with a record-breaking number of victories. Today, Henrik and Charlotte still approve all products that Skagen designs.

## Internal policies

Skagen Designs has its name from the Danish fishing village of Skagen; a popular retreat for artists from around the world. Many say this place has the perfect source of natural light and those who visit find its unique charm to be a mix between nature-given and man-made romanticism. This region has inspired, not only the brand-name, but also the Jorst design philosophy as well. The colours, shapes and simplicity inspire the design team. The design team is on the pulse of current fashions, with regular visits to design centres around the world including

Collection of Skagen watches for men (left) and women (right)

Switzerland, Italy, France, New York and Hong Kong. Skagen Design tries to stay true to its classic design philosophy and is never content to follow established trends.

The Skagen Designs' logo symbolizes the meeting of the Skagerak and the Kattegat seas that surround the village of Skagen.

Charlotte and Henrik have divided the work between them as follows. Charlotte is primarily in charge of sales and marketing, while Henrik is in charge of the company's finance and administration.

In the United States the watches are sold at very competitive prices compared with other design watches: typically at a level of US$100–120.

The core competences of Skagen Designs are assessed as follows:

- Development of new watch concepts following the fashion trend with 'the finger on the pulse'.
- Human resource policy – both Charlotte and Henrik use a lot of time walking around and communicating with employees and to let them feel that Skagen Designs is one big team with the same family-oriented values in all parts of the worldwide organization.
- Quick and flexible management decisions.
- New products are introduced five times a year (November, January, March, May and August) providing retailers with seasonal updates and giving consumers the opportunity to update the style for each season.
- Well-developed partnerships with the 'upstream' specialists in the Far East who are in charge of the production at competitive prices.

## Marketing the watches

In the United States Skagen Design products are launched through fashion papers like *Vogue*, *InStyle* and *Accessories*. TV shows like *Jeopardy* and *Wheel of Fortune* have been sponsored as well as actors in the series *Ally McBeal* and *The Practice*.

The company's national advertising is also placed in major industry publications as well as out-of-home advertising opportunities including billboards, buses and phone kiosks to support peak selling periods such as spring fashion, Mother's Day, Father's Day, fall fashion and Christmas.

In 2006 Skagen Designs became an official sponsor of the professional cycling team CSC. Its wins include some of the most prestigious trophies in the sport of cycling, including a second place in the 2005 Tour de France for Ivan Basso as well as Yellow Jerseys for David Zabriskie

and Jens Voigt. Skagen Denmark's Team CSC watch collection is comprised of six new styles of performance-inspired, Swiss-made watches featuring ultra lightweight and durable titanium cases and water-resistant leather straps. Two of these new styles, the Ivan Basso Special Edition and the Ivan Basso 'Yellow Jersey' Special Edition, are numbered and endorsed with Basso's signature on the dials and case backs. In Spring 2006 Ivan Basso also won 'Tour of Italy' (Italian Giro) and he was one of the top favourites for the 2006 Tour de France. However, just two days before the start of the Tour de France in July 2006, Ivan Basso and Jan Ullrich were excluded from the Tour because of a doping scandal in Spain.

## Competitors

As a fashion company Skagen Designs is competing with all the major international companies designing watches – for example, Calvin Klein, Coach, Guess, Gucci, Swatch, Alfex and Jacob Jensen. Most of these companies possess a financial strength many times larger than Skagen Designs.

## Questions

As an expert in international marketing Charlotte and Henrik have called you in to get valuable input in connection with the international expansion of Skagen Designs. Therefore, you need to answer the following questions. If necessary, make your own conditions and remember to state the reasons for your answers.

1 What screening criteria should Skagen Designs use in connection with its choice of new markets for its watch collection?

2 Make a specific choice of new markets for Skagen Designs. Table 1 and Table 2 can be used to support your argument.

3 Which 'market entry mode' should Skagen Designs use on the chosen markets?

4 Skagen Designs has launched other product lines (e.g. sun glasses, branded items for the home) with varying success. What should be the guidelines for including other product lines in the Skagen Designs collection?

5 Which criteria should Skagen Designs use for its selection of future sponsor partners?

6 Skagen Designs is considering online sale of its watches. What problems and possibilities do you see for the company in this area? On this basis what are your conclusions?

Table 1  Volume of different watch markets, 2005

| | 2000 | 2001 | 2002 | 2003 | 2004 | 2005 | 2000–05 (%) |
|---|---|---|---|---|---|---|---|
| **Retail volume in thousands of units** | | | | | | | |
| Belgium | 624.98 | 515.02 | 714.37 | 739.44 | 778.06 | 819.53 | 31 |
| France | 5,035.20 | 4,913.47 | 4,987.27 | 4,837.80 | 4,827.73 | 4,825.53 | −4 |
| Germany | 7,501.72 | 7,452.94 | 8,217.55 | 10,284.34 | 10,918.50 | 9,859.88 | 31 |
| Italy | 5,712.08 | 5,482.23 | 5,366.33 | 5,874.31 | 6,525.52 | 6,893.24 | 20 |
| Netherlands | 5,613.00 | 5,850.00 | 5,931.00 | 6,073.00 | 6,200.00 | 6,414.00 | 14 |
| Spain | 12,299.70 | 12,018.98 | 11,810.19 | 11,533.47 | 11,308.69 | 10,989.01 | −11 |
| Sweden | 2,491.00 | 2,565.00 | 2,641.00 | 2,719.50 | 2,800.00 | 2,884.00 | 16 |
| United Kingdom | 17,800.00 | 17,900.00 | 18,100.00 | 18,400.00 | 16,000.00 | 15,500.00 | −13 |
| Hungary | 1,106.19 | 1,113.93 | 1,126.19 | 1,134.07 | 1,140.87 | 1,150.00 | 4 |
| USA | 63,954.47 | 55,441.04 | 50,370.68 | 48,500.85 | 51,593.56 | 53,037.50 | −17 |
| Mexico | 35,690.68 | 38,721.57 | 34,946.59 | 47,598.71 | 46,780.14 | 47,851.56 | 34 |
| China | 57,500.00 | 60,000.00 | 61,000.00 | 61,900.00 | 59,725.00 | 64,000.00 | 11 |
| India | 33,469.00 | 35,876.98 | 38,829.72 | 41,778.67 | 47,232.00 | 52,324.80 | 56 |
| Japan | 9,864.95 | 9,751.41 | 9,615.49 | 9,530.93 | 9,431.18 | 9,333.77 | −5 |
| Australia | 3,189.74 | 3,505.84 | 3,604.25 | 3,817.23 | 3,920.20 | 4,001.79 | 25 |
| South Africa | 23,117.73 | 21,081.80 | 26,000.23 | 15,925.30 | 18,117.89 | 16,348.31 | −29 |
| **Number of watches per 1000 people** | | | | | | | |
| Belgium | 61.04 | 50.18 | 69.29 | 71.41 | 74.86 | 78.62 | |
| France | 85.71 | 83.22 | 84.04 | 81.09 | 80.49 | 80.04 | |
| Germany | 91.30 | 90.60 | 99.68 | 124.59 | 132.13 | 119.21 | |
| Italy | 99.03 | 94.78 | 92.51 | 101.03 | 112.03 | 118.17 | |
| Netherlands | 353.82 | 365.92 | 368.26 | 375.06 | 380.97 | 392.24 | |
| Spain | 309.56 | 299.56 | 292.26 | 284.13 | 277.52 | 268.82 | |
| Sweden | 281.11 | 288.76 | 296.44 | 304.19 | 312.12 | 320.36 | |
| United Kingdom | 303.53 | 303.13 | 305.59 | 309.62 | 268.40 | 259.19 | |
| Hungary | 108.22 | 109.21 | 110.68 | 111.82 | 112.85 | 114.08 | |
| USA | 232.45 | 199.78 | 180.02 | 171.95 | 181.46 | 185.06 | |
| Mexico | 363.59 | 388.41 | 345.29 | 463.43 | 448.98 | 452.90 | |
| China | 45.69 | 47.31 | 47.79 | 48.15 | 46.11 | 49.07 | |
| India | 33.19 | 35.00 | 37.28 | 39.51 | 44.00 | 48.05 | |
| Japan | 77.72 | 76.61 | 75.45 | 74.70 | 73.83 | 73.00 | |
| Australia | 166.54 | 180.59 | 183.30 | 192.60 | 195.87 | 198.05 | |
| South Africa | 527.18 | 470.37 | 569.51 | 343.00 | 381.02 | 336.62 | |

Source: Adapted from Euromonitor and trade sources/national statistics.

Table 2  Value of different watch markets, 2005

|  | 2000 | 2001 | 2002 | 2003 | 2004 | 2005 | 2000–05 (%) |
|---|---|---|---|---|---|---|---|
| **(US$ million)** | | | | | | | |
| Belgium | 23.91 | 17.06 | 20.50 | 26.20 | 29.51 | 30.34 | 27 |
| France | 934.22 | 910.42 | 945.84 | 1,097.25 | 1,205.66 | 1,205.42 | 29 |
| Germany | 1,429.95 | 1,519.96 | 1,762.75 | 2,699.99 | 2,846.60 | 2,954.50 | 107 |
| Italy | 951.62 | 918.02 | 934.11 | 1,103.06 | 1,215.72 | 1,311.61 | 38 |
| Netherlands | 189.50 | 191.64 | 204.00 | 250.15 | 275.03 | 284.86 | 50 |
| Spain | 804.77 | 792.48 | 849.75 | 1,027.89 | 1,141.35 | 1,155.92 | 44 |
| Sweden | 214.69 | 198.02 | 218.48 | 273.54 | 312.97 | 318.41 | 48 |
| United Kingdom | 960.77 | 942.91 | 1,064.11 | 1,225.10 | 1,328.51 | 1,359.78 | 42 |
| Hungary | 19.56 | 19.50 | 21.98 | 25.40 | 28.33 | 29.09 | 49 |
| USA | 7,477.65 | 6,486.85 | 6,321.98 | 6,426.05 | 7,118.52 | 7,206.49 | −4 |
| Mexico | 200.44 | 246.59 | 274.57 | 303.69 | 353.17 | 434.30 | 117 |
| China | 405.27 | 500.66 | 518.67 | 544.28 | 604.10 | 655.09 | 62 |
| India | 191.37 | 232.18 | 288.58 | 416.40 | 675.55 | 975.02 | 410 |
| Japan | 4,560.11 | 4,109.99 | 4,077.30 | 4,493.29 | 4,916.32 | 4,901.23 | 8 |
| Australia | 171.92 | 168.72 | 181.51 | 226.99 | 264.75 | 281.81 | 64 |
| South Africa | 245.67 | 221.85 | 235.62 | 228.68 | 323.93 | 451.58 | 84 |
| | | | | | | | |
| **US$ per capita** | | | | | | | |
| Belgium | 2.34 | 1.66 | 1.99 | 2.53 | 2.84 | 2.91 | |
| France | 15.90 | 15.42 | 15.94 | 18.39 | 20.10 | 19.99 | |
| Germany | 17.40 | 18.48 | 21.38 | 32.71 | 34.45 | 35.72 | |
| Italy | 16.50 | 15.87 | 16.10 | 18.97 | 20.87 | 22.49 | |
| Netherlands | 11.95 | 11.99 | 12.67 | 15.45 | 16.90 | 17.42 | |
| Spain | 20.25 | 19.75 | 21.03 | 25.32 | 28.01 | 28.28 | |
| Sweden | 24.23 | 22.29 | 24.52 | 30.60 | 34.89 | 35.37 | |
| United Kingdom | 16.38 | 15.97 | 17.97 | 20.62 | 22.29 | 22.74 | |
| Hungary | 1.91 | 1.91 | 2.16 | 2.50 | 2.80 | 2.89 | |
| USA | 27.18 | 23.38 | 22.59 | 22.78 | 25.04 | 25.15 | |
| Mexico | 2.04 | 2.47 | 2.71 | 2.96 | 3.39 | 4.11 | |
| China | 0.32 | 0.39 | 0.41 | 0.42 | 0.47 | 0.50 | |
| India | 0.19 | 0.23 | 0.28 | 0.39 | 0.63 | 0.90 | |
| Japan | 35.93 | 32.29 | 32.00 | 35.22 | 38.49 | 38.33 | |
| Australia | 8.98 | 8.69 | 9.23 | 11.45 | 13.23 | 13.95 | |
| South Africa | 5.60 | 4.95 | 5.16 | 4.93 | 6.81 | 9.30 | |

Source: Adapted from Euromonitor and trade sources/national statistics.

# Part III

# MARKET ENTRY STRATEGIES

## Contents

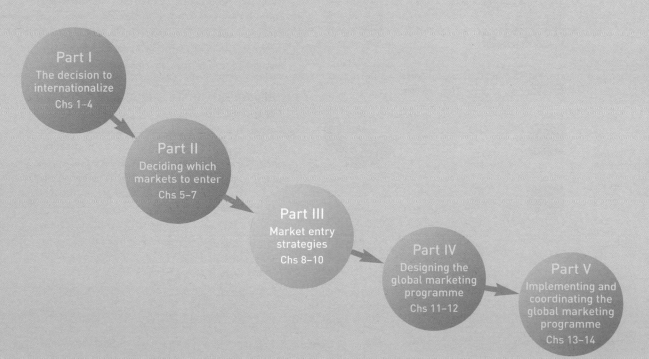

Part I
The decision to internationalize
Chs 1–4

Part II
Deciding which markets to enter
Chs 5–7

Part III
Market entry strategies
Chs 8–10

Part IV
Designing the global marketing programme
Chs 11–12

Part V
Implementing and coordinating the global marketing programme
Chs 13–14

# Tata:
# Which entry modes should be used for Tata Nano – the World's cheapest car

Indian conglomerate Tata Group (**www.tata.com**) employs nearly 300,000 people in 85 countries. The patriarchal company has a history dating back to 1868 and the height of the Victorian Raj. Today the Tata Group is India's largest conglomerate company, with revenues in 2006–07 equivalent to US$28 billion (equal to 3.2 per cent of India's GDP), and a market capitalization of US$73 billion at the end of 2007. The Tata Group comprises 98 companies in seven business sectors. About 66 per cent of the ownership of Tata Group is held by the charitable trust of Tata. Companies that form a major part of the group include Tata Steel, Tata Motors, Tata Consultancy Services, Tata Tea, Tata Power and the Taj Hotels. Tata Motors has a workforce of 22,000 employees working in its three plants and other regional offices across the country.

Tata Nano

Tata Motors' range of passenger cars in still not comprehensive by international standards. In commercial vehicles, Tata Motors commands an imposing 65 per cent market share in the Indian heavy commercial market (buses and trucks). The company is trying to modernize its range of commercial vehicles. Tata Motors has less than 20 per cent share of the Indian passenger car market and has recently been suffering a sales slump. In 2007, it produced 237,343 cars and more than 300,000 buses and trucks. Outside India Tata Motors is selling relatively few cars so its international marketing experience is weak.

Tata Motors has some distinct advantages in comparison to other MNC competitors. There is a definite cost advantage as labour costs are 8–9 per cent of sales as against 30–35 per cent of sales in developed economies. Tata Motors has extensive backward and forward linkages and it is strongly interwoven with machine tools and metals sectors from other parts of the Tata Group. In addition, there are favourable government polices and regulations to boost the auto industry, for example, incentives for R&D.

### Introduction of Tata Nano in January 2008

Measuring just over 10 feet in length and 5 feet in height and width, the Tata Nano is powered by a 623cc two-cylinder petrol engine at the rear giving just 33 horse-power. It has a top speed of about 90 km/hour and will do about 22 km on a litre of petrol. And the basic version is sparce: no air conditioning (other than the wind-down window variety), no power steering, no radio, no passenger-side mirror and only one windscreen wiper. But the makers claim it can carry four passengers plus the driver, with a bit of a squeeze.

Tata website

The Tata Motors factory in West Bengal will initially be able to turn out up to 250,000 cars a year but sales are predicted to top one million within two or three years.

The vehicle is called the 'one lakh' car because it will sell in India for one lakh – or 100,000 rupees – equivalent to about US$2,500 or three times the average national income per annum in India.

Tata Motors insists the car is 'environmentally friendly' and exceeds regulatory standards on safety and pollution. Indian standards for road safety and pollution emissions generally lag behind British and European levels, so the car might not be legal on European roads. It must comply with European standards, which could mean replacing glass, lights, tyres and seatbelts.

The Nano aims to bring the joys of motoring to millions of Indians, doing for the subcontinent what the Volkswagen Beetle did for Germany and the Mini for Britain. But the plan has horrified environmentalists who fear that the demand from India's aspirational and increasingly middle class population – now numbering 50 million in a country with a total 1.1 billion people – for more cars will add to pollution and global warming.

*Watch the video before answering the questions.*

## Questions

1  Which world regions (and specific countries) would you recommend for Tata Nano's international market expansion?

2  Which 'entry mode' would you suggest for the chosen markets (knowing that Tata Motors have taken over Land Rover and Jaguar – see the Video Case Study in the Introduction to Part II)?

Source: Video accompanying the text, www.tata.com

# Introduction to Part III

Once the firm has chosen target markets abroad (see Part II) the question arises as to the best way to enter those markets. In Part III we will consider the major market entry modes and criteria for selecting them. An international market entry mode is an institutional arrangement necessary for the entry of a company's products, technology and human capital into a foreign country/market.

To separate Part III from later chapters, let us take a look at Figure 1. The figure shows the classical distribution systems in a national consumer market.

**Figure 1  Examples of different market entry modes and the distribution decision**

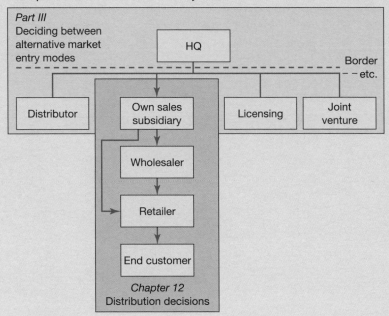

In this context the chosen market entry mode (here, own sales subsidiary) can be regarded as the first decision level in the vertical chain that will provide marketing and distribution to the next actors in the vertical chain. In Chapter 12 we will take a closer look at the choice between alternative distribution systems at the single national level.

Some firms have discovered that an ill-judged market entry selection in the initial stages of its internationalization can threaten its future market entry and expansion activities. Since it is common for firms to have their initial mode choice institutionalized over time, as new products are sold through the same established channels and new markets are entered using the same entry method, a problematic initial entry mode choice can survive through the institutionalization of this mode. The inertia in the shift process of entry modes delays the transition to a new entry mode. The reluctance of firms to change entry modes once they are in place, and the difficulty involved in so doing, makes the mode of entry decision a key strategic issue for firms operating in today's rapidly internationalizing marketplace (Hollensen, 1991).

For most SMEs the market entry represents a critical first step, but for established companies the problem is not how to enter new emerging markets, rather how to exploit opportunities more effectively within the context of their existing network of international operations.

There is, however, no ideal market entry strategy, and different market entry methods might be adopted by different firms entering the same market and/or by the same firm in different markets. Firms often combine modes to enter or develop a specific foreign market (Petersen and Welch, 2002). Such 'mode packages' may take the form of concerted use of several operation modes in an integrated, complementary way (Freeman *et al.*, 2006). In some cases a firm uses a combination of modes that compete with each other. Sometimes this occurs when a firm attempts a hostile takeover of an export market.

As shown in Figure 2, three broad groupings emerge when one looks at the assortment of entry modes available to the firm when entering international markets. There are different degrees of control, risk and flexibility associated with each of these different market entry modes. For example, the use of hierarchical modes (investment modes) gives the firm ownership and thereby high control, but committing heavy resources to foreign markets also represents a higher potential risk. At the same time heavy resource commitment creates exit barriers, which diminish the firm's ability to change the chosen entry mode in a quick and easy way. So the entry mode decision involves trade-offs, as the firm cannot have both high control and high flexibility.

Figure 2  **Classification of market entry modes**

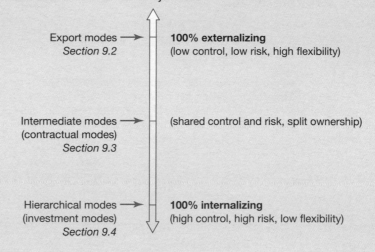

Export modes ⟶ **100% externalizing**
*Section 9.2* (low control, low risk, high flexibility)

Intermediate modes ⟶ (shared control and risk, split ownership)
(contractual modes)
*Section 9.3*

Hierarchical modes ⟶ **100% internalizing**
(investment modes) (high control, high risk, low flexibility)
*Section 9.4*

Figure 3 shows three examples representing the main types of market entry mode. By using hierarchical modes, transactions between independent actors are substituted by intra-firm transactions, and market prices are substituted by internal transfer prices.

Many factors should be considered in deciding on the appropriate market entry mode. These factors (criteria) vary with the market situation and the firm in question.

Chapter 8 will examine the different decision criteria and how they influence the choice among the three main groupings of market entry modes. Chapter 9 will discuss in more detail the three main types of entry mode. A special issue for SMEs is how their internationalization process is related to their much bigger customers and their sourcing and entry mode decisions. This will be discussed further in Chapter 10.

Figure 3  Examples of the different market entry modes in the consumer market

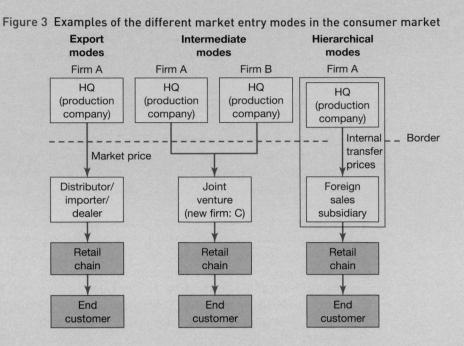

The simple version of the value chain (see Figure 1.7) will be used to structure the different entry modes in Chapter 9.

## References

Freeman, S., Edwards, R. and Schroder, B. (2006) 'How smaller Born-Globals Firms use Networks and Alliances to Overcome Constraints to Rapid Internationalization', *Journal of International Marketing*, Vol. 14, No. 3, pp. 33–63.

Hollensen, S. (1991) 'Shift of market servicing organization in international markets: a Danish case study', in Vestergaard, H. (ed.), *An Enlarged Europe in the Global Economy*, EIBA's 17th Annual Conference, Copenhagen.

Petersen, B. and Welch, L.S. (2002), 'Foreign operation mode combinations and internationalization', *Journal of Business Research*, 55, pp. 157–162.

# 8

# Some approaches to the choice of entry mode

## Contents

## Learning objectives

After studying this chapter you should be able to do the following:

- Identify and classify different market entry modes.
- Explore different approaches to the choice of entry mode.
- Explain how opportunistic behaviour affects the manufacturer/intermediary relationship.
- Identify the factors to consider when choosing a market entry strategy.

## 8.1 Introduction

**Entry modes**
An institutional arrangement necessary for the entry of a company's products and services into a new foreign market. The main types are: export, intermediate and hierarchical modes.

We have seen the main groupings of entry modes which are available to companies that wish to take advantage of foreign market opportunities. At this point we are concerned with the question: what kind of strategy should be used for the entry mode selection?

According to Root (1994) there are three different rules:

1 *Naive rule.* The decision maker uses the same entry mode for all foreign markets. This rule ignores the heterogeneity of the individual foreign markets.
2 *Pragmatic rule.* The decision maker uses a workable entry mode for each foreign market. In the early stages of exporting the firm typically starts doing business with a low-risk entry mode. Only if the particular initial mode is not feasible or profitable will the firm look for another workable entry mode. In this case not all potential alternatives are investigated, and the workable entry may not be the 'best' entry mode.
3 *Strategy rules.* This approach requires that all alternative entry modes are systematically compared and evaluated before any choice is made. An application of this decision rule would be to choose the entry mode that maximizes the profit

contribution over the strategic planning period subject to (a) the availability of company resources, (b) risk and (c) non-profit objectives.

Although many SMEs probably use the pragmatic or even the naive rule, this chapter is mainly inspired by an analytical approach, which is the main principle behind the strategy rule.

## 8.2  The transaction cost approach

The principles of transaction cost analysis have already been presented in Chapter 3 (section 3.3). This chapter will go into further details about 'friction' and opportunism.

The unit of analysis is the transaction rather than the firm. The basic idea behind this approach is that in the real world there is always some friction between the buyer and seller in connection with market transactions. This friction is mainly caused by opportunistic behaviour in the relation between a producer and an export intermediary.

In the case of an agent, the producer specifies sales-promoting tasks that the export intermediary is to solve in order to receive a reward in the shape of commission.

In the case of an importer, the export intermediary has a higher degree of freedom as the intermediary itself, to a certain extent, can fix sales prices and thus base its earnings on the profit between the producer's sales price (the importer's buying price) and the importer's sales price.

No matter who the export intermediary may be, there will be some recurrent elements that may result in conflicts and opportunistic actions:

- stock size of the export intermediary;
- extent of technical and commercial service that the export intermediary is to carry out for its customers;
- division of marketing costs (advertising, exhibition activities, etc.) between producer and export intermediary;
- fixing of prices: from producer to export intermediary, and from the export intermediary to its customers;
- fixing of commission to agents.

### Opportunistic behaviour from the export intermediary

In this connection the export intermediary's opportunistic behaviour may be reflected in two activities:

1 In most producer–export intermediary relations a split of the sales promoting costs has been fixed. Thus statements by the export intermediary of too high sales promotion activities (e.g. by manipulating invoices) may form the basis of a higher payment from producer to export intermediary.
2 The export intermediary may manipulate information on market size and competitor prices in order to obtain lower ex-works prices from the producer. Of course, this kind of opportunism can be avoided if the export intermediary is paid a commission of realized turnover (the agency case).

### Opportunistic behaviour from the producer

In this chapter we have so far presumed that the export intermediary is the one who has behaved opportunistically. The producer may, however, also behave in an opportunistic way, as the export intermediary must also use resources (time and money) on building up the market for the producer's product programme. This is especially the case if the producer wants to sell expensive and technically complicated products.

Thus the export intermediary carries a great part of the economic risk, and will always have the threat of the producer's change of entry mode hanging over its head. If the export intermediary does not live up to the producer's expectations it risks being replaced by another export intermediary, or the producer may change to its own export organization (sales subsidiary), as the increased transaction frequency (market size) can obviously bear the increased costs.

The last case may also be part of a deliberate strategy from the producer: namely, to tap the export intermediary for market knowledge and customer contacts in order to establish a sales organization itself.

### What can the export intermediary do to meet this situation?

Heide and John (1988) suggest that the agent should make a number of further 'offsetting' investments in order to counterbalance the relationship between the two parties. These investments create bonds that make it costly for the producer to leave the relationship: that is, the agent creates 'exit barriers' for the producer (the principal). Examples of such investments are as follows:

- Establish personal relations with the producer's key employees.
- Create an independent identity (image) in connection with selling the producer's products.
- Add further value to the product, such as a BDA (before–during–after) service, which creates bonds in the agent's customer relations.

If it is impossible to make such offsetting investments Heide and John (1988) suggest that the agent reduces its risk by representing more producers.

These are the conditions that the producer is up against, and when several of these factors appear at the same time the theory recommends that the company (the producer) internalizes rather than externalizes.

## 8.3 Factors influencing the choice of entry mode

A firm's choice of its entry mode for a given product/target country is the net result of several, often conflicting forces. The need to anticipate the strength and direction of these forces makes the entry mode decision a complex process with numerous trade-offs among alternative entry modes.

Generally speaking the choice of entry mode should be based on the expected contribution to profit. This may be easier said than done, particularly for those foreign markets where relevant data are lacking. Most of the selection criteria are qualitative in nature, and quantification is very difficult.

As shown in Figure 8.1, four groups of factors are believed to influence the entry mode decision:

1 internal factors;
2 external factors;
3 desired mode characteristics;
4 transaction-specific behaviour.

**Figure 8.1 Factors affecting the foreign market entry mode decision**

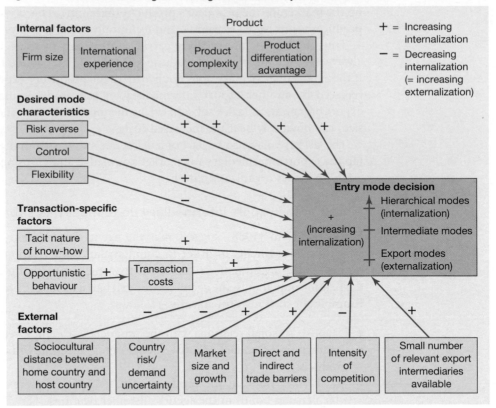

In what follows a proposition is formulated for each factor: how is each factor supposed to affect the choice of foreign entry mode? The direction of influence is also indicated both in the text and in Figure 8.1. Because of the complexity of the entry mode decision the propositions are made under the condition of other factors being equal. If the firm wants to quantify its decision making it may often be necessary to measure the different factors' effect on internalization/externalization on a scale, for example, from −3 to +3 with 0 indicating that the factor would favour intermediate modes.

## 1   Internal factors

### Firm size

Size is an indicator of the firm's resource availability; increasing resource availability provides the basis for increased international involvement over time. Although SMEs may desire a high level of control over international operations and wish to make heavy resource commitments to foreign markets, they are more likely to enter foreign markets using export modes because they do not have the resources necessary to achieve a high degree of control or to make these resource commitments. Export entry modes (market modes), with their lower resource commitment, may therefore be more suitable for SMEs. As the firm grows it will increasingly use the hierarchical model (Sanchez-Peinado *et al.*, 2007). The 'firm size' may e.g. be measured in terms of sales volume or number of employees before the time of foreign entry.

## International experience

Another firm-specific factor influencing mode choice is the international experience of managers and thus of the firm. Experience, which refers to the extent to which a firm has been involved in operating internationally, can be gained from operating either in a particular country or in the general international environment. International experience reduces the cost and uncertainty of serving a market, and in turn increases the probability of firms committing resources to foreign markets.

In developing their theory of internationalization Johanson and Vahlne (1977) assert that uncertainty in international markets is reduced through actual operations in foreign markets (experiential knowledge) rather than through the acquisition of objective knowledge. They suggest that it is direct experience with international markets that increases the likelihood of committing extra resources to foreign markets (Sanchez-Peinado *et al.*, 2007; Chen and Mujtaba, 2007).

## Product/service

The physical characteristics of the product or service, such as its value/weight ratio, perishability and composition, are important in determining where production is located. Products with high value/weight ratios, such as expensive watches, are typically used for direct exporting, especially where there are significant production economies of scale, or if management wishes to retain control over production. Conversely, in the soft drinks and beer industry, companies typically establish licensing agreements, or invest in local bottling or production facilities, because shipment costs, particularly to distant markets, are prohibitive.

The nature of the product affects channel selection because products vary so widely in their characteristics and use, and because the selling job may also vary markedly. For instance, the technical nature of a product (high complexity) may require service both before and after sale. In many foreign market areas marketing intermediaries may not be able to handle such work. Instead firms will use one of the hierarchical modes.

Blomstermo *et al.* (2006) distinguish between *hard* and *soft services*. Hard services are those where production and consumption can be decoupled. For example software services can be transferred into a CD, or some other tangible medium, which can be mass-produced, making standardization possible. With soft services, where production and consumption occur simultaneously, the customer acts as a co-producer, and decoupling is not viable. The soft-service provider must be present abroad from their first day of foreign operations. Blomstermo *et al.* (2006) conclude that there are significant differences between hard- and soft-service suppliers regarding choice of foreign market entry mode. Managers in soft services are much more likely to choose a high control entry mode (hierarchical mode) than hard services. It is important for soft-service suppliers to interact with their foreign customers, thus they should opt for a high degree of control, enabling them to monitor the coproduction of the services.

Products distinguished by physical variations, brand name, advertising and after-sales service (e.g. warranties, repair and replacement policies) that promote preference for one product over another may allow a firm to absorb the higher costs of being in a foreign market. Product differentiation advantages give firms a certain amount of impulse in raising prices to exceed costs by more than normal profits (quasi rent). They also allow firms to limit competition through the development of entry barriers, which are fundamental in the competitive strategy of the firm, as well as serving customer needs better and thereby strengthening the competitive position of the firm compared to other firms. Because these product differentiation advantages represent a 'natural monopoly' firms seek to protect their competitive advantages from dissemination through the use of hierarchical modes of entry.

## 2   External factors

### Sociocultural distance between home country and host country

Socioculturally similar countries are those that have similar business and industrial practices, a common or similar language, and comparable educational levels and cultural characteristics.

Sociocultural differences between a firm's home country and its host country can create internal uncertainty for the firm, which influences the mode of entry desired by that firm.

The greater the perceived distance between the home and host country in terms of culture, economic systems and business practices, the more likely it is that the firm will shy away from direct investment in favour of joint venture agreements. This is because the latter institutional modes enhance firms' flexibility to withdraw from the host market, if they should be unable to acclimatize themselves comfortably to the unfamiliar setting. To summarize, other things being equal, when the perceived distance between the home and host country is great, firms will favour entry modes that involve relatively low resource commitments and high flexibility. This is also supported by Sanchez-Peinado *et al.* (2007).

### Country risk/demand uncertainty

Foreign markets are usually perceived as riskier than the domestic market. The amount of risk the firm faces is a function not only of the market itself but also of its method of involvement there. In addition to its investment the firm risks inventories and receivables. When planning its method of entry the firm must do a risk analysis of both the market and its method of entry. Exchange rate risk is another variable. Moreover, risks are not only economic; there are also political risks.

When country risk is high a firm would do well to limit its exposure to such risk by restricting its resource commitments in that particular national domain. That is, other things being equal, when country risk is high, firms will favour entry modes that involve relatively low resource commitments (export modes).

Unpredictability in the political and economic environment of the host market increases the perceived risk and demand uncertainty experienced by the firm. In turn this disinclines firms to enter the market with entry modes requiring heavy resource commitments; on the other hand, flexibility is highly desired.

### Market size and growth

Country size and rate of market growth are key parameters in determining the mode of entry. The larger the country and the size of its market, and the higher the growth rate, the more likely management will be to commit resources to its development, and to consider establishing a wholly-owned sales subsidiary or to participate in a majority-owned joint venture. Retaining control over operations provides management with direct contact and allows it to plan and direct market development more effectively.

Small markets, on the other hand, especially if they are geographically isolated and cannot be serviced efficiently from a neighboring country, may not warrant significant attention or resources. Consequently they may be best supplied via exporting or a licensing agreement. While unlikely to stimulate market development or maximize market penetration this approach enables the firm to enter the market with minimal resource commitment, and frees resources for potentially more lucrative markets.

### Direct and indirect trade barriers

Tariffs or quotas on the import of foreign goods and components favour the establishment of local production or assembly operations (hierarchical modes).

Product or trade regulations and standards, as well as preferences for local suppliers, also have an impact on mode of entry and operation decisions. Preferences for local suppliers, or tendencies to 'buy national', often encourage a company to consider a joint venture or other contractual arrangements with a local company (intermediate modes). The local partner helps in developing local contacts, negotiating sales and establishing distribution channels, as well as in diffusing the foreign image.

Product and trade regulations and customs formalities similarly encourage modes involving local companies, which can provide information about and contacts in local markets, and can ease access. In some instances, where product regulations and standards necessitate significant adaptation and modification, the firm may establish local production, assembly or finishing facilities (hierarchical modes).

The net impact of both direct and indirect trade barriers is thus likely to be a shift towards performing various functions such as sourcing, production and developing marketing tactics in the local market.

### Intensity of competition

When the intensity of competition is high in a host market firms will do well to avoid internalization, as such markets tend to be less profitable and therefore do not justify heavy resource commitments. Hence, other things being equal, the greater the intensity of competition in the host market the more the firm will favour entry modes that involve low resource commitments (export modes).

### Small number of relevant intermediaries available

In such a case the market field is subject to the opportunistic behaviour of the few export intermediaries, and this will favour the use of hierarchical modes in order to reduce the scope for opportunistic behaviour.

## 3 Desired mode characteristics

### Risk averse

If the decision maker is risk averse they will prefer export modes (e.g. indirect and direct exporting) or licensing (an intermediate mode) because they typically entail low levels of financial and management resource commitment. A joint venture provides a way of sharing risk, financial exposure and the cost of establishing local distribution networks and hiring local personnel, although negotiating and managing joint ventures often absorb considerable management time and effort. However, modes of entry that entail minimal levels of resource commitment and hence minimal risks are unlikely to foster the development of international operations and may result in significant loss of opportunity.

### Control

Mode-of-entry decisions also need to consider the degree of control that management requires over operations in international markets. Control is often closely linked to the level of resource commitment. Modes of entry with minimal resource commitment, such as indirect exporting, provide little or no control over the conditions under which the product or service is marketed abroad. In the case of licensing and contract manufacturing management needs to ensure that production meets its quality standards. Joint ventures also limit the degree of management control over international operations and can be a source of considerable conflict where the goals and objectives of partners diverge. Wholly-owned subsidiaries (hierarchical mode) provide the most control, but also require a substantial commitment of resources (Sanchez-Peinado *et al.*, 2007).

### Flexibility

Management must also weigh up the flexibility associated with a given mode of entry. The hierarchical modes (involving substantial equity investment) are typically the most costly but the least flexible and most difficult to change in the short run. Intermediate modes (contractual agreements and joint ventures) limit the firm's ability to adapt or change strategy when market conditions are changing rapidly.

**Equity**
Some investment of a defined financial value.

## 4   Transaction-specific factors

The transaction cost analysis approach was discussed in Chapter 3 (section 3.3) and earlier in this chapter. We will therefore refer to only one of the factors here.

### Tacit nature of know-how

**Tacit**
Difficult to articulate and express in words – tacit knowledge has often to do with complex products and services, where functionality is very hard to express.

When the nature of the firm-specific know-how transferred is tacit it is by definition difficult to codify and patent, and therefore it is more difficult to transfer through contracts with external partners.

Sanchez-Peinado *et al.* (2007) use the following measures for 'tacit know-how':

* the difficulty in understanding the involved skills and knowledge;
* the difficulty in transferring skills and knowledge;
* the difficulty in valuing *a priori* the exact price of a product/service;
* the difficulty in copying skills and knowledge.

Tacit know-how makes the drafting of a contract (to transfer such complex know-how) very problematic. The difficulties and costs involved in transferring tacit know-how provide an incentive for firms to use hierarchical modes. Investment modes are better able to facilitate the intra-organizational transfer of tacit know-how. By using a hierarchical mode the firm can utilize human capital, drawing upon its organizational routines to structure the transfer problem. Hence, the greater the tacit component of firm-specific know-how, the more a firm will favour hierarchical modes.

## 8.4   Summary

Seen from the perspective of the manufacturer (international marketer), market entry modes can be classified into three groups:

* export modes: low control, low risk, high flexibility;
* intermediate modes (contractual modes): shared control and risk, split ownership;
* hierarchical modes (investment modes): high control, high risk, low flexibility.

**Intermediate modes**
Somewhere between using export modes (external partners) and hierarchical modes (internal modes).

It cannot be stated categorically which alternative is the best. There are many internal and external conditions which affect this choice and it should be emphasized that a manufacturer wanting to engage in global marketing may use more than one of these methods at the same time. There may be different product lines, each requiring a different entry mode.

# Ansell condoms: Is acquisition the right way for gaining market shares in the European condom market?

Ansell Limited is the new name of the company formerly known as Pacific Dunlop Limited.

The company's name was changed in April 2002 as a result of its strategic repositioning to concentrate on its core business, protective products and services in a broad health care context, and following the disposition of a series of other business units that did not fit within the strategy. Ansell Limited is an Australian publicly listed company with its corporate head office located in Richmond, Australia.

In 1905 Eric Ansell, a former Dunlop employee, took the machinery and set up his own company, The Ansell Rubber Company, in Melbourne, Australia, manufacturing toy balloons and condoms. The rest is history, as Ansell made strategic acquisitions and expansions and invested in the research and development necessary to bring a number of products to the world market.

Today Ansell Limited is a global leader in barrier protective products. With operations in the Americas, Europe and Asia, Ansell employs more than 12,000 people worldwide and holds leading positions in the natural latex and synthetic polymer glove and condom markets.

Ansell Condom brands are marketed globally through the Personal Healthcare division of Ansell Healthcare, with main office in Red Bank, NJ, USA. This 100-year-old company has fostered some innovations in latex condoms and gloves. It manufactures and markets a variety of condoms with flavours, colours, spermicide, studded and ribbed features. Ansell markets branded condoms worldwide each with its own unique marketing strategy that has been tailored to the particular country or region. A quick list of their brands around the globe includes: *LifeStyles (for the US market), Mates (for the UK market), KamaSutra (for the Indian market), Contempo, Manix, Primex, Pleasure* and *Chekmate*.

Additionally, the company participates in the public sector market where condoms are supplied through health and social welfare programmes and agencies, mainly in developing countries around the world. Ansell also participates in a broad range of studies and educational activities. Ansell continues to expand their market presence with the introduction of new products. Lifestyle Ultra Sensitive condoms

with spermicide, for instance, were developed to meet demand for a thinner condom that includes a spermicide to maximize protection from sexually transmitted diseases (STDs).

## World market for male condoms

Condoms offer protection against both unwanted pregnancies (contraception) and STDs (prophylaxis). The latter property is unique to condoms. Although there is considerable superficial variation in the types of condoms available (e.g. ribbed, thin and thick) there has been little fundamental change in the latex condom over the years.

Organizations that comprise the 'global public health sector' currently distribute 8 to 10 billion male condoms, mostly free of charge or at a nominal cost, to sexually active people throughout the world, mostly in developing nations. It is estimated that another 3 to 5 billion male condoms are distributed through commercial channels, mostly in developed countries such as the United States, Japan and European nations. The size of the world market for male condoms and how is made up as shown in Table 1.

In 2005, 35 per cent of condoms were purchased by the United Nations Population Fund. The World Health Organization (WHO) also is a buyer.

Besides the direct competitors, described in Table 2, it is essential to emphasize the role of the indirect competitors, which are those with a product of substitution. According to the Durex Sex Survey, the male condom is globally the most popular form of contraception (41 per cent of people use it). Among the 59 per cent non-condom users, 19 per cent of the population uses the pill, 8 per cent natural methods and the rest (75 per cent) use no contraception.

Table 1  World market for male condoms (2005)

|  | Per year (billions) |
|---|---|
| Global public health sector (UN, WHO and local governments) | 8 |
| Commercial channels (mainly in the US, Japan, and European nations) | 4 |
| World market | 12 |

Source: Adapted from different public sources.

In the distribution of male condoms in the commercial sector, there has been a movement from the pharmacies toward the retail chains (supermarkets). For example, in the early 1990s supermarkets accounted for around 25 per cent of the UK retail sales of condoms while pharmacies accounted for over a half. Today, the supermarkets account for around 40 per cent of retail sales, a share mostly drawn from the pharmacies, which have seen their share fall to 30 per cent. Therefore, national retailing chains (supermarkets, Boots and Superdrug) now account for at least 65 per cent of condom sales in the United Kingdom.

## Key competitors (manufacturers) in the world male condom market

### SSL International

In 1929 the London Rubber Company (LRC) registered the DUREX condom trademark, whose name was derived from **Du**rability, **Re**liability and **Ex**cellence. The next important steps as a global condom's provider were in 1951 with the introduction of the first fully-automated production process and two years later with the development of the first electronic testing machines.

In the UK 'home market', during the 1980s, Durex condoms began to be sold in public areas (e.g. supermarket, pubs), due to the AIDS fear. That decade showed a sharp development in marketing with the first Durex poster campaign in 1982, as well as the first condom advertising on television (1987).

Finally, during this past decade, Durex has followed a marketing policy aimed at increasing the awareness of the brand with: the installation of free-standing outdoor Durex vending machines (1992); the sponsorship of MTV's events (1995); the first Durex Sex Survey (1995); the launch of the first selection of

Table 2  Company shares on the world market for male condoms (2005)

| Company | Nationality | Major brands | Key strategies (MS = market share) | Market share (%) |
|---|---|---|---|---|
| Seton Scholl London (SSL) | UK | Durex, Durex Avanti, Durex Pleasure, Durex Fetherlite, Durex Extra Sensitive, etc. | A true global brand with strong positions in all main markets, except US (15% MS) and Japan (5% MS). In UK the Durex MS is 85% | 25 |
| Ansell Limited | Australia/US | LifeStyles, Mates, Contempo, Manix, Primex, KamaSutra, Pleasure and Chekmate | Semi-global company with relatively strong market positions in US, UK, Asian and AUS/NZ markets. Local/regional brands, e.g. LifeStyles for US and Mates for UK | 13 |
| Church & Dwight Co. | US | Trojan, Trojan Magnum, Trojan Pleasure, Trojan Enz | Market leader in US market, minor position in UK | 8 |
| Okamoto Industries | Japan | Beyond Seven, Skinless Skin | Home market oriented: 60% MS of the Japanese market, but with little exports, mainly to US | 10 |
| Others: Sagami Rubber Industries (JP), Fuji Latex Co (JP), DKT Indonesia (Indonesia), Mayer Laboratories (JP) and about 70 other manufacturers around the world |  |  | Domestic and region oriented companies with strong positions in local markets | 44 |

Source: Estimations based on different public sources.

coloured, flavoured and ribbed condom in the same pack (1996); and in 1997 the launch of the first non-latex protection called Avanti.

At the beginning of the twenty-first century, Durex launched **www.Durex.com** over 30 countries. These websites, featuring localized pages, in particular the use of local language, provide sexual information, allow people to question specialists, give details of Durex condoms and any sponsored events.

Durex is nowadays part of SSL International Plc, which was formed in 1999 from the merger of the Seton-Scholl Group and London International, the former owner of LRC. It is a worldwide company producing a range of branded products such as Scholl and Marigold gloves, sold to medical and consumer health care markets.

With a market share of approximately 25 per cent, Durex's position can be defined as the world market leader of the sector. Obviously, at different national levels, rankings can be slightly different with, for example, 80–85 per cent of market share in the United Kingdom, 55–60 per cent in Italy, 10–15 per cent in the United States and around 5 per cent in Japan.

Durex condoms are manufactured in 17 factories worldwide.

### Church & Dwight Company Inc

Armkel, LLC, Church & Dwight's 50/50 joint venture with the private equity group, Kelso & Company, acquired in 2001 the remainder of the Carter-Wallace consumer products businesses, including Trojan Condoms.

The Trojan brand accounts for the largest proportion of condom supplies in the United States (with around 60–70 per cent market share).

The company markets condoms under the Trojan brand name in Canada, Mexico and recently, in limited distribution, in the United Kingdom. In Canada, the Trojan brand has a leading market share. It entered the UK condom market in 2003, but at present has only a small share of this market. The company markets its condoms through distribution channels similar to those of its domestic condom business.

### Okamoto

Okamoto has been in existence since 1934. It holds a remarkable 60 per cent market share in Japan, where condoms are the preferred method of birth control.

In late 1988, Okamoto introduced its condoms to the US market, but without great success until now.

### Latest development – Possible acquisition of an European key condom player

Following financial problems at some European condom manufacturers with relatively strong local brands, Ansell is now considering acquiring one of these manufacturers.

Sources: www.ansell.com; www.durex.com; http://www.churchdwight.com/conprods/personal/; http://www.okamoto-condoms.com/; 'Polish Condom Producer Acquires Condomi', Polish News Bulletin, 21 January 2005; Office of Fair Trading (2006), Condoms – Review of the undertakings given by LRC Products Limited, OFT837, HMSO.

### Questions

1 What are the differences between the global strategies of Ansell and the other three competitors?

2 What are the pros and cons for Ansell acquiring a European competitor? In your opinion, is it a good idea?

For further exercises and cases, see this book's website at **www.pearsoned.co.uk/hollensen**

## Questions for discussion

1 Why is choosing the most appropriate market entry and development strategy one of the most difficult decisions for the international marketer?

2 Do you agree with the view that LSEs use a 'rational analytic' approach ('strategy rule') to the entry mode decision, while SMEs use a more pragmatic/opportunistic approach?

3 Use Figure 8.1 to identify the most important factors affecting the choice of foreign entry mode. Prioritize the factors.

# References

Blomstermo, A., Sharma, D.D. and Sallis, J. (2006) 'Choice of foreign market entry mode in service firms', *International Marketing Review*, 23(2), pp. 211–229.

Chen, L.C and Mujtaba, B. (2007) 'The Choice of Entry Mode Strategies and Decisions for International Market Expansion', *The Journal of American Academy of Business*, Vol. 10 No. 2, pp. 322–337.

Heide, J.B. and John, G. (1988) 'The role of dependence balancing in safeguarding transaction-specific assets in conventional channels', *Journal of Marketing*, 52, January, pp. 20–35.

Johanson, J. and Vahlne, J.E. (1977) 'The internationalization process of the firm – a model of knowledge', *Journal of International Business Studies*, 8(1), pp. 23–32.

Root, F.R. (1994) Entry Strategies for International Markets: Revised and expanded edition, The New Lexington Press, Lexington, MA.

Sanchez-Peinado, E.S., Pla-Barber, J. and Herbert, L. (2007) 'Strategic Variables that Influence Entry Mode Choice in Service Firms', *Journal of International Marketing*, Vol. 17, No. 1, pp. 67–91.

# 9

# Export, intermediate and hierarchical entry modes

## Contents

## Learning objectives

After studying this chapter you should be able to do the following:

- Distinguish between indirect, direct and cooperative export modes.
- Describe and understand the five main entry modes of indirect and direct exporting.
- Discuss how manufacturers can influence intermediaries to be effective marketing partners.
- Describe and understand the main intermediate entry modes.
- Explain the different stages in joint-venture formation.
- Explore the reasons for the 'divorce' of the two parents in a joint-venture constellation.
- Explore different ways of managing a joint venture/strategic alliance.
- Describe and understand the main hierarchical modes.
- Compare and contrast the two investment alternatives: acquisition versus greenfield.
- Explain the different determinants that influence the decision to withdraw investments from a foreign market.

## 9.1 Introduction

**Export modes** (section 9.2) are the most common modes for initial entry into international markets. With export entry modes a firm's products are manufactured in the domestic market or third countries and then transferred either directly or indirectly to the host market.

Exporting can be organized in a variety of ways, depending on characteristics of the host market and the number and types of available intermediaries.

**Intermediate modes** (section 9.3) are distinguished from export modes because they are primarily vehicles for the transfer of knowledge and skills, although they may also create export opportunities. They are distinguished from the hierarchical entry modes in that there is no full ownership (by the parent firm) involved, but ownership and control can be shared between the parent firm and a local partner. This is the case with the (equity) joint venture.

The final group of entry modes is the hierarchical modes (section 9.4), where the firm completely owns and controls the foreign entry mode. Here it is a question of where control in the firm lies. The degree of control that head office can exert on the subsidiary will depend on how many and which value chain functions can be transferred to the market. This again depends on the allocation of responsibility and competence between head office and the subsidiary, and how the firm wants to develop this at an international level.

**Hierarchical modes**
The firm owns and controls the foreign entry mode/organization.

## 9.2 Export modes

In establishing export channels a firm has to decide which functions will be the responsibility of external agents and which will be handled by the firm itself. While export channels may take many different forms, for the purposes of simplicity three major types may be identified: indirect, direct and cooperative export marketing groups.

1 *Indirect export*. This is when the manufacturing firm does not take direct care of exporting activities. Instead another domestic company, such as an export house or trading company, performs these activities, often without the manufacturing firm's involvement in the foreign sales of its products.

2 *Direct export*. This usually occurs when the producing firm takes care of exporting activities and is in direct contact with the first intermediary in the foreign target market. The firm is typically involved in handling documentation, physical delivery and pricing policies, with the product being sold to agents and distributors.

3 *Cooperative export*. This involves collaborative agreements with other firms (export marketing groups) concerning the performance of exporting functions.

In Figure 9.1 the different export modes are illustrated in a value chain.

### Partner mindshare

No matter which of the three export modes the manufacturer uses in a market, it is important to think about what level of 'mindshare', that the manufacturer 'occupies' in the mind of the export-partner. Partner mindshare is a measurement of the strength of a relationship in terms of trust, commitment and cooperation. There is a strong and proven correlation between mindshare levels and how willing an export intermediary is to place one company-brand in front of another, or how likely the intermediary is to defect. Mindshare also expresses itself very clearly in sales performance. Intermediaries who have high mindshare will, typically, sell more than those with low mindshare.

Mindshare can be broken down into three drivers (Gibbs, 2005)

1 commitment and trust;
2 collaboration;
3 mutuality of interest and common purpose.

**Partner mindshare**
The level of mindshare that the manufacturer's product occupies in the mind of the export partner (e.g. agent or distributor).

Figure 9.1 Export modes

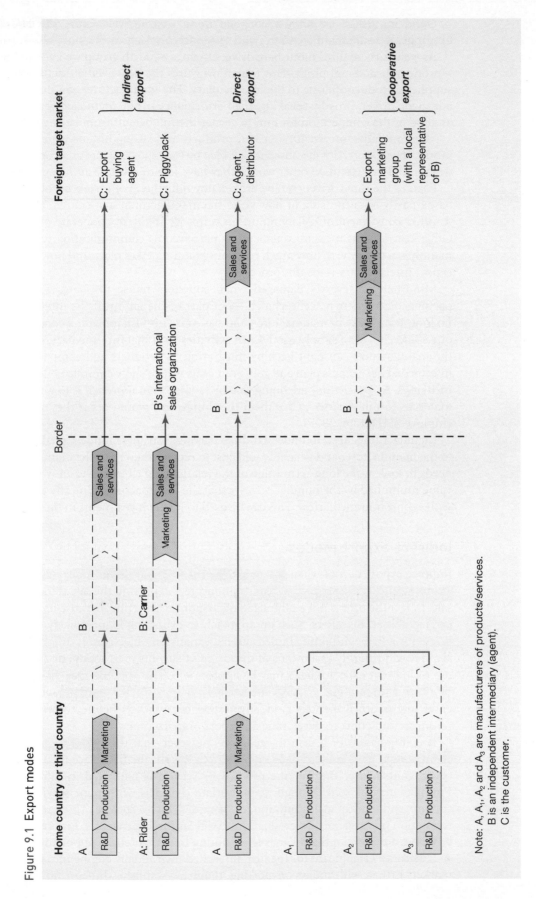

Note: A, A₁, A₂ and A₃ are manufacturers of products/services.
B is an independent intermediary (agent).
C is the customer.

Good mindshare is going to depend upon scoring well across the board. For example, there are manufacturers, who are good communicators, but are not trusted.

As well as these three mindshare drivers there is a fourth group we need to measure – product, brand and profit. This fourth measures the perceived attractiveness of the supplier's product offering to the intermediary. The manufacturer can think of this as a hygiene driver. Broadly speaking, the performance of the manufacturer needs to be as good as the competition for him to garner the full benefit from strong mindshare.

Many manufacturers with excellent products and strong brands which offer good profits, struggle precisely because they are seen by the export partner as arrogant, untrustworthy and unhelpful. In other words, they have low mindshare at the export partner.

Each of the three drivers can be broken down further. For instance, collaboration is based partly on a measure of how good the manufacturer is at cooperating on sales. Another constituent of collaboration measures its ability to cooperate on marketing. Other constituents measure whether it is perceived as communicating relevant information in a timely way, how much real joint planning takes place and how valuable the export intermediary finds this process.

Mindshare is severely damaged when suppliers refuse to share resources with partners. Partners may feel excluded – not part of the family. If the intermediary has no long-term stake in manufacturer, and has more mindshare with a competitor, then one could choose to simply wind down activities with that intermediary. Alternatively, the manufacturer can fight back by integrating its products and campaigns into the intermediary's business plan and going out of its way to show commitment to the intermediaries. At Oracle they are doing that by saying: 'Our approach is to give marketing materials to our partners. Give them the things they would get if they were internal employees' (Hotopf, 2005).

Manufacturers need to understand the partners' business models, goals, their value to the manufacturer and what it would cost to replace them. But the manufacturer also needs to look at the long-term value of the relationship (life time value = year-on-year value multiplied by the number of years that the manufacturer typically does business with export intermediaries). This can be used to justify investments in the relationship.

## Indirect export modes

Indirect export occurs when the exporting manufacturer uses independent organizations *located in the producer's country.* In indirect exporting the sale is like a domestic sale. In fact the firm is not really engaging in global marketing, because its products are carried abroad by others. Such an approach to exporting is most likely to be appropriate for a firm with limited international expansion objectives. If international sales are viewed primarily as a means of disposing of surplus production, or as a marginal, use of indirect export modes may be appropriate. This method may also be adopted by a firm with minimal resources to devote to international expansion, which wants to enter international markets gradually, testing out markets before committing major resources and effort to developing an export organization.

**Indirect export modes**
Manufacturer uses independent export organizations located in its own country (or third country).

It is important for a firm to recognize, however, that the use of agents or export management companies carries a number of risks. In the first place the firm has little or no control over the way the product or service is marketed in other countries. Products may be sold through inappropriate channels, with poor servicing or sales support and inadequate promotion, or be under- or overpriced. This can damage the reputation or image of the product or service in foreign markets. Limited effort may be devoted to developing the market, resulting in lost potential opportunities.

Particularly significant for the firm interested in gradually edging into international markets is that, with indirect exporting, the firm establishes little or no contact with markets abroad. Consequently the firm has limited information about foreign market potential, and obtains little input to develop a plan for international expansion. The firm will have no means to identify potential sales agents or distributors for its products.

While exporting has the advantage of the least cost and risk of any entry method, it allows the firm little control over how, when, where and by whom the products are sold. In some cases the domestic company may even be unaware that its products are being exported.

Moreover, an SME that is already experienced in traditional exporting may have resources that are too limited to open up a great number of export markets by itself. Thus, through indirect export modes the SME is able to utilize the resources of other experienced exporters and to expand its business to many countries.

There are five main entry modes of indirect exporting:

1  export buying agent;
2  broker;
3  export management company/export house;
4  trading company;
5  piggyback (shown as a special case of indirect exporting in Figure 9.1).

## 1  Export buying agent (export commission house)

Some firms or individuals do not realize that their products or services have potential export value until they are approached by a buyer from a foreign organization, which might make the initial approach, purchase the product at the factory gate and take on the task of exporting, marketing and distributing the product in one or more overseas markets.

**Export buying agent**
A representative of foreign buyers who is located in the exporter's home country. The agent offers services to the foreign buyers: such as identifying potential sellers and negotiating prices.

The export buying agent is a representative of foreign buyers who resides in the exporter's home country. As such, this type of agent is essentially the overseas customer's hired purchasing agent in the exporter's domestic market, operating on the basis of orders received from these buyers. Since the export buying agent acts in the interests of the buyer, it is the buyer that pays a commission. The exporting manufacturer is not directly involved in determining the terms of purchase; these are worked out between the export buying agent and the overseas buyer.

The export commission house essentially becomes a domestic buyer. It scans the market for the particular merchandise it has been requested to buy. It sends out specifications to manufacturers inviting bids. Other conditions being equal, the lowest bidder gets the order and there is no sentimentality, friendship or sales talk involved.

From the exporter's point of view, selling to export commission houses represents an easy way to export. Prompt payment is usually guaranteed in the exporter's home country, and the problems of physical movement of the goods are generally taken completely out of its hands. There is very little credit risk and the exporter has only to fulfil the order, according to specifications. A major problem is that the exporter has little direct control over the global marketing of products.

Small firms find that this is the easiest method of obtaining foreign sales but, being totally dependent on the purchaser, they are unlikely to be aware of a change in consumer behaviour and competitor activity, or of the purchasing firm's intention to terminate the arrangement. If a company is intent upon seeking longer-term liability for its export business it must adopt a more proactive approach, which will inevitably involve obtaining a greater understanding of the markets in which its products are sold.

## 2  Broker

Another type of agent based in the home country is the export/import broker. The chief function of a broker is to bring a buyer and a seller together. Thus the broker is a specialist in performing the contractual function, and does not actually handle the products sold or bought. For its services the broker is paid a commission (about 5 per cent) by the principal. The broker commonly specializes in particular products or classes of product. Being a commodity specialist there is a tendency for the broker to concentrate on just one or two products. Because the broker deals primarily in basic commodities, for many potential export marketers this type of agent does not represent a practical alternative channel of distribution. The distinguishing characteristic of export brokers is that they may act as the agent for either the seller or the buyer.

### 3  Export management company/export house

Export houses or export management companies (EMCs) are specialist companies set up to act as the 'export department' for a range of companies. As such the EMC conducts business in the name of each manufacturer it represents. All correspondence with buyers and contracts are negotiated in the name of the manufacturer, and all quotations and orders are subject to confirmation by the manufacturer.

By carrying a large range EMCs can spread their selling and administration costs over more products and companies, as well as reducing transport costs because of the economies involved in making large shipments of goods from a number of companies.

EMCs deal with the necessary documentation, and their knowledge of local purchasing practices and government regulations is particularly useful in markets that might prove difficult to penetrate. The use of EMCs, therefore, allows individual companies to gain far wider exposure of their products in foreign markets at much lower overall costs than they could achieve on their own, but there are a number of disadvantages, too:

- The export house may specialize by geographical area, product or customer type (retail, industrial or institutional), and this may not coincide with the supplier's objectives. So the selection of markets may be made on the basis of what is best for the EMC rather than for the manufacturer.
- As EMCs are paid by commission they might be tempted to concentrate upon products with immediate sales potential, rather than those that might require greater customer education and sustained marketing effort to achieve success in the longer term.
- EMCs may be tempted to carry too many product ranges and as a result the manufacturer's products may not be given the necessary attention from sales people.
- EMCs may carry competitive products that they may promote to the disadvantage of a particular firm.

Manufacturers should therefore take care in selecting a suitable EMC and be prepared to devote resources to managing the relationship and monitoring its performance.

As sales increase the manufacturer may feel that it could benefit from increased involvement in international markets, by exporting itself. However, the transition may not be very easy. First, the firm is likely to have become very dependent on the export house and, unless steps have been taken to build contacts with foreign customers and to build up the firm's knowledge of its markets, moving away from using an EMC could prove difficult. Second, the firm could find it difficult to withdraw from its contractual commitments to the export house. Third, the EMC may be able to substitute products from an alternative manufacturer and so use its existing customer contacts as a basis for competing against the original manufacturer.

### 4  Trading company

Trading companies are part of the historical legacy from colonial days and, although different in nature now, they are still important trading forces in Africa and the Far

East. Although international trading companies have been active throughout the world, it is in Japan that the trading company concept has been applied most effectively. There are thousands of trading companies in Japan involved in exporting and importing, and the largest firms (varying in number from nine to 17 depending upon source of estimate) are referred to as general trading companies or *Soge Shosha*. This group of companies, which includes C. Itoh, Mitsui & Company and Mitsubishi Shoji Kaisha, handle 50 per cent of Japan's exports and 67 per cent of its imports. While the smaller trading companies usually limit their activities to foreign trade, the larger general trading companies are also heavily involved in domestic distribution and other activities.

Trading companies play a central role in such diverse areas as shipping, warehousing, finance, technology transfer, planning resource development, construction and regional development (e.g. turnkey projects), insurance, consulting, real estate and deal making in general (including facilitating investment and joint ventures). In fact it is the range of financial services offered that is a major factor distinguishing general trading companies from others. These services include the guaranteeing of loans, the financing of both accounts receivable and payable, the issuing of promissory notes, major foreign exchange transactions, equity investment and even direct loans.

Another aspect of their operations is to manage counter-trade activities (barter), in which sales into one market are paid for by taking other products from that market in exchange. The essential role of the trading company is to find a buyer quickly for the products that have been taken in exchange. Sometimes this can be a very resource-demanding process.

Counter trade is still a very widespread trading form in Eastern Europe and developing countries because of their lack of 'hard' currency. One of the motivations for western firms to go into counter trade is the low-cost sources of production and raw materials for use in the firm's own production (Okoroafo, 1994).

## 5 Piggyback

**Piggyback**
An abbreviation of 'Pick-a-Back': i.e. choosing a back to ride on. It is about the rider's use of the carrier's international distribution organization.

In piggybacking the export-inexperienced SME, the 'rider', deals with a larger company (the 'carrier') which already operates in certain foreign markets and is willing to act on behalf of the rider that wishes to export to those markets. This enables the carrier to utilize fully its established export facilities (sales subsidiaries) and foreign distribution. The carrier is either paid by commission and so acts as an agent or, alternatively, buys the product outright and so acts as an independent distributor. Piggyback marketing is typically used for products from unrelated companies that are non-competitive (but related) and complementary (allied).

Sometimes the carrier will insist that the rider's products are somewhat similar to its own, in view of the need to deal with technical queries and after-sales service 'in the field'. Branding and promotional policies are variable in piggybacking. In some instances the carrier may buy the products, put its own brand on them, and market them as its own products (private labels). More commonly the carrier retains the brand name of the producer and the two work out promotional arrangements between them. The choice of branding and promotional strategy is a function of the importance of brand to the product and of the degree to which the brand is well established.

Piggybacking has the following advantages/disadvantages for the carrier and the rider.

### Carrier

**Advantages:** A firm that has a gap in its product line or excess capacity in its export operation has two options. One is to develop internally the products necessary to round out its line and fill up its exporting capacity. The other option is to acquire the necessary products outside by piggybacking (or acquisition). Piggybacking may be attractive because the firm can get the product quickly (someone already has it). It is also a low-cost way to get the product because the carrier firm does not have to invest in R&D, production facilities or market testing for the new product. It can just pick up the product from another firm. In this way the firm can broaden its product range without having to develop and manufacture extra products.

**Disadvantages:** Piggybacking can be extremely attractive for the carrier, but some concerns exist about quality control and warranty. Will the rider maintain the quality of the products sold by another firm? This depends in part on whose brand name is on the product. If the rider's name is on the product the quality incentive might be stronger. A second concern is continuity of supply. If the carrier develops a substantial market abroad, will the rider firm develop its production capacity, if necessary? Each of these items should be a subject in the agreement between the two parties. If the piggybacking arrangement works out well there is another potential advantage for the carrier. It might find that the rider is a good acquisition candidate or joint-venture partner for a stronger relationship.

### Rider

**Advantages:** Riders can export conveniently without having to establish their own distribution systems. They can observe carefully how the carrier handles the goods and hence learn from the carrier's experience – perhaps to the point of eventually being able to take over its own export transactions.

**Disadvantages:** For the smaller company this type of agreement means giving up control over the marketing of its products – something that many firms dislike doing, at least in the long run. Lack of commitment on the part of the carrier and the loss of lucrative sales opportunities in regions not covered by the carrier are further disadvantages.

In summary, piggyback marketing provides an easy, low-risk way for a company to begin export marketing operations. It is especially well suited to manufacturers that either are too small to go directly into exports or do not want to invest heavily in foreign marketing.

## Direct export modes

Direct exporting occurs when a manufacturer or exporter sells directly to an importer or buyer located in a foreign market area. In our discussion of indirect exporting we examined ways of reaching foreign markets without working very hard. Indeed, in the indirect approaches, foreign sales are handled in the same way as domestic sales: the producer does the global marketing only by proxy (that is, through the firm that carries its products overseas). However, both the global marketing know-how and the sales achieved by these indirect approaches are limited.

As exporters grow more confident they may decide to undertake their own exporting task. This will involve building up overseas contacts, undertaking marketing research, handling documentation and transportation, and designing marketing mix strategies. Direct export modes include export through foreign-based agents and distributors (independent intermediaries).

The terms 'distributor' and 'agent' are often used synonymously. This is unfortunate because there are distinct differences: distributors, unlike agents, take title to the goods, finance the inventories and bear the risk of their operations, whereas agents do not. Distributors are paid according to the difference between the buying and selling prices rather than by commission (agents). Distributors are often appointed when after-sales service is required, as they are more likely than agents to possess the necessary resources.

**Direct export modes**
Manufacturer sells directly to an importer, agent or distributor located in the foreign target market.

## Distributors

**Distributors (importers)**
Independent company that stocks the manufacturer's product. It will have substantial freedom to choose own customers and price. It profits from the difference between its selling price and its buying price from the manufacturer.

Exporting firms may work through distributors (importers), which are the exclusive representatives of the company and are generally the sole importers of the company's product in their markets. As independent merchants, distributors buy on their own accounts and have substantial freedom to choose their own customers and to set the conditions of sale. For each country exporters deal with one distributor, take one credit risk, and ship to one destination. In many cases distributors own and operate wholesale and retail establishments, warehouses and repair and service facilities. Once distributors have negotiated with their exporters on price, service, distribution and so on their efforts focus on working their own suboperations and dealers.

The distributor category is broad and includes more variations, but distributors usually seek exclusive rights for a specific sales territory and generally represent the manufacturer in all aspects of sales and servicing in that area. The exclusivity is in return for the substantial capital investment that may be required on the part of the distributor in handling and selling products.

## Agents

**Agents**
Independent company that sells on to customers on behalf of the manufacturer (exporter). Usually it will not see or stock the product. It profits from a commission (typically 5–10 per cent) paid by the manufacturer on a pre-agreed basis.

Agents may be exclusive, where the agent has exclusive rights to specified sales territories; semi-exclusive, where the agent handles the exporter's goods along with other non-competing goods from other companies; or non-exclusive, where the agent handles a variety of goods, including some that may compete with the exporter's products.

An agent represents an exporting company and sells to wholesalers and retailers in the importing country. The exporter ships the merchandise directly to the customers, and all arrangements on financing, credit, promotion, etc., are made between the exporter and the buyers. Exclusive agents are widely used for entering international markets. They cover rare geographic areas and have subagents assisting them. Agents and subagents share commissions (paid by the exporter) on a pre-agreed basis. Some agents furnish financial and market information, and a few also guarantee the payment of customers' accounts. The commissions that agents receive vary substantially, depending upon services performed, the market's size and importance, and competition among exporters and agents.

The advantages of both agents and distributors are that they are familiar with the local market, customs and conventions, have existing business contacts and employ foreign nationals. They have a direct incentive to sell through either commission or profit margin, but since their remuneration is tied to sales they may be reluctant to devote much time and effort towards developing a market for a new product. Also, the amount of market feedback may be limited as the agent or distributor may see itself as a purchasing agent for its customers rather than as a selling agent for the exporter. If the agent or distributor is performing well and develops the market it risks being replaced by a subsidiary of the principal. Therefore a long-term strategy is needed whereby it might be useful to include the agent in any new entry mode decision (e.g. advent of a subsidiary) to avoid the disincentive of being replaced.

## Choice of an intermediary

The selection of a suitable intermediary can be a problematic process. But the following sources may help a firm to find such an intermediary:

- asking potential customers to suggest a suitable agent;
- obtaining recommendations from institutions such as trade associations, chambers of commerce and government trade departments;
- using commercial agencies;

- poaching a competitor's agent;
- advertising in suitable trade papers.

In selecting a particular intermediary the exporter needs to examine each candidate firm's knowledge of the product and local markets, experience and expertise, required margins, credit ratings, customer care facilities and ability to promote the exporter's products in an effective and attractive manner.

Figure 9.2 shows the matchmaking of a manufacturer and its 'wish'-profile, and two potential intermediaries and their performance profiles in a particular market.

If Partners 1 and 2 were the only potential candidates for the manufacturer, Partner 2 would probably be chosen because of the better match of profiles between what the manufacturer wants on the market ('wish'-profile) and the performance profile of Partner 2.

The criteria listed in Figure 9.2 would probably not be the only criteria in a selection process. Some other specific desirable characteristics of an intermediary (to be included in the decision-making process) are listed below (Root, 1998):

- size of firm;
- physical facilities;
- willingness to carry inventories;
- knowledge/use of promotion;
- reputation with suppliers, customers and banks;

**Figure 9.2 An example of matchmaking between a manufacturer and two potential distribution partners**

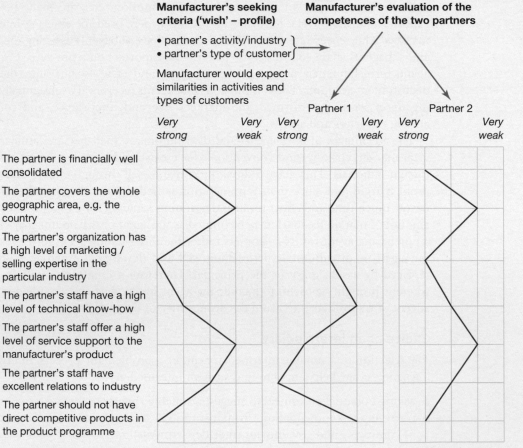

- record of sales performance;
- cost of operations;
- overall experience;
- knowledge of English or other relevant languages;
- knowledge of business methods in manufacturer's country.

When an intermediary is selected by the exporting manufacturer it is important that a contract is negotiated and developed between the parties. The foreign representative agreement is the fundamental basis of the relationship between the exporter and the intermediary. Therefore the contract should clearly cover all relevant aspects and define the conditions upon which the relationship rests. Rights and obligations should be mutually defined and the spirit of the agreement must be one of mutual interest.

For most exporters the three most important aspects of their agreement with foreign representatives are sole or exclusive rights, competitive lines and termination of the agreement. The issue of agreeing territories is becoming increasingly important, as in many markets distributors are becoming fewer in number, larger in size and sometimes more specialized in their activity. The trend to regionalization is leading distributors increasingly to extend their territories through organic growth, mergers and acquisitions, making it more difficult for firms to appoint different distributors in individual neighboring markets.

In general there are some principles that apply to the law of agency in all nations:

- An agent cannot take delivery of the principal's goods at an agreed price and resell them for a higher amount without the principal's knowledge and permission.
- Agents must maintain strict confidentiality regarding their principal's affairs and must pass on all relevant information.
- The principal is liable for damages to third parties for wrongs committed by an agent 'in the course of his or her authority' (e.g. if the agent fraudulently misrepresents the principal's firm).

During the contract period the support and motivation of intermediaries is important. Usually this means financial rewards for volume sold, but there can also be other means:

- significant local advertising and brand awareness development by the supplying firm;
- participation in local exhibitions and trade fairs, perhaps in cooperation with the local intermediary;
- regular field visits and telephone calls to the agent or distributor;
- regular meetings of agents and distributors arranged and paid for by the supplying company in the latter's country;
- competitions with cash prizes, free holidays, etc., for intermediaries with the highest sales;
- provision of technical training to intermediaries;
- suggestion schemes to gather feedback from agents and distributors;
- circulation of briefings about the supplying firm's current activities, changes in personnel, new product developments, marketing plans, etc.

### Evaluating international distribution partners

Even if the firm has been very careful in selecting intermediaries a need can arise to extricate oneself quickly from a relationship that appears to be going nowhere.

In the process of evaluating international distribution partners Figure 9.3 can be used:

Figure 9.3 International partner matrix

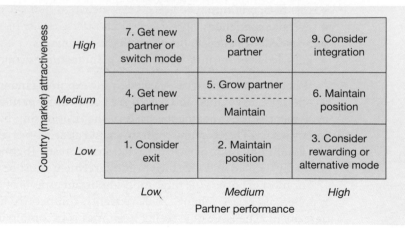

According to Figure 9.3 the two most important criteria for evaluating international distributor partners are:

1  the performance of the distributor partner;
2  the general attractiveness of the market where the partner operates.

Performance can be evaluated by using criteria like achieved turnover and market share, profits generated for the manufacturer, established network to potential customers, etc. The country (market) attractiveness can be evaluated by using criteria like the ones discussed in Chapter 7 (Table 7.2 and Figure 7.5), for example, market size and market growth.

If the partner performance is low combined with a low attractiveness of the country (Cell 1), then the company should consider an exit from that country, especially if the low attractiveness seems to be a long-term phenomenon.

If the partner performance is high, but the country attractiveness is low (Cell 3), then the company could consider better rewarding of the partner or a shift to another entry mode (e.g. a joint venture). In this way the company can prevent dissatisfaction on the partner's side by rewarding it with a bigger part of the created profit pool in such a difficult market (low attractiveness).

If the partner is doing badly on a very attractive market (Cell 7), the partner should be switched with another (and better) one or the company should switch to another mode (e.g. own sales subsidiary) with better control opportunity.

If the market is very attractive and the partner is doing a good job (Cell 9), then the company could consider forward integration, by turning the existing entry mode (distributor) into a subsidiary and promoting the distributor as the new CEO of the subsidiary, provided he or she has got the necessary competences for such a position and is endowed with sufficient management talent.

The other cells of Figure 9.3 are mainly concerned with maintaining current position or 'growing' the existing partner. This can be done by offering training in the company's product/service solutions at HQ, or visiting the partner in the local market in order to show it that you are committed to its selling efforts in that local market.

### Termination of contracts with distribution partners

Cancellation clauses in distribution partner agreements usually involve rights under local legislation and it is best that a contract is scrutinized by a local lawyer before signature, rather than after a relationship has ended and a compensation case is being fought in the courts.

Termination laws differ from country to country, but the European Union situation has been largely reconciled by a Directive regarding agents that has been effective in all EU member states since 1994. Under the Directive, an agent whose agreement is terminated is entitled to the following:

- full payment for any deal resulting from its work (even if concluded after the end of the agency);
- a lump sum of up to one year's past average commission;
- compensation (where appropriate) for damages to the agent's commercial reputation caused by unwarranted termination.

Outside western Europe some countries regard agents as basically employees of client organizations, while others see agents as self-contained and independent businesses. It is essential to ascertain the legal position of agency agreements in each country in which a firm is considering doing business. For example, laws in Saudi Arabia are extremely strong in protecting agents.

## Cooperative export modes/export marketing groups

Export marketing groups are frequently found among SMEs attempting to enter export markets for the first time. Many such firms do not achieve sufficient scale economies in manufacturing and marketing because of the size of the local market or the inad-equacy of the management and marketing resources available. These characteristics are typical of traditional, mature, highly fragmented industries such as furniture and clothing. Frequently the same characteristics are to be found among small, recently established high-technology firms.

Figure 9.1 shows an export marketing group with manufacturers $A_1$, $A_2$ and $A_3$, each having separate upstream functions but cooperating on the downstream functions through a common, foreign-based agent.

One of the most important motives for SMEs to join with others is the opportunity of effectively marketing a complementary product programme to larger buyers. The following example is from the furniture industry.

Manufacturers $A_1$, $A_2$ and $A_3$ have their core competences in the upstream functions of the following complementary product lines:

$A_1$ Living room furniture
$A_2$ Dining room furniture
$A_3$ Bedroom furniture.

Together they form a broader product concept that could be more attractive to a buyer in a furniture retail chain, especially if the total product concept targets a certain lifestyle of the end customers.

The cooperation between the manufacturers can be tight or loose. In a loose cooperation the separate firms in a group sell their own brands through the same agent, whereas a tight cooperation often results in the creation of a new export association. Such an association can act as the exporting arm of all member companies, presenting a united front to world markets and gaining significant economies of scale. Its major functions are the following:

- exporting in the name of the association;
- consolidating freight, negotiating rates and chartering ships;
- performing market research;
- appointing selling agents abroad;
- obtaining credit information and collecting debts;

- setting prices for export;
- allowing uniform contracts and terms of sale;
- allowing cooperative bids and sales negotiation.

Firms in an association can research foreign markets more effectively together, and obtain better representation in them. By establishing one organization to replace several sellers they may realize more stable prices, and selling costs can be reduced. Through consolidating shipments and avoiding duplicated effort firms realize transportation savings, and a group can achieve standardization of product grading and create a stronger brand name, just as the California fruit growers did with Sunkist products.

Considering all the advantages for an SME in joining an export marketing group, it is surprising that so few groups are actually running. One of the reasons for this could be that the firms have conflicting views as to what the group should do. In many SMEs there are strong feelings of independence inspired by their founders and entrepreneurs, which may be contrary, for example, to the common goal setting of export marketing groups. One of the major tasks of the export group is to balance the interests of the different stakeholders in the group.

## 9.3 Intermediate modes

Intermediate entry modes include a variety of arrangements, such as licensing, franchising, management contracts, turnkey contracts, joint ventures and technical know-how or coproduction arrangements. In Figure 9.4 the most relevant intermediate modes are shown in the usual value chain perspective.

Generally speaking, contractual arrangements take place when firms possessing some sort of competitive advantage are unable to exploit this advantage because of resource constraints, for instance, but are able to transfer the advantage to another party. The arrangements often entail long-term relationships between partner firms and are typically designed to transfer intermediate goods such as knowledge and/or skills between firms in different countries.

### Contract manufacturing

Several factors may encourage the firm to produce in foreign markets:

- Desirability of being close to foreign customers. Local production allows better interaction with local customer needs concerning product design, delivery and service.
- Foreign production costs (e.g. labour) are low.
- Transportation costs may render heavy or bulky products non-competitive.
- Tariffs or quotas can prevent entry of an exporter's products.
- In some countries there is government preference for national suppliers.

**Contract manufacturing**
Manufacturing is outsourced to an external partner, specialized in production and production technology.

Contract manufacturing enables the firm to have foreign sourcing (production) without making a final commitment. Management may lack resources or be unwilling to invest equity to establish and complete manufacturing and selling operations. Yet contract manufacturing keeps the way open for implementing a long-term foreign development policy when the time is right. These considerations are perhaps most important to the company with limited resources. Contract manufacturing enables the firm to develop and control R&D, marketing, distribution, sales and servicing of its

Figure 9.4 Intermediate modes

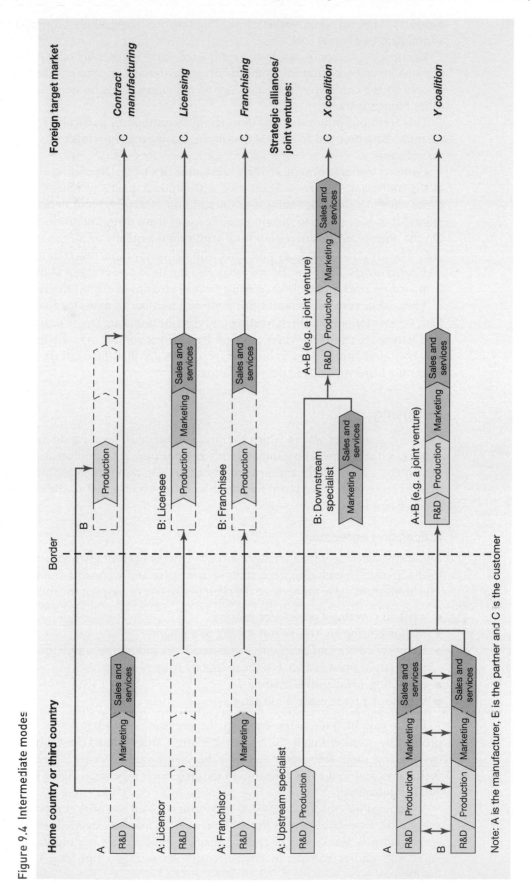

products in international markets, while handing over responsibility for production to a local firm (see Figure 9.4).

Payment by the contractor to the contracted party is generally on a per unit basis, and quality and specification requirements are extremely important. The product can be sold by the contractor in the country of manufacture, its home country, or some other foreign market.

This form of business organization is quite common in particular industries. For example, Benetton and IKEA rely heavily on a contractual network of small overseas manufacturers.

Contract manufacturing also offers substantial flexibility. Depending on the duration of the contract, if the firm is dissatisfied with product quality or reliability of delivery it can shift to another manufacturer. In addition, if management decides to exit the market it does not have to sustain possible losses from divesting production facilities. On the other hand, it is necessary to control product quality to meet company standards. The firm may encounter problems with delivery, product warranties or fulfilling additional orders. The manufacturer may also not be as cost efficient as the contracting firm, or may reach production capacity, or may attempt to exploit the agreement.

Thus, while contract manufacturing offers a number of advantages, especially to a firm whose strength lies in marketing and distribution, care needs to be exercised in negotiating the contract. Where the firm loses direct control over the manufacturing function mechanisms need to be developed to ensure that the contract manufacturer meets the firm's quality and delivery standards.

## Licensing

**Licensing**
The licensor gives a right to the licensee against payment, e.g. a right to manufacture a certain product based on a patent against some agreed royalty.

**Licensing** is another way in which the firm can establish local production in foreign markets without capital investment. It differs from contract manufacturing in that it is usually for a longer term and involves much greater responsibilities for the national firm, because more value chain functions have been transferred to the licensee by the licensor (see Figure 9.4).

### A licensing agreement

A licensing agreement is an arrangement wherein the licensor gives something of value to the licensee in exchange for certain performance and payments from the licensee. The licensor may give the licensee the right to use one or more of the following things:

- a patent covering a product or process;
- manufacturing know-how not subject to a patent;
- technical advice and assistance, occasionally including the supply of components, materials or plant essential to the manufacturing process;
- marketing advice and assistance;
- the use of a trade mark/trade name.

In the case of trade mark licensing the licensor should try not to undermine a product by overlicensing it. For example, Pierre Cardin diluted the value of his name by allowing some 800 products to use the name under license. Overlicensing can increase income in the short run, but in the long run it may mean killing the goose that laid the golden egg.

In some situations the licensor may continue to sell essential components or services to the licensee as part of the agreement. This may be extended so that the total agreement may also be one of cross-licensing, wherein there is a mutual exchange of knowledge and/or patents. In cross-licensing there might not be a cash payment involved.

Licensing can be considered a two-way street because a license also allows the original licensor to gain access to the licensee's technology and product. This is important because the licensee may be able to build on the information supplied by the licensor. Some licensors are very interested in grantbacks and will even lower the royalty rate in return for product improvements and potentially profitable new products. Where a product or service is involved the licensee is responsible for production and marketing in a defined market area. This responsibility is followed by all the profits and risks associated with the venture. In exchange the licensee pays the licensor royalties or fees, which are the licensor's main source of income from its licensing operations and that usually involve some combination of the following elements:

- A lump sum not related to output. This can include a sum paid at the beginning of an agreement for the initial transfer of special machinery, parts, blueprints, knowledge and so on.
- A minimum royalty – a guarantee that at least some annual income will be received by the licensor.
- A running royalty – normally expressed as a percentage of normal selling price or as a fixed sum of money for units of output.

Other methods of payment include conversions of royalties into equity, management and technical fees, and complex systems of counter purchase, typically found in licensing arrangements with eastern European countries.

If the foreign market carries high political risk then it would be wise for the licensor to seek high initial payments and perhaps compress the timescale of the agreement. Alternatively, if the market is relatively free of risk and the licensee is well placed to develop a strong market share, then payment terms will be somewhat relaxed and probably influenced by other licensors competing for the agreement.

The licensing agreement or contract should always be formalized in a written document. The details of the contract will probably be the subject of detailed negotiation and hard bargaining between the parties, and there can be no such thing as a standard contract.

In the following we see licensing from the viewpoint of a *licensor* (licensing out) and a *licensee* (licensing in). This section is written primarily from the licensor's viewpoint, but licensing in may be an important element in smaller firms' growth strategies, and therefore some consideration is given to this issue too.

## Licensing out

Generally there is a wide range of strategic reasons for using licensing. The most important motives for licensing out are as follows:

- The licensor firm will remain technologically superior in its product development. It wants to concentrate on its core competences (product development activities) and then outsource production and downstream activities to other firms.
- The licensor is too small to have financial, managerial or marketing expertise for overseas investment (own subsidiaries).
- The product is at the end of its product life cycle in the advanced countries because of obsolescent technology or model change. A stretching of the total product life cycle is possible through licensing agreements in less developed countries.
- Even if direct royalty income is not high margins on key components to the licensee (produced by the licensor) can be quite handsome.
- If government regulations restrict foreign direct investment or if political risks are high licensing may be the only realistic entry mode.
- There may be constraints on imports into the licensee country (tariff or non-tariff barriers).

**Figure 9.5  Life cycle benefits of licensing**

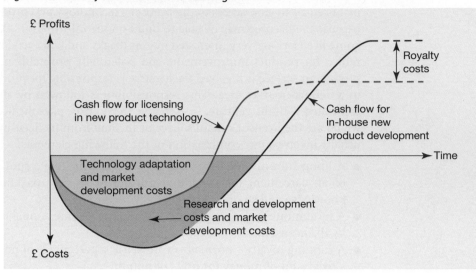

Sources: Lowe and Crawford, 1984; Bradley, 1995, p. 388.

## Licensing in

Empirical evidence shows (Young *et al.*, 1989, p. 143) that many licensing agreements actually stem from approaches by licensees. This would suggest that the licensee is at an immediate disadvantage in negotiations and general relations with the licensor. In other cases licensing in is used as the easy option, with the license being renewed regularly and the licensee becoming heavily dependent on the technology supplier (the licensor).

As Figure 9.5 shows, licensing in can improve the net cash flow position of the licensee, but mean lower profits in the longer term. Because technology licensing allows the firms to have products on the market sooner than otherwise, the firm benefits from an earlier positive cash flow. In addition, licensing means lower development costs. The immediate benefits of quick access to new technology, lower development costs and a relatively early cash flow are attractive benefits of licensing.

Table 9.3 (see the Summary) summarizes the advantages and disadvantages of licensing for the licensor.

## Franchising

**Franchising**
The franchisor gives a right to the franchisee against payment, e.g. a right to use a total business concept/system, including use of trade marks (brands), against some agreed royalty.

The term franchising is derived from the French, meaning 'to be free from servitude'. Franchise activity was almost unknown in Europe until the beginning of the 1970s. The concept was popularized in the United States, where over one-third of retail sales are derived from franchising, in comparison with about 11 per cent in Europe (Young *et al.*, 1989, p. 111).

A number of factors have contributed to the rapid growth rate of franchising. First, the general worldwide decline of traditional manufacturing industry and its replacement by service-sector activities has encouraged franchising. It is especially well suited to service and people-intensive economic activities, particularly where these require a large number of geographically dispersed outlets serving local markets. Second, the growth in popularity of self-employment is a contributory factor to the growth of franchising. Government policies in many countries have improved the whole climate for small businesses as a means of stimulating employment.

A good example of the value of franchising is the Swedish furniture manufacturer IKEA, which franchises its ideas throughout the western world, especially in Europe and North America. In terms of retail surface area and the number of visitors to retail stores, this company has experienced very significant growth through franchising in recent years.

Franchising is a marketing-oriented method of selling a business service, often to small independent investors who have working capital but little or no prior business experience. However, it is something of an umbrella term that is used to mean anything from the right to use a name to the total business concept. Thus there are two major types of franchising:

1 Product and trade name franchising. This is very similar to trade mark licensing. Typically it is a distribution system in which suppliers make contracts with dealers to buy or sell products or product lines. Dealers use the trade name, trade mark and product line. Examples of this type of franchising are soft drink bottlers such as Coca-Cola and Pepsi.
2 Business format 'package' franchising.

The latter is the focus of this section.

International business format franchising is a market entry mode that involves a relationship between the entrant (the franchisor) and a host country entity, in which the former transfers, under contract, a business package (or format) that it has developed and owns, to the latter. This host country entity can be either a franchisee or a master franchisee (subfranchisor). The franchise system can be set up as a direct or indirect system (see Figure 9.6).

In the direct system the franchisor is controlling and coordinating the activities of the franchisees directly. In the indirect system a master franchisee (subfranchisor) is appointed to establish and service its own subsystem of franchisees within its territory.

The advantages of the direct system include access to local resources and knowledge, more adaptation and the possibility of developing a successful master franchisee (subfranchisor) as a tool for selling the concept to other prospective franchisees within the

**Figure 9.6 Direct and indirect franchising models**

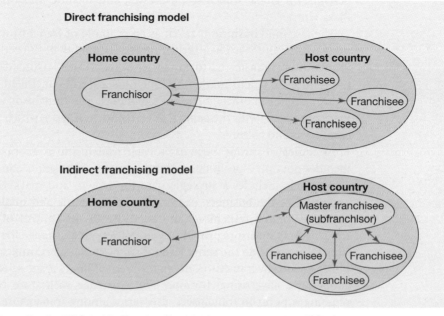

Source: Based on Welsh *et al.* (2006)

country. The indirect system has disadvantages, including monitoring issues because of loss of control. There have been examples of a master franchisee holding the sub-franchisees hostage to compete against the franchisor. Ultimately, the success of the indirect system will be determined by the capabilities and commitment of the master franchisee (Welsh *et al.*, 2006).

The package transferred by the franchisor contains most elements necessary for the local entity to establish a business and run it profitably in the host country in a pre-scribed manner, regulated and controlled by the franchisor. The package can contain the following items:

- trade marks/trade names;
- copyright;
- designs;
- patents;
- trade secrets;
- business know-how;
- geographic exclusivity;
- design of the store;
- market research for the area;
- location selection.

In addition to this package the franchisor also typically provides local entities with managerial assistance in setting up and running local operations. All locally-owned franchisees, can also receive subsupplies from the franchisor or the master franchisees (subfranchisor) and benefit from centrally coordinated advertising. In return for this business package the franchisor receives from the franchisee or subfranchisor an initial fee up front and/or continuing franchise fees, based typically on a percentage of annual turnover as a mark-up on goods supplied directly by the franchisor.

There is still a lively debate about the differences between licensing and franchising, but if we define franchising in the broader 'business format' (as here), we see the differences presented in Table 9.1.

Types of business format franchise include business and personal services, convenience stores, car repairs and fast food. US fast-food franchises are some of the best-known global franchise businesses, and include McDonald's, Burger King and Pizza Hut.

The fast-food business is taken as an example of franchising in the value chain approach of Figure 9.4. The production (e.g. assembly of burgers) and sales and service functions are transferred to the local outlets (e.g. McDonald's restaurants), whereas the central R&D and marketing functions are still controlled by the franchisor (e.g. McDonald's head office in the United States). The franchisor will develop the general marketing plan (with the general advertising messages), which will be adapted to local conditions and cultures.

As indicated earlier, business format franchising is an ongoing relationship that includes not only a product or a service but also a business concept. The business concept usually includes a strategic plan for growth and marketing, instruction on the operation of the business, elaboration of standards and quality control, continuing guidance for the franchisee, and some means of control of the franchisee by the franchisor. Franchisors provide a wide variety of assistance for franchisees, but not all franchisors provide the same level of support. Some examples of assistance and support provided by franchisors are in the areas of finance, site selection, lease negotiation, cooperative advertising, training and assistance with store opening. The extent of ongoing support to franchisees also varies among franchisors. Support areas include central data processing, central purchasing, field training, field operation evaluation,

**Table 9.1 How licensing and franchising differ**

| Licensing | Franchising |
|---|---|
| The term 'royalties' is normally used. | 'Management fees' is regarded as the appropriate term. |
| Products, or even a single product, are the common element. | Covers the total business, including know-how, intellectual rights, goodwill, trade marks and business contacts. (Franchising is all-encompassing, whereas licensing concerns just one part of the business.) |
| Licences are usually taken by well-established businesses. | Tends to be a start-up situation, certainly as regards the franchisee. |
| Terms of 16–20 years are common, particularly where they relate to technical know-how, copyright and trade marks. The terms are similar for patents. | The franchise agreement is normally for 5 years, sometimes extending to 11 years. Franchises are frequently renewable. |
| Licensees tend to be self-selecting. They are often established businesses and can demonstrate that they are in a strong position to operate the licence in question. A licensee can often pass its licence on to an associate or sometimes unconnected company with little or no reference back to the original licensor. | The franchisee is very definitely selected by the franchisor, and its eventual replacement is controlled by the franchisor. |
| Usually concerns specific existing products with very little benefit from ongoing research being passed on by the licensor to its licensee. | The franchisor is expected to pass on to its franchisees the benefits of its ongoing research programme as part of the agreement. |
| There is no goodwill attached to the licence as it is totally retained by the licensor. | Although the franchisor does retain the main goodwill, the franchisee picks up an element of localized goodwill. |
| Licensees enjoy a substantial measure of free negotiation. As bargaining tools they can use their trade muscle and their established position in the marketplace. | There is a standard fee structure and any variation within an individual franchise system would cause confusion and mayhem. |

Sources: Based on Perkins (1987), pp. 22, 157 and Young et al. (1989), p. 148.

newsletters, regional and national meetings, a hotline for advice and franchisor–franchisee advisory councils. The availability of these services is often a critical factor in the decision to purchase a franchise, and may be crucial to the long-term success of marginal locations or marginally prepared owners.

## International expansion of franchising

Franchisors, as other businesses, must consider the relevant success factors in making the decision to expand their franchising system globally. The objective is to search for an environment that promotes cooperation and reduces conflict. Given the long-term nature of a franchise agreement country stability is an important factor.

Where should the international expansion start? The franchising development often begins as a response to a perceived local opportunity, perhaps as an adaptation of a franchising concept already operating in another foreign market. In this case the market focus is clearly local to begin with. In addition, the local market provides a better environment for testing and developing the franchising format. Feedback from the marketplace and franchisees can be obtained more readily because of the ease of communication. Adjustments can be made more quickly because of the close local contact.

A whole variety of minor changes in the format may be necessary as a result of early experience in areas such as training, franchisee choice, site selection, organization of suppliers, promotion and outlet decoration. The early stages of franchise development represent a critical learning process for the franchisor, not just about how to adapt the total package to the market requirements but also regarding the nature of the franchising method itself. Ultimately, with a proven package and a better understanding of its operation, the franchisor is in a better position to attack foreign markets, and is more confident about doing so with a background of domestic success.

## Developing and managing franchisor-franchisee relationships

Franchising provides a unique organizational relationship in which the franchisor and franchisee each bring important qualities to the business. The franchise system combines the advantages of economy of scale offered by the franchisor with the local knowledge and entrepreneurial talents of the franchisee. Their joint contribution may result in success. The franchisor depends on franchisees for fast growth, an infusion of capital from the franchise purchase fee, and an income stream from the royalty fee paid by franchisees each year. Franchisors also benefit from franchisee goodwill in the community and, increasingly, from franchisee suggestions for innovation. The most important factor, however, is the franchisee's motivation to operate a successful independent business. The franchisee depends on the franchisor for the strength of the trade mark, technical advice, support services, marketing resources and national advertising that provides instant customer recognition.

There are two additional key success factors, which rest on the interdependence of the franchisee and the franchisor:

1 integrity of the whole business system;
2 capacity for renewal of the business system.

### 1 Integrity of the business system

The business will be a success in a viable market to the extent that the franchisor provides a well-developed, proven business concept to the franchisee and the franchisee is motivated to follow the system as it is designed, thereby preserving the integrity of the system. Standardization is the cornerstone of franchising: customers expect the same product or service at every location. Deviations from the franchising business concept by individual franchisees adversely affect the franchisor's reputation. The need for the integrity of the system requires that the franchisor exerts control over key operations at the franchise sites (Doherty and Alexander, 2006).

### 2 Capacity for renewal of the business system

Although most franchisors conduct research and development within the parent company, the highest proportion of innovation originates from franchisees in the field. Franchisees are most familiar with customers' preferences. They sense new trends and the opportunity to introduce a new product and service. The issue is getting the franchisee to share new ideas with the parent company. Not all franchisees are willing to share ideas with the franchisor, for a number of reasons. The most common is failure of the franchisor to keep in close contact with the franchisees; the most troubling is a lack of trust in the franchisor. The franchisor needs to promote a climate of trust and cooperation for mutual benefit.

**Handling possible conflicts:** Conflict is inherent in the franchisor–franchisee relationship, since all aspects that are good for the franchisor may not be good for the franchisee. One of the most basic conflicts is failure of either the franchisor or the franchisee to live up to the terms of the legal agreement.

Disagreement over objectives may be the result of poor communication on the part of the franchisor, or failure on the part of the franchisee to understand the franchisor's objectives. Both franchisor and franchisee agree on the need for profits in the business, not only to provide a living but to stay competitive. However, the two parties may disagree on the means of achieving profits. The number of conflicts between franchisors and franchisees may be reduced by establishing extensive monitoring of the franchisee (e.g. computer-based accounting, purchasing and inventory systems). Another way of reducing the number of conflicts is to view franchisors and franchisees as partners in running a business; both objectives and operating procedures have to be in harmony. This view requires a strong common culture with shared values established by the use of intensive communication between franchisor and franchisees in different countries (e.g. cross-national/regional meetings, cross-national/regional advisory councils).

## Joint ventures/strategic alliances

**Joint venture (JV)**
An equity partnership typically between two partners. It involves two 'parents' creating the 'child' (the 'joint venture' acting in the market).

A joint venture (JV) or a strategic alliance is a partnership between two or more parties. In international joint ventures these parties will be based in different countries, and this obviously complicates the management of such an arrangement.

A number of reasons are given for setting up joint ventures, including the following:

- Complementary technology or management skills provided by the partners can lead to new opportunities in existing sectors (e.g. multimedia, in which information processing, communications and the media are merging).
- Many firms find that partners in the host country can increase the speed of market entry.
- Many less developed countries, such as China and South Korea, try to restrict foreign ownership.
- Global operations in R&D and production are prohibitively expensive, but are necessary to achieve competitive advantage.

The formal difference between a joint venture and a strategic alliance is that a strategic alliance is typically a non-equity cooperation, meaning that the partners do not commit equity into or invest in the alliance. The joint venture can be either a contractual non-equity joint venture or an equity joint venture.

In a contractual joint venture no joint enterprise with a separate personality is formed. Two or more companies form a partnership to share the cost of investment, the risks and the long-term profits. An equity joint venture involves the creation of a new company in which foreign and local investors share ownership and control. Thus, according to these definitions, strategic alliances and non-equity joint ventures are more or less the same (Figure 9.7).

The question of whether to use an equity or a non-equity joint venture is a matter of how to formalize the cooperation. Much more interesting is to consider the roles that partners are supposed to play in the collaboration.

In Figure 9.8 two different types of coalition are shown in the value chain perspective. These are based on the possible collaboration pattern along the value chain. In Figure 9.8 we see two partners, A and B, each having its own value chain. Three different types of value chain partnership, appear:

1 *Upstream-based collaboration.* A and B collaborate on R&D and/or production.
2 *Downstream-based collaboration.* A and B collaborate on marketing, distribution, sales and/or service.
3 *Upstream/downstream-based collaboration.* A and B have different but complementary competences at each end of the value chain.

Figure 9.7  Joint ventures and strategic alliance

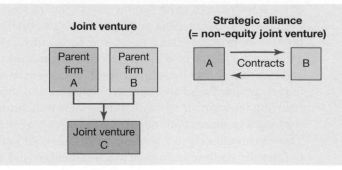

Figure 9.8  Collaboration possibilities for partners A and B in the value chain

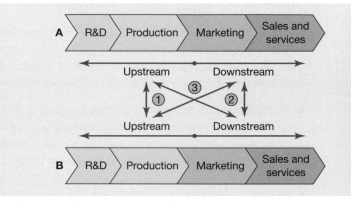

Source: Adapted from Lorange and Roos, 1995, p. 16.

**Y coalition**
Each partner in the alliance/JV contributes with complementary product lines or services. Each partner takes care of all value chain activities within their product line.

**X coalition**
The partners in the value chain divide the value chain activities between them, e.g. the manufacturer (exporter) specializes in up-stream activities, whereas the local partner takes care of the down-stream activities.

Types 1 and 2 represent the so-called Y coalition and type 3 represents the so-called X coalition (Porter and Fuller, 1986, pp. 336–337):

- *Y coalitions.* Partners share the actual performance of one or more value chain activities: for example, joint production of models or components enables the attainment of scale economies that can provide lower production costs per unit. Another example is a joint marketing agreement where complementary product lines of two firms are sold together through existing or new distribution channels, and thus broaden the market coverage of both firms.

- *X coalitions.* Partners divide the value chain activities between themselves: for example, one partner develops and manufactures a product while letting the other partner market it. Forming X coalitions involves identifying the value chain activities where the firm is well positioned and has its core competences. Take the case where A has its core competences in upstream functions but is weak in downstream functions. A wants to enter a foreign market but lacks local market knowledge and does not know how to get access to foreign distribution channels for its products. Therefore A seeks and finds a partner, B, which has its core competences in the downstream functions but is weak in the upstream functions. In this way A and B can form a coalition where B can help A with distribution and selling in a foreign market, and A can help B with R&D or production.

In summary, X coalitions imply that the partners have asymmetric competences in the value chain activities: where one is strong the other is weak and vice versa. In Y coalitions, on the other hand, partners tend to be more similar in the strengths and weaknesses of their value chain activities.

**Figure 9.9   Partner-to-partner relationships creating a joint venture**

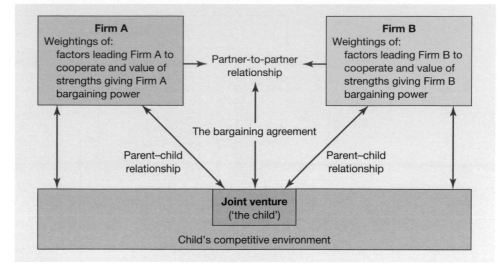

Source: K.R. Harrigan (2003) *Joint Ventures, Alliances and Corporate Strategy*, Pub. Beard Books.

## Managing the joint venture

In recent years we have seen an increasing number of cross-border joint ventures. An alliance or joint venture is able to sustain its structure and remain an efficient mechanism for interfirm transactions as long as partners' economic interests exceed potential costs in managing the alliance. But it is dangerous to ignore the fact that the average lifespan for alliances is only about seven years, and nearly 80 per cent of joint ventures ultimately end in a sale by one of the partners (Wahyuni *et al.*, 2007).

Harrigan's model (Figure 9.9) can be used as a framework for explaining this high 'divorce rate'. As Figure 9.10 shows, the final agreement is determined by the relative bargaining power of both prospective partners.

### Changes in bargaining power

According to Bleeke and Ernst (1994), the key to understanding the 'divorce' of the two parents is changes in their respective bargaining power. Let us assume that we have established a joint venture with the task of penetrating markets with a new product. In the initial stages of the relationship the product and technology provider generally has the most power. But unless those products and technologies are proprietary and unique power usually shifts to the party that controls distribution channels and thus customers.

The bargaining power is also strongly affected by the balance of learning and teaching. A company that is good at learning can access and internalize its partner's capabilities more easily, and is likely to become less dependent on its partner as the alliance evolves. Before entering a joint venture some companies see it as an intermediate stage before acquiring the other partner. By entering a joint venture the prospective buyer of the partner is in a better position to assess the true value of such intangible assets as brands, distribution networks, people and systems. This experience reduces the risk that the buyer will make an uninformed decision and buy an expensive 'lemon' (Nanda and Williamson, 1995).

### Other change stimuli and potential conflicts

**Diverging goals**: As the joint venture progresses the goals of the two partners may diverge. For example, unacceptable positions can develop in the local market when the

Figure 9.10  Model of joint-venture activity

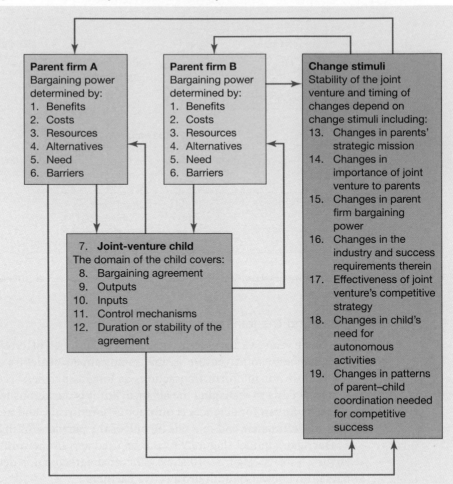

Source: K.R. Harrigan (2003) *Joint Ventures, Alliances and Corporate Strategy*, Pub. Beard Books.

self-interest of one partner conflicts with the interest of the joint venture as a whole, as in the pricing of a single-source input or raw material.

Diverging goals typically arise in the local market entry joint ventures. These joint ventures are created when multinational enterprises (MNEs) take local partners to enter foreign markets. The MNE is usually interested in maximizing its global income, that is, the net income of all of its affiliates, and this means that it is quite willing to run losses on some affiliates if this leads to higher net income for the whole network. The local partner, however, wants to maximize the profits of the specific affiliate of which it is part owner. Conflicts then flare up whenever the two goals are incompatible, as global income maximization is not necessarily compatible with the maximization of the separate profits of each affiliate. For example, conflicts may arise concerning the role given to the joint venture within the MNE network (and particularly on its allocation of export markets). This was the case when General Motors (GM) set up with Daewoo to manufacture subcompact cars for the Korean market and for export to the United States under GM's Pontiac badge. Since GM's Opel subsidiary was selling similar subcompacts in Europe, GM limited the joint venture's export to its US Pontiac subsidiary. Dissatisfied with Pontiac's performance, Daewoo decided to export to Eastern Europe in competition with Opel, a move that contributed to the dissolution of the joint venture (Hennert and Zeng, 2005).

**Double management:** A potential problem is the matter of control. By definition, a joint venture must deal with double management. If a partner has less than 50 per cent ownership that partner must in effect let the majority partner make decisions. If the board of directors has a 50–50 split it is difficult for the board to make a decision quickly if at all.

**Repatriation of profits:** Conflicts can also arise with regard to issues such as repatriation of profits, where the local partner desires to reinvest them in the joint venture while the other partner wishes to repatriate them or invest them in other operations.

**Mixing different cultures:** An organization's culture is the set of values, beliefs and conventions that influence the behaviour and goals of its employees. This is often quite different from the culture of the host country and the partner organization. Thus, developing a shared culture is central to the success of the alliance.

Partnering is inherently very people oriented. To the extent that the cultures of the partners are different, making the alliance work may prove difficult. Cultural differences often result in an 'us versus them' situation. Cultural norms should be consistent with management's vision of the alliance's ideal culture. This may entail creating norms as well as nurturing those that already exist. The key to developing a culture is to acknowledge its existence and to manage it carefully. Bringing two organizations together and letting nature take its course is a recipe for failure. Language differences are also an obvious hurdle for an international alliance.

Ignoring the local culture will almost certainly destroy the chances of it accepting the alliance's product or service. Careful study of the culture prior to embarking on the venture is vital. Again, extensive use of local managers is usually preferred.

### Shared equity

Shared equity may also involve an unequal sharing of the burden. Occasionally, international companies with 50–50 joint ventures believe that they are giving more than 50 per cent of the technology, management skill and other factors that contribute to the success of the operation, but are receiving only half the profits. Of course, the national partner contributes local knowledge and other intangibles that may be underestimated. Nevertheless, some international companies believe that the local partner gets too much of a 'free ride'.

**Developing trust in joint ventures:** Developing trust takes time. The first times that companies work together their chances of succeeding are very slight. But once they find ways to work together all sorts of opportunities appear. Working together on relatively small projects initially helps develop trust and determine compatibility while minimizing economic risk. Each partner has a chance to gauge the skills and contributions of the other, and further investment can then be considered. Of course, winning together in the marketplace on a project of any scale is a great way to build trust and overcome differences. It usually serves as a precursor to more ambitious joint efforts.

**Providing an exit strategy:** As indicated earlier, there is a significant probability that a newly formed joint venture will fail, even if the previously mentioned key principles are followed. The anticipated market may not develop, one of the partner's capabilities may have been overestimated, the corporate strategy of one of the partners may have changed, or the partners may simply be incompatible. Whatever the reason for the failure, the parties should prepare for such an outcome by addressing the issue in the partnership contract. The contract should provide for the liquidation or distribution of partnership assets, including any technology developed by the alliance.

### Other intermediate entry modes

*Management contracting* emphasizes the growing importance of services and management know-how. The typical case of management contracting is where one firm (contractor) supplies management know-how to another company that provides the capital and takes care of the operating value chain functions in the foreign country. Normally the contracts undertaken are concerned with management operating/ control systems and training local staff to take over when the contracts are completed. It is usually not the intention of the contractor to continue operating after the contract expires. Normally it is the philosophy to operate, transfer know-how to the local staff and then depart. This will usually give a strong competitive position to pick up other management contracts in the area.

Management contracts typically arise in situations where one company seeks the management know-how of another company with established experience in the field. The lack of management capability is most evident for developing countries. Normally the financial compensation to the contractor for the management services provided is a management fee, which may be fixed irrespective of the financial performance or may be a percentage of the profit (Luostarinen and Welch, 1990). The advantages and disadvantages of management contracting are listed in Table 9.3 (see the Summary).

## 9.4   Hierarchical modes

An organization that is not wholly-owned (i.e. 100 per cent) will here be viewed as an export mode or an intermediate mode. The following example, though, may suggest some of the problems involved in this sharp division: a majority-owned (e.g. 75 per cent) joint venture is, according to definition, an intermediate mode, but in practice a firm with 75 per cent will generally have nearly full control, similar to a hierarchical mode.

If a producer wants greater influence and control over local marketing than export modes can give it is natural to consider creating own companies in the foreign markets. However, this shift involves an investment, except in the case of the firm having its own sales force, which is considered an operating cost (see Figure 9.11).

As a firm goes through Figure 9.11 it chooses to decentralize more and more of its activities to the main foreign markets. In other words, it transfers the responsibility of performing the value chain functions to the local management in the different countries. While moving through Figure 9.11 the firm also goes from one internationalization stage to another (Perlmutter, 1969):

- *Ethnocentric orientation*, represented by the domestic-based sales representatives. This orientation represents an extension of the marketing methods used in the home country to foreign markets.
- *Polycentric orientation*, represented by country subsidiaries. This orientation is based on the assumption that markets/countries around the world are so different that the only way to succeed internationally is to manage each country as a separate market with its own subsidiary and adapted marketing mix.
- *Regiocentric orientation*, represented by a region of the world (section 9.5).
- *Geocentric orientation*, represented by the transnational organization. This orientation is based on the assumption that the markets around the world consist of similarities and differences and that it is possible to create a transnational strategy which takes advantage of the similarities between the markets by using synergy effects to leverage learning on a worldwide basis.

**Figure 9.11  Hierarchical modes in a value chain perspective**

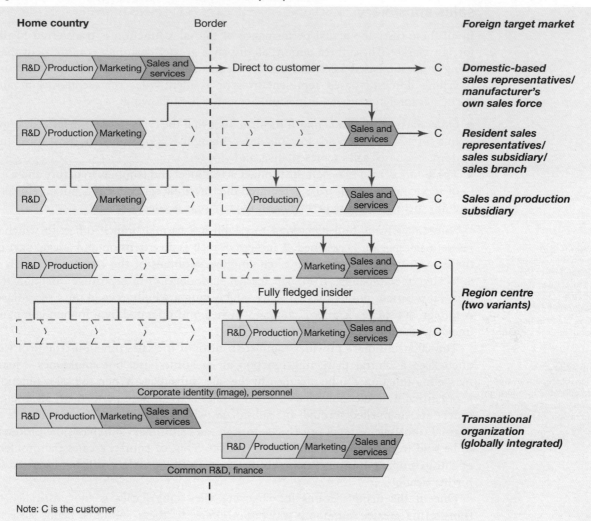

Note: C is the customer

The following description and discussion concerning hierarchical modes takes Figure 9.11 as its starting point.

## Domestic-based sales representatives

**Domestic-based sales representative**
The sales representative resides in the home country of the manufacturer and travels abroad to perform the sales function.

A domestic-based sales representative is one who resides in one country, often the home country of the employer, and travels abroad to perform the sales function. As the sales representative is a company employee better control of sales activities can be achieved than with independent intermediaries. Whereas a company has no control over the attention that an agent or distributor gives to its products or the amount of market feedback provided, it can insist that various activities be performed by its sales representatives.

The use of company employees also shows a commitment to the customer that the use of agents or distributors may lack. Consequently they are often used in industrial markets, where there are only a few large customers that require close contact with suppliers, and where the size of orders justifies the expense of foreign travel. This method of market entry is also found when selling to government buyers and retail chains, for similar reasons.

## Resident sales representatives/foreign sales branch/foreign sales subsidiary

In all these cases the actual performance of the sales function is transferred to the foreign market. These three options all display a greater customer commitment than using domestic-based sales representatives. In making the decision whether to use travelling domestic-based representatives or resident sales representatives in any particular foreign market a firm should consider the following:

- *Order making or order taking.* If the firm finds that the type of sales job it needs done in a foreign market tends towards order taking it will probably choose a travelling domestic-based sales representative, and vice versa.
- *The nature of the product.* If the product is technical and complex in nature and a lot of servicing/supply of parts is required the travelling salesperson is not an efficient entry method. A more permanent foreign base is needed.

**Foreign branch**
An extension of and a legal part of the manufacturer (often called a sales office). Taxation of profits takes place in the manufacturer's country.

**Subsidiary**
A local company owned and operated by a foreign company under the laws and taxation of the host country.

Sometimes firms find it relevant to establish a formal branch office, to which a resident salesperson is assigned. A foreign branch is an extension and a legal part of the firm. A foreign branch also often employs nationals of the country in which it is located as salespeople. If foreign market sales develop in a positive direction the firm (at a certain point) may consider establishing a wholly-owned sales subsidiary. A foreign subsidiary is a local company owned and operated by a foreign company under the laws of the host country.

The sales subsidiary provides complete control of the sales function. The firm will often keep a central marketing function at its home base, but sometimes a local marketing function can be included in the sales subsidiary. When the sales function is organized as a sales subsidiary (or when sales activities are performed) all foreign orders are channelled through the subsidiary, which then sells to foreign buyers at normal wholesale or retail prices. The foreign sales subsidiary purchases the products to be sold from the parent company at a price. This, of course, creates the problem of intra-company transfer pricing. In Chapter 16 this problem will be discussed in further detail.

One of the major reasons for choosing sales subsidiaries is the possibility of transferring greater autonomy and responsibility to these subunits, being close to the customer. However, another reason for establishing sales subsidiaries may be the tax advantage. This is particularly important for companies headquartered in high-tax countries. With proper planning companies can establish subsidiaries in countries having low business income taxes and gain an advantage by not paying taxes in their home country on the foreign-generated income until such income is actually repatriated to them. Of course the precise tax advantages that are possible with such subsidiaries depend upon the tax laws in the home country compared to the host country.

One of the most interesting things to determine for a firm doing business in a foreign market is when to switch from an agent to having its own sales subsidiary and own sales force (Ross *et al.*, 2005). Figure 9.12 shows the total sales and marketing costs associated with using two different entry modes:

- *Agent*: This curve is based on a contract where the agent gets a minimum annual commission independent of annual sales. The agent will get the same percentage in commission independent of how much they will generate in annual sales.
- *Sales subsidiary*: This curve is based on the assumption that the sales force in the sales subsidiary will have a fixed salary per annum (independent of the annual sales), but will be paid an extra bonus if they fulfil certain sales objectives.

Under these circumstances there will be a certain break-even point from where it is more advantageous (from a financial standpoint) to switch from an agent to own sales

Figure 9.12  Break-even shifting from agent to sales subsidiary

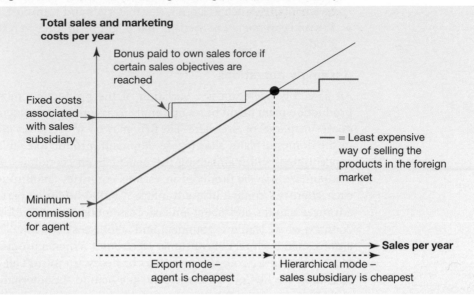

subsidiary. Of course other issues, like control, flexibility and level of investment must be considered before making such a switch.

## Sales and production subsidiary

Particularly in developing countries sales subsidiaries may be perceived as taking money out of the country and contributing nothing of value to the host country in which they are based. In those countries a sales subsidiary will generally not be in existence long before there are local demands for a manufacturing or production base.

Generally, if the company believes that its products have long-term market potential in a politically relatively stable country, then only full ownership of sales and production will provide the level of control necessary to meet fully the firm's strategic objectives. However, this entry mode requires great investment in terms of management time, commitment and money. There are considerable risks, too, as subsequent withdrawal from the market can be extremely costly – not simply in terms of financial outlay but also in terms of reputation in the international and domestic market, particularly with customers and staff.

Japanese companies have used this strategy to build a powerful presence in international markets over a long period of time. Their patience has been rewarded with high market shares and substantial profits, but this has not been achieved overnight. They have sometimes spent more than five years gaining an understanding of markets, customers and competition, as well as selecting locations for manufacturing, before making a significant move.

The main reasons for establishing some kind of local production are as follows:

- *To defend existing business.* Japanese car imports to Europe were subject to restrictions, and as their sales increased so they became more vulnerable. With the development of the single European market Nissan and Toyota set up operations in the United Kingdom.
- *To gain new business.* Local production demonstrates strong commitment and is the best way to persuade customers to change suppliers, particularly in the industrial markets where service and reliability are often the main factors when making purchasing decisions.

- *To save costs.* By locating production facilities overseas costs can be saved in a variety of areas such as labour, raw materials and transport.
- *To avoid government restrictions* that might be in force to restrict imports of certain goods.

## Assembly operations

An assembly operation is a variation of the production subsidiary. Here a foreign production plant might be set up simply to assemble components manufactured in the domestic market or elsewhere. The firm may try to retain key component manufacture in the domestic plant, allowing development, production skills and investment to be concentrated, and maintaining the benefit from economies of scale. Some parts or components may be produced in various countries (multisourcing) in order to gain each country's comparative advantage. Capital-intensive parts may be produced in advanced nations, and labour-intensive assemblies may be produced in a less developed country, where labour is abundant and labour costs are low. This strategy is common among manufacturers of consumer electronics. When a product becomes mature and faces intense price competition it may be necessary to shift all of the labour-intensive operations to LDCs. This is the principle behind the international product life cycle (IPLC).

## Region centres (regional headquarters)

Until now choice of foreign entry mode has mainly been discussed in relation to one particular country. If we suspend this condition, we consider option 3 in Figure 9.13, where 'geographically focused start-up' is an attempt to serve the specialized needs of a particular region of the world. It is very difficult for competitors to imitate a successful coordination of value chain activities in a particular region, as it involves tacit knowledge and is socially complex.

The world is increasingly being regionalized through the formation of such groupings as the European Union, the North American Free Trade Area (NAFTA) and the Association of South-East Asian Nations (ASEAN).

In Figure 9.11 two examples of region centres are shown. The first variant shows that the downstream functions have been transferred to the region. In the second variant even greater commitment is shown to the region because here all the value chain activities are moved to the region, whereby the firm has become a fully fledged insider

**Region centres**
The regional HQ ('lead country') will usually play the role of coordinating and stimulating sales in the whole region.

Figure 9.13  Types of international new venture

| | | Number of countries involved | |
| --- | --- | --- | --- |
| | | *Few* | *Many* |
| **Coordination of value chain activities** | *Few activities coordinated across countries (primarily logistics)* | New international market makers | |
| | | Export/import start-up ① | Multinational trader ② |
| | *Many activities coordinated across countries* | ③ Geographically focused start-up | ④ Global start-up |

Source: Reprinted by permission from Macmillan Publishers Ltd. *Journal of International Business Studies*, Vol. 25, No. 1, Toward a theory of international new ventures, by B.M. Oviatt and P. McDougall, copyright © 1994, Macmillan Publishers Ltd.

**Figure 9.14 The lead country concept**

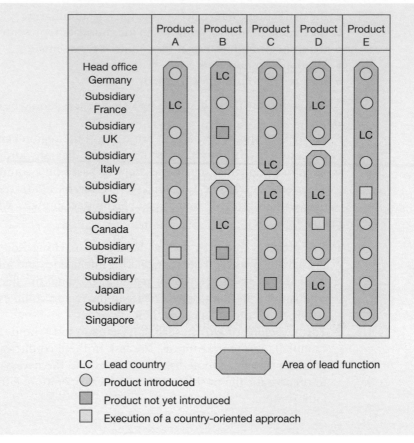

Source: Raffée and Kreutzer, 1989. Published with permission of Emerald Publishing Ltd.; www.emeraldinsight.com.

in the region. At this stage the firm has all the necessary functions in the region to compete effectively against local and regional competitors. At the same time, the firm can respond to regional customer needs. This situation is also illustrated in the lower part of Figure 9.13, where many activities are coordinated across countries.

Formation of region centres implies creation of a regional headquarters or appointment of a 'lead country', which will usually play the role of coordinator and stimulator with reference to a single homogeneous product group (see Figure 9.14).

The coordination role consists of ensuring three things:

1 Country and business strategies are mutually coherent.
2 One subsidiary does not harm another.
3 Adequate synergies are fully identified and exploited across business and countries.

The stimulator role consists of two functions:

1 facilitating the translation of 'global' products into local country strategies;
2 supporting local subsidiaries in their development (Lasserre, 1996).

Figure 9.14 (an example of a multinational company having its head office in Germany) shows that different countries/subsidiaries can have a leading function for different product groups. In the diagram there is a world market such that for products A and E only one country/subsidiary has the coordination function on a global basis (France and the United Kingdom, respectively). For product D there are three regions with a lead country in each region.

The choice of a lead country is influenced by several factors:

● the marketing competences of the foreign subsidiaries;
● the quality of human resources in the countries represented;
● the strategic importance of the countries represented;
● location of production;
● legal restrictions of host countries.

The country with the best 'leading' competences should be chosen for the job as lead country.

Figure 9.15 shows how a firm can develop the region centre concept in the Asia-Pacific area. The countries in the Asia-Pacific area are so different that you have to proceed in a sequential way. The example is based on a country-by-country approach together with developing a regional view (Lasserre, 1995).

One can distinguish four types of country in Asia, which are represented in Figure 9.15:

1 The *platform countries*, such as Singapore or Hong Kong, which can be used in the starting phase as bases for gathering intelligence and initiating first contacts that can later become the centre of regional coordination. For instance, medium-sized companies with no prior experience in the region could establish their presence by setting up a 'listening post' in these countries.

2 The *emerging countries*, such as Vietnam today and Myanmar (Burma) and Cambodia in the near future. The task in these countries is to establish an initial presence through a local distributor and build the necessary relationships in order to prepare for the establishment of a local operation, either directly or through a joint venture.

**Figure 9.15  Developing the region centre concept in Asia-Pacific**

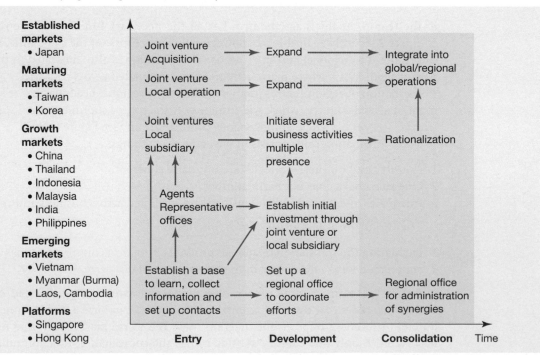

Source: Reprinted from *Long Range Planning*, Vol. 29, No. 1, Lasserre, P. (1996) 'Regional headquarters: the spearhead for Asian Pacific markets', p. 21, Copyright 1996, with permission from Elsevier.

3 The *growth countries*, such as China and the ASEAN countries, where it is becoming urgent to establish a significant presence in order to capitalize on the opportunities generated by rapid economic development.

4 The *maturing* and *established countries*, such as Korea and Taiwan, which already have significant economic infrastructures and well-established local and international competitors. In the entry phase the task here is to find a way to acquire, through massive investment, the necessary operational capability to catch competitors up.

The particular entry and pathway to development will depend upon the company's prior experience and capabilities, and on the particular strategic attractiveness of an industrial sector in a country.

Gradually the firm will start to look at all the countries in one region, because some activities, notably strategic, intelligence, financial, engineering, R&D, training and specialized services, can reap the benefits of economies of scale only by servicing the whole region.

## Transnational organization

In this final stage of internationalization companies attempt to coordinate and integrate operations across national boundaries so as to achieve potential synergies on a global scale. Management views the world as a series of interrelated markets. At this stage the employees tend to identify more strongly with their company than with the country in which they operate.

Common R&D and frequent geographical exchange of human resources across borders are among the characteristics of a transnational organization. Its overall goal will be to achieve global competitiveness through recognizing cross-border market similarities and differences, and linking the capabilities of the organization across national boundaries. One of the relatively few international companies that have reached this stage is Unilever – see also section 7.5.

In summary, managing a transnational organization requires the sensitivity to understand the following:

- when a global brand makes sense or when local requirements should take precedence;
- when to transfer innovation and expertise from one market to another;
- when a local idea has global potential;
- when to bring international teams together fast to focus on key opportunities.

**Transnational organization**
Integration and coordination of operations (R&D, production, marketing, and sales and services) across national boundaries in order to achieve synergies on a global scale.

## Establishing wholly-owned subsidiaries – acquisition or greenfield

All the hierarchical modes presented in this chapter (except domestic-based sales representatives) involve investment in foreign-based facilities. In deciding to establish wholly-owned operations in a country a firm can either acquire an existing company or build its own operations from scratch (greenfield investment).

### Acquisition

Acquisition enables rapid entry and often provides access to distribution channels, an existing customer base and, in some cases, established brand names or corporate reputations. In some cases, too, existing management remains, providing a bridge to entry into the market and allowing the firm to acquire experience in dealing with the local market environment. This may be particularly advantageous for a firm with limited international management expertise, or little familiarity with the local market.

In saturated markets the industry is highly competitive or there are substantial entry barriers, and therefore there is little room for a new entrant. In these circumstances acquisitions may be the only feasible way of establishing a base in the host country.

Acquisitions take many forms. According to Root (1987) acquisition may be horizontal (the product lines and markets of the acquired and acquiring firms are similar), vertical (the acquired firm becomes supplier or customer of the acquiring firm), concentric (the acquired firm has the same market but different technology, or the same technology but different markets) or conglomerate (the acquired firm is in a different industry from that of the acquiring firm). No matter what form the acquisition takes, coordination and styles of management between the foreign investor and the local management team may cause problems.

### Greenfield investment

The difficulties encountered with acquisitions may lead firms to prefer to establish operations from the ground up, especially where production logistics is a key industry success factor, and where no appropriate acquisition targets are available or they are too costly.

The ability to integrate operations across countries, and to determine the direction of future international expansion, is often a key motivation to establish wholly-owned operations, even though it takes longer to build plants than to acquire them. Further motives for green field investment can also include incentives offered by the host country.

Furthermore, if the firm builds a new plant, it can not only incorporate the latest technology and equipment, but also avoid the problems of trying to change the traditional practices of an established concern. A new facility means a fresh start and an opportunity for the international company to shape the local firm into its own image and requirements.

### Location/Relocation of HQ

The starting point is to consider the traditional checklist of HQ site selection criteria (Baaij *et al.* 2005):

- corporate tax advantages;
- investment incentives;
- investment climate;
- company law (internal restriction – the owners' wishes have to be followed);
- operational costs;
- quality, availability and costs of the workforce;
- quality of living (major hotels and restaurants, proximity of quality housing, cultural life and recreation, quality of schools, cultural diversity, safety, crime and health factors, personal taxes, cost of living, etc.);
- level of infrastructure (in particular transportation, communication and IT)
- level of high-level business services (e.g. accounting, legal and management consulting);
- sufficient representative office space;
- the presence of other major corporations.

The main benefit of using this checklist is not to find suitable sites, but to eliminate unsuitable ones. Once these factors have been assessed, more strategic criteria for the right HQ location can be considered.

There are three strategic motives that can affect the HQ location decision:

1 mergers and acquisitions;
2 internationalization of leadership and ownership;
3 strategic renewal.

## 1 Mergers and acquisitions

When companies of equal size merge, they need to find a neutral location for the head-quarters of the merged corporation. In 1987, ASEA from Västerås in Sweden and BBC Brown Boveri of Baden, Switzerland merged to create ABB Asea Brown Boveri. The new headquarters were not situated in either original location, but in Zurich.

## 2 Internationalization of leadership and ownership

In the case of acquisitions, the obvious solution is the most effective – the new headquarters is that of the acquirer, and the acquired corporation relocates (e.g. DaimlerChrysler). The second motive – internationalization of leadership and ownership – makes corporations less sensitive to national sentiments or ties to a specific country. Foreign board executives and shareholders will be less attached to the traditional home country, and less likely to resist a cross-border relocation of the headquarters.

## 3 Strategic renewal

The final reason for relocating headquarters is strategic renewal. This was a key reason for Philips Electronics' relocation to Amsterdam after 106 years of emotional ties to Eindhoven, the town where Philips was founded. Relocation can be a mechanism of change as it symbolises a fresh start and a break with the past.

# Foreign divestment: withdrawing from a foreign market

While a vast theoretical and empirical literature has examined the determinants of entering into foreign direct investments, considerably less attention has been given to the decision to exit from a foreign market.

Most of the studies undertaken show a considerable 'loss' of foreign subsidiaries over time:

● Between 1967 and 1975 the 180 largest US-based multinationals added some 4,700 subsidiaries to their networks, but more than 2,400 affiliates were divested during the same period (Boddewyn, 1979).
● Out of 225 FDIs undertaken by large Dutch multinationals in the period 1966–88, only just over half were still in existence in 1988 (Barkema et al., 1996).

Closing down a foreign subsidiary or selling it off to another firm is a strategic decision, and the consequence may be a change of foreign entry mode (e.g. from a local sales and production subsidiary to an export mode or a joint venture), or a complete withdrawal from a host country.

The most obvious incentive to exit is profits that are too low, which in turn may be due to high costs, permanent decreases in local market demand or the entry into the industry of more efficient competitors. Besides being voluntary, the divestment may also be a result of expropriation or nationalization in the foreign country.

In order to investigate further the question of why foreign divestments take place it is necessary to look at the specific factors that may influence incentives and barriers to exit, and thereby the probability of exiting from a foreign subsidiary. Benito (1996) classifies the specific factors into four main groups (Figure 9.16).

Figure 9.16  Divestment of foreign operation: a framework

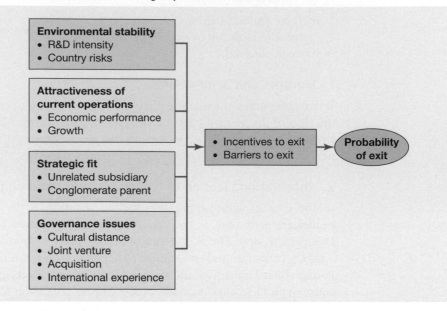

Source: Benito, 1997, pp. 309–34.

## Environmental stability

This is a question of the predictability of the environment – competitively and politically – in which the foreign subsidiary operates:

- *R&D intensity*. Perceived barriers to exit are likely to increase due to large market-specific investments made in R&D and the marketing of the products.
- *Country risks*. These risks are typically outside the firm's scope of control. Political risks may often lead to forced divestment, with the result that expropriation takes place.

## Attractiveness of current operations

- *Economic performance*. Unsatisfactory economic performance (i.e. inability to produce a net contribution to overall profits) is the most obvious reason why particular subsidiaries are sold off or shut down. On the other hand, if the subsidiary is a good economic performer, the owners may see an opportunity to obtain a good price for the unit while it is performing well.
- *Growth*. Economic growth in the host country would normally make FDI even more attractive, thereby increasing the barriers to exit from such a country. However, the attractiveness of the location would make such operations more likely targets for takeovers by other investors.

## Strategic fit

Unrelated expansion (i.e. diversification) increases the governance cost of the business, and economies of scale and scope are also rarely achieved by unrelated subsidiaries. Hence these factors increase the incentives to exit.

The same arguments apply to a conglomerate parent.

## Governance issues

- *Cultural distance.* Closeness between home country and host countries results in easier monitoring and coordination of production and marketing activities in the various locations. Thus culturally close countries increase the barriers to exit and vice versa.
- *Joint venture and acquisition.* A joint venture with a local partner can certainly reduce barriers to the penetration of a foreign market by giving rapid access to knowledge about the local market. On the other hand, whenever a joint venture is set up with a foreign partner, both different national and corporate cultures may have an impact on its success. Joint ventures and acquisitions are put in a difficult situation in the often critical initial phases of the integration process. Thus a lack of commitment in the parent company or companies may increase the incentive to exit.
- *Experience.* Firms learn from experience how to operate in the foreign environment, and how to search for solutions to problems that emerge. As experience is accumulated it becomes easier to avoid many of the problems involved in running foreign subsidiaries and to find workable solutions if problems should arise. This also includes the unpleasant decision to close down a subsidiary.

## 9.5 Summary

The advantages and disadvantages of the three main types of market entry modes are summarized in Tables 9.2 to 9.4.

**Table 9.2 Advantages and disadvantages of the different export modes for the manufacturer**

| Export mode | Advantages | Disadvantages |
|---|---|---|
| *Indirect exporting* (e.g. export buying agent, broker or export management company) | Limited commitment and investment required. High degree of market diversification is possible as the firm utilizes the internationalization of an experienced exporter. Minimal risk (market and political). No export experience required. | No control over marketing mix elements other than the product. An additional domestic member in the distribution chain may add costs, leaving smaller profit to the producer. Lack of contact with the market (no market knowledge acquired). Limited product experience (based on commercial selling). |
| *Direct exporting* (e.g. distributor or agent) | Access to local market experience and contacts with potential customers. Shorter distribution chain (compared to indirect exporting). Market knowledge acquired. More control over marketing mix (especially with agents). Local selling support and services available. | Little control over market price because of tariffs and lack of distribution control (especially with distributors). Some investment in sales organization required (contact from home base with distributors or agents). Cultural differences, providing communication problems and information filtering (transaction costs occur). Possible trade restrictions. |
| *Export marketing groups* | Shared costs and risks of internationalization. Provide a complete product line or system sales to the customer. | Risk of unbalanced relationships (different objectives). Participating firms are reluctant to give up their complete independence. |

**Table 9.3 Advantages and disadvantages of the different intermediate modes**

| Intermediate entry mode | Advantages | Disadvantages |
|---|---|---|
| *Contract manufacturing* (seen from the contractor's viewpoint) | Permits low-risk market entry.<br><br>No local investment (cash, time and executive talent) with no risk of nationalization or expropriation.<br><br>Retention of control over R&D, marketing and sales/after-sales service.<br><br>Avoids currency risks and financing problems.<br><br>A locally made image, which may assist in sales, especially to government or official bodies.<br><br>Entry into markets otherwise protected by tariffs or other barriers.<br><br>Possible cost advantage if local costs (primarily labour costs) are lower.<br><br>Avoids intra-corporate transfer-pricing problems that can arise with a subsidiary. | Transfer of production know-how is difficult.<br><br>Contract manufacture is only possible when a satisfactory and reliable manufacturer can be found – not always an easy task.<br><br>Extensive technical training will often have to be given to the local manufacturer's staff.<br><br>As a result, at the end of the contract, the subcontractor could become a formidable competitor.<br><br>Control over manufacturing quality is difficult to achieve despite the ultimate sanction of refusal to accept substandard goods.<br><br>Possible supply limitation if the production is taking place in developing countries. |
| *Licensing* (seen from the licensor's viewpoint) | Increases the income on products already developed as a result of expensive research.<br><br>Permits entry into markets that are otherwise closed on account of high rates of duty, import quotas and so on.<br><br>A viable option where manufacture is near the customer's base.<br><br>Requires little capital investment and should provide a higher rate of return on capital employed.<br><br>There may be valuable spin-off if the licensor can sell other products or components to the licensee. If these parts are for products being manufactured locally or machinery, there may also be some tariff concessions on their import.<br><br>The licensor is not exposed to the danger of nationalization or expropriation of assets.<br><br>Because of the limited capital requirements, new products can be rapidly exploited, on a worldwide basis, before competition develops.<br><br>The licensor can take immediate advantage of the licensee's local marketing and distribution organization and of existing customer contacts.<br><br>Protects patents, especially in countries that give weak protection for products not produced locally.<br><br>Local manufacture may also be an advantage in securing government contracts. | The licensor is ceding certain sales territories to the licensee for the duration of the contract; should it fail to live up to expectations, renegotiation may be expensive.<br><br>When the licensing agreement finally expires, the licensor may find he or she has established a competitor in the former licensee.<br><br>The licensee may prove less competent than expected at marketing or other management activities. Costs may even grow faster than income.<br><br>The licensee, even if it reaches an agreed minimum turnover, may not fully exploit the market, leaving it open to the entry of competitors, so that the licensor loses control of the marketing operation.<br><br>Danger of the licensee running short of funds, especially if considerable plant expansion is involved or an injection of capital is required to sustain the project. This danger can be turned to advantage if the licensor has funds available by a general expansion of the business through a partnership.<br><br>License fees are normally a small percentage of turnover, about 5 per cent, and will often compare unfavourably with what might be obtained from a company's own manufacturing operation.<br><br>Lack of control over licensee operations.<br><br>Quality control of the product is difficult – and the product will often be sold under the licensor's brand name.<br><br>Negotiations with the licensee, and sometimes with local government, are costly.<br><br>Governments often impose conditions on transferral of royalties or on component supply. |

Table 9.3 continued

| Intermediate entry mode | Advantages | Disadvantages |
|---|---|---|
| *Franchising* (seen from franchisor's viewpoint) | Greater degree of control compared to licensing.<br><br>Low-risk, low-cost entry mode (the franchisees are the ones investing in the necessary equipment and know-how).<br><br>Using highly motivated business contacts with money, local market knowledge and experience.<br><br>Ability to develop new and distant international markets, relatively quickly and on a larger scale than otherwise possible.<br><br>Generating economies of scale in marketing to international customers.<br><br>Precursor to possible future direct investment in foreign market. | The search for competent franchisees can be expensive and time consuming.<br><br>Lack of full control over franchisee's operations, resulting in problems with cooperation, communications, quality control, etc.<br><br>Costs of creating and marketing a unique package of products and services recognized internationally.<br><br>Costs of protecting goodwill and brand name.<br><br>Problems with local legislation, including transfers of money, payments of franchise fees and government-imposed restrictions on franchise agreements.<br><br>Opening up internal business knowledge may create potential future competitor.<br><br>Risk to the company's international profile and reputation if some franchisees underperform ('free riding' on valuable brand names). |
| *Joint venture* (seen from parent's viewpoint) | Access to expertise and contacts in local markets. Each partner agrees to a joint venture to gain access to the other partner's skills and resources. Typically, the international partner contributes financial resources, technology or products. The local partner provides the skills and knowledge required for managing a business in its country. Each partner can concentrate on that part of the value chain where the firm has its core competence.<br><br>Reduced market and political risk.<br><br>Shared knowledge and resources: compared to wholly owned subsidiary, less capital and fewer management resources are required.<br><br>Economies of scale by pooling skills and resources (resulting in e.g. lower marketing costs).<br><br>Overcomes host government restrictions.<br><br>May avoid local tariffs and non-tariff barriers.<br><br>Shared risk of failure.<br><br>Less costly than acquisitions.<br><br>Possibly better relations with national governments through having a local partner (meets host country pressure for local participation). | Objectives of the respective partners may be incompatible, resulting in conflicts.<br><br>Contributions to joint venture can become disproportionate.<br><br>Loss of control over foreign operations. Large investments of financial, technical or managerial resources favour greater control than is possible in a joint venture.<br><br>Completion might overburden a company's staff.<br><br>Partners may become locked into long-term investments from which it is difficult to withdraw.<br><br>Transfer pricing problems as goods pass between partners.<br><br>The importance of the venture to each partner might change over time.<br><br>Cultural differences may result in possible differences in management culture among participating firms.<br><br>Loss of flexibility and confidentiality.<br><br>Problems of management structures and dual parent staffing of joint ventures. Nepotism perhaps the established norm. |
| *Management contracting* (seen from contractor's viewpoint) | If direct investment or export is considered too risky – for commercial or political reasons – this alternative might be relevant.<br><br>As with other intermediate entry modes, management contracts may be linked together with other forms of operation in foreign markets.<br><br>Allows a company to maintain market involvement, so puts it in a better position to exploit any opportunity that may arise.<br><br>Organizational learning: if a company is in its early development stages of internationalization, a management contract may offer an efficient way of learning about foreign markets and international business. | Training future competitors: the management transfer package may in the end create a competitor for the contractor.<br><br>Creates a great demand for key personnel. Such staff are not always available, especially in SMEs.<br><br>Considerable effort needs to be put into building lines of communication at local level as well as back to contractor.<br><br>Potential conflict between the contractor and the local government as regards the policy of the contract venture.<br><br>Little control, which also limits the ability of a contractor to develop the capacity of the venture. |

**Table 9.4 Advantages and disadvantages of different hierarchical entry modes**

| Hierarchical entry mode | Advantages | Disadvantages |
| --- | --- | --- |
| *Domestic-based sales representatives* | Better control of sales activities compared to independent intermediaries.<br><br>Close contact with large customers in foreign markets close to home country. | High travel expenses.<br><br>Too expensive in foreign markets, far away from home country. |
| *Foreign sales, branch/sales and production subsidiary* | Full control of operation.<br><br>Eliminates the possibility that a national partner gets a 'free ride'.<br><br>Market access (sales subsidiary).<br><br>Acquire market knowledge directly (sales subsidiary).<br><br>Reduce transport costs (production subsidiary).<br><br>Elimination of duties (production subsidiary).<br><br>Access to raw materials and labour (production subsidiary). | High initial capital investment required (subsidiary).<br><br>Loss of flexibility.<br><br>High risk (market, political and economic).<br><br>Taxation problems. |
| *Region centres/ transnational organization* | Achieves potential synergies on a regional/global scale.<br><br>Regional/global scale efficiency.<br><br>Leverage learning on a cross-national basis. Resources and people are flexible and can be put into operating units around the world. | Possible threats:<br><br>– increasing bureaucracy.<br><br>Limited national-level responsiveness and flexibility.<br><br>A national manager can feel he or she has no influence.<br><br>Missing communication between head office and region centres. |
| *Acquisition* | Rapid entry to new markets.<br><br>Gaining quick access to:<br>– distribution channels;<br>– a qualified labour force;<br>– existing management experience;<br>– local knowledge;<br>– contacts with local market and government;<br>– established brand names/reputation. | Usually an expensive option.<br><br>High risk (taking over companies that are regarded as part of a country's heritage can raise considerable national resentment if it seems that they are being taken over by foreign interests).<br><br>Possible threats:<br>– lack of integration with existing operation. Communication and coordination problems between acquired firm and acquirer. |
| *Greenfield investment* | Possible to build in an 'optimum' format, i.e. in a way that fits the interests of the firm (e.g. integrating production with home base production).<br><br>Possible to integrate state-of-the-art technology (resulting in increased operational efficiency). | High investment cost.<br><br>Slow entry of new markets (time-consuming process). |

# Lysholm Linie Aquavit: International marketing of the Norwegian Aquavit brand

Aquavit, which translates as 'water of life', a slightly yellow or colourless alcoholic liquor, is produced in the Scandinavian countries by redistilling neutral spirits such as grain or potatoes and flavouring them with caraway seeds. It is often consumed as an aperitif.

The alcohol content in the various aquavits varies somewhat, starting at 37.5 per cent. Most brands contain about 40 per cent alcohol but Lysholm Linie Aquavit has an alcohol content of 41.5 per cent. ('Lysholm' is the name of the distillery in Trondheim where the aquavit is made, and from this point on the name 'Linie Aquavit' is used.)

## The history of Aquavit

Originally, aquavit was used for medicinal purposes, but from the 1700s stills became commonplace in Scandinavian homes.

The definition of aquavit gets slightly complicated when you try to draw the line between it and other spirits popular in the northern climate. The term 'schnapps', for instance, is widely used in Germany, Switzerland and Scandinavia (the Danish say 'snaps') to mean any sort of neutral spirits, flavoured or otherwise. Then there's 'brannvin' a term used similarly in Sweden. (Like the Dutch word 'brandewijn' from which we derive the word 'brandy' it means 'burnt wine'.) The famous Swedish vodka Absolut began life in 1879 as a product called 'Absolut Renat Brannvin' which might be translated as 'absolutely pure schnapps', said to have been distilled ten times. However, when the Swedish government's alcohol monopoly launched Absolut's descendant as an international brand in 1979, it labelled it vodka.

## Making Linie Aquavit

Caraway is the most important herb in aquavit, but the mixture of herbs varies from brand to brand. Linie Aquavit is derived from Norwegian potato alcohol blended with spices and herbal infusions, and caraway and aniseed predominate. After the

alcohol and the herbs have been mixed the aquavit is poured into 500-litre oak barrels, the choice of which has not been left to chance. Norwegian specialists travel to Spain for the express purpose of selecting the best barrels, from those used in the production of Oloroso sherry for several years. Sherry casks are used because they remove the rawer, more volatile aspects of the liquor; the aquavit takes on a golden hue, and the residual sherry imparts a gentle sweetness.

Many theories have been put forward to explain how the man behind Linie Aquavit, Jørgen B. Lysholm, came up with the idea of sending aquavit around the world on sailboats in order to produce a special flavour. History tells us that, in the early 1800s, his family tried to export aquavit to the West Indies, but the ship 'Trondheim's Prøve' returned with its unsold cargo. That is when they discovered the beneficial effects that the long ocean voyage and the special storage had had on the aquavit: the length of the journey, the constant gentle rocking of the boat and the variation in temperature on deck, all helped give Linie Aquavit its characteristic taste. Jørgen B. Lysholm subsequently commercialized his maturation method and this is still how things are done today.

Linie Aquavit has one of Norway's long-established shipping companies as its steady travel partner. The first Wilhelmsen liner vessel carrying Lysholm Linie Aquavit set sail in 1927. Since that time, Wilhelmsen has been the sole carrier of this distinguished product. The barrels are tightly secured in specially designed cribs before being loaded onto containers, which remain on deck during the entire journey. The journey from Norway to Australia and back again takes four and a half months and crosses the equator (or the line, as sailors prefer to call it) twice. In fact, this is where Linie Aquavit gets its name. On the back of each label is the name of the ship and the date that it first crossed the equator.

### International sales of Linie Aquavit

Arcus AS is Norway's sole manufacturer of hard liquor and it is this company which produces Linie Aquavit. The company also taps wine from wine producers all over the world and imports a select range of bottled wines. With a market share of about 30 per cent, Arcus AS is the leading player in the Norwegian wine and spirits market.

The international aquavit markets (primarily Sweden, Norway, Denmark, Germany and the United States) are dominated (except the last) by local Aquavit brands. At present Linie Aquavit is the market leader in Norway with a 20 per cent market share. In Denmark and Sweden the market share is 3–5 per cent. Germany is the most important export market, where Linie Aqavit holds 12 per cent of the aquavit market in competition with brands like Malteserkreutz and Bommerlunde.

Arcus is using export modes (foreign-based intermediaries) in all export markets. In 2000 the main distributors in Germany (Berentzen-Gruppe) and Denmark (Hans Just) became part-owners of Arcus AS, because they wanted to be sole distributors of Linie Aquavit in their countries. In the German market Berentzen offers a whole range of different types of alcoholic drinks. The company ranked number three in spirits in 2001, with a volume share of 7 per cent. Berentzen aims to expand its international spirits business during the next few years, in order to achieve long-term growth.

Sources: www.arcus.no/english/; Christian Brink, Head of Marketing, Sales and R&D at Arcus AS.

### Questions

1 What are the main advantages and disadvantages for Arcus of using export modes, compared to other entry modes, for its Linie Aquavit?

2 What are the advantages for Arcus of having distributors as part-owners?

3 What should be Arcus' main criteria for selecting new distributors, or cooperation partners, for Linie Aquavit in new markets?

4 Would it be possible to pursue an international branding strategy for Linie Aquavit?

For further exercises and cases, see this book's website at **www.pearsoned.co.uk/hollensen**

## ? Questions for discussion

1 Why is exporting frequently considered the simplest way of entering foreign markets and is thus favoured by SMEs?

2 What procedures should a firm follow in selecting a distributor?

3 Why is it difficult – financially and legally – to terminate a relationship with overseas intermediaries? What should be done to prevent or minimize such difficulties?

4 What is the difference between direct and indirect exporting?

5 Discuss the financial and pricing techniques for motivating foreign distributors.

6 Which marketing tasks should be handled by the exporter and which ones by its intermediaries in foreign markets?

7 How can the carrier and the rider both benefit from a piggyback arrangement?

8 'When exporting to a market, you're only as good as your intermediary there.' Discuss.

9 Why are joint ventures preferred by host countries as an entry strategy for foreign firms?

10 Why are strategic alliances used in new product development?

11 Under what circumstances should franchising be considered? How do these circumstances vary from those leading to licensing?

12 Do you believe that licensing in represents a feasible long-term product development strategy for a company? Discuss in relation to in-house product development.

13 Why would a firm consider forming partnerships with competitors?

14 Apart from the management fees involved, what benefits might a firm derive from entering into management contracts overseas?

15 By what criteria would you judge a particular foreign direct investment activity to have succeeded or failed?

16 What are a firm's major motives in deciding to establish manufacturing facilities in a foreign country?

17 Is the establishment of wholly-owned subsidiaries abroad an appropriate international market development for SMEs?

18 What is the idea behind appointing a 'lead country' in a region?

## References

Baaij, M. (2005) 'Rotterdam or anywhere: relocating corporate HQ', *Business Strategy Review*, Summer, pp. 45–48.

Barkema, H.G., Bell, J. and Pennings, J.M. (1996) 'Foreign entry, cultural barriers and learning', *Strategic Management Journal*, 17, pp. 151–166.

Benito, G.R.G. (1997) 'Why are foreign subsidiaries divested? A conceptual framework', in Björkman, I. and Forsgren, M. (eds) *The Nature of the International Firm*, Handelshøjskolens Forlag/Copenhagen Business School Press.

Benito, G. (1996) 'Why are subsidiaries divested? A conceptual framework', Working Paper No. 3793, Institute of International Economics and Management, Copenhagen Business School.

Bleeke, J. and Ernst, D. (1994) Collaborating to Compete: Using strategic alliances and acquisitions in the global marketplace, John Wiley, New York.

Boddewyn, J.J. (1979) 'Foreign divestment: magnitude and factors', *Journal of International Business Studies*, 10, pp. 21–27.

Bradley, F. (1995) *International Marketing Strategy* (2nd edn), Prentice Hall, Hemel Hempstead.

Doherty, A.M. and Alexander, N. (2006) 'Power and Control in International Retail Franchising', *European Journal of Management*, Vol. 40, No. 11/12, pp. 1292–1316.

Gibbs, R. (2005) 'How to measure and master mindshare', *The Routes to Market – Journal (www.viaint.com)*, June, pp. 2–5.

Harrigan, K.R. (2003) *Joint Ventures, Alliances and Corporate Strategy*, Beard Books/Beard Group, Inc., MD.

Hennert, J.-F., Zeng, M. (2005) 'Structural determinants of joint venture performance', *European Management Review*, 2, pp. 105–115.

Hotopf, M. (2005) 'Winning partner mindshare', *The Routes to Market – Journal (www.viaint.com)*, February, pp. 13–16.

Lasserre, P. (1995) 'Corporate strategies for the Asia Pacific region', *Long Range Planning*, 28(1), pp. 13–30.

Lasserre, P. (1996) 'Regional headquarters: the spearhead for Asian Pacific markets', *Long Range Planning*, 29(1), pp. 30–37.

Lorange, P. and Roos, J. (1995) *Strategiske allianser i globale strategier*, Norges Eksportråd, Oslo.

Lowe, J. and Crawford, N. (1984) *Technology Licensing and the Small Firm*, Gower, Aldershot.

Luostarinen, R. and Welch, L. (1990) *International Business Operations*, Helsinki School of Economics, Helsinki.

Nanda, A. and Williamson, P.J. (1995) 'Use joint ventures to ease the pain of restructuring', *Harvard Business Review*, November–December, pp. 119–128.

Okoroafo, S.C. (1994) 'Implementing international countertrade: a dyadic approach', *Industrial Marketing Management*, 23, pp. 229–234.

Oviatt, B.M. and McDougall, P.P. (1994) 'Toward a theory of international new ventures', *Journal of International Business Studies*, 25(1), pp. 45–64.

Perkins, J.S. (1987) 'How licensing and franchising differ', *Les Nouvelles*, 22(4), pp. 155–158.

Perlmutter, H. (1969) 'The torturous evolution of multinational corporations', *Columbia Journal of World Business*, January–February, pp. 9–18.

Porter, M.E. and Fuller, M.B. (1986) 'Coalition and global strategy', in Porter, M.E. (ed.), *Competition in Global Strategies*, Harvard Business School Press, Boston, MA.

Raffée, H. and Kreutzer, R. (1989) 'Organizational dimensions of global marketing', *European Journal of Marketing*, 23(5), pp. 43–57.

Root, F.R. (1987) *Entry Strategies for International Markets*, Lexington Books, Lexington, MA.

Root, F.R. (1998) *Entry Strategies for International Markets: Revised and Expanded Edition*, The New Lexington Press, Lexington, MA.

Ross, W.T., Dalsace, F. and Anderson, E. (2005) 'Should you set up your own sales force or should you outsource it? Pitfalls in the standard analysis', *Business Horizons*, Vol. 48, pp. 23–36.

Wahyuni, S., Ghauri, P.N. and Karsten, L. (2007) 'Important Factors in Strategic Alliance Development: A Study on Alliances Between Dutch–American Companies', *Thunderbird International Business Review*, No. 6, Nov–Dec, pp. 671–687.

Welsh, D.H.B., Alon, I., Falbe, C.M. (2006) 'An examination of international retail franchising in emerging markets', *Journal of Small Business Management*, Vol. 44, No. 1, pp. 130–149.

Young, S., Hamill, J., Wheeler, S. and Davies, J.R. (1989) *International Market Entry and Development*, Harvester Wheatsheaf/Prentice Hall, Hemel Hempstead.

# 10

# International buyer-seller relationships

## Contents

**Case study**

## Learning objectives

After studying this chapter you should be able to do the following:

- Describe the role of subcontractors in the vertical chain.
- Explore the reasons for international outsourcing.
- Explain the development of a buyer–seller relationship.
- Discuss alternative routes of subcontractor internationalization.
- Explain how turnkey contracts differ from conventional subcontracting.

## 10.1 Introduction

Recent studies of subcontracting and competitiveness have emphasized the importance of outsourcing: moving functions or activities out of an organization. Outsourcing is often more efficient, except in the case of the firm's core competences, which are considered central to its success. Thus the issue is whether an organization should perform certain functions itself ('make') or source ('buy') these activities from outside. If LSEs outsource an increasing number of value chain functions this provides business opportunities for SMEs as subcontractors to LSEs (main contractors).

A subcontractor can be defined as a person or a firm that agrees to provide semi-finished products or services needed by another party (main contractor) to perform

Figure 10.1 Subcontractor's position in the vertical chain

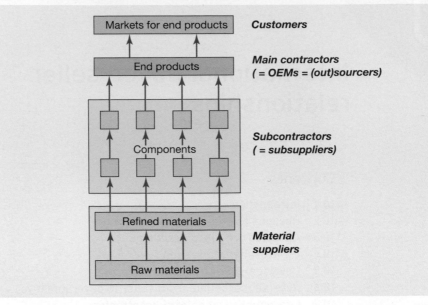

Source: Adapted from Lehtinen, 1991, p. 22.

another contract to which the subcontractor is not a party. According to this definition, the characteristics of subcontractors that distinguish them from other SMEs are as follows:

- Subcontractors' products are usually part of the end product, not the complete end product itself.
- Subcontractors do not have direct contact with the end customers, because the main contractor is usually responsible to the customer.

The position of subcontractors in the vertical production chain is shown in Figure 10.1.

**OEM**
Original equipment manufacturer – the customer of a subsupplier.

In the OEM contract (where OEM stands for original equipment manufacturer), the contractor is called the OEM or 'sourcer', whereas the parts suppliers are regarded as 'manufacturers' of OEM products (= subcontractors = subsuppliers). Typically the OEM contracts are different from other buyer–seller relationships because the OEMs (contractors) often have much stronger bargaining power than the subcontractors. However, in a partner-based buyer–seller relationship the power balance will be more equal. There are cases where a subcontractor improved its bargaining position and went on to become a major force in the market (Cho and Chu, 1994).

The internationalization of the supply chain adds considerable complexity to the coordination tasks performed by the subsuppliers (Andersen and Christensen, 2005).

The structure of the remainder of this chapter is shown in Figure 10.2.

## 10.2 Reasons for international sourcing

More and more international firms are buying their parts, semi-finished components or system solutions from international subcontractors. In most multinational companies there is a tendency to outsource more and more of the upsteam activities to subsuppliers,

Figure 10.2 Structure of Chapter 10

who will then take over more complex coordination tasks, leaving firms to concentrate on their core competences. This will create more business for subsuppliers, but at the same time there is a tendency to decrease the number of subsuppliers (system suppliers) (see the first layer of Figure 10.1) in the vertical chain. This means that there is fierce competition among existing subsuppliers for staying at the first layer level. In this consolidation process, those firms who cannot stay at the first layer level will have to move to the second layer, maybe concentrating on production of more simple components, which will then be sold and handed over to the system suppliers (first layer).

In general, creating competitiveness through the subcontractor is based on the understanding that the supplier could be essential to the buyer (contractor) for a number of reasons.

## Concentration on in-house core competences

A contractor wishes to concentrate management time and effort on those core business activities that make the best use of in-house skills and resources. There may also be special difficulties in obtaining suitably skilled labour in-house.

## Lower product/production costs

In this respect there are two underlying reasons for outsourcing:

1 *Economies of scale.* In many cases the subcontractor produces similar components for other customers, and by use of the experience curve the subcontractor can obtain lower production costs per unit.
2 *Lower wage costs.* The labour costs involved in the domestic country can make the in-house operation uneconomic and motivate international sourcing. For example, 80 per cent of the labour cost of clothing manufacture is in the sewing stage. Short production runs of different sizes of clothes permit only a low degree of mechanization. Moreover, adjusting the tooling for each run is relatively labour intensive (Hibbert, 1993). Therefore a large part of labour-intensive clothing production is moved to low-wage countries in eastern Europe and the Far East.

Figure 10.3  The total cost/value hierarchy model

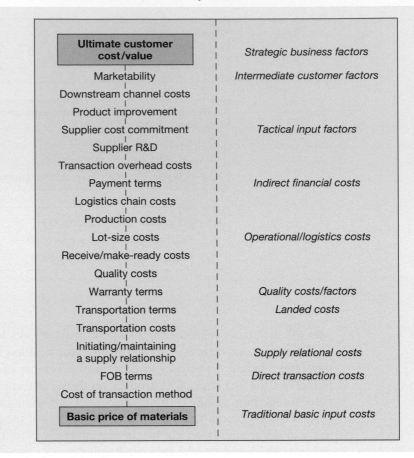

## General cost efficiency

If a firm plans to be more cost efficient than its competitors it has to minimize the total costs towards the end (ultimate) customer. Figure 10.3 shows a model of the different cost elements, from the basic price of materials to the ultimate customer cost.

Each element of the supply chain is a potential candidate for outsourcing. Quality costs, inventory costs (not explicitly mentioned in Figure 10.3) and buyer–supplier transaction costs are examples of costs that should be included in every calculation. However, some of these costs are difficult to estimate and are consequently easily overlooked when evaluating a subcontractor.

For example, the quality of a subcontractor's product or service is essential to the buyer's quality. However, it is not only a question of the quality of the product or service. The quality of the delivery processes also has a major impact on the buyer's performance. Uncertainties, as far as lead times are concerned, have an impact on the buyer's inventory investments and cost efficiency, and they may cause delays in the buyer's own delivery processes. Thus the buyer's own delivery times towards the end customers are determined by the subcontractors and their delivery. Another important fact is that the cost of components and parts is to a large extent already determined at the design stage. Thus, close cooperation between buyer and seller at this stage can give rise to considerable cost advantages in production and distribution.

## Increased potential for innovation

Ideas for innovation can be generated by the subcontractor due to its more in-depth understanding of the component. New ideas can also be transferred from other customers of the subcontractor.

## Fluctuating demand

If the main contractor is confronted with fluctuating demand levels, external uncertainty and short product life cycles, it may transfer some risk and stock management to the subcontractor, leading to better cost and budget control.

Finally, it should be mentioned that, when buying from international sources, fluctuations in exchange rates become particularly important, especially when there is a lag from the time the contract is signed to when payment is made. When the currency in the country of the main contractor is very strong against a particular country this can be an incentive for the main contractor to buy from this country.

In summary, price is a very important reason for (international) outsourcing, but the main contractors increasingly regard cooperation with critical subcontractors as advantageous to the buying firm's competitiveness and profitability.

## 10.3  A typology of subcontracting

Traditionally, a subcontractor has been defined as a firm carrying out day-to-day production based on the specifications of another firm (the main contractor). The variety of subcontracting relationships that are appearing indicates a need for a more differentiated typology.

Figure 10.4 displays a typology of subcontractors based on differences in the contractor–subcontractor relationship. The typology displays the interplay between the degree of coordination needed and the complexity of the tasks to be solved.

**Figure 10.4 Typology of subcontracting**

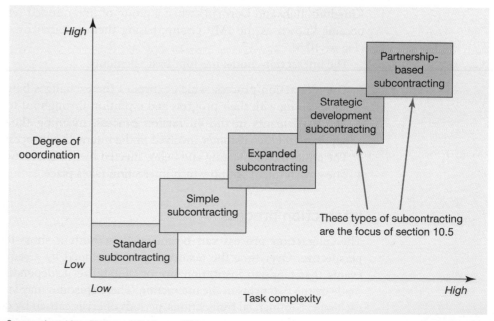

Source: adapted from Blenker and Christensen, 1994.

● *Standard subcontracting.* Economies of scale often operate in the global market with standardized products, in which case no adaptation to specific customers is needed.
● *Simple subcontracting.* Information exchange is simple since the contractor specifies criteria for contribution. The contractor's in-house capacity is often a major competitor.
● *Expanded subcontracting.* There is some mutual specialization between the two parties and exit costs are higher for both parties. Therefore single sourcing (one supplier for a product/component) may replace multisourcing (more suppliers for a product/component).
● *Strategic development subcontracting.* This is very important to the contractor. Subcontractors possess a critical competence of value to the contractor. They are involved in the contractor's long-term planning, and activities are coordinated by dialogue.
● *Partnership-based subcontracting.* This is a relationship based on a strong mutual strategic value and dependency. The subcontractor is highly involved in the R&D activities of the contractor.

There is a certain overlap between the different types of subcontractor and in a specific relationship it can be very difficult to place a subcontractor in a certain typology. Depending primarily on the task complexity, a main contractor may have both standard subcontractors and partnership-based subcontractors. Also a subcontractor may play more than one role in Figure 10.4, but only one at a time.

## 10.4 Buyer–seller interaction

Traditionally, subcontracting has been defined as the production activities that one firm carries out on the day-to-day specification of another firm. Outsourced activities increasingly include R&D, design and other functions in the value chain. Thus what starts with simple transactions (so-called episodes) may, if repeated over time, evolve into a relationship between buyer and seller.

Interaction theory was developed by the Swedes but spread into France, the United Kingdom, Italy and Germany when a group of like-minded researchers formed what became known as the IMP Group, basing their research on the interaction model (Figure 10.5).

The interaction model has four basic elements:

1 The interaction process, which expresses the exchanges between the two organizations along with their progress and evolution throughout time.
2 The participants in the interaction process, meaning the characteristics of the supplier and the customer involved in the interaction process.
3 The atmosphere affecting and being affected by the interaction.
4 The environment within which interaction takes place.

### Interaction process

The interaction process can be analysed in both a short-term and a long-term perspective. Over time the relationship is developed by a sequence of episodes and events that tends to institutionalize or destabilize it, depending on the evaluations made by the two firms in the interaction. These episodes may vary in terms of types of exchange: commercial transactions, periods of crisis caused by delivery, price disputes, new product development stages, etc.

Figure 10.5 The buyer–seller interaction

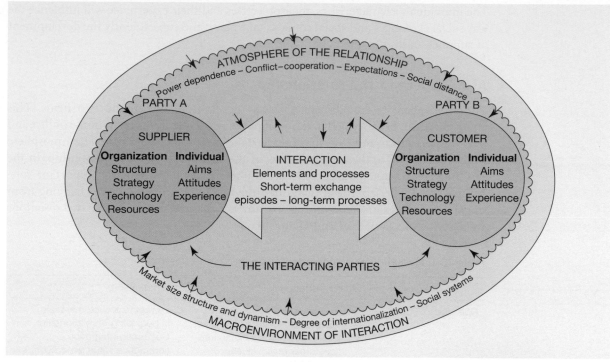

Source: Turnbull and Valla, 1986. Reprinted by permission of Taylor and Francis Books UK.

Through social exchange with the supplier the customer attempts to reduce decision-making uncertainty. Over time and with mutual adaptation a relationship-specific mode of operation emerges and may act as a 'shock absorber' in case of crisis. This mode of operation can take the form of special procedures, mutual developments, communication style between individuals, and more or less implicit rules. These rules are modified through past exchanges and form the framework for future exchanges.

## Interacting parties

The participants' characteristics strongly influence the way they interact. Three analytical perspectives of buyer and seller, at different levels, may be taken into account.

### 1 The social system perspective

Dimensions such as culture – languages, values and practices – and the operating modes of the firm influence the distance between actors that will limit or encourage collaboration.

### 2 The organizational perspective

The relationship between buyer and seller is influenced by three organizational dimensions:

1 The characteristics of each firm's technology (i.e. products and production technology) strongly influence the nature of the interaction between the two organizations.
2 The complexity of products sold, for example, conditions the very nature and the density of the interaction between supplier and customer.
3 Relationship characteristics: a supplier can choose to develop a stable relationship with a customer, or the supplier can regard the relationship as a pure transaction-based exchange where the supplier typically makes 'one-shot' business with a customer purely to increase sales volume and with no further involvement.

### 3 The individual perspective

The individuals' characteristics, their objectives and their experience will influence the way social exchanges and social contacts take place, and subsequently the development of supplier–customer interaction.

## Atmosphere of the relationship

The atmosphere is the 'climate' that has developed between the two firms. This atmosphere can be described in terms of power–dependence, cooperation–conflict and trust–opportunism, and in terms of understanding and social distance. The atmosphere concept is central to the understanding of the supplier–customer relationship. In the case of key account management, atmosphere plays a particularly important role. As buyer and seller approach each other the marketing exchanges are changing from single transactions to a relationship. The further characteristics of these two situations are described in Table 10.1 and Figure 10.6.

**Table 10.1 Marketing exchange understanding**

|  | Transaction | Relationship |
|---|---|---|
| *Objective* | To make a sale (sale is end result and measure of success). Customer needs satisfaction (customer buys values). | To create a customer (sale is beginning of relationship). Customer integration (interactive value generation). |
| *Customer understanding* | Anonymous customer. Independent buyer and seller. | Well-known customer. Interdependent buyer and seller. |
| *Marketers' task and performance criteria* | Assessment on the basis of products and prices. Focus on gaining new customers. | Assessment on the basis of problem-solving competence. Focus on value enhancing of existing customers. |
| *Core aspects of exchange* | Focus on products. Sale as a conquest. Discrete event. Monologue to aggregated broad customer segments. | Focus on service. Sale as an agreement. Continuing process. Individualized dialogue. |

Source: Jüttner and Wehrli 1994. Published with permission of Emerald Publishing Ltd. www.emeraldinsight.com.

**Figure 10.6 Market exchange understanding**

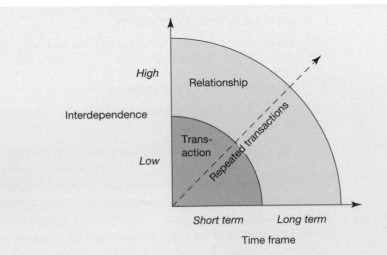

Source: Jüttner and Wehrli 1994. Published with permission of Emerald Publishing Ltd. www.emeraldinsight.com.

## Interaction environment

Supplier–customer relationships evolve in a general macroenvironment that can influence their very nature. The following analytical dimensions are traditionally considered: political and economic context, cultural and social context, market structure, market internationalization and market dynamism (growth, innovation rate).

## 10.5 Development of a relationship

A relationship between two firms begins, grows and develops – or fails – in ways similar to relationships between people. The development of a relationship has been mapped out in a five-phase model: awareness, exploration, expansion, commitment and dissolution. The five phases are shown in Figure 10.7.

Figure 10.7 shows, the initial psychic *distance 1* between a buyer and a seller (both from different countries and cultures) and it is influenced by the psychological characteristics of the buyer and the seller, the firm's organizational culture, and the national and industry culture to which the firm belongs. Figure 10.7 also shows that the initial psychic distance 1 at the beginning of the relationship is reduced to physical *distance 2* through the interaction process of the two partners. However, relationships do not always last forever. The partners may 'move from each other' and the psychic may increase to *distance 3*. If the problems in the relationship are not solved, it may result in a 'divorce'.

Within such a framework one might easily characterize a marketing relationship as a marriage between a seller and a buyer (the dissolution phase being a 'divorce').

**The marriage metaphor**
The process of reducing the psychic distance + increasing dependence between buyer and seller = shared values and joint investments in the relationship.

The use of the marriage metaphor indicates that business relationships involve inter-organizational relationships, but certainly also inter-personal relationships (Mouzas *et al.*, 2007).

Dwyer *et al.* (1987) call the first phase in a relationship *awareness*, which means that the partners recognize each other as potential partners. In other words, in their model the decisions made about cooperating and choosing the partner are combined. Both types of decision making can exist at the beginning of cooperation, but it is difficult to state any definite chronological order between them.

In SMEs it is likely that the decision-making process is reactive, in the way that the SME probably first realizes the existence of a potential partner (maybe 'love at first sight') and then decides to cooperate. The selection process may, however, be better if companies look for three key criteria (Kanter, 1994):

1 *Self-analysis.* Relationships get off to a good start when partners know themselves and their industry, when they have assessed changing industry conditions and decided to seek an alliance. It also helps if executives have experience in evaluating potential partners. They will not be easily attracted by the first good-looking prospect that comes along.

2 *Chemistry.* To highlight the personal side of business relationships is not to deny the importance of sound financial and strategic analysis. But successful relations often depend on the creation and maintenance of a comfortable personal relationship between senior executives. This will include personal and social interests. Signs of managers' interests, commitment and respect are especially important in high-context countries. In China, as well as in Chinese-dominated businesses throughout Asia, the top manager of the western company should show honour and respect to the potential partner's decision by investing his or her personal time.

Figure 10.7 The five-phase relationship model

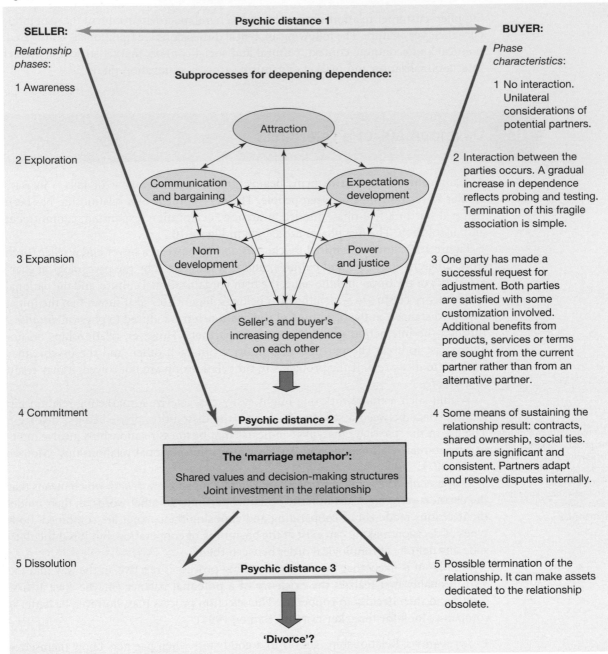

3 *Compatibility*. The courtship period tests compatibility on broad historical, philosophical and strategic grounds: common experiences, values and principles, and hopes for the future. While analysts examine financial viability, managers can assess the less tangible aspects of compatibility. What starts out as personal rapport, philosophical and strategic compatibility, and shared vision between two companies' top executives must eventually be institutionalized and made public ('getting engaged'). Other stakeholders get involved, and the relationship begins to become depersonalized. But success in the engagement phase of a new alliance still depends on maintaining a careful balance between the personal and the institutional.

In the *exploration phase* of Figure 10.7 trial purchases may take place and the exchange outcomes provide a test of the other's ability and willingness to deliver satisfaction. In addition, electronic data interchange can be used to reduce the costly paperwork associated with purchase orders, production schedule releases, invoices and so on.

At the end of the exploration phase it is time to 'meet the family'. The relations between a handful of leaders from the two firms must be supplemented with approval, formal or informal, by other people in the firms and by stake holders. Each partner has other outside relationships that may need to approve the new relationship.

When a party (as is the case in the *expansion phase*) fulfils perceived exchange obligations in an exemplary fashion, the party's attractiveness to the other increases. Hence motivation to maintain the relationship increases, especially because high-level outcomes reduce the number of alternatives that an exchange partner might use as a replacement.

The romance of courtship quickly gives way to day-to-day reality as the partners begin to live together ('setting up house'). In the *commitment phase* the two partners can achieve a level of satisfaction from the exchange process that actually precludes other primary exchange partners (suppliers) that could provide similar benefits. The buyer has not ceased attending other alternative suppliers, but maintains awareness of alternatives without constant and frequent testing. In a buyer–seller relationship with a high conflict potential (e.g. caused by two very different partners) the partners tend to a more close monitoring of the relationship because each partner is afraid that its interests are not fully taken into account. However, the relationship is able to sustain its structure and remain an efficient mechanism for interfirm transactions between buyer and seller, as long as partners' economic benefits exceed potential costs in managing the alliance (Wahyuni *et al.*, 2007).

During the description of the relationship development, the possibility of a withdrawal has been implicit. The dissolution phase may be caused by the following problems:

**Dissolution phase** 'Divorce': termination of the relationship. It can make the assets dedicated to the relationship obsolete.

- Operational and cultural differences emerge after collaboration is under way. They often come as a surprise to those who created the alliance. Differences in authority, reporting and decision-making styles become noticeable at this stage.
- People in other positions may not experience the same attraction as the chief executives. The executives spend a lot of time together both informally and formally. Other employees have not been in touch with one another, however, and in some cases have to be pushed to work with their overseas counterparts.
- Employees at other levels in the organization may be less visionary and cosmopolitan than top managers and less experienced in working with people from different cultures. They may lack knowledge of the strategic context in which the relationship makes sense and see only the operational ways in which it does not.
- People just one or two tiers from the top might oppose the relationship and fight to undermine it. This is especially true in organizations that have strong independent business units.
- Termination of personal relationships, because managers leave their positions in the companies, is a potential danger to the partnership.

Firms have to be aware of these potential problems before they go into a relationship, because only in that way can they take action to prevent the dissolution phase. By jointly analysing the extent and importance of the attenuating factors, the partners will become more aware of the reasons for continuing the relationship, in spite of the trouble they are already in. Moreover, this awareness increases the parties' willingness to engage in restorative actions, thus trying to save the relationship from dissolution (Tähtinen and Vaaland, 2006).

**10.6** # Reverse marketing: from seller to buyer initiative

**Reverse marketing**
The buyer (and not the seller like in traditional marketing) takes the initiatives for searching a supplier that is able to fulfil their needs.

**Reverse marketing** describes how purchasing actively identifies potential subcontractors and offers suitable partners a proposal for long-term cooperation. Similar terms are proactive procurement and buyer initiative (Ottesen, 1995). In recent years the buyer–seller relationship has changed considerably. The traditional relationship, in which a seller takes the initiative by offering a product, is increasingly being replaced by one in which the buyer actively searches for a supplier that is able to fulfil its needs.

Today, many changes are taking place in the utilization of the purchasing function:

- Reduction in the number of subcontractors.
- Shorter product life cycles, which increase the pressure to reduce the time to market (just in time).
- Upgraded demands on subcontractors (zero defects). In addition, firms are demanding that their suppliers become certified. Those that do not comply may be removed from the approved supplier list.
- Purchasing that no longer just serves the purpose of getting lower prices. The traditional arm's-length relationships are increasingly being replaced by long-term partnerships with mutual trust, interdependence and mutual benefits.

Implementing a reverse marketing strategy starts with fundamental market research and with an evaluation of reverse marketing options (i.e. possible suppliers). Before choosing suppliers the firm may include both present and potential suppliers in the analysis as well as current and desired activities (Figure 10.8).

Based on this analysis the firm may select a number of suitable partners as suppliers and rank them in order of preference.

Figure 10.8 **Supplier development strategies**

|  | Current activities | New activities |
|---|---|---|
| **Existing suppliers** | Intensify current activities | Develop and add new activities |
| **New potential suppliers** | Replace existing suppliers Add suppliers: secure deliveries | Develop new activities not covered by existing suppliers |

**10.7** # Internationalization of subcontractors

In Chapter 3 the internationalization process was described as a learning process (the Uppsala school). Generally speaking it is something that can be described as a gradual internationalization. According to this view the international development of the firm is accompanied by an accumulation of knowledge in the hands of management and by growing capabilities and propensities to manage international affairs. The main consequence of this way of thinking is that firms tend to increase their commitment towards foreign markets as their experience grows. The number of adherents to this theory has grown, but there has also been much criticism of it.

The main problem with the model is that it seems to suggest the presence of a deterministic and mechanistic path that firms implementing their internationalization strategy must follow. Sometimes it happens that firms leapfrog one or more stages in the establishment chain; at other times firms stop their internationalization altogether (Welch and Luostarinen, 1988).

Concerning internationalization among contractors and subcontractors, there is a central difference. The internationalization of subcontractors is closely related to their customers. The concept of subcontractor indicates that the strategies of such a firm, including its internationalization strategy, cannot be seen in isolation from the strategies of its partner, the contractor.

Systems supplies result in the development of a new layer of subcontractors (second-tier subcontractors). Through the interaction between a system supplier and a domestic main contractor the system supplier can get access to the network of a global contractor (the dotted line in Figure 10.9) because of the network/contract between the contractor and the global contractor. For example, a Japanese car seat supplier supplies the Japanese Toyota factory (domestic main contractor). This can eventually give the supplier access to other Toyota factories around the world (global contractors) and their global networks.

In many cases the collaboration between the subcontractors will be characterized by exchange of tacit, not easily transferable, knowledge. The reason for this is that the complete subsystem is frequently based on several fields of competence, which have to be coordinated by use of tacit knowledge and communication. In the case of the Japanese car seat supplier, the system supplier should have a tight relationship with the subcontractors (suppliers of leather head rests, etc.) in order to adapt the car seat to the individual car models. (See also Exhibit 10.1.)

**Figure 10.9 Possible internationalization of system suppliers**

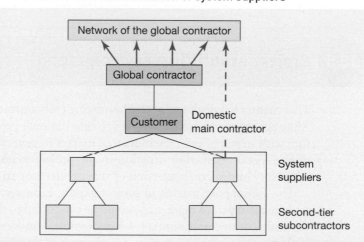

## Exhibit 10.1 An example of Japanese network sourcing: the Mazda seat-sourcing case

Mazda adopts a policy of splitting its seat purchases between two suppliers, Delta Kogyo and the Toyo Seat Company. The present division is approximately 60 per cent to Delta and 40 per cent to Toyo. Each of these companies is responsible for different models of seats. Note that each individual item, such as a seat for the Mazda 626, is single sourced for the product life cycle of typically three to five years, but seat production in general is, in effect, dual sourced.

Both Delta Kogyo and the Toyo Seat Company are informally assured of a certain percentage of the Mazda seat business at any one time. This percentage is approximately one-third of the total Mazda seat purchases for each of them. Thus each firm has an assured long-term share of Mazda's seat business. The last third of the Mazda seat business was available to whichever of the suppliers had performed the best over the life cycle of previous car models.

The two seat makers rely on Mazda for a very high percentage of their business. In the case of Delta Kogyo, Mazda business represents around two-thirds of its total sales. In addition, both suppliers are members of Mazda's *keiretsu* (network) and hence come into direct contact with each other on a regular basis. Additionally, since they are direct competitors for only a third of Mazda's seat business, there is a significant degree of openness between the two firms. This openness in some instances takes the form of cooperation in solving mutual or individual problems, because the other seat supplier is often in a better position to give advice than Mazda itself.

However, competition for the remaining third of the Mazda seat business is very intense, since both firms know that they have only one chance to gain the orders for a new car model every three to five years. Either firm can obtain new business as long as the other does not fall below 33 per cent of Mazda's total seat purchases. A situation has been created in which there is creative tension between cooperation and competition.

Indeed, when one of the suppliers approaches the lower limit of its 33 per cent supply Mazda typically uses its own engineers, and possibly those of the supply competitor, to help the weaker supplier in terms of a joint value analysis/value engineering programme. Because neither supplier wants to be forced into this situation both will work diligently to avoid this fate – and at the same time to enhance their own competitiveness.

Mazda is careful to ensure that neither supplier is forced into a situation of unprofitability, since this would obviously mean that Mazda would suffer in the long term. This is not to say that either supplier is allowed to make excessive profits. Indeed profit as a percentage of sales is roughly equalized throughout the supply network, including the Mazda organization itself. During recessionary periods Mazda and its network of suppliers would make no more than about 2 per cent profit on sales. Thus members of the supply network stand or fall together, increasing the shared bonds and the willingness to help any member of the network.

Source: 'Network Sourcing: A Hybrid Approach', *International Journal of Purchasing and Materials Management*, Hines, P. (1995) Spring, 31(2), pp. 18–24. Copyright © 1995, Blackwell Publishing Ltd.

## 10.8 Project export (turnkey contracts)

This chapter has dealt mainly with sourcing (subcontracting) in the industrial market. Although marketing of subsupplies to international projects has a number of similarities with subsupplies in the industrial market in general, it also has the characteristics of the special marketing situation in the project market: for example, the long and often very bureaucratic selection of subsuppliers for ad hoc supplies.

The subsupplier market in project export, however, is also very internationalized, and the main part of marketing should be conducted in those centres or countries where the main contractor is domiciled. For example, London is the domicile of a number of building contracting businesses, which work in those countries that used to be in the British Empire.

**Project export**
Combination of hardware (e.g. buildings and infrastructure) and software (technology and project know-how), e.g. in the form of a factory for ice cream production.

**Project export** is a very complex international activity, involving many market players. The preconditions for project export are a technology gap between the exporting and importing countries and that the exporter possesses the specific product and technology know-how that is being demanded in the importing country.

Project export involves supplies or deliveries that contain a combination of hardware and software. When the delivery is concluded it will constitute an integrated system that is able to produce the products and/or the services, which the buyer requires. An example of this type of project is the construction of a dairy in a developing country.

*Hardware* is the blanket term for the tangible, material or physical contribution of the project supply. Hardware is composed of buildings, machines, inventory, transport equipment, etc., and is specified in the quotation and contract between buyer and seller in the form of drawings, unit lists, descriptions and so on.

*Software* is the blanket term for the intangible contributions in a project supply. Software includes know-how and service. There are three types of know-how:

1 *technology know-how*, comprising product, process and hardware know-how;
2 *project know-how*, comprising project management, assembly and environmental know-how;
3 *management know-how*, which in general terms involves tactical and operational management, and specifically includes marketing and administrative systems.

Service includes advisory services and assistance in connection with various applications and approvals (environmental approval, financing of the project, planning permission, etc.).

The marketing of projects is different from the marketing of products in the following respects:

- Decision of purchase, apart from local business interests, often involves decision processes in national and international development organizations. This implies the participation of a large number of people and a heavily bureaucratic system.
- The product is designed and created during the negotiation process, where the requirements are put forward.
- It often takes years from the disclosure of needs to the purchase decision being taken. Therefore total marketing costs are very large.
- When the project is taken over by the project buyer, the buyer–seller relations cease. However, by cultivating these relations before, during and after the project, a 'sleeping' relationship can be woken again in connection with a new project (Hadjikhani, 1996).

Financing a project is a key problem for the seller as well as the buyer. The project's size and the time used for planning and implementation result in financial demands that make it necessary to use external sources of finance. In this connection the following main segments can be distinguished. The segments arise from differences in the source of financing for the projects:

- Projects where *multilateral organizations*, such as the World Bank or regional development banks, are a primary source of finance.
- Projects where *bilateral organizations* are a primary or essential source of finance.
- Projects where a *government institution* acts as buyer. This was normal in the command economies, where government companies acted as buyers. However, it can also be found in liberal economies: for example, in connection with the development of social infrastructure or the building of a bridge.
- Projects where a *private person or firm* acts as buyer, as when Unilever builds a factory in Vietnam for the production of ice cream.

For large-scale projects, like a new airport, there may be many partners forming a consortium, where we will have the concept of a 'leader firm', but each partner would undertake financing, organization, supervision and/or construction etc., of a part of the project on the basis of their specific expertise.

Organizing export projects involves establishing an interaction between different firms from the West on the one side, and firms and authorities typically from developing countries on the other. Creating or adapting an organization that is able to function under these conditions is a precondition of project marketing.

## 10.9 Summary

This chapter has analysed the buyer–seller relationship from different angles in the internationalized environment. The advantages and disadvantages for the contractor and subcontractor of going into a relationship are summarized in Table 10.2.

The project export situation differs from the 'normal' buyer–seller relationship in the following ways:

- The buying decision process often involves national and international development organizations. This often results in very bureaucratic selection of subcontractors.
- Financing of the project is a key problem.

Table 10.2 Advantages and disadvantages of buyer–seller relationships for contractor and subcontractor

|  | Advantages | Disadvantages |
|---|---|---|
| *Contractor (buyer)* | The contractor is flexible by not investing in manufacturing facilities. | The availability of suitable manufacturers (subcontractors) cannot be assumed. |
|  | The subcontractor can source the products more cheaply (because of e.g. cheaper labour costs) than by own production. | Outsourcing tends to be relatively less stable than in-house operations. |
|  | The contractor can concentrate on in-house core competences. | The contractor has less control over the activities of the subcontractor. |
|  | Complement of the contractor's product range. | Subcontractors can develop into competitors. |
|  | New ideas for product innovation can be carried over from the subcontractor. | Quality problems of outsourced products can harm the business of the contractor. |
|  |  | Assistance to the subcontractor may increase the costs of the whole operation. |
| *Subcontractor (seller)* | Access to new export markets because of the internationalization of the contractor (especially relevant for the so-called late starters). | Risk of becoming dependent on the contractor because of expanding production capacity and concurrent overseas expansion of sales and marketing activities in order to meet the demands of the contractor. |
|  | Exploits scale economies (lower cost per unit) through better capacity utilization. |  |
|  | Learns product technology of the contractor. |  |
|  | Learns marketing practices of the contractor. |  |

# YouTube: Can YouTube get too many marketing partners?

*'The marketing guys love YouTube and the legal guys hate it'.*

*(Jones and Leamonth, 2007)*

YouTube (**www.youtube.com**) is a video sharing website where users can upload, view and share video clips. YouTube was founded in a garage in February 2005 by three former PayPal employees – Chad Hurley, Steve Chen and Jawed Karim – in the city of San Mateo, California, USA and it was officially launched in December of the same year.

Source: © Roberto Herrett/Alamy.

YouTube started out as a video clone of HotOrNot.com targetting the young adult market. However, the initial site was attracting very little traffic. A site revamp in June 2005 focused on:

- creating a general-purpose video-sharing platform;
- increasing number of views by offering 'related' content;
- encouraging interaction between users;
- offering an external video player that could be embedded on a site like MySpace.com.

Soon after, it became an instant hit among its users. Adobe Flash technology is the preferred choice to play back a wide variety of video content, including movie clips, TV clips and music videos, as well as amateur content such as video blogging and short original videos, thus providing a huge store on the net for keeping video clips and files safe. This is a standard format supported by most browsers, including Internet Explorer, Firefox, Safari and Opera. Videos can be played on some mobile devices and even on the Nintendo Wii game system.

YouTube's video playback technology is based on Macromedia's Flash Player. This technology allows the site to display videos with quality comparable to more established video playback technologies (such as Windows Media Player, QuickTime and RealPlayer) that generally require the user to download and install a web browser plug-in in order to view video. Flash also requires a plug-in, but Adobe considers the Flash 7 plug-in to be present on approximately 90 per cent of online computers.

YouTube officially accepts uploaded videos in .WMV, .AVI, .MOV, MPEG and .MP4 formats and converts videos into .FLV (Adobe Flash Video) format after uploading. The extension is then stripped from the file. The different files are stored in obscurely named subdomains. YouTube also converts content to other formats so that it can be viewed outside the website.

Unregistered users can watch most videos on the site, while registered users are permitted to upload an unlimited number of videos. Some videos (e.g. videos containing potentially offensive content) are available only to users aged 18 plus. The uploading of pornography or videos containing nudity is prohibited. Related videos, determined by title and tags, appear on screen to the right of a given video.

In October 2006, Google Inc. announced that it had reached a deal to acquire the company for US$1.65 billion in Google stock. The deal closed on 13 November 2006. The working arrangement is that Google will focus on the search engine technology and the YouTube team will focus on the video content. Google has helped to make YouTube videos more searchable, including tighter integration into Google's video search product. As cameras become more and more powerful, YouTube video resolution will need to keep pace by encoding videos at higher and multiple bitrates – this is where Google's infrastructure advantages come into play.

A few notable statistics on YouTube at the time of its acquisition by Google are as follows:

- it is the fastest growing website in Internet history;
- on average 100 million videos are streamed every day;
- 65,000 new video clips are uploaded every day;

- there are more than 13 million unique visitors per month;
- an average user spends 30 minutes on YouTube and most uploaders are repeat visitors themselves;
- 58 per cent of Internet videos are watched on Youtube;
- 20–30 per cent of traffic volume is from the United States;
- while there is a wide range of user demographics, the largest segment of users are 18–35 year-olds.

The ability to embed the external player on any web page turned the tide for YouTube. Once MySpace.com users started adopting YouTube *en masse*, MySpace.com blocked video links to YouTube. However, MySpace caved under pressure from MySpace users and reinstated access to YouTube content.

The other key driver to YouTube's user acquisition was the frequency at which popular video content was distributed in a viral manner. Once traffic picked up, roughly every two weeks or so a video would become wildly popular. Soon the time between these super-hit videos started shrinking. The site took off at a scorching pace. Video footage of the South-east Asian tsunami resulted in one of the largest traffic spikes. Other popular clips included Jon Stewart on Crossfire and the infamous Janet Jackson Super Bowl video.

YouTube remains an interesting study in marketing a consumer internet service. While initial responses to the site were tepid, the June 2005 site revamp resulted in viral growth.

Before being purchased by Google, YouTube declared that its business model was advertisement-based, making 15 million dollars per month. Some industry commentators have speculated that YouTube's running costs – specifically the bandwidth required – may be as high as US$5–6 million per month, thereby fuelling criticisms that the company, like many Internet start-ups, did not have a viably implemented business model. Advertisements were launched on the site beginning in March 2006 (Mikew, 2007).

### The copyright balance

YouTube presents perhaps the best example of the fine line video-sharing companies must walk in regard to copyright materials. Besides displaying a fascination with amateur-made videos, YouTube fans have shown they want slicker, professionally crafted content as well. People often upload TV shows or movie clips on YouTube without authorization.

At present, most user-generated sites remove copyright materials once notified by the owner. YouTube, which does not pre-screen any of its videos, is very quick to pull videos once it has confirmed that the rightful owner did not authorize the material to be posted on the site.

### Marketing partnerships

As YouTube started in late 2005, NBC Universal was demanding that clips of its shows be removed from YouTube. Since then, NBC seemes to have changed its mind. In June 2006, NBC and YouTube signed a strategic marketing partnership. NBC would upload promotional video clips of some of its TV shows on YouTube, including *Saturday Night Live* and *The Tonight Show with Jay Leno*. In return NBC would also advertise on YouTube and promote the site on some of its TV shows. The companies also launched a contest where viewers of *The Office* could create and submit their own 20-second promo videos and post them on YouTube.

What NBC was doing was acknowledging the power of YouTube as a marketing vehicle. At the same time, NBC has a vested interest in controlling the marketing message on YouTube.

However, in March 2007, News Corp. and NBC announced that they would create an online video site that would rival the popular YouTube. The site will contain user-generated videos but the emphasis here is on the premium content, showing whole shows and not only video clips as with YouTube. In August 2007, the two companies were finally revealing key details about the joint venture: the site's name is Hulu.

Such deals do not necessarily mean that YouTube and other video-sharing sites will still not run into legal troubles. Also YouTube needs partnerships with professional media companies (entertainment companies) so it can get high-quality content on the site in a legitimate way.

Since June 2006 YouTube has gone into several partnerships (in Europe alone there are now more than 150 YouTube partners), including with the BBC.

BBC content now appears legitimately on YouTube. Whereas shows such as *Top Gear*, for example, were often to be found on the site, content will now appear legitimately. Under the terms of the deal, there will be three officially BBC-branded channels on YouTube featuring promo, entertainment and news content

There will be no full length episodes online, however. Under the non-exclusive partnership, the BBC channels will only contain 'short-form videos'.

On the News channel, around 30 news clips a day are available, providing 'up-to-the-minute news and analysis from around the world', in the words of the BBC. These advertising-funded clips, however, have only been available to users outside the UK.

## Internationalization

Localized versions of YouTube are available in a number of countries (see Table 1).

## Competitors

YouTube now competes with a range of domestic competitors, such as RuTube and Mail.ru in Russia, MyVideo (owned by Pro7Sat.1 media group), Sevenload and RTL's Clipfish in Germany, DailyMotion in France, Tudou in China (see below), Hispavista's Tu.tv, Libero Video in Italy, Brazil's Videolog, French-based Dailymotion, Dutch video sharing sites Filmpjes and 123video.nl, and many others.

### Tudou (www.tudou.com)

**Tudou** is the largest video sharing website in China, where users can upload, view and share video clips. Tudou went live on 15 April 2005 and by September 2007 used the world's largest CDN to serve over 55 million videos each day.

Tudou was founded by Gary Wang and Dutchman Marc van der Chijs, whom Wang met while at Bertelsmann Media Group in China. Like many technology start-ups, Tudou began on a shoestring with a raw technology team, practically in a garage. The name Tudou is Chinese Pinyin (Romanized Chinese) for potato. It was previously known as Toodou.com, and changed its domain name to Tudou.com in August 2006 when that domain became available. According to CEO Wang, the name comes from the English idiom 'couch potato'.

Tudou states it is one of the world's largest bandwidth users, moving more than 1 petabyte per day to 7 million users. YouTube serves more videos per day, but Tudou's content is much longer on average, so its total delivered video is much larger: about 15 billion minutes versus 3 billion for YouTube.

The Shanghai-based service uses Adobe Flash technology to publish more than 20,000 new videos each day, including amateur content such as video-blogging and original videos, movie and TV clips, and music videos. Unregistered users can watch videos on the site, while registered users are permitted to upload an unlimited number of videos, using online and Windows-based upload tools.

Sources: www.youtube.com; www.google.com; Mikew (2007), *Mikew's blog*, http://willy.boerland.com/myblog/youtube_bandwidth_usage_25_petabytes_per_month; Jones, B. and Leamonth, M. (2007) 'Showbiz's site fright/Web seen as both a threat and a gold mine', *Variety*, 10 March.

## Table 1 Localization of YouTube (in chronological order)

| Country | URL | Languages | Launch date |
|---|---|---|---|
| World (USA) | http://www.youtube.com/ | American English | 15 February 2005 |
| Netherlands | http://nl.youtube.com/ | Dutch | 19 June 2007 |
| France | http://fr.youtube.com/ | French | 19 June 2007 |
| Spain | http://es.youtube.com/ | Spanish | 19 June 2007 |
| United Kingdom | http://uk.youtube.com/ | British English | 19 June 2007 |
| Ireland | http://ie.youtube.com/ | Irish English | 19 June 2007 |
| Italy | http://it.youtube.com/ | Italian | 19 June 2007 |
| Japan | http://jp.youtube.com/ | Japanese | 19 June 2007 |
| Brazil | http://br.youtube.com/ | Brazilian Portuguese | 19 June 2007 |
| Hong Kong | http://hk.youtube.com/ | Traditional Chinese | 17 October 2007 |
| Republic of China (Taiwan) | http://tw.youtube.com/ | Traditional Chinese | 18 October 2007 |
| Australia | http://au.youtube.com/ | Australian English | 22 October 2007 |
| Germany | http://de.youtube.com/ | German | 8 November 2007 |
| South Korea | http://kr.youtube.com/ | | 23 January 2008 |
| India | http://in.youtube.com/ | | 7 May 2008 |

## Questions for discussion

1 What are the reasons for the increasing level of outsourcing to international subcontractors?

2 Describe the typology of subcontractors based on the differences in the contractor/subcontractor relationship.

3 Explain the shift from seller to buyer initiative in subcontracting.

4 Explain the main differences between the US and the Japanese subsupplier systems.

5 How are project exports/turnkey projects different from general subcontracting in the industrial market?

6 Project export is often characterized by a complex and time-consuming decision-making process. What are the marketing implications of this for the potential subcontractor?

## References

Andersen, P.H. and Christensen, P.R. (2005) 'Bridges over troubled water: suppliers as connective nodes in global supply networks', *Journal of Business Research*, Vol. 58, pp. 1261–1273

Blenker, P. and Christensen, P.R. (1994) 'Interactive strategies in supply chains: a double-edged portfolio approach to SME', *Subcontractors Positioning Paper* presented at the 8th Nordic Conference on Small Business Research.

Cavinato, J.L. (1992) 'A total cost/value model for supply chain competitiveness', *Journal of Business Logistics*, 13(2), pp. 285–301.

Cho, Dong-Sung and Chu, Wujin (1994) 'Determinants of bargaining power in OEM negotiations', *Industrial Marketing Management*, 23, pp. 342–355.

Dwyer, R.F., Schurr, P.H. and Oh, S. (1987) 'Developing buyer–seller relationships', *Journal of Marketing*, 51, April, pp. 11–27.

Ghauri, P., Wahyuni, S. and Karsten, L. (2007) 'Managing international strategic alliance relationships', *Thunderbird International Business Review* 49(6) (Nov–Dec), pp. 671–687.

Hadjikhani, A. (1996) 'Project marketing and the management of discontinuity', *International Business Review*, 5(3), pp. 319–336.

Hibbert, E.P. (1993) 'Global make or buy decisions', *Industrial Marketing Management*, 22, pp. 67–77.

Hines, P. (1995) 'Network sourcing: a hybrid approach', *International Journal of Purchasing and Materials Management*, 31(2), Spring, pp. 18–24.

Jüttner, U. and Wehrli, H.P. (1994) 'Relationship marketing from a value system perspective', *International Journal of Service Industry Management*, 5, pp. 54–73.

Kanter, R.M. (1994) 'Collaborative advantage', *Harvard Business Review*, July–August, pp. 96–107.

Lehtinen, U. (1991) 'Alihankintajarjestelma 1990-luvulla [Subcontracting system in the 1990s]', *Publications of SITRA*, 114, Helsinki.

Mouzas, S., Henneberg, S. and Naudé, P. (2007) 'Trust and reliance in business relationships', *European Journal of Marketing*, Vol. 41, No. 9/10, pp. 1016–1032.

Ottesen, O. (1995) 'Buyer initiative: ignored, but imperative for marketing theory', Working Paper, Department of Business Administration, Stavanger College, Norway.

Tähtinen, J. and Vaaland, T. (2006) 'Business relationships facing the end: why restore them?', *Journal of Business & Industrial Marketing*, 21(1), pp. 14–23.

Turnbull, P.W. and Valla, J.P. (1986) *Strategies for International Industrial Marketing*, Croom Helm, London.

Welch, L.S. and Luostarinen, R. (1988) 'Internationalization: evolution of a concept', *Journal of General Management*, 14(2), pp. 36–64.

# IKEA:
## Expanding through franchising to the South American market?

At the beginning of 2007 Ingvar Kamprad, founder of the Swedish furniture retailing giant IKEA, is concerned 'his' firm may be growing too quickly. He used to be in favour of rapid expansion, but he has now become worried that the firm may be forced to close stores in the event of a sustained economic downturn.

Although IKEA is one of Sweden's best-known exports, it has not in a strict legal sense been Swedish since the early 1980s. The store has made its name by supplying Scandinavian designs at Asian prices. It has managed its international expansion without stumbling. Indeed, its brand – which stands for clean, green and attractive design and value for money – is as potent today as it has been at any time in more than 50 years in business.

The parent of all IKEA companies – the operator of 207 of the 235 worldwide IKEA stores – is Ingka Holding, a private Dutch-registered company. Ingka Holding (which is named after the first and last name of the founder) belongs entirely to Stichting Ingka Foundation. This is a Dutch-registered, tax-exempt, non-profit-making legal entity, which was given the shares of Ingvar Kamprad in 1982. *Stichtingen*, or foundations, are the most common form of not-for-profit organization in the Netherlands; tens of thousands of them are registered.

Most Dutch *stichtingen* are tiny, but if Stichting Ingka Foundation were listed it would be one of the Netherlands' ten largest companies by market value. Its main asset is the Ingka Holding group, which is conservatively financed and highly profitable.

Valuing the Ingka Holding Group is awkward, because IKEA has no direct competitors that operate globally. Shares in Target, a large, successful chain of stores in the United States that makes a fifth of its sales from home furnishings, are priced at 20 times the store's latest full-year earnings. Using that price/earnings ratio, the Ingka Holding Group is worth €28 billion ($36 billion).

Now Ingvar Kamprad has heard that the top management of the IKEA Group plans to make a further international expansion, into South America, because of the growth opportunities there. Kamprad is very scep-

tical about these plans and his personal assistant has asked you, as an international marketing specialist, to get an expert opinion about the plans . . .

### IKEA – the story
IKEA Svenska AB, founded in 1943, is the world's largest furniture retailer and specializes in stylish but inexpensive Scandinavian designed furniture.

### *Brief timeline*

1943   The founder of IKEA, Ingvar Kamprad from Agunnaryd, Sweden, registers the name IKEA. The name was formed from the founder's initials (IK) plus the first letters of Elmtaryd and Agunnaryd, the farm and village where he grew up.

1950   Furniture enters the IKEA product range for the first time.

1951   The first IKEA catalogue is published.

1953   The first IKEA furniture showroom is opened in Älmhult, Sweden, to better display the products' quality.

1955   IKEA begins to design its own furniture.

1956   IKEA introduces self-assembly furniture in flat packs.

1958   The first IKEA store opens in Älmhult, Sweden.

1963   The second IKEA store is opened in Oslo, Norway.

1965   The IKEA Stockholm store opens. The self-service, open warehouse is introduced.

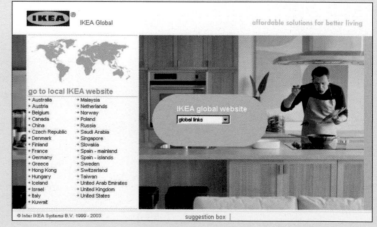

1969  The first IKEA store in Denmark opens.

1973  The first store outside Scandinavia is opened in Spreitenbach, Switzerland.

1974  The first IKEA store opens in Germany, in Munich.

1975  The first IKEA store in Australia.

1976  The first IKEA store in Canada.

1977  The first IKEA store in Austria.

1978  The first IKEA store in Singapore.

1979  The first IKEA store in the Netherlands.

1980  The first IKEA store in the Canary Islands.

1981  The first IKEA stores in France and Iceland.

1983  The first IKEA store in Saudi Arabia.

1984  The first IKEA stores in Belgium and Kuwait.

1985  The first IKEA store in the United States.

1987  The first IKEA stores in the United Kingdom and Hong Kong.

1989  The first IKEA store in Italy.

1990  The first IKEA stores in Hungary and Poland.

1991  The first IKEA stores in the Czech Republic and the United Arab Emirates.

1992  The first IKEA stores in Mallorca and Slovakia.

1994  The first IKEA store in Taiwan.

1996  The first IKEA stores in Finland, Malaysia and mainland Spain.

1997  IKEA appears on the Internet with the World Wide Living Room website.

1998  The first IKEA store in mainland China.

2000  First IKEA store opens in Russia (Moscow).

2001  First stores in Israel (Netanya) and Greece (Thessaloniki).

2004  First stores in Portugal (Lisbon).

2005  First stores in Turkey (Istanbul).

2006  First stores in Ireland (Dublin).

2007  First stores in Romania (Bucharest).

## About corporate IKEA

IKEA has grown into the world's largest furniture retailer, with 237 stores in 35 countries (2007) and a workforce of some 90,000 people since its first outlet opened in Älmhult in 1958. The firm is noted for its rapid international expansion and has recently set up stores in Eastern Europe and Russia.

IKEA's success in the retail industry can be attributed to its vast experience in the retail market, product differentiation and cost leadership. The company is one of the world's most successful multinational retailing firms, operating as a global organization, with its unique concept that its furniture is sold in kits that are assembled by the customer at home.

The firm, which remains in private ownership, racked up sales of nearly €15 billion in 2002.

There are about 12,000 products in the total IKEA product range. Each store carries a selection of these 12,000 products depending on store size. The core range is the same worldwide.

IKEA accounts for just 5 per cent to 10 per cent of the furniture market in each country in which it operates. More important is that the awareness of the IKEA brand is much bigger than the size of the company because IKEA is far more than a furniture merchant. It sells a Scandinavian lifestyle that customers around the world embrace.

The IKEA business idea is to offer a wide range of home furnishing items of good design and function, excellent quality and durability, at prices so low that the majority of people can afford them. The company targets the customer who is looking for value and is willing to do a little bit of work serving themselves, transporting the items home and assembling the furniture. The typical IKEA customer is a young low-to middle-income family.

As mentioned, IKEA's retailing, is based on a franchise system. Inter IKEA Systems B.V., located in Delft (the Netherlands), is the owner and franchisor of the IKEA concept. The IKEA Group is a private group of companies owned by a charitable foundation in the Netherlands. It is active in developing, purchasing, distributing and selling IKEA products. The IKEA experience is more than just products, however, it is a retail concept. For the concept to work all aspects must be in place. IKEA products are therefore sold only in IKEA stores franchised by Inter IKEA Systems B.V. However, most of the global product policy (including product development) and the global marketing is centralized to the Swedish part of the company, IKEA of Sweden.

## Product development

The team behind each product consists of designers, product developers and purchasers who get together to discuss design, materials and suitable suppliers. Everyone contributes with their specialist knowledge. Purchasers, for example, use their contacts with suppliers all over the world via IKEA Trading Service Offices. Who can make this product of the best quality for the right price at the right time? Products are often developed in close cooperation with suppliers and often only one supplier is appointed to supply all the stores around the world.

IKEA does not have its own manufacturing facilities but uses subcontracted manufacturers all over the world. In order to keep costs low, IKEA shoppers are prosumers – half producers and half consumers. In other words, they have to assemble the products themselves. To facilitate shopping, IKEA provides catalogues, tape measures, shopping lists and an internet website to help the consumer with fitting the furniture into the room. Car roof racks are available for purchase at cost and

IKEA pick-up vans/mini-trucks are available to rent. IKEA's success is based on the relatively simple idea of keeping the cost between manufacturers and customers down. Costs are kept under control starting at the design level of the value-added chain. IKEA also keeps costs down by packing items compactly in flat standardized packaging and stacking them as high as possible to reduce storage space during and after distribution.

Effective marketing through catalogues is what usually attracts the customer first; what keeps customers coming back is good service. IKEA believes that a strong in-stock position, in which the most popular style and design trends are correctly anticipated, is crucial to keep customers satisfied. For that IKEA depends on leading-edge technology and the company has developed its own global distribution network. By utilizing control points in the distribution cycle the firm is able to insure timely delivery of products to retail stores all over the world.

IKEA thinks that consumer tastes are merging globally. To take one example, IKEA, which has been exporting the 'streamlined and contemporary Scandinavian style' to the United States since 1985, found several opportunities to export US style to Europe, as Europeans picked up on some US furnishing concepts. To respond to this new demand IKEA now markets 'American-style' furnishings in Europe.

Bureaucracy is fought at all levels in the organization. Kamprad believes that simplicity and common sense should characterize planning and strategic direction. In addition, the culture emphasizes efficiency and low cost, which is not to be achieved at the expense of quality or service. Symbolic policies, such as only flying economy class and stay at economical hotels, employing young executives and sponsoring university programmes, have been integrated into the corporate culture and have further inspired the spirit of entrepreneurship in the organization. For instance, all design teams enjoy complete autonomy in their work, but are expected to design new and appealing products regularly.

IKEA has improved its value chain by a cooperative focus on suppliers and customers. The firm emphasizes centralized control and standardization of the product mix.

In order to maintain cost leadership in the market, internal production efficiencies must be greater than those of competitors. Under IKEA's global strategy suppliers are usually located in low-cost nations, with close proximity to raw materials and reliable access to distribution channels. These suppliers produce highly standardized products intended for the global market, which size provides the firm with the opportunity to take advantage of economies of scale. IKEA's role is not only to globally integrate operations and centrally design products, but also to find an effective combination of low cost, standardization, technology and quality.

In the case of IKEA, a standardized product strategy does not mean complete cultural insensitivity. The company is, rather, responding to globally emerging consumer tastes and preferences. Retail outlets all over the world carry the basic product range, which is universally accepted, but also place great emphasis on the product lines that appeal to local customer preferences.

IKEA has modified the value chain approach by integrating the customer into the process and introducing a two-way value system between customers, suppliers and IKEA's headquarters. In this global sourcing strategy the customer is a supplier of time, labour, information, knowledge and transport. On the other hand, the suppliers are customers, receiving technical assistance from IKEA's corporate technical headquarters through various business services. The company wants customers to understand that their role is not to consume value, but rather to create it.

IKEA's role in the value chain is to mobilize suppliers and customers to help them further add value to the system. Customers are clearly informed in the catalogues of what the firm's business systems provide, and what they are expected to add to the final process.

In order to furnish the customer with good quality products at a low cost, the firm must be able to find suppliers that can deliver high-quality items at low cost per unit. The company's headquarters provides carefully selected suppliers with technical assistance, leased equipment and the necessary skills needed to produce high-quality items. This long-term supplier relationship not only produces superior products, but also adds internal value to the suppliers. In addition, this value chain modification differentiates IKEA from its competitors.

Directly linked to its mission statement, IKEA has built its cost leadership position on these processes. It furnishes the customer with a quality product with components derived from all over the world utilizing multilevel competitive advantages, low cost logistics, and large simple retail outlets in suburban areas. Furthermore, cost leadership has been effectively incorporated into the organization's culture through symbols and efficient processes. In return for high sales volumes IKEA accepts low profit margins. In addition, IKEA's marketing emphasis on budget prices and good value clearly communicates cost leadership to customers. IKEA's strategy demonstrates that the perception that cost leadership equals poor quality in products and services is incorrect. High quality is associated with input and process variables. Cost reduction, on the other hand, does not mean reducing the quality of these variables, but rather doing things better, and more efficiently. Cost leadership is a part of the management process and culture.

From this discussion it is possible to conclude that IKEA effectively aligns its cost leadership platform, focusing on the needs of its target market segment. Differentiation, as indicated in the modification of the value chain, also focuses on this particular segment.

## The internationalization of IKEA

IKEA has applied a conservative policy to internationalization. As a general rule, the firm does not enter a new potential market by opening a retail outlet. Instead, a supplier link with the host nation is established. This is a strategic, risk-reducing approach in which local suppliers can provide valuable input on political and legal, cultural, financial and other issues that provide opportunities and/or threats to the IKEA concept. In the 1970s and 1980s IKEA concentrated its international expansion in Europe and in North America mainly through company-owned subsidiaries. On the other hand, over the past 20 years franchising has been extensively utilized in expanding to other areas of the world.

### Expansion by franchising

IKEA approaches unknown, relatively small and high risk markets by franchising. Franchises are granted by Inter IKEA Systems B.V. as part of a detailed international expansion plan. Serious applicants are carefully researched and evaluated and franchises are granted only to companies and/or individuals with strong financial backing and a proven record in retail. Franchisees have to carry basic items, but have the freedom to design the rest of the product mix to fit local market needs. The basic core items number approximately 12,000 simple and functional products. The centralized head office is actively involved in the selection processes and provides advice. In addition, all products have to be purchased from IKEA's product lines. In order to maintain service, quality and logistic standards, individual franchisees are periodically audited and compared to overall corporate performance. Extensive training and operational support is provided from headquarters. All franchisees pay franchise fees to IKEA Holdings. All catalogues and promotional advertising is the responsibility of headquarters. Franchising has been used as a vehicle for the company's generic focus strategy.

### Balance of autonomy and strategic direction

As IKEA continues to expand overseas the significance of centralized strategic direction will increase. Naturally rapid internationalization will trigger a range of challenges imposed on the headquarters, such as the following:

- The complexity of the logistics system will increase.
- It will be more difficult to respond to national needs and cultural sensitivity issues.
- Franchisees may demand more control over operations.
- Emerging demographic trends will force the organization to broaden its focus strategy to respond to varying nation-level consumer groups.

With all these challenges emerging it might be very difficult to maintain a central organizational structure. The best way to meet these challenges is to find the proper balance between country level autonomy and centralized intervention. With reference to IKEA's long-term relationship and control over its suppliers in exchange for quality assurance, technology transfers and economies of scale factors may trigger potential suppliers to integrate forward and produce competitive products for IKEA's local competitors. With logistics complications and long lead times IKEA is forced to maintain high control levels over its suppliers. For instance, if the supplier responsible for the screws component to a table cannot deliver on time, the supplier of the table-top has to adapt its production to the new scenario. Without IKEA's centralized logistics system this example could lead to severe store shortages, leading to losses in sales.

## The Brazilian market for furniture

According to the Brazilian Association of Furniture Manufacturers (ABIMOVEL), the Brazilian furniture market was estimated at approximately $3.6 billion in 2000, of which about $111 million were imports. The market can be broken down into three main categories: residential (60 per cent), office (25 per cent), and institutional organizations, such as schools, hospitals and hotels (15 per cent).

Brazil has 4.6 million hectares of planted forests, almost all of which is located in the south of the country. Wood from such forests is mainly used in the production of furniture, pulp and paper. The main furniture production centres, as well as the most important markets, are also located in southern Brazil.

The production of particleboard, which was 494,000 m$^3$ in 1990, jumped to 1.3 million m$^3$ in 1998, an annual growth rate of 13 per cent. This pattern is expected to continue in the near future. Approximately 80 per cent of Brazil's particleboard production is consumed by the furniture sector. A smaller volume is marketed by resellers and destined for small furniture manufacturers.

As the Brazilian furniture market continues to reap more and more of its profits from exports, production is increasingly tailored to satisfy market niches that demand differentiated products. To meet this need the Brazilian industry is investing more in design and development, although investments are smaller in comparison to investments made in the United States, Italy and Germany. Brazil is also importing state-of-the-art equipment to address quality issues mandated by foreign markets, e.g. the US, Italian and German ones. Today the segment requires import of equipment such as wood-drying machinery, finishing machinery and tools.

According to the Brazilian Furniture Association there are approximately 13,500 Brazilian furniture manufacturers, most of which are small. These firms are typically family-owned companies whose capital is exclusively Brazilian. Historically, the greater proportion of Brazilian manufacturers have been concentrated in areas of large population density in southern Brazil.

The process of trade liberalization initiated in 1990 introduced significant changes in Brazil's trade regime, resulting in a more open and competitive economy.

The Brazilian economy was deeply affected by the crises in the Asian and Russian markets. As a consequence the currency suffered deeply from the devaluation in January 1999. Brazilian imports of furniture were also seriously affected by this devaluation, and the industry is currently suffering from the unfavourable (for Brazilians) *real*–dollar exchange rate.

US exports of furniture to Brazil reached $43 million in 2000 (39 per cent of total Brazilian furniture imports) and are expected to decrease to $36 million in 2001. US exports to Brazil were particularly strong in the area of seats, new-design office furniture, and high-end, high-value-added residential furniture. Market analysts estimate that in the next three to four years imports of institutional furniture, such as that used in hospitals and hotels, will increase considerably, mainly imports from the United States.

### Imports

Brazilian furniture imports totalled $111 million in 2000, and decreased to $96 million in 2001. This represents 3 per cent of the total furniture market in Brazil. The USA holds 39 per cent of the imported furniture market, followed by Germany with 36 per cent, Italy with 10 per cent, and other countries with 15 per cent.

### End-user analysis

Different industry segments, such as automotive, aviation and furniture (residential, commercial and institutional) make up the Brazilian market. Each of those areas has its own purchasing approach. For example, the automotive industry may import directly from its headquarters and, in the case of the furniture industry, the end user might be an importer or a store chain.

It is important to mention that there are no major distributor chains in Brazil. Most furniture imports are made through direct importers and, in a smaller proportion, local manufacturers wishing to complement their product line.

High-end furniture and mattresses are commonly imported into Brazil by direct importers or furniture stores. Interior decorators and architects are also considered decision makers, since they are the ones who recommend brands and styles to their final clients.

### Import climate

Brazil has a tariff-based import system and has simplified the process for obtaining import licences. Import tariffs are levied *ad valorem* on the CIF value of the imports. Import tax (IPI – See below) for furniture varies from 5–15 per cent.

The industrial products tax (IPI) is a federal tax levied on most domestic and imported manufactured products. It is assessed at the point of sale by the manufacturer or processor in the case of domestically produced goods, and at the point of customs clearance in the case of imports. The tax rate varies by product and is based on the product's CIF value plus duties.

Interest rates in Brazil are high (estimated at 18.3 per cent per year in June 2001) and discourage demand for bank loans. The few sources of funds available for long-term financing are provided by the National Bank for Economic and Social Development (BNDES), through leasing operations and by foreign government export agencies.

### Distribution and business practices

Major end users of furniture will only purchase from well-known and reliable suppliers. Although large end users may import directly from foreign suppliers, they are always concerned with after-sales service. Technical assistance and availability of replacement parts are considered important factors in the purchasing decision. In some segments, such as commercial and institutional, this factor may determine from whom the end user will purchase. A physical presence in the market, either through an agent or a manufacturing plant, increases the end user's trust in the supplier's commitment to this market and facilitates the sale.

### The retail scene in Brazil

For many years the popular wisdom in Brazil was that shopping malls were only for rich people. The 1984 opening of Center Norte mall in São Paulo changed all that. It is strategically placed next to a subway and a bus terminal. Proximity to mass transit is essential, since many low-income consumers do not own cars. Center Norte was followed by other shopping malls in other cities, such as Rio de Janeiro and Belo Horizonte.

Economic instability, difficulties in obtaining financing at reasonable interest rates and customs barriers for certain imports have slowed down the the entry of foreign retailers to Brazil. Among the international chains that have been attracted by Brazil's 80 million consumers are JC Penney, Zara and the Dutch chain

C&A, that leads the fashion sector in Brazil. International franchisors such as Benetton, Lacoste, Hugo Boss, Polo Ralph Lauren and McDonald's operate in Brazilian shopping centres, some on a large scale.

Those who have set up shops in Brazil have varied results directly related to their ability to adapt to local conditions. Sears, for example, had extremely negative results, due to the centralization of decision making in Chicago. Similarly, Zara tried to bring to Brazil its European management policy and market approach and is now facing poor financial results. The contrast is the excellent performance of C&A, whose policies and procedures were defined in Brazil for the local market. JC Penney acquired a local chain (Renner) and accelerated its expansion with good results (ICSC Worldwide Commission, 2000).

Sources: IKEA Annual Report 2002 (preliminary results); www.ikea.com; BBC News (2003), news.bbc.co.uk, 'IKEA founder worried over growth', 3 January; ICSC Worldwide Commission (2000), 'Shopping centres: a world of opportunities', www.icsc.org.

## Questions

1 Until now IKEA international marketing strategy has been tightly and centrally controlled by corporate headquarters. However, high local pressures emerging due to demographic and cultural differences might force the local IKEA shops to take strategic initiatives to respond to local market needs. In this connection discuss the regional headquarters and transnational organization (presented in Chapter 9) as hierarchical 'entry mode' alternatives to the very centralized strategy emanating from IKEA's headquarters.

2 IKEA has not yet explored joint venture and strategic alliances strategies. Evaluate the pros and cons regarding these two entry strategies versus the traditional IKEA entry mode of franchising.

3 Should IKEA penetrate the South American market by establishing a shop in Brazil?

4 In the light of the political and economic situation in South America, outline the sourcing concept that should be implemented in the South American market.

# Autoliv Air Bags:
## Transforming Autoliv into a global company

Chief executive officer of Autoliv Inc., Lars Westerberg, is in the middle of a board of directors' meeting in Stockholm in September 2006, discussing how it is possible to further globalize Autoliv. He takes out a situation report for the business area of air bags. As there are a couple of new members on the board Lars takes the opportunity to give a broader introduction to the business area than he usually does. The following is Lars Westerberg's status report.

## Situation report for the business area of air bags

### Business concept

Autoliv Inc., which is a Fortune 500 company, is the world's largest automotive safety supplier with sales to all the leading car manufacturers in the world. Autoliv's shares are listed on the New York Stock Exchange and on the Stockholm Stock Exchange. The company develops, markets and manufactures airbags, seat belts, safety electronics, steering wheels, anti-whiplash systems, seat components and child seats. Autoliv has 80 subsidiaries (production plants) and joint ventures in 30 vehicle-producing countries, with over 40,000 employees. In addition, Autoliv has technical centres in nine countries with 20 crash test tracks – more than any other automotive safety supplier.

Autoliv aims to develop, manufacture and market systems and components worldwide for *personal safety* in automobiles. This includes the mitigation of injuries to autombile occupants and pedestrians and the avoidance of accidents. In this aspect, Autoliv wants to be the systems supplier and the development partner to car producers that satisfy all the needs in the area of personal safety. To fulfil its business concept Autoliv has strong product lines:

- frontal and side-impact airbags (including all key components such as inflators with initiators, textile cushions, electronics with sensors and software, steel and plastic parts);
- seat belts (including all key components such as webbing, retractors and buckles);
- seat belt features (including pretensioners, load limiters, height adjusters and belt grabbers);
- seat SubSystems (including anti-whiplash systems);
- steering wheels (including integrated driver airbags);

- roll-over protection (including sensors, pretensioners and airbag curtains).

In 2006 the penetration rate of curtain airbags in new cars was 50 per cent in Europe, 35 per cent in North America, 20 per cent in Japan and 10 per cent in the rest of the world.

The following concentrates on the business area of air bags.

### Production strategy

Autoliv has final assembly of restraint systems, located close to major customers' plants for just-in-time supply (see Figure 1). Most of the component production (textiles and stamped metal components, etc.) has been outsourced during the past five years.

Since major automobile manufacturers are continually expanding production into more countries, it is also Autoliv's strategy to have manufacturing capacity where the major vehicle manufacturers have or are likely to set up production facilities. As a consequence Autoliv has more plants for automotive safety products in more countries than any other supplier.

## The product: the air bag

Even the best belt designs cannot prevent all head and chest injuries in serious head-on crashes. This is where air bags help, by creating an energy-absorbing cushion between an occupant's upper body and the steering wheel, instrument panel or windshield. Independent research has shown that driver deaths in head-on crashes are about 20 per cent lower in cars with frontal air bags than in similar cars with belts only. In all kinds of crash deaths are down by about 15 per cent over and above lives already being saved by belts.

Although air bags may seem complicated they are in fact relatively simple. In moderate and severe head-on crashes sensors signal inflators to fill the bags with harmless gas. The bags fill in a fraction of a second and begin deflating the instant they cushion people, but in the United States a few occupants have died of broken necks. Peak inflation is in less than $^d/_{20}$th of a second, faster than the blink of an eye. The speed and force of air bag inflation may occasionally cause injuries, mostly minor abrasions or bruises, but in the United States some occupants have died of broken necks caused by air bags that inflated with great force. Those at the greatest risk of injury caused by an air bag are those who drive or ride unbelted, small children, short or obese adults, and certain disabled people.

Injury risk from the bag itself can be reduced by choosing a driving or passenger position that does not put your face or chest close to the steering wheel or instrument panel. The combination of seat belt and air bag provides maximum protection in all kinds of crash.

Together with Volvo Autoliv has also developed the first side air bags to protect drivers and front-seat passengers in side-impact crashes. These bags are typically smaller than frontal air bags and they inflate more quickly. Volvo was the first manufacturer to offer side air bags in its 850 model in 1994. Volvo's bag is mounted on the outside of driver and front-seat passenger seat backs. Since 1996 side bags have been standard in all Volvo models.

The history of air bags goes back to the early 1950s. The product idea was patented in 1951 by Walter Linderer from Munich. It was in the United States, however, that the concept came into existence, driven by the North Americans' reluctance to use seat belts and hindered by the car manufacturers, which initially ridiculed the idea. In 1981 only 2,636 air bag systems were produced.

However, in late 1989 automatic restraint systems became compulsory in all passenger cars in the United States on the driver's side and, while this included automatically fastening seat belts, it seemed that the air bag had at last arrived. By 1992, 10 million air-bag-equipped cars had been delivered to the United States. In 1993 came the requirement that all new light vehicles of model year 1999 produced in the United States had to be fitted with frontal air bags for the driver and the front-seat occupant. The next stage will be the compulsory fitting of air bags to both the driver and front passenger sides.

Autoliv introduced its first air bag system in 1990. It was designed to meet US requirements, where not all states have laws on wearing seat belts. The air bag therefore had to be relatively large. Autoliv has developed a special system (the Eurobag system) for markets where wearing a seat belt is compulsory. In this system the air bags have less volume (but they are still effective) and therefore the price can be kept at a lower level than some of the competitors. In the Eurobag system the air bags are 30–45 litres on the driver's side and 60–100 litres on the passenger's side. Furthermore, the Eurobag system is lighter and less bulky.

An air bag system consists of an electronic control unit and an air bag module. The electronic control unit contains (among other things) a sensor, while the module essentially consists of a gas generator, a nylon bag and a cover for the steering wheel centre or the instrument panel, depending on where the air bag module is placed. Autoliv typically supplies entire systems adapted to individual car models.

## Organization

In France, Germany, Spain, Sweden, the United Kingdom and the United States, local management is regionally responsible for Autoliv's operations in countries other than their own. As a result the main customers have the advantage of dealing with Autoliv both in their home market and when they have or are going to establish production in other markets. Together with two regional coordination offices this organization contributes to low corporate overheads and short response times for the customers. (Autoliv's global headquarters has only 40 employees.) Autoliv's business directors and their organizations coordinate all activities with major customers on a global basis.

## The world market for air bags

With its successful growth strategy, Autoliv has become the global leader in the $20 billion automobile occupant restraint market. Airbags account for just over 50 per cent of that market, seat belts for almost 30 per cent and electronics for nearly 20 per cent.

The global steering wheel market, which Autoliv entered in 1995 to promote the integration of driver air bags into steering wheels, amounts to over $1.5 billion.

The world market for air bags was an area of spectacular growth during the 1990s. In 2005 the number of frontal air bag units was almost 125 million and the number of side-impact air bags nearly 50 million.

Figure 1 Autoliv's corporate structure

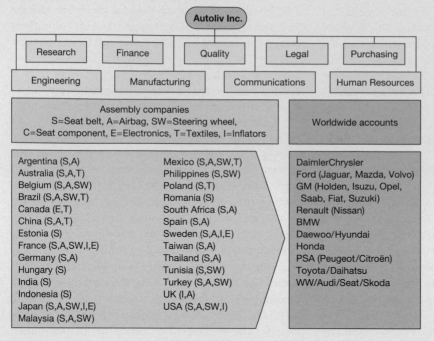

optional accessories in many cars – at least initially – until the car producers have had time to evaluate the reaction from the market.

Autoliv estimates that it currently has approximately one-third of the global market for car occupant restraint products and that it has a somewhat larger global market share for air bags than for seat belts. For side air bags, which were invented by Autoliv and introduced in 1994, Autoliv's global market share is still more than 40 per cent (see also Table 2). For other recent safety improvements, such as seat belt pretensioners and load limiters, Autoliv's global market position is strong.

In North America, Autoliv estimates that in 2001 it accounted for a little less than one-third the air bag products market and the same for the seat belt market compared with just over 10 per cent in 1999. (Autoliv did not sell seat belts in the United States until 1993.) Autoliv made its big entry into the North American market in 1996 when it acquired

In the United States frontal air bags – both on the driver and the passenger side – are compulsory under federal law in all new light vehicles sold after 1 September 1998. The US market for frontal air bags therefore fluctuates with the car production cycle, but sales of side air bags are now about to take off. Their penetration rate was less than 20 per cent among new US light vehicles in 2001. Both Ford and General Motors have announced aggressive plans for curtain side air bags such as Autoliv's Inflatable Curtain. In addition, new regulations in the United States will require vehicle manufacturers to phase in more valuable 'advanced air bags' during a three-year period starting on 1 September 2003.

In Europe, Autoliv estimates that more or less all new vehicles have dual airbags. Installations of side impact air bags began in 1994, but in 2001 two-thirds of all new vehicles in Europe had such systems for chest protection. In addition, 25 per cent had a separate side impact air bag for head protection (such as the inflatable curtain).

In Japan, where development started later than in Europe, penetration rates for frontal air bags are nearly as high as in Europe, while the penetration rate for side air bags is clearly below the level in Europe.

In the rest of the world, penetration rates vary greatly from country to country, but the average is still less than 50 per cent for both driver and passenger air bags (see Table 1). Installations of side air bags has just started.

The potential market for side air bags is difficult to assess. This is because side impact air bags will be

Table 1 The world market for frontal air bags (2005)

| | Production of light vehicles (millions) | Percentage of vehicles equipped with air bags (dual air bags, both driver and passenger) | Total market for frontal air bags (driver + passenger) (millions) |
|---|---|---|---|
| Europe | | | 44 |
| East | 6 | | |
| West | 16 | 100% with dual bags | |
| USA | 18 | 100% with dual bags | 36 |
| Asia | | | |
| Japan | 11 | | |
| China | 5 | 70% with driver's air bag | 34 |
| South Korea | 4 | 50% with dual air bags | |
| Others | 10 | 50% with driver's air bag 30% with dual air bags | 11 |
| Total | 60 | | 125 |

Source: Autoliv Financial Report 2005; Autoliv PowerPoint presentations.

Table 2 Autoliv's global market shares (%) in main product categories, 2005

| Product | North America | Europe | Japan | Global |
|---|---|---|---|---|
| Seat belts | 28 | 62 | 19 | 41 |
| Frontal airbags | 28 | 42 | 11 | 28 |
| Side airbags | 41 | 52 | 32 | 41 |

Morton Automotive Safety Products, which at that time was North America's largest air bag producer. The air bag business has given Autoliv an opportunity to expand its seat belt business now as complete systems sourcing takes place. In 2000 Autoliv acquired the North American seat belt business of NSK. Autoliv's market share for seat belts also increased as a result of new contracts, and the increasing number of new United States vehicles with seat belt pretensioners. Steering wheel sales in the United States commenced in 1998. Based on orders received so far, Autoliv expects its steering wheel market share to approach 10 per cent in just a couple of years.

In Europe, Autoliv estimates its market share to be about 50 per cent with a somewhat higher market share for seat belts than for air bags. The market share for steering wheels is approximately 15 per cent. In Asia, Autoliv's market share is not more than approximately 10 per cent for frontal air bags.

In Japan, Autoliv has a strong position in the air bag inflator market and rapidly growing sales of air bag modules. Local assembly of air bag modules began in 1998. In 2000 Autoliv acquired the second largest Japanese steering wheel company with a market share exceeding 20 per cent, and 40 per cent of NSK's Asian seat belt operations with the option to acquire the remaining shares in two steps in 2002 and 2003. Including NSK's sales, Autoliv accounts for approximately a fifth of the Japanese seat belt market.

In other countries, such as Argentina, Australia, China, India, Malaysia, New Zealand, South Africa and Turkey, where Autoliv established production early, the company has achieved strong market positions in several places.

## Competitors

In the late 1990s the number of major suppliers of occupant restraint systems was reduced from nine to four. As a result of the consolidation among producers of light vehicles the new entities that have been formed require suppliers to be cost efficient and have the capability to deliver the same products to all the companies' plants worldwide.

The four leading car occupant restraint suppliers now account for approximately 80 per cent of the world market (worth $16 billion) as opposed to 50 per cent

five years ago. During this period Autoliv has increased its share to slightly more than 30 per cent and has replaced TRW (a US publically traded company) as the market leader. Another important auto safety supplier is Takata (a privately owned Japanese company). Both TRW and Takata have about 25 per cent market share. Delphi (the world's largest automotive components supplier) and Key Safety Systems, formerly Breed (a US company that in 2000 emerged from bankruptcy) have less than 5 per cent each.

## Customers

Several of the world's largest car producers are among Autoliv's customers (see Table 3). Autoliv typically accounts for between 25 and 75 per cent of customers' purchases of seat belts and air bags. Autoliv supplies all major car makers in the world and most car brands. In the development of a new car model, a process that takes several years, Autoliv in many cases functions as a development partner for the car manufacturer. This typically means that Autoliv gives advice on new safety-enhancing products and assists in adaptation and conduct testing (including full-scale crash tests with the vehicle) of the safety systems.

No customer accounts for more than 21 per cent of Autoliv's sales. Most of these car makers can be characterized as Autoliv's global accounts (GAs) – see also Chapter 20. The contracts are generally divided among a car maker's different car models, with each contract usually running for the life of the car model. No contract accounts for more than 5 per cent of consolidated sales. Of the 2005 total sales in Table 4, Europe accounts for 54 per cent, North America 26 per cent, Japan 9 per cent and the rest of the world 11 per cent.

Table 3 Autoliv's customer mix (2005)

| Car manufacturer | Share of global vehicle production (70 million vehicles) (%) | Share of Autoliv's total sales ($6.2 billion) (%) |
|---|---|---|
| General Motors | 14 | 13 |
| Renault/Nissan | 9 | 14 |
| Ford | 12 | 21 |
| Daimler/Chrysler | 7 | 7 |
| PSA (Citroën and Peugeot) | 6 | 9 |
| VW | 8 | 9 |
| Toyota | 15 | 7 |
| BMW | 2 | 4 |
| Hyundai | 6 | 4 |
| Honda | 6 | 6 |
| Others | 15 | 6 |
| Total | 100 | 100 |

Table 4 **Three years of economic development at Autoliv Inc.**

| Key figures | 2005 | 2004 | 2003 |
|---|---|---|---|
| Sales ($million) | 6,205 | 6,144 | 5,301 |
| Pre-tax profit ($million) | 293 | 326 | 268 |

The total number of employees (whole Autoliv Group, including subsidiaries) in December 2005 was about 400,000.

With this positive news Lars Westerberg finishes his presentation of Autoliv's position in the air bags market. He would like a discussion of the following, to which you are asked to contribute.

## Questions

1 Describe Autoliv's role as a subsupplier for large auto manufacturers in a market that is characterized by consolidation.

2 Which car manufacturer should Autoliv target to strengthen its global competitive position?

3 What strategic alternative does Autoliv have to strengthen its competitive position outside Europe?

# DESIGNING THE GLOBAL MARKETING PROGRAMME

## Contents

**Part I**
The decision to
internationalize
Chs 1–4

**Part II**
Deciding which
markets to enter
Chs 5–7

**Part III**
Market entry
strategies
Chs 8–10

**Part IV**
Designing the
global marketing
programme
Chs 11–12

**Part V**
Implementing and
coordinating the
global marketing
programme
Chs 13–14

# Electrolux:
## Trying to establish a global brand identity

Electrolux is a global leader in home appliances and appliances for professional use, selling more than 40 million products to customers in 150 countries. The company has production and/or production subsidiaries in approximately 60 countries. In Europe, Electrolux has factories located in Italy, Germany, Sweden, the United Kingdom and France, and is currently growing fast in eastern and central Europe. In 2007, Electrolux has sales of SEK105 billion (€11 billion), operating profits of SEK3 billion (€0.33 billion) and 55,000 employees. Electrolux products include refrigerators, dishwashers, washing machines, vacuum cleaners and cookers sold under well-known brands such as Electrolux, AEG-Electrolux, Zanussi, Eureka and Frigidaire.

**Electrolux website**

In 2003–04 the worldwide consolidation of its brands began, with Electrolux continuing as the main brand. Also an accelerated and a consumer insight driven product development process was initiated. Global communication is focused on creating a global image of Electrolux, in every product category and in every geographical market. The share of products sold under the Electrolux brand has risen from 16 per cent of sales in 2002 to approximately 45 per cent in 2006.

Electrolux sells its products to its end-customers through distributors and retailers. Many of the retailers that sell Electrolux's products are part of huge cross-border retail chains. These retail chains have been consolidating in recent years and an increasing number of Electrolux's products are being sold through them. The trend towards consolidation is particularly apparent in the market for major appliances in the United States, where the four largest retail chains account for almost 66 per cent of the total sales of major appliances for all manufacturers. In Europe, there has been no such clear consolidation of the retail chains, but consolidation is in progress in specific countries, such as France, the United Kingdom and the Netherlands.

**Electrolux fitted kitchen**

Electrolux's most important competitors when selling to the different regions are:

- Europe – Bosch-Siemens, Miele, SEB Group
- North America – Whirlpool, General Electric
- Latin America – Whirlpool, General Electric, Mabe
- Asia/Pacific – LG, Samsung, Haier.

*Watch the video before answering the questions.*

## Questions

1  Why and how is Electrolux trying to establish a global brand identity?

2  What is the purpose of Electrolux having eight design studios around the world in Europe, North America, Latin America and Asia/Pacific?

3  Please give examples from the video where cultural differences had an effect on the design and product development of adapted Electrolux products.

4  How can the Internet help Electrolux with the global marketing and selling of its products?

Source: Video accompanying the text, **www.electrolux.com**

# Introduction to Part IV

Once the firm has decided how it will enter the international market(s) (see Part III), the next issue is how to design the global marketing mix.

Part IV is based mainly on the traditional 4P marketing mix:

- Chapter 11: Product and pricing decisions
- Chapter 12: Distribution and communication decisions

The original 4P marketing mix was primarily derived from research on manufacturing B2C companies, where the essence of the marketing mix concept is the idea of a set of controllable variables or a 'tool kit' (the 4Ps) at the disposal of marketing management that can be used to influence customers. However, especially in B2B marketing, the marketing mix is also influenced by the interaction process itself between buyer and seller, so that the influence process is negotiation/interaction and not persuasion as implied by the traditional 4P mix (Håkansson and Waluszewski, 2005). Furthermore there has been concern that the classic 4Ps model does not incorporate the characteristics of services – namely inherent intangibility, perishability, heterogeneity (variability), inseparability and ownership.

## The extended marketing mix

The most influential of the alternative frameworks is, however, Booms and Bitner's (1981) **7Ps mix** where they suggest that the traditional 4Ps need to be extended also to include an additional three Ps: **participants**, **physical evidence** and **process**. Their framework is discussed below.

## Participants

Any person coming into contact with customers can have an impact on overall satisfaction. Participants are all human actors who play a part in service delivery, namely the firm's personnel and other customers. Because production and consumption is simultaneous, the firm's personnel occupy a key position in influencing customer perceptions of product quality. That is especially the case in 'high-contact' services, such as restaurants, airlines and professional consulting services. In fact, the firm's employees are part of the product and hence product quality is inseparable from the quality of the service provider. It is important, therefore, to pay particular attention to the quality of employees and to monitor their performance. This is especially important in services because employees tend to be variable in their performance, which can lead to variable quality.

The participant concept also includes the customer who buys the service and other customers in the service environment. Marketing managers therefore need to manage not only the service provider–customer interface but also the actions of other customers. For example, the number, type and behaviour of people will partly determine the enjoyment of a meal at a restaurant.

## Process

This is the process involved in providing a service to the customers. It concerns the procedures, mechanisms and flow of activities by which the service is acquired and delivered. The process of obtaining a meal at a self-service, fast-food outlet such as McDonalds, is clearly different from that at a full-service restaurant. Furthermore, in a service situation customers are likely to have to queue before they can be served and the service delivery itself is likely to take a certain length of time. Marketers have to ensure that customers understand the process of acquiring a service and that the queuing and delivery times are acceptable to them.

## Physical evidence

Unlike a product, a service cannot be experienced before it is delivered, which makes it intangible. This therefore means that potential customers perceive greater risk when deciding whether or not to use a service. To reduce the feeling of risk, thus improving success, it is often vital to offer customers some tangible clues to assess the quality of the service provided. This is done by providing physical evidence, such as case studies or testimonials. The physical environment itself (i.e. the buildings, furnishings, layout, etc.) is instrumental in customers' assessment of the quality and level of service they can expect, for example in restaurants, hotels, retailing and many other services. In fact, the physical environment is part of the product itself.

It can be argued that there is no need to amend or extend the 4Ps, as the extensions suggested by Booms and Bitner can be incorporated into the existing framework. The argument is that consumers experience a bundle of satisfactions and dissatisfactions that derive from all dimensions of the product whether tangible or intangible. The process can be incorporated in the distribution. Buttle (1989), for example, argues that the product and/or promotion elements may incorporate participants (in the Booms and Bitner framework) and that physical evidence and processes may be thought of as being part of the product. In fact, Booms and Bitner (1981) themselves argue that product decisions should involve the three extended elements in their proposed mix.

Therefore Part IV of this text still uses the structure of the 4Ps, but at the same time the three extended Ps will be incorporated in Chapters 11 to 12.

## Globalization

Since the beginning of the 1980s the term 'globalization' has increasingly become a matter of debate. In 'The globalization of markets' (1983) Levitt provoked much controversy concerning the most appropriate way for companies to become international. Levitt's support of the globalization strategy received both support and criticism. Essentially the two sides of this debate represented local marketing versus global marketing and focused on the central question of whether a standardized, global marketing approach or a country-specific, differentiated marketing approach has the most merits. In Part IV we learn that there are different forces in the international environment that may favour either 'increasing globalization' or 'increasing adaptation' of a firm. The starting point is illustrated by the existing balance point on the scale illustrated in Figure 1. Which force will win not only depends on the environmental forces but also on the specific international marketing strategy that the firm might favour. Figure 2 shows the extremes of these two strategies.

Hence, a fundamental decision that managers have to make regarding their global marketing strategy is the degree to which they should standardize or adapt their global marketing mix. The following three factors provide vast opportunities for marketing standardization (Meffert and Bolz, 1993):

**Figure 1** Environmental factors influencing the balance between standardization and adaptation

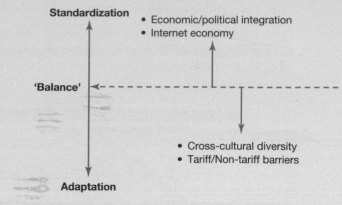

**Figure 2** Standardization and adaptation of the international marketing mix

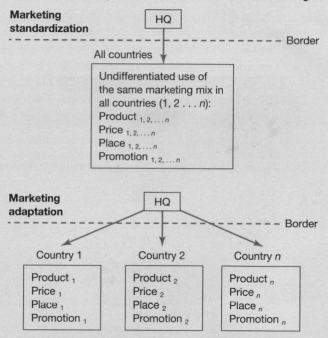

Each country/market has its own marketing mix

1 *Globalization of markets*. Customers are increasingly operating on a worldwide basis and are characterized by an intensively coordinated and centralized purchasing process. As a countermeasure, manufacturers establish a global key account management in order to avoid individual country subsidiaries being played off against each other in separate negotiations with, for example, global retailers.

2 *Globalization of industries*. Many firms can no longer depend on home markets for sufficient scale economies and experience curve effects. Many industries, such as computers, pharmaceuticals and automobiles, are characterized by high R&D costs that can be recouped only via worldwide, high-volume sales.

3 *Globalization of competition*. As a consequence of the worldwide homogenization of demand, the different markets are interrelated. Therefore firms can plan their activities on a worldwide scale and attempt to establish a superior profile vis-à-vis

other global competitors. Hence, country subsidiaries no longer operate as profit centres, but are viewed as parts of a global portfolio.

The standardized marketing concept can be characterized by two features:

1 Standardization of marketing processes is mainly concerned with a standardized decision-making process for cross-country marketing planning. By standardizing the launch of new products, controlling activities, etc., rationalization of the general marketing process is sought.
2 Standardization of marketing programmes and the marketing mix is concerned with the extent to which individual elements of the 4Ps can be unified into a common approach for different national markets.

These two characteristics of standardization are often interrelated: for many strategic business units process-oriented standardization is the precondition for the implementation of standardized marketing programmes.

Many writers discuss standardization and adaptation as two distinct options. The commercial reality, however, is that few marketing mixes are totally standardized or adapted. Instead it is more relevant to discuss *degrees* of standardization. Therefore Figure 3 shows a standardization-potential profile for two different products by the same company (Procter & Gamble).

The results indicate that there are different ways of realizing a standardized concept within the marketing mix. In the case of both products it is possible to standardize the package at least on an average level. Difficulties arise as far as the price policy is concerned. Here it is possible to reach a standardized price positioning only for disposable nappies. So Procter & Gamble selects only those markets that possess the

Figure 3 **Analysis of a company's standardization potential**

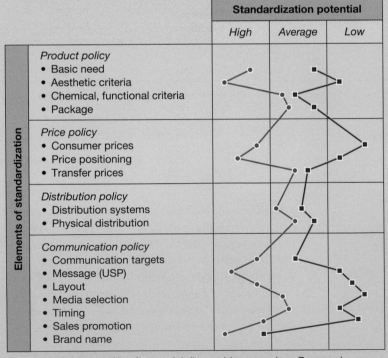

● Standardization profile of a special disposable nappy (e.g. Pampers)
■ Standardization profile of a special drink (e.g. Johnny Walker)

Source: Adapted from Kreutzer, 1988. Reproduced with kind permission from Emerald Group Publishing Ltd.

Table 1 **Main factors favouring standardization versus adaptation**

| Factors favouring standardization | Factors favouring adaptation |
|---|---|
| ● Economies of scale in R&D, production and marketing (experience curve effects) | ● Local environment-induced adaptation: government and regulatory influences (no experience curve effects) |
| ● Global competition | ● Local competition |
| ● Convergence of tastes and consumer needs (consumer preferences are homogeneous) | ● Variation in consumer needs (consumer needs are heterogeneous because of cultural differences) |
| ● Centralized management of international operations (possible to transfer experience across borders) | ● Fragmented and decentralized management with independent country subsidiaries |
| ● A standardized concept is used by competitors | ● An adapted concept is used by competitors |
| ● *High* degree of transferability of competitive advantages from market to market | ● *Low* degree of transferability of competitive advantages from market to market |
| *Further issues:* | *Further issues:* |
| ● Easier communication, planning and control (through Internet and mobile technology) | ● Legal issues – differences in technical standards |
| ● Stock cost reduction | |

necessary purchasing power to pay a price within the target price range. In the case of alcoholic drinks it is nearly impossible to gain a standardized price positioning due to legal constraints. In Denmark, for example, consumers have to pay twice as much for the same Johnny Walker whisky as they do in Germany because of tax regulations. In many cases it is possible to use one brand name on a worldwide basis. There are negative effects connected with particular names in only a few cases; e.g. you have to change brand names to avoid these unintentional images.

We end this introduction to Part IV by listing in Table 1 the main factors favouring standardization versus adaptation of the global marketing programme.

Since 'competitive advantages' play a critical role in the global marketing strategy, similarity in the nature of competitive advantages across international markets would favour the use of similar strategies across markets, facilitating a standardization of the strategy. Competitive advantages arise from core competences (see also Chapter 4), so firms possessing core competences would be in a better position to standardize their marketing strategies than firms that do not possess core competences (Viswanathan and Dickson, 2007).

## References

Booms, B.H. and Bitner, M.J. (1981), 'Marketing strategies and organization structures for service firms', in Donnelly, J.H. and George, W.R. (eds), *Marketing of Services*, American Marketing Association, Chicago, IL, pp. 47–51.

Buttle, F. (1989), 'Marketing services', in Jones, P. (eds), *Management in Service Industries*, Pitman, London, pp. 235–259.

Håkansson, Håkan and Waluszewski, A. (2005) 'Developing a new understanding of markets: reinterpreting the 4Ps', *Journal of Business & Industrial Marketing*, Vol. 20, No. 3, pp. 110–117.

Kreutzer, R. (1988) 'Marketing mix standardization: an integrated approach in global marketing', *European Journal of Marketing*, 22(10), pp. 19–30.

Levitt, T. (1983) 'The globalization of markets', *Harvard Business Review*, May–June, pp. 92–102.

Meffert, H. and Bolz, J. (1993) 'Standardization of marketing in Europe', in Halliburton, C. and Hünerberg, R. (eds), *European Marketing: Readings and cases*, Addison-Wesley, Wokingham, England.

Viswanathan, N.K. and Dickson, P.R. (2007) 'The fundamentals of standardizing global marketing strategy', *International Marketing Review*, Vol. 24, No. 1, pp. 46–63.

## Further reading

Berman, B. (2002) 'Should your firm adopt a mass customization strategy?', *Business Horizons*, July–August, pp. 51–60.

Biemans, W. (2001) 'Designing a dual marketing program', *European Management Journal*, 19(6), December, pp. 670–677.

Solberg, C.A. (2000) 'Educator insights: standardization or adaptation of the international marketing mix: the role of the local subsidiary/representative', *Journal of International Marketing*, 8(1), pp. 78–98.

# 11

# Product and pricing decisions

## Contents

**Case study**

## Learning objectives

After studying this chapter you should be able to do the following:

- Discuss the influences that lead a firm to standardize or adapt its products.
- Explore how international service strategies are developed.
- Discuss the challenge of developing new products for foreign markets.
- Explain and illustrate the alternatives in the product communication mix.
- Define and explain the different branding alternatives.
- Explain what is meant by a 'green' product.
- Discuss alternative environmental management strategies.
- Explain how internal and external variables influence international pricing decisions.
- Explain why and how prices escalate In export selling.
- Discuss the strategic options in determining the price level for a new product.
- Explain the necessary sales volume increase as a consequence of a price decrease.
- Explain what is meant by experience curve pricing.
- Explore the special roles and problems of transfer pricing in global marketing.
- Discuss how varying currency conditions challenge the international marketer.

## 11.1 Introduction

The product decision is among the first decisions that a marketing manager makes in order to develop a global marketing mix. This chapter examines product-related issues and suggests conceptual approaches for handling them. Also discussed are international brand (labelling) strategies and service policies.

The pricing decision must be integrated with the other three Ps of the marketing mix. Price is the only area of the global marketing mix where policy can be changed rapidly without large direct cost implications. This characteristic, plus the fact that overseas consumers are often sensitive to price changes, results in the danger that pricing action may be resorted to as a quick fix instead of changes being made in other areas of the firm's marketing programme. It is thus important that management realizes that constant fine-tuning of prices in overseas markets should be avoided and that many problems are not best addressed by pricing action.

Generally, pricing policy is one of the most important yet often least recognized of all the elements of the marketing mix. The other elements of the marketing mix all lead to costs. The only source of profit to the firm comes from revenue, which in turn is dictated by pricing policy. In this chapter we focus on a number of pricing issues of special interest to international marketers.

## 11.2 The dimensions of the international product offer

In creating an acceptable product offer for international markets it is necessary to examine first what contributes to the 'total' product offer. Kotler (1997) suggests five levels of the product offer that should be considered by marketers in order to make the product attractive to international markets. In the product dimensions of Figure 11.1

**Figure 11.1** The three levels of a product

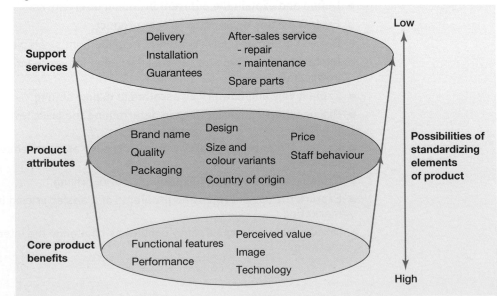

we include not just the core physical properties, but also additional elements such as packaging, branding and after-sales service that make up the total package for the purchaser.

We can also see from Figure 11.1 that it is much easier to standardize the core product benefits (functional features, performance, etc.) than it is to standardize the support services, which often have to be tailored to the business culture and sometimes to individual customers, i.e. personalization (Vesanen, 2007).

## 11.3 Developing international service strategies

We have seen from the definition of a product that services often accompany products, but products are also an increasingly important part of our international economy in their own right. As Figure 11.2 shows, the mix of product and service elements may vary substantially.

## Characteristics of services

Before considering possible international service strategies it is important to consider the special nature of global service marketing. Services are characterized by the following features:

- *Intangibility*. As services such as air transport or education cannot be touched or tested, the buyers of services cannot claim ownership or anything tangible in the

**Figure 11.2** Scale of elemental dominance

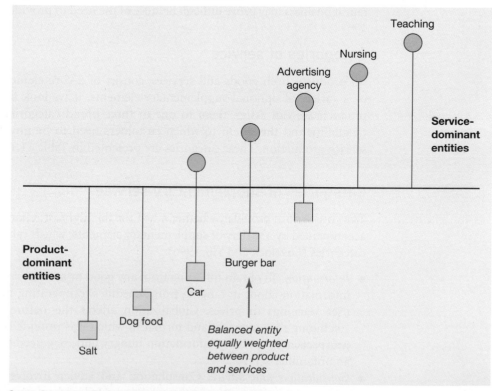

Source: Czinkota and Ronkainen, *International Marketing*, 4th edn, (1995), p. 526.

traditional sense. Payment is for use or performance. Tangible elements of the service, such as food or drink on airlines, are used as part of the service in order to confirm the benefit provided and to enhance its perceived value.

- *Perishability*. Services cannot be stored for future use – for example, unfilled airline seats are lost once the aircraft takes off. This characteristic causes considerable problems in planning and promotion in order to match supply and demand. To maintain service capacity constantly at levels necessary to satisfy peak demand will be very expensive. The marketer must therefore attempt to estimate demand levels in order to optimize the use of capacity.

- *Heterogeneity*. Services are rarely the same because they involve interactions between people. Furthermore, there is high customer involvement in the production of services. This can cause problems of maintaining quality, particularly in international markets where there are quite different attitudes towards customer service.

- *Inseparability*. The time of production is very close to or even simultaneous with the time of consumption. The service is provided at the point of sale. This means that economies of scale and experience curve benefits are difficult to achieve, and supplying the service to scattered markets can be expensive, particularly in the initial setting-up phase.

## Global marketing of services

There are some specific problems in marketing services internationally. There are particular difficulties in achieving uniformity of the different marketing parameters in remote locations where exerting control can be especially problematic. Pricing, too, can be extremely difficult, because fixed costs can be a very significant part of the total service costs. Consumers' ability to buy and their perceptions of the service they receive may vary considerably between markets, resulting in significantly different prices being set and profits generated. Moreover, preserving customer loyalty in order to obtain repeat business may prove difficult because of the need to provide personalized services.

## Categories of service

All products, both goods and services, consist of a core element that is surrounded by a variety of optional supplementary elements. If we look first at the core service products we can assign them to one of three broad categories depending on their tangibility and the extent to which customers need to be physically present during service production. These categories are presented in Table 11.1.

## Categories of supplementary service

The core service provider, whether a bed for the night or a bank account, is typically accompanied by a variety of supplementary elements, which can be grouped into eight categories (Lovelock and Yip, 1996):

- *Information*. To obtain full value from any good or service, customers need relevant information about it, ranging from schedules to operating instructions, and from user warnings to prices. Globalization affects the nature of that information (including the languages and format in which it is provided). New customers and prospects are especially information hungry and may need training in how to use an unfamiliar service.

- *Consultation and advice*. Consultation and advice involve a dialogue to probe customer requirements and then develop a tailored solution. Customers' need for

Table 11.1 Three categories of service

| Categories of service | Characteristics | Examples (service provider) | Possibilities of worldwide standardization (hence utilizing economies of scale, experience effects, lower costs) |
| --- | --- | --- | --- |
| People processing | Customers become part of the production process. The service firm needs to maintain local geographic presence. | Education (schools, universities). Passenger transport (airlines, car rental). Health care (hospitals). Food service (fast-food, restaurants). Lodging service (hotel). | No good possibilities: because of 'customer involvement in production' many local sites will be needed, making this type of service very difficult to operate globally. |
| Possession processing | Involves tangible actions to physical objects to improve their value to customers. The object needs to be involved in the production process, but the owner of the object (the customer) does not. A local geographic presence is required. | Car repair (garages). Freight transport (forwarding agent). Equipment installation (e.g. electrician). Laundry service (launderette). | Better possibilities: compared to people-processing services, this involves a lower degree of contact between the customer and the service personnel. This type of service is not so culture sensitive. |
| Information-based services | Collecting, manipulating, interpreting and transmitting data to create value. Minimal tangibility. Minimal customer involvement in the production process. | Telecommunication services (telephone companies). Banking. News. Market analysis. Internet services (producers of homepages on the WWW, database providers). | Very good possibilities: of worldwide standardization from one central location (single sourcing) because of the 'virtual' nature of these services. |

advice may vary widely around the world, reflecting such factors as level of economic development, nature of the local infrastructure, topography and climate, technical standards and educational levels.

- *Order taking*. Once customers are ready to buy suppliers need to make it easy for them to place orders or reservations in the language of their choice, through telecommunications and other channels, at times and in locations that are convenient to them.

- *Hospitality: taking care of the customer*. Well-managed businesses try, at least in small ways, to treat customers as guests when they have to visit the supplier's facilities (especially when, as is true for many people-processing operations, the period extends over several hours or more). Cultural definitions of appropriate hospitality may differ widely from one country to another, such as the tolerable length of waiting time (much longer in Brazil than in Germany) and the degree of personal service expected (not much in Scandinavia, but lavish in Indonesia).

- *Safekeeping: looking after the customer's possessions*. When visiting a service site customers often want assistance with their personal possessions, ranging from car parking to packaging and delivery of new purchases. Expectations may vary by country, reflecting culture and levels of affluence.

- *Exceptions*. Exceptions fall outside the routine of normal service delivery. They include special requests, problem solving, handling of complaints/suggestions/compliments, and restitution (compensating customers for performance failures). Special requests are particularly common in people-processing services, such as in the travel and lodging industries, and may be complicated by differing cultural norms. International airlines, for example, find it necessary to respond to an array of medical and dietary needs, sometimes reflecting religious and cultural values.

Problem solving is often more difficult for people who are travelling overseas than it would be in the familiar environment of their native country.

- *Billing.* Customers need clear, timely bills that explain how charges are computed. With abolition of currency exchange restrictions in many countries bills can be converted to the customer's home currency. Hence currencies and conversion rates need to be clarified on billing statements. In some instances prices may be displayed in several currencies, even though this policy may require frequent adjustments in the light of currency fluctuations.

- *Payment.* Ease and convenience of payment (including credit) are increasingly expected by customers when purchasing a broad array of services. Major credit cards and travellers cheques solve the problem of paying in foreign funds for many retail purchases, but corporate purchasers may prefer to use electronic fund transfers in the currency of their choice.

Not every core service is surrounded by all eight supplementary elements. In practice the nature of the product, customer requirements and competitive pressures help to determine which supplementary service must be offered. In many cases the provider of the supplementary services can be located in one part of the world and the services delivered electronically to another. For example, order taking/reservations and payment can be handled through telecommunication channels, ranging from voice telephone to the Web. As long as appropriate languages are available many such service elements could be delivered from almost anywhere.

In summary, the information-based services offer the best opportunities of global standardization. The two other types of service (people processing and possession processing) both suffer from their inability to transfer competitive advantages across borders. For example, when Euro Disneyland in Paris opened Disney suffered from not being able to transfer the highly motivated staff of its US parks to Europe.

The accelerating development within information technology (the Internet/the Web) has resulted in the appearance of new types of information service (e.g. information on international flight schedules), which offer great opportunities for standardization.

## Service in the business-to-business market

Business-to-business markets differ from customer markets in many ways:

- fewer and larger buyers, often geographically concentrated;
- a derived, fluctuating and relatively inelastic demand;
- many participants in the buying process;
- professional buyers;
- a closer relationship;
- absence of intermediaries;
- technological links.

For services in consumer markets an alternative for dissatisfied consumers is always to exit from the supplier–consumer relationship, as the number of firms offering the same kind of products is usually high. Therefore it is easy to switch between products and firms.

In the business-to-business market, however, bonds between the buyer and seller make the firms more unwilling to break the relationship. Of course the exit opportunity also exists to some extent in the business-to-business market, but the loss of investment in bonds and commitment tends to create exit barriers, because the costs of changing supplier are high. Furthermore, it can be difficult to find a new supplier.

Professional service firms, such as consulting engineering firms, have similarities with typical business-to-business service firms, but they involve a high degree of customization and have a strong component of face-to-face interaction. The service frequently takes the form of a hundred-million-dollar project and is characterized by the development of long-term relationships between firms, but also the management of day-to-day relationships during the project. When a professional service firm (whether it be an accountant, architect, engineer or management consultant) sells to its clients it is less the services of the firm than the services of specific individuals that it is selling. As a consequence professional service firms require highly skilled individuals.

Filiatrault and Lapierre (1997) made a study of the cultural differences in consulting engineering projects between Europe (France) and North America (Canada). In North America the consulting engineering firms are generally smaller and they work in an economic environment closer (than in Europe) to pure competition. The contracts in Europe are very large and often awarded by governments. The French consultants recognize that there is more flexibility in managing in North America than in Europe. Subcontracting also appears to be more popular in North America.

## 11.4 The product communication mix

Having decided upon the optimum standardization/adaptation route and the newness of the product, the next most important (and culturally sensitive) factor to be considered is that of international promotion.

Product and promotion go hand in hand in foreign markets and together are able to create or destroy markets in very short order. We have considered above the factors that may drive an organization to standardize or adapt its product range for foreign markets. Equally important are the promotion or the performance promises that the organization makes for its product or service in the target market. As with product decisions, promotion can be either standardized or adapted for foreign markets.

Keegan (1995) has highlighted the key aspects of marketing strategy as a combination of standardization or adaptation of the product and promotion of elements of the mix, and offers five alternative and more specific approaches to product policy. These approaches are shown in Figure 11.3.

Figure 11.3 Product/communication mode

|  |  | **Product** | | |
|---|---|---|---|---|
|  |  | *Standard* | *Adapt* | *New* |
| **Promotion** | *Standard* | Straight extension | Product adaptation | Product invention |
|  | *Adapt* | Promotion adaptation | Dual adaptation | |

Source: Based on Keegan, 1995, pp. 489–94 and p. 498, Table 13.1.

## Straight extension

This involves introducing a standardized product with the same promotion strategy throughout the world market (one product, one message worldwide). By applying this strategy successfully major savings can be made on market research and product development. Since the 1920s Coca-Cola has adopted a global approach, which has allowed the company to make enormous cost savings and benefits from continual reinforcement of the same message. While a number of writers have argued that this will be the strategy adopted for many products in the future, in practice only a handful of products might claim to have achieved this already. A number of firms have tried and failed. Campbell's soups, for example, found that consumers' taste in soup was by no means international.

An example of successful extension is Unilever's worldwide introduction of Organics Shampoo, which was first launched in Thailand in late 1993 after joint development work by Unilever's Hair Innovation Centres in Bangkok and Paris. By 1995 the brand was sold in over 40 countries, generating sales of £170 million. You can see below a two-page advertisement from a magazine, used during the product's introduction into Argentina. The basic advertising concept all over the world (including Argentina) has been 'Organics – the first ever root-nourishing shampoo'.

## Promotion adaptation

Use of this strategy involves leaving a product unchanged but fine-tuning promotional activity to take into account cultural differences between markets. It is a relatively cost-effective strategy as changing promotion messages is not as expensive as adapting products. An example of this strategy is illustrated in the following Lux example.

### LUX soap (Unilever): the United Kingdom versus India

The UK version of the LUX advertisement is based on the classic transborder advertising campaign, 'the beauty soap of film stars', which has been standardized to a high degree. In India the LUX campaign has been given a special local touch.

'Straight extension' of Organics Shampoo to Argentina

**Advertisements for Lux in UK and India**

The Indian version is one of three advertisements that trace LUX's association with film stars from the past era to the current stars of today and the potential film stars of tomorrow. The advertisement focuses on three past legendary beauties of Indian cinema who have endorsed the brand. The creative statement is in a cinema poster style, keeping the brand image in mind, and in a sepia colour tone to give it a nostalgic feel.

## Product adaptation

By modifying only the product a manufacturer intends to maintain the core product function in the different markets. For example, electrical appliances have to be modified to cope with different electrical voltages in different countries. A product can also be adapted to function under different physical environmental conditions. Exxon changed the chemical composition of petrol to cope with the extremes of climate, but still used the 'Put a tiger in your tank' campaign unchanged around the world.

## Dual adaptation

By adapting both product and promotion for each market the firm is adopting a totally differentiated approach. This strategy is often adopted by firms when one of the previous three strategies has failed, but particularly if the firm is not in a leadership position and is therefore reacting to the market or following competitors. It applies to the majority of products in the world market. The modification of both product and promotion is an expensive but often necessary strategy.

An example of dual adaptation is shown below, with the launch of Kellogg's Basmati Flakes in the nascent breakfast cereal market in India. This product was specially created to suit Indian tastes, India being a large rice-eating country. The advertising campaign was a locally adapted concept based on international positioning. Note that the product is available only in the Bombay area.

Kellogg's dual adaptation for the Indian market

## Product invention

Product invention is adopted by firms usually from advanced nations that are supplying products to less developed countries. Products are specifically developed to meet the needs of the individual markets. Existing products may be too technologically sophisticated to operate in less developed countries, where power supplies may be intermittent and local skills limited. Keegan (1995) uses a hand-powered washing machine as a product example.

## 11.5 Product positioning

Product positioning is a key element in the successful marketing of any organization in any market. The product or company that does not have a clear position in the customer's mind consequently stands for nothing and is rarely able to command more than a simple commodity or utility price. Premium pricing and competitive advantage are largely dependent upon the customer's perception that the product or service on offer is markedly different in some way from competitive offers. How can we achieve a credible market position in international markets?

Since it is the buyer/user perception of benefit-generating attributes that is important, product positioning is the activity by which a desirable 'position' in the mind of the customer is created for the product. Positioning a product for international markets begins with describing specific products as comprising different attributes that are capable of generating a flow of benefits to buyers and users.

The global marketing planner puts these attributes into bundles so that the benefits generated match the special requirements of specific market segments. This product design problem involves not only the basic product components (physical, package, service and country of origin) but also brand name, styling and similar features.

Viewed in a multidimensional space (commonly denoted as 'perceptual mapping'), a product can be graphically represented at a point specified by its attributes. The location of a product's point in perceptual space is its 'position'. Competitors' products are similarly located (see also Johansson and Thorelli, 1985). If points representing other products are close to the point of the prototype then these other products are close competitors of the prototype. If the prototype is positioned away from its closest competitors in some international markets and its positioning implies important features for customers, then it is likely to have a significant competitive advantage.

## Country-of-origin effects

The country of origin of a product, typically communicated by the phrase 'made in [country]', has a considerable influence on the quality perception of that product. Some countries have a good reputation and others have a poor reputation for certain products. For example, Japan and Germany have good reputations for producing cars. The country-of-origin effects are especially critical among eastern European consumers. A study (Ettensén, 1993) examined the brand decision for televisions among Russian, Polish and Hungarian consumers. These consumers evaluated domestically produced television products much lower than western-made products, regardless of brand name. There was a general preference for televisions manufactured in Japan, Germany and the United States.

| Exhibit 11.1 | Chinese piano manufacturers are experiencing the 'Country Of Origin' (COO) effect |
|---|---|

The Chinese piano industry is a useful example to show the opportunities and challenges facing Chinese brands. China has overtaken Japan and South Korea to become the world's largest piano-producing nation. One of the brand manufacturers, Pearl River, has become the world's largest piano manufacturer with annual sales of about 100,000 units. As piano making is still a labour-intensive industry, Chinese manufacturers enjoy a big cost and price advantage. This also motivates international dealers to stock Chinese pianos, because of a larger profit margin. However, the biggest branding dilemma facing Chinese piano manufacturers is negative perceptions of 'made in China' as a label. It is difficult for individual firms to change this perception and requires the country to change its image in general, which may take a generation. It has taken Japanese Yamaha more than 30 years to change its image from a cheap 'me-too' product to a leading global brand. An important buying influence also comes from music teachers, and many of them advise their students not to buy Chinese-made instruments.

To overcome this difficulty, Chinese manufacturers could try to link their brands to Western-oriented values and names. For example, Longfeng Piano could emphasize that its Kingsburg model is designed by the world-renowned German designer Klaus Fenner.

Sources: Adapted from Fan (2007)

The country of origin is more important than the brand name and can be viewed as good news for western firms that are attempting to penetrate the eastern European region with imports whose brand name is not yet familiar. Another study (Johansson et al., 1994) showed that some products from eastern Europe have done well in the West, despite negative country-of-origin perceptions. For example, Belarus tractors have sold well in Europe and the United States not only because of their reasonable price but also because of their ruggedness. Only the lack of an effective distribution network has hindered the firm's ability to penetrate western markets to a greater degree.

When considering the implications of product positioning it is important to realize that positioning can vary from market to market, because the target customers for the product differ from country to country. In confirming the positioning of a product or service in a specific market or region it is therefore necessary to establish in the consumer's perception exactly what the product stands for and how it differs from existing and potential competition. In developing a market-specific product positioning the firm can focus upon one or more elements of the total product offer, so the differentiation might be based upon price and quality, one or more attributes, a specific application, a target consumer or direct comparison with one competitor.

## 11.6  Brand equity

A study by Citibank and Interbrand in 1997 found that companies basing their business on brands had outperformed the stock market for 15 years. The same study does, however, note the risky tendency of some brand owners to have reduced investments in brands in the mid-1990s with negative impacts on their performance (Hooley *et al.*, 1998, p. 120).

The following two examples show that brands add value for customers:

1 The classic example is that in blind test 51 per cent of consumers prefer Pepsi to Coca-Cola, but in open tests 65 per cent prefer Coca-Cola to Pepsi: soft drink preferences are based on brand image, not taste (Hooley *et al.*, 1998, p. 119).

2 Skoda cars have been best known in the United Kingdom as the butt of bad jokes, reflecting a widespread belief that the cars are of very low quality. In 1995 Skoda was preparing to launch a new model in the United Kingdom, and did 'blind and seen' tests of the consumers' judgement of the vehicle. The vehicle was rated as better designed and worth more by those who did not know the make. With the Skoda name revealed perceptions of the design were less favourable and estimated value was substantially lower. This leads us from the reputation of the company to branding (Hooley *et al.*, 1998, p. 117).

---

### Exhibit 11.2  Madame Tussauds – a brand which brings people closer to celebrities on a global basis

The attraction's history is a rich and fascinating one with roots dating back to the Paris of 1770. It was here that Madame Tussaud learnt to model wax likenesses under the tutelage of her mentor, Dr Philippe Curtius. Her skills were put to the test during the French Revolution when she was forced to prove her allegiance making the death masks of executed aristocrats. It was in the early 19th century that she came to Britain, bringing with her a travelling exhibition of revolutionary relics and effigies of public heroes and rogues.

The Tussauds Group strategy is to develop an international entertainment business of successful visitor attractions that are special, imaginative and offer exceptional visitor value.

With over 13 million guests a year, the Tussauds Group is today Europe's largest operator and developer of visitor attractions and is sixth largest in the world. In 1998 the Group was acquired by Charterhouse Development Capital after 20 years of ownership by Pearson plc.

In March 2005 the Tussauds Group, that owns Madame Tussauds, was sold to Dubai International Capital, a private equity firm backed by the Dubai government and the Crown Prince of Dubai. They paid £800 million to take control.

#### Brand experience
The future for brands is about building memorable consumer experiences. Experience-oriented companies like Madame Tussauds need to have something that goes beyond the product. Madame Tussauds' selling point is not about waxworks, it is about bringing people closer to celebrities and what they do in life.

**Robbie Williams (London) and the local Chinese popstars (Twins) (Shanghai)**
Sources: Madame Tussauds London (left) and Madame Tussauds Shanghai (right).

## Choice of new location

The choice of a new location is based on many different criteria. Madame Tussauds has a product development team that investigates how many tourists visit a city, whether they fit the profile of the attraction's visitors and whether there's enough space. Detailed research is vital to take a concept into a new market. After opening in Hong Kong Madame Tussauds recently opened its second Asian branch in Shanghai. As China's largest and wealthiest city with over 13 million residents and nearly 40 million tourists a year, Shanghai represents a good opportunity for Madame Tussauds.

## Interactivity with the waxwork figures

The new Shanghai branch has the most interactivity of all the attractions, with fewer waxwork figures and more to do around them. The Tiger Woods exhibit allows visitors to putt on the green and see their scores come up. The latest guest to have a hole-in-one is recorded on the leaderboard. Visitors can also go into a karaoke booth with models of some famous Chinese popstars, called Twins (see the photo), sing with them and view themselves on video. People can also dress up like Charlie Chaplin and see themselves on a movie screen in black and white.

## Balancing local and global branding

The research of Madame Tussauds shows a 98 per cent brand recognition in the UK maket. However, in Asia, the term 'madame' sometimes implies a bar or club to many consumers, and saying that the brand is a 'wax attraction' does not mean anything in the Asian market as there is no tradition of that type of museum there.

For Madame Tussauds it is important to make sure the brand maintains a good mix of local and global content. This is a delicate balance: too much local content does not fit with the idea of a global brand, while too little emphasis on global figures can disappoint international customers. The new Chinese venue overwhelmingly features local faces, such as actor Ge You, kung fu king Jackie Chan, the pop-group Twins and basketball superstar Yao Ming; it also has global figures such as David Beckham, Michael Jackson and Brad Pitt. The London attraction has a wide range of global figures such as Angelina Jolie, Beyonce Knowles and Robbie Williams (see the photo), but international tourists also love Margaret Thatcher, Princess Diana, Winston Churchill and the Queen. The photos illustrate the Madame Tussauds mixture of global content (like Robbie Williams) and local content (like the Twins).

Expanding the Madame Tussauds brand on a global scale is a challenge, but when it comes down to the essentials, Madame Tussauds is not about waxworks – it is about consumer experiences and bringing people into interaction with the celebrities.

Sources: With kind permission from Madame Tussauds Group, especially Global Marketing Director Nicky Marsh from London (www.madame-tussauds.com) and Cathy Wong, External Affairs Consultant from Shanghai (www.madame-tussauds.com.cn); Marsh, N. (2006) 'Translating experiences across the world', *Brand Strategy*, June, p. 11; Macalister, T. (2005) 'Madame Tussauds to open in Shanghai', *The Guardian* (London), 19 September, p. 20.

## Definitions of 'brand equity'

Although the definition of brand equity is often debated, the term deals with the brand value, beyond the physical assets associated with it manufacture.

David Aaker of the University of California at Berkeley, one of the leading authorities on brand equity, has defined the term as 'a set of *brand assets and liabilities* linked to the brand, its name and symbol, that add to or subtract from the value provided by a product or service to a firm or to the firm's customers (Aaker, 1991, p. 15).

Aaker has clustered those assets and liabilities into five categories:

1 *Brand loyalty*. Encourages customers to buy a particular brand time after time and remain insensitive to competitors' offerings.
2 *Brand awareness*. Brand names attract attention and convey images of familarity. May be translated to: how big a percentage of the customers know the brand name.
3 *Perceived quality*. 'Perceived' means that the customers decide upon the level of quality, not the company.
4 *Brand associations*. The values and the personality linked to the brand.
5 *Other proprietary brand assets*. Include trademarks, patents and marketing channel relationships.

Brand equity can be thought of as the additional cash flow achieved by associating a brand with the underlying values of the product or service. In this connection it is useful (although incomplete) to think of a brand's equity as *the premium a customer/consumer would pay for the branded product or service compared to an identical unbranded version of the same product/service.*

Hence brand equity refers to the strength, depth and character of the consumer–brand relationship. A strong equity implies a positive force that keeps the consumer and the brand together, in the face of resistance and tension. The strength, depth and character of the customer–brand relationship is referred to as the *brand relationship quality* (Marketing Science Institute, 1995).

## 11.7  Branding decisions

Closely linked to product positioning is the question of branding. The basic purposes of branding are the same everywhere in the world. In general, the functions of branding are as follows:

● to distinguish a company's offering and differentiate one particular product from its competitors;
● to create identification and brand awareness;
● to guarantee a certain level of quality and satisfaction;
● to help with promotion of the product.

All of these purposes have the same ultimate goals: to create new sales (market shares taken from competitors) or induce repeat sales (keep customers loyal).

As seen from Figure 11.4 there are four levels of branding decisions. Each alternative at the four levels has a number of advantages and disadvantages, which are presented in Table 11.2. We will discuss these options in more detail below.

Figure 11.4 Branding decisions

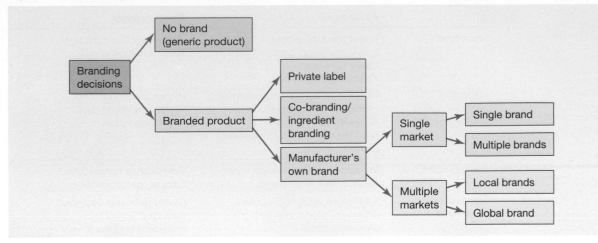

Source: Adapted from Onkvisit and Shaw, 1993, p. 534.

---

Exhibit 11.3   **Unilever's Snuggle fabric softener – an example of local brands in multiple markets**

An effective example of promotion adaptation is illustrated by Unilever's Snuggle Fabric softener. The product was initially launched in Germany as an economy brand in a category dominated by Procter and Gamble. In order to counteract the negative quality inferences associated with low price, Unilever emphasized softness as the product's key point of difference. The softness association was communicated through the name, 'Kuschelweich', which means 'enfolded in softness', and this was illustrated through a picture of a teddy bear on the package. When the product was launched in France, Unilever kept the brand positioning of economy and softness but changed the name to 'Cajoline', meaning softness in French. In addition, the teddy bear that had been inactive in Germany now took the centre stage in the French advertising as the brand symbol for softness and quality. Success in France led to global expansion and in each case the brand name was changed to connote softness in the local language while the advertising featuring the teddy bear remained virtually identical across global markets. By the 1990s, Unilever marketed the fabric softener around the globe with over a dozen brand names, all with the same product positioning and advertising support. More importantly, the fabric softener was generally number 1 or number 2 brand in each market.

Source: Adapted from Keller and Sood (2001).

---

## Brand versus no brand

Branding is associated with added costs in the form of marketing, labelling, packaging and promotion. Commodities are 'unbranded' or undifferentiated products. Examples of products with no brand are cement, metals, salt, beef and other agricultural products.

## Private label versus co-branding versus manufacturer's own brand

These three options can be graded as shown in Figure 11.5.

The question of consumers having brand loyalty or shop loyalty is a crucial one. The competitive struggle between the manufacturer and the retailer actualizes the need for

**Table 11.2 Advantages and disadvantages of branding alternatives**

| | Advantages | Disadvantages |
|---|---|---|
| *No brand* | Lower production cost. Lower marketing cost. Lower legal cost. Flexible quality control. | Severe price competition. Lack of market identity. |
| *Branding* | Better identification and awareness. Better chance for production differentiation. Possible brand loyalty. Possible premium pricing. | Higher production cost. Higher marketing cost. Higher legal cost. |
| *Private label* | Possibility of larger market share. No promotional problems. | Severe price competition. Lack of market identity. |
| *Co-branding/ ingredient branding* | Adds more value to the brand. Sharing of production and promotion costs Increases manufacturer's power in gaining access to retailers' shelves. Can develop into long-lasting relationships based on mutual commitment. | Consumers may become confused. Ingredient supplier is very dependent on the success of the final product. Promotion cost for ingredient supplier. |
| *Manufacturer's own brand* | Better price due to higher price inelasticity. Retention of brand loyalty. Better bargaining power. Better control of distribution. | Difficult for small manufacturer with unknown brand. Requires brand promotion. |
| *Single market, single brand* | Marketing efficiency. Permits more focused marketing. Eliminates brand confusion. Good for product with good reputation (halo effect). | Assumes market homogeneity. Existing brand's image harmed when trading up/down. Limited shelf space. |
| *Single market, multiple brands* | Market segmented for varying needs. Creates competitive spirit. Avoids negative connotation of existing brand. Gains more retail shelf space. Does not harm existing brand's image. | Higher marketing cost. Higher inventory cost. Loss of economies of scale. |
| *Multiple markets, local brands (see also Exhibit 11.4)* | Meaningful names. Local identification. Avoidance of taxation on international brand. Allows variations of quantity and quality across markets. | Higher marketing cost. Higher inventory cost. Loss of economies of scale. Diffused image. |
| *Multiple markets, global brand* | Maximum marketing efficiency. Reduction of advertising costs. Elimination of brand confusion. Good for culture-free product. Good for prestigious product. Easy identification/recognition for international travellers. Uniform worldwide image. | Assumes market homogeneity. Problems with black and grey markets. Possibility of negative connotation. Requires quality and quantity consistency. LDCs' opposition and resentment. Legal complications. |

Source: Adapted from Onkvisit and Shaw 1989. Published with permission from Emerald Publishing Ltd. www.emeraldinsight.com

a better understanding of shopping behaviour. Both actors need to be aware of determinants of shop choice, shopping frequency and in-store behaviour. Where manufacturers pay little attention to the shopping behaviour of their consumers, this helps to anticipate the increasing power of certain retail chains.

Figure 11.5 **The three brand options**

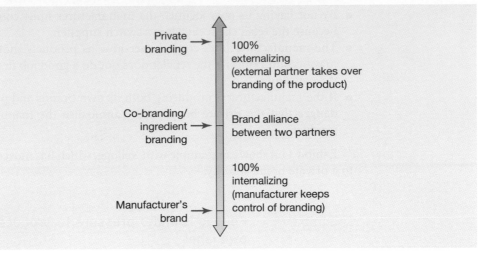

## Private label

Private labelling is most developed in the United Kingdom, where Marks & Spencer, for instance, only sell own-label (private label) products. At Sainsbury's own labels account for 60 per cent of the sales. Compared with the high share of private labelling in northern Europe, the share in southern Europe (e.g. Spain and Portugal) is no higher than 10 per cent.

**Private label**
Retailers own brand, e.g. Marks & Spencer's St Michael.

### *The retailer's perspective*

For the retailer there are two main advantages connected with own-label business:

1 *Own labels provide better profit margins.* The cost of goods typically makes up 70–85 per cent of a retailer's total cost (*The Economist*, 4 March 1995, p. 10). So if the retailer can buy a quality product from the manufacturer at a lower price this will provide a better profit margin for the retailer. In fact private labels have helped UK food retailers to achieve profit margins averaging 8 per cent of sales, which is high by international standards. The typical figure in France and the United States is 1–2 per cent.

2 *Own labels strengthen the retailer's image with its customers.* Many retail chains try to establish loyalty to their particular chain of shops by offering their own quality products. In fact premium private-label products (e.g. Marks & Spencer's St Michael) that compete in quality with manufacturers' top brands have seen a growth in market share, whereas the share of cheap generics is tiny and declining.

### *The manufacturer's perspective*

Although private brands are normally regarded as threats for manufacturers there may be situations where private branding is a preferable option (Herstein and Gamliel, 2006):

● Since there are no promotional expenses associated with private branding for the producer, the strategy is especially suitable for SMEs with limited financial resources and limited competences in the downstream functions.

● The private brand manufacturer gains access to the shelves of the retail chains. With increasing internationalization of the big retail chains this may also result in export business for the SME that has never been in international markets.

There are also a number of reasons why private branding is bad for the manufacturer:

- By not having its own identity, the manufacturer must compete mainly on price, because the retail chain can always switch supplier.
- The manufacturer loses control over how its products should be promoted. This may become critical if the retailer does not do a good job in pushing the product to the consumer.
- If the manufacturer is producing both its own brands and private brands there is a danger that the private brands will cannibalise the manufacturer's brand-name products.

Exhibit 11.4 shows an example with Kellogg, which has moved from a brand strategy to a private brand strategy.

### Exhibit 11.4  Kellogg is under pressure to produce under Aldi's own label

In February 2000 Kellogg (the cereal giant) made an own-label deal with German supermarket chain Aldi. It is the first time that Kellogg has supplied own label.

A slogan on Kellogg's cereal packets claims: 'If you don't see Kellogg's on the box . . . it isn't Kellogg's in the box.' But now Kellogg has negotiated a deal with Aldi to supply products in Germany bearing a different brand name. Reports in Germany say that the deal was made after Aldi announced it would no longer pay brand suppliers' prices and threatened to cut top brands from its shelves.

Source: Adapted from various public media.

Quelch and Harding (1996) argue that many manufacturers have over reacted to the threat of private brands. Increasing numbers of manufacturers are beginning to make private-label products to take up excess production capacity. According to Quelch and Harding (1996), more than 50 per cent of US manufacturers of branded consumer packaged goods already make private-label goods as well.

Managers typically examine private-label production opportunities on an incremental marginal cost basis. The fixed overhead costs associated with the excess capacity used to make the private-label products would be incurred anyway. But if private-label manufacturing were evaluated on a full-cost basis rather than on an incremental basis it would, in many cases, appear much less profitable. The more private-label production grows as a percentage of total production, the more an analysis based on full costs becomes relevant (Quelch and Harding, 1996).

### Manufacturer's own brand

From the Second World War until the 1960s brand manufacturers managed to build a bridge over the heads of the retailers to the consumers. They created consumer loyalty for their particular brand by using sophisticated advertising (culminating in TV advertising) and other promotional techniques. Developing a global brand is not an easy task. Firms must decide how to manage brands that span different geographic regions and product lines and determine who should control the positioning and marketing of such brands. B2B brands are also good candidates for global branding. Often it is the seller's reputation combined with the buyer's own level of awareness and degree of loyalty shown to the manufacturer (seller), that are important considerations in the purchasing decisions (Beverland *et al.*, 2007; Kotler and Pfoertsch, 2007).

Since the 1960s various sociological changes (notably the car) have encouraged the rise of large, efficient retailers. Nowadays the distribution system is being turned upside down. The traditional supply chain, powered by manufacturer 'push', is becoming a demand chain, driven by consumer 'pull'. Retailers have won control over distribution not just because they decide the price at which goods are sold, but also because both individual shops and retail companies have become much bigger and more efficient. They are able to buy in bulk and to reap economies of scale, mainly due to advances in transport and, more recently, in information technology. Most retail chains have not only set up computer links between each store and distribution warehouses, they are also hooked up with the computers of the firm's main suppliers, through an (electronic data interchange) system.

After some decades of absence private labels reappeared in the 1970s as generic products pioneered by Carrefour in France but were soon adopted by UK and US retailers. Ten years ago there was a distinct gap in the level of quality between private-label and brand-name products. Today the gap has narrowed: private-label quality levels are much higher than ever before, and they are more consistent, especially in categories historically characterized by little product innovation.

### Co-branding/ingredient branding

Despite the similarities between co-branding and ingredient branding there is also an important difference, as we shall see below.

### *Co-branding*

**Co-branding**
Form of cooperation between two or more brands, which can create synergies that create value for both participants, above the value they would expect to generate on their own.

Co-branding is a form of cooperation between two or more brands with significant customer recognition, in which all the participants' brand names are retained. It is of medium to long-term duration and its net value creation potential is too small to justify setting up a new brand and/or legal joint venture. The motive for co-branding is the expectation of synergies that create value for both participants, above the value they would expect to generate on their own (Bengtsson and Servais, 2005).

In the case of co-branding, the products are often complementary, in the way that one product can be used or consumed independently of the other (e.g. Bacardi Rum and Coca-Cola). Hence co-branding may be an efficient alternative to traditional brand extension strategies (Figure 11.6).

Figure 11.6 Illustration of co-branding and ingredient branding

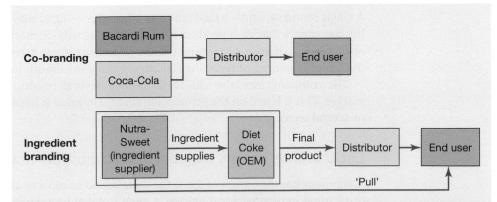

---

Exhibit 11.5 **Shell's co-branding with Ferrari and Lego**

In 1999–2000 Shell ran a £50 million co-branding campaign with Ferrari and LEGO. Some people might have thought that this was an attempt to persuade people, mainly in the West, that Shell's controversial attempt to dump the Brent Spar oil platform in the North Sea was not a true reflection of the company.

However, it may be more accurate to say that Shell was seeking a 'brand image transfer'. In the petrol retailer market traditionally driven by price and more price promotions, Shell wanted both Ferrari's sexy, sporty image and the family values of LEGO. Furthermore Shell was and is no longer only in the petroleum and oils business, where price promotions are the main focus of marketing activity. The company is also involved in food retailing, where loyalty programmes are important.

What were the benefits for Ferrari and LEGO? Ferrari gained sponsorship and royalty income from model car sales, while LEGO got improved global distribution. The co-branding strategy involved the use of ten exclusive small boxed toys and a big Ferrari LEGO car carrying a Shell logo. Shell wanted to sell between 20 and 40 million units of LEGO globally. It made Shell one of the world's largest toy distributors.

Source: Adapted from various public media.

### Ingredient branding

Normally the marketer of the final product (OEM) creates all of the value in the consumer's eyes. But in the case of Intel and NutraSweet the ingredient supplier is seeking to build value in its products by branding and promoting the key component of an end product. When promotion ('pull' strategy: see Figure 11.6) of the key component brand is initiated by the ingredient supplier the goal is to build awareness and preference among consumers for that ingredient brand. Simultaneously, it may be the manufacturer (OEM) that seeks to benefit from a recognized ingredient brand. Some computer manufacturers are benefiting from the quality image of using an Intel chip.

However, ingredient branding is not suitable for every supplier of components. An ingredient supplier should fulfil the following requirements:

**Ingredient branding**
The supplier delivers an important key component to the final OEM-product, e.g. Intel delivers its processor to the major PC-manufacturers.

- The ingredient supplier should be offering a product that has a substantial advantage over existing products. DuPont's Teflon, NutraSweet, Intel chips and the Dolby noise reduction system are all examples of major technological innovations, the result of large investments in R&D.
- The ingredient should be critical to the success of the final product. NutraSweet is not only a low-calorie sweetener, but has a taste that is nearly identical to that of sugar.

### Single brand versus multiple brands (single market)

A single brand or family brand (for a number of products) may be helpful in convincing consumers that each product is of the same quality or meets certain standards. In other words, when a single brand in a single market is marketed by the manufacturer, the brand is assured of receiving full attention for maximum impact.

The company may also choose to market several (multiple) brands in a single market. This is based on the assumption that the market is heterogeneous and consists of several segments.

### Local brands versus a global brand (multiple markets)

A company has the option of using the same brand in most or all of its foreign markets or of using individual, local brands. A single, global brand is also known as an international or universal brand. A Eurobrand is a slight modification of this approach, as it is a single product for a single market of 15 or more European countries, with an emphasis on the search for intermarket similarities rather than differences.

A global brand is an appropriate approach when a product has a good reputation or is known for quality. In such a case a company would be wise to extend the brand name to other products in the product line. Examples of global brands are Coca-Cola, Shell and the Visa credit card. Although it is possible to find examples of global brands, local brands are probably more common among big multinational companies than people realize. Boze and Patton (1995) have studied the branding practices in 67 countries all over the world of six multinational companies:

1 Colgate-Palmolive – headquartered in the United States.
2 Kraft General Foods (now part of Philip Morris) – headquartered in the United States.
3 Nestlé – headquartered in Switzerland.
4 Procter & Gamble – headquartered in the United States.
5 Quaker Oats – headquartered in the United States.
6 Unilever – headquartered in the United Kingdom and the Netherlands.

The findings of the research are summarized in Table 11.3. Of the 1,792 brands found in the 67 countries, 44 per cent were only marketed in one country. Only 68 brands (4 per cent) could be found in more than half of the countries. Of these 68 brands, only the following six were found in all 67 countries: Colgate, Lipton, Lux, Maggi, Nescafé and Palmolive. Hence these were the only true world brands.

Surprisingly, each of the six multinationl corporations (MNCs) seems to follow the practice of multiple brands in a single market. No official explanation was offered for this strategy, but a Nestlé manager explained 'that he believed it is a very important marketing advantage to provide a brand name not found in any other country, especially those adjacent to the nation or bigger than it' (Boze and Patton, 1995, p. 24).

The use of umbrella brands varies a lot among the MNCs examined. Of the six MNCs Colgate is the most intensive user of its two company names:

1 *Colgate*. Mostly dental products: toothpaste, tooth powder, toothbrushes, dental floss, mouthwash, and shaving cream.
2 *Palmolive*. Hair products, shaving products, hand lotion, talc, deodorant, sun screen, toilet soap, bath products, liquid detergent (dishes and fine fabrics) and automatic dishwasher detergent.

It should be emphasized that the big MNCs prefer to acquire some local brands instead of using a global brand.

**Table 11.3  Brands of six multinational companies in 67 countries**

| Company | Total no. of brands | Brands found in 50% or more countries | | Brands in only one country | |
|---|---|---|---|---|---|
| | | Number | % of total | Number | % of total |
| Colgate | 163 | 6 | 4 | 59 | 36 |
| Kraft GF | 238 | 6 | 3 | 104 | 44 |
| Nestlé | 560 | 19 | 4 | 250 | 45 |
| P & G | 217 | 18 | 8 | 80 | 37 |
| Quaker | 143 | 2 | 1 | 55 | 38 |
| Unilever | 471 | 17 | 4 | 236 | 50 |
| Total | 1,792 | 68 | 4 | 784 | 44 |

Source: Boze and Patton, 1995, p. 22. Reproduced with kind permission from the *Journal of Consumer Marketing*, Emerald Group Publishing Ltd.

## 11.8 Implications of the Internet for collaboration with customers on product decisions

Firms are realizing the importance of collaboration for creating and sustaining competitive advantage. Collaboration with partners and even competitors has become a strategic imperative for firms in the networked world of business. More recently, scholars in strategy and marketing have focused on collaboration with customers to cocreate value (Prahalad and Ramaswamy, 2004).

The Internet is an open, cost-effective and ubiquitous network. These attributes make it a global medium with unprecedented reach, contributing to reduce constraints of geography and distance. The Internet enhances the ability of firms to engage customers in collaborative innovation in several ways. It allows firms to transform episodic and one-way customer interactions into a persistent dialogue with customers. Internet-based virtual environments allow the firm to engage in interaction with a much larger number of customers without significant compromises on the richness of the interaction (Evans and Wuster, 2000).

### Customization and closer relationships

The new business platform recognizes the increased importance of customization of products and services. Increased commoditization of standard features can only be countered through customization, which is most powerful when backed up by sophisticated analysis of customer data.

Mass-marketing experts such as Nike are experimenting with ways of using digital technology to enable customization. Websites that can display three-dimensional images, for example, will certainly boost the attractiveness of custom tailoring.

The challenge is clear: to use IT to get closer to customers. There are already many examples of this. Dell is building a closer relationship with its end customer by letting them design their own PCs on the Internet. Customers who have ordered their computers from Dell can then follow their computers along the various stages of the production process in real time on their personalized website. Such experimentation is advisable because the success of 'build-to-order' models such as Dell's represents a challenge to current 'build-to-stock' business platforms, which Compaq generally uses. A comparison of the business models of Dell and HP shows that Dell's basic business principle is the close relationship between the PC manufacturer and the end customer, without further intermediaries in the distribution channel. This allows Dell to individualize the computers to customers' specific needs.

Computers can also be remotely diagnosed and fixed over the network today; this may soon be true of many other appliances. Airlines now communicate special fares to preferred customers through e-mails and special websites. Cars will soon have Internet protocol addresses, which will make possible a range of personal, in-vehicle information services.

Customers can also be involved in the early stages of product development so that their inputs can shape product features and functionality. Pharmaceutical companies are experimenting with the possibility of analysing patients' genes to determine precisely what drugs should be administered in what dosages.

The transformation in the business platform can be seen in university textbook publishing. This industry – which has seen little innovation since the advent of the printing press – is now in the midst of major changes. Publishers are creating supplementary website links to provide additional ways for students and lecturers to be connected during courses (e.g. **www.pearsoneduc.com** and **www.wiley.com**). The publisher's role, which traditionally was selling textbooks at the beginning of term, is becoming that of an educational consultant or value-adding partner throughout the term.

---

**Exhibit 11.6    Ducati motorcycles – product development through web communities**

Founded in 1926, Italian Ducati builds racing-inspired motorcycles characterized by unique engine features, innovative design, advanced engineering and overall technical excellence. The company produces motorcycles in six market segments which vary in their technical and design features and intended customers: Superbike, Supersport, Monster, Sport Touring, Multistrada and the new SportClassic. The company's motorcycles are sold in more than 60 countries worldwide, with a primary focus in western European, Japanese and North American markets. Ducati has won 13 of the last 15 World Superbike Championship titles and more individual victories than the competition put together.

Ducati was quick to realize the potential of using the Internet to engage customers in its new product development efforts. The company set up a web division and a dedicated website, **www.ducati.com**, in early 2000, inspired by the internet sales of the MH900 evolution, a limited-production motorcycle. Within 30 minutes, the entire year's production was sold out, making Ducati a leading international e-commerce player. Since then, Ducati has evolved its site to create a robust virtual customer community that had 160,000 registered users as of July 2004. Community management has become so central at Ducati that management has replaced the words 'marketing' and 'customer' with the words 'community' and 'fan'. Ducati considers the community of fans to be a major asset of the company and it strives to use the Internet to enhance the 'fan experience'. Ducati involves its fans on a systematic basis to reinforce the places, the events and the people that express the Ducati life style and Ducati's desired brand image. The community function is tightly connected with the product development and the fan involvement in the community directly influences product development.

Virtual communities play a key role in helping Ducati to explore new product concepts. Ducati has promoted and managed ad hoc online forums and chat rooms for over three years to harness a strong sense of community among Ducati fans.

Ducati also realized that a significant number of its fans spend their leisure time not only riding their bikes, but also maintaining and personalizing them. As a result, Ducati fans have deep technical knowledge that they are eager to share with other fans. To support such knowledge sharing, the company has created the 'Tech Café', a forum for exchanging technical knowledge. In this virtual environment, fans can share their projects for customizing motorcycles, provide suggestions to improve Ducati's next generation products, and even post their own mechanical and technical designs, with suggestions for innovations in aesthetic attributes as well as mechanical functions.

While not all fans participate in the online forums, those who do participate provide rich inputs for exploring new product concepts and technical solutions. These forums also help Ducati to enhance customer loyalty, because its fans are more motivated to buy products they helped to create.

Ducati managers also monitor vertical portals created for bikers, including Motorcyclist.com and Motoride.com; and Ducati monitors other virtual communities that have lifestyle associations with the Ducati brand. For instance, Ducati has entered into a partnership with the fashion company DKNY to tap into its community and interact with its members.

To validate its insights, Ducati uses online customer surveys to test product concepts and to quantify customer preferences. As a testimony to the ability of Ducati to create an ongoing customer dialogue and create a sense of engagement with its fans, Ducati gets extraordinary response rates, often in excess of 25 per cent when it surveys its customers. Ducati uses customer feedback for activities that go beyond product development.

Exhibit 11.6 continued

Ducati also pursues Internet-based customer collaboration at the back end of its NPD process. Virtual communities play an important role at the product design and market testing stages. For instance, in early 2001, the community managers of Ducati.com identified a group of customers on its website that had particularly strong relationships with the company. They decided to transform such customers into active partners, involving them in virtual teams that cooperate with Ducati professionals from R&D, Product Management and Design. These virtual teams of customers work with the company's engineers to define attributes and technical features for the 'next bike'.

Within the virtual community, current and future Ducati bike owners discuss and review proposed product modifications that can be tested online in the form of virtual prototypes. They can even vote to reject proposed modifications, personalize products to their preferences, and can ask Ducati technicians for suggestions on personalizing their bikes to individual taste.

Source: adapted from www.ducati.com and Sawhney *et al.* (2005). Images from Ducati.

## Dynamic customisation of product and services

The second stage of the customer interaction vector focuses on the opportunities and challenges in dynamically customizing products and services. Competitive markets are rapidly eroding margins due to price-based competition, and companies are seeking to enhance margins through customized offerings. Dynamic customization is based on three principles: modularity, intelligence, and organization.

1 *Modularity*: An approach for organizing complex products and processes efficiently. Product or service modularity requires the partitioning of a task into independent modules that function as a whole within overall architecture.
2 Intelligence: Continuous information exchange with consumers allows companies to create products and processes using the best possible modules. Website operators can match buyer and seller profiles and make recommendations based on their shared interests. The result is intelligent sites that learn their visitors' (potential buyers') tastes and deliver dynamic, personalised information about products and services.
3 *Organization*: Dynamic customisation of products and services requires a customer-oriented and flexible approach that is fundamentally committed to operating in this new way.

## How can the Internet be integrated in the future product innovation?

Figure 11.7 shows some of the implications of the Internet on future product innovation. The Internet is seen as the medium through which each 'box' communicates with the R&D function in the company.

- *Design*. Data is gathered directly from the product and is part of designing and developing the product. New product features (such as new versions of software programs) may be built into the product directly from the Internet.
- *Service and support*. The service department can perform troubleshooting and correction directly through the Internet set-up. For example a Mercedes car driving on the highway may be directly connected to the Mercedes service department. It will monitor the main functions of the car and if necessary make online repairs of, for example, the software of the car.

Figure 11.7 Product innovation through the Internet

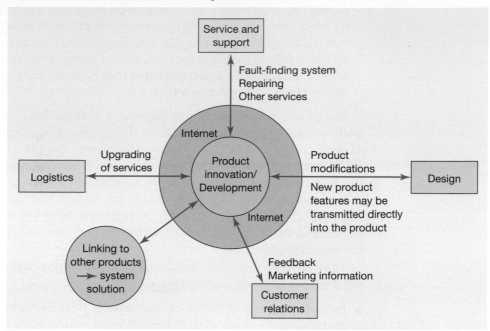

- *Customer relations.* Data gathered from the product may form part of statistics, comparisons between customers, etc. In this way the customer can compare the performance of their product (e.g. a car) with other customers' product (a kind of benchmarking). This may also strengthen an existing customer relationship.
- *Logistics.* Concurrently with increasing demands for just-in-time deliveries, the Internet will automatically find the distribution and transport that will take the goods from the subsupplier to the producer and then to the customers in the cheapest and most efficient way (and on time).

A fundamental shift in thinking is to replace the term 'supply chain' with 'demand chain'. The critical difference is that demand-chain thinking starts with the customers and works backwards. This breaks away from parochial approaches that focus solely on reducing transport costs. It supports a 'mass customization' viewpoint, in which bundles of goods and services are offered in ways that support customers' individual objectives.

This does not necessarily imply product differentiation. In fact the service aspects often require differentiation. For example, a company such as Unilever will provide the same margarine to both Tesco and Sainsbury's. However, the ways in which the product is delivered, transactions are processed and other parts of the relationship are managed, can and should be different, since these two competing supermarket chains each have their own ways of evaluating performance. The information systems required to coordinate companies along the demand chain require a new and different approach to that required within individual companies. Some managers believe that if they and their suppliers choose the same standard software package, such as SAP, they will be able to integrate their information systems.

- *Link to other products.* Sometimes a product is used as a subcomponent in other products. Through links in the Internet such subcomponents may be essential inputs for more complex product solutions. The car industry is an example of an industry that already makes a targeted effort in this direction. New 'stylish' cars are linked together by the Internet. In the wake of this development a new industry is created, the purpose of which is to provide integrated transport. In this new industry developing and producing cars is only one of several important services. Instead systems are to be developed that can diagnose cars (and correct the error) while the car is running, systems for regulation of traffic, interactive systems that enable drivers to have the desired transport at their disposal when and where they want it without tiresome rental agreements, etc.

The music industry is also undergoing a change. Today you can buy portable 'players' that can download music from the Internet using the MP3 format, and subsequently play the music that is stored in the 'player'. The CD is skipped – and so is the whole distribution facility. The music industry will become completely altered through the different economic conditions. The struggle will be about creating the best portal to the Internet, where the consumer can find the best information on music and the largest selection of music. The problems regarding rights are, however, still being discussed, and the lawyers and politicians have to find a final solution before the market can increase significantly.

Thus innovative product development of the future demands that a company possesses the following characteristics:

- *Innovative product development and strategic thinking.* Product development will contain much technology and demand an interdisciplinary, strategic overview and knowledge in order to find out what new services are worth aiming at.
- *Management of alliances.* Few companies have all the necessary qualifications themselves – innovative product development and the resulting services demand that companies enter into alliances very dynamically and yet in a structured way.
- *New customer relations.* The above-mentioned car industry example clearly shows that the customers are not car buyers any longer but *buyers of transport services*, and that is quite another matter. This means that companies have to focus on understanding the customers' needs in a quite different way.

## Developing brands on the Internet

Clearly consumer product companies such as Procter & Gamble, Colgate, Kraft Foods, and consumer durables and business-to-business companies such as General Motors, General Electric, Allied Signal and Caterpillar have crafted their business strategies by leveraging physical assets and developing powerful global brands supported by mass advertising and mass distribution. But remote links with customers apply equally well to these companies. Remote and continuous links with customers become critical as the concepts of brand identity and brand equity are redefined by the Internet.

Kraft Interactive Kitchen (**www.kraftfoods.com**) is an example of a consumer products company keeping in touch with its consumers by providing information-based services such as meal planners, recipes, tips and cooking techniques. Kraft's intention is to have remote connections and interactions with consumers in new ways.

However, some companies find it difficult to translate a strong offline brand (such as Nike and Levi's) to the Internet, because many of the well-known brands are based on an extensive 'physical' retail distribution system, and many of the retailers are reluctant to support online brands because of the fear of disintermediation (see section 11.5 for more discussion of this issue).

In fact many sites that are run by top brands register minimal online traffic, according to a report by Forrester Research. Forrester studied brand awareness and web surfing behaviour among 16–22-year-olds, whom advertisers consider to be strongly brand conscious.

Companies are taking a broad approach to branding, integrating it with an overall advertising and marketing strategy. On the net branding is more than logos and colour schemes; it is about creating experiences and understanding customers. Consequently web brand building is not cheap. Building a brand requires a persistent online presence. For some brands that entails a mass-appeal site; for others brand building requires a combination of initiatives, from banner ads to sponsorships.

## 11.9 Green marketing strategies

As understanding grows about the impact of human activity on the earth's ecosystems, consumer concern about the environment and its links to health and safety will intensify. At the same time, humankind's passion for consumption will persist. The challenge for companies will be to devise business practices and products that are friendly to the environment while also meeting the needs of consumers.

Environmentalists were once considered the only people concerned about the depletion of natural resources, waste accumulation and pollution. Environmentalists around the world are now becoming global in their scope and scale of operations. Their aim is to increase people's awareness of the importance of environmental preservation on a global scale and how the lack of it will have a harmful effect on our planet.

Because ecological grassroot campaigns gain widespread recognition and support, and global media networks such as CNN continue to report on environmental issues and disasters, today's consumer is becoming more environmentally conscious. Various polls and surveys reveal that many consumers are taking environmental issues into consideration as they buy, consume and dispose of products. Consequently there is a direct connection between a company's ability to attract and keep consumers and its ability to develop and execute environmentally sound strategies.

As consumer preferences and government policies increasingly favour a balanced business approach to the environment, managers are paying more attention to the strategic importance of their environmental decisions. Irresponsible behaviour by some firms has led to consumer boycotts, lengthy lawsuits and large fines. Such actions may have harmed firms in less direct ways, such as negative public relations, diversion of management attention and difficulty in hiring top employees.

In Europe particularly the green consumer movement is large and growing, and certain countries can be considered leaders and standard setters in green awareness. Of German consumers, for instance, 80 per cent are willing to pay premiums for household goods that are recycled, recyclable and non-damaging to the environment; in France 50 per cent of consumers will pay more at the supermarket for products they perceive as being environmentally friendly. This trend is growing elsewhere too: according to a European study, consumers throughout the OECD area are willing to pay more for green goods (Vandermerwe and Oliff, 1991).

**Green marketing**
Integrating business practices and products that are friendly to the environment while also meeting the needs of the consumers.

Several retailers have also committed themselves to marketing green products (green marketing). Clearly, failing to consider the environmental impact of strategic decisions may affect the financial stability of the firm and the ability of that firm to compete with others in the industry.

### Strategic options

Businesses realize that they must be prepared to provide their customers with information on the environmental impact of their products and manufacturing processes.

Figure 11.8 **Types of environmental strategic posture**

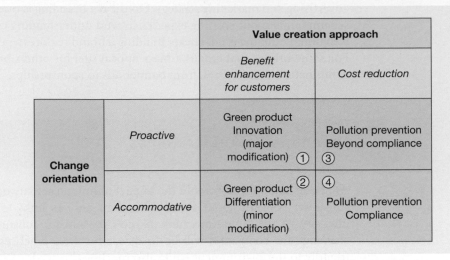

Source: Adapted from Starik *et al.*, (1996), 'Growing an environmental strategy', *Business Strategy and the Environment*, 5, p. 17.

Figure 11.8 presents four strategic options that are available for the firm with environmental concerns. The choice of strategic environmental posture will depend on how an organization wants to create value for its green customers and how change oriented its approach is.

As can be seen from Figure 11.8, if a firm is more oriented to cost reduction than to benefit enhancement for customers, pollution prevention strategies (options 3 and 4) would probably be chosen in preference to the development of green products: for example by using natural or recycled materials. If a firm is more proactive than accommodative, it tends to be more innovative than otherwise (options 1 and 3).

Although going beyond compliance (i.e. doing more than required according to environmental legislation) is generally perceived as highly desirable, SMEs may not have the resources to act proactively, and hence need to focus on compliance and minor product modification (options 2 and 4).

However, because consumers buy products and services primarily to fulfil individual needs and wants, companies should continue to highlight the direct benefits of their products. They should not forget to emphasize the traditional product attributes of price, quality, convenience and availability and make only a secondary appeal to consumers on the basis of environmental attributes (Ginsberg and Bloom, 2004).

## Green alliances between business and environmental organizations

Strategic alliances with environmental groups (e.g. Greenpeace) can provide five benefits to marketers of consumer goods (Mendleson and Polonsky, 1995):

1 *They increase consumer confidence in green products and their claims*. It can be assumed that, if an environmental group supports a firm, product or service, consumers are more likely to believe the product's environmental claims.

2 *They provide firms with access to environmental information*. It is in their role as an information clearing house that environmental groups may be of immense benefit to organizations with which they form strategic alliances. Manufacturers facing environmental problems may turn to their strategic partners for advice and information. In some cases environmental partners may actually have technical staff who can be used to assist in solving organizational problems or implementing existing solutions.

3 *They give the marketer access to new markets.* Most environmental groups have an extensive support base, which in many cases receives newsletters or other group mailings. Their members receive catalogues marketing a variety of licensed products, all of which are less environmentally harmful than other commercial alternatives. Environmental group members represent a potential market that can be utilized by producers, even if these groups do not produce specialized catalogues. An environmental group's newsletter may discuss how a firm has formed a strategic alliance with the group, as well as the firm's less environmentally harmful products. Inclusion of this information in a newsletter is a useful form of publicity.

4 *They provide positive publicity and reduce public criticism.* Forming strategic alliances with environmental groups may also stimulate increased publicity. When the Sydney Olympic Bid Committee announced that Greenpeace was the successful designer for the year 2000 Olympic Village the story appeared in all major newspapers and on the national news. It is highly unlikely that this publicity would have been generated if a more conventional architect had been named as the designer of the village. Once again the publicity associated with the alliance was positive and credible.

5 *They educate consumers about key environmental issues for the firm and its product(s).* Environmental groups are valuable sources of educational information and materials. They educate consumers and the general public about environmental problems and also inform them about potential solutions. In many cases the public views these groups as credible sources of information, without a vested interest. Marketers can also play an important role as providers of environmental information through their marketing activities. In doing so they create environmental awareness of specific issues, their products and their organizations. For example, Kelloggs in Norway educated consumers and promoted its environmental concern by placing environmental information on the packaging of its cereals relating to various regional environmental problems (World Wide Fund for Nature, 1993).

Choosing the correct alliance partner is not a simple task, as environmental groups have different objectives and images. Some groups may be willing to form exclusive alliances, where they partner only one product in a given product category. Other groups may be willing to form alliances with all products that comply with their specific criteria.

The marketer must determine what capabilities and characteristics an alliance partner can bring to the alliance. As with any symbiotic relationship, each partner must contribute to the success of the activity. Poor definition of these characteristics may result in the firm searching out the wrong partner.

McDonald's offers an example of a company that gained credibility through collaboration. The company's collaboration with EDF (Environmental Defense Fund) in the early 1990s over its decision to move from Styrofoam to paper packaging similarly allowed the company to increase its credibility on environmental issues with consumers (Argenti, 2004).

## 11.10 Factors influencing international pricing decisions

An SME exporting for the first time, with little knowledge of the market environment that it is entering, is likely to set a price that will ensure that the sales revenue generated at least covers the costs incurred. It is important that firms recognize that the cost structures of products are very significant, but they should not be regarded as sole determinants when setting prices.

Pricing policy is an important strategic and tactical competitive weapon that, in contrast to the other elements of the global marketing mix, is highly controllable and inexpensive to change and implement. Therefore pricing strategies and action should be integrated with the other elements of the global marketing mix.

Figure 11.9 presents a general framework for international pricing decisions. According to this model, factors affecting international pricing can be broken down into two main groups (internal and external factors) and four subgroups, which we will now consider in more detail.

Figure 11.9 **International pricing framework**

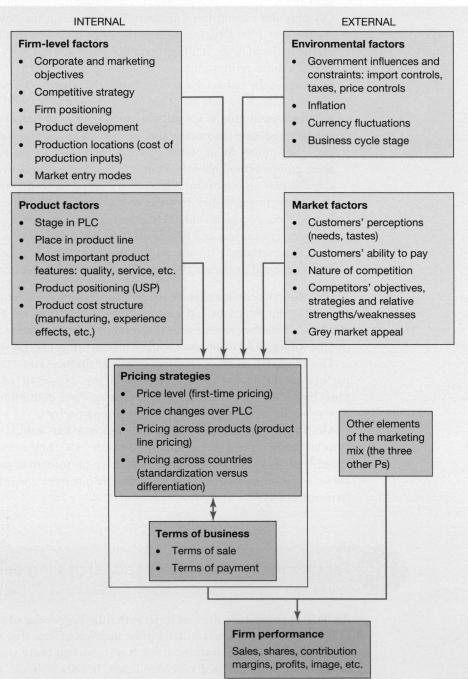

## Firm-level factors

International pricing is influenced by past and current corporate philosophy, organization and managerial policies. The short-term tactical use of pricing in the form of discounts, product offers and reductions is often emphasized by managers at the expense of its strategic role, and yet pricing over recent years has played a very significant part in the restructuring of many industries, resulting in the growth of some businesses and the decline of others. In particular, Japanese firms have approached new markets with the intention of building market share over a period of years by reducing price levels, establishing the brand name, and setting up effective distribution and servicing networks. The market share objectives of the Japanese firms have usually been accomplished at the expense of short-term profits, as international Japanese firms have consistently taken a long-term perspective on profit. They are usually prepared to wait much longer for returns on investments than some of their western counterparts.

The choice of foreign market entry mode also affects the pricing policy. A manufacturer with a subsidiary in a foreign country has a high level of control over the pricing policy in that country.

## Product factors

Key product factors include the unique and innovative features of the product and the availability of substitutes. These factors will have a major impact on the stage of the product life cycle, which will also depend on the market environment in target markets. Whether the product is a service or a manufactured or commodity good sold into consumer or industrial markets is also significant.

The extent to which the organization has had to adapt or modify the product or service, and the level to which the market requires service around the core product, will also affect cost and thereby have some influence on pricing.

Costs are also helpful in estimating how rivals will react to the setting of a specific price, assuming that knowledge of one's own costs helps in the assessment of competitors' reactions. Added to the above is the intermediary cost, which depends on channel length, intermediary factors and logistical costs. All these factors add up and lead to price escalation.

**Price escalation**
All cost factors (e.g. firms' net ex-works price, shipping costs, tariffs, distributor mark-up) in the distribution channel add up and lead to price escalation. The longer the distribution channel, the higher the final price in the foreign market.

The example in Table 11.4 shows that, due to additional shipping, insurance and distribution charges, the exported product costs some 21 per cent more in the export market than at home. Through the use of an additional distribution link (an importer), the product costs 39 per cent more abroad than at home.

Many exporters are not aware of rapid price escalation; they are preoccupied with the price they charge to the importer. However, the final consumer price should be of vital concern because it is on this level that the consumer can compare prices of different competitive products and it is this price that plays a major role in determining the foreign demand.

Price escalation is not a problem for exporters alone. It affects all firms involved in cross-border transactions. Companies that undertake substantial intracompany shipment of goods and materials across national borders are exposed to many of the additional charges that cause price escalation.

The following management options are available to counter price escalation:

- *Rationalizing the distribution process.* One option is to reduce the number of links in the distribution process, either by doing more in-house or by circumventing some channel members.
- *Lowering the export price from the factory* (firm's net price), thus reducing the multiplier effect of all the mark-ups.

Table 11.4 **Price escalation (examples)**

| | Domestic channel (a) | Foreign marketing channel (b) | (c) |
|---|---|---|---|
| | Firm ↓ Wholesaler ↓ Retailer ↓ Consumer | Firm ↓ ----Border Wholesaler ↓ Retailer ↓ Consumer | Firm ↓ ----Border Importer ↓ Wholesaler ↓ Retailer ↓ Consumer |
| | £ | £ | £ |
| Firm's net price | 100 | 100 | 100 |
| Insurance and shipping costs | – | 10 | 10 |
| Landed cost | – | 110 | 110 |
| Tariff (10% of landed cost) | – | 11 | 11 |
| Importer pays (cost) | – | – | 121 |
| Importer's margin/mark-up (15% of cost) | – | – | 18 |
| Wholesaler pays (cost) | 100 | 121 | 139 |
| Wholesaler'/mark-up (20% of cost) | 20 | 24 | 28 |
| Retailer pays (cost) | 120 | 145 | 167 |
| Retail margin/mark-up (40% of cost) | 48 | 58 | 67 |
| Consumer pays (price) (exclusive of VAT) | 168 | 203 | 234 |
| % price escalation over domestic channel | – | 21 | 39 |

- *Establishing local production of the product* within the export market to eliminate some of the cost.
- *Pressurizing channel members to accept lower profit margins.* This may be appropriate if these intermediaries are dependent on the manufacturer for much of their turnover.

It may be dangerous to overlook traditional channel members. In Japan, for example, the complex nature of the distribution system, which often involves many different channel members, makes it tempting to consider radical change. However, existing intermediaries do not like to be overlooked, and their possible network with other channel members and the government may make it dangerous for a foreign firm to attempt to cut them out.

## Environmental factors

The environmental factors are external to the firm and thus uncontrollable variables in the foreign market. The national government control of exports and imports is usually based on political and strategic considerations.

Generally speaking, import controls are designed to limit imports in order to protect domestic producers or reduce the outflow of foreign exchange. Direct restrictions commonly take the form of tariffs, quotas and various non-tariff barriers. Tariffs directly increase the price of imports unless the exporter or importer is willing to absorb the tax and accept lower profit margins. Quotas have an indirect impact on prices. They restrict supply, thus causing the price of the import to increase.

Since tariff levels vary from country to country there is an incentive for exporters to vary the price somewhat from country to country. In some countries with high customs duties and high price elasticity the base price may have to be lower than in other countries if the product is to achieve satisfactory volume in these markets. If demand is quite inelastic the price may be set at a high level, with little loss of volume, unless competitors are selling at lower prices.

Government regulations on pricing can also affect the firm's pricing strategy. Many governments tend to have price controls on specific products related to health, education, food and other essential items. Another major environmental factor is fluctuation in the exchange rate. An increase (revaluation) or decrease (devaluation) in the relative value of a currency can affect the firm's pricing structure and profitability.

## Market factors

One of the critical factors in the foreign market is the purchasing power of the customers (customers' ability to pay). The pressure of competitors may also affect international pricing. The firm has to offer a more competitive price if there are other sellers in the market. Thus the nature of competition (e.g. oligopoly or monopoly) can influence the firm's pricing strategy.

Under conditions approximating pure competition price is set in the marketplace. Price tends to be just enough above costs to keep marginal producers in business. Thus, from the point of view of the price setter, the most important factor is cost. The closer the substitutability of products, the more nearly identical the prices must be, and the greater the influence of costs in determining prices (assuming a large enough number of buyers and sellers).

Under conditions of monopolistic or imperfect competition the seller has some discretion to vary the product quality, promotional efforts and channel policies in order to adapt the price of the total product to serve preselected market segments. Nevertheless the freedom to set prices is still limited by what competitors charge, and any price differentials from competitors must be justified in the minds of customers on the basis of differential utility: that is, perceived value.

When considering how customers will respond to a given price strategy, Nagle (1987) has suggested nine factors that influence the sensitivity of customers to prices:

1 More distinctive product.
2 Greater perceived quality of products.
3 Consumers less aware of substitutes in the market.
4 Difficulty in making comparisons (e.g. in the quality of services such as consultancy or accountancy).
5 The price of a product represents a small proportion of total expenditure of the customer.
6 The perceived benefit for the customer increases.
7 The product is used in association with a product bought previously, so that, for example, components and replacements are usually extremely highly priced.
8 Costs are shared with other parties.
9 The product or service cannot be stored.

Price sensitivity is reduced in all these nine cases.

In the following sections we discuss the different available pricing strategies.

## 11.11  International pricing strategies

In determining the price level for a new product the general alternatives are as shown in Figure 11.10.

### Skimming

In this strategy a high price is charged to 'skim the cream' from the top end of the market, with the objective of achieving the highest possible contribution in a short time. For a marketer to use this approach the product has to be unique, and some segments of the market must be willing to pay the high price. As more segments are targeted and more of the product is made available the price is gradually lowered. The success of skimming depends on the ability and speed of competitive reaction.

Products should be designed to appeal to affluent and demanding consumers, offering extra features, greater comfort, variability or ease of operation. With skimming the firm trades off a low market share against a high margin.

Problems with skimming are as follows:

- Having a small market share makes the firm vulnerable to aggressive local competition.
- Maintenance of a high-quality product requires a lot of resources (promotion, after-sales service) and a visible local presence, which may be difficult in distant markets.
- If the product is sold more cheaply at home or in another country grey marketing (parallel importing) is likely.

### Market pricing

If similar products already exist in the target market, market pricing may be used. The final customer price is based on competitive prices. This approach requires the exporter to have a thorough knowledge of product costs, as well as confidence that the product life cycle is long enough to warrant entry into the market. It is a reactive approach and may lead to problems if sales volumes never rise to sufficient levels to produce a satisfactory return. Although firms typically use pricing as a differentiation tool the global marketing manager may have no choice but to accept the prevailing world market price.

From the price that customers are willing to pay it is possible to make a so-called retrograde calculation where the firm uses a 'reversed' price escalation to calculate backwards (from market price) to the necessary (ex-factory) net price. If this net price can create a satisfactory contribution margin then the firm can go ahead.

Figure 11.10  **Strategies for pricing a new product**

## Penetration pricing

A penetration pricing policy is used to stimulate market growth and capture market shares by deliberately offering products at low prices. This approach requires mass markets, price-sensitive customers and reduction in unit costs through economies of scale and experience curve effects. The basic assumption that lower prices will increase sales will fail if the main competitors reduce their prices to a correspondingly low level. Another danger is that prices might be set so low that they are not credible to consumers. There exist 'confidence levels' for prices below which consumers lose faith in the product's quality.

Motives for pricing at low levels in certain foreign markets might include the following:

- Intensive local competition from rival companies.
- Lower income levels of local consumers.
- Some firms argue that, since their R&D and other overhead costs are covered by home sales, exporting represents a marginal activity intended merely to bring in as much additional revenue as possible by offering a low selling price.

Japanese companies have used penetration pricing intensively to gain market share leadership in a number of markets, such as cars, home entertainment products and electronic components.

## Price changes

Price changes on existing products are called for when a new product has been launched or when changes occur in overall market conditions (such as fluctuating foreign exchange rates).

Table 11.5 shows the percentage sales volume increase or decrease required to maintain the level of profit. An example (the figure in bold type in Table 11.5) shows how the table functions. A firm has a product with a contribution margin of 20 per cent. The firm would like to know how much the sales volume should be increased as a consequence of a price reduction of 5 per cent, if it wishes to keep the same total profit contribution. The calculation is as follows:

*Before price reduction*

| Per product | sales price | £100 |
| | variable cost per unit | £80 |
| | contribution margin | £20 |

Total contribution margin: 100 units @ £20 = £2,000

*After price reduction (5%)*

| Per product | sales price | £95 |
| | variable cost per unit | £80 |
| | contribution margin | £15 |

Total contribution margin: 133 units @ £15 = £1,995

As a consequence of a price reduction of 5 per cent, a 33 per cent increase in sales is required.

If a decision is made to change prices, related changes must also be considered. For example, if an increase in price is required it may be accompanied, at least initially, by increased promotional efforts.

When reducing prices the degree of flexibility enjoyed by decision makers will tend to be less for existing products than for new products. This follows from the high probability that the existing product is now less unique, faces stronger competition and is

Table 11.5 Sales volume increase or decrease (%) required to maintain total profit contribution

| Price reduction (%) | Profit contribution margin (price – variable cost per unit as % of the price) | | | | | | | | |
| | 5 | 10 | 15 | 20 | 25 | 30 | 35 | 40 | 50 |
| | Sales volume increase (%) required to maintain total profit contribution | | | | | | | | |
|---|---|---|---|---|---|---|---|---|---|
| 2.0 | 67 | 25 | 15 | 11 | 9 | 7 | 7 | 5 | 4 |
| 3.0 | 150 | 43 | 25 | 18 | 14 | 11 | 9 | 8 | 6 |
| 4.0 | 400 | 67 | 36 | 25 | 19 | 15 | 13 | 11 | 9 |
| 5.0 | | 100 | 50 | **33** | 25 | 20 | 17 | 14 | 11 |
| 7.5 | | 300 | 100 | 60 | 43 | 33 | 27 | 23 | 18 |
| 10.0 | | | 200 | 100 | 67 | 50 | 40 | 33 | 25 |
| 15.0 | | | | 300 | 150 | 100 | 75 | 60 | 43 |

| Price increase (%) | Profit contribution margin (price – variable cost per unit as % of the price) | | | | | | | | |
| | 5 | 10 | 15 | 20 | 25 | 30 | 35 | 40 | 50 |
| | Max. sales volume reduction (%) required to maintain total profit contribution | | | | | | | | |
|---|---|---|---|---|---|---|---|---|---|
| 2.0 | 29 | 17 | 12 | 9 | 7 | 6 | 5 | 5 | 4 |
| 3.0 | 37 | 23 | 17 | 13 | 11 | 9 | 8 | 7 | 6 |
| 4.0 | 44 | 29 | 21 | 17 | 14 | 12 | 10 | 9 | 7 |
| 5.0 | 50 | 33 | 25 | 20 | 17 | 14 | 12 | 11 | 9 |
| 7.5 | 60 | 43 | 33 | 27 | 23 | 20 | 18 | 16 | 13 |
| 10.0 | 67 | 50 | 40 | 33 | 29 | 25 | 22 | 20 | 17 |
| 15.0 | 75 | 60 | 50 | 43 | 37 | 33 | 30 | 27 | 23 |

aimed at a broader segment of the market. In this situation the decision maker will be forced to pay more attention to competitive and cost factors in the pricing process.

The timing of price changes can be nearly as important as the changes themselves. For example, a simple tactic of time lagging competitors in announcing price increases can produce the perception among customers that you are the most customer-responsive supplier. The extent of the time lag can also be important.

In one company an independent survey of customers (Garda, 1995) showed that the perception of being the most customer-responsive supplier was generated just as effectively by a six-week lag in following a competitor's price increase as by a six-month lag. A considerable amount of money would have been lost during the unnecessary four-and-a-half-month delay in announcing a price increase.

## Experience curve pricing

**Experience curve pricing**
Combination of the experience curve (lowering costs per unit with accumulated production of the product) with typical market price development within an industry.

Price changes usually follow changes in the product's stage in the life cycle. As the product matures more pressure will be put on the price to keep the product competitive because of increased competition and less possibility of differentiation.

Let us also integrate the cost aspect into the discussion. The experience curve has its roots in a commonly observed phenomenon called the learning curve, which states that as people repeat a task they learn to do it better and faster. The learning curve applies to the labour portion of manufacturing cost. The Boston Consulting Group extended the learning effect to cover all the value-added costs related to a product – manufacturing plus marketing, sales, administration and so on.

The resulting experience curves, covering all value chain activities (see Figure 11.11), indicate that the total unit costs of a product in real terms can be reduced by a certain percentage with each doubling of cumulative production. The typical decline in cost is 30 per cent (termed a 70 per cent curve), although greater and lesser declines are observed (Czepiel, 1992, p. 149).

Figure 11.11 **Experience curves of value chain activities**

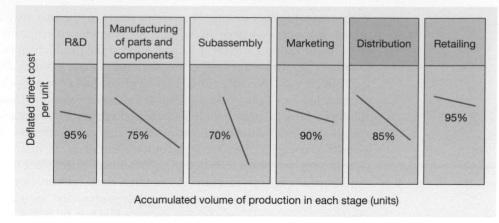

Source: Czepiel, 1992, *Competitive Marketing Strategy*, pub. Prentice-Hall, p. 154.

If we combine the experience curve (average unit cost) with the typical market price development within an industry we will have a relationship similar to that shown in Figure 11.12.

Figure 11.12 shows that after the introduction stage (during part of which the price is below the total unit cost), profits begin to flow. Because supply is less than demand prices do not fall as quickly as costs. Consequently the gap between costs and prices widens, in effect creating a price umbrella, attracting new competitors. However, the competitive situation is not a stable one. At some point the umbrella will be folded by one or more competitors reducing the prices in an attempt to gain or retain market share. The result is that a shake-out phase will begin: inefficient producers will be shaken out by rapidly falling market prices, and only those with a competitive price/cost relationship will remain.

Figure 11.12 **Product life cycle stages and the industry price experience curve**

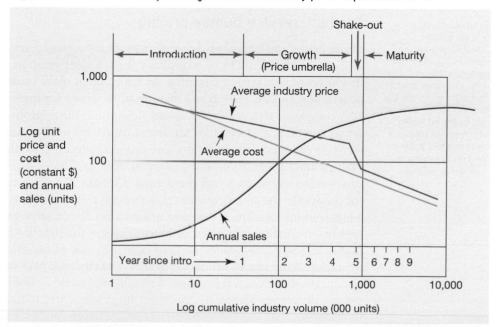

Source: Czepiel, 1992, *Competitive Marketing Strategy*, pub. Prentice-Hall, p. 167.

## Pricing across products (product line pricing)

With across-product pricing the various items in the line may be differentiated by pricing them appropriately to indicate, for example, an economy version, a standard version and a top-of-the-range version. One of the products in the line may be priced to protect against competitors or to gain market share from existing competitors.

Products with less competition may be priced higher to subsidize other parts of the product line, so as to make up for the lost contribution of such 'fighting brands'. Another strategy is price bundling (total 'package' price), where a certain price is set for customers who simultaneously buy several items within the product line (one price for a personal computer package with software and printer). In all such cases a key consideration is how much consumers in different countries want to save money, to spend time searching for the 'best buy' and so forth. Furthermore, some items in the product line may be priced very low to serve as loss leaders and induce customers to try the product. A special variant of this is the so-called buy in–follow on strategy (Weigand, 1991). A classic example of this strategy is the razor blade link where Gillette, for example, uses a penetration price on its razor (buy in) but a skimming pricing (relatively high price) on its razor blades (follow on). Thus the linked product or service – the follow on – is sold at a significant contribution margin. This inevitably attracts hitchhikers who try to sell follow-on products without incurring the cost of the buy in.

The buy in–follow on strategy is different from a low introductory price, which is based on the hope that the customer (of habit) will return again and again at higher prices. With the buy in–follow on strategy sales of two products or services are powerfully linked by factors such as legal contracts, patents, trade secrets, experience curve advantages and technological links.

Other examples of the strategy are as follows:

- The price of a Polaroid instant camera is very low, but Polaroid hopes that this will generate sales of far more profitable films for many years.
- The telephone companies sell mobile (cellular) telephones at a near giveaway price, hoping that the customer will be a 'heavy' user of the profitable mobile telephone network.

## Product-service bundle pricing

**Product-service bundle pricing**
Bundling product and services together in a system-solution product. If the customer thinks that entry price is a key barrier, service contracts can be priced higher, which allows for lower entry product pricing – the practice in many software businesses.

The structure and level of pricing is perhaps the most crucial design choice in embedded *services*. To get pricing right, a company needs a clear grasp of its strategic intent and its sources of competitive advantage and must often make trade-offs between product penetration and the growth and margins of its *service* business.

A company's strategic intent largely determines the appropriate extent of product-*service* bundling and the *value* attributed to *services* in such bundles. Companies that focus on enhancing or protecting core products should price their *services* to improve their product penetration. The pricing strategy to achieve such product pull-through varies according to customer purchasing decisions. Companies can raise the *value* of the product in use and increase its pull-through by bundling products and *services* into a higher-*value* solution. If the entry price is a key factor, *service* contracts can be priced higher, which allows for lower product pricing – the practice in many software businesses. In some cases, companies can raise the price of maintenance *service* contracts to accelerate the rate of product upgrades. The strategic goal of product pull-through also means that sales and field agents should have some flexibility and authority in the pricing of *services*. However, companies must still actively manage pricing discipline by ensuring that these salespeople are accountable for the total profitability of the bundles they sell.

By contrast, companies aiming to create an independent, growth-oriented *service* business should price their offerings to achieve profitable growth and set pricing targets as close to the *service's value* to customers as competitive alternatives permit. These companies should set pricing guidelines and delegate authority centrally, with relatively limited freedom for sales and field personnel and clear rules for discounting. Bundling prices for *services* and products is usually a bad idea for a growth platform in *services*, since within any given customer's organization, the person who buys the *service* might not be the one who buys the product. It is also difficult to bundle prices while holding both product and *service* business units accountable for their independent sales and margin targets.

The source of competitive advantage – scale or skill – mainly affects pricing structures. If economies of scale drive a business, its pricing should be based on standard units (such as terabytes of storage managed) and it should offer volume discounts to encourage growth in usage. Such companies ought to make the price of any customized variation from their standard *service* offerings extremely high, since these exceptions push up costs throughout the business.

By contrast, if a *service* business relies mostly on special skills, it should base its prices on the costs its customers avoid by using its *services* or on the cost of the next-best alternative. Such *value*-based pricing requires a sophisticated analysis of a customer segment's total cost of ownership and a deep understanding of the cost structure of the *service* business. Competitive benchmarks and the cost of deploying the skills should determine the respective upper and lower bounds for these price levels. In the best case, companies can package this intelligence into pricing tools that allow sales and field agents to estimate customer *value* more accurately and thus improve field-level pricing decisions (Auguste *et al.*, 2006).

## Pricing across countries (standardization versus differentiation)

A major problem for companies is how to coordinate prices between countries. There are two essential opposing forces: first, to achieve similar positioning in different markets by adopting largely standardized pricing; and second, to maximize profitability by adapting pricing to different market conditions. In determining to what extent prices should be standardized across borders two basic approaches appear:

1 *Price standardization.* This is based on setting a price for the product as it leaves the factory. At its simplest it involves setting a fixed world price at the headquarters of the firm. This fixed world price is then applied in all markets after taking account of factors such as foreign exchange rates and variance in the regulatory context. For the firm this is a low-risk strategy, but no attempt is made to respond to local conditions and so no effort is made to maximize profits. However, this pricing strategy might be appropriate if the firm sells to very large customers, who have companies in several countries. In such a situation the firm might be under pressure from the customer only to deliver at the same price to every country subsidiary, throughout the customer's multinational organization. In Figure 11.13 this is exemplified, for example, by the international activities of large retail organizations. Another advantage of price standardization includes the potential for rapid introduction of new products in international markets and the presentation of a consistent (price) image across markets.

2 *Price differentiation.* This allows each local subsidiary or partner (agent, distributor, etc.) to set a price that is considered to be the most appropriate for local conditions, and no attempt is made to coordinate prices from country to country. Cross-cultural empirical research has found significant differences in customer characteristics,

Figure 11.13 Structural factors of standardized versus differentiated pricing in European consumer goods markets

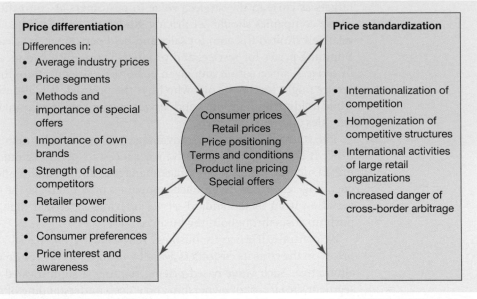

Source: Reprinted from *European Management Journal*, Vol. 12, No. 2, Diller. H. and Bukhari, I. (1994) 'Pricing conditions in the European Common Market', p. 168, Copyright 1994, with permission from Elsevier.

preference and purchasing behaviour among different countries (Theodosiou and Katsikeas, 2001). The weakness with 'price differentiation' is the lack of control that the headquarters has over the prices set by the subsidiary operations or external partner. Significantly different prices may be set in adjacent markets, and this can reflect badly on the image of multinational firms. It also encourages the creation of parallel importing/grey markets, whereby products can be purchased in one market and sold in another, undercutting the established market prices in the process.

The underlying forces favouring standardization or differentiation are shown in Figure 11.13.

## An international pricing taxonomy

As we discussed previously, pricing decisions in the international environment tend to be a function of the interplay between the external, market-related complexities that shape firm operations and the capabilities of the firm to respond effectively to these contingencies. Solberg's (1997) framework captures this interface in a meaningful way and leads to sufficiently important consequences for the export pricing behaviour of firms in foreign markets. Solberg suggests that firms' international strategic behaviour is shaped primarily by two dimensions: (a) the degree of globalism of the firm's industry (a measure of the market related factors) and (b) its degree of preparedness for internationalization (a measure of the firm's abilities to respond to these factors). These two dimensions are discussed in Chapter 1 (Figure 1.2) with the purpose of suggesting under which circumstances the firm should 'stay at home', 'strengthen the global position' or something in between. In Figure 11.14 an international pricing taxonomy is proposed along these two dimensions (Solberg *et al.*, 2006).

A global industry is dominated by a few, large major competitors that 'rule' their categories in world markets within their product category. Thus, the degree of globalism along the industry globalism dimension is considered to vary between two extremes: a monopoly at one end (the right) and atomistic competition at the other (the left).

**Figure 11.14 A taxonomy of international pricing practices**

Source: Adapted from Solberg *et al.*, 2006, p. 31. In the original article Solberg has used the concept 'Globality' instead of 'Globalism'.

The strategic implication of this perspective is that the monopolistic and oligopolistic global player would be the price setter, whereas the firm in the atomistic (multilocal) market setting would be exposed to local market forces, finding itself needing to follow market prices in every case. Although most firms fall into intermediate positions along this continuum, we believe that the leverage of the individual international firm in setting its pricing strategy will be greatly influenced by the globalism of the competitive environment in which it will operate.

On the other dimension, *preparedness for internationalization*, experienced firms find international pricing to be a more complicated matter, even though they devote additional resources to collecting and processing greater amounts of information. These firms are found to have the international preparedness that is necessary to offset the effects of reduced prices when they penetrate new markets or respond to competitive attacks, to be more self-confident in setting pricing strategies, and, in general, to enjoy higher market shares in the export market. In contrast, smaller and more inexperienced firms seem to be too weak both in relation to their local counterparts and in terms of generating local market insight to be able to determine effective price levels for their products in foreign markets. Therefore, they tend to possess smaller shares in their markets and to follow the pricing practices of their competitors or segment leaders.

Looking through the lens of this framework we assume that large, internationally experienced exporters will be likely to centralize their pricing decisions and will prefer higher degrees of control over those decisions, whereas smaller, often new-to-export, and internationally inexperienced firms will be likely to experiment with decentralized and often opportunistic modes of price-setting behaviour in their market.

The following discusses the characteristics of each of the four strategic prototypes in Figure 11.14.

## Prototype 1: The local price follower firm

In this cell the firm (manufacturer) will only have limited international experience, and consequently, the firm's local export intermediate (agent or distributor) will serve as the key informant for the firm. This information asymmetry bears the danger that the export intermediate might mislead the exporter by exercising opportunism or by pursuing goals that are in conflict with those of the exporter. That may cause further transaction costs, and lead to internalization (see section 3.3 on transaction cost analysis).

Because of the limited market knowledge the exporter is prone to calculate its prices crudely and most likely on the basis of cost and the (sometimes insufficient or biased) information from its local export intermediary. In the extreme case such an exporter would respond only to unsolicited offers from abroad, and will tend following a pricing procedure based on internal cost information, thus missing potential international business opportunities.

### Prototype 2: The global price follower firm

Firms that fall into the global price follower cell have limited preparedness for internationalization. In contrast, however, global price follower firms are often more motivated in expanding their international market involvement, as they are 'pushed' by the global market. Firms in this cell are expected to charge a standardized price in all countries because the interconnected international markets have more or less the same price level.

Given their marginal position in global markets, such firms have limited bargaining leverage and may be compelled to adopt the price level set by global market leaders, often very large global customers. The Prototype 2 firms are typically under constant pressure from their more efficient distribution and globally branded counterparts to adjust their prices.

### Prototype 3: The multilocal price setter firm

Firms in this cell are well-prepared international marketers with well-entrenched positions in local markets. Typically they are capable of assessing local market conditions through in-depth analyses and evaluation of market information, established market intelligence systems and/or deeply rooted market knowledge. They tend to have a tight control of their local market distribution networks through information and feedback systems. Prototype 3-firms adapt their prices from one market to the next in light of the differentiated requirements of each local market and manage the different market and pricing structures they cope with in their many (multidomestic) markets with relatively high sophistication.

In contrast to their local price follower counterparts (Prototype 1), however, these firms are often the pricing leaders in their local markets and base their pricing strategy primarily on local market conditions in each market. Given their multidomestic orientation, these firms tend to shift pricing decision-making authority to local subsidiary managers, even though their headquarters personnel closely monitors sales trends in each local market. Firms in this cell face challenges from grey market imports in their local markets that are motivated by the opportunity for cheaper producers to exploit price differences across markets.

### Prototype 4: The global price leader firm

Firms in this cell hold strong positions in key world markets. They manage smoothly functioning marketing networks, operating mainly through hierarchical entry modes or in combination with intermediate modes like joint ventures or alliances in major world markets. Prototype 4-firms compete against a limited number of competitors in each major market, similar to a global (or a regional) oligopoly. Typical of oligopoly players, they tend to be challenged by the cross-border transparency of the price mechanism; manage global (or regional) constraints, such as demand patterns and market regulation mechanisms; and set prices pan-regionally (i.e. across the EU). Global price leaders tend to maintain relatively high price levels in their markets, though possibly not as effectively as their multilocal counterparts. Compared with the global price leader firm, the multilocal price setter more effectively erects local entry barriers, such as brand leadership, has closer relationships with its local distributors and a deeper understanding of local conditions in each local market, thus protecting itself from the downside of international price competition (Solberg *et al.*, 2006).

## Establishing global-pricing contracts (GPCs)

**Global pricing contract**
A customer requiring one global price (per product) from the supplier for all its foreign SBUs and subsidiaries.

As globalization increases the following sentence is heard frequently among global suppliers and global customers: 'Give me a global-pricing contract (GPC) and I'll consolidate my worldwide purchase with you.' Increasingly, global customers are demanding such contracts from suppliers. For example, in 1998 General Motor's Powertrain Group told suppliers of components used in GM's engines, transmissions and subassemblies to charge GM the same for parts from one region as they did for parts from another region.

Suppliers do not need to lose out when customers globalize. The most attractive global-pricing opportunities are those that involve suppliers and customers working together to identify and eliminate inefficiencies that harm both. Sometimes, however, suppliers do not have a choice – they cannot afford to shut themselves out of business with their largest and fastest-growing customers.

Suppliers and customers have different advantages and disadvantages with global-pricing contracts and Table 11.6 illustrates some of these.

**Table 11.6 Global pricing contracts (GPCs): advantages and disadvantages**

| | Customers | Suppliers |
|---|---|---|
| *Advantages* | Lower prices worldwide coupled with higher levels of service. | Easily gain access to new markets and grow the business. |
| | Standardization of products and services offered across markets. | Consolidate operations and achieve economies of scale. |
| | Efficiencies in all processes, including new product development, manufacturing, inventory, logistics and customer service | Work with industry leaders and influence market development by using them as showcase accounts. |
| | Faster diffusion of innovations globally. | Collaborate with customers and develop strong relationships that are difficult for potential competitors to break into. |
| | | Rectify price and service anomalies in a customer relationship across country markets. |
| *Disadvantages* | Customer might be less adaptable to local market variance and changes over time. | Local managers sometimes resist change, and supplier may get caught in the crossfire between customer's HQ and country managers. |
| | Supplier might not have capabilities to provide consistent quality and performance across markets. | Supplier might lose the ability to serve other attractive customers. |
| | Supplier might use customer's over-dependence to extract higher prices. | Customer might not be able to deliver on promises. |
| | Local managers might resist global contracts and prefer dealing with local suppliers. | Customer might take advantage of cost information shared in the relationship. |
| | Costs of monitoring global contracts might outstrip the benefits. | Supplier might become over-dependent on one customer, even when there are other more attractive customers to serve. |
| | | Supplier might have a conflict with existing channels of distribution in the new markets. |

Source: Adapted from Narayandas *et al.*, 2000, pp. 61–70.

One chemicals manufacturer concentrated on relationships with a few select customers. It had decided that its strength lay in value-added services but that potential customers in emerging markets were fixated on price. The select customers, however, were interested in money-saving supply and inventory management initiatives developed jointly with the supplier.

Global customers' demands for detailed cost information can also put suppliers at risk. Toyota, Honda, Xerox and others force suppliers to open their books for inspection. Their stated objectives: to help suppliers identify ways to improve processes and quality while reducing costs – and to build trust. But in an economic downturn the global customer might seek price reductions and supplementary services.

### European pricing strategy

In 1991 price differentials for identical consumer goods across Europe were around 20 per cent on average, but much greater differences were apparent in certain products (Simon and Kucher, 1993). In another study (Diller and Bukhari, 1994) there were also considerable price differences for identical take-home ice-cream products.

The causes of price differentials are differences in regulations, competition, distribution structures and consumer behaviour, such as willingness to pay. Currency fluctuations can also influence short-term price differences. The pressures of regionalization are accelerating the move to uniform pricing, but Simon and Kucher (1993) warn that this is a potential time bomb, as the pressure is for uniform pricing to be at the lowest pricing levels.

Europe was a price differentiation paradise as long as markets were separated. But it is becoming increasingly difficult to retain the old price differentials. There are primarily two developments that may force companies to standardize prices across European countries:

1　International buying power of cross-European retail groups.
2　Parallel imports/grey markets. Because of differentiated prices across countries, buyers in one country are able to purchase at a lower price than in another country. As a result there will be an incentive for customers in lower-price markets to sell goods to higher-price markets in order to make a profit.

Simon and Kucher (1993) suggest a price 'corridor' (Figure 11.15). The prices in the individual countries may only vary within that range. Figure 11.15 is also interesting in the light of the euro, which had been fully implemented by January 2002. However, price differences that can be justified by transportation costs and short-term competitive conditions, etc., may still be maintained. They recommend that business in smaller countries should be sacrificed, if necessary, in order to retain acceptable pricing levels in the big markets such as France, Germany, the United Kingdom and Italy. For example, for a pharmaceutical manufacturer it is more profitable not to sell in the Portuguese pharmaceutical market than to accept a price reduction of 10 per cent in the German market due to parallel imports from Portugal.

### Transfer pricing

**Transfer pricing**
Prices charged for intra-company movement of goods and services. While transfer prices are internal to the company, they are important externally for cross-border taxation purposes.

Transfer prices are those charged for intracompany movement of goods and services. Many purely domestic firms need to make transfer-pricing decisions when goods are *transferred* from one domestic unit to another. While these transfer prices are internal to the company they are important externally because goods being transferred from country to country must have a value for cross-border taxation purposes.

The objective of the corporation in this situation is to ensure that the transfer price paid optimizes corporate rather than divisional objectives. This can prove difficult

Figure 11.15 Development of prices in Europe

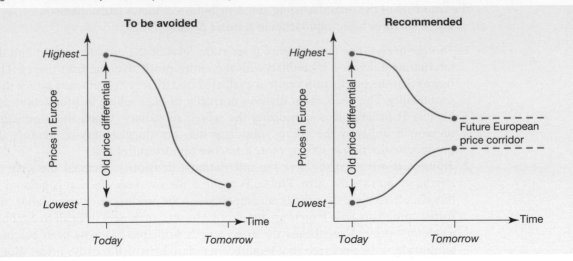

Source: Simon and Kucher, 1993, p. 26. Copyright ESOMAR.

when a company internationally is organized into profit centres. For profit centres to work effectively a price must be set for everything that is transferred, be it working materials, components, finished goods or services. A high transfer price – for example, from the manufacturing division to a foreign subsidiary – is reflected in an apparently poor performance by the foreign subsidiary (see the high mark-up policy in Table 11.7), whereas a low price would not be acceptable to the domestic division providing the goods (see the low mark-up policy in Table 11.7). This issue alone can be the cause of much mistrust between subsidiaries.

The 'best' of Table 11.7's two mark-up policies seen from the consolidated point of view is to use a high mark-up policy, since it generates a net income of $550, as against

Table 11.7 Tax effect of low versus high transfer price on net income ($)

|  | Manufacturing affiliate (division) | Distribution/selling affiliate (subsidiary) | Consolidated company total |
|---|---|---|---|
| **Low mark-up policy** |  |  |  |
| Sales | 1,400 | 2,000 | 2,000 |
| Less cost of goods sold | 1,000 | 1,400 | 1,000 |
| **Gross profit** | **400** | **600** | **1,000** |
| Less operating expenses | 100 | 100 | 200 |
| **Taxable income** | **300** | **500** | **800** |
| Less income taxes (25%/50%) | 75 | 250 | 325 |
| Net income | 225 | 250 | 475 |
| **High mark-up policy** |  |  |  |
| Sales | 1,700 | 2,000 | 2,000 |
| Less cost of goods sold | 1,000 | 1,700 | 1,000 |
| **Gross profit** | **700** | **300** | **1,000** |
| Less operating expenses | 100 | 100 | 200 |
| **Taxable income** | **600** | **200** | **800** |
| Less income taxes (25%/50%) | 150 | 100 | 250 |
| Net income | 450 | 100 | 550 |

Note: Manufacturing affiliate pays income taxes at 25%. Distribution affiliate pays income taxes at 50%.

Source: Adapted from Eiteman and Stonehill, 1986. *Multinational Business Finance*, 4th edn, pub. Addison Wesley.

$475 from using a low mark-up policy. The 'best' solution depends on the tax rates in the countries of the manufacturing and distribution affiliates (subsidiaries).

There are three basic approaches to transfer pricing:

1 *Transfer at cost.* The transfer price is set at the level of the production cost and the international division is credited with the entire profit that the firm makes. This means that the production centre is evaluated on efficiency parameters rather than profitability. The production division normally dislikes selling at production cost because it believes it is subsidizing the selling subsidiary. When the production division is unhappy the selling subsidiary may get sluggish service, because the production division is serving more attractive opportunities first.

2 *Transfer at arm's length.* Here the international division is charged the same as any buyer outside the firm. Problems occur if the overseas division is allowed to buy elsewhere when the price is uncompetitive or the product quality is inferior, and further problems arise if there are no external buyers, making it difficult to establish a relevant price. Nevertheless the arm's-length principle has now been accepted worldwide as the preferred (not required) standard by which transfer prices should be set (Fraedrich and Bateman, 1996).

3 *Transfer at cost plus.* This is the usual compromise, where profits are split between the production and international divisions. The actual formula used for assessing the transfer price can vary, but usually it is this method that has the greatest chance of minimizing executive time spent on transfer-price disagreements, optimizing corporate profits and motivating the home and international divisions. A senior executive is often appointed to rule on disputes.

A good transfer-pricing method should consider total corporate profile and encourage divisional cooperation. It should also minimize executive time spent on transfer-price disagreements and keep the accounting burden to a minimum.

## Currency issues

A difficult aspect of export pricing is the decision about what currency the price should be quoted in. The exporter has the following options:

- the foreign currency of the buyer's country (local currency);
- the currency of the exporter's country (domestic currency);
- the currency of a third country (usually US dollars);
- a currency unit such as the euro.

If the exporter quotes in the domestic currency then not only is it administratively much easier, but also the risks associated with changes in the exchange rate are borne by the customer, whereas by quoting prices in the foreign currency the exporter bears the exchange rate risk. However, there are benefits to the exporter in quoting in foreign currency:

- Quoting in foreign currency could be a condition of the contract.
- It could provide access to finance abroad at lower interest rates.
- Good currency management may be a means of gaining additional profits.
- Customers normally prefer to be quoted in their own currency in order to be able to make competitive comparisons and know exactly what the eventual price will be.

Another difficult problem that exporters face is caused by fluctuating exchange rates. A company in a country with a devalued currency can (all other things being equal) strengthen its international competitive position. It can choose to reduce prices in foreign currencies or it can leave prices unchanged and instead increase profit margins.

When the Italian lira dropped by 15–20 per cent in value against the German mark it gave the Italian car producer Fiat a competitive advantage in pricing. The German car exporters, such as Volkswagen, were adversely affected and had to lower its list prices. In this respect the geographic pattern of a firm's manufacturing and sales subsidiaries compared with those of its main competitors becomes very important, since a local subsidiary can absorb most of the negative effects of a devaluation.

## 11.12 Implications of the Internet for pricing across borders

Europe's single currency, the euro (http://europa.eu.int/euro/) has finally become a reality after more than a decade of planning and preparation. In one stroke the single currency has created the largest single economy in the world, with a larger share of global trade and a greater number of consumers than in the United States.

The implication is that Europe suddenly became a single market by the end of 2000, and people can purchase from another country as easily as they can from a shop across the road. The same currency will be used; only the language issue remains. Opinion in Europe is that, as more of the population goes online, and as Europe starts using its new single currency, online shopping will experience a tremendous growth.

Most of this growth has been fuelled by aggressive price cutting from internet service providers (ISPs). A number of UK companies, for example, are now offering free internet access or pay-as-you-go models, which have encouraged new sections of the population to try the Internet for the first time.

A European single currency was a long-held ambition for members of the European Union. The idea was first considered in the 1970s, but knocked off-course by oil price rises. It re-emerged in the early 1980s and was finally agreed to in the 1992 Maastricht Treaty. There were many accounting criteria to be met by each country, such as the control of the rate of inflation and the debt/GDP ratio. Most countries have met these criteria and were permitted to join the European Monetary Union.

The euro is now the currency of 13 European Union member states: Belgium, Germany, Greece, Spain, France, Ireland, Italy, Luxembourg, the Netherlands, Austria, Portugal, Finland and Slovenia. Other member states are looking to adopt the euro in the near future.

The United Kingdom being outside the euro region will be quite inconvenient for many US companies who trade heavily with UK companies or have UK subsidiaries.

The main detailed implications of the euro will be that it will:

- lower prices for consumers by making prices transparent across Europe;
- create a real single market by reducing 'friction' to trade caused by high transaction costs and fluctuating currencies;
- enhance competition by forcing companies to concentrate on price, quality and production instead of hiding behind weak currencies;
- benefit SMEs and consumers by making it easier for the former to enter 'foreign' markets and allowing the latter, increasingly via the internet, to shop in the lowest priced markets;
- establish inflation and interest rate stability via the new European Central Bank; and
- lower the costs of doing business through lower prices, lower interest rates, no transaction costs or loss through exchanging currencies, and the absence of exchange rate fluctuations.

In short, the single currency will significantly increase competition, lower transaction costs, and bring about greater certainty. These new forces will bring about structural reforms in Europe. Almost every aspect of Europe's business and political environment will be affected.

Perhaps most importantly, marketing and pricing strategies need rethinking. Because the euro will allow easy price comparison across Europe (especially via the Internet), it will reveal the differences between higher and lower priced markets.

For those selling via the Internet the euro will make it easier to do business and give encouragement to companies selling to European customers. Since Europeans will now be able to shop and compare prices at the click of a mouse they will also be more favourably inclined towards e-commerce.

In any single European country there is not usually much competition for a given product, since purchasing habits have always been local (in one's own country). Now that Europeans will be able to shop internationally via the Internet they will become aware of other choices and prices for the same product that were not previously known. Competition will heat up for the buyer's euro, and this should put a downward pressure on prices.

However, recent research has also shown that the Internet is not creating a state of perfect competition with decreasing prices as a result. In fact, in some cases, online prices are higher than those of conventional retail outlets. Research has also shown that online consumers are not as price sensitive as had previously been thought. Consumers become less price sensitive and more loyal as the level of quality information on a site increases (Kung and Monroe, 2002).

## 11.13 Summary

In deciding the product policy abroad, it is important to decide what parts (product levels) should be standardized and what parts should be adapted to the local environment. This chapter has discussed the variety of factors that are relevant to this decision.

A very important issue is the question of branding. Different branding alternatives have been discussed. For example, because large (often transnational) retail chains have won control over distribution, they try to develop their own labels. For the retailer, private labels provide better profit margins and strengthen the retailer's image with its customers. Because of the power shift to the retailers the percentage of retail grocery sales derived from private brands has increased in recent years.

This chapter has also discussed issues that are experiencing increasing interest: for example, green marketing strategies, including the need for product adaptation in a 'green' direction. Consumers, shareholders and society at large all stand to benefit when a company integrates environmental friendliness into its marketing strategy. If properly implemented, green marketing can help to increase the emotional connection between consumers and brands. Being branded a green company can generate a more positive public image, which can, in turn, enhance sales and increase stock prices. A green image may also lead consumers to have an increased affinity for a company or a specific product, causing brand loyalty to grow.

The major pricing issues covered in this chapter include the determinants of price, pricing strategy, how foreign prices are related to domestic prices, price escalation, the elements of price quotation, and transfer pricing.

Several factors must be taken into consideration in setting price, including cost, competitors' prices, product image, market share/volume, stage in the product life cycle and number of products involved. The optimum mix of these ingredients varies by product, market and corporate objectives. Price setting in the international context is further complicated by such factors as foreign exchange rates, different competitive situations in each export market, different labour costs and different inflation rates in various countries. Also local and regional regulations and laws in setting prices have to be considered.

## CASE STUDY 11.1

## Zippo Manufacturing Company: Has product diversification beyond the lighter gone too far?

### History

Zippo (www.zippo.com) was founded in Bradford, Pennsylvania in 1932 when George G. Blaisdell decided to create a lighter that would look good and be easy to use. Blaisdell obtained the rights for an Austrian windproof lighter with a removable top, and redesigned it to his own requirements. He made the case rectangular and attached the lid to the bottom with a welded hinge, and surrounded the wick with a windhood. Fascinated by the sound of the name of another recent invention, the zipper, Blaisdell called his new lighter 'Zippo', and backed it with a Lifetime Guarantee. The 70-year old brand's fame took off during the Second World War, when Zippo's entire production was distributed through commercial outlets run by the US military.

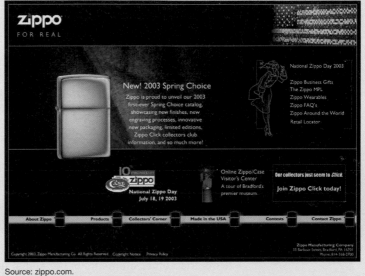

Source: zippo.com.

### Today

Zippo has produced over 375 million windproof lighters since its founding in 1932. Except for improvements in the flint wheel and modifications in case finishes, Blaisdell's original design remains virtually unchanged. The Lifetime Guarantee that accompanies every Zippo lighter still guarantees that 'It works or we fix it free™'.

Although the windproof lighter is the most popular Zippo product, Zippo has been hurt by the anti-smoking campaigns. Its business is fundamentally tied to smokers, and it has suffered from US tobacco regulations. Cigarette makers order thousands of Zippos to promote their brands, distributing them to smokers in exchange for coupons. One of the company's recent advertising campaigns suggested 101 ways to use your Zippo. Warming your hands and de-icing car locks were on the list; lighting a cigarette was not.

The success of this product led Zippo to expand the line to its current product family of tape measures, pocket knives, money clips, writing instruments, key holders and its newest product, the Multi-Purpose Lighter. All of these items can be imprinted with company logos or trademarks.

In 1993 Zippo licensed its name to Itochu Fashion System Co., a large clothing manufacturer in Japan. Zippo leather jackets, Zippo jeans and Zippo gloves are now available in Tokyo, and Zippo may license clothes in the United States too. Today Japan is still the biggest export market for Zippo.

Zippo has expanded its sales operations nationally and internationally through a wide network of sales representatives. In more than 120 countries throughout the world Zippo is synonymous with US-made quality and craftsmanship.

Zippo windproof lighters enjoy a widespread and enviable reputation as valuable collectibles. The company produces the *Zippo Lighter Collectors' Guide*, containing illustrations of the lighters and descriptions of the series, as well as an explanation of the date code found on the bottom of every Zippo lighter. Clubs for lighter collectors have been organized in the United Kingdom, Italy, Switzerland, Germany, Japan and the United States. Zippo also sponsors it own collectors club, Zippo Click.

### Questions

1 What are the pros and cons of the product diversification strategy that Zippo has been following recently?

2 On **www.sramarketing.com/experience/outdoor/ case_studies/zippo_casestudy.cfm** you will find a case story, where Zippo in the late 1990s was repositioned as an essential tool for avid outdoorsmen. However the outdoor market was entirely new to the Zippo salesforce, who were accustomed to calling on tobacconists and convenience stores. How would you use the PLC concept for this case story?

3 What obstacles would Zippo Manufacturing Company face if it repeated the outdoor campaign in other countries?

For further exercises and cases, see this book's website at **www.pearsoned.co.uk/hollensen**

## Questions for discussion

1 How would you distinguish between services and products? What are the main implications of this difference for the global marketing of services?

2 To what degree should international markets be offered standardized service and warranty policies that do not differ significantly from market to market?

3 Why is the international product policy likely to be given higher priority in most firms than other elements of the global marketing mix?

4 What are the requirements that must be met so that a commodity can effectively be transformed into a branded product?

5 Discuss the factors that need to be taken into account when making packaging decisions for international product lines.

6 What are the distinguishing characteristics of services? Explain why these characteristics make it difficult to sell services in foreign markets.

7 Identify the major barriers to developing international brands.

8 Discuss the decision to add or drop products to or from the product line in international markets.

9 What are the characteristics of a good international brand name?

10 What are the major causes of international price escalation? Suggest possible courses of action to deal with this problem.

11 Explain how exchange rate and inflation affect the way you price your product.

12 In order to protect themselves, how should marketers price their product in a country with high inflation?

13 International buyers and sellers of technology frequently disagree on the appropriate price for knowledge. Why?

**14** What methods can be used to compute a transfer price (for transactions between affiliated companies)?

**15** Why is it often difficult to compute fair arm's-length transfer prices?

## References

Aaker, D. (1991) *Managing the Brand Equity: Capitalizing on the Value of the Brand Name*, The Free Press, New York.

Argenti, P.A. (2004) 'Collaborating with activists: how Starbucks works with NGOs', *California Management Review*, 47(1), pp. 91–116.

Auguste, B.G., Harmon, E.P. and Pandit, V. (2006) 'The right service strategies for product companies', *McKinsey Quarterly*, 1, March, pp. 10–15.

Bengtsson, A. and Servais, P. (2005) 'Co-branding on industrial markets', *Industrial Marketing Management*, 34, pp. 706–713.

Beverland, M., Napoli, J. and Lindgreen, A. (2007) 'Industrial global brand leadership: A capabilities view', *Industrial Marketing Management*, Vol. 36, pp. 1082–1093

Boze, B.V. and Patton, C.R. (1995) 'The future of consumer branding as seen from the picture today', *Journal of Consumer Marketing*, 12(4), pp. 20–41.

Czepiel, J.A. (1992) *Competitive Marketing Strategy*, Prentice-Hall, Englewood Cliffs, NJ.

Czinkota, M.R. and Ronkainen, I.A. (1995) *International Marketing* (4th edn), Dryden Press, Fort Worth, TX.

Diller, H. and Bukhari, I. (1994) 'Pricing conditions in the European Common Market', *European Management Journal*, 12(2), pp. 163–170.

Eiteman, D.K. and Stonehill, A.I. (1986) *Multinational Business Finance* (4th edn), Addison-Wesley, Reading, MA.

Ettensén, R. (1993) 'Brand name and country of origin: effects in the emerging market economies of Russia, Poland and Hungary', *International Marketing Review*, 5, pp. 14–36.

Evans, P.B. and Wuster, T.S. (2000), *Blown to Bits: How the new economics of information transforms strategy*, Harvard Business School Press, Boston.

Fan, Y. (2007) 'Marque in the making', *Brand Strategy*, June 2007, pp. 52–54.

Filiatrault, P. and Lapierre, J. (1997) 'Managing business-to-business marketing relationships in consulting engineering firms', *Industrial Marketing Management*, 26, pp. 213–222.

Fraedrich, J.P. and Bateman, C.R. (1996) 'Transfer pricing by multinational marketers: risky business', *Business Horizons*, 39(1), pp. 17–22.

Garda, R.A. (1995) 'Tactical pricing', in Paliwoda, S.J. and Ryans, J.K. (eds), *International Marketing Reader*, Routledge, London.

Ginsberg, J.M. and Bloom, P.N. (2004) 'Choosing the right green marketing strategy', *MIT Sloan Management Review*, Fall, pp. 79–84.

Herstein, R. and Gamliel, E. (2006) 'Striking a balance with private branding', *Business Strategy Review*, Autumn, 39–43.

Hooley, G.J., Saunders, J.A. and Piercy, N. (1998) *Marketing Strategy and Competitive Positioning* (2nd edn), Prentice Hall, Hemel Hempstead.

Johansson, J.K. and Thorelli, H.B. (1985) 'International product positioning', *Journal of International Business Studies*, 16, Fall, pp. 57–75.

Johansson, J.K., Ronkainen, I.A. and Czinkota, M.R. (1994) 'Negative country-of-origin effects: the case of the new Russia', *Journal of International Business Studies*, 25, 1st quarter, pp. 1–21.

Keegan, W.J. (1995) *Global Marketing Management* (5th edn), Prentice-Hall, Englewood Cliffs, NJ.

Keller, K.L. and Sood, S. (2001) 'The ten commandments of global branding', 8(2), pp. 1–12.

Kotler, P. (1997) *Marketing Management: Analysis, planning, implementation and control* (9th edn), Prentice-Hall, Englewood Cliffs, NJ.

Kotler, P. and Pfoertsch, W. (2007) 'Being known or being one of many: the need for brand management for business-to-business (B2B) companies', *Journal of Business & Industrial Marketing*, Vol. 22, No. 6, pp. 357–362.

Kung, M. and Monroe, K.B. (2002) 'Pricing on the Internet', *Journal of Product & Brand Management*, 11(5), pp. 274–287.

Lovelock, C.H. and Yip, G.S. (1996) 'Developing global strategies for service business', *California Management Review*, 38(2), pp. 64–86.

Marketing Science Institute (1995) *Brand Equity and Marketing Mix: Creating customer value*, Conference Summary, Report no. 95–111, September, p. 14.

Mendleson, N. and Polonsky, M.J. (1995) 'Using strategic alliances to develop credible green marketing', *Journal of Consumer Marketing*, 12(2), pp. 4–18.

Nagle, T.T. (1987) *The Strategies and Tactics of Pricing*, Prentice-Hall, Englewood Cliffs, NJ.

Narayandas, D., Quelch, J. and Swartz, G. (2000) 'Prepare your company for global pricing', *Sloan Management Review*, Fall, pp. 61–70.

Onkvisit, S. and Shaw, J.J. (1989) 'The international dimension of branding: strategic considerations and decisions', *International Marketing Review*, 6(3), pp. 22–34.

Onkvisit, S. and Shaw, J.J. (1993) *International Marketing: Analysis and strategy* (2nd edn), Macmillan, London.

Prahalad, C.K. and Ramaswamy V. (2004) *The Future of Competition: Co-creating Unique Value with Customers*, Harvard Business School Press, Boston.

Quelch, J.A. and Harding, D. (1996) 'Brands versus private labels: fighting to win', *Harvard Business Review*, January–February, pp. 99–109.

Sawhney, M., Verona, G. and Prandelli, E. (2005) 'Collaborating to create: The Internet as a platform for customer engagement in product innovation', *Journal of Interactive Marketing*, Vol. 19, No. 4, pp. 4–17.

Simon, H. and Kucher, E. (1993) 'The European pricing bomb – and how to cope with it', *Marketing and Research Today*, February, pp. 25–36.

Solberg, C.A. (1997) 'A framework for analysis of strategy development in globalizing markets', *Journal of International Marketing*, 5(1), pp. 9–30.

Solberg, C.A., Stöttinger B. and Yaprak, A. (2006) 'A taxonomy of the pricing practices of exporting firms: evidence from Austria, Norway and the United States', *Journal of International Marketing*, 14(1), pp. 23–48.

Starik, M., Throop, G.M., Doody, J.M. and Joyce, M.E. (1996) 'Growing on environmental strategy', *Business Strategy and the Environment*, 5, pp. 12–21.

Theodosiou, M. and Katsikeas, C.S. (2001) 'Factors influencing the degree of international pricing strategy standardization of multinational corporations', *Journal of International Marketing*, 9(3), pp. 1–18.

Vandermerwe, J. and Oliff, M.D. (1991) 'Corporate challenges for an age of reconsumption', *Columbia Journal of World Business*, 26(3), pp. 6–25.

Vesanen, J. (2007) 'Commentary: What is personalization? A conceptual framework', *European Journal of Marketing*, Vol. 41, No. 5/6, pp. 409–418.

Weigand, R.E. (1991) 'Buy in–follow on strategies for profit', *Sloan Management Review*, Spring, pp. 29–38.

World Wide Fund for Nature (1993) *Corporate Relationships*, Sydney.

# 12

# Distribution and communication decisions

## Contents

## Learning objectives

After studying this chapter you should be able to do the following:

- Explore the determinants of channel decisions.
- Discuss the key points in putting together and managing global marketing channels.
- Discuss the factors influencing channel width (intensive, selective or exclusive coverage).
- Explain what is meant by integration of the marketing channel.
- Define and classify the different types of communication tool.
- Describe and explain the major steps in advertising decisions.
- Describe the techniques available and appropriate for setting the advertising budget in foreign markets.
- Discuss the possibilities of marketing via the Internet.
- Explain how important personal selling and sales force management are in the international marketplace.
- Define and explain the concept of 'viral marketing'.
- Discuss how standardized international advertising has both benefits and drawbacks.

## 12.1 Introduction

Access to international markets is a key decision area facing firms into the 2000s. In Part III we considered the firm's choice of an appropriate market entry mode that could assure the entry of a firm's products and services into a foreign market. After the firm has chosen a strategy to get its products into foreign markets the next challenge (and the topic of this chapter: see Figure 12.1) is the distribution of the products within those foreign markets. The first part of this chapter concerns the structure and management of foreign distribution. The second part is concerned with the management of international logistics.

Distribution channels typically account for 15–40 per cent of the retail price of goods and services in an industry.

Over the next few years the challenges and opportunities for channel management will multiply, as technological developments accelerate channel evolution. Data networks are increasingly enabling end users to bypass traditional channels and deal directly with manufacturers and service providers.

The following presents a systematic approach to the major decisions in international distribution. The main channel decisions and their determinants are illustrated in Figure 12.1. Distribution channels are the links between producers and final customers. In general terms, an international marketer distributes either directly or indirectly. As we saw in Chapter 9, direct distribution amounts to dealing with a foreign firm, while the indirect method means dealing with another home country firm that serves as an intermediary. Figure 12.1 shows that the choice of a particular channel link will be strongly influenced by various characteristics of the host markets. We will now consider these in more detail.

**Figure 12.1 Channel decisions**

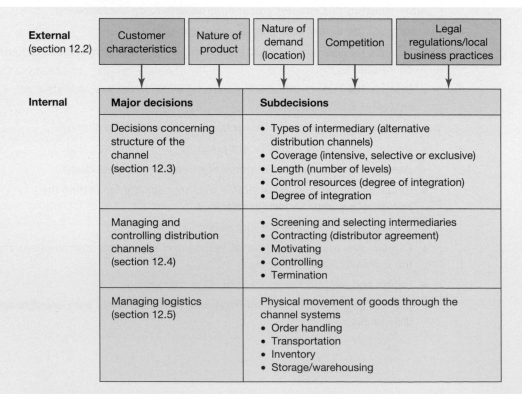

Communication is the fourth and final decision to be made about the global marketing programme. The role of communication in global marketing is similar to that in domestic operations: to communicate with customers so as to provide information that buyers need to make purchasing decisions. Although the communication mix carries information of interest to the customer, in the end it is designed to persuade the customer to buy a product – at the present time or in the future.

To communicate with and influence customers, several tools are available. Advertising is usually the most visible component of the promotion mix, but personal selling, exhibitions, sales promotions, publicity (public relations) and direct marketing (including the Internet) are also part of a viable international promotion mix.

One important strategic consideration is whether to standardize worldwide or to adapt the promotion mix to the environment of each country. Another consideration is the availability of media, which varies around the world.

## 12.2 External determinants of channel decisions

### Customer characteristics

The customer, or final consumer, is the keystone in any channel design. Thus the size, geographic distribution, shopping habits, outlet preferences and usage patterns of customer groups must be taken into account when making distribution decisions.

Consumer product channels tend to be longer than industrial product channels because the number of customers is greater, the customers are more geographically dispersed, and they buy in smaller quantities. Shopping habits, outlet preferences and usage patterns vary considerably from country to country and are strongly influenced by sociocultural factors.

### Nature of product

Product characteristics play a key role in determining distribution strategy. For low-priced, high-turnover convenience products, the requirement is an intensive distribution network. On the other hand it is not necessary or even desirable for a prestigious product to have wide distribution. In this situation a manufacturer can shorten and narrow its distribution channel. Consumers are likely to do some comparison shopping and will actively seek information about all brands under consideration. In such cases limited product exposure is not an impediment to market success.

Transportation and warehousing costs of the product are also critical issues in the distribution and sale of industrial goods such as bulk chemicals, metals and cement. Direct selling, servicing and repair, and spare parts warehousing dominate the distribution of such industrial products as computers, machinery and aircraft. The product's durability, ease of adulteration, amount and type of customer service required, unit costs and special handling requirements (such as cold storage) are also significant factors.

### Nature of demand/location

The perceptions that the target customers hold about particular products can force modification of distribution channels. Product perceptions are influenced by the customer's income and product experience, the product's end use, its life cycle position and the country's stage of economic development.

The geography of a country and the development of its transportation infrastructure can also affect the channel decision.

## Competition

The channels used by competing products and close substitutes are important because channel arrangements that seek to serve the same market often compete with one another. Consumers generally expect to find particular products in particular outlets (e.g. speciality stores), or they have become accustomed to buying particular products from particular sources. In addition, local and global competitors may have agreements with the major wholesalers in a foreign country that effectively create barriers and exclude the company from key channels.

Sometimes the alternative is to use a distribution approach totally different from that of the competition and hope to develop a competitive advantage.

## Legal regulations/local business practices

A country may have specific laws that rule out the use of particular channels or intermediaries. For example, until recently all alcoholic beverages in Sweden and Finland had to be distributed through state-owned outlets. Other countries prohibit the use of door-to-door selling. Channel coverage can also be affected by law. In general, exclusive representation may be viewed as a restraint of trade, especially if the product has a dominant market position. EU antitrust authorities have increased their scrutiny of exclusive sales agreements. The Treaty of Rome prohibits distribution agreements (e.g. grants of exclusivity) that affect trade or restrict competition.

Furthermore, local business practices can interfere with efficiency and productivity and may force a manufacturer to employ a channel of distribution that is longer and wider than desired. Because of Japan's multitiered distribution system, which relies on numerous layers of intermediaries, foreign companies have long considered the complex Japanese distribution system as the most effective non-tariff barrier to the Japanese market.

Figure 12.2 shows how the complex Japanese distribution system escalates prices with a factor 5 through both vertical transactions and horizontal transactions (e.g. from one wholesaler to another wholesaler).

**Figure 12.2  A hypothetical channel sequence in the Japanese consumer market**

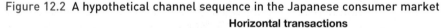

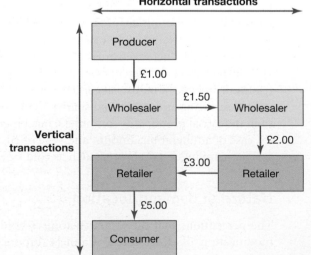

Source: Pirog and Lancioni, 1997, p. 57. Adapted with kind permission from *International Journal of Physical Distribution and Logistics Management*, Emerald Group Publishing Ltd.

Let us now return to the major decisions concerning the structure of the distribution channel (Figure 12.1).

## 12.3 The structure of the channel

### Market coverage

**Market coverage**
Coverage can relate to geographical areas or number of retail outlets. Three approaches are available: intensive, selective or exclusive coverage.

The amount of market coverage that a channel member provides is important. Coverage is a flexible term. It can refer to geographical areas of a country (such as cities and major towns) or the number of retail outlets (as a percentage of all retail outlets). Regardless of the market coverage measure(s) used the company has to create a distribution network (dealers, distributors and retailers) to meet its coverage goals.

As shown in Figure 12.3, three different approaches are available:

1. *Intensive coverage.* This calls for distributing the product through the largest number of different types of intermediary and the largest number of individual intermediaries of each type.
2. *Selective coverage.* This entails choosing a number of intermediaries for each area to be penetrated.
3. *Exclusive coverage.* This involves choosing only one intermediary in a market.

Channel coverage (width) can be identified along a continuum ranging from wide channels (intensive distribution) to narrow channels (exclusive distribution). Figure 12.4 illustrates some factors favouring intensive, selective and exclusive distribution.

Figure 12.3 Three strategies for market coverage

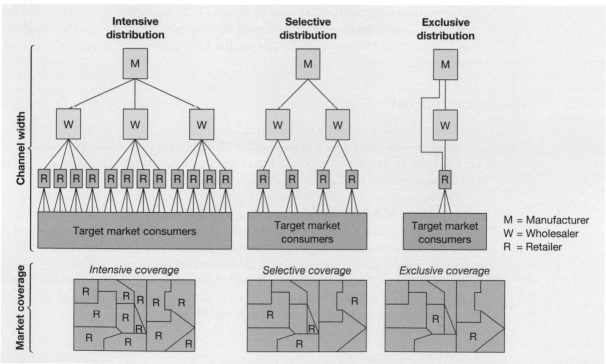

Source: Lewison, 1996, p. 271.

Figure 12.4  Factors influencing channel width

| | | **Channel width** | | |
|---|---|---|---|---|
| | | *Intensive distribution* ←→ | *Selective distribution* ←→ | *Exclusive distribution* |
| **Factor** | *Product type* | Convenience products | ←——————→ | Speciality products |
| | *Product life cycle stage* | Mature products | ←——————→ | New products |
| | *Product price* | Low-price products | ←——————→ | High-price products |
| | *Brand loyalty* | Brand-preferred products | ←——————→ | Brand-insisted products |
| | *Purchase frequency* | Frequently purchased products | ←——————→ | Infrequently purchased products |
| | *Product uniqueness* | Common products | ←——————→ | Distinctive products |
| | *Selling requirement* | Self-service products | ←——————→ | Personal-selling products |
| | *Technical complexity* | Non-technical products | ←——————→ | Technical products |
| | *Service requirements* | Limited-service products | ←——————→ | Extensive-service products |

Source: Adapted from Lewison, 1996, p. 279.

## Channel length

**Channel length**
Number of levels (middlemen) in the distribution channel.

This is determined by the number of levels or different types of intermediaries. Longer channels, those with several intermediaries, tend to be associated with convenience goods and mass distribution. As seen in Exhibit 12.1, Japan has longer channels for convenience goods because of the historical development of its system. One implication is that prices increase considerably for the final consumer (price escalation: see section 12.3).

## Control/cost

The 'control' of one member in the vertical distribution channel means its ability to influence the decisions and actions of other channel members. Channel control is of critical concern to international marketers wanting to establish international brands and a consistent image of quality and service worldwide.

The company must decide how much control it wants to have over how each of its products is marketed. The answer is partly determined by the strategic role assigned to each market. It is also a function of the types of channel member available, the regulations and rules governing distribution activity in each foreign market, and to some extent the roles traditionally assigned to channel members.

Normally a high degree of control is provided by the use of the firm's own sales force in international markets. The use of intermediaries will automatically lead to loss of some control over the marketing of the firm's products.

An intermediary typically performs certain functions:

- carrying of inventory;
- demand generation, or selling;

- physical distribution;
- after-sales service;
- extending credit to customers.

In getting its products to end-user markets a manufacturer must either assume all of these functions or shift some or all of them to intermediaries. As the old saying goes, 'You can eliminate the intermediary, but not the functions of the intermediary.'

In most marketing situations there is a trade-off between a producer's ability to control important channel functions and the financial resources required to exercise that control. The more intermediaries involved in getting a supplier's product to user customers, the less control the supplier can generally exercise over the flow of its product through the channel and the way it is presented to customers. On the other hand, reducing the length and breadth of the distribution channel usually requires that the supplier perform more functions itself. In turn this requires the supplier to allocate more financial resources to activities such as warehousing, shipping, credit, field selling or field service.

In summary, the decision to use an intermediary or to distribute via a company-owned sales force requires a major trade-off between the desire to control global marketing efforts and the desire to minimize resource commitment costs.

## Degree of integration

Control can also be exercised through integration. Channel integration is the process of incorporating all channel members into one channel system and uniting them under one leadership and one set of goals. There are two different types of integration:

**Vertical integration**
Seeking control of channel members at different levels of the channel, e.g. the manufacturer's acquisition of the distributor.

1 **vertical integration** seeking control of channel members at different levels of the channel;

2 **horizontal integration**: seeking control of channel members at the same level of the channel (i.e. competitors).

**Horizontal integration**
Seeking control of channel members at the same level of the channel, e.g. the manufacturer's acquisition of the competitor.

Integration is achieved either through acquisitions (ownership) or through tight cooperative relationships. Getting channel members to work together for their own mutual benefit can be a difficult task. However, today cooperative relationships are essential for efficient and effective channel operation.

Figure 12.5 shows an example of vertical integration.

**Figure 12.5 Vertical integration**

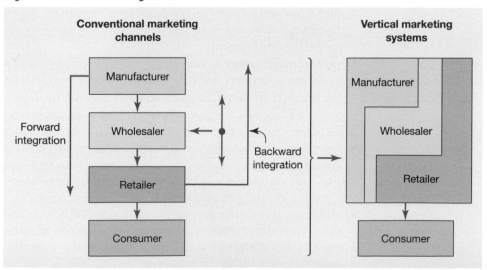

The starting point in Figure 12.5 is the conventional marketing channels, where the channel composition consists of isolated and autonomous participating channel members. Channel coordination is here achieved through arm's-length bargaining. At this point, the vertical integration can take two forms – forward and backward.

- The manufacturer can make forward integration when it seeks control of businesses of the wholesale and retail levels of the channel.
- The retailer can make backward integration, seeking control of businesses at wholesale and manufacturer levels of the channel.
- The wholesaler has two possibilities: both forward and backward integration.

The result of these manoeuvres is the vertical marketing system (Figure 12.5). Here the channel composition consists of integrated participating members, where channel stability is high due to assured member loyalty and long-term commitments.

## 12.4  Managing and controlling distribution channels

In the beginning of a market entry, partnerships with local distributors make good sense: Distributors know the distinctive characteristics of their market, and most customers prefer to do business with local partners. Arnold (2000) propose the following guidelines to the international marketer (manufacturer) in order to anticipate and correct potential problems with international distributors:

- *Select distributors – do not let them select you:* Typically, manufacturers are approached by potential distributors at international fairs and exhibitions, but the most eager potential distributors are often the wrong people to partner with.
- *Look for distributors capable of developing markets, rather than those with a few obvious contacts:* This means sometimes bypassing the most obvious choice – the distributor who has the right customers and can generate quick sales – in favour of a partner with a greater willingness to make long-term investments and an acceptance of an open relationship.
- *Treat the local distributors as long-term partners, not temporary market-entry vehicles:* Many companies actively signal to distributors that their intentions are only for the short term, drawing up contracts that allow them to buy back distribution rights after a few years. Under such a short-term agreement the problem is that the local distributor does not have much incentive to invest in the necessary long-term marketing development.
- *Support market entry by committing money, managers, and proven marketing ideas:* Many manufacturers are reluctant to commit resources at the early stages of a market entry. However, to retain strategic control, the international marketer must commit adequate corporate resources. This is especially true during market entry, when companies are least certain about their prospect in new countries.
- *From the start, maintain control over marketing strategy:* An independent distributor should be allowed to adapt the manufacturer's strategy to local conditions. However, only companies providing solid leadership for marketing will be in a position to exploit the full potential of a global marketing network.
- *Make sure distributors provide you with detailed market and financial performance data:* Most distributors regard data like customer identification and local price levels as key sources of power in the relationship with the manufacturer. But the manufacturer's ability to exploit its competitive advantages in the international

market depends heavily on the quality of information it obtains from the market. Therefore a contract with the distributor must include the exchange of such information, like detailed market and financial performance data.

● *Build links among national distributors at the earliest opportunity:* The links may take form of creating an independent national distributor council or a regional corporate office. The transfer of ideas within local markets can improve performance and result in greater consistency in the execution of international marketing strategies because links to other national distributor networks could be established. This could lead to a cross-national transfer of efficient marketing tools.

Once the basic design of the channel has been determined the international marketer must begin to fill it with the best available candidates, and must secure their cooperation.

## Screening and selecting intermediaries

Figure 12.6 shows the most important criteria (qualifications) for selecting foreign distributors, grouped in five categories.

After listing all important criteria (like in Figure 12.6), some of these must then be chosen for a more specific evaluation, where the potential candidates are compared and contrasted against determining criteria.

The example in Table 12.1 uses the first two criteria in each of Figure 12.6's five categories for screening potential channel members, in total ten criteria. The specific criteria to be used depend on the nature of a firm's business and its distribution objectives in given markets. The list of criteria should correspond closely to the marketer's own determinants of success – all the things that are important to beating the competition.

**Figure 12.6** Criteria for evaluating foreign distributors

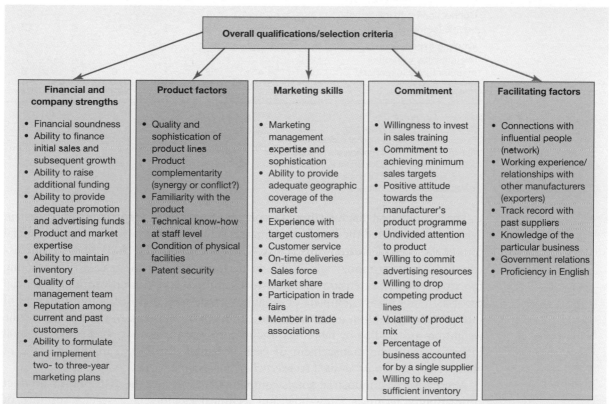

Source: Adapted from Cavusgil *et al.* (1995).

Table 12.1 An example of distributor evaluation by the use of selection criteria from Figure 12.6

| Criteria (no ranking implied) | Weight | Distributor 1 | | Distributor 2 | | Distributor 3 | |
|---|---|---|---|---|---|---|---|
| | | Rating | Score | Rating | Score | Rating | Score |
| **Financial and Company strengths:** | | | | | | | |
| Financial soundness | 4 | 5 | 20 | 4 | 16 | 3 | 12 |
| Ability to finance initial sales and subsequent growth | 3 | 4 | 12 | 4 | 12 | 3 | 9 |
| **Product factors:** | | | | | | | |
| Quality and sophistication of product lines | 3 | 5 | 15 | 4 | 12 | 3 | 9 |
| Product complementarity (synergy or conflict?) | 3 | 3 | 9 | 4 | 12 | 2 | 6 |
| **Marketing skills:** | | | | | | | |
| Marketing management expertise and sophistication | 5 | 4 | 20 | 3 | 15 | 2 | 10 |
| Ability to provide adequate geographic coverage of the market | 4 | 5 | 20 | 4 | 16 | 3 | 12 |
| **Commitment:** | | | | | | | |
| Willingness to invest in sales training | 4 | 3 | 12 | 3 | 12 | 3 | 12 |
| Commitment to achieving minimum sales targets | 3 | 4 | 12 | 3 | 9 | 3 | 9 |
| **Facilitating Factors:** | | | | | | | |
| Connections with influential people (network) | 3 | 5 | 15 | 4 | 12 | 4 | 12 |
| Working experience/ relationships with other manufacturers (exporters) | 2 | 4 | 8 | 3 | 6 | 3 | 6 |
| **Score** | | | **143** | | **122** | | **94** |

Scales:

| *Rating* | *Weighting* |
|---|---|
| 5 Outstanding | 5 Critical success factor |
| 4 Above average | 4 Prerequisite success factor |
| 3 Average | 3 Important success factor |
| 2 Below average | 2 Of some importance |
| 1 Unsatisfactory | 1 Standard |

The hypothetical manufacturer (a consumer packaged goods company) used in Table 12.1 considered the distributor's marketing management expertise and financial soundness to be of greatest importance. These indicators will show whether the distributor is making money and is able to perform some of the necessary marketing functions such as extension of credit to customers and risk absorption. Financial reports are not always complete or reliable, or may lend themselves to differences of interpretation, pointing to the need for a third-party opinion. In order to make the weighting and grading in Table 12.1, the manufacturer must have had some personal interviews with the management of each potential distributor. In the example of Table 12.1, *Distributor 1 would be selected by the manufacturer*.

Alternatively, an industrial goods company may consider the distributor's product compatibility, technical know-how and technical facilities, and service support, of high importance, and the distributor's infrastructure, client performance and attitude towards its products of low importance. Quite often global marketers find that the most desirable distributors in a given market are already handling competitive products and are therefore unavailable.

A high-tech consumer goods company, on the other hand, may favour financial soundness, marketing management expertise, reputation, technical know-how, technical facilities, service support and government relations. In some countries religious or ethnic differences might make an agent suitable for one part of the market coverage but unsuitable for another. This can result in more channel members being required in order to give adequate market coverage.

## Contracting (distributor agreements)

When the international marketer has found a suitable intermediary a foreign sales agreement is drawn up. Before final contractual arrangements are made it is wise to make personal visits to the prospective channel member. The agreement itself can be relatively simple but, given the numerous differences in the market environments, certain elements are essential. These are listed in Figure 12.7.

The long-term commitments involved in distribution channels can become particularly difficult if the contract between the company and the channel member is not carefully drafted. It is normal to prescribe a time limit and a minimum sales level to be achieved, in addition to the particular responsibilities of each party. If this is not carried out satisfactorily the company may be stuck with a weak performer that either cannot be removed or is very costly to buy out from the contract.

*Contract duration* is important, especially when an agreement is signed with a new distributor. In general, distribution agreements should be for a specified, relatively short period (one or two years). The initial contract with a new distributor should stipulate a trial period of either three or six months, possibly with minimum purchase requirements. Duration is also dependent on the local laws and their stipulations on distributor agreements.

*Geographic boundaries* for the distributor should be determined with care, especially by smaller firms. Future expansion of the product market might be complicated if a distributor claims rights to certain territories. The marketer should retain the right to distribute products independently, reserving the right to certain customers.

The *payment section* of the contract should stipulate the methods of payment as well as how the distributor or agent is to draw compensation. Distributors derive

**Figure 12.7 Items to include in an agreement with a foreign intermediary (distributor)**

- Names and addresses of both parties.
- Date when the agreement goes into effect.
- Duration of the agreement.
- Provisions for extending or terminating the agreement.
- Description of sales territory.
- Establishment of discount and/or commission schedules and determination of when and how paid.
- Provisions for revising the commission or discount schedules.
- Establishment of a policy governing resale prices.
- Maintenance of appropriate service facilities.
- Restrictions to prohibit the manufacture and sale of similar and competitive products.
- Designation of responsibility for patent and trade mark negotiations and/or pricing.
- The assignability or non-assignability of the agreement and any limiting factors.
- Designation of the country and state (if applicable) of contract jurisdiction in the case of dispute.

Source: From Jain, S.C. (1996) *International Marketing Management*, 5th edn, pub. South-Western, p. 523. Reprinted by permission of Subhash C. Jain.

compensation from various discounts, such as the functional discount, whereas agents earn a specific commission percentage of net sales (typically 10–20 per cent). Given the volatility of currency markets the agreement should also state the currency to be used.

*Product and conditions of sale* need to be agreed on. The products or product lines included should be stipulated, as well as the functions and responsibilities of the intermediary in terms of carrying the goods in inventory, providing service in conjunction with them, and promoting them. Conditions of sale determine which party is to be responsible for some of the expenses (e.g. marketing expenses) involved, which will in turn have an effect on the price to the distributor. These conditions include credit and shipment terms.

*Means of communication* between the parties must be stipulated in the agreement if a marketer–distributor relationship is to succeed. The marketer should have access to all information concerning the marketing of its products in the distributor's territory, including past records, present situation assessments and marketing research.

## Motivating

Geographic and cultural distance make the process of motivating channel members difficult. Motivating is also difficult because intermediaries are not owned by the company. Since intermediaries are independent firms they will seek to achieve their own objectives, which will not always match the objective of the manufacturer. The international marketer may offer both monetary and psychological rewards. Intermediaries will be strongly influenced by the earnings potential of the product. If the trade margin is poor and sales are difficult to achieve intermediaries will lose interest in the product. They will concentrate upon products with a more rewarding response to selling efforts, since they make their sales and profits from their own assortment of products and services from different companies.

It is important to keep in regular contact with agents and distributors. A consistent flow of all relevant types of communication will stimulate interest and sales performance. The international marketer may place one person in charge of distributor-related communications and put into effect an exchange of personnel so that both organizations gain further insight into the workings of the other.

## Controlling

Control problems are reduced substantially if intermediaries are selected carefully. However, control should be sought through the common development of written performance objectives. These performance objectives might include some of the following: sales turnover per year, market share growth rate, introduction of new products, price charged and marketing communications support. Control should be exercised through periodic personal meetings.

Evaluation of performance has to be done against the changing environment. In some situations economic recession or fierce competition activity prevents the possibility of objectives being met. However, if poor performance is established, the contract between the company and the channel member will have to be reconsidered and perhaps terminated.

## Termination

Typical reasons for the termination of a channel relationship are as follows:

- The international marketer has established a sales subsidiary in the country.
- The international marketer is unsatisfied with the performance of the intermediary.

Open communication is always needed to make the transition smooth. For example, the intermediary can be compensated for investments made, and major customers can be visited jointly to assure them that service will be uninterrupted.

Termination conditions are among the most important considerations in the distribution agreement. The causes of termination vary and the penalties for the international marketer may be substantial. It is especially important to find out what local laws say about termination and to check what type of experience other firms have had in the particular country.

In some countries terminating an ineffective intermediary can be time consuming and expensive. In the European Union one year's average commissions are typical for termination without justification. A notice of termination has to be given three to six months in advance. If the cause for termination is the manufacturer's establishment of a local sales subsidiary, then the international marketer may consider engaging good employees from the intermediary as, for example, managers in the new sales subsidiary. This can prevent a loss of product know-how that has been created at the intermediary's firm. The international marketer could also consider an acquisition of this firm if the intermediary is willing to sell.

## 12.5 Implications of the Internet for distribution decisions

The Internet has the power to change drastically the balance of power among consumers, retailers, distributors, manufacturers and service providers. Some participants in the distribution chain may experience an increase in their power and profitability. Others will experience the reverse; some may even find that they have been bypassed and have lost their market share.

Physical distributors and dealers of goods and services that are more conveniently ordered and/or delivered online are indeed subject to increasing pressure from e-commerce. This *disintermediation* process, with increasing direct sales through the Internet, leads manufacturers to compete with their resellers, which may also result in *channel conflict*. The reality is that the Internet may eliminate the traditional 'physical' distributors, but in the transformation process of the value chain new types of intermediaries may appear. So the disintermediation process has come to be balanced by a re-intermediation force – the evolution of new intermediaries tailor-made for the online world (Figure 12.8).

The transformation of any industry structure in the Internet economy is likely to go through the intermediation–disintermediation–reintermediation (IDR) cycle – as shown in Figure 12.8. The IDR cycle will occur because new technologies are forcing change in the relationships among buyers, suppliers and middlemen. Intermediation occurs when a firm begins as a middleman between two industry players (e.g. buyer–supplier, buyer–established intermediary or established intermediary–supplier). Disintermediation occurs when an established middleman is pushed out of the value chain. Reintermediation occurs when a once disintermediated player is able to re-establish itself as an intermediary.

### Distinction between e-marketing and m-marketing

A key distinction between e-marketing and m-marketing (mobile marketing) lies in the different enabling technologies. Most notably, the facilitative mode for traditional e-marketing, the PC, is a relatively large and cumbersome device that is probably

Figure 12.8 **Disintermediation and reintermediation**

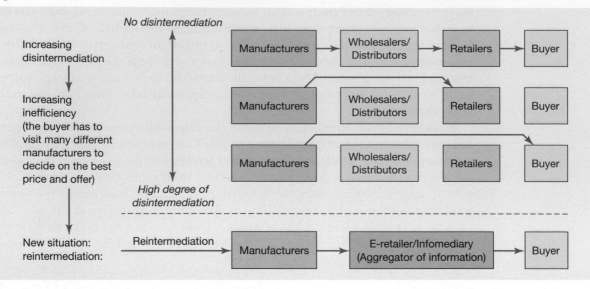

deskbound and equipped with a Web browser through standard connectivity. Even when configured as a laptop it is not easy to move. M-marketing is faced with the challenge of developing capabilities in a much more diverse technical context, albeit within the single framework of mobility. Mobile devices currently vary in terms of the network to which they are connected – the 'European' standard or the North American standard.

Rapidly emerging innovations will deliver the possibility of smart phones able to use product bar codes to access product-related information and phones able to act as e-wallets, as either a prepaid card for small purchases or a fully functioning credit/debit card unit.

## Benefits of m-marketing

The introduction of m-marketing should bring a series of benefits to consumers, merchants and telecommunication companies. As with all technologies, many benefits will arise in the future that are not yet even imagined. Some benefits that are apparent now, however, include the following:

### For consumers

- Comparison shopping: Consumers can access on demand, at the point of purchase, the best prices in the marketplace. This can be done now without mobility, with services such as pricescan.com.
- *Bridge the gap between bricks and clicks*: Services permitting users to examine merchandise in a store and still shop electronically for the best price.
- *Opt-in searches*: Customers may receive alerts from merchants when products they are looking for become available.
- *Travel*: Ability to change and monitor scheduled travel any time, any place.

### For merchants

- *Impulse buying*: Consumers may buy discounted products from a Web page promotion or a mobile alert, increasing their willingness to buy as they are right near or even inside the store, and thus increasing merchants' sales.
- *Drive traffic*: Companies will guide their customers to where it is easier to carry out the transaction, to either online or offline stores, due to the time-sensitive, location-based and personalized characteristics of the mobile device.

- *Education of consumers*: Companies will send information to customers about product benefits or new products.
- *Perishable products*: This is especially important for products that do not retain their value when unused, such as service-based products. For example, the use of an aeroplane seat, that, when unused, generates no revenue and is lost value. This will enable companies to better manage inventory.
- *Drive efficiency*: Companies will save time with their clients. Because information is readily available on the mobile device they will not have to talk about the benefits of the different products or about prices.
- *Target market*: Companies will be better able to target their products and promotions to those in a given geographic area at a specific time.

For telecommunication companies the advantages are primarily more airtime used by the consumers and higher fees charged to content providers for each m-commerce transaction. M-marketing requires direct marketers to rethink their strategies to tap into already existing communities – such as sports fans, surfers and music fans; time-context communities such as spectators at sports events and festivals; and location-sensitive communities such as gallery visitors and small shoppers – and develop ways to get them to opt in to m-marketing. Applications must be responsive to location, customer needs and device capabilities. For example, time and location-sensitive applications, such as travel reservations, cinema tickets and banking will be excellent vehicles for young, busy and urban people.

Finally, as highlighted, m-marketing enables distribution of information to the consumer at the most effective time, place and in the right context. This suggests that m-marketing, via mobile devices, will cement further the interactive marketing relationship.

## 12.6 The communication process

In considering the communication process we normally think about a manufacturer (sender) transmitting a message through any form of media to an identifiable target segment audience. Here the seller is the initiator of the communication process. However, if the seller and the buyer have already established a relationship it is likely that the initiative in the communication process will come from the buyer. If the buyer has positive post-purchase experience with a given offering in one period of time this may dispose the buyer to rebuy on later occasions: that is, take initiatives in the form of making enquiries or placing orders (so-called reverse marketing).

The likely development of the split between total sales volume attributable to buyer and seller initiatives is shown in Figure 12.9. The relative share of sales volume attributable to buyer initiative will tend to increase over time. Present and future buyer initiatives are a function of all aspects of a firm's past market performance: that is, the extent, nature and timing of seller initiative, the competitiveness of offerings, post-purchase experience, the relationships developed with buyers as well as the way in which buyer initiative has been dealt with (Ottesen, 1995).

### Key attributes of effective communication

The rest of the chapter will be devoted to the communication process and communicative tools based on seller initiatives. All effective marketing communication has

Figure 12.9  **The shift from seller initiative to buyer initiative in buyer/seller relationships**

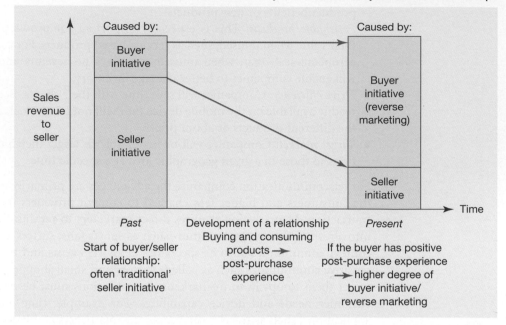

four elements: a sender, a message, a communication channel and a receiver (audience). The communication process in Figure 12.10 highlights the key attributes of effective communication.

To communicate in an effective way the sender needs to have a clear understanding of the purpose of the message, the audience to be reached and how this audience will interpret and respond to the message. However, sometimes the audience cannot hear clearly what the sender is trying to say about its product because of the 'noise' of rival manufacturers making similar and often contradictory claims about their products.

Another important point to consider in the model of Figure 12.10 is the degree of 'fit' between medium and message. For example, a complex and wordy message would be better for the press than for a visual medium such as television or cinema.

## Other factors affecting the communication situation

### Language differences

A slogan or advertising copy that is effective in one language may mean something different in another language. Thus the trade names, sales presentation materials and advertisements used by firms in their domestic markets may have to be adapted and translated when used in other markets.

There are many examples of unfortunate translations of brand names and slogans. General Motors has a brand name for one of its models called the Vauxhall Nova – this does not work well in Spanish-speaking markets because there it means 'no go'. In Latin America 'Avoid embarrassment – Use Parker Pens' was translated as 'Avoid pregnancy – Use Parker Pens'. Scandinavian vacuum manufacturer Electrolux used the following in a US ad campaign: 'Nothing sucks like an Electrolux.'

A Danish company made up the following slogan for its cat litter in the UK market: 'Sand for Cat Piss.' Unsurprisingly, sales of the firm's cat litter did not increase! Another Danish company translated 'Teats for baby's bottles' as 'Loose tits'. In Copenhagen Airport the following poster could be seen until recently: 'We take your baggage and

Figure 12.10 Elements of the intentional communication process

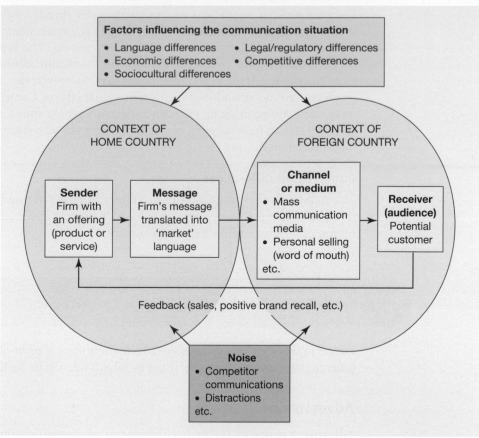

send it in all directions.' A slogan thus used to express the desire to give good service might cause concern as to where the baggage might end up (Joensen, 1997).

## Economic differences

In contrast to industrialized countries, developing countries may have radios but not television sets. In countries with low levels of literacy written communication may not be as effective as visual or oral communication.

## Sociocultural differences

Dimensions of culture (religion, attitudes, social conditions and education) affect how individuals perceive their environment and interpret signals and symbols. For example, the use of colour in advertising must be sensitive to cultural norms. In many Asian countries white is associated with grief; hence an advertisement for a detergent where whiteness is emphasized would have to be altered for promotional activities in, say, India.

---

### Exhibit 12.1    In Muslim markets only God is great

One of the major car manufacturers was using Muhammad Ali in one of its Arab advertising campaigns. Muhammad Ali is very popular in the Middle East, but the theme was him saying 'I am the greatest', which offended people because the Muslims regard only God as great.

Source: Harper, 1986.

### Legal and regulatory conditions

Local advertising regulations and industry codes directly influence the selection of media and content of promotion materials. Many governments maintain tight regulations on content, language and sexism in advertising. The type of product that can be advertised is also regulated. Tobacco products and alcoholic beverages are the most heavily regulated in terms of promotion. However, the manufacturers of these products have not abandoned their promotional efforts. Camel engages in corporate-image advertising using its Joe Camel. Regulations are found more in industrialized economies than in developing economies, where the advertising industry is not yet as highly developed.

### Competitive differences

As competitors vary from country to country in terms of number, size, type and promotional strategies used, a firm may have to adapt its promotional strategy and the timing of its efforts to the local environment.

## 12.7 Communication tools

Earlier in this chapter we mentioned the major forms of promotion. In this section the different communication tools, listed in Table 12.2, will be further examined.

### Advertising

Advertising is one of the most visible forms of communication. Because of its wide use and its limitations as a one-way method of communication advertising in international markets is subject to a number of difficulties. Advertising is often the most important part of the communications mix for consumer goods, where there are a large number of small-volume customers who can be reached through mass media. For most business-to-business markets advertising is less important than the personal selling function.

Table 12.2 Typical communication tools (media)

| One-way communication ⟵ | | | ⟶ Two-way communication | |
|---|---|---|---|---|
| Advertising | Public relations | Sales promotion | Direct marketing | Personal selling |
| Newspapers | Annual reports | Rebates and price discounts | Direct mail/ database marketing | Sales presentations |
| Magazines | Corporate image | Catalogues and brochures | Internet marketing (WWW) | Sales force management |
| Journals | House magazines | Samples, coupons and gifts | Telemarketing | Trade fairs and exhibitions |
| Directories | Press relations | Competitions | Viral marketing | |
| Radio | Public relations | | | |
| Television | Events | | | |
| Cinema | Lobbying | | | |
| Outdoor | Sponsorship | | | |

Figure 12.11 **The major international advertising decisions**

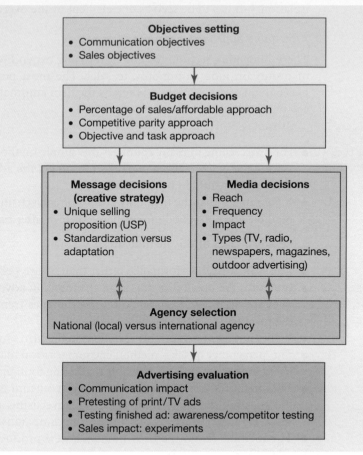

The major decisions in advertising are shown in Figure 12.11. We will now discuss these different phases.

## Objectives setting

Although advertising methods may vary from country to country the major advertising objectives remain the same. Major advertising objectives (and means) might include some of the following:

- *Increasing sales from existing customers* by encouraging them to increase the frequency of their purchases; maintaining brand loyalty via a strategy that reminds customers of the key advantages of the product; and stimulating impulse purchases.
- *Obtaining new customers* by increasing consumer awareness of the firm's products and improving the firm's corporate image among a new target customer group.

### Budget decisions

Controversial aspects of advertising include determining a proper method for deciding the size of the promotional budget and its allocation across markets and over time.

In theory the firm (in each of its markets) should continue to put more money into advertising, as an amount of money spent on advertising returns more than an amount of money spent on anything else. In practice it is not possible to set an optimum advertising budget. Therefore firms have developed more practical guidelines.

The manager must also remember that the advertising budget cannot be regarded in isolation, but has to be seen as one element of the overall marketing mix.

### Affordable approach/percentage of sales

These budgeting techniques link advertising expenditures directly to some measure of profits or, more commonly, to sales. The most popular of these methods is the percentage of sales method, whereby the firm automatically allocates a fixed percentage of sales to the advertising budget.

Advantages of this method are as follows:

**Percentage of sales method**
The firm will automatically allocate a fixed percentage of sales to the advertising budget.

- For firms selling in many countries this simple method appears to guarantee equality among the markets. Each market seems to get the advertising it deserves.
- It is easy to justify in budget meetings.
- It guarantees that the firm only spends on advertising as much as it can afford. The method prevents 'good money being thrown after bad'.

Disadvantages of this method are as follows:

- It uses historical performance rather than future performance.
- It ignores the possibility that extra spending on advertising may be necessary when sales are declining, in order to reverse the sales trend by establishing a 'recycle' on the product life cycle curve (see section 11.4).
- It does not take into account variations in the firm's marketing goals across countries.
- The 'percentage of sales' method encourages local management to maximize sales by using the easiest and most flexible marketing tool: price (that is, lowering the price).
- The method's convenience and simplicity encourage management not to bother investigating the relationships between advertising and sales or analysing critically the overall effectiveness of its advertising campaigns.
- The method cannot be used to launch new products or enter new markets (zero sales = zero advertising).

### Competitive parity approach

**Competitive parity approach**
Duplicating the amounts spent on advertising by major rivals.

Competitive parity approach involves estimating and duplicating the amounts spent on advertising by major rivals. Unfortunately, determining the marketing expenditures of foreign-based competitors is far more difficult than monitoring home country businesses, whose financial accounts (if they are limited companies) are open to public inspection and whose promotional activities are obvious the moment they occur. Another danger in following the practice of competitors is that they are not necessarily right.

Furthermore, the method does not recognize that the firm is in different situations in different markets. If the firm is new to a market its relationships with customers are different from those of existing domestic companies. This should also be reflected in its promotion budget.

### Objective and task approach

**Objective and task approach**
Determining the advertising objectives and then ascertaining the tasks needed to attain these objectives.

The weaknesses of the above approaches have led some firms to follow the objective and task approach, which begins by determining the advertising objectives and then ascertaining the tasks needed to attain these objectives. This approach also includes a cost/benefit analysis, relating objectives to the costs of achieving them. To use this method the firm must have good knowledge of the local market.

A research study (Hung and West, 1991) showed that only 20 per cent of companies in the United States, Canada and the United Kingdom used the objective and task approach. Although it is the 'theoretically correct' way of determining the promotion budget it is sometimes more important to be operational and to use a 'percentage of sales' approach. This is not necessarily a bad method if company experience shows it to be reasonably successful. If the percentage is flexible it allows different percentages in different markets.

### Message decisions (creative strategy)

**USP**
Unique selling proposition is the decisive sales argument for customers to buy the product.

This concerns decisions about what unique selling proposition (USP) needs to be communicated, and what the communication is intended to achieve in terms of consumer behaviour in the country concerned. These decisions have important implications for the choice of advertising medium, since certain media can better accommodate specific creative requirements (use of colour, written description, high definition, demonstration of the product, etc.) than others.

An important decision area for international marketers is whether an advertising campaign developed in the domestic market can be transferred to foreign markets with only minor modifications, such as translation into the appropriate languages. Complete standardization of all aspects of a campaign over several foreign markets is rarely attainable. Standardization implies a common message, creative idea, media and strategy, but it also requires that the firm's product has a USP that is clearly understood by customers in a cross-cultural environment.

Standardizing international advertising can lead to a number of advantages for the firm. For example, advertising costs will be reduced by centralizing the advertising campaign in the head office and transferring the same campaign from market to market, as opposed to running campaigns from different local offices.

However, executing an advertising campaign in multiple markets requires a balance between conveying the message and allowing for local nuances. The adaptation of global ideas can be achieved by various tactics, such as adopting a modular approach, adapting international symbols and using international advertising agencies.

## Media decisions

The selection of the media to be used for advertising campaigns needs to be done simultaneously with the development of the message theme. A key question in media selection is whether to use a mass or target approach. The mass media (television, radio and newsprint) are effective when a significant percentage of the general public are potential customers. This percentage varies considerably by country for most products, depending on, for example, the distribution of incomes in different countries.

**OTS**
Opportunity to see – total number of people in the target market exposed to at least one ad in a given time period ('reach').

The selection of the media to be used in a particular campaign typically starts with some idea of the target market's demographic and psychological characteristics, regional strengths of the product, seasonality of sales, and so on. The media selected should be the result of a careful fit of local advertising objectives, media attributes and target market characteristics. Furthermore, media selection can be based on the following criteria:

**Frequency**
Average number of times within a given timeframe that each potential customer is exposed to the same ad.

- Reach. This is the total number of people in a target market exposed to at least one advertisement in a given time period ('opportunity to see', or OTS).
- Frequency. This is the average number of times within a given time period that each potential customer is exposed to the same advertisement.
- Impact. This depends on compatibility between the medium used and the message. *Penthouse* magazine continues to attract advertisers for high-value-added consumer durables, such as cars, hi-fi equipment and clothes, which are geared primarily to a high-income male segment.

**Impact**
Depends on the compatibility between the medium used and the message (the 'impact' on the consumer's brain).

High reach is necessary when the firm enters a new market or introduces a new product so that information about, for example, the new product's availability is spread to the widest possible audience. A high level of frequency is appropriate when brand awareness already exists and the message is about informing the consumer that a campaign is under way. Sometimes a campaign should have both a high frequency and extensive reach, but limits on the advertising budget often create the need to trade off frequency against reach.

**GRPs**
Gross rating points –
Reach multiplied by
frequency. GRPs may be
estimated for individual
media vehicles. Media
planning is often based
on 'cost per 1,000 GRPs'.

A media's gross rating points (GRPs) are the result of multiplying its reach by the frequency with which an advertisement appears within the media over a certain period. Hence it contains duplicated exposure, but indicates the 'critical mass' of a media effort. GRPs may be estimated for individual vehicles, for entire classes of media or for a total campaign.

The cost of running a media campaign also has to be taken into consideration. Traditionally media planning is based on a single measure, such as 'cost per thousand GRPs'. When dealing with two or more national markets the selection of media also has to take the following into account:

- differences in the firm's market objectives across countries;
- differences in media effectiveness across countries.

Since media availability and relative importance will not be the same in all countries plans may require adjustment in cross-border campaigns.

As a way of distributing advertising messages through new communication channels, co-promotion has a strong foothold.

Let us now take a closer look at the main media types.

### Television

Television is an expensive but commonly used medium in attempting to reach broad national markets. In most developed countries coverage is no problem. However, television is one of the most regulated of communications media. Many countries have prohibited the advertising of cigarettes and alcohol other than beer. In other countries (e.g. in Scandinavia) there are limits on the number of minutes that TV advertising is permitted. Some countries also prohibit commercial breaks in TV programmes.

---

### Exhibit 12.2 Mercedes uses Janis Joplin's hit to market its cars in the United States

> 'Oh, Lord, won't you buy me a Mercedes Benz.
> My friends all drive Porsches, I must make amends.
> Worked hard all my lifetime. No help from my friends.
> So, Lord, won't you buy me a Mercedes Benz.'

Some 30 years ago rock singer Janis Joplin begged the Lord for a Mercedes Benz. The vocal version of a poor woman's evening prayer was a hit then and is still played frequently on radio stations all over the world.

#### Buying power of the generation of 1968

The generation of 1968 have now reached an age with purchasing power, and the German car company has decided to let the prayer be heard as part of a huge advertising campaign. Mercedes Benz has bought the rights to use the song in its advertisements in coming years. The campaign has already been launched on US TV, where Joplin's 'whisky' voice accompanies the delicate pictures of two of Mercedes' newest luxury models. Many classic rock hits from the 1950s and 1960s have been used commercially in advertisements during recent years. But Joplin's hit is different in two ways. First, it mentions the product directly. Second, the song was originally a satire of the poor's dream that happiness was found in one of the day's most materialistic status symbols.

'It was never meant to be taken seriously,' songwriter Bob Neuwirth recollects, who back in 1970 helped Joplin fabricate the song in a break between two concerts. He has nothing to do with the song today and has not been asked for advice. 'But I am surprised that it took them so long to think of the idea,' he says, and maintains that Joplin had no desperate personal need for an expensive status symbol.

### Drove a Porsche

In those days, Joplin owned a Porsche. Mercedes Benz has chosen Joplin as part of an attempt to reach a younger audience through advertisements that, according to the director for Mercedes' North American department Andrew Goldberg, create an instant emotional and physical connection to the product.

The reactions of a test audience have documented that the song produced warm, nostalgic feelings and created a more positive attitude towards Mercedes. 'What she meant by the song 25 years ago can be freely interpreted by anyone. But when a customer sees the advertisement it is solely about emotions and not sociology,' says Goldberg.

Janis Joplin became a world name with the group Big Brother and the Holding Co. at the end of the 1960s, but died from an overdose of heroin on 4 October 1970. Six months later her solo LP *Pearl* was released. It contained among others the Mercedes song, which a chuckling Joplin finishes with the words 'That's it,' after the famous refrain: 'So Lord won't you buy me a Mercedes Benz.' Exactly as she is doing now a quarter of a century later in the advertisement.

Source: Translated from an article by Jan Lund in the Danish newspaper *Jyllands-posten*, 24 March 1995.

### Radio

Radio is a lower-cost broadcasting activity than television. Commercial radio started several decades before commercial television in many countries. Radio is often transmitted on a local basis and therefore national campaigns have to be built up on an area-by-area basis.

### Newspapers (print)

In virtually all urban areas of the world the population has access to daily newspapers. In fact the problem for the advertiser is not having too few newspapers, but rather having too many of them. Most countries have one or more newspapers that can be said to have a truly national circulation. However, in many countries newspapers tend to be predominantly local or regional and, as such, serve as the primary medium for local advertisers. Attempting to use a series of local papers to reach a national market is considerably more complex and costly.

Many countries have English-language newspapers in addition to local-language newspapers. For example, the aim of the *Asian Wall Street Journal* is to supply economic information in English to influential Asian business people, politicians, top government officials and intellectuals.

### Magazines (print)

In general, magazines have a narrower readership than newspapers. In most countries magazines serve to reach specific segments of the population. For technical and industrial products magazines can be quite effective. Technical business publications tend to be international in their coverage. These range from individual businesses (e.g. beverages, construction, textiles) to worldwide industrial magazines covering many industries.

Marketers of international products have the option of using international magazines that have regional editions (e.g. *Newsweek*, *Time* and *Business Week*). In the case of *Reader's Digest*, local-language editions are distributed.

### Cinema

In countries where it is common to subsidize the cost of showing films by running advertising commercials prior to the feature film, cinema advertising has become an important medium. India, for example, has a relatively high level of cinema attendance per capita (few have television at home). Therefore cinema advertisements play a much greater role in India than in, for example, the United States.

Cinema advertising has other advantages, one of the most important being that it has a truly captive audience (no channel hopping!). The problem, of course, is that people know that commercials will be shown before the film. So they will not turn up until the main feature begins.

### Outdoor advertising

Outdoor advertising includes posters/billboards, shop signs and transit advertising. This medium shows the creative way in which space can be sold to customers. In the case of transit advertising, for example, a bus can be sold as an advertising medium. In Eastern Europe transit advertising is very effective. The use of transit media is expanding rapidly in China as well. Outdoor posters/billboards can be used to develop the visual impact of advertising. France is a country associated with the effective use of poster/ billboard advertising. In some countries legal restrictions limit the poster space available.

## Agency selection

Confronted with the many complex problems that international advertising involves, many businesses instinctively turn to an advertising agency for advice and practical assistance. Agencies employ or have instant access to expert copywriters, translators, photographers, film makers, package designers and media planners who are skilled and experienced in the international field. Only the largest of big businesses can afford to carry such people in-house.

If the international marketer decides to outsource the international advertising functions they have a variety of options including the following:

- Use different national (local) agencies in the international markets where the firm is present.
- Use the services of a big international agency with domestic overseas offices.

In Table 12.3 the different factors favoring a national or an international agency are listed. The single European (pan-European) market is used as an example of an international agency.

The criteria relevant to the choice of a national or an international agency include the following:

- *Policy of the company*. Has the company got any realistic plans for a more standardized advertising approach?
- *Nature of the advertising to be undertaken*. Corporate image advertising might be best undertaken by a single large multinational agency that operates throughout the world via its own subsidiaries. For niche marketing in specialist country sectors a local agency might be preferred.

Table 12.3 European agency selection: national (local) or pan-European (international)

| National (local) | Pan-European (international) |
|---|---|
| Supports national subsidiary. | Reflects new European reality and trends. |
| Investment in existing brand best handled nationally. | Economies of scale in new product development and branding. |
| Closer to marketplace. | Uniformity of treatment across Europe. |
| Smaller size more conducive to personalized service and greater creativity. | Resources and skills of major European or global agency. |
| Diversity of ideas. | Easier to manage one agency group. |

Source: Adapted from Lynch, (1994), *European Marketing*, Table 11-4 pub. Irwin Professional Publishing.

● *Type of product.* The campaign for an item that is to be presented in a standardized format, using the same advertising layouts and messages in all countries, might be handled more conveniently by a single multinational agency.

### Advertising evaluation

Advertising evaluation and testing is the final stage in the advertising decision process shown in Figure 12.11. Testing advertising effectiveness is normally more difficult in international markets than in domestic markets. An important reason for this is the distance and communication gap between domestic and foreign markets. Thus it can be very difficult to transfer testing methods used in domestic ones to foreign ones. For example, the conditions for interviewing people can vary from country to country. Consequently, many firms try to use sales results as a measure of advertising effectiveness, but awareness testing is also relevant in many cases, for example, brand awareness is of crucial importance during the early stages of a new product launch.

Testing the impact of advertising on sales is very difficult because it is difficult to isolate the advertising effect. One way to solve this problem is to use a kind of *experiment*, where the markets of the firm are grouped according to similar characteristics. In each group of countries, one or two are used as test markets. Independent variables to be tested against the sales (dependent variable) might include the amount of advertising, the media mix, the unique selling proposition and the frequency of placement.

This kind of experiment is also relevant for testing other types of communication tool mentioned in Table 12.2.

---

**Exhibit 12.3** **Baileys Irish Cream liqueur: sales expansion with market and product development**

In 1993 R&A Bailey and Co. decided to increase sales of its brand in Europe by expanding usage of the drink. A cross-border television advertising campaign, 'Baileys with ice', was developed to reinforce the contemporary all-year-round image of the drink and to distinguish it from the 'stuffy' image of traditional liqueurs with their mainly after-dinner role. The appeal was to younger consumers to drink Bailey's on a greater number of occasions. Special promotional packs were also developed, consisting of a one-litre bottle together with two free liqueur glasses.

In early 1993 Baileys was also launched on the Japanese market after a period of test marketing. The regular brand was offered in addition to a specially developed brand for the Japanese called Baileys Gold, which was developed with ten-year-old malt whiskey to appeal to the Japanese taste for premium-quality spirits. This Baileys Gold was also priced at double the price of the regular brand.

Source: MacNamee and McDonnell, 1995. Baileys® Irish Cream Liqueur Image by permission of Diageo.

---

## Public relations

Word-of-mouth advertising is not only cheap, it is very effective. Public relations (PR) seeks to enhance corporate image building and influence favourable media treatment. PR (or publicity) is the marketing communications function that carries out programmes designed to earn public understanding and acceptance. It should be viewed as an integral part of the global marketing effort.

Table 12.4 Target groups for public relations

| Publics or target groups: domestic markets | Extra international dimensions: international markets |
| --- | --- |
| *Directly connected with the organization* Employees | Wider range of cultural issues |
| Shareholders | The degree of remoteness of the corporate headquarters |
| *Suppliers of raw materials and components* Providers of financial services | Is this to be handled on a country-by-country basis, or is some overall standardization desirable? |
| Providers of marketing services (e.g. marketing research, advertising, media) | |
| *Customers of the organization* Existing customers | May have less knowledge of the company |
| Past customers | The country-of-origin effect will influence communications |
| Those capable of becoming customers | |
| *Environment* The general public | Wide range of general publics |
| Government: local, regional, national | Host governments |
| Financial markets generally | Regional grouping (e.g. EU), world groupings |

Source: Phillips *et al.*, 1994, p. 362. Reprinted by permission of Thomson Publishing Services Ltd.

PR activities involve both internal and external communication. Internal communication is important to create an appropriate corporate culture. The target groups for public relations are shown in Table 12.4.

The range of target groups is far wider in public relations than it is for the other communications tools. Target groups are likely to include the main stakeholder groups of employees, customers, distribution channel members and shareholders. For companies operating in international markets this gives a very wide range of communication tasks. Internal communications in different country subsidiaries, employing people from a number of different countries, with different cultural values, will be particularly challenging.

In a more market-oriented sense, the PR activity is directed towards an influential, though relatively small, target audience of editors and journalists who work for newspapers/magazines, or towards broadcasting aimed at the firm's customers and stakeholders.

Since the target audience is small it is relatively inexpensive to reach. Several methods can be used to gain PR. Such methods include the following:

● Contribution of prizes at different events.
● Sponsorship of events (sporting, cultural, etc.).
● Press releases of news about the firm's products, plant and personnel.
● Announcements of the firm's promotional campaigns.
● Lobbying (government).

The degree of control of the PR messages is quite different. Journalists can use PR material to craft an article of so many words, or an interview of so many seconds. How material is used will depend on the journalist and the desired story line. On occasions a thoroughly negative story can result from a press release that was designed to enhance the company image.

Hence PR activity includes anticipating criticism. Criticisms may range from general ones against all multinational corporations to more specific ones. They may also be based on a market: for example, doing business with prison factories in China.

## Sales promotion

Sales promotion is defined as those selling activities that do not fall directly into the advertising or personal selling category. Sales promotion also relates to so-called below-the-line activities such as point-of-sale displays and demonstrations, leaflets, free trials, contests and premiums such as 'two for the price of one'. Unlike media advertising, which is 'above the line' and earns a commission, below-the-line sales promotion does not. To an advertising agency 'above the line' means traditional media for which they are recognized by the media owners, entitling them to commission.

Sales promotion is a short-term effort directed primarily to the consumer and/or retailer, in order to achieve specific objectives:

- consumer product trial and/or immediate purchase;
- consumer introduction to the shop;
- encouraging retailers to use point-of-purchase displays for the product. E.g. perfume manufacturer, Chanel, focuses heavily on in-store point-of-purchase information displays like wall displays and seasonal floor displays (Marber and Wellen, 2007).
- encouraging shops to stock the product.

Especially in the United States, the sales promotion budgets for fast-moving consumer goods (FMCG) manufacturers are larger than the advertising budgets. Factors contributing to the expansion of sales promotion activities include the following:

- greater competition among retailers, combined with increasingly sophisticated retailing methods;
- higher levels of brand awareness among consumers, leading to the need for manufacturers to defend brand shares;
- improved retail technology (e.g. electronic scanning devices that enable coupon redemptions, etc., to be monitored instantly);
- greater integration of sales promotion, public relations and conventional media campaigns.

In markets where the consumer is hard to reach because of media limitations the percentage of the total communication budget allocated to sales promotions is also relatively high. Here are some of the different types of sales promotion:

- *Price discounts.* These are very widely used. A variety of different price reduction techniques is available, such as cash-back deals.
- *Catalogues/brochures.* The buyer in a foreign market may be located at quite a distance from the closest sales office. In this situation a foreign catalogue can be very effective. It must be able to close the gap between buyer and seller in the way that the potential buyer is supplied with all the necessary information, from prices, sizes, colours and quantities to packing, shipping time and acceptable form of payment. In addition to catalogues, brochures of various types are useful for salespersons, distributors and agents. Translations should be done in cooperation with overseas agents and/or distributors.
- *Coupons.* Coupons are a classic tool for FMCG brands, especially in the United States. A variety of coupon distribution methods exists: door-to-door, on pack, in newspapers. Coupons are not allowed in all European countries.
- *Samples.* A sample gives the potential foreign buyer an idea of the firm and quality of product that cannot be attained by even the best graphic picture. Samples may prevent misunderstandings over style, sizes, models and so on.
- *Gifts.* Most European countries have a limit on the value of the premium or gift given. Furthermore, in some countries it is illegal to offer premiums that are conditional

on the purchase of another product. The United States does not allow alcoholic beer to be offered as a free sample.

● *Competitions.* This type of sales promotion needs to be communicated to the potential customers. This can be done on the pack, in stores via leaflets or through media advertising.

The success of sales promotion depends on local adaptation. Major constraints are imposed by local laws, which may not permit premiums or free gifts to be given. Some countries' laws control the amount of discount given at retail level; others require permits for all sales promotions. Since it is impossible to know the specific laws of each and every country, international marketers should consult local lawyers and authorities before launching a promotional campaign.

## Direct marketing

According to Onkvisit and Shaw (1993, p. 717), direct marketing is the total of activities by which products and services are offered to market segments in one or more media for informational purposes or to solicit a direct response from a present or prospective customer or contributor by mail, telephone or personal visit.

Direct marketing covers direct mail (marketing database), telephone selling and marketing via the Internet as in the light of the development in Internet technologies it is highly relevant to consider the Web as a direct marketing tool.

## Personal selling

The differences between advertising and personal selling were indicated in Table 12.2. Advertising is a one-way communication process that has relatively more 'noise', whereas personal selling is a two-way communication process with immediate feedback and relatively less 'noise'. Personal selling is an effective way to sell products, but it is expensive. It is used mainly to sell to distribution channel members and in business-to-business markets. However, personal selling is also used in some consumer markets – for example, for cars and for consumer durable products. In some countries labour costs are very low and here personal selling will be used to a greater extent than in high-cost countries.

If personal selling costs on business-to-business markets are relatively high it is relevant to economize with personal selling resources, and use personal selling only at the end of the potential customer's buying process (Figure 12.12). Computerized database marketing (direct mail, etc.) is used in a customer screening process, to point out possible customers, who will then be 'taken over' by salespersons. Their job is to turn 'hot' and 'very hot' customer candidates into real customers.

### The international sales force organization

In international markets firms often organize their sales forces similarly to their domestic structures, regardless of differences from one country to another. This means that the sales force is organized by geography, product, customer or some combination of these (Table 12.5).

A number of firms organize their international sales force along simple geographical territories within a given country or region. Firms that have broad product lines and large sales volume, and/or operate in large, developed markets may prefer more specialized organizations, such as product or customer assignment. The firm may also organize the sales force based upon other factors such as culture or languages spoken in the targeted foreign markets. For example, firms often divide Switzerland into different regions reflecting French, Italian and German language usage.

Expatriates and third country nationals are seldom used in sales capacities for long periods of time. They are used for three main reasons: to upgrade a subsidiary's selling performance, to fill management positions and to transfer sales policies, procedures and techniques. However, most companies use local nationals as their sales personnel. They are familiar with local business practices and can be managed accordingly.

### Trade fairs and exhibitions

A trade fair (TF) or exhibition is a concentrated event at which manufacturers, distributors and other vendors display their products and/or describe their services to current and prospective customers, suppliers, other business associates and the press.

Trade fairs can enable a company to reach in a few days a concentrated group of interested prospects that might otherwise take several months to contact. Potential buyers can examine and compare the outputs of competing firms in a short period at the same place. They can see the latest developments and establish immediate contact with potential suppliers. TFs also offer international firms the opportunity to gather vital information quickly, easily and cheaply. For example, within a short period a firm can learn a considerable amount about its competitive environment, which would take much longer and cost much more to get through other sources (e.g. secondary information).

Whether a marketer should participate in a trade fair depends largely on the type of business relationship it wants to develop with a particular country. A company looking only for one-off or short-term sales might find the TF expense prohibitive, but a firm looking for long-term involvement may find the investment worthwhile.

## 12.8 International advertising strategies in practice

In the introduction to Part IV the question of standardization or adaptation of the whole marketing mix was discussed. Standardization allows the realization of economies of scale in the production of advertising materials, reducing advertising costs and increasing profitability. On the other hand, since advertising is based largely on language and images, it is mostly influenced by the sociocultural behaviour of consumers in different countries.

In reality it is not a question of either/or. For the internationally oriented firm it is more a question of the degree of standardization/localization. A study by Hite and Frazer (1988) showed that a majority (54 per cent) of internationally oriented firms were using a combination strategy (localizing advertising for some markets and standardizing advertising for others). Only 9 per cent of the firms were using totally standardized advertising for all foreign markets, much lower than in previous studies (Sorenson and Weichman, 1975; Boddewyn *et al.*, 1986). This could indicate a trend towards less standardization. A total of 37 per cent of the firms reported that they were using only localized advertising. Many of the global companies using standardized advertising are well known (e.g. Coca-Cola, Intel, Philip Morris/Marlboro).

The Cathay Pacific advertisements show that the company uses a standardized strategy in the South-East Asian area. The only element of adaptation is the translation of the English text into Japanese.

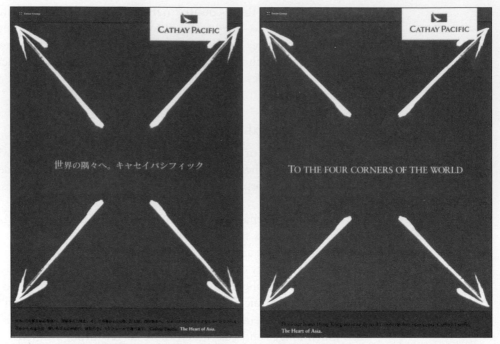

Standardized advertisements from Cathay Pacific

## Examples of adaptation (localization) strategies

### Courvoisier Cognac: Hong Kong/China versus Europe

The Chinese love affair with western alcohol goes back a long way. The first imported brandy arrived in Shanghai in 1859 when Hennessy unloaded its first cargo. Then in 1949 the favourite drink of 'the Paris of the East' suddenly became a symbol of western capitalist decadence; alcohol shipments came to an abrupt halt and did not resume for the next 30 years. However, when foreign liquor once again became

Habits of cognac drinking in Western Europe and Asia

available in the late 1970s, cognac quickly resumed its place as a guest at the Chinese banquet table.

Today cognac and brandy still account for about 80 per cent of all imported spirits in China. Most of the imported brandy goes through Hong Kong via grey markets (see also section 12.8). Chinese awareness of brand and category of cognac is particularly high in the South, where the drinking habits of visiting Hong Kong businessmen set a strong example. This impact is reinforced by alcohol advertising on Hong Kong television, available to millions of viewers in Guangdong province.

The key to Chinese consumption patterns lies in the importance of 'face'. Whatever the occasion, be it the father of the bride toasting his son-in-law's family in Beijing or a Shenzhen entrepreneur's night out on the town, brandy is of paramount importance. Unlike their western counterparts, who like to curl up on the couch with a snifter of brandy, the Chinese consider cognac drinking an extremely social – and conspicuous – pastime.

Two different Courvoisier advertisements are shown: the one for the western European market shows couples drinking cognac with their coffee; the Asian advertisement shows people drinking cognac from beer glasses during the meal.

Folklore as much as marketing has propelled the growth of cognac sales. Cognac has long had the inestimable commercial benefit of being widely regarded by the Chinese as enhancing a man's sexual prowess. And much to the delight of the liquor companies, the Chinese believe that the older (and pricier) the cognac, the more potent its effect.

Source: adapted from *Business Week*, 1984; Balfour, 1993.

### Prince cigarettes: UK versus Germany

The Danish cigarette company House of Prince has high market share (50–90 per cent) in Scandinavian countries, but outside this area its market share is very low, typically 1–2 per cent.

The House of Prince cigarettes images show advertisements used in the UK and Germany. The UK version is based on an invitation to try the product ('I go for Prince'). The target group is also above average in education and income. The German advertisement is somewhat different. Prince is promoted as an 'original import from Denmark'. Apparently there is no 'buy German' mentality working against the use of this slogan. In the German consumer's mind Danish cigarettes are strongly positioned compared to light German cigarettes. Therefore the product's position is emphasized as 'men's business', with Viking associations and ideas of freedom. Incidentally, the two products Prince and Prince Denmark are not identical. The German Prince Denmark has a milder taste than does Prince.

### Gammel Dansk (Danish Distillers/Danisco): Denmark versus Germany

The Danish bitter Gammel Dansk has a 75 per cent share of the bitter market in Denmark. Thus the product has a high degree of recognition there (nearly all Danish adults know the label). The objective of the Danish advertisement has therefore primarily been to maintain Gammel Dansk's high degree of recognition.

Although the market share in Denmark is very high, Gammel Dansk does not have any position worth mentioning outside Denmark. In Germany the situation is totally different. Here the knowledge (and trial share) is at a minimum. The Germans have their own Jägermeister and competition is tough. The strategy behind the German campaign has therefore been to make people try Gammel Dansk by letting them fill out a coupon. By sending it in they receive a little bottle of Gammel Dansk and two original Gammel Dansk glasses.

Advertisements for Prince cigarettes in the UK and Germany

Advertisements for Gammel Dansk in Denmark and Germany (Danisco Distillers Berlin GmbH).

## LEGO FreeStyle: Europe versus the Far East

The LEGO images show European and Far Eastern versions of an advertisement for LEGO FreeStyle. The Asian version, 'Build your child's mind', appeals to Asian parents' desire for their children to do well in school.

The Asian educational system is very competitive and only those with the highest grades are admitted to university. In many places in Asia it is a defeat for parents if their

Advertisement for LEGO® FreeStyle in the Far East, © 1997
Source: © 2008 The LEGO Group, used by permission.

Advertisement for LEGO® FreeStyle in Europe, © 1997
Source: © 2008 The LEGO Group, used by permission.

child does not do well in school. The Asian version has been run in Hong Kong, Taiwan and Korea (preferably in the local languages because the majority of consumers do not understand English). In Hong Kong the advertisements are run in English or Chinese (depending on the language of the magazine).

The European version implies creativity when playing with the different FreeStyle bricks: 'What will your child make of it?'

## 12.9 Implications of the Internet for communication decisions

In the physical marketplace different communication tools are used in the buying process of customers (see Figure 12.13). Traditional mass communication tools (print advertising, TV and radio) can create awareness and this can result in consumers' identification of new needs. From then on other elements of the communication mix take over, such as direct marketing (direct marketing, personal selling) and in-store promotion. Unlike marketing in the physical marketplace the Internet/e-commerce encompasses the entire 'buying' process. Of course, the online markets also make use of traditional mass advertising in order to get potential customers into the online buying process (from the left in Figure 12.13)

**Figure 12.13 The role of Internet communication in the buying process of customers**

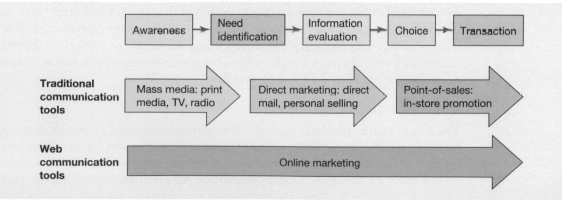

Market communication strategies change dramatically in the online world. On the Internet it is easier than ever to actually *communicate* a message to large numbers of people. However, in many cases, it is much harder for your message to be heard above the noise by your target audience. Various strategies for conducting online marketing have been developed in the past several years – from the most common (website linking) to the most expensive (banner advertising) to the most offensive (e-mail spamming), and everything in between. It is almost certain that a continual stream of new market communication strategies will emerge as the Internet medium evolves.

How, then, can a web audience be created? One of the new possibilities in this field is Viral Marketing:

## Viral Marketing

Global selling and buying is part of a social process. It involves not only a one-to-one interaction between the company and the customer but also many exchanges of information and influence among the people who surround the customer.

For example, diffusion occurs when an innovation is communicated through certain channels among members of a social system. An innovation is an idea, practice, or object that an individual or unit of adoption perceives as new (Rogers, 1995). According to Rogers, mass media channels are relatively more important for learning about an innovation, whereas interpersonal communication is especially important for persuasion. Thus, consumers communicating via e-mail may be persuadeal more readily than those via mass media advertising.

Passing along e-mail is even easier than writing comments. Beyond this, pass-along e-mail seems particularly well suited for the spread of images and/or verbal content that is too detailed to be disseminated via word of mouth.

The Internet has radically changed the concept of word-of-mouth, so much so that the term viral marketing was coined by venture capitalist Steve Jurvetson in 1997. The term was used to describe Hotmail's e-mail practice of appending advertising for itself to outgoing mail from its users. In the Hotmail case each e-mail sent arrived with the appended message 'Get your private, free e-mail from Hotmail at http://www.hotmail.com'.

The assumption is that if such an advertisement reaches a 'susceptible' user, that user will become 'infected' (i.e. sign up for an account) and can then go on to infect other susceptible users.

**Viral marketing**
Online word-of-mouth is a marketing technique that seeks to exploit existing social networks to produce exponential increases in brand awareness.

### Definition

Viral marketing can be defined as a marketing technique that seeks to exploit pre-existing social networks to produce exponential increases in brand awareness, through viral processes similar to the spread of an epidemic. It is word-of-mouth delivered and enhanced online; it harnesses the network effect of the Internet and can be very useful in reaching a large number of people rapidly. From a marketing perspective, it is the process of encouraging individuals to pass along favourable or compelling marketing information they receive in a hypermedia environment: information that is favourable or compelling either by design or by accident.

### Motives for viral marketing

The creation of technologies such as SMS technology, satellite radio and Internet ad blocking software are driving a fundamental shift in the way the public consumes media and the advertising often tied to it. Television ads, radio spots, online ads and even e-mails are facing increasing competition for effectively capturing the viewer's attention and provide positive ROI for the marketer. Additionally, consumers are becoming increasingly immune to mass marketing and advertising, so this form of marketing offers something that does not feel like they are being sold to, making them more receptive to the offer.

This competition, coupled with the rising cost of media buys, has caused marketers to search for an alternative means to reach the customer. Viral marketing is an attractive solution because it utilizes the free endorsement of the individual rather than purchasing mass media to spread the word. Because the distribution model is free, viral can potentially be lower cost and more effective than traditional media.

### Advantages of viral marketing

- It incurs very little expense since the individual passing on the referral carries the cost of forwarding the brand message. Viral marketing offers SMEs the opportunity to target a whole new set of customers while keeping distribution costs to a minimum.
- Unlike traditional advertising viral is not an interruptive technique. Instead, viral campaigns work the Internet to deliver exposure via peer-to-peer endorsement. Viral campaigns, whether ultimately liked or disliked, are often welcomed by the receiver. The act of forwarding electronic messages containing advertising is voluntary rather than a paid testimonial or a mass ad campaign and thus may be viewed more favourably by the recipient. The focus is on campaigns containing material that consumers want to spend time interacting with and spreading proactively.
- Those forwarding the messages will be more likely to know which of their friends, family members and work colleagues have similar interests and are thus more likely to read the message: hence, more effective targeting. Here, the term 'interests' refers not only to the narrow sense of just the product or service but also includes the way the message is presented, such as the humour, the artwork, or the medium itself.

### Disadvantages of viral marketing

Viral marketing, like all marketing is hit or miss. However, viral marketing by nature is often more risky or controversial than traditional marketing. If done improperly viral marketing can backfire and create negative buzz:

- If particular software is needed that is not widely used, then people will not be able to open or view the message
- Many people receive viral marketing messages while at the office, and company anti-virus software or firewalls can prevent people from receiving or viewing such attachments
- For a viral marketing campaign to be successful, it must be easy to use. For example, if the promotion is some sort of game or contest, then asking for referrals should be an option immediately after the game, not as a condition to play.

### Developing a viral marketing campaign

Viral marketing is by no means a substitute for a comprehensive and diversified marketing strategy. In employing viral marketing to generate peer-to-peer endorsement, the technique should not be considered as a standalone miracle worker.

While the messaging and strategy ranges radically from campaign to campaign, most successful campaigns contain some commonly used approaches. These approaches are often used in combination to maximize the viral effect of a campaign.

Successful viral campaigns are easily spread. The key is to get your customers to do the hard work for you by recommending your company or its promotional offers to friends and colleagues, who in turn will recommend it to their friends and so on. An effective viral marketing campaign can get your marketing message out to thousands of potential customers at phenomenal speeds.

When creating a campaign marketers should evaluate how people will communicate the message or campaign to others.

### 1 Creating compelling content

Creating quality content can often be more expensive than simply offering a free product, but the results are often better. Fun is often a vital part of any viral marketing campaign. The general rule of thumb is that the content must be compelling, it must evoke a response on an emotional level from the person viewing it. This fact alone has allowed many smaller brands to capitalize on content-based viral campaigns. Traditionally, larger brands are more reserved and risk adverse to the possibility of negative reaction. Central to the success of these campaigns is one or more of the following: their entry timing (early), their visibility or the simplicity of the idea.

### 2 Targeting the right audience

If a campaign is skewed towards a certain audience or certain regions (countries), marketers should make sure they seed towards that audience. Failure to due so may kill a campaign before it ever gets off the ground.

The influence and, in some cases, the power of reference groups or opinion leaders in individual decision making is significant.

### 3 Campaign seeding

'Seeding' the original message is a key component of a viral campaign. Seeding is the act of planting the campaign with the initial group who will then go on to spread the campaign to others. The Internet provides a wide array of options for seeding, including:

- e-mail/SMS
- online forums (Google groups)
- social networks (Facebook.com, MySpace.com)
- chatroom environment (MSN Messenger)
- blogs
- podcasts.

When determining where to seed it is important that marketers consider the audience they are aiming for. Is the target audience using the above-mentioned media (technologies) and to what degree?

Companies often use a combination of technologies to 'spread the virus'. Many use SMS. An example of an SMS campaign is that of Heineken, which linked an SMS promotion with the British pub tradition of playing quiz games. Heineken combined both online and offline promotions through point-of-sale signs in pubs, inviting customers to call from their mobile phones, type in the wordplay and receive a series of multiple-choice questions to answer. Food and beverage prizes were awarded for correct answers. From a promotional perspective, the idea was successful as customers told others what they were doing, prompting them to call in too.

### 4 Control/measuring results

The goal of a viral campaign is explosive reach and participation. To measure the success of a viral marketing campaign, establish specific and obtainable goals within a timeframe. For example, you would like to see a 20 per cent increase in traffic to a website within three months or to double your subscriber rate to an e-mail newsletter in one year.

Marketers should also be adequately prepared to meet the needs of participants in the event that the campaign is successful. Server space, bandwidth, support staff, fulfilment and stocking should be taken into consideration well in advance of campaign launch. The marketer should have the ability to capitalize on the full success of the campaign.

---

**Exhibit 12.4**  *Cloverfield*: promotion of a Paramount Pictures movie by a viral marketing campaign in January 2008

The film is presented as a video file recovered by the United States Department of Defense from a digital hand-held camera. At the start of the film, it is stated the camera was 'found in US-447, area formerly known as Central Park'.

The film follows five young New Yorkers who throw their friend a going-away party on the same night that a gigantic monster attacks the city.

The film was shot and edited to look like it was filmed with one hand-held camera, including jump cuts similar to ones found in home movies. What the audience is watching is a home movie that turns into something other than planned.

The film was provisionally entitled *Cloverfield* from the beginning, but this changed frequently throughout

Source: © Frank Trapper/Corbis.

production – due to the hype caused by the 'teaser trailer' – before it was finalized as the title. The excitement spread to such a degree that the producers suddenly couldn't use the name anymore, so they started to refer to it as *Slusho* and *Cheese*.

The filmmakers decided to create a teaser trailer that would be a surprise compared to commonplace media saturation; and they put it together during the preparation stage of the production process. The teaser trailer for *Cloverfield* showed the release date of 18 January 2008 but not the title, and this fuelled media speculation over the film's plot. For example, *USA Today* reported the possibilities of the film being based on the works of H. P. Lovecraft, a live-action adaptation of *Voltron*, a new film about Godzilla, or a spin-off of the TV show *Lost*.

A second trailer was then released on 16 November 2007, which published the real title, *Cloverfield*.

In early April 2008, a video-oriented contest website, 'Where Were You When *Cloverfield* Hit?', was launched to promote the release of the DVD, which allowed fans to upload their own enactments of the *Cloverfield* experience. The DVD was released on 22 April 2008 in two versions: the standard single-disc edition and an exclusive 'steel-book' special edition.

### The financial outcome

With no expensive actors, the production costs of *Cloverfield* could be kept at $25 million. *Cloverfield* opened in 3,411 theaters on 18 January 2008 and grossed a total of nearly $17 million on its opening day in the United States and Canada. It made $40 million on its opening weekend. Up to May 2008 it has worldwide grossed $170 million (www.boxofficemojo.com/movies/?id=cloverfield.htm). Forty-seven per cent of this came from United States, and 53% come from abroad.

Sources: Adapted from: www.cloverfieldmovie.com/; www.imdb.com/title/tt1060277/; www.boxofficemojo.com/movies/?id=cloverfield.htm;www.moviesonline.ca/movienews_12553.html (*JJ Adams talks Cloverfield*); other public sources.

## 12.10  Summary

In this chapter we have examined the management of international distribution channels and logistics. The main structure of this chapter was given in Figure 12.1, and from the discussion it is evident that the international marketer has a broad range of alternatives for selecting and developing an economical, efficient and high-volume international distribution channel.

The fear of cannibalizing existing distribution channels and potential channel conflict requires manufacturers to trade off existing sales through the traditional distribution network and potential future sales through the Internet. Unfortunately, history suggests that most companies tend to stay with declining distribution networks for too long.

Five ingredients of international communication have been presented in this chapter:

1  advertising;
2  public relations;
3  sales promotion;
4  direct marketing;
5  personal selling.

As international marketers manage the various elements of the promotions mix in differing environmental conditions decisions must be made about what channels are to be used in the communication, the message, who is to execute or help execute the programme, and how the results of the communication plan are to be measured. The trend is towards greater harmonization of strategy, at the same time allowing for flexibility at the local level and early incorporation of local needs into the communication plans.

Hence an important decision for international marketers is whether the different elements of the communication should be standardized worldwide or localized. The main reasons for seeking standardization are as follows:

● Customers do not conform to national boundaries.
● The company is seeking to build an international brand image.
● Economies of scale can be achieved.
● The few high-quality creative ideas can be exploited as widely as possible.
● Special expertise can be developed and exploited.

However, some communication tools, especially personal selling, have to be localized to fit conditions of individual markets. Another reason for the localization of the personal selling tool is that distribution channel members are normally located firmly within a country. Consequently decisions concerning recruitment, training, motivation and evaluation of salespeople have to be made at the local level.

The process of selecting agencies has also been considered. The requisite blend of local knowledge, cultural understanding and management expertise across international markets is elusive. Too much centralization and standardization results in inappropriate marketing communications.

A very important communication tool for the future is the Internet. Any company eager to take advantage of the Internet on a global scale must select a business model for its Internet ventures and estimate how information and transactions delivered through this new direct marketing medium will influence its existing distribution and communication system.

Viral marketing is by no means a substitute for a comprehensive and diversified marketing strategy. Viral marketing is a credible marketing tactic that can deliver positive ROI when properly executed as a component of an overarching strategic plan. Marketers should utilize viral marketing when the messaging can coincide and support a measurable business goal.

## CASE STUDY 12.1

## De Beers: Forward integration into the diamond industry value chain

Since the late 1800s the South African multinational De Beers (**www.debeers.com**) has regulated both the industrial and gemstone diamond markets and effectively maintained an illusion of diamond scarcity. It has developed and nurtured the belief that diamonds are precious, invaluable symbols of romance. Every attitude consumers hold today about diamonds exists – at least in part – because of the persistent efforts of De Beers.

Moreover, by monitoring the supply and distribution of diamonds throughout the world, De Beers has introduced and maintained an unprecedented degree of price stability for a surprisingly common mineral: compressed carbon. Such unique price stability lies within the cartel's tight control over the distribution of diamonds. De Beers' operating strategy has been pure and simple: to restrict the number of diamonds released into the market in any given year and to perpetuate the myth that they are scarce and should therefore command high prices.

De Beers spends about $200 million a year to promote diamonds and diamond jewellery. 'A diamond is forever' and the firm controls nearly 70 per cent of the rough diamond market.

De Beers controls a producer's cartel that operates as a quantity-fixing entity by setting production quotas for each member (as does OPEC). De Beers has successfully convinced the producers that the diamond supply must be regulated in order to maintain favourably high prices and profits.

During the early part of the last century much of the diamond cartel's strength rested with De Beers' control of the South African mines. Today the source

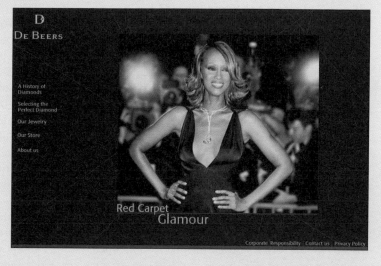

of power no longer comes from rough diamond production alone, but from a sophisticated network of production, marketing sales and promotion arrangements, all administered by De Beers.

It is interesting to note that diamond prices have little or no relation to the cost of extraction (production).

Table 1 shows average or 'normal' price mark-ups on gemstones along the channel of distribution.

Table 1 **Mark-ups on diamonds**

| Stage of distribution | Mark-up (%) | Average value of 0.5 carat gem ($/carat) |
| --- | --- | --- |
| Cost of mining | – | 100 |
| Mine sales | 67 | 167 |
| Dealers of rough gems | 20 | 200 |
| Cutting units | 100 | 400 |
| Wholesaler dealers | 15 | 460 |
| Retail | 100 | 920 |

Source: adapted from Ariovich, 1985 and Bergenstock and Maskula, 2001.

A diamond that may cost $100 to mine can end up costing a consumer $920 at a local jewellery store. Business cycles and individual commercial practices may positively or negatively influence these figures, together with the gemstone quality. Diamond sales, known in the trade as 'sights', are held ten times a year in London, in Lucerne, Switzerland, and in Kimberley, South Africa. The sales are limited to approximately 160 privileged 'sightholders', primarily owners of diamond-cutting factories in New York, Tel Aviv, Mumbai and Antwerp, who then sell to the rest of the diamond trade.

Diamond output from De Beers' self-owned and self-operated mines constitutes only 43 per cent of the total world value of rough diamonds. Because it is not the sole producer of rough stones in the world De Beers has had to join forces with other major diamond-producing organizations, forming the international diamond cartel that controls nearly three-quarters of the world market.

De Beers has constructed a controlled supply and distribution chain whereby all cartel producers are contracted to sell the majority of their entire output to a single marketing entity: the De Beers-controlled Central Selling Organization (CSO) (see Figure 12.14).

The total rough diamond supply controlled by the CSO comes from three sources: De Beers/Centenary-owned mines, outside suppliers contracted to the CSO (cartel members) and open market purchases via buying offices in Africa,

Antwerp and Tel Aviv (rough output purchased from countries that have not signed an agreement with De Beers). De Beers functions as the sole diamond distributor. In any given year approximately 75 per cent of the world's diamonds pass through the CSO to cutters and brokers.

The economic success of the cartel depends highly on strict adherence to their rules, written or unwritten. Clients who follow the rules are rewarded with consistent upgrades in the quality and quantity of rough stones in their boxes, while those who circumvent them find progressively worse allocations and risk not being invited back to future sights.

### De Beers' 'forward integration' decision

Until 2001 De Beers concentrated on supplying its diamonds to brand manufacturers, such as Cartier. The core business of the De Beers Group remains the mining and marketing of rough diamonds. However, in January 2001 the De Beers Group, the world's premier diamond group, and LVMH Moet Hennessy Louis Vuitton, the world's leading luxury products group, agreed to establish an independently managed joint venture, De Beers LV, to develop the global consumer brand potential of the De Beers name.

LVMH Moet Hennessy Louis Vuitton is the home of premier brands in the categories of fashion and leather goods, watches and jewellery, wine and spirits, cosmetics and perfumes. LVMH will contribute with

**Figure 12.14  De Beers' diamond distribution**

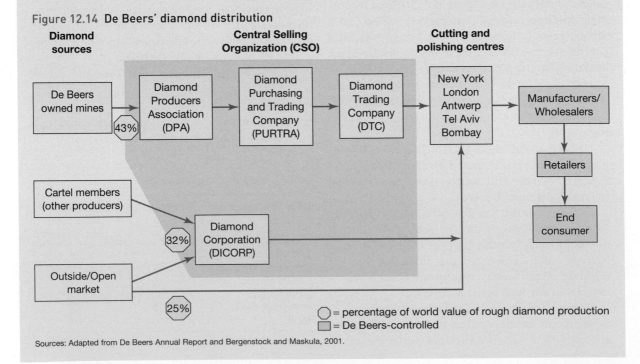

Sources: Adapted from De Beers Annual Report and Bergenstock and Maskula, 2001.

its extensive experience in both developing luxury brands and rolling out premium retail concepts.

The 'mother' company, De Beers SA, contributes to the joint venture with its over 100 years of experience in the form of technology and individual experts to allow for the selection of the most beautiful diamonds.

As part of the joint venture agreement De Beers SA has transferred to De Beers LV the worldwide rights to use the De Beers brand name for luxury goods in consumer markets. From now on, De Beers will design, manufacture and sell premium diamond jewellery under its own brand name. The diamonds bearing De Beers brand name will be sold exclusively through De Beers stores. De Beers has opened a flagship store in London (Oxford Street) and have plans for further openings in New York and Paris.

Source: information and news on www.diamonds.net.

### Questions

1 What could be De Beers' motives for making this 'forward integration' into the retail and consumer market?

2 Is it a wise decision?

3 How should De Beers develop its Internet strategy following this 'forward integration' strategy?

4 Would it be possible for De Beers, with its branded diamonds, to standardize the international marketing strategy across borders.

For further exercises and cases, see this book's website at **www.pearsoned.co.uk/hollensen**

# ? Questions for discussion

1 Discuss current distribution trends in world markets.

2 What are the factors that affect the length, width and number of marketing channels?

3 In attempting to optimize global marketing channel performance, which of the following should an international marketer emphasize: training, motivation or compensation? Why?

4 When would it be feasible and advisable for a global company to centralize the coordination of its foreign market distribution systems? When would decentralization be more appropriate?

5 Compare domestic communication with international communication. Explain why 'noise' is more likely to occur in the case of international communication processes.

6 Why do more companies not standardize advertising messages worldwide? Identify the environmental constraints that act as barriers to the development and implementation of standardized global advertising campaigns.

7 Explain how personal selling may differ overseas from how it is used in the home market.

8 What is meant by saying that advertising regulations vary around the world?

9 Evaluate the 'percentage of sales' approach to setting advertising budgets in foreign markets.

10 Explain how the multinational firm may have an advantage over local firms in training the sales force and evaluating its performance.

11 Identify and discuss problems associated with allocating the company's promotion budget across several foreign markets.

# References

Arnold, D. (2000) 'Seven rules of international distribution', *Harvard Business Review*, Nov–Dec, pp. 131–137.

Ariovich, G. (1985) 'The Economics of diamond price movements', *Managerial Decision Economics*, 6(4), pp. 234–240.

Balfour, F. (1993) 'Alcohol industry: companies in high spirits', *China Trade Report*, June, pp. 4–5.

Bergenstock, D.J. and Maskula, J.M. (2001) 'The De Beers story: are diamonds forever?', *Business Horizons*, 44(3), May–June 2001, pp. 37–44.

Boddewyn, J.J., Soehl, R. and Picard, J. (1986) 'Standardization in international marketing: is Ted Levitt in fact right?', *Business Horizons*, pp. 69–75.

*Business Week* (1984) 'Advertising Europe's new Common Market', July, pp. 62–65.

Cavusgil, S.T., Yeoh, P.-L. and Mitri, M. (1995) 'Selecting foreign distributors – an expert systems approach', *Industrial Marketing Management*, 24, pp. 297–304.

Harper, T. (1986) 'Polaroid clicks instantly in Moslem markets', *Advertising Age* (special report on 'Marketing to the Arab world'), 30 January, p. 12.

Hite, R.E. and Frazer, C. (1988) 'International advertising strategies of multinational corporations', *Journal of Advertising Research*, 28, August–September, pp. 9–17.

Honeycutt, E.D. and Ford, J.B. (1995) 'Guidelines for managing an international sales force', *Industrial Marketing Management*, 24(2), pp. 135–144.

Hung, C.L. and West, D.C. (1991) 'Advertising budgeting methods in Canada, the UK and the USA', *International Journal of Advertising*, 10, pp. 239–250.

Jain, S. (1996) *International Marketing Management* (5th edn), South-Western College Publishing, Cincinnati, OH.

Joensen, S. (1997) 'What hedder it now on engelsk?', *Politikken* (Danish newspaper), 24 April.

Lewison, D.M. (1996) *Marketing Management: An overview*, The Dryden, Press/Harcourt Brace College Publishers, Fort Worth, TX.

Lynch, R. (1994) *European Marketing: A Strategic Guide to the New Opportunities*, Irwin Professional Publishing.

Lynch, R. (1994) *European Marketing*, Irwin, Homewood, IL.

MacNamee, B. and McDonnell, R. (1995) *The Marketing Casebook*, Routledge, London.

Onkvisit, S. and Shaw, J.J. (1993) *International Marketing: Analysis and strategy* (2nd edn), Macmillan, London.

Ottesen, O. (1995) 'Buyer initiative: ignored, but imperative for marketing management – towards a new view of market communication', *Tidsvise Skrifter*, 15, avdeling for Økonomi, Kultur og Samfunnsfag ved Høgskolen i Stavanger.

Phillips, C., Poole, I. and Lowe, R. (1994) *International Marketing Strategy: Analysis, development and implementation*, Routledge, London/New York.

Pirog III, S.F. and Lancioni, R. (1997) 'US–Japan distribution channel cost structures: is there a significant difference?', *International Journal of Physical Distribution and Logistics Management*, 27(1), pp. 53–66.

Rogers, E.M. (1995) *Diffusion of Innovations* (4th ed), New York: The Free Press.

Sorenson, R.Z. and Weichman, V.E. (1975) 'How multinationals view marketing standardization', *Harvard Business Review*, May–June, pp. 38–56.

*The Economist* (2006) 'The Cutting edge – A Moore's law for razor blades', 16 March.

*WorldNetDaily.com* (2005) 'Razor wars: 15-blade fever', 26 November.

# Guinness:
## How can the iconic Irish beer brand compensate for declining sales in the home market?

Beer is a alcoholic beverage made by brewing and fermenting cereals, especially malted barley, usually with the addition of hops as a flavouring agent and stabilizer. One of the oldest of alcoholic beverages (there is archaeological evidence dating to c.3000 BC), beer was well known in ancient Egypt, where it may have been made from bread. At first brewed chiefly in the household and monastery, it became in late medieval times a commercial product and is now made by large-scale manufacture in almost every industrialized country. Although British, European, and American beers can differ markedly in flavour and content, brewing processes are similar. A mash, prepared from crushed malt (usually barley), water, and, often, cereal adjuncts such as rice and corn, is heated and rotated in the mash tun to dissolve the solids and permit the malt enzymes to convert the starch into sugar. The solution, called wort, is drained into a copper vessel, where it is boiled with the hops (which provide beer with its bitter flavour), then run off for cooling and settling. After cooling, it is transferred to fermenting vessels where yeast is added, converting the sugar into alcohol. Modern beers contain about 3 per cent to 6 per cent alcohol. After brewing, the beer is usually a finished product. At this point the beer is kegged, casked, bottled, or canned. Beers fall into two broad categories:

- *Lighter beer (lagers)*. These are made with yeast that ferments more quickly at warmer temperatures and tends to rise to the surface. Lagers use yeast that ferments more slowly at cooler temperatures and tends to settle, and they are aged at cold temperatures for weeks or months, hence the name (German, Lager = storage place). Lagers are the most commonly-consumed beer in the world, with brands like Budweiser, Heineken, Fosters, Carlsberg, Becks, Carling, Kronenbourg and Stella Artois.
- *Darker beer*. Included in this broad category are ales, stout and porters. Stout (and porter) are dark beers made using roasted malts or roast barley. Porter is a strong and dark beer brewed with the addition of roasted malt to give flavour and colour. Stout (today more or less identical to Guinness) is normally darker and maltier than porter, has a more pronounced hop aroma. Porter was first recorded as being made and sold in London in the 1730s. It

became very popular in the British Isles, and was responsible for the trend toward large regional breweries with tied pubs. Originally, the adjective 'stout' meant 'proud' or 'brave', but later, after the fourteenth century, 'stout' came to mean 'strong'. The first known use of the word *stout* about beer was in 1677, the sense being that a stout beer was a strong beer. The expression *Stout-Porter* was applied during the 1700s for strong versions of porter, and was used by Guinness of Ireland in 1820, although Guinness had been brewing porters since 1759. 'Stout' still meant only 'strong' and it could be related to any kind of beer, as long as it was strong: in the United Kingdom it was possible to find 'stout pale ale', for example. Later 'stout' was eventually associated only with porter, becoming a synonym of dark beer. During the end of the nineteenth century, stout porter beer (especially the so-called 'milk stout' – a sweeter version) got the reputation of being a healthy strengthening drink, so it was used by athletes and nursing women, while doctors often recommended it to help recovery. Stouts can be classed into two main categories, sweet and bitter, and there are several kinds of each. Irish stout or Dry stout is the original product, equivalent to the Guinness beer. It is very dark in colour and it often has a 'toast' or coffee-like taste. Major brands in this broad category include Murphy's (Heineken), Castle Milk Stout (SAB Miller) and of course Guinness (Diageo).

### Diageo

UK-based Diageo was formed in 1997 through the merger of Guinness and Grand Metropolitan. Both companies were themselves products of earlier mergers and acquisitions – Guinness had acquired Distillers in 1986 while Grand Metropolitan had diversified from its origins as a hotel chain into spirits (IDV), food (Pillsbury), restaurants (Burger Kings) and pubs. Diageo quickly in to pick up as many brands it could. Pillsbury and Burger King were sold off; and the Guinness business was integrated into the global spirits organization. Today Diageo is a Fortune 500 Company listed on both the New York Stock Exchange and the London bourse. The firm is the world's leading premium drinks enterprise, with a broad selection of brands. It currently occupies a 30 per cent share of the

Table 1  **Key financial figures of Diageo, 2003–05**

|                        | 2003 £m | 2004 £m | 2005 £m |
| ---------------------- | ------- | ------- | ------- |
| Total net sales        | 9,281   | 8,891   | 9,036   |
| Profit before taxations | 1,955   | 1,969   | 1,822   |

global market, and owns nine of the world's top 20 spirit brands, including Smirnoff vodka, Bushmills Irish whiskey, Johnnie Walker Scotch whisky, Captain Morgan rum, Gordon's dry gin, J&B Scotch whisky, Crown Royal whiskey and Baileys cream liqueur. The portfolio also includes Guinness stout. The company has over 25,000 employees, and trades in over 180 markets around the world. Its annual turnover in fiscal year 2005 reached £9 billion, with a total market capitalization of over £20 billion. The financial development of Diageo during the last three years is illustrated in Table 1.

Diageo Plc has one major beer brand: Guinness, which is the world's leading stout brand. However, in the world beer market the stout only accounts for 1.1 per cent of the world beer sales (see Table 2). As a result of Guinness' status, Diageo Plc's beer performance is heavily reliant on the fortunes of the Guinness brand. However, cracks have started to appear in the brand as an aggressive price increases policy was employed to mask volume declines in key markets. Diageo Plc fails to disclose operating profit figures for its beer sector or for the flagship Guinness stout brand. However, it is estimated that beer accounts for 20 per cent of company sales, while its contribution to profits is thought to be smaller, at around 15 per cent.

Diageo top-management has growing concern over the company's principal beer brand, Guinness. The company reported a volume sales decline of 2 per cent for the brand in 2005, with value sales growth of 5 per cent only being achieved as a result of aggressive price increases in its main markets. The adoption of such a strategy has raised doubts of the sustainability of brand profitability. The Guinness brand has suffered on a number of levels, being hit by deteriorating demographics, with younger drinkers turning away from stout in general, a growing preference for wine and spirits, and a shift towards off-trade consumption (buying beers in the shops and drink them at home), which puts the on-trade (pubs and bars) skewed Guinness at a distinct disadvantage.

One of the reasons for this shift away from traditional pub consumption towards home drinking experiences is the banning of smoking in public places, both in United Kingdom and Ireland. Nowhere have these trends been more evident than in the brand's key markets of the United Kingdom and Ireland. In general, Diageo Plc in 2005 reported a 2 per cent decline in Guinness worldwide volume sales, while in the United Kingdom and Ireland the fall was steeper, at 3 per cent. Nevertheless, on the back of notable price rises, value growth of 4 per cent was achieved in both markets.

## Guinness – an iconic Irish brand

As an adopted Irish national icon (though it is actually not Irish-owned), the Guinness brand is readily recognized throughout the world, even by non-consumers. Indeed, it is one of only a few truly global beer brands, possessing a geographic coverage that spans all international regions. Brewed in over 50 countries, the Guinness recipe is modified to suit different market tastes in type and strength, with around 20 different variants sold worldwide. Its prime line is Guinness Draught, launched in 1959 and marketed in over 70 countries. This subbrand accounts for around 55 per cent of all Guinness sold worldwide.

Widget technology saw Guinness Draught move into cans in 1989, and into bottles in 1999. To entice younger lager drinkers to stout, Guinness Draught Extra Cold was added to its range in its core markets of the UK and Ireland in 1998. The subbrand actually comes from the same barrel as Guinness draught but goes through a super cooler on the way to the glass, and is served at a temperature around one-third lower than regular Guinness. This product is generally served in more modern outlets, where people prefer their beer cooler than standard.

Other line extensions include Guinness Bitter, a dark beer primarily sold in the United Kingdom, Guinness

Extra Stout, which is mainly distributed in Europe in bottles and cans and Guinness Foreign Extra Stout. The latter is a higher strength, carbonated stout with a strong oaky flavour and no head, which is distributed throughout Africa, Asia and the Caribbean. Malta Guinness, an alcohol-free beer sold in Africa, and Guinness Extra Smooth, a smoother and creamy variation on traditional Guinness Draught, complete the Guinness portfolio.

## The world market for beer and stout

Although Guinness is holding 55 per cent of the world stout market the brand accounts for less than 1 per cent of the total world beer market (see Table 2).

Guinness's market share has declined slightly, however, falling from 58 per cent in 2000. This was caused mainly by the South African Breweries/Miller merger in 2001, which gave impetus to brands such as Castle Milk Stout and Tyskie Porter, which have encroached on Guinness.

## Competitors

Despite recent regional declines, the global strength of Diageo Plc's Guinness brand has left little room for other major brands to become established in stout. Its main international rivals are SAB Miller's Castle Milk Stout, Heineken with its Murphy's brand and, to a lesser extent, Scottish & Newcastle's Beamish.

Table 2 **World market for beer and stout, 2005**

| Beer/stout 2005 | Western Europe | Eastern Europe | North America | Latin America | Asia Pacific | Australia and Asia | Africa and Middle East | World total |
|---|---|---|---|---|---|---|---|---|
| Beer volume sales (million litres) | 30,290 | 19,543 | 26,154 | 21,918 | 43,656 | 2,075 | 6,961 | 150,596 |
| Stout volume sales (million litres) | 637 | 121 | 122 | 21 | 88 | 25 | 720 | 1,734 (1.1% of total beer sales) |
| **Brand (company) market shares of stout** | % | % | % | % | % | % | % | % |
| Guinness (Diageo) | 80 | 12 | 86 | 2 | 64 | 66 | 30 | 55 |
| Murphy's (Heineken) | 8 | 6 | 3 | | | | | 5 |
| Zywiec Porter (Heineken) | | 14 | | | | | | 2 |
| Kelt (Heineken) | | 8 | | | | | | 1 |
| Beamish (Scottish & Newcastle) | 4 | 1 | | | | | | 3 |
| Carlsberg (Carlsberg) | 1 | 1 | | | | | | 1 |
| Okocim Porter (Carlsberg) | | 4 | | | | | | 1 |
| Danish Royal Stout (Carlsberg) | | | | | 5 | | | |
| Lvivske (BBH) | | 12 | | | | | | 1 |
| Baltica 6 Porter (BBH) | | 5 | | | | | | |
| Tyskie Porter (SAB Miller) | | 10 | | | | | | 1 |
| Castle Milk Stout (SAB Miller) | | | | | | | 64 | 20 |
| Morenita (CCU) | | | | 97 | | | | 1 |
| Speight's (Lion Nathan) | | | | | | 12 | | |
| Monteith's (Asia Pacific Breweries) | | | | | | 12 | | |
| Hite Stout (Hite Brewery) | | | | | 10 | | | 1 |
| Others | 7 | 27 | 11 | 1 | 21 | 10 | 6 | 8 |
| Total | 100 | 100 | 100 | 100 | 100 | 100 | 100 | 100 |
| **Beer distribution** | % | % | % | % | % | % | % | % |
| On-trade (bars, pubs etc.) | 48 | 22 | 25 | 39 | 33 | 26 | 34 | 34 |
| Off-trade (retail) | 52 | 78 | 75 | 61 | 67 | 74 | 66 | 66 |
| Total | 100 | 100 | 100 | 100 | 100 | 100 | 100 | 100 |

Source: Adapted from Euromonitor.

### Castle Milk Stout (SAB Miller)

Castle Milk Stout is only present in South Africa but it is very strongly placed here. This country has a considerable base, equivalent in size to the US stout environment, and, combined with relatively low consumption of stout on a global level, this means that Castle Milk Stout had a heavy influence on the global market, with a volume share of 20 per cent in 2005. The product's performance of late has been dramatic. Under the guidance of SAB Miller, the brand is by far the leading stout product in South Africa, with a share of 89 per cent, a notable leap from the 74 per cent posted in 2003. It appears that Diageo Plc's decision to cut back marketing spend and implement aggressive price increases has backfired in South Africa.

### Murphy's (Heineken)

Murphy's features in most markets across Western and Eastern Europe and North America, but most significantly it holds a 7 per cent volume share of the largest stout market: the United Kingdom. Here, Murphy's has exerted limited pressure on Guinness in recent years, although its own share is partially under threat, facing similar problems in appealing to younger demographics. Conversely, notable brand growth in 2004 was evident in Slovakia, while forward momentum was maintained in Italy, France, the Netherlands, Norway and Russia.

### Beamish (Scottish & Newcastle)

Beamish remains the most popular stout after Guinness in Ireland, posting a notable increase in volume share in 2004, up from 7 per cent to 8 per cent. Beamish is less of a threat in the United Kingdom, and is also present in the smaller stout markets of Canada, Portugal, France, Spain and the Ukraine. In 2003, Beamish was also introduced to the Finnish off-trade environment. Carlsberg is another international player in stout, but its competitive position is diluted by the fragmentation of its brand portfolio, which includes Carlsberg, Danish Royal Stout and Okocim Porter.

### Local brand competition

Other local brands that generate reasonable volumes include Zywiec Porter in Poland and Kelt in Slovakia. Both of these brands are owned by Heineken and contributed to the company retaining its position as the number three player in stout, with a volume share of 8 per cent in 2004. That said, it remains some way behind the two leaders. Asahi Stout and Kirin Stout in Japan are also strong localized brands. Across eastern Europe, Asia-Pacific, Australasia and Africa and the Middle East, Guinness has to contend with strong local brands. Aside from Castle Milk Stout, SAB Miller's other key brand is Tyskie Porter, which is hugely popular in

The Guinness Surger

Poland. Overall, SAB Miller sits in second place in global sales of stout, reflecting the strong performance of Castle Milk Stout in its domestic market.

### Guinness market shares across regions

As seen in Table 2, Guinness is the market leader in four of the seven regions: western Europe, North America, Asia Pacific and Australia and Asia. In the remaining three regions Guinness is No. 2 or 3.

### Western Europe

Focusing on stout, in Western Europe, Diageo Plc led every national market with the exception of Denmark and Greece. Despite this strength, the company experienced its second successive year of volume sales decline in the region. At the heart of this downward trend in 2005 was a notable volume sales decline in Ireland, at 5 per cent and stagnation in the United Kingdom. Also the other markets in the region are declining. Key to this decline is the ageing profile of stout drinkers, with younger consumers failing to connect with the product. In addition, wine and spirits have grown in popularity, taking share from beer, and momentum behind the off-trade sector has grown, placing the on-trade-focused Guinness brand at a disadvantage.

### Eastern Europe

The strength of local brands also poses a problem to Guinness in Eastern Europe, with limited market shares in markets such as Poland (10 per cent in 2005), the Ukraine (3 per cent) and Slovakia (4 per cent). Guinness' volume share of stout is at 12 per cent in the region, its second lowest showing, with only its presence in Latin America smaller. Notably, Diageo posted a steady increase in its volume share of stout between 2004 and 2005 as consumers enjoyed rising disposable income levels and looked to trade up from low-to-middle end local brands. In contrast, Heineken, in pole position with its standard brand (Zywiec Porter), steadily lost share over the same period.

### North America

Guinness also suffered a decline in North America, with sales volume falling in 2005. Poor US beer market conditions, with a price war taking place among leading players, were the main reason behind the downbeat performance, as performance in Canada was stronger. Nevertheless, the company remained the dominant force in stout in the region, with a volume share of 86 per cent in 2005.

### Latin America

In Latin America a relatively new arrival in stout is Cía de Cervecerías Unidas SA (CCU) in Chile, although its global presence is negligible. CCU's entry with its Morenita brand has knocked Guinness off the top spot.

### Asia-Pacific

Demand for stout is underdeveloped in Asia-Pacific, where an almost total lack of demand in the populous markets of China and India is a notable barrier to growth. The Guinness sales volume declined in Hong Kong as well as a marked dip for Guinness in Indonesia and Thailand. A key force behind Diageo Plc's decline was the success of local player Hite Brewery Company Ltd, whose Hite Stout products quickly and confidently gained volume share of stout following its entry in 2000. Given its performance to date, this product comprises a considerable threat to Diageo Plc in the region. In addition, other local players performed well in recent years, negatively affecting Diageo Plc's regional position. Despite the dip in volume share, Diageo Plc remained the number 1 player in stout, even maintaining the top spot in Hong Kong, where decline was at its steepest. Another source of positive momentum in 2004 was Japan, where the company took its volume share to over 40 per cent. This growth was a notable achievement given the extent of local competition from Asahi and Kirin, which both have rival products to Guinness (Asahi Stout and Kirin Stout) and both enjoy significant price advantages.

### Australia and Asia

This region is one of the strongest markets for Guinness, which enjoys a market share of 66 per cent in the region as a whole.

### Africa and Middle East

This region is one of the most important for the company in terms of growth potential as the level of stout consumption is among the highest in the world and much growth is expected in the short term. At the centre of Guinness' troubles in Africa and the Middle East is the growing strength of SAB Miller and its Castle Milk Stout brand, in particular in South Africa, where Guinness saw its market volume share decline from 20 per cent in 2004 to 12 per cent in 2005. Elsewhere, Nigeria is a major market for Guinness, as is Cameroon, where it has invested in increased production and distribution, and dominated sales.

## The international marketing strategy

In the following, Guinness' initiatives within the international marketing mix will be explained.

### New product innovation/packaging

Diageo Plc moved its Guinness Draught into bottles in late 1999 following the development of a new 'rocket widget', which enabled Guinness to retain its distinctive foamy white head when consumed from its packaging. Presented in long-neck bottles, this line positioned Guinness alongside premium lagers and flavoured alcoholic beverages, such as Diageo Plc's popular Smirnoff Ice.

The beer market in the United Kingdom is seeing a dynamic shift away from traditional pub consumption towards home drinking experiences, partially due to the banning of smoking in public places. The impact of banning smoking in pubs in Ireland and the United Kingdom was indicating a switch from on-trade (pubs, bars) into off-trade as more people opted to smoke and drink at home.

In February 2006 the Guinness Surger was launched. It is a plug-in unit promising to deliver the perfect pint at home by sending ultra-sonic sound waves through the special Guinness Draught Surger beer. By releasing this new product, Diageo is aiming to recreate the 'pub experience' in consumers' own homes, as the idea of pubs in which people can smoke will be a thing of the past. Consumers purchasing drinks for at-home occasions want to mimic the on-trade experience as much as possible, particularly in terms of presentation and quality (Carey, 2006). The new Surger gadget delivers exactly this, as well as having a 'shareability' factor to enhance consumers' at home drinking experience through the novelty of using the ultrasound device. The price in the United Kingdom is £17 for the starter kit which includes one Surger, a pint glass and two cans of Surger Beer.

Guinness Draught Surger could help Diageo to capitalize on the growing movement towards the off-trade. The product has already been released with success in Japan and Singapore, and will be the focus of a £2.5 million marketing campaign in the UK.

### Distribution

Diageo Plc handles its own distribution as a rule. However, in many countries, stout occupies a very small niche in the beer environment, making it uneconomical for Guinness to set up its own production and distribution network. It therefore operates in partnership with a number of local and international brewers. Sometimes the company appoints third party distributors or agrees a joint venture for the purpose.

Distribution agreements most often include licensing and distribution agreements for beer. These include both Guinness and rival brands. For example, with Carlsberg it is allowing them the production of their beer in Ireland. In return Carlsberg helps Guinness with distribution in some countries. Japanese Sapporo beer is also produced in the Guinness breweries. As compensation, Guiness gets access to Japanese distribution.

Diageo has also entered into a three-way joint venture with Heineken and Namibia Breweries Limited in southern Africa, called Brandhouse, to take advantage of the consumer shift towards premium brands. The company is also aiming to merge its business in Ghana (Guinness Ghana Limited) with Heineken's Ghana Breweries Limited, to achieve operational synergy benefits.

Diageo terminated its rights agreement for the distribution of Bass Ale in the United States with effect from 30 June 2003. According to the original agreement Diageo had the rights to distribute Bass Ale in the US until 2016. After negotiation, the distribution rights reverted to the global brand owner, Interbrew, for £69 million.

### Advertising of Guinness

Guinness advertising spend has been reduced in recent years, falling in both 2004 and 2005. In the latter, it stood at £1,023 million, compared to £1,039 million, a fall of 2 per cent. Whether this caution is a wise move in times of increased competition remains to be seen. As a largely unique product that leads its category, Guinness has historically been supported by a high degree of creative and ground-breaking marketing and advertising, beginning with the 'Guinness for Strength' girder-man in 1934, and its long-surviving Toucan character, which ran from 1935 to 1982. Guinness has increasingly developed below-the-line campaigns to target existing and potential consumers with the development of customer relationship marketing (CRM). However, above-the-line spend in 2002 was notable, with Guinness's first ever global campaign entitled 'believe'. This focused on the concept of 'self belief' and 'belief in Guinness', and was created by BBDO. The campaign featured a logo with the V in 'believe' replaced with the Guinness harp, and was designed to reinforce brand loyalty among existing consumers and, of course, attract new ones.

### Advertising in the United Kingdom and Ireland

Especially in the United Kingdom and Ireland, the Guinness marketing campaigns have been very high profiled, turning the brand into one of the most successful fast-moving consumer goods in the UK, with very strong top-of-mind recall awareness. In Ireland, however, repeated attempts to reinvigorate the Guinness brand have met with limited success. In February 2004, Diageo Plc launched a new advertising campaign for Guinness in the UK called 'Out of Darkness Comes Light'. The first advert in the series – Moth – represented the start of a campaign marking a new chapter in the heritage of Guinness advertising. This advert was followed up by the Mustang execution, which has all the epic drama and scale characteristic of Guinness advertising. It was supported by a total media spend of £15 million, and first appeared on national TV in September 2004.

In 2005, Diageo Plc launched a new advertising campaign for the core Guinness brand in the United Kingdom and Ireland late in the year. The 'Evolution' campaign features an advert depicting three men in a bar taking a sip of Guinness and then being transported back in time, going back through the main stages of evolution. The new advert had a more contemporary and youthful feel than previous showings, suggesting that Diageo Plc has responded to the problem of deteriorating demographics affecting the brand.

As the biggest growth markets for Guinness are African countries, the greatest marketing innovation generated by Diageo Plc are being implemented here. Guinness spent more than £25 million on advertising in Africa, where the brand commands premium pricing through its reputation. Following on from Saatchi & Saatchi's 1999 creation of character Michael Power in a series of five-minute action thriller advertisements, the concept has culminated in a full-length promotional film production shown across Africa. Guinness Nigeria shot a new Michael Power film, which was screened in 2004. In a further display of commitment to this growth region, Guinness Nigeria has worked with local communities to provide them with clean, safe water. Royalties from the Guinness-sponsored feature film 'Critical Assignment', which highlights the need for clean drinking water, have helped fund a Water of Life project.

### How to attract young consumer

Despite its previous marketing successes, Guinness is suffering from a lack of take-up among younger consumers in preference for more fashionable lagers and FABs. An interesting trend in Diageo Plc's marketing strategy was a further change in the way the company marketed its flagship Guinness brand. For a period on its Guinness.com website, the company actively encouraged consumers to mix Guinness with other products to produce various 'cocktails'. This was clearly a further effort to appeal to the youth segment given that many consumers in this age group find the taste of Guinness too bitter. Examples of mixers suggested by the company included champagne, blackcurrant juice, lime juice or curacao, cacao and Dubonnet.

### Sponsoring

In 2005, Guinness made a notable investment in sports sponsorship, putting its name to the 2005 tour of the British and Irish Lions rugby union team to New Zealand and paying £20 million to sponsor the 2005/2006 season of top league domestic rugby union in the United Kingdom. In addition, the brand was the sponsor of the G8 Summit in Gleneagles, Scotland.

### Investments in a new Irish-theme pub concept

Guinness consumption rose partly because of the development of the Irish-theme pub. In the UK, Diageo Plc invested £13 million in 2001 in developing a new bar concept that it encouraged independent owners of Irish-theme pubs to adopt.

The idea was to make traditional pubs less cluttered and more contemporary, lighter and cleaner, and thereby more appealing to women. This new concept also put a stronger focus on spirits rather than draught beer, thereby signalling that Diageo Plc saw its spirits brands driving future revenue growth rather than Guinness beer.

The top management in Diageo is really in doubt, what to do about the Guinness in future. Should they continue the 'milking strategy' by withdrawing marketing resources (lowering costs) and increasing revenues (by increasing the end-consumer prices)? At least that would maximize profits over a shorter term and Diageo could use the financial resources in acquiring other beer brands. Or should Diageo instead make a long term investment in developing the brand, by implementing new global marketing initiatives?

Sources: Muzellec, L. and Lambkin, M. (2007) 'Does Diageo make your Guinness taste better', *Journal of Product & Brand Management*, Vol. 16, No. 5, pp. 321–333; Wiggins, J. (2006) 'Guinness still posing slow sales problems at Diageo', *Financial Times*, 30 June; Choueke, M. (2006) 'Dark times for the black stuff?', *Marketing Week*, 15 June; Carey, B. (2006) 'Is Guinness still good for Diageo?' *Sunday Times* (London), 9 April; www.diageo.com www.euromonitor.com. Guiness® brand images by permission of Diageo.

## Questions

As an international marketing consultant you are asked to give an independent assessment of Guinness' opportunities in the world beer market. You are specifically asked the following questions:

1  How would you explain the Guinness pricing strategy and the underlying assumptions about consumer behaviour when Diageo reports for 2005 that in the United Kingdom and Ireland the Guinness sales volume fell by 3 per cent, but a value growth of 4 per cent was achieved in both markets, mainly due to price increases?

2  Motivated by the success of this pricing strategy should Diageo continue to increase the price of Guinness?

3  In Choueke (2006) an anonymous beer retail buyer comments on Guinness' decreasing sales volume:

> 'Guinness has an older profile of drinker and with an ever-increasing availability of continental lagers and a fast-growing range of alcopops, the younger generation of drinkers simply haven't bought into it. Innovation – widgets and gadgets – will keep the brand alive for a while but where else can Diageo go? Flavored Guinness? No thanks. It is in decline and Diageo's best minds can't do much about it. The brand may have only a couple of decades worth of life in it and I would milk it for everything before getting rid of it and concentrating on spirits'

Do you agree with this statement? Explain your reasons.

4  What elements of the Guinness international marketing strategy would you do differently, in order to increase both global sales volume, value and profits.

# Dyson Vacuum Cleaner:
## Shifting from domestic to international marketing with the famous bagless vacuum cleaner

### The Dyson history

It is impossible to separate the very British Dyson vacuum cleaner from its very British inventor. Together they are synonymous with innovation and legal battles against established rivals.

James Dyson was born in Norfolk in 1947. He studied furniture design and interior design at the Royal College of Art from 1966 to 1970 and his first product, the Sea Truck, was launched while he was still studying.

Dyson's foray into developing vacuum cleaner technology happened by chance. In 1978, while renovating his 300-year-old country house, Dyson became frustrated with the poor performance of his conventional vacuum cleaner. Whenever he went to use it, there was poor suction. One day he thought he would find out what was wrong with the design. He noted that the appliance worked by drawing air through the bag to create suction, but when even a fine layer of dust got inside, it clogged its pores, stopping the airflow and suction.

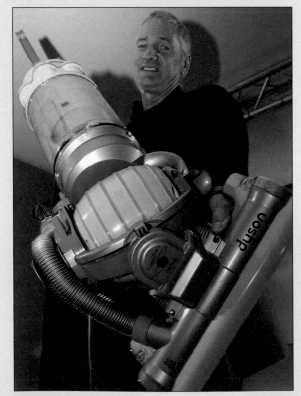

Source: Matthew Fearn/PA/EMPICS.

In his usual style of seeking solutions from unexpected sources, Dyson notice how a nearby sawmill used a cyclone – a 30-foot-high cone that spun dust out of the air by centrifugal force – to expel waste. He reasoned that a vacuum cleaner that could separate dust by cyclonic action and spin it out of the airstream which would eliminate the need for both bag and filter. James Dyson set out to replicate the cyclonic system.

Over the next eight years, Dyson tried to license his Dual Cyclone concept to established vacuum manufacturers, only to be turned down. At least two of these initial contacts forced him to file patent infringement lawsuits, which he won in out-of-court and in-court settlements. Finally in 1985, a small company in Japan contacted him out of the blue after seeing a picture of his vacuum cleaner in a magazine. Mortgaged to the hilt and on the brink of bankruptcy, Dyson took the cheapest flight to Tokyo to negotiate a deal. The result was the G Force vacuum cleaner, priced at $2,000, which became the ultimate domestic appliance status symbol in Japan.

In June 1993, using money from the Japanese licence, Dyson opened a research centre and factory in Malmesbury, Wiltshire. Here he developed the Dyson Dual Cyclone and within two years it was the fastest-selling vacuum cleaner in the UK.

Dyson was nearly bankrupted by the legal costs of establishing and protecting his patent. It took him more than 14 years to get his first product into a shop and it is on display in the Science Museum. Other products can be seen in the Victoria & Albert Museum, the San Francisco Museum of Modern Art and the Georges Pompidou Centre in Paris.

Dyson went on to develop the Root 8 Cyclone, which removes more dust by using eight cyclones instead of two. In 2000, he launched the Contrarotator washing machine, which uses two drums spinning in opposite directions and is said to wash faster and with better results than traditional washing machines.

In 2005 the company's sales reached £470 million, roughly two-thirds of which came from outside the United Kingdom, while pre-tax profit for the year was £103 million, up 32 per cent on 2004. Almost all the sales come from vacuum cleaners – a product in which Dyson has built large sales in the United States, Japan and Australia.

## Marketing of the Dyson vacuum cleaner

Dyson believes the most effective marketing tool is by word of mouth, and today the company claims 70 per cent of its vacuum cleaners are sold on personal recommendation. An enthusiastic self-publicist, Dyson believes that if you make something, you should sell it yourself, so he often appears in his own advertisements.

When a Belgian court banned Dyson from denigrating old-style vacuum cleaner bags, he was pictured wearing his trademark blue shirt and holding a Dyson vacuum cleaner in a press advertisement that had the word 'bag' blacked out several times. A note at the bottom said: 'Sorry, but the Belgian courts won't let you know what everyone has a right to know'.

Dyson has sometimes shunned advertising altogether. For example, in 1996–97 the company spent its marketing budget sponsoring Sir Ranulph Fiennes' solo expedition to Antarctica, and gave £1.5 million to the charity Breakthrough Breast Cancer.

As rivals started to manufacture their own bagless cleaners, Dyson knew he would have to advertise more aggressively and in 2000 he appointed an advertising agency to promote the £2 million business. The marketing strategy, however, remains true to Dyson's original principles, with an emphasis on information and education rather than brand-building. Moreover, it seems to be working, one in every three vacuum cleaners bought in Britain today is a Dyson. See also Table 1.

### Table 1 Vacuum cleaners: market volume and market shares (2005)

| Market/%/ Manufacturers (brands) | Germany | Italy | Sweden | France | Spain | UK | Netherlands | Total Western Europe | United States |
|---|---|---|---|---|---|---|---|---|---|
| **Total market** | | | | | | | | + others 3.0 | |
| Volume (mio. units) | 7.2 | 1.8 | 0.4 | 3.0 | 0.7 | 4.8 | 0.9 | =21.8 | 26.6 |
| **% – types:** | | | | | | | | | |
| Cylinder | 67 | 50 | 94 | 88 | 73 | 34 | 80 | 65 | 9 |
| Upright | 13 | 30 | 1 | 5 | 2 | 62 | 5 | 25 | 66 |
| Hand-held | 20 | 20 | 5 | 7 | 25 | 4 | 15 | 10 | 25 |
| Total | 100 | 100 | 100 | 100 | 100 | 100 | 100 | 100 | 100 |
| **Market shares (%):** | | | | | | | | | |
| BSH (Bosch-Siemens Hausgeräte) | 18 | – | 9 | – | – | – | 28 | 8 | |
| Electrolux (Eureka in US) | 16 | – | 51 | 19 | – | 19 | 9 | 14 | 22 |
| Miele | 15 | – | 12 | 9 | – | 3 | 23 | 9 | |
| Dyson Appliances | 2 | 1 | 2 | 1 | 1 | 34 | 2 | 9 | 4 |
| SEB Group (Rowenta + Moulinex) | – | 18 | – | 22 | 19 | – | 8 | 7 | |
| Maytag (Hoover) | – | – | – | – | – | – | – | – | 20 |
| Candy SpA (Hoover) | 5 | 12 | – | – | – | 11 | – | 6 | |
| Philips | 8 | – | 2 | – | 7 | – | 10 | 4 | |
| De Longhi | – | 15 | – | – | – | – | – | 2 | |
| Matsushita (Panasonic) | – | – | 8 | – | 21 | – | – | 2 | |
| Daewoo Group | – | 8 | – | – | – | – | – | 1 | |
| Samsung | – | 6 | – | – | – | – | – | 1 | |
| Electromomésticos Solac SA | – | – | – | – | 10 | – | – | 1 | |
| Private label | 8 | – | 15 | 2 | – | 3 | 3 | 4 | 10 |
| Others | 28 | 40 | 1 | 47 | 37 | 30 | 17 | 33 | 44 |
| Total | 100 | 100 | 100 | 100 | 100 | 100 | 100 | 100 | 100 |

Comments:

Two different companies in Europe and United States own the Hoover-brand. In United States the brand is now owned by the Whirlpool, but in 1995 Maytag sold its European operations to Italian Candy Spa, which owns the brand in Europe.

The SEB group took over the Rowenta brand in 1988. In 2001 the SEB Group took over Moulinex SA and the SEB Group now markets the Moulinex vacuum cleaner.

Source: Author's own work, based on Euromonitor.

## The world market for vacuum cleaners

The use of vacuum cleaners is largely related to national preferences for carpets rather than floor tiles. In many warm countries instead of carpets floor tiles are more usual, and these can be swept rather than vacuumed. In countries where houses are predominantly carpeted, such as in Northern Europe, Eastern Europe and North America, the number of households owning vacuum cleaners is high. In 2005 app. 95 per cent of households owned vacuum cleaners in Belgium, Germany, Japan, the Netherlands, Sweden, the United States and the United Kingdom. Many Belgian households possess more than one vacuum cleaner, as traditional vacuum cleaners are often complemented with hand-held cleaners (cleanettes). In parts of Eastern Europe, it is also common to carpet walls, which provides additional demand for vacuum cleaners.

Few vacuum cleaners are sold in China and India. Vacuum cleaners have only been available in China for ten years, but ownership has not become widespread. In India many of the rural population do not have the means for such appliances and power supply is erratic. The Asia-Pacific market for vacuum cleaners (not shown in Table 1) is 11.1 million units per year.

The world market for vacuum cleaners is fairly mature and stable. As average prices fell throughout 2000–05, value growth amounted to only 2 per cent overall. In 2005 the number of vacuum cleaners sold throughout the world was 74 million units. Demand is driven mainly by replacement purchases at the end of a product's life cycle (the commercial lifetime of a vacuum cleaner is about 8 years), although new product developments such as bagless models spurred growth in some markets.

The most sold vacuum cleaner types are the upright and the cylinder types. The distinction between upright and cylinder vacuum cleaners became less clear in recent years, with the addition of hoses and tools to the upright version and cylinders mimicking uprights by adding turbo brushes to eradicate dust from carpets.

Cylinder, or canister, vacuum cleaners make up the majority of the global market, but do not take a strong lead, accounting for 65 per cent of European volume sales in 2005, compared with 25 per cent for upright models (see Table 1). As upright vacuum cleaners are more expensive, their share is higher by value, amounting to 33 per cent of the market by value.

Generally, the sales of upright vacuum cleaners grew faster than cylinders over the five-year period from 2000 to 2005. This largely reflected trends in the US, which was the world's leading market for vacuum cleaners (especially upright vacuum cleaners). Here, the addition of new features fuelled the upright subsector, including bagless operation, HEPA (High Efficiency Particulate Air) filtration and self-propulsion, which are available in various combinations on models selling for less than US$200.

In other markets, such as in Eastern Europe, cylinder vacuum cleaners are the most popular type, as they are more practical for use on wall carpets, which are common for example, in Russia.

The handheld vacuum cleaners do not play an important role in the market, so they are neglected in the rest of this case.

The market for vacuum cleaners tends to be dominated by leading white goods manufacturers. Electrolux was uncontested world leader in this sector with a volume share of 14 per cent in 2005, through its brands Eureka and Electrolux.

In recent years one of the most significant developments in the market was that of bagless technology. Dyson UK pioneered its dual cyclone technology back in 1993, Dyson's technology is protected by patent, but other manufacturers were quick to develop bagless versions. In the United States, bagless vacuum cleaners increased their unit share from just 2.6 per cent in 1998 to over 20 per cent in 2005.

Electrolux owes its global dominance to its leadership in both Western Europe and North American markets, though in the latter market its position is strongly contested by Maytag and Royal Appliance Manufacturing (under 'others' in Table 1). Between them, these three manufacturers accounted for 60 per cent of the North American market in 2005. Electrolux also led the emerging market in Africa and the Middle East, and ranked second in Latin America behind Swiss manufacturer Koblenz Electrica.

The Western European market is more fragmented. Dyson was some way behind Electrolux with a share of 9 per cent (see Table 1), closely followed by the premium appliance manufacturer Miele, while BSH and Candy also had strong shares. Though Dyson's overall market share is not high it used to be one of the dominating brands in the high-priced segment.

The Asia-Pacific market for vacuum cleaners is highly concentrated, with the top five players accounting for 80 per cent of sales in 2005. These were all Japanese companies, led by Matsushita. The latter also led the Australasian market, slightly ahead of Dyson. Interestingly, Samsung did not rank among the top five Asian manufacturers in 2002, although it led the eastern European market.

In the United States Dyson now sells 1 million units, equal to a total market share of 4 per cent. However, in the high-priced segment ($400 – plus) Dyson (in 2005) pushed Hoover to a second place with 21 per cent of the market against Hoover's 15 per cent. Dyson is taking market shares in the high-end, which Hoover used to dominate, and at the same time Hoover lost the low-cost market to non-brand Asian competitiors.

## Competitors

The following describes the five most important players in the world vacuum cleaner industry:

### BSH (Bosch-Siemens Hausgeräte)

Bosch-Siemens Hausgeräte (www.bsh-group.com) was established in 1967 by the merger of the domestic appliance divisions of Robert Bosch Hausgeräte and Siemens. During the 1990s, the company was largely geared towards improving its international presence. This was achieved mainly through organic growth, with a cautious approach taken towards acquisitions (e.g. Ufesa).

Ufesa is the leading manufacturer in Spain and Portugal of small appliances such as vacuum cleaners, irons and coffee makers, and has a good export network to Latin America. The acquisition allowed BSH to improve its production and distribution arrangements.

Bosch-Siemens Hausgeräte (BSH) is entirely focused on the production and servicing of domestic electrical appliances, including large kitchen appliances and small electrical appliances. Total revenue for the group amounted to €6,289 million in 2002, of which a small proportion (4 per cent) was derived from customer services. The rest came from electrical appliances. The operating profit in 2002 was €434 million.

The company is involved in all five sectors of the large kitchen appliances market, in which cooking appliances are the most important with 28 per cent of sales in 2002. This is followed by refrigeration/freezing appliances and washing/drying appliances, which each took 20 per cent of the total. Dishwashing appliances accounted for a further 16 per cent. Other business activities centred on the production of consumer products, including small kitchen appliances such as food processors and coffee makers and small appliances such as vacuum cleaners and hair dryers.

BSH remains highly focused on Western Europe, especially its domestic German market. Germany alone accounted for 28 per cent of total sales in 2002, which was down from 30 per cent the previous year. This was due to the difficult trading environment, which led to a 4 per cent decline in sales in this market.

The rest of western Europe took a further 54 per cent of sales in 2002, up by two percentage points on 2001 as sales in the region rose by 8 per cent. This was due to particular growth in France (8 per cent), the United Kingdom (10 per cent), Spain (8 per cent) and Italy (11 per cent). Turkey also continued to see very high growth of 9 per cent, despite the impact of economic and political turmoil in this market.

Sales in markets outside western Europe were minimal, with North America, eastern Europe and Asia-Pacific each accounting for 6 per cent of the total, and Latin America just 3 per cent. Eastern Europe recorded above-average growth rates, especially Russia with over 21 per cent.

Sales in Latin America continued to decline, due to the ongoing economic crisis in Argentina, and both Brazil and Argentina causing significant foreign-exchange-related losses. However, double-digit growth was achieved in China, where the company saw sales rise for the fourth consecutive year.

### Electrolux

Electrolux (headquarters in Sweden) www.electrolux.com is the world's second largest manufacturer of large kitchen appliances behind American Whirlpool, in terms of revenue derived from this activity. The company produces a wide range of large kitchen appliances, as well as vacuum cleaners, and heating and cooling equipment. In addition, Electrolux manufactures products outside the scope of this report, such as garden equipment, food service equipment and chainsaws.

Electrolux dates back to 1901 when its predecessor, Lux AB was formed in Stockholm as a manufacturer of kerosene lamps. The company changed its name to Electrolux AB in 1919, following collaboration between Lux AB and Svenska Elektron AB. The company shifted into electrical appliances in 1912, when it introduced its first household vacuum cleaner, the Lux 1. In 1925, this was followed by the launch of the first Electrolux absorption refrigerator. The company was quick to expand internationally, and by the 1930s was selling refrigerators and vacuum cleaners across the globe.

Between the 1940s and the 1980s, Electrolux expanded into all areas of the large kitchen appliances, floor care and garden equipment sectors through a wide range of acquisitions. In the 1990s the company worked to expand its appliance business internationally.

From 1997, Electrolux entered into a restructuring programme to improve profitability. In line with this, several divestments were made, including industrial products, sewing machines, agricultural implements, interior decoration equipment, recycling, kitchen and bathroom cabinets, professional cleaning equipment, heavy-duty laundry equipment, leisure appliances, baking equipment and electric motors. Furthermore, the programme aimed to streamline the product portfolio down to a smaller number of well-defined brands. Concurrently, the company made some further notable acquisitions in core areas.

The company is divided into two major business areas:

1 Consumer durables, including large kitchen appliances and air conditioners, floor care products (vacuum cleaners) and garden equipment (such as lawn mowers, garden tractors and lawn trimmers).

2 Professional products, including foodservice equipment, laundry equipment for apartment/house laundry rooms, laundrettes, hotels and institutions, components such as compressors, forestry equipment such as chainsaws and clearing saws, and other products such as landscape maintenance equipment, turf-care equipment and professional-use power cutters.

In 2002 the Electrolux Group had a total sales of €14,500 million, of which €800 million was left for operating profit. Consumer durables accounted for 84 per cent of total sales, and 7 per cent came from vacuum cleaners.

Electrolux's business is largely split between Europe and North America, which together accounted for 87 per cent of sales in the consumer durables division in 2002. The company has achieved a good balance between these regions, with similar sales levels.

## Miele

Miele (www.mielevacuums.com) is a German-based, family-run company, which produces a range of premium household appliances (e.g. vacuum cleaners), commercial appliances, components and fitted kitchens.

Carl Miele and Reinhard Zinkann established Miele in Gütersloh, Germany in 1899. The company has, since its inception, been focused on producing high-quality appliances at the premium end of the market.

The company began producing washing machines in 1900, with vacuum cleaners and dishwashers added to the product portfolio in the 1920s. During the 1950s and 1960s the company began to produce fully automatic washing machines and dishwashers, as well as tumble dryers. The 1970s saw further advances in technology, with the launch of built-in washing machines and condenser dryers and microcomputer-controlled appliances.

Since then, the company has produced a number of innovative appliances including washing machines with hand wash programmes for woollens, and during the 1990s, vacuum cleaners with the HEPA filter and Sealed System.

Over the past decade, Miele has focused on expanding its business overseas, especially in eastern Europe and Asia-Pacific. The company opened a branch office in Hong Kong in 1998, followed by offices in Poland and Russia. In 1999, Miele opened its US headquarters in Princeton, New Jersey and in 2001 it opened sales offices in Singapore and Mexico.

Miele has made few significant acquisitions through its history. Its largest acquisition was that of Imperial in 1990, a German company specialising in built-in appliances and catering equipment.

Miele products are marketed throughout Europe and also in the United States, Canada, South Africa, Australia, Japan and Hong Kong, through subsidiaries, and elsewhere in the world via authorized importers.

The company's range of domestic electrical appliances covers vacuum cleaners, large kitchen appliances such as home laundry appliances, refrigeration appliances, large cooking appliances, microwaves and dishwashers, and other small appliances such as rotary irons and coffee makers. The company specializes in producing innovative products within these sectors.

As a private company, Miele does not release detailed financial results. In 2002, company revenue reached €2,200 million, up by 3.2 per cent on the previous year. This occurred despite a difficult operating environment, particularly in its domestic market of Germany.

Miele does not publish detailed financial results by geographic region. However, for the 2002 financial year, the company reported that sales in Germany fell back by 1 per cent to reach €800 million. Outside Germany, sales increased by a strong 6 per cent to reach €1.4 billion. As a result, international sales accounted for 65 per cent of total sales in 2002.

The company lists its highest gross overseas market as the Netherlands, followed by Switzerland, France, Austria, the United Kingdom and the United States. The United States recorded especially swift growth at double-digit rates. Double-digit growth was also achieved in Greece, Finland and Ireland, while other markets showing above average growth, included the United Kingdom and Norway. Russia also showed extremely good growth, although to date the company has only focused on Moscow and St Petersburg.

## SEB Group

SEB Group of France (www.seb.com) is one of the world's leading producers of small domestic equipment. The company is entirely focused on this area, manufacturing household goods (cookware), as well as small electrical appliances such as cooking appliances (steam cookers, toasters, coffeemakers, and grills), home appliances (vacuum cleaners and fans), and personal care appliances (hair dryers, scales, and electric toothbrushes). SEB's key brands include T-Fal/Tefal, Rowenta, Krups and SEB. The total sales of SEB Group in 2002 were €2,496 million.

Groupe SEB's origins date back to 1857, when the tinware company Antoine Lescure was founded. The company gradually expanded its activities to include products such as kitchen utensils and zinc tubs, beginning to mechanize its production at the beginning of the 20th century. In 1953, the company launched the first pressure cooker.

The company has since grown by acquisition. This began with Tefal in 1968, a company specialising in nonstick cookware, and continued with the acquisition of the Lyon company, Calor, a maker of irons, hair dryers, small washing machines and portable radiators in 1972. In 1973, a group structure was formed under a lead holding company, SEB SA, which was listed on the Paris Stock Exchange two years later.

Groupe SEB made a significant push into international markets when it acquired Rowenta in 1988, a German manufacturer of irons, electric coffee makers, toasters and vacuum cleaners. In 1992 and 1993, it took advantage of the opening up of Eastern Europe, setting up marketing operations to make inroads in these countries and gain a foothold in the Russian market.

In 1997–98, Groupe SEB entered South America with the acquisition of Arno, Brazil's market leader in small electrical appliances. Arno specializes in the manufacture and sale of food preparation appliances (mixers/blenders), non-automatic washing machines and fans.

In September 2001, Groupe SEB's main domestic rival, Moulinex, filed for bankruptcy. The company submitted an offer for a partial takeover of the business assets of Moulinex, for which it finally received approval by both the European Commission and the French Finance Ministry in 2002. Moulinex had purchased one of Europe's leading brands, Krups, in the early 1990s, and was a good fit with Groupe SEB's existing businesses.

Examples of new SEB vacuum cleaners introduced in 2002 are:

- The new Neo vacuum cleaner, with a futuristic and compact design and very high performance which heralded the arrival of a new ultra-modern range.
- The relaunch of Moulinex vacuum cleaners in all market segments, including the Boogy supercompact vacuum cleaner with an automatic bag ejection system; and the Alto high-power compact vacuum cleaner.

Groupe SEB is one of the few small electrical appliance manufacturers to have achieved a truly global presence. Furthermore, the company has a good geographical balance of sales. Although its domestic market in France accounted for the highest proportion of sales, 26.4 per cent in 2002, a further 30.6 per cent of revenues was derived from other EU countries. The Americas represented 23.2 per cent of sales, with the rest of the world accounting for the remaining 19.8 per cent.

Groupe SEB has stated its intention to expand in emerging markets which offer high growth potential, such as Brazil, Korea, the CIS countries and China, although it also sees potential for development of high added-value niche products in developed markets such as the EU, North America and Japan.

Growth was achieved in all regions in 2002, which was largely due to the partial acquisition in that year of Moulinex-Krups.

### Whirlpool

In 2006 Whirlpool announced that it had taken over Maytag's Hoover vacuum cleaner division. Whirlpool closed its takeover of Maytag in March, after passing an extended Justice Department antitrust review. Hoover was acquired as part of its $1.68 billion purchase of Maytag Corp. The company operates under the premium brands Maytag, Jenn-Air, and the lower-end brands Magic Chef, Amana and Admiral. It operates mainly in the United States, but has sales subsidiaries in Canada, Australia, Mexico, Puerto Rico and the United Kingdom.

Maytag Corp traces its roots back to 1893 when FL Maytag began manufacturing farm implements in Newton, Iowa. In order to offset seasonal slumps in demand he introduced a wooden-tub washing machine in 1907. The company diversified into cooking appliances and refrigerators after the Second World War in 1946. It introduced its first automatic washing machine in 1949, and its first portable dishwashers in 1966.

One of the most famous brands in the vacuum cleaner industry – Hoover – dates back to 1907, when it was developed by the Hoover family in Canton, Ohio. The Hoover Company began selling its products worldwide in 1921. Maytag took over the Hoover brand in 1989 when they merged with Chicago Pacific Corporation. In 1995, Maytag sold the European Hoover operations to Italian appliance manufacturer, Candy.

In the vacuum cleaner sector, Whirlpool operates only under the Hoover brand, which has a strong heritage and is the leading brand in the US market. Hoover manufactures a wide range of vacuum cleaners, including uprights, canisters, stick and handheld vacuums, hard surface cleaners, extractors and other home care products.

In mid-2006 Whirlpool Corp. announced that it planned to sell the Hoover vacuum cleaner business. The Hoover brand, with its 3,000 employees, does not fit with Whirlpool's core products – laundry, refrigeration and kitchen equipment.

### Distribution of vacuum cleaners

The situation in Dyson's domestic market, the UK, is as follows:

Department stores are the most popular source of small electrical goods in the UK, with many trusted names (e.g. Co-op Home Stores and John Lewis) who are able to stock a sufficient variety of competitively priced goods to attract consumer loyalty. Their share has increased slightly over recent years, as department stores in general have become more fashionable again.

Specialist multiples have the second largest share, although not far behind are the independents which have a larger share of the small electrical appliances market than they do of large appliances. Smaller high street stores in small and medium-sized towns attract buyers of small electrical appliances, like vacuum cleaners, since consumers are less motivated to drive to a retail park for these items, than they are say, for a fridge.

Grocery multiples, such as Tesco and Asda, sell vacuum cleaners and generally offer advantageous deals on a narrow range of goods. Catalogue showrooms such as Argos also benefited from increasing their range and from low pricing and online shopping facilities.

Distribution of vacuum cleaners has become hugely extensive, with supermarkets and grocery stores stocking the cheaper to mid-end of the market. For electrical retailers still selling smaller items, their domain lies more in the pricier, higher-end of the market.

The distribution of vacuum cleaners in most other major countries is limited principally to specialist 'household appliance' store chains and department stores.

Huge retail chains like Electric City, Best Buy and Sears more and more dominate the distribution of vacuum cleaners in United States.

## Latest development

During the last years, Dyson has decided to move most of its vacuum cleaner production from the United Kingdom to the Far East (Malaysia).

Although Dyson is still a leading vacuum cleaner brand, it is beginning to lose out to cheaper machines that have developed their own bagless technology.

The dilemma Dyson faces is dropping its own prices or reinforcing the power and quality of its brand. The loyalty of Dyson's customers has dropped off and the company's market share in UK by volume has also decreased.

Besides vacuum cleaners Dyson is also trying to make headway in washing machines, an industry with global annual sales of £15 billion and with big competitors including Whirlpool of the United States and Japan's Matsushita.

Dyson gained success in vacuum cleaners through high price and stylish machines that featured a new way of sucking up dirt without a bag, which appealed to consumers' desire to try something new. Then in 2000 Dyson unveiled a novel type of washing machine – called the 'Contrarotator' because it featured two drums spinning in opposite directions. Most industry analysts say that the complexity of manufacturing washing machines, which feature a host of sophisticated mechanisms including pumps and motors that have to work reliably, is a lot higher than for the relatively simple design of a vacuum cleaner. Dyson's washing machine is very expensive, retailing at more than £500, or twice the price of a standard washing machine sold in the United Kingdom. And whether consumers will pay significantly extra for a new design – even if its performance is better – is open to question.

Even in its best year for sales in 2002 the Contrarotator accounted for sales of only 18,000 units in the United Kingdom, out of total washing machine sales of some 2.2 million a year. In 2005, the number of Contrarotators sold slumped to 2,500.

Counting only those sales of 'up-market' washing machines retailing at above £500, the Dyson product chalked up a creditable 21 per cent share of the market in 2002. But by 2005, when the machine was quietly withdrawn, this figure had fallen to 2 per cent.

Dyson insists that a new type of washing machine – now being worked on by a research and development team at Dyson's headquarters in Malmesbury, Wiltshire – will be better than the first one. He says: 'We will develop a new machine and then see how many people want to buy it. I am sure it can be a success.' (Marsh, 2006)

Sources: www.dyson.com; www.electrolux.com; www.mielevacuums.com; www.seb.com; www.hoover.com; http://news.bbc.co.uk Marsh, P. (2006), 'A 10-year struggle to clean up in the appliance market', *Financial Times*, 27 June, p. 26.

## Questions

1  Until now Dyson has concentrated its efforts in the United Kingdom, the United States, Japan and Australia. In your opinion, which new international markets should be allocated more marketing resources, in order to develop them into future Dyson growth markets?

2  In the US market Dyson achieved its market share by moving into the mass retail channels, like Electric City and Best Buy. Some industry specialists are critical towards this the long-term strategy for Dyson's high-priced product. Evaluate the Dyson distribution strategy in the US market.

3  Do you think that James Dyson can repeat the international vacuum cleaner success with the new washing machine? Why? Why not?

# Part V

# IMPLEMENTING AND COORDINATING THE GLOBAL MARKETING PROGRAMME

## Contents

Part V Video case study

Royal Enfield: Trying to establish an international brand identity

Introduction to Part V

## Part V Case studies

Part I
The decision to internationalize
Chs 1–4

Part II
Deciding which markets to enter
Chs 5–7

Part III
Market entry strategies
Chs 8–10

Part IV
Designing the global marketing programme
Chs 11–12

Part V
Implementing and coordinating the global marketing programme
Chs 13–14

# Royal Enfield:
## Trying to establish an international brand identity

Royal Enfield (**www.royalenfield.com**) was a brand of the British Enfield Cycle Company from 1890, and today it is one of the oldest existing motorcycle manufacturers in the world.

The company established a satellite licence factory in India in 1955, to help meet demand from the Indian Army. When the UK factory closed in 1970 (because of increasing competition from Japanese bikes), production continued in India. Royal Enfield entered into a strategic alliance with Indian Eicher and in 1994 it became a part of the Eicher Group (**www.eicherworld.com**), which has interests in commercial vehicles (trucks and buses), automotive gears and engineering software, motorcycles, and automotive gears and components. Eicher has around 2,500 employees located in four manufacturing facilities in India.

**Royal Enfield Electra 5S**

The head office of Royal Enfield is located in Chennai (formerly Madras) and has marketing offices across India in both the metropolitan and state capitals. With a workforce of around 800 employees, its market network includes more than 200 dealers/spare parts distributors and several authorized service centres.

Royal Enfield exports its bikes to over 25 countries including developed countries such as the United States, Japan, the United Kingdom and several European countries. In the United Kingdom Royal Enfield has been ranked among the top 10 selling brands in the 125–500 cc category. The most famous Royal Enfield brand 'Bullet' is still essentially hand-made utilizing very little assembly line activity. First introduced in Britain in 1949 this classic single cylinder motorcycle has seen only minor modifications since it was first produced in India in 1955. The demand for this old motorcycle has never stopped. Every year the company is producing over 20,000 'Bullet' motorcycles.

In 1999 Watsonian-Squire, the world's longest established sidecar manufacturer (founded in 1912) took over UK distribution of Royal Enfield motorcycles. Located close to the original factory, the company has worked closely with the factory in Chennai to help develop several new models for the European market.

**Royal Enfield website**

*Watch the video before answering the questions.*

## Questions

1 What are the differences in Royal Enfield's brand image and marketing strategy from India to Europe? Explain why these differences occur.

2 Which cross-cultural difficulties would Royal Enfield experience if it started negotiating with potential US partners with the aim of further penetration of its motorcycles into the US market?

3 What kind of organizational structure should Royal Enfield's mother-company, Eicher Group, use for its global activities?

Source: Video accompanying the text, www.royalenfield.com

# Introduction to Part V

While the first four parts of this book have considered the set-up necessary to carry out global marketing activities, Part V will discuss the implementation and coordination phase.

An essential criterion for success in selling and negotiating internationally is to be able to adapt to each business partner, company and situation. Chapter 13 therefore discusses how the international negotiator should cope with the different cultural background of its counterparts. A part of this chapter will also deal with how knowledge and learning can be transferred across borders within the company and between cooperation partners.

As companies evolve from purely domestic firms to multinationals their organizational structure, coordination and control systems must change to reflect new global marketing strategies. Chapter 14 is concerned with how organizational structures and marketing budgets (including other control systems) have to be adjusted as the firm itself and market conditions change.

# 13

# Cross-cultural sales negotiations

## Contents

## Learning objectives

After studying this chapter you should be able to do the following:

- Discuss why intercultural selling through negotiation is one of the greatest challenges in global marketing.

- Explain the major phases in a cross-cultural negotiation process.

- Discuss how learning and knowledge transfer across borders can increase international competitiveness.

- Discuss the implications of Hofstede's research for the firm's cross-cultural negotiation.

- Explain some important aspects of intercultural preparation.

- Discuss opportunities and pitfalls with global multicultural project groups.

- Explain the complexity and dangers of transnational bribery.

## 13.1 Introduction

Culture is a dimension that intervenes at each stage of the negotiation. It plays a role in the way people conceive of the situation even before any discussion starts because it contributes to structuring the problem. It influences the strategic approach developed in terms of competition or cooperation.

To remain competitive and to flourish in the complex and fast-changing world of international business companies must look worldwide not only for potential markets but also for sources of high quality but less expensive materials and labour. Even small business managers who never leave their home countries will deal with markets and a workforce whose cultural background is increasingly diverse. Those managers with the skills to understand and adapt to different cultures are better positioned to succeed in these endeavours and to compete successfully in the world market.

Culture contributes to orchestrating behaviours, drawing a line between what is desirable and what is not acceptable. It conditions perception in providing meaning to what is observed, organizing and codifing communication. It influences the choice of norms for fairness that will seal the final agreement. By the importance and significance that it gives to the context, culture directly influences the negotiation process. Fundamentally, negotiation as a process which is intended to reach a goal, is a process of strategic nature, taking place in a cultural context and conducted by people who are themselves cultural vectors. It would be quite unrealistic not to take this into account. Culture is the variable that distinguishes international negotiation from any other type. Before engaging in such a lengthy and complex negotiation process as establishing a joint venture, it is essential for an international negotiator, whether buyer or seller, to assimilate basic elements of the counterpart's culture. Such a task will enable a better understanding of what really goes on around the negotiation table and in the immediate environment, to avoid misunderstandings, to communicate more effectively, to be better equipped to solve deadlocks that may surface and to be able to diagnose the real problems.

Consequently, conducting business with people from other cultures will never be as easy as doing business at home.

In the early stages of internationalization SMEs may treat cross-cultural markets as purely short-term economic opportunities to be pursued in order to maximize short-term profit.

However, learning more about the nature of culture and how it affects business practices can increase the chances of success, even in the early cross-cultural business negotiations. When people from two different cultures are conducting business making assumptions about another culture is often detrimental, and can result in miscommunication. The managers in SMEs should develop realistic assumptions based on a truthful appreciation of the culture and should refrain from any thoughts of cultural stereotyping. Exhibit 13.1 shows that cultural influences can be difficult to predict.

---

### Exhibit 13.1    Giving gifts in China and Japan

A US businessman once presented a clock to the daughter of his Chinese counterpart on the occasion of her marriage, not knowing that clocks are inappropriate gifts in China because they are associated with death. His insult led to the termination of the business relationship. It is also bad to give one's Japanese counterpart gifts of greater value than those received.

Source: Hendon *et al.* 1999.

---

All successful international marketers have personal representation abroad. Face-to-face negotiations with the customer are the heart of the sales job. Negotiations are necessary to reach an agreement on the total exchange transaction, comprising such issues as the product to be delivered, the price to be paid, the payment schedule and the service agreement.

International sales negotiations have many characteristics that distinguish them from negotiations in the domestic setting. First and foremost, the cultural background of the negotiating parties is different. Successful negotiations therefore require some understanding of each party's culture and may also require the adoption of a negotiating strategy that is consistent with the other party's cultural system. It is interesting to note that Japanese negotiators, among other things, routinely request background information on US companies and key negotiators. Japanese negotiators therefore often know in advance the likely negotiating strategies and tactics of the other side.

## 13.2   Cross-cultural negotiations

Faced with different customs, perceptions and language the most common human tendency is to stereotype the other party in a negative way. A crucial perception is knowing what to look for and thoroughly researching the characteristics of a culture before conducting negotiations. Understanding other cultures is often based on tolerance. Trust and respect are essential conditions for several cultures, for example, the Japanese, Chinese, Mexican, and most Latin American cultures. The Japanese may require several meetings before actual negotiation issues are discussed, while North Americans and North Europeans are inclined to do business as soon as possible. Culture affects a range of strategies, including the many ways they are implemented. The Israeli prefers direct forms of negotiation, and the Egyptian prefers an indirect form. The Egyptians interpret Israeli directness as aggressive, and are insulted, while the Israelis view Egyptian indirectness with impatience, and consider it insincere. This cultural difference endangers any negotiation between business people in the two countries.

Even the language of negotiation can be deceptive. Compromise for North Americans and western Europeans is equal to morality, good faith and fair play. To the Mexicans and other Latin Americans compromise means losing dignity and integrity; in Russia and the Middle East it is a sign of weakness. Furthermore, members of other cultures may regard the common western ideal of a persuasive communicator as aggressive, superficial and insincere.

### The cross-cultural negotiation process

**Negotiation process**
A process in which two or more entities come together to discuss common and conflicting interests in order to reach an agreement of mutual benefit.

A negotiation process can be defined as 'a process in which two or more entities come together to discuss common and conflicting interests in order to reach an agreement of mutual benefit' (Harris and Moran, 1987, p. 55). The negotiation process is significantly influenced by the cultures within which the negotiators (typically a buyer and a seller) have been socialized and educated. Cultural differences prevalent in the international sales negotiation process can have a tremendous impact upon the process itself as well as its outcome.

The cross-cultural negotiation process can be divided into two different parts: namely, the non-task related interaction and task related interaction (see Figure 13.1) – each part is discussed in the following sections (Simintiras and Thomas, 1998; Simintiras and Reynolds, 2001).

Figure 13.1 shows that the cross-cultural negotiation process is very much influenced by the cultural 'distance' between seller and buyer. This perspective is further developed in Figure 13.2 later.

### Non-task related interaction

The non-task related aspects of the sales negotiation process (status distinction, impression formation accuracy and interpersonal attractiveness) are considered first as it is these factors that are more relevant when establishing a relationship with the buyer; that is, *approaching* the buyer:

**Figure 13.1 The cross-cultural negotiation process is influenced by the cultural distance between buyer and seller**

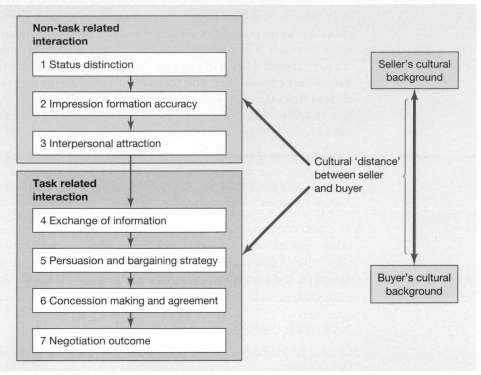

Source: Adapted from Simintiras, A.C. and Thomas, A.H. (1998) and Simintiras, A.C. and Reynolds, N. (2001).

### 1  Status distinction

In cross-cultural negotiations it is critical that sellers and buyers understand status distinction. Status distinction is defined by interpersonal rank, age, gender, education, the position of an individual in the company and the relative position of one's company. Different cultures attach different degrees of importance to status in negotiations. High-context cultures are status-oriented and the meaning of communication is internalized in the person. The words used by negotiators in high-context cultures are not as important as the negotiator's status. The status distinctions of negotiators between high- and low-context are sources of potential problems. For example, a seller from a high-context culture negotiating with a buyer from a low-context culture is likely to attach importance to the status of the buyer. The seller expects the buyer to reciprocate this respect, but this will rarely take place.

### 2  Impression formation accuracy

This stage refers to initial contact between negotiators. The first two minutes that a salesperson spends with a prospect are the most important (the 'moment of truth'). Meeting someone for the first time, individuals have immediate feelings that precede rationalized thought processes; these feelings lead to the formation of instant opinions that are often based on minimal information. As the perceptions of the individuals from dissimilar cultures differ, the likelihood of a negotiator forming accurate impressions of the counterpart is reduced. A bad impression based on an inaccurate impression formation may also have negative effects on subsequent stages of negotiation.

### 3 Interpersonal attraction

This stage refers to the immediate face-to-face impression influenced by the feelings of attraction or liking between the buyer and seller. Interpersonal attraction can have either a positive or negative influence on the negotiation outcome. Similarity between negotiators can induce trust which leads, in turn, to interpersonal attraction. Individuals who are attracted are likely to make concessions in the bargaining process. Thus an individual negotiator may give up economic rewards for the rewards of the satisfaction derived from the relationship with an attractive partner. Zhang and Dodgson (2007) give an interesting character sketch of the founder of a Korean start-up IT-company, Mr. Lee:

> We found Mr. Lee was influenced by his partners, and sometimes followed their advice – even though he knew they were not necessarily right, because he could not face losing connections within his personal networks. Mr. Lee's biggest problem is he cannot separate business relations from his personal networks (p. 345).

This also confirms that Korean negotiation culture is based on Confucianism and its values permeate every aspect of society, providing a basis for morality and social norms. Like other Asian countries, Korea is a society where group harmony within social networks, and company loyalty and commitment, are greatly appreciated collectivistic attributes.

## Task related interaction

Once a relationship has successfully been established between buyer and seller, the task related aspects of the cross-cultural negotiation process are going to be more important. However, it should be remembered that even though the non-task related factors are not of prime importance at this stage, they could still have an impact on the negotiation process and the final outcome.

### 4 Exchange of information

At this point in the process a clear understanding of the negotiator's needs and expectations is essential as a point of departure for an effective communication flow between the partners. More specifically, there is an emphasis on the participants' expected utilities of the various alternatives open to them. The amount of information that has to be exchanged explicitly will vary from culture to culture, and with the extra complexity of several thousand languages and local dialects in the world, communication in cross-cultural negotiations through verbal means is complex and difficult. Even in cases when participants understand each other and are mutually fluent, the meaning of the information exchanged can be lost as a result of different meanings of words and across cultures. In addition to difficulties with verbal communication, cross-cultural sales negotiations are subject to non-verbal problems, such as body language, which can reduce the possibility that the negotiators will accurately understand their differences and their similarities.

### 5 Persuasion and bargaining strategy

This phase of the negotiation process refers to a negotiator's attempts to modify the performance expectations of the other party through the use of various persuasive tactics. There are various styles of persuasion and each culture has its own style of persuasion. According to Anglemar and Stern (1978), there are two basic strategies used in the negotiation process. These are *representational* and *instrumental strategies*.

When *representational strategies* are used communication is based on identification of problems, a search for solutions and the selection of the most appropriate course of action; for example, the salesperson may cooperate with the buyer and seek information on the buyer's views of the situation.

When *instrumental strategies* are used, communication involves affecting the other party's behaviour and attitudes; for example, a salesperson may influence the buyer with persuasive promises, commitments, rewards and punishments. The existence of a friendly and cooperative negotiation climate favours the use of the representational bargaining strategy.

### 6 Concession making and agreement

This stage refers to the manoeuvring of negotiators from their initial position to a point of agreement on what is being negotiated. Negotiators from different cultures have different approaches to concession making. For example, while in low-context cultures negotiators are likely to use logic, individuals in high-context cultures are more likely to use personalized arguments.

### 7 Negotiation outcome

Agreement is the last stage of the negotiation process. The agreement should be the starting point for the development of a 'deeper' relationship between buyer and seller. The final agreement of a negotiation process may take the form of a gentleman's agreement, which is common in high-context cultures, or more formal contracts, which are more prevalent in 'low-context' countries.

## Implications of Hofstede's work

From Hofstede's work we see that there are differences (gaps) between national cultures. Each of four dimensions is reflected in the corporate culture patterns exhibited across countries (Hofstede, 1983). In the following, implications of Hofstede's four dimensions on the firm's international negotiation strategies will be discussed (Rowden, 2001; McGinnis, 2005).

## Masculinity/femininity

Masculine cultures value assertiveness, independence, task orientation and self-achievement. Masculine culture's strategy for negotiation is usually competitive, resulting in a win–lose situation. Conflict is usually resolved by fighting rather than compromising, reflecting an ego-boosting manner. In this situation the person with the most competitive behaviour is likely to gain the most. On the other hand, feminine cultures value cooperation, nurturing, modesty, empathy and social relations, and prefer a collaborative or a compromising style or strategy to assure the best possible mutually accepting solution to obtain a win–win situation.

When negotiating, individuals from masculine countries are more likely to focus on the specifics of the agreement and not show much concern for its overall impact on the other party. Negotiators from feminine cultures are more likely to be concerned with the agreement's aesthetics and longer-range effects; they feel that the details can be worked out later.

## Uncertainty avoidance

This dimension refers to the comfort level of a person in an unclear or risky situation. High uncertainty avoidance cultures have formal bureaucratic negotiation rules, rely on rituals and standards, and trust only family and friends. They require clearly defined structure and guidelines. Low uncertainty avoidance cultures prefer to work informally with flexibility. They disfavour hierarchy, and are likely to seek resolving solutions and compromises rather than the status quo.

Negotiators from high-risk avoidance cultures are likely to seek specific commitments in terms of volume, timing and requirements. Their counterparts from low-uncertainty avoidance cultures are likely to be comfortable with rough estimates of volume and timing and with constantly changing requirements. During the negotiating process, discussions around delays in new product availability, for example, might cause great concern to those high on uncertainty avoidance. On the other hand, it would be regarded as an opportunity to creatively improvise by those who are low on uncertainty avoidance.

## Power distance

This dimension refers to the acceptance of authority differences between those who have power and those affected by power. High power distance is authoritarian, and protocol formality and hierarchy are considered important. In 'high power distance' cultures the CEO of the company is often directly involved in the negotiations and is the final decision maker.

Business negotiations between equals (low power distance) are basically a western concept and are not found in status-oriented societies such as Japan, Korea or Russia. Western Europeans and North Americans are normally informal and downplay status by using first names, dressing in casual attire, etc.

The Japanese dress conservatively – they always prefer dark business suits; to be dressed casually during negotiations with the Japanese would, therefore, be inappropriate. The Japanese do not believe in using first names unless in the very best of personal relationships. In Asia honours, titles and status are extremely important: address your counterparts by their proper titles. Frankness and directness are important in the western world, but are not desirable in Asia.

The valued European handshake is often out of place in Japan, where bowing is customary. When meeting a devout Muslim, never shake with the left hand or utilize the left hand for any purpose – it is considered rude and a personal affront.

When a person from a high masculine culture negotiates with a high power distance culture then conflict will most likely result if neither party makes an effort to understand the cultural balance. Competence is valued over seniority, which yields a consultative management style. Dealings between cultures with low masculinity and low power distance usually result in more cooperative and creative behaviour.

Negotiators from low power distance cultures may be frustrated by the need of negotiators from high power distance cultures to seek approvals from their supervisors. On the other hand, negotiators from high power distance cultures may feel pressured by the pace imposed by those from low power distance cultures. The key here is to understand the power distance mindset of the people that you are negotiating with. That understanding is the first step toward closing the deal and setting realistic expectations for the relationship that follows.

## Individualism/collectivism

Individualistic cultures tend to put tasks before relationships and value independence highly. These cultures tolerate open conflict and place the needs of the individual over the needs of a group, community or society. In negotiations the individualistic society expects the other party to have the authority to make decisions unilaterally. In a highly individualist country such as the United States it is considered socially acceptable to pursue one's own ends without understanding the benefits for others. In contrast managers from a collectivistic culture, such as China, will seek a stable relationship with a long-term orientation, stressing above all the establishment of a personal relationship. A collectivistic society values solidarity, loyalty and strong interdependence among individuals, and the members define themselves in terms of their membership within groups. Collectivist managers assume that details in the negotiation process can be worked out and show more concern for the needs of the other party by focusing on group goals. Members of collectivist societies are irritated when members from individualistic societies promote their own positions and ideas during negotiations.

On the other hand, negotiators from individualistic societies are more likely to focus on the short term, make extreme offers and view negotiations from a competitive perspective. A critical factor in such negotiations is for each party to understand the other's main interests rather than just focusing solely on its own.

### Different organizational models

The British model of organization seems to be that of a village market with no decisive hierarchy, flexible rules and a resolution of problems by negotiating. The German model is more like a well-oiled machine. The exercise of personal command is largely unnecessary because the rules settle everything. The French model is more of a pyramidal hierarchy held together by a united command issuing strong rules. If we look at international buyer–seller relations, the national culture is only one level in the cultural hierarchy that will influence the behaviour of the individual buyer or seller. When members of different cultures come together to communicate, whether within the sales organization or in buyer–seller encounters, they typically do not bring the same shared values, thought patterns and actions to the situation. Common ground is typically limited. This increases the degree of uncertainty about the outcome of the interaction and can limit the efficiency and effectiveness of communication. To reduce uncertainty communicators must accurately predict how others will behave and be able to explain the behaviours of others (Bush and Ingram, 2001).

## The gap model in international negotiation

In negotiation situations the most fundamental gap influencing the interaction between buyer and seller is the difference between their respective cultural backgrounds (gap 1 in Figure 13.2). This cultural distance can be expressed in terms of differences in communication and negotiation behaviour, the concepts of time, space or work patterns, and the nature of social rituals and norms (Madsen, 1994). The cultural distance between two partners tends to increase the transaction costs, which may be quite high in cross-cultural negotiations.

Cultural influence on persons, and thereby international negotiations, can be analysed at various levels of society. Furthermore there is a learning 'effect' in the way that a person's cultural identity formed in one specific cultural setting will affect how they view other situations in other cultural settings. Both seller and buyer are influenced by (at least) the national and organizational culture they belong to. As seen in Chapter 6 (Figure 6.2) there are probably more levels in the understanding of individual negotiation behaviour.

The level of adaptation that is necessary is dependent on how culturally similar the seller and buyer are in the first place. However, the cultural differences between buyer and seller are likely to be less than the cultural differences between their two nations, as, to a certain extent, they will share a 'business' culture.

### The influence of national culture

The national culture is the macro/societal culture that represents a distinct way of life of a group of citizens in a certain country. This national culture is composed of the norms and values that members hold, as well as their level of, for example economic

Figure 13.2 Gap analysis in a cross-cultural negotiation

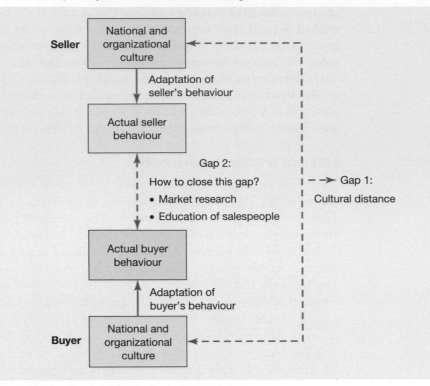

development, education system, national laws and other parts of the regulatory environment (Harvey and Griffith, 2002). All these factors play an important role in socializing individuals in a specific pattern of belief (Andersen, 2003). Therefore it is typical that when individuals encounter cultural differences in their international interactions/ relationships, they tend to view people from different national cultures as strangers, that is unknown people who belong to different groups. This feeling of distance can directly impact upon trust and personal bonding, which increases the probability of conflict between seller and buyer in the negotiation process. The discussion earlier of the four dimensions of Hofstede's research gives several examples of differences in national culture and how they may affect intercultural negotiations between two partners.

## The influence of organizational culture

Organizational culture is the pattern of shared behaviour, values and beliefs that provides a foundation for understanding the organizational functioning processes (Schein, 1985). When two or more organizations are negotiating with each other the relative level of consistency of core elements between organizational cultures can directly influence the effectiveness of communication and negotiation.

The overall complexity of a firm's communication environment will vary tremendously when elements of national culture and organizational culture are examined. In instances where a high level of national culture distance exists between buyer and seller and the organizational cultures are inconsistent (i.e. high inter-organizational distance), then the negotiation environment will be highly complex, necessitating careful planning and monitoring of the firm's intercultural negotiation strategies. Alternatively, when the national cultural distance is low and the cultures of buyer's and seller's organizations are consistent, both partners will find it easier to employ effective negotiation strategies without too much adaptation (Griffith, 2002).

In the case of a certain national and organizational cultural 'distance' between buyer and seller, both the buyer and especially the seller will try to adapt their own behaviour in such a way that they think is acceptable to the other party. In this way the initial gap 1 may be reduced to gap 2, through adaptation of behaviour. To what extent the seller can adjust his behaviour to another culture's communication style is a function of their skills and experience. The necessary skills include the ability to handle stress, initiate conversation and establish a meaningful relationship.

But neither the seller nor the buyer obtains full understanding of the other party's culture, so the final result will often still be a difference between the cultural behaviour of the seller and the buyer (gap 2). This gap can create friction in the negotiation and exchange process and hence give rise to transaction costs.

Gap 2 can be reduced through market research and the education of salespeople (see next section). However, salespeople bring different 'baggage' with them in the form of attitudes and skills that result in different stages of intercultural awareness. The different stages of intercultural prepareness are highlighted in the next section. For example, if a trainer chooses to give a basic cultural awareness exercise to salespeople who are already at the acceptance stage and willing to learn about behaviour strategies, then they are likely to be bored and not see the value of some types of diversity training.

Furthermore, face-to-face communication skills remain an important topic in international sales training. This is especially true in consultative selling, where questioning and listening skills are essential in the global marketing context. However, learning about cultural diversity through training programmes should help salespeople and marketing executives be better prepared to predict the behaviours they encounter with diverse customers or coworkers. Yet many salespeople are sceptical of training and question its value. In fact employees may view diversity training as simply a current 'fad' or the 'politically correct thing to do'. However, if not prepared many salespeople may not realize the impact of cultural diversity until they encounter an unfamiliar cultural situation.

---

**Exhibit 13.2    Euro Disney becomes Disneyland Resort Paris – Disney learns to adapt to European cultures**

The Walt Disney Company began scouting locations for a European theme park in the mid-1980s, with France and Spain emerging as the strongest possibilities. The city of Marne-la-Vallée (about 20 miles east of Paris) eventually won the battle for the new mouse house, and in 1987 Disney created subsidiary Euro Disney. It broke ground on the $4.4 billion project the next year, and in 1989 Euro Disney went public (Walt Disney retained a 49 per cent stake).

In preparing the opening of Euro Disney in 1992, Euro Disney's first chairman proudly announced that his company would 'help change Europe's chemistry'.

However, some cross-cultural blunders occurred:

- Prior to opening the park, Disney insisted employees comply with a detailed written code

Source: Copyright © Disney. Euro Disney Associés, S.C.A.

regarding clothing, jewellery, and other aspects of personal appearance. Women were expected to wear 'appropriate undergarments' and keep their fingernails short. Disney defended its move, noting that similar codes were used in its other parks. The goal was to ensure that guests received the kind of experience

Exhibit 13.2 continued

associated with the Disney name. Despite such statements the French considered the code to be an insult to French culture, individualism and privacy.

- The extension of Disney's standard 'no alcohol' policy from the United States meant that wine was not available at Euro Disney. This, too, was deemed inappropriate in a country renowned for its production and consumption of wine.

It took a series of adaptations, such as renaming the park 'Disneyland Resort Paris' and the addition of some special attractions, to make the park profitable as of 1996.

Euro Disney owns and operates the Disneyland Resort Paris theme park, Europe's top tourist attraction. Attendance at the Disneyland Resort Paris has surpassed the Eiffel Tower as Europe's No. 1 tourist destination with more than 12 million visits per year.

In the fiscal year 2006, Disneyland Paris drew about 12.8 million visitors: 40 per cent were from France, with 15 per cent from Belgium, Luxembourg and the Netherlands, 20 per cent from the United Kingdom, 9 per cent from Spain and 5 per cent from Germany.

For the year 2006 Disneyland Resort Paris reported revenues of €1,087.7 million with consolidated net losses of €89 million. Of the total revenues 53.2 per cent came from the theme parks, 37.9 per cent came from the hotels and Disney Village, and the remaining 8.9 per cent came from real estate and other things.

Disneyland Resort Paris features some 50 rides and attractions, more than 60 restaurants, 54 shops, and plenty of live entertainment. The company also runs seven hotels, two convention centres, and the Disney Village entertainment complex that links the park to the on-site hotels. Its newest park, Walt Disney Studios Park, opened in 2002. Euro Disney pays royalty and management fees to Walt Disney.

Euro Disney restructured its debt in early 2005 and is renewing its focus on sales and marketing efforts. It is also planning a wide variety of upgrades to its hotels and rides: it revamped Space Mountain roller coaster in late 2005 to reopen as Space Mountain; Mission 2 and the Toy Story 2-themed ride Buzz Lightyear Laser Blast were inaugurated in 2006.

In 2007, Disneyland Resort Paris will mark its 15th anniversary with an exceptional celebration. Guests will enjoy *Le Chateau de la Belle au Bois Dormant*, which will be specially decorated for the event. And Disney stories will come to life in new ways with special character experiences and new attractions and shows. In 2008, the Twilight Zone Tower of Terror will open at the Walt Disney Studios Park. But first, in 2007, two exciting attractions are debuting in the new land called Toon Studio at the Walt Disney Studios Park. They are:

- **Crush's Coaster** – Guests step through the soundstage set of Sydney Harbour, from the hit Disney/Pixar film 'Finding Nemo', and into an adventure onboard a spinning turtle shell, surfing the East Australian Current.
- **Cars Quatre Roues Rallye** – Guests take a spin through the desert landscape on a wild, figure-8 racecourse. It's a rigorous test drive for the guests and their rookie cars, but on hand with racing tips and encouragement are the stars of the hit Disney/Pixar film 'Cars' – Lightning McQueen and Mater – cheering from the sidelines over the roar of the engines.

Over the years the company has learned to cater more to European tastes, for example, by serving such foods and beverages as sausage and wine. Also on Disney Studios' virtual tour guides are European actors.

Sources: Tagliabue, J., 2000; Della Cava, M.R., 1999, www.eurodisney.com, Hoovers Company Records: Euro Disney S.C.A, December 2006.

One of the main problems frequently encountered in providing salespeople with meaningful educational experience that includes cultural diversity (distance) is the inability routinely to provide on-location experiential learning opportunities. This is due to lack of time and resources. Although desirable, in many instances one cannot beforehand take the salesperson to the culture to analyse and learn from their reactions. A viable alternative to this dilemma is to expose trainees to a simulated culturally diverse experience. The advantages of this approach are that it is more efficient and requires the active involvement of individuals resulting in experiential learning. Simulations based on role-plays and result-oriented learning have been very successful in teaching salespeople and managers (Bush and Ingram, 2001).

## Negotiating strategies

Basic to negotiating is, of course, knowing your own strengths and weaknesses, but also knowing as much as possible about the other side, understanding the other's way of thinking and recognizing their perspective. Even starting from a position of weakness there are strategies that a salesperson can pursue to turn the negotiation to their advantage.

## 13.3 Intercultural preparation

Many salespeople may be aware that cultural diversity is an important issue in their work environment. However, as evidenced by many stories of cultural 'blunders' (see the example in Exhibit 13.2) salespeople may not realize the impact of diversity on their ability to predict behaviour in a selling situation. Thus individuals may progress through a kind of self-revelation about their own perceived skills and how these skills impact on their interactions with coworkers or buyers of culturally diverse backgrounds. Participating in such an experimental exercise can help sales and marketing personnel begin to understand the impact of cultural diversity in different ways.

### General intercultural preparation

The following five-step approach is proposed to help firms with preparing their salespeople for coping with cultural diversities when entering different international markets (Bush and Ingram, 2001):

1 Build awareness about how cultural differences impact upon them in the sales organization.
2 Motivate salespeople and managers to 'rethink' their behaviour and attitude towards customers.
3 Allow salespeople to examine their own biases in a psychologically safe environment.
4 Examine how stereotypes are developed, and how they can create misunderstandings between buyers and sellers.
5 Identify diversity issues that need to be addressed in the international sales organization.

This simulation may be perceived as a valuable starting point for learning about communication styles and cultural differences. Most firms realize that cultural diversity training requires much more time than expected. One of the difficulties in educating individuals about communicating between cultures or subcultures is that individuals can not be handled in only a two-hour session. Respecting and successfully interacting with members of diverse cultures is a long-term process. By participating in a long-term exercise salespeople may begin to realize that the concept of diversity goes beyond 'the right thing to do' or satisfying affirmative action requirements. Valuing diversity can also impact the bottom line of an organization.

### Specific evaluation of partner's intercultural communication and negotiation competences

To address the issues involved with the fit and reduction of 'gaps' in negotiation processes a firm must be proactive and develop specific strategies to enhance communication effectiveness. Most organizations have not formalized their management of cross-cultural communication but at least three steps are necessary in order to improve the selling firm's cross-cultural communication and negotiation competences:

1   *Assessing communication competences of salespersons:* Given the importance of a salesperson's communication competences for relationship success, it is critical that selling firms assess these persons' competences. Once the technical level (e.g. technical and standard language competences) is assessed the firm could use the above-mentioned simulation and experiential methods to gauge behavioural competences.

2   *Assessing communication competences of negotiators in the buying firm:* If possible the same procedure as in (1) above should be done for the buyers in the foreign culture. However, it might be difficult to get this information about the negotiators in the buying firm.

3   *Matching communication and negotiation competences of buying and selling firm:* Only if there is a match (and not too large a 'gap') between the communication competences of the two firms can they realistically expect success in the international negotiation and in the possible future relationship. Of course it should be noted that the selling firm is only able to control its internal competences, and not those of the buying firm.

This issue of communication assessment can also be integrated into the firm's partner selection and retention criteria. As the selling firm begins to integrate these communication competences into its partner selection and retention criteria it is also important that it shows flexibility and willingness to improve the existing competences in relation to its partner (the buying firm).

## 13.4   Coping with expatriates

**Expatriates**
Employees sent out from the HQ to work for the company in the foreign markets, often in its subsidiaries.

The following discussion can be applied not only to expatriate salespeople but also to other jobs in the firm based in a foreign country (e.g. an administrative position in a foreign subsidiary). Expatriate salespeople negotiating in foreign cultures often experience a culture shock when confronted with a buyer. Culture shock is more intensely experienced by expatriates whose cultures are most different from the ones in which they are now working. What can the management of the international firm do to minimize the risk of culture shock? The following areas should be considered (Guy and Patton, 1996).

### The decision to employ an expatriate salesperson

The first major decision to make is whether the use of home country expatriates is the best choice for entering and serving foreign markets. The firm should first examine its own past experience with culture shock and sales rep adjustment in other cultures. Inexperienced firms would probably be best advised to evaluate possible agents and distributors rather than using home country expatriates. Other options for firms with their own sales force are host country or third country nationals (see also section 12.7).

The firm should try to identify the elements in the expatriate sales job that suggest potential problems with culture shock. If the job is highly technical, is located in an area with other home country nationals, and involves similar tastes and lifestyles as in the home country, then the expatriate sales force may be appropriate.

If, however, the job places the expatriate salesperson in an unfamiliar job with conflicting expectations, the firm should consider other options. The chances of greater culture shock and adjustment problems increase with greater cultural distance. The greater the high context/low context contrast, the greater is the chance of difficulty. When entering a different culture many familiar symbols and cues are missing. The removal of these everyday reassurances can lead to feelings of frustration, stress and anxiety.

## Selection of expatriates

Since being an expatriate salesperson is a critical task the selection process should be given considerable thought and should not be decided too quickly. The selection should not be based primarily on the technical competence of the salesperson. Substantial emphasis must also be placed on the following attributes:

● foreign-language skills;
● general relational abilities;
● emotional stability;
● educational background;
● past experience with the designated culture;
● ability to deal with stress.

Previous research (Guy and Patton, 1996) suggests that the following characteristics of the expatriate are associated with a lower level of cultural shock:

● open-mindedness;
● empathy;
● cultural sensitivity;
● resilience;
● low ego identity.

An assessment of the potential expatriate alone is not sufficient if the person has a family that will be making the move as well. Family issues that must be considered include marital stability, the overall emotional stability of family members, and family cohesiveness. In-depth interviews with at least the rep's spouse and preferably other family members as well can be very useful in determining the status of these variables.

## Training

Selecting the most appropriate training programme for each expatriate requires methods for classifying people into various levels of intercultural skills. Each level needs a different training programme. The initial requirement is to train the expatriate, and any accompanying family member, to know the main sociocultural, economic, political, legal and technological factors in the assigned country.

The training activities may include the following:

● area/country description;
● cultural assimilation training;
● role playing;
● handling critical incidents;
● case studies;
● stress reduction training;
● field experience;
● extensive language training.

Obviously many firms will not be able to provide all the training needed in-house or through a single source, but they may need to coordinate a variety of methods and external programmes for their expatriates to take place before and during the foreign assignment.

## Support

It is very important to provide a solid support network from the head office so that the expatriate is not simply left alone to 'sink or swim'. Support during expatriate assignment may include a number of elements:

- Adequate monetary compensation or other benefits.
- Constant communication from the home base regarding ongoing operations at head office and in the assigned country/area.
- Providing opportunities for periodic travel to the home country to maintain contacts and relationships within the firm. The home base could also send copies of forthcoming job postings in which the expatriate may be interested.

The expatriate should identify and contact individuals in the host country who can become a part of the expatriate's social network. It is also important that the expatriate's spouse and family are included in a social support network.

## Repatriation

Companies employing expatriates should develop an integrated career plan, identifying likely subsequent job positions and career progression. If the expatriates, during their careers, are exposed to a series of international assignments, each assignment should be selected to develop their awareness of different cultures. For example, for a UK company the first non-UK assignment would be a culturally similar or proximate country, say Germany or the United States, the next assignment might be South Africa or Australia, the next Hong Kong, then Japan and so on. In this way cultural shock is minimized, since the process encourages the ability to manage situations in more and more distant cultures.

The return of the expatriate to the home country is sometimes difficult. Lack of job guarantees is one of the most critical challenges faced by expatriates. Some months prior to return an internal position search should be started with a home visit arranged for the expatriate to meet with appropriate managers. An internal sponsor in the head office should be appointed to maintain ongoing contact and to help the expatriate secure a desirable position upon return.

Sometimes expatriated families also experience a culture shock upon returning to the home country. Therefore some support is needed during repatriation. This includes spouse job-finding assistance and time to readjust before going back to work.

## 13.5  Knowledge management and learning across borders

Managing global knowledge that crosses the lines between business units, subsidiaries and departments that are dispersed geographically across continents is highly complex and requires consideration of different issues and factors. The global strategy exploits the knowledge of the parent organization (headquarters) through worldwide diffusion and adaptation. The global strategy strives to achieve the slogan, 'think globally but act

Figure 13.3 'Bottom-up' learning in global marketing

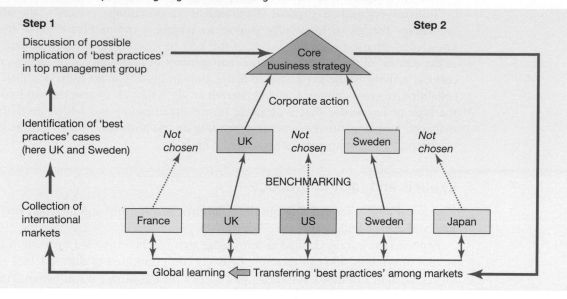

locally', through dynamic interdependence between the headquarters and the subsidiaries. Organizations following such a strategy coordinate efforts, ensuring local flexibility while exploiting the benefits of global integration and efficiencies, as well as ensuring worldwide diffusion of innovation (Desouza and Evaristo, 2003).

A key element in knowledge management is the continuous learning from experience (Stewart, 2001). In practical terms the aim of knowledge management, as a learning-focused activity across borders, is to keep track of valuable capabilities used in one market that could be used elsewhere (in other geographic markets), so that firms can continually update their knowledge without 'reinventing the wheel'. See also the example in Figure 13.3 for a systematic approach to global learning from transferring 'best practices' in the firm's different international markets.

The steps in transferring the firm's 'best practices' to other international markets are as follows:

1 By benchmarking (comparing) the different procedures in the firm's international markets the firm should be able to pick up best practices – in Figure 13.3 the best practices are found in the United Kingdom and Sweden. Subsequently, the possible implications of the 'best practices' are discussed in the 'top management' group.
2 After the procedures for diffusion of the 'best practices' have been established in the top management group the next step is to see if these 'best practices' can be used elsewhere in the firm's international markets. In order to disseminate global knowledge and 'best practices', meetings (with representatives from all international markets) and global project groups should be established. If done successfully the benchmarking could result in a global learning process, where the different international marketing managers would select the most usable elements from the presented 'best practices' and adapt these in the local markets.

However, as noted earlier in this chapter, knowledge developed and used in one cultural context is not easily transferred to another. The lack of personal relationships, the absence of trust and 'cultural distance' all conspire to create resistance, frictions and misunderstandings in cross-cultural knowledge management (Bell *et al.*, 2002).

With globalization becoming a centrepiece in the business strategy of many firms – be it firms engaged in product development or providing services – the ability to manage the 'global knowledge engine' to achieve a competitive edge in today's knowledge-intensive economy is one of the keys to sustainable competitiveness. But in the context of global marketing the management of knowledge is *de facto* a cross-cultural activity, whose key task is to foster and continually make more sophisticated collaborative cross-cultural learning (Berrell *et al.*, 2002). Of course the kind and/or the type of knowledge that is strategic for an organization and which needs to be managed for competitiveness varies depending on the business context and the value of different types of knowledge associated with it.

## Explicit and tacit knowledge

New knowledge is created through the synergistic relationship and interplay between *tacit* and *explicit* knowledge.

*Explicit knowledge* is defined as knowledge that can be expressed formally using a system of symbols, and can therefore be easily communicated or diffused. It is either object based or rule based. It is object based when the knowledge is codified in symbols (e.g. words, numbers, formulas) or in physical objects (e.g. equipment, documents, models). Object-based knowledge may be found in examples such as product specifications, patents, software codes, computer databases, technical drawings, etc. Explicit knowledge is rule based when the knowledge is codified into rules, routines, or standard operating procedures (Choo, 1998).

*Tacit knowledge* is the implicit knowledge used by organizational members to perform their work and to make sense of the world. It is knowledge that is uncodified and difficult to diffuse across borders and subsidiaries. It is hard to verbalize because it is expressed through action-based skills and cannot be reduced to rules and recipes. Instead tacit knowledge is learned through extended periods of experiencing and doing a task, during which the individual develops a feel for and a capacity to make intuitive judgements about the successful execution of the activity. Tacit knowledge is vital to an organization because organizations can only learn and innovate by somehow levering on the implicit knowledge of its members. Tacit knowledge becomes substantially valuable when it is turned into new capabilities, products, services or even new markets for the firm. Organizational knowledge creation is a process that organizationally amplifies the knowledge created by individuals in different countries and subsidiaries and crystallizes it as a part of the international knowledge network of the company. There are two sets of dynamics that drive the process of international knowledge amplification (Nonaka and Takeuchi, 1995):

1 converting tacit knowledge into explicit knowledge;
2 moving knowledge from the individual level to the group, organizational and inter-organizational levels (across subsidiaries in different countries).

A central issue in internationalized firms concerns where knowledge is created and diffused. Because of the capabilities in creating knowledge centres of excellence may be formed in certain subsidiaries, for example, regarding specific functions such as product development or international marketing.

## Global project groups

Today's business with its growing emphasis on globalization increasingly requires people to collaborate in workgroups that cross cultural and geographic boundaries. The trend to multicultural workgroups emerged as a reaction to changed economic conditions, forcing organizations to develop new structures in order to minimize costs and maximize flexibility. One consequence of these changes is that as a result of rapid knowledge growth and increasingly complex work environments more and more tasks can only be accomplished in international project groups by cooperation of functionally and culturally different experts. Based on the assumption of diversity creating value and therefore competitive advantage by bringing together different ideas and pooling knowledge, multicultural project groups have become a prevailing tendency in multinational organizations. However, the use of such groups in practice often turns out to be a lot more problematic than expected. It seems that the cognitive advantages which can be gained by a diverse workforce are counterbalanced by relational problems such as miscommunication and distrust, and therefore high turn-over rates (Wolf, 2002). Nevertheless, with today's economy facing an ever increasing need to cross all kinds of borders, the existence of culturally diverse project groups has become inevitable.

Given the communication problems and trust issues that plague ad hoc global project groups, structuring the project team is particularly critical to success. The following three questions need attention from the top management of the firm (Govindarajan and Gupta, 2001):

1   *Is the objective clearly defined?* One of the first concerns for any global project team must be explicitly to discuss the group's agenda and ensure that the objective/ problem is defined clearly and correctly. Many project groups do not fully resolve and discuss the issues involved and they immediately run into problems. Different framing of the same problem can produce different outcomes. Because the project group typically has members from different subsidiaries that usually compete with one another for scarce corporate resources they tend to have a high degree of internal conflict, combined with a low level of trust. As a result it is generally best to frame the problem of the project group in terms of the company's position vis-à-vis the external marketplace instead of emphasizing internal issues. An external focus encourages benchmarking, fosters creativity and provides a compelling rationale for making the tough decisions inherent in any manufacturing rationalization and workforce reduction. Given the possible communication problems in the global project group it is imperative that the members understand the agenda of the project group: the scope of the project, the expected deliverables and the timeline. Cultural and language differences may complicate the task of getting group members to agree on the agenda and the problems to be solved. Clarity is essential to promoting commitment and accountability.

2   *Choosing group members*: Another key to creating a successful global team is choosing the right group members. Two issues are of particular importance: how do you balance diversity within the team and what should be the size of the group? Normally we will see high levels of diversity. Why? First, members come from diverse cultural and national backgrounds – this refers to so-called *behavioural diversity*. Second, members generally represent subsidiaries whose agenda may not be congruent. Third, because members often represent different functional units and departments, their priorities and perspectives may differ. The last two issues refer to so-called *cognitive diversity*.

    *Let us take a closer look at an example of behavioural diversity*: consider, for example, a cross-border project group in a Swedish–Chinese joint venture. The norm in most Chinese teams is that the most senior member presents the team's perspective, but in a Swedish team the most junior member typically does so. Unless the members of the team are sensitized to such differences misunderstandings can easily emerge and block communication. So behavioural diversity is best regarded as a necessary evil: something that no global project group can avoid but the effects of which the group must attempt to minimize through training in cultural sensitivity.

*Let us also take a closer look at an example of cognitive diversity*: this diversity refers to differences in the substantive content of how members perceive the group's challenges and opportunities. Differences in functional backgrounds can account for substantive cognitive differences on issues of 'market pull' (preferred by people in marketing departments) and 'technology push' (preferred by people in engineering departments). Because no single member can ever have a monopoly on wisdom cognitive diversity is almost always a source of strength. Divergent perspectives foster creativity and a more comprehensive search for and assessment of options. But the group must be able to integrate the perspectives and come to a single solution.

3  *Selection of team leadership*: structuring the leadership of a global project team involves critical decisions around three roles: the *project leader*, the *external coach* and *the internal sponsor*. The *project leader* plays a pivotal role in cross-border project groups. They must contribute to the development of trust between the members and maybe have the biggest stake in the outcome of the project. They must possess conflict-resolution and integration skills; and expertise in process management, including diagnosing problems, assessing situations and generating and evaluating options. An *external coach* serves as an ad hoc member of the project group and is an expert in process more than content. The need for such a coach is likely to be high when the process-management skills of the best available project leader are inadequate. This might happen if the appointed leader has some major stake in the project's outcome, for example if a cross-border task force has to rationalize and decrease the number of subsidiaries around the world by 30 per cent. The *internal sponsor* of a global project group is typically a senior level executive with a strong interest in the success of the team. Among the responsibilities of the sponsor are to provide ongoing guidelines and to facilitate access to resources.

At any given time a global company will typically have many project groups working on different cross-border coordination issues. Therefore it makes sense for the company to undertake initiatives to create interpersonal familiarity and trust among key managers of different subsidiaries. For example, Unilever uses several approaches to do this – such as bringing together managers from different subsidiaries in executive development education programmes.

**Bribery**
Involving a company from an industrialized country offering an illicit payment to a developing country's public official with perceived or real influence over contract awards. Bribery may range from gifts to large amounts of money.

When a project group consists of members with distinct knowledge and skills drawn from different subsidiaries in different countries the potential for cognitive diversity is high, and this can also be a source of competitive strength. But intellectual diversity will almost always bring with it some degree of interpersonal incompatibility and communication difficulty. Process mechanisms that recognize and anticipate such pitfalls – and integrate the best of individuals' ideas and contributions – are needed to help the project group reconcile diverse perspectives and arrive at better, more creative and novel solutions.

## 13.6  Transnational bribery in cross-cultural negotiations

On first consideration bribery is both unethical and illegal. But a closer look reveals that bribery is not really a straightforward issue. The ethical and legal problems associated with bribery can be quite complex. Thus the definition of bribery can range from the relatively innocuous payment of a few pounds to a minor official or business manager in order to expedite the processing of papers or the loading of a truck, to the extreme of paying millions of pounds to a head of state to guarantee a company preferential treatment. Scott *et al.* (2002) generally define bribery as 'involving a company from an industrialized country offering an illicit payment to a developing country's public official with perceived or real influence over contract awards' (p. 2).

The difference between lubrication and bribery must be established. Lubrication payments accompany requests for a person to do a job more rapidly or more efficiently. They involve a relatively small cash sum, gift or service made to a low-ranking official in a country where such offerings are not prohibited by law, the purpose being to facilitate or expedite the normal, lawful performance of a duty by that official. This practice is common in many countries. Bribery, on the other hand, generally involves large sums of money, which are frequently not properly accounted for, and is designed to entice an official to commit an illegal act on behalf of the one paying the bribe.

Another type of payment that can appear to be a bribe, but may not be, is an agent's fee. When a businessperson is uncertain of a country's rules and regulations an agent may be hired to represent the company in that country. This person will do a more efficient and thorough job than someone unfamiliar with country-specific procedures.

There are many intermediaries (attorneys, agents, distributors and so forth) who function simply as channels for illegal payments. The process is further complicated by legal codes that vary from country to country: what is illegal in one country is winked at in another and legal in a third. In some countries illegal payments can become a major business expense. Hong Kong companies report that bribes account for about 5 per cent of the cost of doing business in China. In Russia the cost is 15–20 per cent, and in Indonesia as high as 30 per cent (Gesteland, 1996, p. 93).

The answer to the question of bribery is not an unqualified one. It is easy to generalize about the ethics of political pay-offs and other types of payment; it is much more difficult to make the decision to withhold payment of money when not making the payment may affect the company's ability to do business profitably or at all. With the variety of ethical standards and levels of morality which exist in different cultures the dilemma of ethics and pragmatism that faces international business cannot be resolved until more countries decide to deal effectively with the issue.

---

**Exhibit 13.3    Does bribery also cover sexual favours? The case of Lockheed Martin and a South Korean defence contract**

A US court has ruled that arms maker Lockheed Martin can be sued for allegedly using sexual favours and bribes to win a South Korean defence contract. Lockheed Martin has denied the allegations.

The case was filed by the Korea Supply Company (KSC) after it lost a contract to Lockheed subsidiary Loral for the supply of an aircraft radar system to South Korea in 1996.

KSC's lawsuit claims a Loral employee, Linda Kim – a former model and singer – bribed South Korean military officers and offered sexual favours to the country's defence minister, Lee Yang Ho. He has admitted to having an 'inappropriate relationship' with Ms Kim but denies it influenced his decision making. Ms Kim's love letters to the defence minister made headline news in South Korea after they were implicated in another bribery scandal.

The US Foreign Corrupt Practises Act forbids US companies from bribing foreign officials to influence an official act or decision.

Source: adapted from BBC News, 'Lockheed sex suit to go ahead', 3 May 2003, news.bbc.co.uk/go/pr/fr/-/2/hi/business/2,820,939.stm.

## 13.7   Summary

When marketing internationally negotiation skills are needed. Negotiation skills and personal selling skills are related. Personal selling typically occurs at the field sales force level and during formal negotiation processes. Cultural factors are critical to understanding the negotiation style of foreigners.

The negotiation process is significantly influenced by the cultures within which the negotiators (typically a buyer and a seller) have been socialized and educated. Cultural differences prevalent in the international sales negotiation process can have a tremendous impact upon the process itself as well as its outcome.

The cross-cultural negotiation process can be divided into two different parts: namely, the *non-task related interaction* and *task related interaction*. The *non-task related* aspects of the sales negotiation process (status distinction, impression formation accuracy and interpersonal attractiveness) are considered first as it is these factors that are more relevant when approaching the buyer. Once a contact has successfully been established, the *task related* aspects of the sales negotiation process (exchange of information, persuasion and bargaining strategies and concession making and agreement).

Prior to the negotiation process between two partners there is a cultural distance between them. This cultural distance causes some transaction costs, which may be quite high. To reduce the cultural distance training of the negotiators is required.

The culture shock felt by expatriates indicates that sending negotiators and salespeople to foreign markets is often difficult and complex to implement successfully. Five important areas of implementation include: (1) making the initial decision to employ an expatriate sales force, (2) identifying and selecting qualified candidates, (3) providing adequate training, (4) maintaining ongoing support and (5) achieving satisfactory repatriation.

In global knowledge management a key element is the continuous learning from experiences in different markets. In practical terms, the aim of knowledge management as a learning-focused activity across borders is to keep track of valuable capabilities used in one market that could be used elsewhere (in other geographic markets), so that firms can continually update their knowledge without 'reinventing the wheel'.

The ethical question of what is right or appropriate poses many dilemmas for international marketers. Bribery is an issue that is defined very differently from country to country. What is acceptable in one country may be completely unacceptable in another.

---

**CASE STUDY 13.1**

## Mecca Cola: Marketing of a 'Muslim' cola to the European market

Until now the cola war has mainly been going on in North America and Europe. But a French Tunisian, in January 2003, opened up a second front – by producing a carbonated drink named Mecca Cola, a new soft drink designed to cash in on anti-US sentiment, mainly in European markets. The new drink will be marketed in bottles of 1.5 litres and 330 ml cans.

### Mecca Cola – a political choice

The new brand, which has a striking resemblance to Coca-Cola, is specifically intended to make a political statement. Its French label and advertising slogan translates as 'No more drinking stupid – Drink with commitment'.

The creator of Mecca Cola, prominent French political activist Taoufiq Mathlouthi, claims the

Welcome to the world of Mecca Cola

Mecca Cola World Company
PO BOX 18 687 - Jebel Ali FZ - Dubai
Tel : + 971 488 733 88

## Zam Zam Cola

It is not the first time Coca-Cola has been the target of a 'buy Muslim' challenge. Zam Zam Cola, an Iranian drink named after a holy spring in Mecca, has won an enthusiastic reception in Saudi Arabia and Bahrain.

US companies such as McDonald's, Starbucks, Nike and the two cola giants admit the campaign is wounding them. Sales of Coca-Cola have dropped between 20 and 40 per cent in some countries. In Morocco, a government official estimates sales of Pepsi and Coca-Cola could fall by half in the north, which is a stronghold of Islamic groups. In the United Arab Emirates, sales of the local Star Cola are up by 40 per cent over the past three months.

Zam Zam, which also produces non-alcoholic 'Islamic beer', has a long pedigree in Iran, where it was founded in 1954 and today has 47 per cent of the domestic market. For many years it was the Iranian partner of Pepsi Cola until their contract was ended after the 1979 revolution.

A Saudi firm owned by one of the kingdom's princes, Turki Abdallah al-Faisal, in January 2003 signed an agreement with the Zam Zam Group, giving the Saudi company exclusive distribution rights in Saudi Arabia, Egypt and a number of other Arab countries.

Zam Zam was taken over by the Foundation of the Dispossessed, a powerful state charity run by clerics, and today it employs more than 7,000 people in its 17 factories in Iran. It is now planning to build factories in the Persian Gulf.

Its cola is already exported to Saudi Arabia, Bahrain, Qatar, the United Arab Emirates, Oman, Kuwait, Afghanistan and Iraq, and the company says it will soon ship its drinks to Lebanon, Syria and Denmark – its first European client.

## The marketing and internationalization of Mecca Cola

Other firms in the Middle East have tried creating different cola drinks, but none has turned its drink into a political weapon. The first businesses to sell Mecca Cola were what Mr Mathlouthi described as 'small ethnic shops in Muslim areas'. Now the drink can be found on the shelves of large cash and carry supermarkets in France, Belgium and Germany. The

drink is not competition for Coke and that his campaign is not anti-American. Instead, he says, each bottle sold is a protest against the Bush administration's foreign policy. Mathlouthi promises that 10 per cent of profits will go to Palestinian causes, humanitarian aid for Palestinian children, education and preserving their heritage. Mathlouthi hopes to make Mecca Cola the soft drink of choice for anti-globalists everywhere and thus push out that icon of US capitalism Coca-Cola.

Mr Masood Shadjareh, Chairman of the London-based Islamic Human Rights Commission, which is backing calls to shun US brands, predicted huge interest in the new cola. He told the *Guardian*: 'The Muslim community is targeting Coca-Cola because people feel that the only thing they can do is hit America economically. It is not only an issue for someone like me who is an activist. I bought some fizzy drinks and my children, who are ten and twelve, found out they were products of Coca-Cola and refused to drink them. I told them I'd already paid for them, but my daughter said "Look Daddy, it just won't go down".'

Meanwhile, some religious fundamentalists object to the use of the name of the Muslim holy city on a soft drink. There is no indication Mecca Cola or any other boycott product will do long-term harm to US multinationals, Coca-Cola and Pepsi-Cola. But some US manufacturers admit the boycott is having an impact on sales. And no one denies how easy it is for consumers to express their politics by simply switching brands. Coca-Cola's comment was: 'Ultimately it is the consumer who will make the decision'. Coca-Cola insists that it is 'not affiliated with any religion or ethnic group' and does not engage in politics.

company behind Mecca Cola says the United Kingdom is also a huge market and already has orders to send about 2 million bottles a month to Britain.

Mecca Cola was originally targeted at France's Muslim community but now several major hypermarket chains in France are stocking the soft drink.

While Coca-Cola's revenues in the Middle East represent less than 2 per cent of its global business, it is galling for Coke to lag behind Pepsi in the region. Britain's 1.8 million Muslims have only recently begun to discover a collective voice and it remains unclear whether a boycott or a 'buy Muslim' campaign will occur.

In Muslim areas of Paris the soft drink is sold for £1.20 per 1.5 litre bottle, approximately the same as its US rival Coke.

### Latest developments

Riding on anti-western anger over issues like Palestine, Iraq, Iran and Afghanistan, and also the Danish Muhammed cartoons (January–February 2006), Mecca Cola has achieved impressive sales in several Muslim countries. Pakistan, Algeria, Yemen, Malaysia and France are Mecca Cola's top markets. In 2006 the demand for Mecca Cola is estimated to be 1.5 million cans per month in the Gulf region alone.

Mecca Cola (with its HQ in the United Arab Emirates) says it will now launch coffee shops under the brand name Mecca Café to provide an alternative to established western outlets in Muslim countries. The first coffee shop is ready to be opened at Dubai Healthcare City. The Dubai opening will be followed by coffee shops in Kuala Lumpur in Malaysia and Pakistan's Islamabad.

Mecca Cola plans to have at least one coffee shop in every Muslim capital. After that it will discuss franchising arrangements with partners for expanding the chain. The company has also launched a new energy drink called 'Mecca Power'. This drink is based purely on halal ingredients (Husain, 2006).

Sources: www.mecca-cola.com; Husain, S. (2006) 'Mecca Cola Rides Anti-West Wave With Café Chain Plan', Gulf News, 22 February.

### Questions

1 What are the main reasons for the success of Mecca Cola?

2 What are the criteria for the successful implementation of Mecca Cola's international marketing strategies?

3 How should Tawfiq Mathlouthi prepare his sales force 'culturally' for selling Mecca Cola to European supermarket chains?

4 Can Tawfiq Mathlouthi repeat the international 'Mecca Cola' success with the new coffee shop chain and new energy drink 'Mecca Power'?

For further exercises and cases, see this book's website at **www.pearsoned.co.uk/hollensen**

 ## Questions for discussion

1 Explain why the negotiation process abroad may differ from country to country.

2 You are a European preparing to negotiate with a Japanese firm for the first time. How would you prepare for the assignment if it is taking place: (a) in the Japanese headquarters; (b) in one of its European subsidiaries?

3 Should expatriate personnel be used? What are some of the difficulties they may encounter overseas? What can be done to minimize these problems?

4 Compare and contrast the negotiating styles of Europeans and Asians. What are the similarities? What are the differences?

5 What are your views on lobbying efforts by foreign firms?

6 Why is it so difficult for an international marketer to deal with bribery?

# References

Andersen, P.H. (2003) 'Relationship marketing in cross-cultural contexts', in Rugimbana, R. and Nwankwo, S. (eds), *Cross-cultural Marketing*, Thomson, London.

Anglemar, R. and Stern, L.W. (1978) 'Development of a content analytical system for analysis of bargaining communication in marketing', *Journal of Marketing Research*, February, pp. 93–102.

Bell, D.B., Giordano, R. and Putz, P. (2002) 'Inter-firm sharing of process knowledge: exploring knowledge markets', *Knowledge and Process Management*, 9(1), pp. 12–22.

Berrell, M., Gloet, M. and Wright, P. (2002) 'Organizational learning in international joint ventures: implications for management development', *Journal of Management Development*, 21(2), pp. 83–100.

Bush, V.D. and Ingram, T. (2001) 'Building and assessing cultural diversity skills: implications for sales training', *Industrial Marketing Management*, 30, pp. 65–76.

Choo, C. (1998) *The Knowing Organization*, Oxford University Press, New York.

Della Cava, R.R. (1999) 'Magic Kingdoms, new colonies: theme parks are staking bigger claims in Europe', *USA Today*, 17 February.

Desouza, K. and Evaristo, R. (2003) 'Global knowledge management strategies', *European Management Journal*, 21(1), pp. 62–67.

Gesteland, R.R. (1996) *Cross-cultural Business Behaviour*, Copenhagen Business School Press, Copenhagen.

Govindarajan, V. and Gupta, A.K. (2001) 'Building an effective global business team', *MIT Sloan Management Review*, Summer, pp. 63–71.

Griffith, D.A. (2002) 'The role of communication competencies in international business relationship development', *Journal of World Business*, 37(4), pp. 256–265.

Guy, B.S. and Patton, P.W.E. (1996) 'Managing the effects of culture shock and sojourner adjustment on the expatriate industrial sales force', *Industrial Marketing Management*, 25, pp. 385–393.

Harvey, M.G. and Griffith, D.A. (2002) 'Developing effective intercultural relationships: the importance of communication strategies', *Thunderbird International Business Review*, 44(4), pp. 455–476.

Harris, P.R. and Moran, R.T. (1987) *Managing Cultural Differences*. 1st edn. Gulf Publishing Company.

Hendon, D.W., Hendon, R.A. and Herbig, P. (1999) *Cross-cultural Negotiations*, Praeger Publishers, Westport, CT.

Hofstede, G. (1983) 'The cultural relativity of organizational practices and theories', *Journal of International Business Studies*, Fall, pp. 75–89.

Madsen, T.K. (1994) 'A contingency approach to export performance research', *Advances in International Marketing*, 6, pp. 25–42.

McGinnis, M.A. (2005) 'Lessons in cross-cultural negotiations', *Supply Chain Management Review*, April, pp. 9–10.

Nonaka, I. and Takeuchi, H. (1995) *The Knowledge Creating Company*, Oxford University Press, New York.

Rowden, R.W. (2001) 'Research note: how a small business enters the international market', *Thunderbird International Business Review*, 43(2), pp. 257–268.

Schein, E.H. (1985) *Organizational culture and leadership*. 1st edn. Jossey-Bass Publishers, San Francisco.

Scott, J., Gilliard, D. and Scott, R. (2002) 'Eliminating bribery as a transnational marketing strategy', *International Journal of Commerce & Management*, 12(1), pp. 1–17.

Simintiras, A.C. and Reynolds, N. (2001) 'Toward an understanding of the role of cross-cultural equivalence in international personal selling', *Journal of Marketing Management*, 16(8), pp. 829–851.

Simintiras, A.C. and Thomas, A.H. (1998) 'Cross-cultural sales negotiations: a literature review and research propositions', *International Marketing Review*, 15(1), pp. 10–28.

Stewart, D. (2001) 'Reinterpreting the learning organization', *The Learning Organization*, 8(4), pp. 141–152.

Tagliabue, J. (2000) 'Lights, action in France for Second Disney Park', *New York Times*, 13 February.

Wolf, J. (2002) 'Multicultural workgroups', *Management International Review*, 42(1), pp. 3–4.

Zhang, M.Y. and Dodgson, M. (2007) 'A roasted duck can still fly away: A case study of technology, nationality, culture and the rapid and early internationalization of the firm', *Journal of World Business*, Vol. 42, pp. 336–349.

# 14

# Organization and control of the global marketing programme

## Contents

## Learning objectives

After studying this chapter you should be able to do the following:

- Examine how firms build their organizational structure internationally and what roles headquarters can play.
- Identify the variables that affect the reorganization design.
- Describe and evaluate functional, geographic, product and matrix organizations as the key international structural alternatives.
- Explain pitfalls and opportunities with 'global account management'.
- Describe the key elements of the marketing control system.
- List the most important measures for marketing performance.
- Explain how a global marketing budget is established.
- Understand the steps in developing the global marketing plan.

## 14.1 Introduction

The overall objective of this chapter is to study intra-organizational relationships as part of the firm's attempt to optimize its competitive response in areas most critical to its business. As market conditions change, and companies evolve from purely domestic entities to multinationals, their organizational structure, coordination and control systems must also change.

First, this chapter will focus on the advantages and disadvantages of the main organizational structures available as well as their appropriateness at various stages of internationalization. Then the chapter will outline the need for a control system to oversee the international operations of the company.

## 14.2 Organization of global marketing activities

The way in which a global marketing organization is structured is an important determinant of its ability to exploit effectively and efficiently the opportunities available to it. It also determines the capacity for responding to problems and challenges. Companies operating internationally must decide whether the organization should be structured along functions, products, geographical areas or combinations of the three (matrix). The evolutionary nature of organizational changes is shown in Figure 14.1. The following pages discuss the different organizational structures.

### Functional structure

**Functional structure**
Here the next level after top management is divided into functional departments, e.g. R&D, sales and marketing, production, and finance.

Of all the approaches, the functional structure (Figure 14.2) is the simplest. Here management is primarily concerned with the functional efficiency of the company.

Many companies begin their international business activities as a result of having received enquiries from abroad. The company, being new to international business, has no international specialist and typically has few products and few markets. In this early stage of international involvement the domestic marketing department may have the responsibility for global marketing activities. But as the international involvement intensifies an export or international department may become part of the organizational structure. The export department may be a subdepartment of the sales and marketing

**Figure 14.1 Structural evolution of international operations**

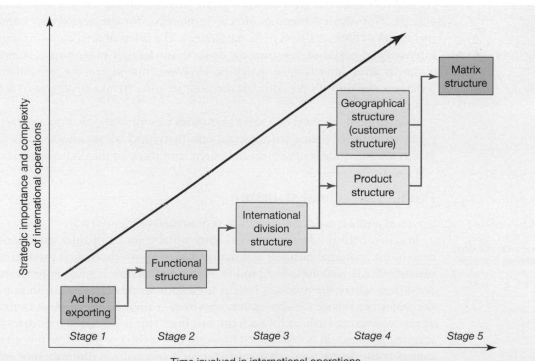

439

Figure 14.2  **Example of the functional structure**

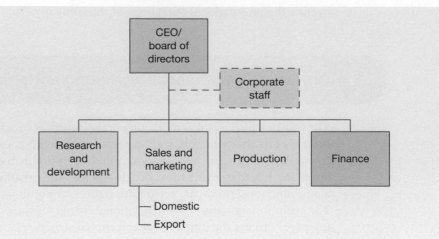

department (as in Figure 14.2) or may have equal ranking with the other functional departments. This choice will depend on the importance assigned to the export activities of the firm. Because the export department is the first real step in internationalizing the organizational structure it should be a fully fledged marketing organization and not merely a sales organization. The functional export department design is particularly suitable for SMEs, as well as larger companies, that are manufacturing standardized products and are in the early stages of developing international business, having low product and area diversities.

## International divisional structure

**International divisional structure**
As international sales grow, at some point the international division may emerge at the same level as the functional departments.

As international sales grow, at some point an international divisional structure may emerge. This division becomes directly responsible for the development and implementation of the overall international strategy. The international division incorporates international expertise, information flows about foreign market opportunities, and authority over international activities. However, manufacturing and other related functions remain with the domestic divisions in order to take advantage of economies of scale.

International divisions best serve firms with new products that do not vary significantly in terms of their environmental sensitivity, and whose international sales and profits are still quite insignificant compared with those of the domestic divisions.

## Product divisional structure

**Product divisional structure**
The next level after top management is divided into product division, e.g. Product A, B, C and D.

A typical product divisional structure is presented in Figure 14.3.

In general, the product structure is more suitable for companies with more experience in international business and marketing, and with diversified product lines and extensive R&D activities. The product division structure is most appropriate under conditions where the products have potential for worldwide standardization. One of the major benefits of the approach is improved cost efficiency through centralization of manufacturing facilities for each product line. This is crucial in industries in which competitive position is determined by world market share, that in turn is often determined by the degree to which manufacturing is rationalized (utilization of economies of scale). The main disadvantages of this type of structure are as follows:

Figure 14.3 **Example of the product structure**

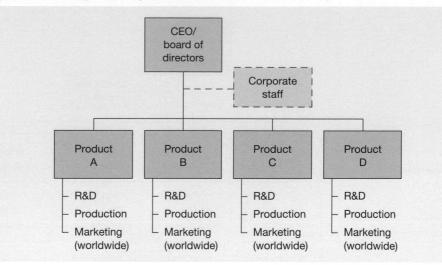

- It duplicates functional resources: you will find R&D, production, marketing, sales force management, etc. in each product division.
- It underutilizes sales and distribution facilities (subsidiaries) abroad. In the 'product structure' there is a tendency that marketing of products is taken care of, centrally from the homebase ('Marketing (worldwide)'). Therefore there is less need for the facilities in the local sales subsidiary.
- The product divisions tend to develop a total independence of each other in world markets. For example, a global product division structure may end up with several subsidiaries in the same foreign country reporting to different product divisions, with no one at headquarters responsible for the overall corporate presence in that country.

## Geographical structure

**Geographical structure**
The next level after top management is divided into international divisions, e.g. Europe, North America, Latin America, Asia/Pacific and Africa/Middle East.

If market conditions with respect to product acceptance and operating conditions vary considerably across world markets, then the geographical structure is the one to choose. This structure is especially useful for companies that have a homogeneous range of products (similar technologies and common end-use markets), but at the same time need fast and efficient worldwide distribution. Typically, the world is divided into regions (divisions), as shown in Figure 14.4.

Many food, beverage, car and pharmaceutical companies use this type of structure. Its main advantage is its ability to respond easily and quickly to the environmental and market demands of a regional or national area through minor modifications in product design, pricing, market communication and packaging. Therefore the structure encourages adaptive global marketing programmes. Moreover, economies of scale can be achieved within regions. Another reason for the popularity of this structure is its tendency to create area autonomy. However, this may also complicate the tasks of coordinating product variations and transferring new product ideas and marketing techniques from one country to another.

Hence the geographical structure ensures the best use of the firm's regional expertise, but it means a less than optimal allocation of product and functional expertise. If each region needs its own staff of product and functional specialists, duplication

Figure 14.4  Example of the geographical structure

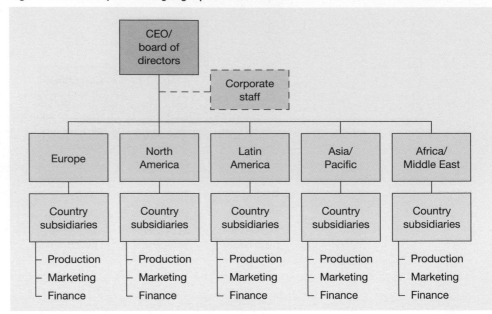

and also inefficiency may be the result. As indicated in Figure 14.4, the geographical structure may include both regional management centres (Europe, North America, etc.) and country-based subsidiaries.

## Regional management centres

There are two main reasons for the existence of regional management centres (RMCs):

1  When sales volume in a particular region becomes substantial there need to be some specialized staff to focus on that region, to realize more fully the potential of an already growing market.
2  Homogeneity within regions and heterogeneity between them necessitate treating each important region separately. Therefore a regional management centre becomes an appropriate organizational feature.

## Country-based subsidiaries

Instead of or parallel to a regional centre, each country has its own organizational unit. Country-based subsidiaries are characterized by a high degree of adaptation to local conditions. Since each subsidiary develops its own unique activities and its own autonomy, it is sometimes relevant to combine local subsidiaries with an RMC: for example, to utilize opportunities across European countries.

Firms may also organize their operations using a customer structure, especially if the customer groups they serve are very different: for example, businesses and governments. Catering to these diverse groups may require the concentration of specialists in particular divisions. The product may be the same, but the buying processes of the various customer groups may differ. Governmental buying is characterized by bidding, in which price plays a larger role than when businesses are the buyers. Much of what has been said about the geographical structure also applies to the customer structure.

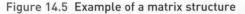

**Figure 14.5 Example of a matrix structure**

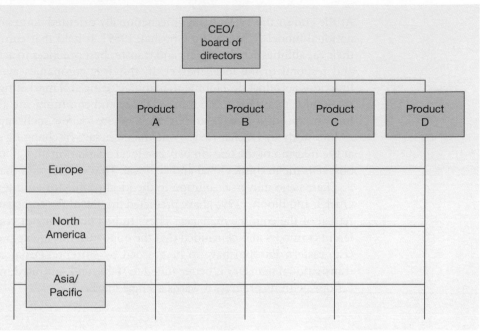

## Matrix structure

The product structure tends to offer better opportunities to rationalize production across countries, thus gaining production cost efficiencies. On the other hand, the geographical structure is more responsive to local market trends and needs, and allows for more coordination in a whole region.

Some global companies need both capabilities, so they have adopted a more complex structure: the matrix structure. The international matrix structure consists of two organizational structures intersecting with each other. As a consequence there are dual reporting relationships. These two structures can be a combination of the general forms already discussed. For example, the matrix structure might consist of product divisions intersecting with functional departments, or geographical areas intersecting with global divisions. The two intersecting structures will largely be a function of what the organization sees as the two dominant aspects of its environment.

The typical international matrix structure is the two-dimensional structure that emphasises product and geography (Figure 14.5). Generally, each product division has worldwide responsibilities for its own business, and each geographical or area division is responsible for the foreign operations in its region. If national organizations (subsidiaries) are involved they are responsible for operations at the country level.

Because the two dimensions of product and geography overlap at the affiliate level, both enter into local decision-making and planning processes. It is assumed that area and product managers will defend different positions. This will lead to tensions and 'creative' conflict. Area managers will tend to favour responsiveness to local environmental factors, and product managers will defend positions favouring cost efficiencies and global competitiveness. The matrix structure deliberately creates a dual focus to ensure that conflicts between product and geographical area concerns are identified and then analysed objectively.

The structure is useful for companies that are both product diversified and geographically spread. By combining a product management approach with a market-oriented approach one can meet the needs both of markets and of products.

**Matrix structure**
The next level after top management consists of two organizational structures (product and geographical areas) intersecting with each other. Results in dual reporting relationships.

## The future role of the international manager

At the end of the 1980s many internationally oriented companies adopted the transnational model (Bartlett and Ghoshal, 1989). It held that companies should leverage their capabilities across borders and transfer best practices to achieve global economies and respond to the local market. In this way companies avoided duplicating their functions (product development, manufacturing and marketing). However, it required that senior managers could think, operate and communicate along three dimensions: function, product and geography. Surely there are few such 'supermanagers' around!

In a study by Quelch (1992) one manager says of changing managerial roles: 'I am at the fulcrum of the tension between local adaptation and global standardization. My boss tells me to think global and act local. That's easier said than done' (p. 158).

There is no universal solution to the ideal profile for an international manager, but Quelch and Bloom (1996) have predicted the 'fall of the transnational manager and the return of the country manager'. They studied behaviour of country managers in different countries and concluded that the opportunities in expanding emerging markets (e.g. eastern Europe) have to be grasped by entrepreneurial country managers. The transnational manager is better suited to stable and saturated markets, such as western Europe, with its progress towards a single market.

## 14.3 The global account management (GAM) organization

**Global account management (GAM)**
A relationship-oriented marketing management approach focusing on dealing with the needs of an important global customer (= account) with a global organization (foreign subsidiaries all over the world).

Global account management (GAM) can be understood as a relationship-oriented marketing management approach focusing on dealing with the needs of an important global customer (= account) in the business-to-business market.

GAM can be defined as an organizational form (a person or a team) in a global supplier organization used to coordinate and manage worldwide activities, by servicing an important customer centrally from headquarters (Harvey *et al.*, 2002).

A global account is a customer that is of strategic importance to the achievement of the supplier's corporate objectives, pursues integrated and coordinated strategies on a worldwide basis and demands a globally integrated product/service offering (Wilson and Millman, 2003).

A global account manager is the person in the selling company who represents that company's capabilities to the buying company, the buying company's needs to the selling company, and brings the two together.

The importance of GAM strategies will grow in future (Harvey *et al.*, 2002; Shi *et al.*, 2004; Shi *et al.*, 2005) because of the consolidation (M&As and global strategic alliances) which take place in most industries. This development means that big multinational customers are getting even bigger and more powerful with increasing buying power. Multinational customers continue to be the increasing importance of GAM. These companies realize that when purchasing is centralized and local subsidiaries can no longer negotiate their own deals, prices become more transparent. In addition, by consolidating and centralizing orders a buyer can demand bigger volume discount. However, very often the multinational customer's national subsidiaries often resist abiding by a global contract that requires them to give all their business to a single supplier. Furthermore, research done by Yip and Bink (2007) conclude that the suppliers' globally consistent service performance is more important than lower prices to the global customers. So suppliers adopting the GAM can build relationships with their global customers that go far beyond price discounts.

Successful GAM often requires an understanding of the logic of both product and service management. Moreover, excellent operational level capabilities are useless if strategic level management is inferior, and vice versa – the GAM approach combines strategic and operational level marketing management.

The starting point for the following is the firm that wishes to implement GAM. Afterwards the development of GAM is regarded in a dyadic perspective.

## Implementation of GAM

The firm that wants to implement successful GAM with suitable global accounts may go through the following four steps (Ojasalo, 2001):

1  identifying the selling firm's global accounts;
2  analysing the global accounts;
3  selecting suitable strategies for the global accounts;
4  developing operational level capabilities to build, grow and maintain profitable and long-lasting relationships with global accounts.

### 1   Identifying the selling firm's global accounts

This means answering the following question: Which existing or potential accounts are of strategic importance to us now and in the future?

The following criteria can be used to determine strategically important customers:

● sales volume;
● age of the relationship;
● the selling firm's share of customers' purchase: the new relationship marketing (RM) paradigm measures success in terms of long-term gains in its share of its customers' business, unlike mass marketing that counts wins or losses in terms of market share increases that may well be temporary (Peppers and Rogers, 1995);
● profitability of the customer to seller;
● use of strategic resources: extent of executive/management commitment.

There is a positive relation (correlation) between the criteria and the likelihood of customers' being identified as global accounts (strategic customers).

### 2   Analysing global accounts

This includes activities such as analysing the following:

● *The basic characteristics of a global account*: Includes assessing the relevant economic and activity aspects of their internal and external environment. This, for example, includes the account's internal value chain inputs, markets, suppliers, products and economic situation.
● *The relationship history*: Involves assessing the relevant economic and activity aspects of the relationship history. This includes volume of sales, profitability, global account's objectives, buying behaviour (the account's decision-making process), information exchange, special needs, buying frequency and complaints. Among the above-mentioned aspects, knowing/estimating relationship value plays a particularly important role. The revenues from each global account (customer lifetime value) should exceed the costs of establishing and maintaining the relationship within a certain time span.
● *The level and development of commitment to the relationship*: The account's present and anticipated commitment to the relationship is important, since the extent of the business with the account depends on that.
● *Goal congruence of the parties*: Goal congruence, or commonality of interests between buyer and seller, greatly affects their cooperation both at the strategic and

operational levels. Common interests and relationship value together determine whether two companies can be partners, friends or rivals that aims it sights lower than the sort of partnership relationship an account is looking for risks losing long-term share of that account's business.

● *Switching costs*: It is useful to estimate both the global account's and the selling company's switching costs in the event that the relationship dissolves. Switching costs are the costs of replacing an existing partner with another. These may be very different for the two parties and thus affect the power position in the relationship. Switching costs are also called transaction costs and are affected by irretrievable investments in the relationship, the adaptations made and the bonds that have developed. High switching costs may prevent a relationship from ending even though the global account's accumulated satisfaction with the selling company may be non-existent or negative.

## 3 Selecting suitable strategies for the global accounts

This depends greatly on the power positions of the seller and the global account. The power structure within different accounts may vary significantly. Thus the selling company may typically not freely select the strategy – there is often only one strategic alternative to be chosen if there is a desire to retain the account.

Maybe the selling firm might prefer to avoid very powerful accounts. Sometimes the selling firm realizes that accounts, which are less attractive today, may become attractive in future. Thus, in the case of certain accounts, the objective of the strategy may be merely to keep the relationship alive for future opportunities.

## 4 Developing operational level capabilities

This refers to customization and development of capabilities related to the following:

### Product/service development and performance

Joint R&D projects are typical between a selling company and a global account in industrial and high-tech markets. In addition, information technology (IT) applied in just-in-time production and distribution channels increases the possibilities of customizing the offering in consumer markets as well.

New products developed in a partnership are not automatically more successful than those developed in-house. However, R&D projects may bring other kinds of long-term benefits, such as access to account organization and learning. Improving capabilities for providing services to global accounts is extremely important, because even when the core product is a tangible good it is often the related services that differentiate the selling company from its competitors and provide competitive advantage.

### Organizational structure

The selling company's *organizational ability* to meet the global account's needs can be developed, for example, by adjusting the organizational structure to correspond to the global account's global and local needs and by increasing the number of interfaces between the selling company and the account, and thus also the number of interacting persons. Organizational capabilities can also be developed by organizing teams, consisting of people with the necessary competences and authorities, to take care of global accounts.

### Individuals (human resources)

A company's capabilities related to individuals can be developed by selecting the right people as global account managers and for global account teams, and by developing their skills. The global account manager's responsibilities are often complex and varied, and therefore require a large number of skills and qualifications, which should be taken into account in the selection and development of global account managers.

It is quite common to find that the current set of global account managers may be good at maintaining their own relationships with their contacts in the account but lack the total set of skills required to lead an account team through a transition in the account relationship. Therefore an assessment of the total desired interfaces between the seller and the customer needs to be considered. It may be that a change is required by moving the relationship from a dependency on a 1:1 relationship (between the global account manager and the chief buyer) to a network of organizational relationships spanning many different projects, functions and countries.

### Information exchange

Information exchange between the selling company and a global account is particularly important in GAM. An important relationship-specific task is to search, filter, judge and store information about the organizations, strategies, goals, potentials and problems of the partners. However, this mainly depends on the mutual trust and attitudes of the parties, and on the technical arrangements. A global account's trust is something that the selling company has to earn over time by its performance, whereas the technical side can be developed, for example with IT.

### Company and individual level benefits

Successful long-term GAM in a business-to-business context always requires the ability to offer both company and individual level benefits to global accounts.

Company level benefits are rational and may be either short or long term, direct or indirect, and typically contribute to the global account's turnover, profitability, cost savings, organizational efficiency and effectiveness, and image. Individual level benefits in turn may be rational or emotional. From the relationship management point of view the global individual(s) is/are the one(s) with the power to continue or terminate the relationship. Rational individual level benefits contribute, for example, to the individual's own career, income and ease of job. Emotional individual level benefits include friendship, a sense of caring and ego enhancement.

## The dyadic development of GAM

The Millman-Wilson model in Figure 14.6 describes and demonstrates the typical dyadic progression of a relationship between buyer and seller through five stages – Pre-GAM, Early-GAM, Mid-GAM, Partnership-GAM and Synergistic-GAM (Wilson and Millman, 2003).

*Pre-GAM* describes preparation for GAM. A buying company is identified as having key account potential, and the selling company starts to focus resources on winning some business with that prospect. Both seller and buyer are sending out signals (factual information) and exchanging messages (interactions) prior to the decision to engage in transactions. There is a need to develop networks of contacts, to gain knowledge about the customer's operations and to begin to assess the potential for relational development.

*Early-GAM*: at this stage the selling company is concerned with identifying the opportunities for account penetration once the account has been won. This is probably the most typical sales relationship, the classic 'bow-tie'.

Adapted solutions are needed, and the key account manager will be focused on understanding more about their customer and the market in which that customer is competing. The buying company will still be market testing other selling companies.

Figure 14.6  Relational development model

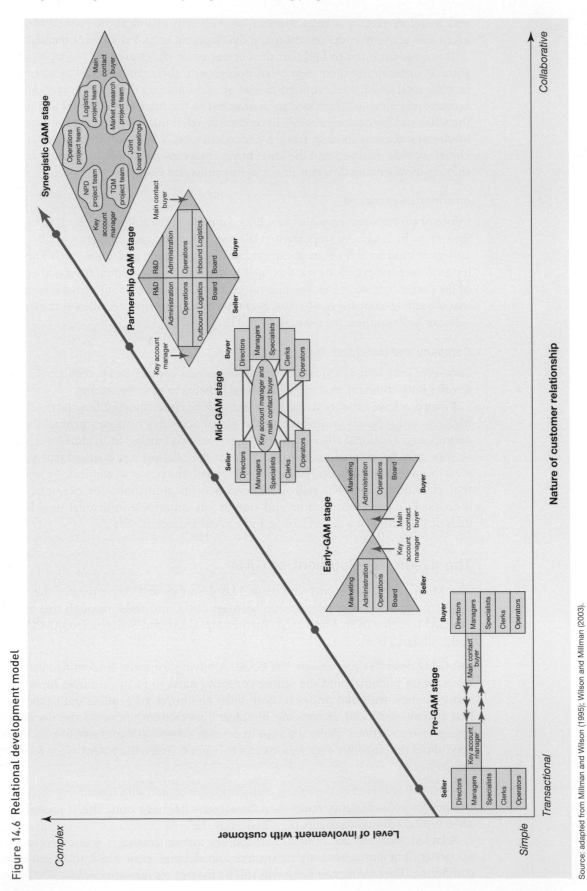

Source: adapted from Millman and Wilson (1995); Wilson and Millman (2003).

Figure 14.7 Development of GAM

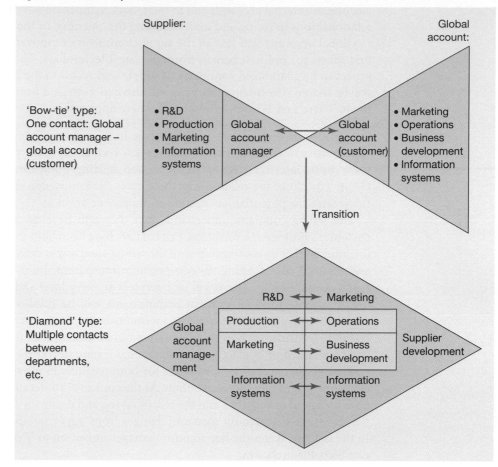

Detailed knowledge of the global customer and their core competences, the depth of the relationship and the potential for creating relation-specific entrepreneurial value are all limited at this stage. There is an increasing need for political skills to be applied as the potential of the account is identified and the global account manager is called upon to ensure that the resources of the supplier configure to best serve the needs of the customer (Wilson and Millman, 2003). The selling company must concentrate hard on product, service and intangibles – the buying company wants recognition that the product offering is the prime reason for the relationship – and expects it to work.

*Mid-GAM stage*: this is a transition stage between the classic 'bow-tie' and the 'diamond' of the partnership GAM stage (see Figure 14.7).

At this stage the selling company has established credibility with the buying company. Contacts between the two organizations increase at all levels and assume greater importance. Nevertheless, buying companies still feel the need for alternative sources of supply. This may be driven by their own customers' desire for choice. The selling company's offering is still periodically market tested, but is reliably perceived to be good value. The selling company is now a 'preferred' supplier.

*Partnership-GAM*: this is the stage where benefits should start to flow. When partnership-GAM is reached the selling company is seen by the buying company organization as a strategic external resource. The two companies will be sharing sensitive information and engaging in joint problem solution. Pricing will be long term and stable, but it will have been established that each side will allow the other to make a profit.

If a major disadvantage of the 'bow-tie' of early-GAM was the denial of access to customers' internal processes and to their market, the main advantage of the 'diamond' relationship is in seeing and understanding the 'opening' of the 'global account'.

Global accounts will test all the supplier company's innovations so that they have first access to, and first benefit from, the latest technology. The buying company will expect to be guaranteed continuity of supply and access to the best material. Expertise will be shared. The buying company will also expect to gain from continuous improvement. There may be joint promotions, where appropriate.

*Synergistic-GAM*: this is the ultimate stage in the relational development model. The experience gained at the partnership stage – coordinating the team-sell, coaching the team on its interface roles – will be a good starting point for moving to synergistic GAM. The closer the relationship, the greater the knowledge about the customer and the greater the potential for creating entrepreneurial value.

The selling company understands that they still have no automatic right to the customer's business. Nevertheless, exit barriers have been built up. The buying company is confident that its relationship with the selling company is delivering improved quality and reduced cost. Costing systems become transparent. Joint research and development will take place. There will be interfaces at every level and function between the organizations. Top management commitment will be fulfilled through joint board meetings and reviews. There will be a joint business plan, joint strategies, joint market research. Information flow should be streamlined and information systems integration will be planned or in place as a consequence. Transaction costs will be reduced.

Though there are clear advantages for both partners in moving through the different GAM-stages there are also pitfalls. As the contacts proliferate through the stages, so does the speed of activity – and the risk of saying and doing the wrong things. Through the stages the key account manager changes from 'super salesperson' to 'super coach'. In the last two stages the key account manager moves on to a 'super coordinator', who conducts the orchestra.

If the key account manager does not move along then the potential of losing control is great, resulting in well-meaning but misdirected individuals following their own quite separate courses.

Key account management requires process excellence and highly skilled professionals to manage relationships with strategic customers. For most companies this represents a number of revolutions. A revolution is needed in the way activity is costed and costs are attributed, from product or geographical focus to customer focus. Currently few financial or information systems in companies are sophisticated enough to support the higher levels of key account management. A transformation is needed in the way the professional with responsibility for a customer relationship is developed, from an emphasis on selling skills to management skills, including cross-cultural management skills (McDonald *et al.*, 1997).

We end this section by assessing the advantages and disadvantages by going into GAM, seen from the supplier's (seller's) point of view:

**Supplier's (seller's) advantages with GAM**
- Provides a better fulfilment of the customer's global need for having only one supplier of certain products and services.
- Creating barriers for competitors – given the high switching costs global competitors (to the supplier) will have difficulty in displacing the existing supplier. If the supplier becomes the preferred supplier, the customer becomes dependent on the supplier shifting power in the relationship.

- Increased sales of existing products and services through a closer relationship with the key customer.
- Facilitating the introduction of new products/services – the global account (GA) is perceived to be more willing to take on new product trials and carry a more complete product line.
- Coordination of marketing/selling activities across borders may increase the total worldwide sales value to this customer – the GAM strategy enables the supplier to coordinate global marketing programmes (i.e. standardization) while at the same time permit local adaptation to individual country environment.
- Perceived high potential for profit increase – due to the increased sales and global coordination – development of a strategic 'fit' between the supplier and the customer, increases the effectiveness of the supplying organization.
- By using the learning effects the supplier has the ability to reduce the marginal cost of creating adapted programmes for every new country/region. In this way 'economies of scale' as well as 'economies of scope' can be utilized through the GAM strategy.
- Through the global network of the customer the supplier might get access to new customers around the world.

**Supplier's (seller's) disadvantages with GAM**

- The supplier will feel pressure from the global customers to improve global consistency – they may force the supplier to institute GAM to maintain their global 'preferred' supplier status.
- Pressure to 'standardize' pricing on a global basis – the global customer may attempt to use GAM as a means to lower prices globally through telling that there should be equity/commonality of pricing throughout the global network of the customer's subsidiaries.
- Pressure to 'standardize' all terms of trade on a global basis, and not just price. So GA increasingly demand uniformity in such issues as volume discounts, transportation charges, overheads, special charges and so forth.
- The supplier's loss of GA due to major competitors utilizing the GAM strategy – by this the supplier may feel compelled to form a GAM team to match or counteract the strategy of key customers.
- Most often a GAM strategy is connected to the use of some kind of matrix organization. Consequently there may be multiple decision makers in the supplier organization making the same decision from different perspectives (e.g. global vs local perspective). The cost of managing may increase due to the parallel structures at global and local levels. Moreover, the parallel structures might slow down the decision-making process.

## The organizational set-up of global account management

According to Figure 14.8 three different organizational models will be presented.

### 1 Central HQ-HQ negotiation model

This model shows a situation where the product in question is standardized. The customer HQ will collect the demands from the different subsidiaries around the world. Thereafter the customer will meet with the supplier and the HQ-to-HQ negotiations will take place. In this situation the customer will typically exercise significant buying power, because the supplier will not have any international organization that can offset

Figure 14.8 The organizational set-up in GAM

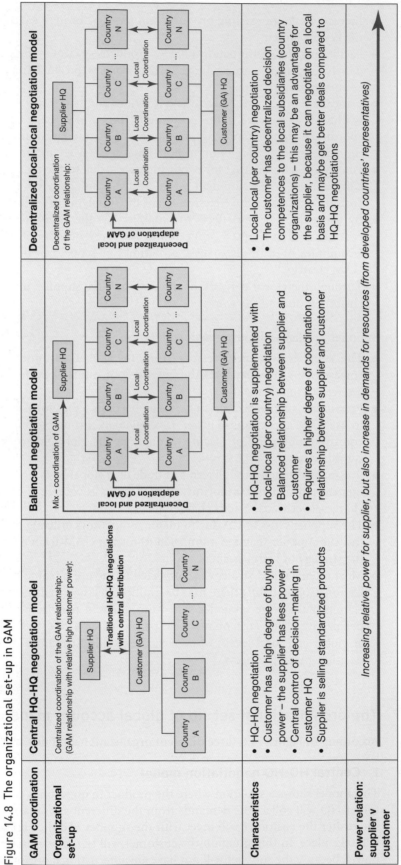

this buying power. For the supplier, a standardized (high) quality is the condition for being invited to the discussions with the customer HQ. Subsequently, the discussion will quickly come down to a question of the 'right' price. The supplier will always be under pressure to lower the price and cut costs of producing the product package (including services).

IKEA (turnover in 2004 of €13,570 million, achieved through its 201 IKEA shops around the world), is an example of a customer that puts its furniture suppliers under constant pressure to reduce their prices and make their production more efficient, in order to reduce costs. Recently IKEA planned to reduce its distribution warehouse costs by 10 per cent per year. In order to achieve this goal IKEA runs weekly batch global-demand forecasts for each of its three major regions: North America, Asia and EMEA (Europe, Middle East and Africa). The fulfilment solution will balance demand forecasts with inventory levels and replenish accordingly through IKEA's ordering system (Scheraga, 2005). Orders may be sent to IKEA's suppliers weekly or daily, depending on how active they are with the retailer. IKEA suppliers are pressurized to deliver furniture to IKEA more frequently and more directly to its stores around the world. If a European subsupplier of furniture wants to be a global supplier to IKEA it must now consider establishing production and assembling factories in the other two main regions of the world: North America and Asia.

## 2 Balanced negotiation model

In this situation the central HQ to HQ negotiation is supplemented with some decentralized and local negotiations on a country basis. Typically this will take place in the form of negotiations between the local subsidiaries of the customers and the different partners (e.g. agents) or subsidiaries of the supplier. The HQ to HQ negotiations will set the possible range of outcomes for the following negotiations on a local basis. This will allow for some degree of price differentiation across the involved countries, dependent on the degree of necessary product adaptation to local conditions. Sauer-Danfoss (www.sauer-danfoss.com) is an example of a subsupplier working to this model (see Exhibit 14.1).

### Exhibit 14.1 Sauer-Danfoss's GAM

Sauer-Danfoss is one of the world's leading companies for the development, production and sale of hydraulic power transmission systems – primarily for use in mobile work vehicles. Sauer-Danfoss, with more than 7,000 employees worldwide and revenue of approximately $1.3 billion (2004), has sales, manufacturing, and engineering capabilities in Europe, the Americas and the Asia-Pacific region. Sauer-Danfoss' key global customers (GAs) are John Deere, Case New Holland, Ingersoll-Rand, Agco and Caterpillar (see also Case 6.2).

One of Sauer-Danfoss's main global accounts (OEM customers), Case New Holland (CNH) is the number one manufacturer of agricultural tractors and combines in the world and the third largest maker of construction equipment. Revenue in 2004 totalled $12 billion. Based in the United States, CNH's network of dealers and distributors operates in over 160 countries. CNH agricultural products are sold under the Case IH, New Holland and Steyr brands. CNH construction equipment is sold under the Case, FiatAllis, Fiat Kobelco, Kobelco, New Holland and O&K brands.

As a result of a merger in 1999 CNH is an example of consolidation on the OEM customer side. The consequence of this consolidation is that fewer than the ten largest OEM customers will represent more than half of Sauer-Danfoss's potential sales over the medium to long term. There is no doubt that the price-down pressure will continue worldwide. The global business culture trend is leading towards a more professional buying process on the customer side. This development requires a new way of structuring the Sauer-Danfoss organization, and the answer is GAM. As illustrated in the figure below. Sauer-Danfoss has met the requirements of CNH's worldwide production units by forming local production locations and GAM team groups in India, China, Poland, North

**Exhibit 14.1 continued**

America, Italy, Brazil, Germany and the United Kingdom. In partnership with CNH the GAM teams try to find more cost-effective solutions, rather than simply reduce prices. Sauer-Danfoss is following CNH into low-cost manufacturing countries, such as India and China. At all of CNH's worldwide production units there is pressure for a higher degree of outsourcing and a request for value added packages. Sauer-Danfoss tries to fulfil this requirement by supplying pre-assembled kit packages and delivering more system solutions to CNH.

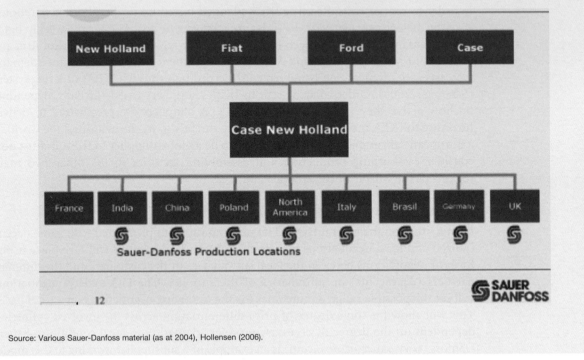

Source: Various Sauer-Danfoss material (as at 2004), Hollensen (2006).

## 3 Decentralized local-local negotiation model

According to this model the negotiations will only take place on a local basis, partly because the supplier is often selling system solutions, which require a high degree of adaptation to the different markets (countries). This means that the HQs are disconnected from the negotiation processes. A consolidation process in the customer's industry may cause this outcome. If the customer has been involved in several M&As, it will have difficulties in understanding the overall picture of the decision structures in the new merged multinational company. In such a situation the customer will tend to decentralize even important decisions to the country subsidiaries, because it has lost its overview of the whole multinational company. It can be really difficult to control and coordinate decision processes in recently merged companies. For that reason top managers will often refer the buying decisions to local decision makers in local country subsidiaries.

This will give the supplier better opportunities for sub-optimization by negotiating only locally with a customer's country-based organizations. By using this approach the supplier may be in a better relative negotiation position and may also achieve better (higher) prices in some markets by using this model. However, the supplier may have higher costs connected to fulfilling the different requirements of the customer's local subsidiaries. Also this model requires that the supplier has an established network of subsidiaries or partners (e.g. agents) who are familiar with the product solutions of the supplier and who can offer local adapted product solutions for the customer's subsidiaries in the different countries (see Exhibit 14.2).

AGRAMKOW (www.agramkow.com) is an example of a company working to this model. AGRAMKOW (Denmark) has a goal to become one of the world's leading developers and suppliers of filling equipment for fluid refrigerants, which are used, for example, in refrigerators or in automotive air conditioners. In 2004 GRAMKOW's total sales were approximately $35 million, of which 95 per cent was realized outside the home country (Denmark). The total number of employees is 150. AGRAMKOW's global customers (GAs) are big multinational companies like Whirlpool (USA), Electrolux (Sweden), Samsung (Korea), Haier (China), Siemens (Germany) and General Electric (USA).

It is a fact that global customers are getting fewer and bigger by mergers and acquisitions. For example, AGRAMKOW's process fluid fill system is fitted into the total production line of the refrigerator manufacturer, Electrolux. AGRAMKOW has 'only' three or four subsidiaries around the world, but instead of having several subsidiaries to support the local production units of the major GAs (like in the Sauer-Danfoss case), it has transferred the values of AGRAMKOW to distributors and agents in order to turn them into partners with internalized AGRAMKOW values. The AGRAMKOW management has implemented this partner-strategy by inviting all the potential partners to common seminars and meetings at the AGRAMKOW HQ in Denmark. The purpose of these meetings are to increase:

- common team spirit and commitment to the AGRAMKOW shared values and goals – this has also been achieved by including some common social activities (e.g. sport activities);
- sales skills for winning local GA business;
- technical competence for installation, integration, maintenance and repair of AGRAMKOW equipment/solutions;
- understanding of the necessity for constant feedback to AGRAMKOW on performance and other market activities (e.g. competitor activity).

Afterwards the individual partner and their organization (e.g. the Chinese partner) is in a better position to take care of customized products, local service and customer care directed towards the local GA unit (e.g. the local Electrolux refrigerator production unit in China). This also means that AGRAMKOW has increased its relative power on the local basis towards one of its important GAs, Electrolux.

Despite this positive development there has been some difficulties in the process of turning the distributors and agents into partners. Those organizations with small turnovers of AGRAMKOW products and services have been somewhat reluctant to take part in this process (Hollensen, 2006).

In summary, the importance of GAM strategies will grow in the future because of consolidation in most industries across the world. The development of relational contracting with a large, global customer – the cooperation between a customer and a supplier into a long-term global relationship – has a number of positive outcomes. However, a great deal of learning is necessary when deciding to implement a GAM strategy because high stakes and high exit barriers accompany the implementation.

## 14.4    Controlling the global marketing programme

The final, but often neglected stage of international market planning, is the control process. Not only is control important to evaluate how we have performed, but it completes the circle of planning by providing the feedback necessary for the start of the next planning cycle.

Figure 14.9 illustrates the connection between the marketing plan, the marketing budget and the control system.

After building the global marketing plan, its quantification appears in the form of budgets. The budget is the basis for the design of the marketing control system that may give the necessary feedback for a possible reformulation of the global marketing

Figure 14.9 The firm's budget and control system

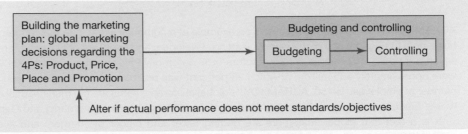

plan. The marketing budgets should represent a projection of actions and expected results, and they should be capable of accurate monitoring and controlling. Indeed, measuring performance against budget is the main (regular) management review process, which may cause the feed back in Figure 14.9.

The purpose of a marketing budget is to pull all the revenues and costs involved in marketing together into one comprehensive document. It is a managerial tool that balances what needs to be spent against what can be afforded and helps make choices about priorities. It is then used in monitoring the performance in practice. The marketing budget is usually the most powerful tool with which you think through the relationship between desired results and available means. Its starting point should be the marketing strategies and plans that have already been formulated in the marketing plan itself. In practice, the strategies and plans will run in parallel and will interact.

Unfortunately, however, 'control' is often viewed by the people of an organization as being negative. If individuals fear that the control process will be used not only to judge their performance, but as a basis for punishing them, then it will be feared and reviled.

The evaluation and control of global marketing probably represents one of the weakest areas of marketing practice in many companies. Even the organizations that are otherwise strong in their strategic marketing planning have poor control and evaluation procedures for their global marketing. There are a number of possible reasons for this: primarily, there is no such thing as a 'standard' system of control for marketing.

The function of the organizational structure is to provide a framework in which objectives can be met. However, a set of instruments and processes is needed to influence the behaviour and performance of organization members to meet the goals. The critical issue is the same as with organizational structures: what is the ideal amount of control? On the one hand, headquarters needs information to ensure that international activities contribute maximum benefit to the overall organization. On the other hand, controls should not be construed as a code of law.

The global question is to determine how to establish a control mechanism capable of early interception of emerging problems. Considered here are various criteria appropriate for the evaluation process, control styles, feedback and corrective action. These concepts are important for all businesses, but in the international arena they are vital.

## Design of a control system

In designing a control system management must consider the costs of establishing and maintaining it and trade them off against the benefits to be gained. Any control system will require investment in a management structure and in systems designs.

The design of the control system can be divided into two groups dependent on the objective of control:

1 output control (typically based on financial measures);

2 behavioural controls (typically based on non-financial measures).

**Output control**
Regular monitoring of output, like profits, sales figures and expenditures (typically based on financial measures).

**Behavioural controls**
Regular monitoring of behaviour, like sales people's ability to interact with customers (typically based on non-financial measures).

Output control may consist of expenditure control, which involves regular monitoring of expenditure figures, comparison of these with budget targets, and taking decisions to cut or increase expenditure where any variance is believed to be harmful. Measures of output are accumulated at regular intervals and typically forwarded from the foreign subsidiary to headquarters, where they are evaluated and criticised based on comparison to the plan or budget.

Behavioural controls require the exercise of influence over behaviour. This influence can be achieved, for example, by providing sales manuals to subsidiary personnel or by fitting new employees into the corporate culture. Behavioural controls often require an extensive socialisation process, and informal, personal interaction is central to the process. Substantial resources must be spent to train the individual to share the corporate culture: that is, 'the way things are done at the company'.

To build common vision and values managers at the Japanese company Matsushita spend a substantial amount of their first months in what the company calls 'cultural and spiritual training'. They study the company credo, the 'Seven Spirits of Matsushita', and the philosophy of the founder, Kanosuke Matsushita.

However, there remains a strong tradition of using output (financial) criteria. A fixation with output criteria leads companies to ignore the less tangible behavioural (non-financial) measures, although these are the real drivers of corporate success. However, there is a weakness in the behavioural performance measures. To date there has been little success in developing explicit links from behaviour to output criteria. Furthermore, companies and managers are still judged on financial criteria (profit contribution). Until a clear link is established it is likely that behavioural criteria will continue to be treated with a degree of scepticism.

We will now develop a global marketing control system based primarily on output controls. Marketing control is an essential element of the marketing planning process because it provides a review of how well marketing objectives have been achieved. A framework for controlling marketing activities is given in Figure 14.10.

The marketing control system begins with the company setting some marketing activities in motion (plans for implementation). This may be the result of certain objectives and strategies, each of which must be achieved within a given budget. Hence budgetary control is essential.

The next step in the control process is to establish specific performance standards that will need to be achieved for each area of activity if overall and subobjectives are to be achieved. For example, in order to achieve a specified sales objective, a specific target of performance for each sales area may be required. In turn this may require a specific standard of performance from each of the salespeople in the region with respect to, for example, number of calls, conversion rates and, of course, order value. Table 14.1 provides a representative sample of the types of data required. Marketing performance measures and standards will vary by company and product according to the goals and objectives delineated in the marketing plan.

The next step is to locate responsibility. In some cases responsibility ultimately falls on one person (e.g. the brand manager); in others it is shared (e.g. the sales manager and sales force). It is important to consider this issue, since corrective or supportive action may need to focus on those responsible for the success of marketing activity.

In order to be successful the people involved and affected by the control process should be consulted in both the design and implementation stages of marketing control. Above all they will need to be convinced that the purpose of control is to improve their own levels of success and that of the company. Subordinates need to be involved

Figure 14.10  The marketing control system

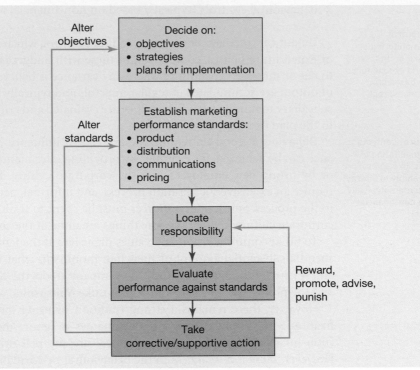

Table 14.1  Measures of marketing performance

| Product | Distribution |
|---|---|
| ● Sales by market segments<br>● New product introductions each year<br>● Sales relative to potential<br>● Sales growth rates<br>● Market share<br>● Contribution margin<br>● Product defects<br>● Warranty expense<br>● Percentage of total profits<br>● Return on investment | ● Sales, expenses and contribution margin by channel type<br>● Percentage of stores carrying the product<br>● Sales relative to market potential by channel, intermediary type and specific intermediaries<br>● Percentage of on-time delivery<br>● Expense-to-sales ratio by channel, etc.<br>● Order cycle performance by channel, etc.<br>● Logistics cost by logistics activity by channel |

| Pricing | Communication |
|---|---|
| ● Response time to price changes of competitors<br>● Price relative to competitor<br>● Price changes relative to sales volume<br>● Discount structure relative to sales volume<br>● Bid strategy relative to new contacts<br>● Margin structure relative to marketing expenses<br>● Margins relative to channel member performance | ● Advertising effectiveness by type of media (e.g. awareness levels)<br>● Actual audience/target audience ratio<br>● Cost per contact<br>● Number of calls, enquiries and information requests by type of media<br>● Sales per sales call<br>● Sales per territory relative to potential<br>● Selling expenses to sales ratio<br>● New accounts per time period<br>● Lost accounts per time period |

Source: Adapted from Jobber, D. (1995) *Principles and Practice of Marketing*, published by McGraw-Hill. Reproduced with the kind permission of the McGraw–Hill Publishing Company.

in setting and agreeing their own standards of performance, preferably through a system of management by objectives.

Performance is then evaluated against these standards, which relies on an efficient information system. A judgement has to be made about the degree of success and failure achieved and what corrective or supportive action is to be taken. This can take various forms:

- Failure that is attributed to the poor performance of individuals may result in the giving of advice regarding future attitudes and actions, training and/or punishment (e.g. criticism, lower pay, demotion, termination of employment). Success, on the other hand, should be rewarded with praise, promotion and/or higher pay.
- Failure that is attributed to unrealistic marketing objectives and performance may cause management to lower objectives or lower marketing standards. Success that is thought to reflect unambitious objectives and standards may cause them to be raised in the next period.

Many firms assume that corrective action needs to be taken only when results are less than those required or when budgets and costs are being exceeded. In fact both 'negative' (underachievement) and 'positive' (overachievement) deviations may require corrective action. For example, failure to spend the amount budgeted for, say, sales force expenses may indicate that the initial sum allocated was excessive and needs to be reassessed, and/or that the sales force is not as 'active' as it might be.

It is also necessary to determine such things as the frequency of measurement (e.g. daily, weekly, monthly or annually). More frequent and more detailed measurement usually means more cost. We need to be careful to ensure that the costs of measurement and the control process itself do not exceed the value of such measurements and do not overly interfere with the activities of those being measured.

The impact of the environment must also be taken into account when designing a control system:

- The control system should measure only dimensions over which the organization has control. Rewards or sanctions make little sense if they are based on dimensions that may be relevant for overall corporate performance, but over which no influence can be exerted (e.g. price controls). Neglecting the factor of individual performance capability would send the wrong signals and severely impair the motivation of personnel.
- Control systems should harmonize with local regulations and customs. In some cases, however, corporate behavioural controls have to be exercised against local customs even though overall operations may be affected negatively. This type of situation occurs, for example, when a subsidiary operates in markets where unauthorized facilitating payments are a common business practice.

## Feedforward control

Much of the information provided by the firm's marketing control system is feedback on what has been accomplished in both financial (profits) and non-financial (customer satisfaction, market share) terms. As such, the control process is remedial in its outlook. It can be argued that control systems should be forward looking and preventive, and that the control process should start at the same time as the planning process. Such a form of control is feedforward control (Figure 14.11).

Feedforward control would continuously evaluate plans, monitoring the environment to detect changes that would call for revising objectives and strategies. Feedforward control monitors variables other than performance; variables that may change before performance itself changes. The result is that deviations can be controlled before their

**Feedforward control**
Monitors variables other than performance – variables that may change before performance itself. In this way deviations can be controlled proactively before their full impact has been felt.

Figure 14.11  Adjustment of global marketing strategy

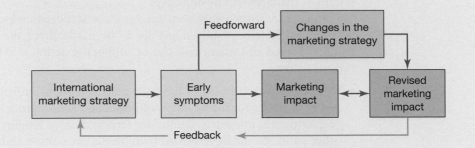

Source: Samli *et al.*, 1993, *International Marketing: Planning and Practice*, p. 425. Pearson Education, Inc., Upper Saddle River, NJ.

Table 14.2  Some key early performance indicators

| Early performance indicators | Market implication |
| --- | --- |
| Sudden drop in quantities demanded | Problem in marketing strategy or its implementation |
| Sharp decrease or increase in sales volume | Product gaining acceptance or being rejected quickly |
| Customer complaints | Product not debugged properly |
| A notable decrease in competitors' business | Product gaining acceptance quickly or market conditions deteriorating |
| Large volumes of returned merchandise | Problems in basic product design |
| Excessive requests for parts or reported repairs | Problems in basic product design, low standards |
| Sudden changes in fashions or styles | Product (or competitors' product) causing a deep impact on the consumers' lifestyles |

Source: Samli *et al.*, 1993, *International Marketing: Planning and Practice*, p. 421 Pearson Education, Inc., Upper Saddle River, NJ.

full impact has been felt. Such a system is proactive in that it anticipates environmental change, whereas after-the-fact and steering control systems are more reactive in that they deal with changes after they occur. Examples of early symptoms (early performance indicators) are presented in Table 14.2.

Feedforward control focuses on information that is prognostic: it tries to discover problems waiting to occur. Formal processes of feedforward control can be incorporated into the business marketer's total control programme to enhance its effectiveness considerably. Utilization of a feedforward approach would help ensure that planning and control are treated as concurrent activities.

## Key areas for control in marketing

Kotler (1997) distinguishes four types of marketing control, each involving different approaches, different purposes and a different allocation of responsibilities. These are shown in Table 14.3. Here we will focus on annual plan control and profit control, since they are the most obvious areas of concern to firms with limited resources (e.g. SMEs).

### Annual plan control

The purpose of annual plan control is to determine the extent to which marketing efforts over the year have been successful. This control will centre on measuring and evaluating sales in relation to sales goals, market share analysis and expense analysis.

Table 14.3 **Types of marketing control**

| Type of control | Prime responsibility | Purpose of control | Examples of techniques/approaches |
|---|---|---|---|
| Strategic control | Top management Middle management | To examine if planned results are being achieved | Marketing effectiveness ratings Marketing audit |
| Efficiency control | Line and staff management Marketing controller | To examine ways of improving the efficiency of marketing | Sales force efficiency Advertising efficiency Distribution efficiency |
| Annual plan control | Top management Middle management | To examine if planned results are being achieved | Sales analysis Market share analysis Marketing expenses to sales ratio Customer tracking |
| Profit control (budget control) | Marketing controller | To examine where the company is making and losing money | Profitability by e.g. product, customer group or trade channel |

Source: Adapted from *Marketing Management: Analysis, Planning, Implementation and Control*, 9th edition, by Kotler, P., p. 765. Pearson Education, Inc., Upper Saddle River, NJ.

Figure 14.12 **The hierarchy of sales and control**

Sales performance is a key element in annual plan control. Sales control consists of a hierarchy of standards on different organizational control levels. These are interlinked, as shown in Figure 14.12.

We can see from the diagram that any variances in achieving sales targets at the corporate level are the result of variances in the performance of individual salespeople at the operational level. At every level of sales control variances must be studied with a view to determining their causes. In general, variances may be due to a combination of variances in volume and/or price.

## Profit control

In addition to the previously discussed control elements, all international marketers must be concerned to control their profit. The budgetary period is normally one year because budgets are tied to the accounting systems of the company. In the following section we will further explore how global marketing budgets are developed, the starting point being the GAM organization and the country-based structure of the company.

## 14.5 The global marketing budget

The classic quantification of a global marketing plan appears in the form of budgets. Because these are so rigorously quantified they are particularly important. They should represent a projection of actions and expected results, and they should be capable of accurate monitoring. Indeed performance against budget is the main (regular) management review process.

Budgeting is also an organization process that involves making forecasts based on the proposed marketing strategy and programmes. The forecasts are then used to construct a budgeted profit-and-loss statement (i.e. profitability). An important aspect of budgeting is deciding how to allocate the last available dollars across all of the proposed programmes within the marketing plan.

Recognizing the *customer* as the primary unit of focus, a market-based business will expand its focus to customers and countries/markets, not just products or units sold. This is an important strategic distinction because there is a finite number of potential customers, but a larger range of products and services can be sold to each customer. A business's volume is its customer share in a market with a finite number of customers at any point in time, not the number of units sold.

Global marketing strategies that affect customer volume include marketing strategies that achieve the following:

- attract new customers to grow market share;
- grow the market demand by bringing more customers into a market;
- enter new markets to create new sources of customer volume.

All marketing strategies require *some* level of marketing effort to achieve a certain level of market share. Expenses associated with sales effort, market communications, customer service and market management are required to implement a marketing strategy designed to obtain a certain customer volume. The cost of this marketing effort are the *marketing expenses* and they must be deducted from the total contribution to produce a *net marketing contribution*.

Figure 14.13 illustrates the traditional marketing budget (per country or customer group) and its underlying determinants. From Figure 14.13 the most important measures of marketing profitability may be defined as:

$$\text{Contribution margin in \%} = \frac{\text{Total contribution}}{\text{Total revenue}} \times 100$$

$$\text{Marketing contribution margin \%} = \frac{\text{Total marketing contribution}}{\text{Total revenue}} \times 100$$

$$\text{Profit margin \%} = \frac{\text{Net profit (before taxes)}}{\text{Total revenue}} \times 100$$

If we have information about the size of assets (accounts receivable + inventory + cash + plant + equipment) we could also define:

$$\text{Return on assets (ROA)} = \frac{\text{Net profit (before taxes)}}{\text{Assets}}$$

ROA is similar to the well-known measure: ROI = return on investment.

Table 14.4 presents an example of a global marketing budget for a manufacturer of consumer goods. Included in the budget are those marketing variables that can be

Figure 14.13 Marketing budget 200X and its underlying determinants

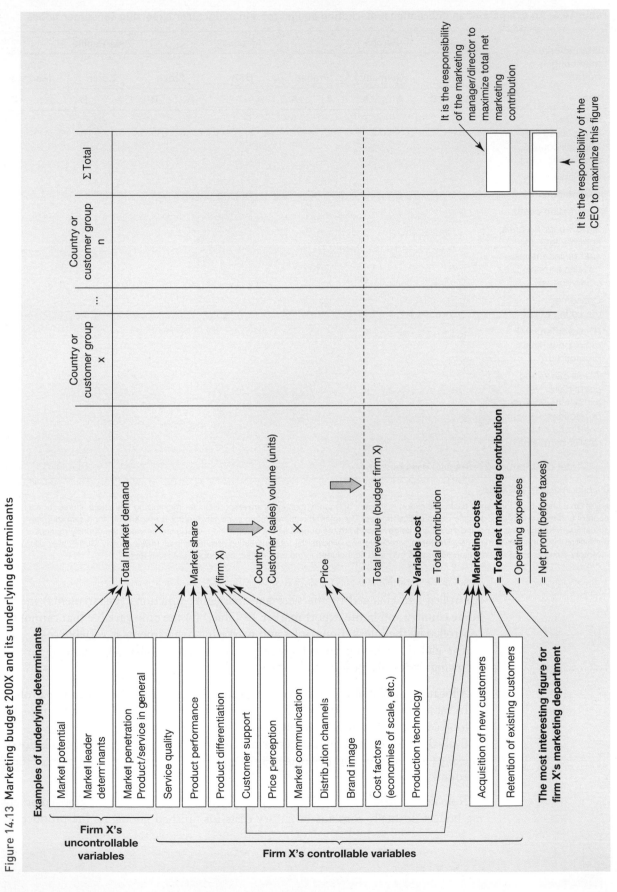

**Table 14.4** An example of an international marketing budget for a manufacturer exporting consumer goods

| International marketing budget | Europe | | | | | | America | | Asia/Pacific | | | | | |
| | UK | | Germany | | France | | USA | | Japan | | Korea | | Other Markets | |
| Year = _____ | A | B | A | A | A | A | A | B | A | B | A | B | A | B |
|---|---|---|---|---|---|---|---|---|---|---|---|---|---|---|
| Net sales (gross sales less trade discounts, allowances, etc.) | | | | | | | | | | | | | | |
| ÷ Variable costs | | | | | | | | | | | | | | |
| = Contribution 1 | | | | | | | | | | | | | | |
| ÷ Marketing costs: | | | | | | | | | | | | | | |
| *Sales costs* (salaries, commissions for agents, incentives, travelling, training, conferences) | | | | | | | | | | | | | | |
| Consumer marketing costs (TV commercials, radio, print, sales promotion) | | | | | | | | | | | | | | |
| *Trade marketing costs* (fairs, exhibitions, instore promotions, contributions for retailer campaigns) | | | | | | | | | | | | | | |
| = Σ **Total contribution 2** (marketing contribution) | | | | | | | | | | | | | | |

B = budget figures; A = actual.

Note: On a short-term (one-year) basis, the export managers or country managers are responsible for maximizing the actual figures for each country and minimizing their deviation from budget figures. The international marketing manager/director is responsible for maximizing the actual figure for the total world and minimizing its deviation from the budget figure. Cooperation is required between the country managers and the international marketing manager/director to coordinate and allocate the total marketing resources in an optimum way. Sometimes certain inventory costs and product development costs may also be included in the total marketing budget (see main text).

controlled and changed by the sales and marketing functions (departments) in the home country and in the export market. In Table 14.4 the only variable that cannot be controlled by the international sales and marketing departments is variable costs.

The global marketing budget system (as presented in Table 14.4) is used for the following (main) purposes:

- Allocation of marketing resources among countries/markets to maximize profits. In Table 14.4 it is the responsibility of the global marketing director to maximize the total contribution 2 for the whole world.
- Evaluation of country/market performance. In Table 14.4 it is the responsibility of export managers or country managers to maximize contribution 2 for each of their countries.

Note that besides the marketing variables presented in Table 14.4 the global marketing budget normally contains inventory costs for finished goods. As the production sizes of these goods are normally based on input from the sales and marketing department, the inventory of unsold goods will also be the responsibility of the international marketing manager or director. Furthermore, the global marketing budget may also contain customer-specific or country-specific product development costs, if certain new products are preconditions for selling in certain markets.

In contrast to budgets, long-range plans extend over periods from two to ten years, and their content is more qualitative and judgemental in nature than that of budgets. For SMEs shorter periods (such as two years) are the norm because of the perceived uncertainty of diverse foreign environments.

## 14.6 The process of developing the global marketing plan

The purpose of the marketing plan is to create sustainable competitive advantages in the global marketplace. Generally, firms go through some kind of mental process in developing global marketing plans. In SMEs this process is normally informal; in larger organizations it is often more systematized. Figure 1.1 at the start of this book offers a systematized approach to developing a global marketing plan.

## 14.7 Summary

Implementation of a global marketing programme requires an appropriate organizational structure. As the scope of a firm's global marketing strategy changes its organizational structure must be adequately modified in accordance with its tasks and technology and the external environment. Five ways of structuring an international organization have been presented: functional structure, international divisional structure, product structure, geographical structure (customer structure) and matrix structure. The choice of organizational structure is affected by such factors as the degree of internationalization of the firm, the strategic importance of the firm's international operations, the complexity of its international business and the availability of qualified managers.

Control is the process of ensuring that global marketing activities are carried out as intended. It involves monitoring aspects of performance and taking corrective action where necessary. The global marketing control system consists of deciding marketing objectives, setting performance standards, locating responsibility, evaluating performance against standards, and taking corrective or supportive action.

In an after-the-fact control system, managers wait until the end of the planning period to take corrective action. In a feedforward control system, corrective action is taken during the planning period by tracking early performance indicators and steering the organization back to desired objectives if it goes out of control.

The most obvious areas of control relate to the control of the annual marketing plan and the control of profitability. The purpose of the global marketing budget is mainly to allocate marketing resources across countries to maximize worldwide total marketing contribution.

# iPhone: Apple's entry into the global mobile phone business

The iPhone was introduced in the United States on 29 June 2007. Apple sold 270,000 iPhones on the first two days of their US launch. As a consequence it set up new budget figures for the next two years. For the 2007 calendar year Apple was expected to sell 2 million iPhones (up from a sales estimate of 1 million before the launch) and for 2008, 7 million (up from 5 million before the launch). CEO Steve Jobs' three-year goal is to achieve a minimum of 1 per cent market share of the world market of 1,000 million mobile phones per annum.

In July 2007 everything looked very promising with regards to future iPhone sales. But then problems occurred. The problems had already begun when Steve Jobs announced plans to spread some iPhone holiday cheer in August 2007 by cutting the price from $599 to $399 for the top-of-the-line 8-gigabyte device. He also discontinued a 4-gigabyte version that was originally $499. Of course, a drop in phone prices after launch is pretty common in the telecom business, but this is Apple, which built its reputation at least in part on high pricing and an absence of discounting. This move was not only risky, but also suggested to some that Apple was worried about sales.

The problems continued when iPhone was launched in Europe before Christmas 2007. The first sales signals from the United Kingdom and Germany were not strong enough in order to fulfil the expectations and budget figures. However, at the beginning of 2008 there were also some positive signals from the number 2 market (according to sales figures) in the world, China. The only two cellular operators, both of them state-owned (China Mobile and China Unicom), were both very interested in distributing and selling the iPhone. The Chinese market is so big that if Apple gets 1 per cent of the Chinese mobile phone market it could see revenues of $600 million a year.

So, all in all, the future for iPhone is somewhat unpredictable, but still Apple's management has to create a sales forecast for iPhone as an input for the three-year budget. So how should the CMO (Chief Marketing Officer) of iPhone, Bill Peach, approach the problem?

Source: Cathal McNaughton/PA Wire/PA Photos.

## Key data about Apple

College dropouts Steve Jobs and Steve Wozniak founded Apple in 1976 in California's Santa Clara Valley. After Jobs' first sales call brought an order for 50 units, the duo built the Apple I in his garage and sold it without a monitor, keyboard or casing. Demand convinced Jobs there was a distinct market for small computers, and the company's name (a reference to Jobs' stint on an Oregon farm) and the computer's user-friendly look and feel set it apart from others.

By 1977 Wozniak added a keyboard, colour monitor and eight peripheral device slots (which gave the machine considerable versatility and inspired numerous third-party add-on devices and software). Sales jumped from $7.8 million in 1978 to $117 million in 1980, the year Apple went public. In 1983 Wozniak left the firm and Jobs hired PepsiCo's John Sculley as President. Apple rebounded from failed product introductions that year by unveiling the Macintosh in 1984. After tumultuous struggles with Sculley, Jobs left in 1985 and founded NeXT Software, a designer of applications for developing software.

In 1997 Apple bought NeXT, and Jobs returned to Apple. In 1998 Apple jumped back into the race with its colourful cocktail of iMacs, and its first server software, the Mac OS X. That year the company also revamped its profitable Claris unit (by cutting 300 employees, shifting most operations to Apple, and renaming it FileMaker) and stopped making its Newton handheld device and printer products.

Apple opened 2001 with another round of product upgrades, including faster processors, components such as CD and DVD burners, and an ultraslim version of its Powerbook, called Titanium. The company also made a move to reclaim some of its slipping share in the education market, purchasing software maker PowerSchool. Soon Apple confirmed a long-rumoured plan to open a small chain of retail stores in the United States. The company then acquired DVD authoring software maker Spruce Technologies. In line with its strategy to market Macs as 'digital hubs' for devices such as cameras and other peripherals, Apple closed the year with the introduction of a digital music player called the iPod.

Since debuting the iPod in 2001, Apple has provided regular feature updates, including touch-screen displays and wireless capabilities. In 2003 Apple announced the launch of an online music service called the iTunes Music Store that lets computer users purchase and download songs for 99 cents each. Apple has since expanded the offerings to include music videos, audiobooks, television shows and other content. In 2006 the company launched an online movie service and previewed a device called iTV for watching downloaded content on televisions. Apple announced availability of its television device, redubbed Apple TV, early the following year.

In 2002 Apple introduced a new look for its iMac line featuring a half-dome base and a flat-panel display supported by a pivoting arm. The redesign was the first departure from the original (and, at the time, radical) all-in-one design since iMac's debut in 1998. Looking to reclaim market share in the education sector, Apple then introduced the eMac – a computer similar to the iMac to be sold only to students and educators (Apple later introduced a retail version). It continued its new product push that year with the announcement that it would begin offering a rack-mount server called Xserve. In 2004,

Apple debuted a streamlined iMac design powered by its G5 processor.

Apple announced it would begin incorporating Intel chips into its PC lines in 2005 and the transition was completed the following year. Late in 2005 Apple, Motorola, and Cingular Wireless (now AT&T Mobility) announced the debut of a mobile phone with iTunes functionality. Apple also unveiled the iPod nano, an updated (and even smaller) version of its miniature iPod model, as well as an iPod capable of playing video.

**Table 1 Apple's 2007 sales by geographical areas**

|  | $m | % of total |
|---|---|---|
| USA | 14,128 | 59 |
| Europe | 5,460 | 23 |
| Asia/Pacific | 1,753 | 7 |
| Japan | 1,082 | 5 |
| Other | 1,583 | 6 |
| Total | 24,006 | 100 |

Source: www.apple.com

**Table 2 Apple's 2007 sales by product**

|  | $m | % of total |
|---|---|---|
| *Music-related products:* |  |  |
| iPod | 8,305 | 35 |
| iTunes Music Store and other | 2,496 | 10 |
| *Computers:* |  |  |
| Portable | 6,294 | 26 |
| Desktop and server | 4,020 | 17 |
| Peripherals and other hardware | 1,260 | 5 |
| *Miscellaneous:* |  |  |
| iPhone and related products and services | 123 | 1 |
| Software, services and other | 1,508 | 6 |
| Total | 24,006 | 100 |

Source: www.apple.com

To reflect the growing breadth of its product portfolio the iPhone was unveiled in 2007. This mobile phone combines features of a high-end handset with those of an iPod. AT&T was named the exclusive carrier for the phone in the US market. Also in 2007 the company changed its name from Apple Computer to simply Apple.

### Apple entering the mobile phone business

Already back in April 2003 at the 'D: All Things Digital' executive conference Steve Jobs expressed his belief that tablet PCs and traditional PDAs were not good choices as high-demand markets for Apple to enter, despite many requests made to him that Apple create another PDA. He did believe that cell phones were going to become important devices for portable information access.

Shortly after Steve Jobs' 9 January 2007 announcement that Apple would be selling a product called iPhone in June 2007, Cisco issued a statement that it had been negotiating trademark licensing with Apple and expected Apple to agree to the final documents that had been submitted the night before. On 10 January 2007 Cisco announced it had filed a lawsuit against Apple over the infringement of the trademark iPhone, seeking an injunction in a federal court to prohibit Apple from using the name. On 20 February 2007 Cisco and Apple reached an agreement. Both companies were allowed to use the 'iPhone' name in exchange for 'exploring interoperability' between their security, consumer and business communications products.

The iPhone device is slightly larger than an average mobile phone, but comes with a 90 mm touchscreen that covers the majority of the front plate of the device. At 11.6 mm, it is not the thinnest phone out there, but it is thin enough to be able to escape the definition of being bulky. Standard equipment includes 4 GB or 8 GB of flash memory storage, Bluetooth and Wi-Fi connectivity, a web browser and push e-mail (with Yahoo e-mail).

Pricing for the phone was originally set at $500 for the 4 GB version and $600 for the 8 GB model.

## Launch in Europe – late 2007

Right after the US launch, Apple officially started making concrete steps toward the iPhone's much-anticipated European market debut. It was important for Apple to launch iPhone in time for the all-important holiday season. It was also important (at least for the UK version) that iPhone would have capabilities to work on 3G wireless networks.

O2, the leading wireless carrier in the United Kingdom, became the exclusive UK carrier for the iPhone when it made its UK debut on 9 November 2007. In the United Kingdom the iPhone was available in an 8 GB model for about $539 (£269). For the German market, Apple announced that T-Mobile would be the exclusive German carrier of Apple's iPhone when it mades its debut there, which was also scheduled for 9 November. In Germany, the iPhone was priced at around $557 (€399). At the start of 2008 iPhone's sales figures accounted for a mere

2 per cent of the total number of all cell phones sold by T-mobile.

France Telecom started marketing the iPhone in France through its wireless arm Orange.

## Competitor reaction – Nokia

Nokia managers would never admit to being influenced by the Apple iPhone, which mobile phone industry insiders regard as clever but technologically unimpressive. 'We don't determine strategy based on the competition,' insists Anssi Vanjoki, Nokia executive Vice-president and General Manager for multimedia. 'The consumer is our compass.' (Ewing, 2007)

Yet Nokia announced a new initiative on 4 December 2007 that seems aimed squarely at Apple. At the start of 2008, higher-end Nokia phones came with a built-in music service offering unlimited downloads of songs for a year. Nokia signed up Universal Music to provide its catalogue, including top contemporary musicians such as Amy Winehouse and Kanye West. And the handset giant is already negotiating with other major music companies.

Nokia is also revamping the software in its high-end handsets, adding a so-called 'scrollable' panels interface. Menus for music, photos, contacts, games and other content appear on floating surfaces that rotate into view and are supposed to make it easier for users to keep track of all the media they have collected on their phones. The interface somewhat resembles that of the iPhone.

But Nokia disappointed anyone waiting for it to introduce a handset to compete directly with the iPhone. Nokia managers say their strategy is to offer a wide range of handsets, targeting special groups of users such as tech freaks or young people. 'It's not one size fits all,' said Mr. Kai, Nokia Executive Vice-president and General Manager for mobile phones, in an obvious dig at the iPhone (Ewing, 2007).

## Iphone enters the the Chinese market

Roughly 500 million of the world's mobile phones (or about half of the global total) were produced in China in 2007. Some 80 per cent, or 400 million of those devices, were exported. There are currently 38 companies in China making mobile handsets (Einhorn and Tschang, 2007).

With more than 180 million Chinese surfing the Internet regularly, it is easy for people to follow the latest trends in the United States. Moreover, many upscale Chinese regularly upgrade their phones to the latest high-end model. And there's now nothing more high-end than iPhone: it is considered by many

Chinese to be the best phone out there. The challenge for Apple is how to capitalize on that popularity. Seduced by the lure of 1.3 billion potential customers, other western tech companies have been focusing on China for years. China, after all, is already the world's largest cellular market, with 528 million mobile users. It is the number 2 PC market, behind only the United States. The United States is also the only country with more Internet users than China. Companies like Dell, Hewlett-Packard, Nokia and Motorola have made selling in China one of their top priorities.

In beginning of 2008 Apple were having talks with the country's number 1 cellular operator, China Mobile, regarding the iPhone. In China, though, Apple does not have many choices. The government allows only two cellular operators, both of them state-owned:

- **China Mobile** is the bigger of the two and with a 70 per cent market share and 369 million subscribers has a thumping lead over longtime laggard China Unicom. China Mobile increased its subscriber base by 23 per cent in 2007 compared to 2006.
- **China Unicom** has finally received the long delayed licences for its 3G service.

China Mobile does face some challenges, though. Its average revenue per user is declining, falling 1.5 per cent this year, as the company finds budget-minded subscribers in poor rural and inland areas. An alliance with Apple would help the company draw more money from affluent customers in the big cities.

All in all, Apple may need China more than China Mobile or China Unicom needs it. Rather than relying on the big Chinese distributors to sell the iPhone, Apple may also plan to open its own stores in China in 2008.

### Questions

As a global marketing specialist you have been hired by CMO, Bill Peach, as a consultant to help with the set up of the global marketing organization and the global marketing budget for iPhone.

1 What were Apple's motives in entering the mobile phone market?

2 Which global organizational structure would you recommend for iPhone?

3 How should Apple build up it global marketing budget for iPhone (by region, country, etc)?

4 Which distribution channel should Apple use in China: China Mobile / China Unicom or should it rely on its own stores? Why?

Sources: Ewing, J. (2007) 'Nokia Won't Play iPhone's Tune', *Business Week Online*, 5 December; Taylor, C. (2007) 'Apple inks deals for Europe iPhone launches', *Electronic News*, 8 October, Vol. 53, Issue 41; Einhorn, B. and Tschang, C.C. (2007) 'China's iPhone Fans Find a Way', *Business Week Online*, 5 December.

For further exercises and cases, see this book's website at **www.pearsoned.co.uk/hollensen**

## Questions for discussion

1 This chapter suggests that the development of a firm's international organization can be divided into different stages. Identify these stages and discuss their relationship to the international competitiveness of the firm.

2 Identify appropriate organizational structures for managing international product development. Discuss key features of the structure(s) suggested.

3 What key internal/external factors influence the organizational structure? Can you think of additional factors? Explain.

4 Discuss the pros and cons of standardizing the marketing management process. Is a standardized process of more benefit to the company pursuing a national market strategy or a global market strategy?

5 Discuss to what degree the choice of organizational structure is essentially a choice between headquarters centralization and local autonomy.

6 Discuss how the international organization of a firm may affect its planning process.

7 Discuss why firms need global marketing controls.

8 What is meant by performance indicators? Why does a firm need them?

9 Performance reviews of subsidiary managers and personnel are required rarely, if at all, by headquarters. Why?

10 Identify the major weaknesses inherent in the international division structure.

11 Discuss the benefits gained by adopting a matrix organizational structure.

## References

Bartlett, C. and Ghoshal, S. (1989) *Managing Across Borders: The transnational solution*, Harvard University Press, Boston, MA.

Harvey, M., Myers, M.B. and Novicevic, M.M. (2002) 'The managerial issues associated with Global Account Management', *Thunderbird International Business Review*, 44(5), pp. 625–647.

Hollensen, S. (2006) 'Global Account Management (GAM): two case studies illustrating the organizational set-up', *The Marketing Management Journal*, 16(1), pp. 244–250.

Jobber, D. (1995) *Principles and Practice of Marketing*, McGraw-Hill, New York.

Kotler, P. (1997) *Marketing Management: Analysis, Planning, Implementation and Control* (9th edn), Prentice-Hall, Englewood Cliffs, NJ.

McDonald, M., Millman, T. and Rogers, B. (1997) 'Key account management: theory, practice and challenges', *Journal of Marketing Management*, 13, pp. 737–757.

Millman, T. and Wilson, K. (1995) 'From key account selling to key account management', *Journal of Marketing Practice: Applied Marketing Science*, 1, pp. 9–21.

Ojasalo, J. (2001) 'Key account management at company and individual levels in B-t-B relationships', *The Journal of Business and Industrial Marketing*, 16(3), pp. 199–220.

Peppers, D. and Rogers, M. (1995) 'A new marketing paradigm: share of customer, not market share.' *Harvard Business Review*, July–August, pp. 105–113.

Quelch, J.A. (1992) 'The new country managers', *The McKinsey Quarterly*, 4, pp. 155–165.

Quelch, J.A. and Bloom, H. (1996) 'The return of the country manager', *The McKinsey Quarterly*, 2, pp. 30–43.

Samli, A.C., Still, R. and Hill, J.S. (1993) *International Marketing: Planning and practice*, Macmillan, London.

Scheraga, P. (2005) 'Balancing act at IKEA', *Chain Store Age*, 81(6) (June), pp. 45–46.

Shi, Linda, H., Zou, Shaoming and Cavusgil, S. Tamer (2004) 'A conceptual framework of global account management capabilities and firm performance', *International Business Review*, 13, pp. 539–553.

Shi, Linda, H., Zou, Shaoming, White, J. Cris, McNally, Regina, C. and Cavusgil, S. Tamer (2005) 'Executive insights: global account management capability: insights from leading suppliers', *Journal of International Marketing*, 13(2), pp. 93–113.

Wilson, K. and Millman, T. (2003) 'The global account manager as political entrepreneur', *Industrial Marketing Management*, 32, pp. 151–158.

Yip, G.S. and Bink, A.J.M. (2007) 'Managing Global Accounts', *Harvard Business Review*, September, pp. 103–111.

# Sony BMG:
## New worldwide organizational structure and the marketing, planning and budgeting of Dido's new album

On a sunny December day in 2006 the Executive Vice President Marketing for Sony-BMG, Tim Prescott, gets on a plane from New York bound for London where, among other things, he is going to meet megastar Dido about the marketing campaign of her new CD release in Spring 2007. Dido was one of BMG's best-selling artists, and Tim is looking forward to meeting the star personally.

New in his job as Executive Vice President, Tim uses the plane trip over the Atlantic to study the global music industry more thoroughly. After the merger between Sony and BMG in 2004 Sony-BMG is now No. 2 in the global music industry, with a world market share of 24 per cent (Universal Music has 25 per cent). But Sony-BMG cannot relax – the competitors (EMI and Warner Music) are not far behind.

After landing in London Tim hurries to the meeting with Dido, but on the way he thinks about the new global organizational structure of Sony-BMG.

In spring 2003 SONY-BMG introduced a new organizational strategy for its music labels and corporate staff that would allow the company to focus on creating global music superstars who reach across geographical boundaries. The streamlining of the organization eliminates regional corporate groups in Europe, Asia and Latin American regions, and creates four new strategic groups within BMG: Office of the Chairman, Label Group, Territory Management and Corporate Center. All management from the groups will report directly to the Office of the Chairman, led by Schmidt-Holtz.

Sony-BMG wants to strengthen relationships with its artists. The top management of the company thinks this structure allows its creative executives to be closer to artists, while allowing managers to better support their creative executives. Sony-BMG wants an organization built on record labels with global reach. The labels and the creative executives should be able to work more closely with artists while being able to rely on effective global marketing capabilities.

Label Group will consist of US-based record labels including Arista Records, RCA Music Group, Jive/Zomba and RLG-Nashville, as well as Music Publishing.

Territory Management will consist of major territories and country groups, such as Japan, Germany/Switzerland/Austria, the United Kingdom, Australia, and South Africa.

Reporting to the Office of the Chairman, Tim Prescott will serve as the company's highest-ranking marketing executive, overseeing global marketing campaigns for Sony-BMG artists. Also reporting to the Office of the Chairman are Human Resources, Strategy and New Technology and Corporate Communications. One of Tim's first tasks in the summer of 2003 was to create the worldwide marketing plan for the UK-singer Dido and her new album, 'Life for rent' released in September 2003. Hence, Tim's meeting with Dido in London. They agree that the launch of Dido's CD should start in the United Kingdom in an effort to get to the top of the charts as quickly as possible.

First some general information about the development in the music industry.

A handful of music companies (operating through several hundred subsidiaries and over a thousand labels) account for most records sold in the advanced economies. Music publishing – production and licensing of intellectual property rights – is even more concentrated.

## Evolution in the music industry

Over the past 100 years we have seen the 'music industry' evolve through three basic stages, characterized by different technologies and different publishing organizations. Prior to the gramophone, when sheet music was the primary vehicle for disseminating popular music, the industry was dominated by music publishing houses. With the rise of recording (and subsequently broadcasting, which was driven by the availability of 'canned content'), those publishers were displaced by the record companies.

Today, increasingly the industry has involved entertainment groups that bring together a broad range of content distribution and repackaging activities – broadcast, film, video, booking and performance management agencies, records, music licensing, print publishing.

See also the value chain of the music recording industry in Figure 1.

Next some further information about the artist, Dido.

Figure 1 The value chain in the music industry

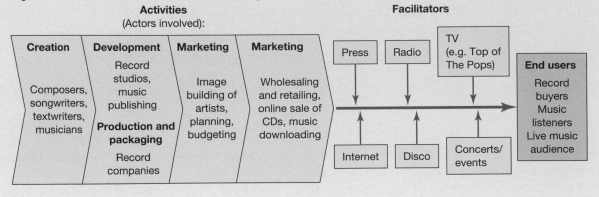

## Dido – one of the best UK-selling artists

The singer and songwriter Dido (Armstrong) was born in London on Christmas Day in 1971. She was christened Florian Cloud De Bounevialle Armstrong. Dido lived with her poet mother and publisher father in London.

At 16 she became enthralled with the music of jazz singer Ella Fitzgerald and her brother Rollo's music collection. Rollo played in the group Faithless, and Dido appeared on the group's five-million selling debut album 'Reverence' in 1995 on the tracks 'Flowerstand Man' and 'Salva Mea'. Dido later appeared on another Faithless album, 'Sunday 8 pm' in 1998 on the tracks 'Postcards' and 'Hem of his Garment'.

In between recording those two albums Dido met producer Clive Davis in 1997, after he had heard demos of some of her own tracks. Dido was later signed to the record company Arista (a Sony-BMG label) and began recording her debut album 'No Angel'. Dido was also involved in the production side of her album. 'Bad boy'

rapper Eminem borrowed part of her song 'Thank You' for his hit 'Stan' and she appeared as his wife in the video. The combination of Dido's angelic voice, soft acoustic guitars and great song writing, with a dash of electronica, has been a big hit with fans around the world.

The album 'No Angel' was released in the United States in 1999 and about a year later in October in the United Kingdom. Two tracks from the album have appeared in a TV show and in a film. 'Thank You' appeared in the film 'Sliding Doors' and 'Here With Me' was the theme tune to *Roswell*, a hit US science-fiction TV show, which has also been doing well in the United Kingdom. This exposure helped make 'No Angel' a huge success.

A special edition of 'No Angel' was released in January 2001 with enhanced videos of 'Here With Me' and 'Thank You'. It also included a bonus track 'Take My Hand' and a picture gallery. The album went to number 1 in United Kingdom and stayed there for several weeks. It has sold more than 20 million copies worldwide.

'No Angel' was the best UK-selling album of 2001 and sold more than 2 million copies during the year. It got to number 1 in 13 countries and was the bestselling album in the world. In total 'No Angel' has sold around 10 million copies around the world. In February 2002 Dido won Best British Female and Best British Album for 'No Angel' at the Brit Awards 2002.

Dido's second official album *Life for Rent* was eventually released on 30 September 2003 and became one of the fastest selling albums in UK music history, debuting at no. 1 in the UK, Ireland, France, Denmark, Switzerland, South Africa, Australia, Greece, Mexico, Hong Kong, Malaysia and Thailand, and in the top four in the USA, Italy, New Zealand, The Netherlands, Germany and Austria. This was preceded by the no. 2 hit single from the album, 'White Flag', which went

**Dido**

Source: Sony BMG. Music Entertainment (UK) Ltd.

on to sell over 400,000 in the first week. Three further singles were lifted from the album: 'Life for Rent', 'Don't Leave Home' and 'Sand in My Shoes'. *Life for Rent* spent many weeks at the top of the UK album charts. 'The Life for Rent Tour' was performed around the world in 2004. A DVD from the tour, entitled 'Dido Live' was released in 2005. In 2004, Dido also won the Brit Award for Best Female Artist and Best British Single ('White Flag').

Dido's third album is expected in August/September 2008.

## The typical value chain for a CD
The following shows how the 'value added' of a typical CD album is split among the various players in the value chain:

| | £ |
|---|---|
| Retail price to consumers | 12 |
| Price to retail | 9 |
| Price to distributor | 6 |
| Price to distributor (exclusive of artist royalty) | 5 |

For a CD single the full retail price to consumers is about £2. But when a record is being pushed hard by the record label retailers are offered big discounts in an attempt to shift units in the all-important first week. In such circumstances singles can retail for as little as 99p.

### Development
In the music industry record labels will actively seek to sign up bands and artistes on long-term exclusive contracts. A key to success in development is to spot talent and to sign it up early.

### Production
Production is relatively cheap in the music industry, and the cost of digital recording equipment and production of CDs is falling rapidly. Some consumers do not understand why the sale price of a CD is so much higher than the cost of producing the actual physical disc. But as described below there are many different activities and costs involved in creating songs and marketing the end result, the CD.

### Distributors
Major distributors have a global network of branch offices to handle the sales, marketing and distribution process. Sometimes the distributors may outsource the physical distribution process.

### Retail
Retailers put in orders to the wholesalers as and when albums and singles are required. In the United Kingdom the retail chains are dominated by HMV, Virgin/Our Price/Smiths, Tower, etc. These chains account for about 80 per cent of the market.

## The costs of a hit
Singles are released with the purpose of getting to the top of the charts. The financial risks involved in mounting an attack on the UK charts have never been greater. According to research carried out by BBC News Online, securing a top ten hit in the United Kingdom in the current climate is likely to cost a minimum of £125,000. Ever increasing amounts of financial resources are being thrown at marketing and promotion in the hope that a single will be picked up by MTV, radio and, perhaps most importantly, the major retailers, in order to secure the highest chart entry.

### Biggest cost categories
Of course the most important component of a CD is the artist's effort that goes into developing the music. Artists spend a large portion of their creative energy on writing song lyrics and composing music or working with producers and A&R executives to find great songs from great writers. This task can take weeks, months, or even years. The creative ability of these artists to produce the music, combined with the time and energy they spend throughout that process, is in itself priceless. But while the creative process is priceless, it must be compensated. Artists receive royalties on each recording, which vary according to their contract, and the songwriter gets royalties too. In addition, the label incurs the costs of finding and signing new artists.

Once an artist or group has songs composed they then go into a studio and begin recording. The costs of recording, including studio fees, musicians, sound engineers, producers and others, must all be recovered by the price of the CD.

Then come marketing and promotion costs – perhaps the most expensive part of the music business today. They include increasingly expensive video clips, public relations, tour support, marketing campaigns and promotion to get the songs played. Labels make investments in artists by paying for both the production and the promotion of the album. New technology such as the Internet offers new ways for artists to reach music fans, but it still requires that some entity, whether a traditional label or another kind of company, market and promote the artist so that fans are aware of new releases.

For every album released in a given year a marketing strategy was developed to make that album stand out from the others hitting the market. Artwork must be designed for the CD box, and promotional materials (posters, store displays and music videos) developed and produced. For many artists a costly concert tour is essential to promote their recordings.

Another factor commonly overlooked in assessing CD prices is to assume that all CDs are equally profitable. In fact the vast majority are never profitable; for example, in the United States, 27,000 new releases hit the market every year. Most of these CDs never sell enough to recover costs. In the end, less than 10 per cent are profitable and, in effect, it is these recordings that finance the rest.

### Marketing and promotion costs

Singles are essentially 3–4 minute adverts for CD albums. Singles' sales guarantee chart places and, in turn, radio play – and that is why music label companies persist with them. They are a kind of loss-leader for albums, where the real money is made.

The biggest expense is normally the promotional video, which for a mainstream artist starts at about £40,000 and can cost anything up to £1 million (however, this is quite exceptional). If the music video is to be shown on, say, MTV it has to comply with a number of requirements, which are set out by MTV (use of alcohol, sex, etc.).

It is common practice for the big retailers, HMV, Our Price and Virgin, to charge music label companies for promoting a single in their shops. This comes in form of a 'singles pack', which guarantees a prominent position for the product in the shop. There are also bonuses to be paid to the sales force to check that the single is being properly promoted in-store.

The singles chart – compiled each week by different organizations and TV stations, such as *Top of the Pops* on the BBC, has always been the cornerstone of the UK music industry. More singles are sold in United Kingdom than anywhere in the world – including the United States, where the album remains king. In 2000 it took an average of 118,700 sold singles to secure a number one spot in the UK chart. Since 2005 the UK single's chart has combined actual release sales with legal online downloads. Initially the proportion of digital sales to physical sales was relatively low, but now (2007) more than 50 per cent of single sales take place online. Sales via mobile phones and video downloads are also now counted.

Here are some of the basic costs for a 'typical' UK top ten single:

| | £ |
|---|---|
| Recording | 3,500 |
| Promotion video | 100,000–150,000 |
| Remixes (of the original single) | 5,000–10,000 |
| Merchandising | 15,000 |
| Posters | 10,000 |
| Stickers | 5,000 |
| PR (Press) | 5,000 |
| Promotion copies to radio stations, etc. | 8,000 |
| Website | 20,000 |
| Manufacturing costs (20p per CD) | 10,000 |
| *Optional costs*: | |
| Press ads | 15,000 |
| Billboard campaign | 50,000 |
| TV/radio/Internet advertising | 200,000 |

Because of the high costs involved combined with the general decline in the sales of CDs and singles (because of the trend towards online downloading of songs), many industry insiders think the singles market can not continue in its current form. One possible escape route is the radio-only release, where a track from an album is promoted to radio stations, but is not actually available to buy. This often happens in the United States, where there is less emphasis on singles' sales, and the singles chart is largely based on radio play.

Sources: adapted from: www.sonybmg.com; RIAA, 'The costs of a CD', www.riaa.com/MD-US-7.cfm, 2003; BMG press release, New York, 23 January 2003; BBC News, 'Sony and BMG merger backed by EU', 19 July; BBC News, 'Sony BMG deal under new scrutiny', 13 July 2006.

### Questions

1 What do you think of the change in BMG's organizational structure, from a geographical structure to an artiste-driven organization?

2 How would you produce a sales and marketing budget for Dido's forthcoming single and album?

3 How would you control your budgets? What key figures would you monitor?

4 How would increasing digital distribution and the piracy of MP3 music files influence your budgeting and control?

5 Which marketing mix would you suggest to increase BMG's share in the UK market?

6 Discuss acquisition as a possible growth strategy.

# Philips Shavers:
## Maintaining shaving leadership in the world market

### The shaving history

With over 450 million shavers sold, the Philips shaver is the best-sold electric shaver worldwide. The many millions of men who shave themselves with Philips are a fitting testimony of the quality of this excellent shaving system. Since 1939, several generations of electric shavers have been developed and introduced.

In October 1937, a Philips employee in the US wrote to the Netherlands that an electric shaver could be an interesting over-the-counter product that would fit perfectly in the Philips product range and could be sold through the radio trade. To study the idea in more detail a box filled with shavers was sent to a group of engineers in the Netherlands. When Alexandre Horowitz evaluated the electric shavers brought over from the United States, he saw possibilities for Philips and said: 'Let us see if we can make a rotating version'.

This marked the beginning of Philishave, the shaver with the one round head. The first Philishave was presented to the public at the Spring exhibition in Utrecht, the Netherlands on the 14 March 1939. The brand 'Philishave' was first registered on 5 April 1939 and the first patent was filed 31 May 1939. But before the Philishave project was well and truly off the ground, the Second World War broke out and sales fell drastically.

After the Second World War, Philishave began its slow march forward, although there was not yet a sign of a real breakthrough. Great efforts were made to prepare the market. Shaving demonstrations ensured that more and more people could experience in person the benefits of this new system. A larger shaving head and a new design improved the product and the number of people choosing the electric shaver with the rounded head increased daily. However, the main problem of the single-headed shaver was that shaving took too long because of the shaver's relatively small surface area.

In their quest for shaving perfection, the developers chose the most logical solution: a model with two shaving heads, called the 'egg'. The great breakthrough came in the early fifties with this two-headed Philishave. Sales soared to unprecedented heights with the United States as undisputed leader. The new production centre in the Dutch town of Drachten was working at full speed to keep up with the explosive growth.

The 'egg' had been a great triumph, but was old fashioned by the end of the Fifties. A new model was needed

Source: Philips DAP/Shaving & Beauty.

to boost sales further, which was a difficult task to say the least, as success does not repeat itself easily. The most obvious innovation was the development of a shaver with three heads. However after a pilot in the test market New Zealand, Philips cancelled the test. A new two-head shaver nicknamed 'the pipe' became a worthy successor.

In the sixties, decade of boundless prosperity, the demand for cars, televisions and refrigerators seemed insatiable. Philishave also profited from this surge in prosperity as production and sales soared to new heights. In addition to the standard electric shave, a new exclusive model made its entry. The wider range meant that the consumer could choose from several models and price ranges.

In 1966, the retail trade was in desperate need of a new Philishave that would surpass competition. With the Philishave '3', Philips set the tone for another generation of shavers. The milestone of the 100th millionth

**Why hide the irritation when you can prevent it?**

COOL SKIN

PHILIPS
sense and simplicity

Source: Philips DAP/Shaving & Beauty.

shaver produced was reached as early as 1970. Despite good results, the market share was regularly threatened in the Seventies. The 'Battle of the Shavers' was raging hard. Global annual figures continued to increase, because new markets were being found, but sales in the most important countries fell catastrophically. Next to the competitive intensity and deteriorating economy, Philips discovered that the electric shaver was no longer number 1 on the wish lists of men. Management faced the difficult task to ensure a long-term top position in the market.

The solution was found in the philosophy of the wheel. This entailed a price increase, so that more money could be spent on research and promotion. More support to the retail trade and drastic product improvements would increase sales so that more money could be used for research and promotion. This was the 'philosophy of the wheel' in a nutshell. Sales rocketed in 1975, the battle of the shavers had been decided in the favour of the triple headed Philishave.

The eighties heralded a new period of growth with the Double Action System giving a tangible better result. Electronics paved the way to greater comfort and cordless ease. Consumers were given an even wider choice as result of a significant expansion of the product line. And with special models, Philips started targeting southeast Asia and the young, the shaving generations of the future.

The fall of the Berlin Wall symbolized the coming of a new era in the Nineties: an era of freedom, economic boom and opening borders. New ideas in design, development, production and marketing went further than ever before. To celebrate the production of the 300 millionth Philishave, Philips introduced a special edition with a walnut print.

In 1998 on the eve of a new millennium, Philips crossed the border between dry and wet shaving with Cool Skin. The Cool Skin was a new way of shaving with an integrated moisturising shaving emulsion. This

additive from Nivea for Men prepares skin and stubble, which results in a close shave.

Between the first Philishave and the latest Philips SmartTouch-XL lie 67 eventful years; years of innovation, unprecedented growth and triumphed setbacks. Furthermore a new milestone is expected: the sale of the 500,000,000th shaver in 2007.

## The world market for shaving

The world market for male shaving can be split into two main segments: electric shaving and wet shaving. The electric shaving market is dominated by Philips, followed at a distance by Braun. The wet shaving category is dominated by Gillette followed at distance by Wilkinson.

The total male shaving market worldwide is estimated at €4 billion in 2004. The wet shaving market worldwide is about twice the size of the electric shaving market. On world basis about 40 per cent mostly use dry shaving and 60 per cent mostly wet shaving. In the western world wet shaving is mainly popular among younger men whereas dry shaving is preferred by the elderly (Euromonitor).

Electric shaving is largely accepted by many millions of users because it makes you feel good and the skin really well cared for with no irritation, nicks or cuts. Furthermore, it is convenient and saves time and money.

The market for electric shaving in 2004 is estimated at €1.3 billion in 2004. The main regions are Europe (where Germany, the United Kingdom and France are key countries) and Asia (with China and Japan as key countries) both regions with 34 per cent of sales. The third largest region is North America with 26 per cent. Latin America and Middle East and Africa close the loop with respectively 4 per cent and 2 per cent. See Figure 1.

**Figure 1 Electric shaving sales per region, 2004**

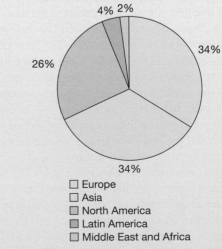

- ☐ Europe
- ☐ Asia
- ☐ North America
- ☐ Latin America
- ☐ Middle East and Africa

Source: Philips DAP/Sharing & Beauty.

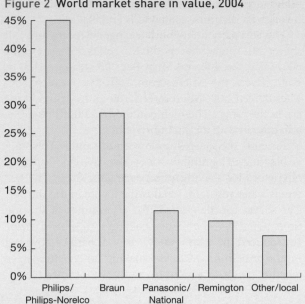

Figure 2 World market share in value, 2004

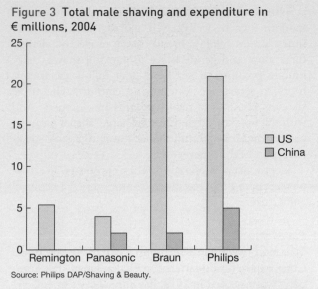

Figure 3 Total male shaving and expenditure in € millions, 2004

Source: Philips DAP/Shaving & Beauty.

## Competitors

Philips dominated the electronic shaving market with a 44 per cent global market share in 2004. Braun, Remington and Panasonic follow at a distance. In each of the markets local brands compete which have been clustered in the 'other/local' category. See Figure 2.

Philips and Braun are the two truly global brands competing in each of the continents, but their electric shavers are based on two different technologies. Philips only sells and markets *rotary shavers*, whereas Braun only markets *foil shavers*. Philips dominates the markets in four continents only to be the No. 2 player in Asia Pacific. Braun is No. 2 in Europe, Latin America, and Middle East and Africa and the No. 3 in North America and Asia Pacific. For Remington the North American market is key, where it has a No. 2 position, as the company does not commend a substantial market position outside this region. Remington competes in both the foil and rotaty segments. Panasonic competes mainly in the Asia Pacific region where it has a No. 1 position. Local competition is also the strongest in Asia Pacific. See Table 1.

Table 1 Geographical percentage shares

|  | Europe | Asia Pacific | North America | Latin America | Middle East and Africa |
|---|---|---|---|---|---|
| Philips | 54 | 27 | 47 | 78 | 79 |
| Braun | 38 | 24 | 23 | 18 | 13 |
| Panasonic | 3 | 29 | 1 | – | – |
| Remington | 4 | 2 | 28 | – | 4 |
| Other | 1 | 18 | 1 | 4 | 4 |

Source: Philips DAP/Shaving & Beauty.

The general picture is that Philips is the global market leader, but there are regional differences. In the eastern part of Europe, Philips and Braun have a head-on competition, each having about 40 per cent of the market, whereas Philips is the clear market leader in western Europe. Also in Australia the competitive situation is different from the general trend: here Remington is the market leader.

The general trend is that Philips is gaining market share in North America at the expense of Braun and Remington. In the following there is a description of the three most important competitors.

Figure 3 looks at the advertisement budget in two key countries for Remington, Panasonic, Braun and Philips.

### Braun

Braun (www.braun.com) was founded in 1921 in Frankfurt by Max Braun. The companies headquarters of Braun GmbH are in Kronberg, Germany. From 1967 to 2005 Braun was part of the Gillette Company, which has been acquired by Procter & Gamble. Braun employs around 9,000 employees worldwide and had net sales in 2004 of $1,392 million. Its profit from operations in 2004 was $99 million.

The company's product range consists of 200 small electrical appliances in ten categories: electric shavers, epilators, food processors, coffeemakers, irons, infrared ear thermometers, blood pressure monitors, hair care appliances, electric oral care products, clocks and calculators. Braun is market leader in foil shavers, epilators, hand blenders, infrared ear thermometers and electric oral care products. Its production takes place in seven plants in five countries: Germany, Ireland, Spain, Mexico and China. Its key shaving products are Activator, Syncro, Flex, CruZer.

With innovative solutions, Braun helps millions of modern men be well-shaved and well-groomed at all times. Braun offers a broad choice of electric shavers for a close and gentle shave. Braun foil shavers have unique pivoting shaver heads that follow facial contours to guarantee top shaving comfort. The triple shaving system sets new standards in closeness. And with the breakthrough 'Clean&Charge' shaver cleaning centre, Braun has found the ideal way to assure spick-and-span freshness every day.

Its product portfolio consists of six products: 360 complete, Syncro Pro, FreeGlider, Contour series, Tricontrol and Cruzer.

### Panasonic

Panasonic (www.panasonic.com) is part of the Matsushita Corporation headquartered in Osaka, Japan. The company was founded in 1918, has annual sales of $62,331 million and employs 290,000 people. The global brand slogan 'Panasonic ideas for life' represents the commitment of Matsushita employees around the world, from R&D and manufacturing, to marketing and services, in providing products and services with value-added ideas, which enrich lives and advance society.

Wet or dry, get a close shave every morning, with the fastest shaver that features the sharpest blades. Panasonic focuses on its pivot action shaving system that claims to have a more comfortable shave, the sharpest blades for precise and accurate shaving and a linear motor that offers a frictionless shave.

Panasonic has no global line up as it offers different products in ranges and different range names in countries. Its product portfolio consists of six products: Lamdash, Linear smoother, Mild smoother, System smoother, TwinEx and Super razor.

### Remington

Remington (www.remingtonproducts.com) is part of Spectrum Brands since 2003. Earlier the name of the company was Rayovac Corporation. The company's mission is to seek long-term growth in both sales and profits by providing innovative, high-quality products that create significant value for customers, combined with establishing long-term partnerships with customers, suppliers and employees.

The company aims to globalize and diversify by expanding distribution in all served markets and aims to generate growth through aggressive pricing, product design and marketing innovation.

Remington introduces the world's first rotary cleaning system with titanium-coated blades. The only shaver that combines the sharpness of titanium coated trimmer blades, with the technology to clean itself. It could just make all other shavers obsolete. This product

offers an incredible close and comfortable shave through its titanium-coated foils and blades.

The company offers both a range of rotary and foil shavers. In rotary shavers the Microflex 800, Microflex 600, Microflex 400 and Microflex 200 are key series. In Foil shavers the Microscreen 700, Microscreen 500, Microscreen 300, Microscreen 100 and a travel razor are in the range. The high end model of both ranges is also offered with a cleaning system.

Recently the sharp line between dry and wet shaving is blurring. The Philips Cool Skin system dispenses Nivea for Men shaving lotion during the shave. The system is water resistant, so allowing its use in the shower. The shaver can be charged for 40 minutes of shaving time. On the other side, Gillette's M3Power razor (introduced in May 2004), uses a battery-powered motor to help lift whiskers, making for a better shave whether the razor is used in the shower or not.

## Seasonal sales and distribution channels

Given the high price tags slapped on electric shavers and as new product developments tend to be concentrated in the premium end, sales of electric shavers tend to be focused over the Christmas period and in connection with Father's Day. It is estimated that approximately 45 per cent of value sales are focused over the fourth quarter and these are mainly bought as gifts. Of this, it is estimated that females who purchase the products as gifts for males make 40 per cent of purchases and appealing to female consumers is, therefore, crucial over this time period. While traditional channels dominate retail distribution, volume sales through non-traditional channels such as supermarkets/hypermarkets, electrical stores and the internet are important growth areas, particularly over the festive season (Euromonitor).

## Marketing of the Philips shavers

When Philips started selling shavers, the company used small adverts in newspapers, and postcards (a first form of direct mail). However the key element was demonstrating, demonstrating and demonstrating. Furthermore Philips has always put quality before turnover.

The flying start of the two-header in the 1950s was followed up with more advertising activities. In addition to dealer adverts in local newspapers, full page adverts began to appear in leading magazines. Radio and TV commercials further stimulated interest, as so did sponsored programmes. Even in Hollywood, the shaver made its appearance in the motion picture 'The Long Wait', where actor Anthony Quinn shaved himself for an entire scene with the two headed egg, a first form of product placement that has become normal today.

In the sixties and fully in line with expectations, the largest group of buyers was made up of well established

**Make every stroke count.**

**Philips Norelco SmartTouch-XL.** Three does more than one. In rowing.
And in shaving. The SmartTouch XL has three shaving rings in each of the three shaving heads, not one. So it's designed to shave more with every stroke. And it actually pivots to stay on your face and neck, catching even tricky hairs. Make your mornings more efficient. Make every stroke count.

**Join us on our journey at www.philips.com/simplicity**

**PHILIPS**
sense and simplicity

**NORELCO**

North America

**Make every stroke count.**

**Philips SmartTouch-XL.** You want a close shave every morning, but it doesn't make sense to go over your face again and again just to get it. So SmartTouch-XL was designed to shave more with each stroke, with three shaving rings in each of the three shaving heads. It actually pivots to stay on your face and neck, catching even tricky hairs. Make your morning shave more efficient.

**Join us on our journey at www.philips.com/simplicity**

**PHILIPS**
sense and simplicity

United Kingdom

**Cada pasada cuenta.**

**Philips SmartTouch-XL.** Cada mañana deseas un afeitado apurado, pero no tiene sentido que para conseguirlo tengas que dar una pasada tras otra. SmartTouch-XL ha sido diseñada para afeitar más en cada movimiento, gracias a las tres cuchillas que hay en cada uno de sus tres cabezales. De hecho, se ajusta a tu rostro y cuello alcanzando hasta el vello más difícil. Haz tu afeitado más eficaz.

**Descubre un mundo más sencillo en www.philips.com/simplicity**

**PHILIPS**
sense and simplicity

Spain

Source: Philips DAP/Shaving & Beauty.

**Jeder Zug zählt.**

**Philips SmartTouch-XL.** Sie wünschen sich eine gründliche Rasur. Und je weniger Züge Sie dafür benötigen, desto besser. Das macht Sinn, oder? Der SmartTouch-XL wurde entwickelt, um mit jedem Zug mehr zu rasieren – mit drei Scherringen pro Scherkopf statt nur einem. Durch die innovative SmartTouch Konturenanpassung bietet er optimalen Hautkontakt und entfernt mühelos sogar schwer zu erreichende Barthaare. Machen auch Sie Ihre morgendliche Rasur effizient.

**Kommen Sie mit uns auf die Reise unter www.philips.com/simplicity**

**PHILIPS**
sense and simplicity

Germany

Another example is the Norelco gift advertisements for the North American market

Source: Philips DAP/Shaving & Beauty.

Germany

Korea

Source: Philips DAP/Shaving & Beauty.

users of electric shavers that were ready for their second or third Philishave, the best shaver money could buy. Furthermore, market researchers discovered that the more expensive shavers were especially popular among female buyers that bought the shaver as a fitting gift for their boyfriends or husbands. All in all the product range extensions were a success.

During the 1970s neither money nor effort were spared to promote the electric shaver. In the United States, Philips Norelco, would broadcast commercials around the most popular television programmes like Ed Sullivan. Advertisements appeared in trend-setting magazines like *Time* and *Sports Illustrated*. Even the landing on the moon formed the basis of a publicity stunt. Next to shavers for the home, Philips also introduced the Carshaver to increase its potential usage.

In the 1980s Philips continued segmentation and targeted specific customer segments like the younger generations with 'New Wave Junior'. In the United States a new advertising campaign was launched, in which various sports heroes claimed that Philipshave and Norelco were tough on your beard, not on your face. In Japan, Philishave leveraged its sponsorship of Roger Moore in the James Bond movie 'A View to a Kill'.

In the nineties, shaving was marketed as an emotion, a daily ritual. The worldwide advertisement campaign 'For The Man Inside' emphasised this emotional side of the modern man. The famous Cobra artist Corneille painted a giant Reflex Action model in 1996. The shaver drew large crowds in a number of European cities during the Philishave moving art tour. Cool Skin is yet another striking example of the innovative power of Philishave. The products and the marketing are constantly on the move.

Philishave as a brand has undergone the necessary development. In addition to electric shavers and Cool Skin, Philips introduced beard and hair trimmers in the Nineties and moved from 'electric shaver with the round head' to a brand for male shaving and grooming.

The marketing of the latest innovation, the SmartTouch-XL, is part of the Philips brand campaign. Here a mix of online and traditional media has been used including the F1 game at (www.williamsf1.philips.com). Examples of the SmartTouch-XL campaigns from different regions are shown.

From March 2006, all Philishave products will be rebranded with the Philips brand name. Philishave is one of the world's most successful brands in electric shaving. However, when a consumer enters a shop looking to buy a shaver, they tend to have Philips rather than Philishave in mind. In fact, recent research has shown that consumers' perception of the Philishave brand is different from how they think of Philips as a whole. In consumer tests on awareness levels, purchase intent and performance against brand pillars, the Philips brand received more positive feedback than Philishave. The Philishave sub-brand does not sufficiently reflect Philips' brand values today.

## Latest development – a sponsor-partnership with WilliamsF1

In 2006, Philips, has set up a partnership with Formula One (F1) team WilliamsF1. It is one of the most important names in sport. Both brands share a long history of innovation and technical expertise and a passion for marketing.

Frank Williams had been running various operations in Formula 1 prior to creating his own team in 1977. After meeting Patrick Head, the two formed what was then called Williams Grand Prix Engineering, now WilliamsF1. The team debuted in the 1977 Spanish Grand Prix. The team became very successful during the 1980s and 1990s, winning nine F1 Constructors' Championships and seven Drivers' Championships and becoming one of the so-called F1 'Big Three' teams (who have achieved over 100 race victories) alongside Ferrari and McLaren.

As well as new driver, Nico Rosberg, the WilliamsF1 Team has now joined forces with Philips, naming the brand as official Male Shaving Partner (www.williamsf1.philips.com).

Source: 'Philishave, generations of shaving excellence, an impression of 60 years of Philishave', a publication marking the 60th anniversary of Philishave, Philips DAP Groningen, 1998; GFK, NPD and import/export figures 2004.

## Questions

1 What are the key success factors (KSFs) in the male shaving market? How are they different from the female shaving market?

2 How can Philips increase the worldwide share of 'dry shaving'?

3 How will you characterize and explain the cross-national advertising 'rowing boat' campaign?

4 Who are the target groups for the:

(a) 'rowing boat' advertising campaign
(b) 'gift' advertising campaign
(c) WilliamsF1 advertising campaign?

5 What is the difference in the cooperative relationship that Philips has with Nivea (Cool Skin) and that with WilliamsF1?

# Index